Scotland

THIS EDITION WRITTEN AND RESEARCHED BY

Neil Wilson

Andy Symington

Contents

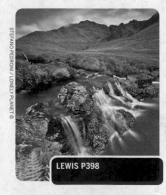

STEFANO PEDRONI / LONELY PLANET ©

LEWIS P398

JUSTIN FOULKES / LONELY PLANET ©

RING OF BRODGAR, ORKNEY
P419

Contents

Welcome to Scotland

Despite its small size, Scotland has many treasures crammed into its compact territory – big skies, lonely landscapes, spectacular wildlife, superb seafood and hospitable, down-to-earth people.

Outdoor Adventure

Scotland harbours some of the largest areas of wilderness left in Western Europe, a wildlife haven where you can see golden eagles soar above the lochs and mountains of the northern Highlands, spot otters tumbling in the kelp along the shores of the Outer Hebrides, and watch minke whales breach through shoals of mackerel off the coast of Mull. It's also an adventure playground where you can tramp the tundra plateaus of the Cairngorms, sea-kayak among the isles of the Outer Hebrides, and take a speed-boat ride into the surging white water of the Corryvreckan whirlpool.

Turbulent History

Scotland is a land with a rich, multilayered history, a place where every corner of the landscape is steeped in the past – a deserted croft on an island shore, a moor that was once a battlefield, a cave that once sheltered Bonnie Prince Charlie. Hundreds of castles, from the plain but forbidding tower houses of Hermitage and Smailholm to the elaborate machicolated fortresses of Caerlaverock and Craigmillar, testify to the country's often turbulent past. And battles that played a pivotal part in the building of a nation are brought to life at sites such as Bannockburn and Culloden.

The Culture

Be it the poetry of Robert Burns, the crime fiction of Ian Rankin or the songs of Emeli Sandé, Scotland's cultural exports are appreciated around the world every bit as much as whisky, tweed and tartan. But you can't beat reading Burns' poems in the village where he was born, enjoying an Inspector Rebus novel in Rankin's own Edinburgh, or catching the latest Scottish bands at the T in the Park festival. Museums such as Glasgow's Kelvingrove, Dundee's Discovery Point and Aberdeen's Maritime Museum recall the influence of Scottish artists, engineers, explorers, writers and inventors in shaping the world.

A Taste of Scotland

Scotland's restaurants have shaken off their old reputation for deep-fried food and unsmiling service and can now compete with the best in Europe. A new-found respect for top-quality local produce means that you can feast on fresh seafood mere hours after it was caught, beef and venison that was raised just a few miles away from your table, and vegetables that were grown in your hotel's own organic garden. And top it all off with a dram of single malt whisky – rich, evocative and complex, the true taste of Scotland.

Why I Love Scotland

by Neil Wilson, Author

It's the weather. Yes, seriously. We get four proper seasons here (sometimes all of them in one day) and that means that you get to enjoy the same landscapes over and over again in a range of different garbs – August hills clad in purple heather, native woodlands gilded with autumn colours, snowpatched winter mountains, and Hebridean machair sprinkled with a confetti of spring wildflowers. And the unpredictability of the weather means that even the wettest day can be suddenly transformed by parting clouds and slanting shafts of golden light. Sheer magic.

For more about our authors, see page 496

Scotland

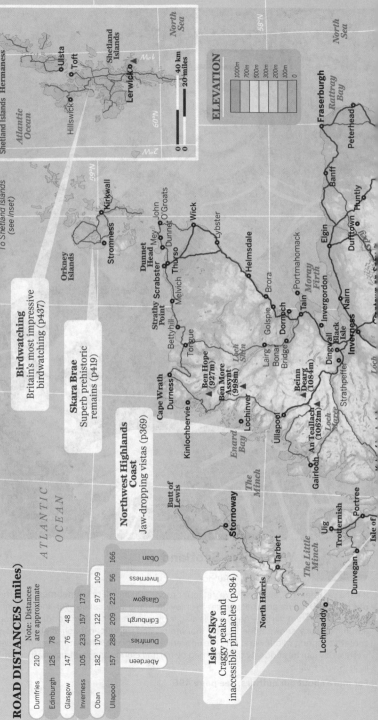

ROAD DISTANCES (miles)
Note: Distances are approximate

	Aberdeen	Dumfries	Edinburgh	Glasgow	Inverness	Oban
Dumfries	210					
Edinburgh	125	78				
Glasgow	147	76	48			
Inverness	105	233	157	173		
Oban	182	170	122	97	109	
Ullapool	157	288	209	223	56	166

Birdwatching
Britain's most impressive birdwatching (p437)

Skara Brae
Superb prehistoric remains (p419)

Northwest Highlands Coast
Jaw-dropping vistas (p369)

Isle of Skye
Craggy peaks and inaccessible pinnacles (p384)

ELEVATION
1000m
700m
500m
300m
200m
100m
0

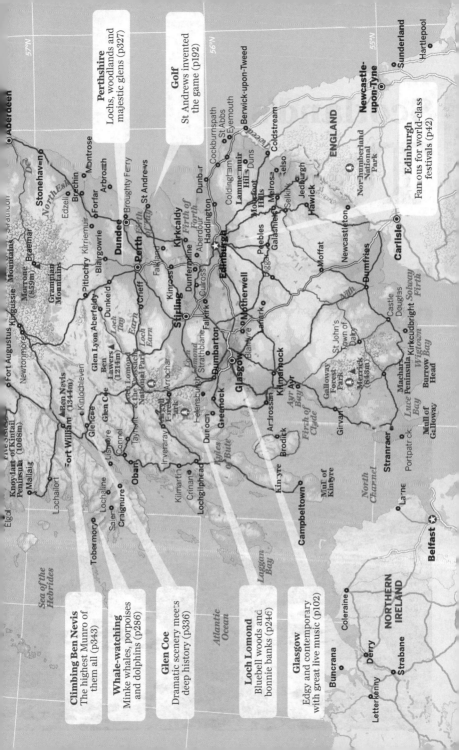

Perthshire
Lochs, woodlands and majestic glens (p327)

Golf
St Andrews invented the game (p192)

Edinburgh
Famous for world-class festivals (p42)

Climbing Ben Nevis
The highest Munro of them all (p343)

Whale-watching
Minke whales, porpoises and dolphins (p286)

Glen Coe
Dramatic scenery meets deep history (p336)

Loch Lomond
Bluebell woods and bonnie banks (p246)

Glasgow
Edgy and contemporary with great live music (p102)

Scotland's
Top 16

1

Isle of Skye

1 In a country famous for stunning scenery, the Isle of Skye (p384) takes top prize. From the craggy peaks of the Cuillins and the bizarre pinnacles of the Old Man of Storr and Quiraing to the spectacular sea cliffs of Neist Point, there's a photo opportunity at almost every turn. Walkers can share the landscape with red deer and golden eagles, and refuel at the end of the day in convivial pubs and top seafood restaurants. Below left: Cuillin Hills (p391)

Edinburgh

2 Scotland's capital may be famous for its festivals, but there's much more to it than that. Edinburgh (p42) is a city of many moods: visit out of season to see the Old Town silhouetted against a blue spring sky and a yellow haze of daffodils; or on a chill December morning with the fog snagging the spires of the Royal Mile, rain on the cobblestones and a warm glow beckoning from the window of a pub.

PHIL HABER PHOTOGRAPHY / GETTY IMAGES ©

2

GEORGE CLERK / GETTY IMAGES ©

Loch Lomond

3 Despite being less than an hour's drive from the bustle and sprawl of Glasgow, the bonnie banks and bonnie braes of Loch Lomond (p246) – immortalised in the words of one of Scotland's best-known songs – comprise one of the most scenic parts of the country. At the heart of Scotland's first national park, the loch begins as a broad, island-peppered lake in the south, its shores clothed in bluebell woods, narrowing in the north to a fjord-like trench ringed by 900m-high mountains.

Walking the West Highland Way

4 The best way to really get inside Scotland's landscapes is to walk them. Despite the wind, midges and drizzle, walking here is a pleasure, with numerous short- and long-distance trails, hills and mountains begging to be tramped. Top of the wish list for many hikers is the 96-mile West Highland Way (p32) from Milngavie (near Glasgow) to Fort William, a challenging week-long walk through some of the country's finest scenery, finishing in the shadow of its highest peak, Ben Nevis.

Climbing Ben Nevis

5 The allure of Britain's highest peak is strong – around 100,000 people a year set off up the summit trail, though not all make it to the top. Nevertheless, the highest Munro of them all is within the reach of anyone who's reasonably fit. Treat Ben Nevis (p343) with respect and your reward (weather permitting) will be a truly magnificent view and a great sense of achievement. Real walking enthusiasts can warm up by hiking the 96-mile West Highland Way first.

Marine Wildlife Watching

6 Scotland is one of the best places in Europe for seeing marine wildlife. In the high season (July and August) many cruise operators on the west coast can almost guarantee sightings of minke whales and porpoises, and the Moray Firth is famous for its resident population of bottlenose dolphins. Basking sharks – at up to 12m, the biggest fish to be found in British waters – make another common sighting. Tobermory and Easdale (near Oban) are top departure points.

Glasgow

7 Scotland's biggest city (p102) lacks Edinburgh's classical beauty, but more than makes up for it with a barrelful of things to do and a warmth and energy that leave every visitor impressed. Edgy and contemporary, it's a great spot to browse art galleries and museums, and to discover the works of local hero Charles Rennie Mackintosh. Add what is perhaps Britain's best pub culture and one of the world's best live-music scenes, and the only thing to do is live it. Above: Glasgow School of Art (p103)

KATHY COLLINS / GETTY IMAGES ©

Perthshire – Big Tree Country

8 Blue-grey lochs shimmer, reflecting the changing moods of the weather; swaths of noble woodland clothe the hills; majestic glens scythe their way into remote wildernesses; and salmon leap upriver to the place of their birth. In Perthshire the heart of the country, picturesque towns bloom with flowers, distilleries emit tempting malty odours and sheep graze in impossibly green meadows. There's a feeling of the bounty of nature that no other place in Scotland can replicate. Above: beech trees near Crieff (p206)

Golf

9 Scotland invented the game of golf and is still revered as its spiritual home by hackers and champions alike. Links courses are the classic experience here – bumpy coastal affairs where the rough is heather and machair and the main enemy is the wind, which can make a disaster of a promising round in an instant. St Andrews (p192), the historic Fife university town, is golf's headquarters, and an alluring destination for anyone who loves the sport.

Northwest Highlands

10 The Highlands abound in breathtaking views, but the far northwest (p369) is truly awe-inspiring. The coastal road between Durness and Kyle of Lochalsh offers jaw-dropping scenes at every turn: the rugged mountains of Assynt, the desolate beauty of Torridon and the remote cliffs of Cape Wrath. These and the nooks of warm Highland hospitality found in classic rural pubs make this an unforgettable corner of the country. Opposite top: Plockton (p381) and the Torridon Hills

Glen Coe

11 Scotland's most famous glen (p336) combines those two essential qualities of Highlands landscape: dramatic scenery and deep history. The peacefulness and beauty of this valley today belie the fact that it was the scene of a ruthless 17th-century massacre, when the local MacDonalds were murdered by soldiers of the Campbell clan. Some of the glen's finest walks – to the Lost Valley, for example – follow the routes used by the clanspeople trying to flee their attackers, and where many perished in the snow. Right: Buachaille Etive Mor (p336)

ANTHONY CLING / GETTY IMAGES ©

MONTY RAKUSEN / GETTY IMAGES ©

Whisky

12 Scotland's national drink – from the Gaelic *uisge bagh*, meaning 'water of life' – has been distilled here for more than 500 years. More than 100 distilleries are still in operation, producing hundreds of varieties of single malt. Learning to distinguish the smoky, peaty whiskies of Islay from, say, the flowery, sherried malts of Speyside has become a hugely popular pastime. Many distilleries offer guided tours, rounded off with a tasting session, and ticking off the local varieties is a great way to explore the whisky-making regions.

Birdwatching in Shetland

13 Sparsely populated, and with large areas of wild land, Scotland is an important sanctuary for all sorts of wildlife. Amazing birdwatching is on offer throughout the country, but the seabird cities of the Shetland Islands take first prize. From their first arrival in late spring to the raucous feeding frenzies of high summer, the vast colonies of gannets, guillemots, puffins and kittiwakes at Hermaness (p436), Noss (p431) and Sumburgh Head (p434) provide one of British birdwatching's most impressive experiences.
Top right: Atlantic puffin

Skara Brae

14 When visiting ancient sites it can be difficult to feel the gulf of years or sense a connection with the people that built them, but Scotland's superb prehistoric remains have an immediate impact. Few places offer a better glimpse of everyday Stone Age life than Skara Brae (p419) in Orkney, with its carefully constructed fireplaces, beds, cupboards and water cisterns. Buried in coastal sand dunes for centuries, it can feel as though the inhabitants have just slipped out to go fishing, and could return at any moment.

Castles

15 Desolate stone fortresses looming in the mist, majestic castles towering over historic towns, or luxurious palaces built on expansive grounds by lairds more concerned with pampering than with defence: Scotland has a full range of castles that reflect its turbulent history and tense relations with its southern neighbour. Most castles have a story (or 10) to tell of plots, intrigues, imprisonments and treachery – as well as a ghost rumoured to stalk their halls. Top: Eilean Donan (p383)

Island Hopping

16 Much of the unique character of western and northern Scotland is down to its expansive vistas of sea and islands – there are more than 700 islands off Scotland's coast, of which almost 100 are inhabited. A network of ferries link these islands to the mainland and each other; buying an Island Rover ticket (unlimited ferry travel for 15 days) provides a fascinating way to explore. It's possible to hop all the way from Arran or Bute to the Outer Hebrides, touching the mainland only at Kintyre and Oban. Bottom: Oban (p280)

Need to Know

For more information, see Survival Guide (p467)

Currency
Pounds Sterling (£)

Language
English, Gaelic and Lallans

Money
ATMs widely available; credit cards widely accepted.

Visas
Generally not needed for stays of up to six months. Not a member of the Schengen Zone.

Mobile Phones
Uses the GSM 900/1800 network. Local SIM cards can be used in European and Australian phones.

Time
UTC/GMT +1 hour during summer daylight saving time, UTC/GMT +0 the rest of the year.

Driving
Drive on the left; steering wheel on right-hand side of car.

When to Go

Cool to mild summers, cold winters

Lerwick
GO mid-May–mid July

Stornoway
GO May–Sep

Inverness
GO May–Sep

Fort William
GO May–Sep

Edinburgh
GO All year

High Season
(Jul & Aug)

➡ Accommodation prices 10%–20% higher (book in advance if possible).

➡ Warmest time of year, but often wet.

➡ Midges at their worst in Highlands and islands.

Shoulder Season (May, Jun & Sep)

➡ Wildflowers and rhododendrons bloom in May and June.

➡ Statistically, best chance of dry weather, minus midges.

➡ June evenings have daylight till 11pm.

Low Season
(Oct–Apr)

➡ Rural attractions and accommodation often closed.

➡ Snow on hills November to March.

➡ Gets dark at 4pm in December.

➡ Can be very cold and wet November to March.

Useful Websites

Lonely Planet (lonelyplanet.com/scotland) Destination information, forums, hotel bookings.

VisitScotland (www.visitscotland.com) Offical tourism site; booking services.

Internet Guide to Scotland (www.scotland-info.co.uk) Best online tourist guide to Scotland.

Traveline (www.travelinescotland.com) Up-to-date public transport timetables.

ScotlandsPeople (www.scotlandspeople.gov.uk) Official genealogical website that lets you search the indexes to Old Parish Registers and Statutory Registers, as well as census returns, on a pay-per-view basis.

Important Numbers

Country code	☎ +44
International access code	☎ 00
Ambulance	☎ 112 or ☎ 999
Fire	☎ 112 or ☎ 999
Police	☎ 112 or ☎ 999

Exchange Rates

Australia	A$1	£0.58
Canada	C$1	£0.56
Euro zone	€1	£0.80
Japan	¥100	£0.59
New Zealand	NZ$1	£0.51
USA	US$1	£0.62

For current exchange rates, see www.xe.com.

Daily Costs

Budget: Less than £35

➡ Dorm beds: £12–22

➡ Wild camping: free

Midrange: £40–120

➡ Double room at midrange B&B: £50–100

➡ Bar lunch: £10; dinner at midrange restaurant: £25

➡ Car hire: £35 per day

➡ Petrol costs: around 15p per mile

Top End: More than £120

➡ Double room at high-end hotel: £130–250

➡ Dinner at high-end restaurant: £40–60

➡ Flights to islands: £65–130 each way

Opening Hours

Opening hours may vary throughout the year, especially in rural areas where many places have shorter hours, or close completely, from October or November to March or April.

Banks 9.30am to 4pm or 5pm Monday to Friday; some are open 9.30am to 1pm Saturday

Pubs & Bars 11am to 11pm Monday to Thursday, 11am to 1am Friday and Saturday, 12.30pm to 11pm Sunday

Shops 9am to 5.30pm (or 6pm in cities) Monday to Saturday, and often 11am to 5pm Sunday

Restaurants Lunch noon to 2.30pm, dinner 6pm to 9pm or 10pm

Arriving in Scotland

Edinburgh Airport

Trams To Edinburgh city centre every 8 to 10 minutes from 6.15am to 10.45pm (£5).

Buses Every 10 to 15 minutes from 4.30am to midnight (£4).

Night buses Every 30 minutes from 12.30am to 4am (£3.50).

Taxis Cost £16–22; about 20 minutes to the city centre.

Glasgow Airport

Buses To Glasgow city centre every 10 to 15 minutes from 6am to 11pm (£6).

Night buses Hourly 11pm to 4am, half-hourly 4am to 6pm (£6).

Taxis Cost £22–26; about 30 minutes to city centre.

Getting Around

Transport in Scotland can be expensive; bus and rail services are sparse in the more remote parts. For timetables, check out Traveline Scotland (www.travelinescotland.com).

Car Useful for travelling at your own pace, or for visiting regions with minimal public transport. Cars can be hired in every town or city. Drive on the left.

Train Relatively expensive, with extensive coverage and frequent departures in central Scotland, but only a few lines in the northern Highlands and southern Scotland.

Bus Cheaper and slower than trains, but useful for more remote regions that aren't serviced by trains.

Boat A network of car ferries link the mainland to the western and northern Scotland.

For much more on **getting around**, see p477.

First Time Scotland

For more information, see Survival Guide (p467)

Checklist

☐ Make sure your passport is valid for at least six months past your arrival date

☐ Make all necessary bookings (for accommodation, events and travel)

☐ Check the airline baggage restrictions

☐ Inform your debit- and credit-card company of your travels

☐ Arrange appropriate travel insurance

☐ Check if you can use your mobile/cell phone

What to Pack

☐ Passport

☐ Drivers licence

☐ Good walking shoes or boots

☐ Waterproof jacket

☐ Camera

☐ UK electrical adapter

☐ Insect repellent

☐ Binoculars

☐ Hangover cure (all that whisky, you know)

Top Tips for Your Trip

➡ Quality rather than quantity should be your goal, so pick a handful of destinations and give yourself time to linger. The most memorable experiences in Scotland are often the ones where you do very little.

➡ If you're driving, get off the main roads when you can. Some of the country's most stunning scenery is best enjoyed on smaller roads that wind their narrow way through standout photo ops.

➡ Make the effort to meet the locals whose helpfulness, friendliness and fun has not been exaggerated.

➡ Be prepared for midges – tiny biting flies that can make life a misery in summer in the Highlands. Bring along insect repellent, antihistamine cream, and long-sleeved shorts and trousers.

What to Wear

Scotland is a fairly casual destination and you can wear pretty much whatever you like. No restaurant will insist on jackets or ties, nor will any theatre or concert hall – smart casual is fine. Summer days can be warm but rarely hot, so be prepared for when the inevitable cool sets in. The weather will determine your outfit so a light, waterproof jacket should always be close at hand, preferably one that you can fold into a shoulder bag.

Sleeping

Booking your accommodation in advance is recommended, especially in summer, at weekends and on islands (where options are often limited). Book at least two months ahead for July and August. See p468 for more information.

➡ **B&Bs** These small, family-run houses generally provide good value. More luxurious versions are more like a boutique hotel.

➡ **Hotels** Scottish hotels range from half-a-dozen rooms above the pub to restored country houses and castles, with a commensurate range in rates.

➡ **Hostels** There's a good choice of both institutional and independent hostels, many housed in rustic and/or historic buildings.

Money

ATMs can generally be found throughout Scotland. If not, it's often possible to get 'cash back' at a hotel or shop in remote areas – ie make a payment by debit card and get some cash back. Credit and debit cards can be used almost everywhere except for some rural B&Bs that only accept cash. Make sure bars or restaurants will accept cards before you order as some don't. The most popular cards are Visa and MasterCard; American Express is only accepted by the major chains, and virtually no one will accept Diners or JCB. Chip-and-PIN is the norm for card transactions; only a few places will accept a signature. Banks, post offices and some of the larger hotels will change cash and travellers cheques.

Bargaining

A bit of mild haggling is acceptable at flea markets and antique shops, but everywhere else you're expected to pay the advertised price.

Tipping

➡ **Hotels** £1 per bag is standard; gratuity for cleaning staff at your discretion.

➡ **Pubs** Not expected unless table service is provided, then £1 for a round of drinks.

➡ **Restaurants** For decent service 10% and up to 15% at more expensive places. Check to see if service has been added to the bill already (most likely for large groups).

➡ **Taxis** Taxis are expensive, and locals rarely tip; generally rounded up to nearest pound.

IZZET KERIBAR / GETTY IMAGES ©

Inside a busy Edinburgh pub

Etiquette

Although largely informal in their everyday dealings, the Scots do observe some rules of etiquette.

➡ **Greetings** Shake hands with men, women and children when meeting for the first time and when saying goodbye. Scots expect a firm handshake with eye contact.

➡ **Conversation** Generally friendly but often reserved, the Scots avoid conversations that might embarrass.

➡ **Language** The Scots speak English with an accent that varies in strength – in places such as Glasgow and Aberdeen it can often be indecipherable. Oddly, native Gaelic speakers often have the most easily understood accent when speaking English.

➡ **Buying your round at the pub** Like the English, Welsh and Irish, Scots generally take it in turns to buy a round of drinks for the whole group, and everyone is expected to take part. The next round should always be bought before the first round is finished.

Eating

It's wise to book ahead for mid-range restaurants in Scotland, especially at weekends. Top-end restaurants should be booked at least a couple of weeks in advance.

➡ **Restaurants** Scotland's restaurants range from cheap-and-cheerful to Michelin-starred, and cover every cuisine.

➡ **Cafes** Open during daytime (rarely after 6pm), cafes are good for a casual breakfast or lunch, or simply a cup of coffee.

➡ **Pubs** Most of Scotland's pubs serve reasonably priced meals, and many can compete with restaurants on quality.

What's New

Edinburgh Trams

After six years of street closures, traffic chaos, ballooning costs and accusations of mismanagement, trams finally returned to Edinburgh's streets on 31 May 2014 after an absence of 58 years. Several hundred million pounds over budget, several years behind schedule, and half the length originally planned, the new tram line runs for 8.7 miles from Edinburgh Airport to York Place in the New Town, passing Murrayfield Stadium, Haymarket and Princes St.

The Kelpies

The regeneration of post-industrial Falkirk continues apace, with the spectacular Falkirk Wheel joined by the even more spectacular Kelpies – a pair of giant equine sculptures framing the entrance to the Forth & Clyde Canal. (p188)

The Hydro

Glasgow's Clyde waterfront gained a new 13,000-seat live-performance arena, The Hydro, christened in 2013 with a Rod Stewart concert and host to the 2014 Commonwealth Games gymnastics and netball events. (p132)

Cheaper Ferries

The Scottish government announced that the Road Equivalent Tariff scheme – which reduces the cost of taking a vehicle on a ferry – will gradually be extended to all west coast and Clyde ferry routes by 2016.

Bannockburn Visitor Centre

To mark the 700th anniversary of the Battle of Bannockburn in 2014, the National Trust for Scotland unveiled a revamped, high-tech heritage centre on the site of the battlefield. (p184)

New Distilleries

The ever-increasing demand for single malt whisky around the world means that there are at least two dozen new distilleries being built around Scotland, including ones at Ardnamurchan (p345), Harris (p401) and Gartbreck. (p276)

Raasay House

Having been gutted by fire in 2009, a multimillion-pound restoration project saw Raasay House reopen in 2013 to provide outdoor activity courses, hostel bunks and luxury B&B accommodation. (p396)

Abbotsford

Sir Walter Scott's magnificent country home at Abbotsford now sports an award-winning new visitor centre with an exhibition celebrating the life of Scotland's greatest historical novelist. (p144)

BikeGlenlivet MTB Trails

Scotland's reputation as a world-class mountain-biking destination has been enhanced with several new trail centres, including the excellent BikeGlenlivet near Tomintoul. (p322)

For more recommendations and reviews, see
lonelyplanet.com/Scotland

If You Like...

Castles

The clash and conflict of Scotland's colourful history has left a legacy of military strongholds scattered across the country, from the border castles raised against English incursions to the island fortresses that controlled the seaways for the Lords of the Isles.

Edinburgh Castle The biggest, the most popular, the Scottish capital's reason for being. (p45)

Stirling Castle Perched on a volcanic crag at the top of the town, this historic royal fortress and palace has the lot. (p179)

Craigievar Castle The epitome of the Scottish Baronial style, all towers and turret. (p235)

Culzean Castle Enormous, palatial 18th-century mansion in a romantic coastal setting. (p162)

Eilean Donan Castle Perfect lochside location conveniently located just by the main road to Skye makes this the Highlands' most photographed fortress. (p383)

Hermitage Castle Bleak and desolate borderland fortress speaking of turbulent times with England. (p148)

Wild Beaches

Nothing clears a whisky hangover like a walk along a wind-whipped shoreline, and Scotland is blessed with a profusion of wild beaches. The west coast in particular has many fine strands of blinding white sands and turquoise waters that could pass for Caribbean beaches if it wasn't for the weather.

Kiloran Bay A perfect curve of deep golden sand – the perfect vantage point for stunning sunsets. (p279)

Sandwood Bay A sea stack, a ghost story and 2 miles of windblown sand – who could ask for more? (p373)

Bosta A beautiful and remote cove filled with white sand beside an Iron Age house. (p400)

Durness A series of pristine sandy coves and duney headlands surrounds this northwestern village. (p371)

Scousburgh Sands Shetland's finest beach is a top spot for birdwatching as well as a bracing walk. (p433)

Orkney's Northern Islands Most of these islands, especially Sanday, Westray and North Ronaldsay, have spectacular stretches of white sand with seabirds galore and seals lazing on the rocks. (p435)

Good Food

Scotland's chefs have an enviable range of quality meat, game, seafood and vegetables at their disposal. The country has shaken off its once dismal culinary reputation as the land of deep-fried Mars Bars, and now boasts countless regional specialities, farmers markets, artisan cheesemakers, smokeries and microbreweries.

Ondine Sustainably sourced seafood in one of Edinburgh's finest restaurants. (p82)

Café 1 International menu based on quality Scottish produce at this Inverness bistro. (p305)

Café Fish Perched on Tobermory waterfront, and serving fresh seafood and shellfish straight off the boat. (p290)

Monachyle Mhor Utterly romantic location deep in the Trossachs and utterly wonderful food with sound sustainable principles. (p257)

Peat Inn One of Scotland's most acclaimed restaurants sits in a hamlet amid the peaceful Fife countryside. (p199)

Albannach Fabulous gourmet retreat in the northwest; a real haven for relaxation. (p374)

Outdoor Adventures

Scotland is one of Europe's finest outdoor adventure playgrounds. The rugged mountain terrain and convoluted coastline of the Highlands and islands offer unlimited opportunities for hiking, mountain biking, surfing and snowboarding.

Fort William The self-styled Outdoor Capital of the UK, centre for hiking, climbing, mountain biking, and winter sports.(p339)

Shetland One of Scotland's top coastlines for sea kayaking, with an abundance of bird and sea life to observe from close quarters. (p427)

7Stanes Mountain-biking trails for all abilities in the forests of southern Scotland. (p173)

Cairngorms Winter skiing and summer walking amid the epic beauty of this high, subarctic plateau. (p316)

Thurso Right up the top of Scotland, this is an unlikely surfing mecca, but once you've got the wetsuit on the waves are pretty good. (p368

Live Music & Festivals

Scotland's festival calendar has seen an explosion of events in the last decade, with music festivals especially springing up in the most unlikely corners. The ones that have stood the test of time are full of character, with superb settings and a smaller, more convivial scale than monster gigs like Glastonbury and Reading.

RockNess Music Festival Regularly praised as the most beautiful festival in the world,

Top: Crossing a river in the Cairngorms (p316)
Bottom: Culzean Castle (p162)

held in June with scenic Loch Ness as a backdrop. (p313)

Arran Folk Festival June sees the fiddles pulled out all over this scenic island. (p270)

T in the Park The country's biggest rock festival kicks off in mid-July, at Strathallan Castle near Gleneagles. (p201)

King Tut's Wah Wah Hut Live music nightly at this legendary Glasgow venue. (p131)

Rural Museums

Every bit as interesting as the 'big picture' history involving Mary, Queen of Scots and Bonnie Prince Charlie, the history of rural communities is preserved in a wide range of fascinating museums, often in original farm buildings and historic houses.

Arnol Blackhouse Preserved in peat smoke since its last inhabitant left in the 1960s, a genuine slice of 'living history'. (p399)

Highland Folk Museum Fascinating outdoor museum populated with real historic buildings reassembled here on site. (p321)

Scottish Crannog Centre Head back to the Bronze Age in this excellent archaeological reconstruction of a fortified loch house. (p335)

Tain Through Time Really entertaining local museum with a comprehensive display on Scottish history and Tain's silversmithing tradition. (p360)

Pubs

No visit to Scotland is complete without a night in a traditional Scottish hostelry, supping real ales, sipping whisky and tapping your toes to traditional music. The choice of pubs is huge, but in our opinion the old ones are the best.

Drover's Inn A classic Highland hostelry with kilted staff, candlelight and a stuffed bear. (p248)

Sandy Bell's A stalwart of the Edinburgh folk scene, with real ale and live trad music. (p88)

Glenelg Inn The beer garden here *is* actually a garden. What's more, it's got sensational views across the water to Skye. (p384)

Horse Shoe This place – all real ales and polished brass – is Glasgow's best traditional pub. (p128)

Stein Inn A lochside pub in Skye with fine ales, fresh seafood and a view to die for. (p394)

Shopping

Scotland offers countless opportunities for shopping, from designer frocks and shoes in city malls, to local art, handmade pottery and traditional textiles in Highland and island workshops.

Glasgow The centre of Glasgow is a shopper's paradise, with everything from designer boutiques to secondhand records. (p133)

Barras Glasgow's legendary flea market is a boisterous and intriguing place to browse for a taste of the city. (p133)

Edinburgh Competes with Glasgow as the country's shopping epicentre, with its Harvey Nicks, malls, cashmere, tartan and quirky little gift shops. (p90)

Wigtown An amazing array of secondhand and specialist bookshops cluster around the square in this small, out-of-the-way village. (p174)

Classic Walks

Scotland's wild, dramatic scenery and varied landscape has made hiking a hugely popular pastime. There's something for all levels of fitness and enthusiasm, but the really keen hiker will want to tick off some (or all) of the classic walks.

West Highland Way The granddaddy of Scottish long-distance walks, the one everyone wants to do. (p32)

Glen Affric to Shiel Bridge A classic two-day cross-country hike, with a night in a remote hostel. (p309)

Southern Upland Way Crosses Southern Scotland's hills from coast to coast; longer and harder than the WHW. (p150)

Ben Lawers One of central Scotland's classic hill walks, with super views over Loch Tay. (334)

Fife Coastal Path Seascapes and clifftops galore on this picturesque route right around the 'Kingdom'. (p188)

Hidden Gems

For those who enjoy exploring off the beaten track, Scotland is littered with hidden corners and remote road-ends where you feel as if you are discovering the place for the first time.

Glen Clova The loveliest of the Angus glens lies hidden away on the quiet side of the Cairngorms National Park. (p327)

Falls of Clyde Normally associated with shipbuilding, the River

Old Man of Hoy (p422)

Clyde reveals the bucolic side of its character further upstream. (p154)

Benmore Botanic Garden Tucked away in a fold of the hills in the heart of the Cowal peninsula, this Victorian garden is a riot of colour in spring and early summer. (p259)

Scotland's Secret Bunker It's back to the Cold War in this chilling but fascinating nuclear hideout hidden beneath a field in the middle of rural Fife. (p200)

Islands

Scotland has more than 700 islands scattered around its shore. While the vast majority of visitors stick to the larger, better-known ones such as Arran, Skye, Mull and Lewis, it's often the smaller, lesser-known islands that provide the real highlights.

Iona Beautiful, peaceful (once the day trippers have left) and of huge historic and cultural importance, Iona is the jewel of the Hebrides. (p293)

Eigg The most intriguing of the Small Isles, with its miniature mountain, massacre cave and singing sands. (p351)

Jura Wild and untamed, with more deer than people, and a dangerous whirlpool at its northern end. (p277)

Isle of May Just a mile long, this spot off the Fife coast erupts to the clamour of tens of thousands of puffins in spring and summer. (p199)

Natural Wonders

Scotland's stunning landscapes harbour many awe-inspiring natural features, including spectacular sea stacks and rock formations, thundering waterfalls, impressive gorges and swirling tidal whirlpools.

Old Man of Hoy While most of the Orkneys is fairly flat, Hoy is rugged and rocky; its spectacular west coast includes Britain's tallest sea stack. (p422)

Corryvreckan Whirlpool One of the world's three most powerful tidal whirlpools, squeezed between Jura and Scarba. (p279)

Falls of Measach A trembling suspension bridge provides a scary viewpoint for one of Scotland's most impressive waterfalls. (p378)

Quiraing This postglacial jumble of pinnacles and landslip blocks in northern Skye is one of the weirdest landscapes in the country. (p395)

Month by Month

January

The nation shakes off its Hogmanay hangover and gets back to work, but only until Burns Night comes along. It's still cold and dark, but the skiing can be good.

🍴 Burns Night

Suppers all over the country (and the world for that matter) are held on 25 January to celebrate the anniversary of national poet Robert Burns, with much eating of haggis, drinking of whisky and reciting of poetry.

🎆 Celtic Connections

Glasgow hosts the world's largest winter music festival, a celebration of Celtic music, dance and culture, with participants from all over the globe. Held mid- to late January. See www.celticconnections.com.

🎆 Up Helly Aa

Half of Shetland dresses up with horned helmets and battleaxes in this spectacular re-enactment of a Viking fire festival, with a torchlit procession leading to the burning of a full-size Viking longship. Held in Lerwick on the last Tuesday in January. See www.uphellyaa.org.

February

The coldest month of the year is usually the best for hill walking, ice-climbing and skiing. The days are getting longer now, and snowdrops begin to bloom.

🏉 Six Nations Rugby Tournament

Scotland, England, Wales, Ireland, France and Italy battle it out in this prestigious tournament, held February to March; home games played at Murrayfield, Edinburgh. See www.rbs6nations.com.

🎆 Fort William Mountain Festival

The UK's Outdoor Capital celebrates the peak of the winter season with ski and snowboard learning workshops, talks by famous climbers, kids' events and a festival of mountaineering films. See www.mountain-filmfestival.co.uk.

April

The bluebell woods on the shores of Loch Lomond come into flower, ospreys arrive at their Loch Garten nest. Weather improving, though heavy showers are still common.

🏉 Rugby Sevens

A series of weekend, seven-a-side rugby tournaments held in various towns throughout the Borders region in April and May, kicking off with Melrose in early April. Fast and furious rugby (sevens was invented here), crowded pubs and great craic. See www.melrose7s.com.

May

Wildflowers on the Hebridean machair, hawthorn hedges in bloom and cherry blossom in city parks – Scottish weather is often at its best in May.

✨ Burns an' a' That

Ayrshire towns are the venues for performances of poetry and music, children's events, art exhibitions and more in celebrations of the Scottish bard. See www.burnsfestival.com.

✨ Spirit of Speyside

Based in the Moray town of Dufftown, this festival of whisky, food and music involves five days of distillery tours, knocking back the 'water of life', cooking, art and outdoor activities; held late April to early May in Moray and Speyside. See www.spiritofspeyside.com.

June

Argyllshire is ablaze with pink rhododendron blooms as the long summer evenings stretch on till 11pm. Border towns are strung with bunting to mark gala days and Common Ridings.

✨ Common Ridings

Following the age-old tradition that commemorates the ancient conflict with England, horsemen and -women ride the old boundaries of common lands, along with parades, marching bands and street parties. Held in various Border towns; Jedburgh (www.jethartcallantsfestival.com) is one of the biggest and best.

✨ Glasgow Festivals

June is Glasgow's version of the Edinburgh festival, when the city hosts three major events – **West End Festival** (www.westendfestival.co.uk), Glasgow's biggest music and arts

event; **Glasgow International Jazz Festival** (www.jazzfest.co.uk); and **Glasgow Mela** (www.glasgowmela.com), a celebration of the city's Asian community.

July

School holidays begin, as does the busiest time of year for resort towns. High season for Shetland birdwatchers.

✨ T in the Park

Held annually since 1994, and headlined by world-class acts such as the Who, REM, Eminem and Kasabian, this major music festival is Scotland's answer to Glastonbury; held over a mid-July weekend at Strathallan Castle, near Gleneagles. See www.tinthepark.com.

August

Festival time in Edinburgh and the city is crammed with visitors. On the west coast, this is the peak month for sighting Minke whales and basking sharks.

✨ Edinburgh Festivals

You name it, Edinburgh has a festival event that covers it – books, art, theatre, music, comedy, dance, and the **Military Tattoo** (www.edintattoo.co.uk). The overlapping **International Festival** and **Fringe** keep the city jumping from the first week in August to the first week in September. See www.edinburghfestivals.co.uk.

September

School holidays are over, midges are dying off, wild brambles are ripe for picking in the hedgerows, and the weather is often dry and mild – an excellent time of year for outdoor pursuits.

☉ Braemar Gathering

The biggest and most famous Highland Games in the Scottish calendar, traditionally attended by members of the Royal Family. Highland dancing, bagpipe-playing and caber-tossing; held early September in Braemar, Royal Deeside. See www.braemargathering.org.

December

Darkness falls mid-afternoon as the shortest day approaches. The often cold and wet weather is relieved by Christmas and New Year festivities.

🏃 Hogmanay

Christmas celebrations in Edinburgh (www.edinburghschristmas.com) culminate in a huge street party on Hogmanay (31 December). The fishing town of Stonehaven echoes an ancient, pre-Christian tradition with its procession of fireball-swinging locals who parade to the harbour and fling their blazing orbs into the sea (www.stonehavenfireballs.co.uk).

Itineraries

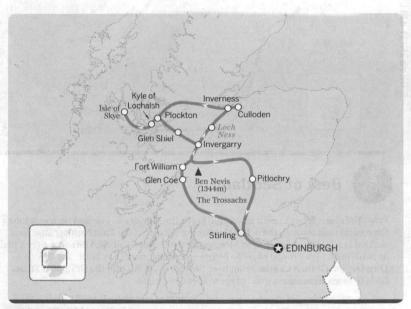

 A Highland Fling

No trip to Scotland would be complete without a visit to **Edinburgh**, and even if your Scottish trip lasts only a week, the capital is worth two days of your time. On day three, head northwest to **Stirling** to see Scotland's other great castle, then on to the **Trossachs** for your first taste of Highland scenery (overnight in Callander).

Day four starts with a scenic drive north via Crianlarich, **Glen Coe** and **Fort William**, then along the Great Glen to **Loch Ness** in time for an afternoon visiting Urquhart Castle and the Loch Ness Centre & Exhibition. An evening cruise on Loch Ness rounds off the day before spending the night in **Inverness**, on picturesque River Ness.

On day five, spend the morning visiting **Culloden Battlefield**, then drive west via Achnasheen and **Plockton** to **Kyle of Lochalsh** and cross the bridge to the **Isle of Skye**. Devote day six to exploring Skye – there will be time for a visit to Dunvegan Castle and a tour of the Trotternish peninsula.

Day seven is the long drive back south – the scenic route goes via **Glen Shiel**, Invergarry, Spean Bridge (pause at the Commando Monument), Laggan and then south on the A9 to Edinburgh, with a stop in **Pitlochry**.

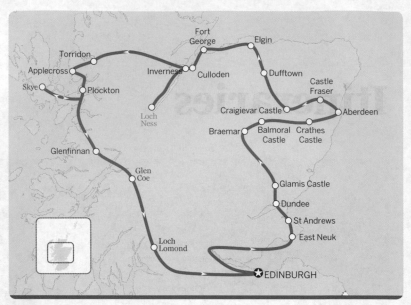

 Best of Scotland

From **Edinburgh** head north across the Forth Road Bridge to Fife and turn east along the coastal road through the delightful fishing villages of the **East Neuk** (pause for a seafood lunch at Anstruther or St Monans) to the home of golf, **St Andrews**. Stay a night or two – heck, play a round of golf – before continuing north across the Tay Bridge to **Dundee** and **Glamis Castle**. From here the A93 leads through the Grampian Mountains to reach **Braemar**, a good place to spend the night.

A feast of castles lies ahead as you make your way east along Royal Deeside – take your time and visit (at the very least) the royal residence of **Balmoral Castle** and the fairy tale **Crathes Castle**. Then overnight at the granite city of **Aberdeen**.

Now strike west again along the A944, making small detours to visit **Castle Fraser** and **Craigievar Castle** before turning north to **Dufftown** in the heart of Speyside. Base yourself here for at least a day while you explore the many whisky distilleries nearby – also try the Quaich whisky bar at the nearby Craigellachie Hotel.

Head northwest to **Elgin** and its magnificent ruined cathedral, then west on the A96 visiting **Fort George** and **Culloden** on the way to Inverness (with maybe a stopover in Nairn). **Inverness** itself is worth a night or two and there's the opportunity for a side trip to **Loch Ness** (Drumnadrochit for monster spotters, Dores Inn for foodies).

Now for a glorious drive from Inverness to **Torridon** via Kinlochewe through some of the country's finest mountain scenery; try to spend a night at the Torridon hotel. Then head south via **Applecross** and the pretty village of **Plockton** to Kyle of Lochalsh and the bridge to **Skye**.

Spend two days exploring Scotland's most famous island before taking the ferry from Armadale to Mallaig, and follow the Road to the Isles in reverse, stopping to visit **Glenfinnan**, where Bonnie Prince Charlie raised his Highland army in 1745. Overnight at Fort William, and drive back to Edinburgh via the scenic road through **Glen Coe** and and along the bonnie banks of **Loch Lomond**.

Top: South Uist (p404)

Bottom: Loch Torridon (p380)

BILLY CURRIE PHOTOGRAPHY / GETTY IMAGES ©

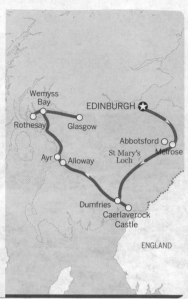

Island Hopscotch
1 WEEK

This route is usually done by car, but it also makes a brilliant cycling tour (270 miles, including the 60 miles from Ullapool to Inverness train station, making both start and finish accessible by rail).

From **Oban** it's a five-hour ferry crossing to **Barra**; book a night's stay here. Then, after a visit to Kisimul Castle and a tour around the island, take the ferry to **South Uist**. Walk the wild beaches of the west coast, sample the local seafood and perhaps go fishing on the island's trout lochs. Continue through Benbecula and **North Uist**, prime birdwatching country.

Overnight at **Lochmaddy** on North Uist (if you're camping or hostelling, a night at **Berneray** is a must) before taking the ferry to **Harris**, whose west coast has some of the most spectacular beaches in Scotland. The road continues north from **Tarbert** (good hotels) through rugged hills to **Lewis.**

Loop west via the **Callanish Standing Stones** and **Arnol Blackhouse museum**. Spend your final night in **Stornoway** (eat at Digby Chick), then take the ferry to Ullapool for a scenic drive to **Inverness**.

Border Raid
5 DAYS

From **Edinburgh** your first objective should be a visit to Sir Walter Scott's former home at **Abbotsford**, followed by a traipse around the beautiful Border abbeys of **Melrose** and nearby Dryburgh; Melrose is a charming place to stay the night, with a choice of good hotels and eating places.

Next morning head west along the A708 to Moffat, passing through glorious scenery around St Mary's Loch. Continue to **Dumfries** (and stop for the night), where you can visit the first of several sights related to Scotland's national poet Robert Burns, and make a short side trip to see spectacular **Caerlaverock Castle**.

Take the A76 northwest towards Ayr, and spend the rest of day three in **Alloway** visiting the birthplace of Robert Burns (and other Burns-related sites); nearby **Ayr** has plenty of accommodation options.

North now to **Wemyss Bay** and the ferry to **Rothesay** on the Isle of Bute, where you can visit stunning Mount Stuart, one of Scotland's most impressive stately homes. Spend the night on the island, then return to the mainland and head east to **Glasgow**.

Plan Your Trip

Walking in Scotland

Scotland's wild, dramatic scenery and varied landscape has made walking a hugely popular pastime for locals and tourists alike. There really is something for everyone, from after-breakfast strolls to the popular sport of Munro bagging.

Planning

For gentle walks along clearly defined tracks, the most planning you'll need to do is take a look at the weather forecast and decide how many layers you'll need to wear. Highland hikers should be properly equipped and cautious, as the weather can become vicious at any time of year. After rain, peaty soil can become boggy, so always wear stout shoes or boots and carry extra food and drink – many unsuspecting walkers have had to survive an unplanned night in the open. Don't depend on mobile phones (although carrying one with you is a good idea, and can be a lifesaver if you get a signal). If necessary, leave a note with your route and expected time of return on the dashboard of your car.

When to Go

The best time of year for hill walking is usually May to September, although snow can fall on the highest summits even in midsummer. Winter walking on the higher hills of Scotland requires the use of an ice axe and crampons and is for experienced mountaineers only.

Access & Rights of Way

There is a tradition of relatively free access to open country in Scotland, a

Essential Hill-Walking Gear

☐ Good waterproofs

☐ Spare warm clothing

☐ Map and compass

☐ Mobile phone (but don't rely on it)

☐ First-aid kit

☐ Head torch

☐ Whistle (for emergencies)

☐ Spare food and drink

☐ Bivvy bag

Safety Checklist

☐ Check the weather forecast first

☐ Let someone know your plans

☐ Set your pace and objective to suit the slowest member of your party

☐ Don't be afraid to turn back if it's too difficult

tradition that was enshrined in law in the 2003 Land Reform (Scotland) Bill, popularly known as 'the right to roam'. The **Scottish Outdoor Access Code** (www.outdooraccess-scotland.com) states that everyone has the right to be on most land and inland waters, providing they act responsibly. You should avoid areas where you might disrupt or disturb wild-life, lambing (generally mid-April to the end of May), grouse shooting (from 12 August to the third week in October) or deer stalking (1 July to 15 February, but the peak period is August to October). You can get up-to-date information on deer stalking in various areas through the **Heading for the Scottish Hills** (www.outdooraccess-scotland.com/hftsh) service. You are also free to pitch a tent almost anywhere that doesn't cause inconven-ience to others or damage to property, as long as you stay no longer than two or three nights in any one spot, take all litter away with you, and keep well away from houses and roads. (Note that this right does not extend to the use of motor-ised vehicles.)

Local authorities aren't required to list and map rights of way, so they're not shown on Ordnance Survey (OS) maps of Scotland, as they are in England and Wales. However, the **Scottish Rights of Way & Access Society** (☎0131-558 1222; www.scotways.com; 24 Annandale St, Edinburgh EH7 4AN) keeps records of these routes, provides and maintains signpost-ing, and publicises them in its guidebook, *Scottish Hill Tracks*.

Best Walks
West Highland Way

This classic hike – the country's most popular long-distance path – stretches for 96 miles through some of Scotland's most spectacular scenery, from Milngavie (mull-guy), on the northwestern fringes of Glasgow, to Fort William.

The route begins in the Lowlands but the greater part of the trail is among the mountains, lochs and fast-flowing rivers of the western Highlands. After following the eastern shore of Loch Lomond and pass-ing Crianlarich and Tyndrum, the route crosses the vast wilderness of Rannoch Moor and reaches Fort William via Glen Nevis, in the shadow of Britain's highest peak, Ben Nevis.

The path is easy to follow, making use of old drovers roads (along which Highland cattle were once driven to Lowland mar-kets), an old military road (built by troops to help subdue the Highlands in the 18th century) and disused railway lines.

Best done from south to north, the walk takes about six or seven days. Many people round it off with an ascent of Ben Nevis. You need to be properly equipped with good boots, waterproofs, maps, a compass, and food and drink for the north-ern part of the walk. Midge repellent is also essential.

It's possible to do just a day's hike along part of the trail. For example, the Loch Lomond Water Bus allows you to walk the section from Rowardennan to Inversnaid, returning to your starting point by boat.

OFFICIAL LONG-DISTANCE FOOTPATHS

WALK	DISTANCE	FEATURES	DURATION	DIFFICULTY
Fife Coastal Path	78 miles	Firth of Forth, undulating country	5-6 days	easy
Great Glen Way	73 miles	Loch Ness, canal paths, forest tracks	4 days	easy
Pilgrims Way	25 miles	Machars peninsula, standing stones, burial mounds	2-3 days	easy
St Cuthbert's Way	62 miles	follows the path of a famous saint	6-7 days	medium
Southern Upland Way	212 miles	remote hills & moorlands	9-14 days	medium-hard
Speyside Way	66 miles	follows river, whisky distilleries	3-4 days	easy-medium
West Highland Way	96 miles	spectacular scenery, mountains & lochs	6-8 days	medium

TOP 10 SHORT WALKS

→ **Quiraing** (Isle of Skye) One to two hours; bizarre rock pinnacles.

→ **Steall Meadows** (Glen Nevis) One to two hours; waterfall beneath Ben Nevis.

→ **Lost Valley** (Glen Coe) Three hours; impressive mountain scenery.

→ **Conic Hill** (Loch Lomond) Two hours; views over Loch Lomond.

→ **Loch an Eilein** (Aviemore) One hour; lovely lochan amid Scots pines.

→ **Linn of Quoich** (Braemar) One hour; rocky gorge and waterfall.

→ **Plodda Falls** (Cannich) One hour; dizzying viewpoint above waterfall.

→ **Duncansby Head** (John O'Groats) One hour; spectacular sea stacks.

→ **Stac Pollaidh** (Coigach) Two to four hours; ascent of miniature mountain.

→ **Old Man of Hoy** (Orkney) Three hours; Britain's tallest sea stack.

The West Highland Way Official Guide by Bob Aitken and Roger Smith is the most comprehensive guidebook, while the Harveys map *West Highland Way* shows the entire route in a single waterproof map sheet.

Accommodation shouldn't be too difficult to find, though between Bridge of Orchy and Kinlochleven it's limited. At peak times (May, July and August), book accommodation in advance. There are some youth hostels and bunkhouses on or near the path, and it's possible to camp in some parts. A list of accommodation is available from tourist offices.

For more information check out the website www.west-highland-way.co.uk.

Speyside Way

This long-distance footpath follows the course of the River Spey, one of Scotland's most famous salmon-fishing rivers. It starts at Buckie and first follows the coast to Spey Bay, east of Elgin, then runs inland along the river to Aviemore in the Cairngorms (with branches to Tomintoul and Dufftown).

The 66-mile route has been dubbed the 'Whisky Trail' as it passes near a number of distilleries, including The Glenlivet and Glenfiddich, which are open to the public. If you stop at them all, the walk may take considerably longer than the usual three or four days! The first 11 miles from Buckie to Fochabers makes a good half-day hike (allow four to five hours).

The Speyside Way, a guidebook by Jacquetta Megarry and Jim Strachan, describes the route in detail. Check out the route at www.speysideway.org.

Isle of Skye

Skye is a walker's paradise, criss-crossed with trails both easy and strenuous that lead you through some of the country's most spectacular scenery.

The Quiraing (3.5 miles; two to three hours) Start at the parking area at the highest point of the minor road between Staffin and Uig. A clear path leads northeast towards the obvious pinnacles, but after 200m or so strike north up the hill to reach another path that leads across the summit of Meall na Suiramach with fantastic views down into the Quiraing. The path continues to a saddle and break in the cliffs where you can descend and return to your starting point through the midst of the pinnacles.

Kilmarie to Coruisk (11 miles; at least six hours) This is one of the most spectacular and challenging of Skye's low-level walks. Begin at a parking area just south of Kilmarie, on the Broadford to Elgol road. A stony track leads over a hill pass to the gorgeous bay of Camasunary, and continues on the far side of the Camasunary River – at low tide you can cross on stepping stones, but if the tide is high you'll have to splash across further upstream. The notorious Bad Step is opposite the north end of the little island in Loch na Cuilce; it's a rock slab that drops straight into the sea, where you scramble out onto a shelf and along a rising crack (the secret is to drop down leftward when you reach a niche in the crack). There are no further obstacles, and 15 minutes later you arrive at Loch Coruisk, one of the wildest and most remote spots in Scotland. Return by the same route, or arrange in advance to be picked up by one of the tour boats from Elgol.

STEVEN FALLON: CHAMPION MUNRO BAGGER

Steven Fallon (☎07795 146400; www.stevenfallon.co.uk; per person from £50), a hill walker, fell runner and mountain guide who lives in Edinburgh, is the world's most prolific Munro bagger, having climbed all of Scotland's 282 Munros (peaks of 3000ft and higher) no fewer than 15 times.

Do you have a favourite Munro? Practically anything in the northwest Highlands could feature – they tend to be pointy with great views. I'd single out Slioch by Loch Maree; Beinn Alligin, Liathach and Beinn Eighe in Torridon; the Five Sisters of Kintail; and all of the mountains in the Cuillin of Skye. However, my most-most-favourite has to be Ladhar Bheinn in the Knoydart Peninsula. It's pretty remote and to reach it requires a long walk-in along the southern shore of Loch Hourn. It's just so beautiful there. The mountain itself is complex with corries and ridges, and the summit has great views over Eigg to Skye and beyond.

Which is the easiest Munro, and which is the hardest? With only 430m of ascent over 5km, the easiest Munros have to be the Cairnwell and Carn Aosda from the Glenshee ski resort. Good paths and ski-tows make for simple navigation over these two peaks, and if you time it right, you'll be back at the cafe in time for something to eat. The most technically difficult has to be the aptly named Inaccessible Pinnacle in the Cuillin Hills on Skye. It's a clamber up a long fin of rock with sensational, tremble-inducing exposure, followed by an abseil down a short but vertical drop. Most Munro-baggers will need the help of their rock-climbing friends or hire a guide.

Check out Steven's website for the 10 easiest Munro walks (click on Hill Lists and Maps/Munros/Easiest Munros).

Munro Bagging

At the end of the 19th century an eager hill walker, Sir Hugh Munro, published a list of Scottish mountains over 3000ft (914m) and over time his name has become used to describe any Scottish mountain over 3000ft. Many keen hill walkers now set themselves the target of reaching the summit of (or bagging) all of Scotland's 282 Munros.

To the uninitiated it may seem odd that Munro baggers see venturing into mist, cloud and driving rain as time well spent. However, for those who can add one or more ticks to their list, the vagaries of the weather are part of the enjoyment, at least in retrospect. Munro bagging is, of course, more than merely ticking off a list – it takes you to some of the wildest and most beautiful corners of Scotland.

Once you've bagged all the Munros you can move on to the Corbetts – hills over 2500ft (700m), with a drop of at least 500ft (150m) on all sides – and the Donalds, lowland hills over 2000ft (610m). And for connoisseurs of the diminutive, there are the McPhies: 'eminences in excess of 300ft (90m)' on the Isle of Colonsay.

Further Information

Every tourist office has leaflets (free or for a nominal charge) of suggested walks that take in local points of interest. Lonely Planet's *Walking in Scotland* is a comprehensive resource, covering short walks and long-distance paths; its *Walking in Britain* guide covers Scottish walks, too. For general advice, VisitScotland produces a **Walking Scotland** (http://walking.visitscotland.com) website that describes numerous routes in various parts of the country, and also offers safety tips and other useful information.

Other useful resources:

Mountaineering Council of Scotland (www.mcofs.org.uk)

Ordnance Survey (www.ordnancesurvey. co.uk)

Ramblers' Association Scotland (www. ramblers.org.uk/scotland)

Scottish Mountaineering Club (www.smc. org.uk)

WalkHighlands (www.walkhighlands.co.uk) Online database of more than 1500 walks complete with maps and detailed descriptions.

Plan Your Trip

Golf

A round in the home of golf isn't about nostalgia: the sport is part of Scotland's fabric. Playing here is a unique experience; you're almost guaranteed heart-stopping scenery and a friendly atmosphere. Scotland's tradition of public courses means that outstanding golf is usually accompanied by sociable moments and warm hospitality.

History

The first known mention of golf is from 1457, when James II banned it to prevent archery, crucial for military reasons, being ignored as an activity. The oldest course is at Musselburgh and the oldest club is the Honourable Company of Edinburgh Golfers (1744), at Muirfield. In 1754, the Royal and Ancient of St Andrews, which became the game's governing body, was born.

Modern golf really evolved in the late 19th and early 20th centuries. Legendary figures such as James Braid and Old Tom Morris designed courses across Britain; the latter was a founding figure of the Open Championship and won it four times.

Scotland is also very much at the forefront of international professional golf, with high-profile events such as the 2014 Ryder Cup, 2015 Open and 2018 Open held at Gleneagles, St Andrews, and Royal Troon respectively.

Where to Play

With more golf courses per capita than any other country, Scotland offers a bewildering choice. A selection of world golf's most iconic courses offers some of the sport's most famous holes, with deep, challenging bunkers where you might only get out backwards, if at all. But there's also great pleasure to be had on simpler, local

When to Play

Summer is most enjoyable – long daylight hours mean you can tee off at 6am or 7pm. Courses are busy in these months though: a good compromise is to play in May or September.

Resources

www.visitscotland.com/golf Useful, and also details discount golf passes. VisitScotland publishes Golf in Scotland, a free annual brochure listing courses, costs and accommodation information.

www.scotlands-golf-courses.com Good for investigating courses to play

Costs

A round at an unfashionable rural course may cost as little as £10. Showpiece courses charge green fees of £160 to £230 in high season.

It's more economical in winter, it's often cheaper midweek, and 'twilight' rates (teeing off after 4pm or so) can save you up to 50% at some clubs.

fairways eked out by small Highland-or-island communities where you have to hope the sheep or deer nibbling at the green understand your cry of 'Fore!'.

Practical Tips

➡ Handicap certificates are often unnecessary, but bring one, along with an introduction letter from your home club, for more upmarket clubs. Some courses have a minimum handicap requirement.

➡ Links present unique challenges with their undulating fairways, unforgiving rough, vertical bunkers and enormous greens. Exposed and unprotected, they are at the mercy of wind and weather: a healthy sea breeze means that approaches into scarily-angled greens need meticulous execution. Listen to locals.

➡ Dress regulations aren't generally too rigorous – think smart casual as a norm. Most places prohibit jeans, trainers and T-shirts, and several don't look kindly on shorts. Mobile-phone use on course is frowned upon. Stricter dress regulations may apply for the clubhouse.

➡ Club hire is usually available, but it's not cheap (up to £70 on elite courses), so if you'll play a few rounds, it's worth bringing your own.

➡ Motorised carts are widely available, but are less used than in the USA or Australia. They tend to be hired mostly by people with mobility difficulties and are prohibited on some courses.

➡ Book rounds at desirable courses well ahead – many months in the case of prestige links such as the Old Course at St Andrews.

➡ Caddies can help greatly. They know the layout, and will advise when to attack the pin and when caution is best. Their local lore and fund

---

CATRIONA MATTHEW, SCOTTISH PROFESSIONAL GOLFER, WINNER OF THE 2009 WOMEN'S BRITISH OPEN

Your favourite course in Scotland? And why? St Andrews is my favourite. The course gets better every time you play it. It is easy to appreciate how naturally it fits into the land with bunkers positioned perfectly and the history associated with the course makes it a thrill to play for every level of golfer.

What's different about golf in Scotland compared with other countries? Golf in Scotland is all about playing courses that fit into the natural landscape, that are designed to be played in all types of challenging weather conditions. The welcome received is always second to none and virtually every course in the country is accessible to visitors.

Scotland's most scenic course? I believe North Berwick West Links. It also happens to be my home course and the views in my opinion are even better than Pebble Beach in California.

Where would you recommend for a high handicapper who wants to experience Scottish golf without posting 130? An ideal course for a high handicapper not wanting to post a huge score is Gullane No 3. It is a great little course with par around 65. The views are as good as the main course (No 1) and it is still challenging.

For someone that's never played a links course, what would be your words of advice? Take a local caddie to help you. Most clubs have members who caddy in the summer and they are very knowledgeable and make the round both more interesting and fun.

One golden tip to an amateur to help us reach the clubhouse in better shape? Don't try and swing any harder when playing in wind. The golden rule is to take one club more than you think and swing it easier.

Any etiquette tips for someone who's never played golf in Britain? Please take your hats off when you go into the clubhouse after your round. Let quicker groups behind you play through. Those two tips will make you popular both on and off the course!

Where's Scotland's best 19th hole? The Old Clubhouse in Gullane is a great place after a round of golf at either Gullane or North Berwick. A warm and friendly pub with great selection of food.

TEN OF THE BEST

➜ **St Andrews** (www.standrews.org.uk; Golf Pl) The public Old Course is the game's spiritual home and you can't help but be awed by the history and atmosphere here. The 17th – the Road Hole – is famous for its blind drive, nasty bunker and seriously sloping green. Several other courses for all abilities make this Scotland's premium golfing destination. Open venue in 2015.

➜ **Turnberry** (☑01655-331000; www.turnberry.co.uk; Maidens Rd, Turnberry) Marvellous views out to Ailsa Craig make this resort one of Scotland's finest. Pack a spare for the nasty 9th on the Ailsa course, where your ball will sleep with the fish unless you manage the 200-yard carry off the tee. Luckily there's the renowned Halfway Hut to drown your sorrows before taking on the 10th.

➜ **Carnoustie** (☑01241-802270; www.carnoustiegolflinks.co.uk; 20 Links Parade, Carnoustie, Angus) Widely known as Scotland's toughest challenge and nicknamed Car-nasty, as much for near-constant winds as for the course itself. It ain't over till it's over here: the Barry Burn on the 18th has undone many a leader in social games and Open Championships alike.

➜ **Loch Lomond** (☑01436-655555; www.lochlomond.com; Luss) On the shores of the famous loch, this – not a links – has a picturesque, romantic location – including an impressive clubhouse and a ruined castle by the 18th green – but is a real test, with plenty of water hazards and cunningly placed sand traps.

➜ **Royal Troon** (☑01292-311555; www.royaltroon.com; Craigend Rd, Troon; ⊗mid-Apr–mid-Oct) Making its way along the dunes, this classic seaside venue could define a links course. The short 8th is known as the Postage Stamp for its tiny, well-protected green. Open venue in 2016.

➜ **Royal Dornoch** (☑01862-810219; www.royaldornoch.com; Golf Rd, Dornoch; summer green fee £120) Up north, the sumptuous championship course rewards the journey with picture-perfect links scenery and a quieter pace to things. If this was near the southern population centres, many would rate it Scotland's best.

➜ **Machrihanish** (☑01586-810000; www.machrihanishdunes.com; Campbeltown; green fee around £70) On the Kintyre peninsula, this Old-Tom-Morris-designed course is one of Scotland's most scenic. There's no easing into your round here; strike long and clean on the 1st or you'll be on the beach – literally.

➜ **Muirfield** (☑01620-842123; www.muirfield.org.uk; Duncur Rd, Muirfield, Gullane) Handy for Edinburgh, this private course on land reclaimed from the sea allocates some public tee times. It's one of Scotland's more traditional – and many would say outrageously sexist – institutions.

➜ **Gleneagles** (☑01764-662231; www.gleneagles.com/golf; Auchterarder, Perthshire) Three brilliant courses and a five-star hotel with truly excellent service make this legendary Perthshire destination a great choice for golfing breaks. Plenty on offer for golf widowers, widows and/or kids. Ryder Cup venue in 2014.

➜ **Trump International** (☑01358-743300; www.trumpgolfscotland.com; Balmedie, Aberdeenshire) Environmentally-controversial course near Aberdeen featuring spectacular high-dune scenery.

of anecdotes also makes for a special Scottish experience. Caddies should be booked, though you may be able to hire one on the day. Think around £50 plus tip for the round.

➜ Some courses have starters, whose job is to get your group out on time. It's worth chatting to these savvy folk for tips on not embarrassing yourself off the 1st tee with everyone watching.

➜ Solo players may be put into existing groups. Some busier courses won't allow single players to book, allocating places in twosomes or threesomes on a first-come, first-served basis.

Regions at a Glance

Which regions of Scotland you choose to visit will naturally depend on how much time you have, and whether you've been here before. First-time visitors will want to squeeze in as many highlights as possible, so could try following the well-trodden route through Edinburgh, the Trossachs, Pitlochry, Inverness, Loch Ness and the Isle of Skye.

It takes considerably more time to explore the further-flung corners of the country, but ruined abbeys and castles of the Borders, the jaw-dropping scenery of the northwest Highlands and the gorgeous white-sand beaches of the Outer Hebrides are less crowded and ultimately more rewarding. The long journey to Orkney or Shetland means that you'll want to devote more than just a day or two to these regions.

Edinburgh

Culture
History
Food

Festival City

The Scottish capital is a city of high culture where, each summer, the world's biggest arts festival gets rave reviews and box-office records.

Scotland's Capital

Perched on a brooding black crag overlooking the city centre, Edinburgh Castle has played a pivotal role in Scottish history. The growth of the city from its medieval origins and the parallel development of Scottish nationhood is documented in its excellent museums.

Eating Out

Edinburgh has more restaurants per head of population than any city in the UK. Eateries range from stylish but inexpensive bistros and cafes to gourmet restaurants with Michelin stars.

p42

Glasgow

Museums
Music
Design

Kelvingrove Art Gallery & Museum

Glasgow's mercantile, industrial and academic history has left the city with the grand Victorian cathedral of culture, Kelvingrove, boasting a bewildering variety of exhibits.

King Tut's Wah Wah Hut

Glasgow is the star of Scotland's live-music scene, with legendary venues such as King Tut's Wah Wah Hut staging gigs from local start-ups to top international acts.

Charles Rennie Mackintosh

With Charles Rennie Mackintosh's iconic buildings, the centre's grand Victorian architecture, fashion boutiques of the Italian Centre and design exhibitions at the Lighthouse, Glasgow is Scotland's most stylish city.

p102

Southern Scotland

Historic Buildings
Stately Homes
Activities

The Great Abbeys

Ruined abbeys dot Scotland's southern border. The Gothic ruins of Melrose, Jedburgh, Dryburgh and Sweetheart and the martial towers of Hermitage Castle, Caerlaverock Castle and Smailholm are testimony to a turbulent past.

Dumfries House

This region is rich in Adam-designed mansions such as Culzean Castle, Paxton House, Floors Castle and Mellerstain House, but Dumfries House takes top place.

Mountain Biking

The rounded hills of the Southern Uplands can't compete with the Highlands for scenery but the 7stanes trail centres offer some of the UK's best and most challenging mountain biking.

p138

Central Scotland

Golf
Fishing Villages
Castles

St Andrews

Scotland is the home of golf, and the Old Course at St Andrews is on every golfer's wish list. The game has been played here for more than 600 years; the Royal & Ancient Golf Club, the game's governing body, was founded in 1754.

East Neuk of Fife

The scenic coastline of the East Neuk of Fife is dotted with picturesque harbours and quaint fishing villages, their history recounted in the excellent Scottish Fisheries Museum in Anstruther.

Stirling Castle

Some say that Stirling has the finest castle in the country, but the region has plenty of others, including Scone Palace, Kellie Castle, Doune Castle and St Andrews Castle.

p178

Northeast Scotland

Whisky
Castles
History

Speyside Distilleries

Don't leave Scotland without visiting a whisky distillery; the Speyside region, around Dufftown in Moray, is the epicentre of the industry. More than 50 distilleries open during the Spirit of Speyside festival; many open all year.

Scottish Baronial Style

Aberdeenshire and Moray have the greatest concentration of Scottish Baronial castles in the country, from the turreted splendour of Craigievar and Fyvie to the elegance of Crathie and Balmoral.

Pictish Stones

The Picts carved mysterious stones (dating from the 7th and 8th centuries) which can be seen in places such as Aberlemno and St Vigeans Museum (near Arbroath).

p212

Southern Highlands & Islands

Wildlife
Islands
Food

Whales and Eagles

See some of Scotland's most spectacular wildlife, from magnificent white-tailed sea eagles in Mull, to minke whales and basking sharks cruising the west coast. Beavers have also been re-introduced into the wild here.

Island-Hopping

Island-hopping is one of the best ways to explore the western seaboard, and the cluster of islands here – Islay, Jura, Mull, Iona, Colonsay, Coll and Tiree – provide a brilliant introduction.

Seafood

Whether you dine at a top restaurant in Oban or Tobermory, or eat with your fingers on the harbourside, the seafood is one of the region's biggest drawcards.

p244

Inverness & the Central Highlands

Activities
Royalty
Legends

Hiking & Skiing

The Cairngorm towns of Aviemore and Fort William offer outdoor adventure galore. Be it climbing, walking, biking or skiing, there's something for everyone.

Royal Deeside

The valley of the River Dee between Ballater and Braemar has been associated with the royal family since Queen Victoria acquired Balmoral Castle.

Loch Ness Monster

Scotland's most iconic legend, the Loch Ness monster, lurks here. You might not spot Nessie, but the magnificent scenery of the Great Glen makes a visit worthwhile, as does Culloden battlefield, the undoing of another Scottish legend, Bonnie Prince Charlie.

p299

Northern Highlands & Islands

Scenery
Activities
History

Mountains & Lochs

From the peaks of Assynt and Torridon, to the rock pinnacles of the Cuillin Hills, to the beaches of the Outer Hebrides, the big skies and landscapes of the northern Highlands and islands are the very essence of Scotland.

Kayaking

The northwest's vast spaces are one huge playground for hikers, bikers, climbers and kayakers, providing the chance to see some of the UK's most spectacular wildlife.

The Clearances

The abandoned rural communities of the north teach much about the Clearances, especially Skye Museum of Island Life. Prehistoric remains include the famous standing stones of Callanish.

p356

Orkney & Shetland Islands

History
Wildlife
Music

Skara Brae

These islands have a fascinating Viking heritage and unique prehistoric villages, tombs and stone circles. Skara Brae is northern Europe's best-preserved prehistoric village; Maes Howe is one of Britain's finest Neolithic tombs.

Birdwatching

Shetland is a birdwatcher's paradise, its cliffs teeming in summer with gannets, fulmars, kittiwakes, razorbills and puffins, and Europe's largest colony of Arctic terns.

Folk Tradition

The pubs of Kirkwall, Stromness and Lerwick are fertile ground for exploring the traditional-music scene. Both Orkney and Shetland host annual festivals of folk music.

p408

On the
Road

**Orkney &
Shetland**
p408

**Northern Highlands
& Islands**
p356

**Northeast
Scotland**
p212

**Inverness &
the Central Highlands**
p299

**Southern
Highlands &
Islands**
p244

**Central
Scotland**
p178

Edinburgh
p42

Glasgow
p102

**Southern
Scotland**
p138

Edinburgh

POP 460,400

Includes ➡

Best Places to Eat

➡ Castle Terrace (p82)

➡ Gardener's Cottage (p82)

➡ The Dogs (p82)

➡ Ondine (p82)

➡ Fishers Bistro (p84)

➡ Timberyard (p80)

Best Places to Stay

➡ Witchery by the Castle (p74)

➡ Hotel Missoni (p74)

➡ Sheridan Guest House (p76)

➡ Southside Guest House (p77)

➡ Malone's Old Town Hostel (p73)

Why Go?

Edinburgh is a city that begs to be explored. From the vaults and wynds (narrow lanes) that riddle the Old Town to the urban villages of Stockbridge and Cramond, it's filled with quirky, come-hither nooks that tempt you to walk just a little bit further. And every corner turned reveals sudden views and unexpected vistas – green sunlit hills, a glimpse of rust-red crags, a blue flash of distant sea.

But there's more to Edinburgh than sightseeing – there are top shops, world-class restaurants and a bacchanalia of bars to enjoy. This is a city of pub crawls and impromptu music sessions, mad-for-it clubbing and all-night parties, overindulgence and wandering home through cobbled streets at dawn.

All these superlatives come together at festival time in August, when it seems as if half the world descends on Edinburgh for one enormous party. If you can possibly manage it, join them.

When to Go
Edinburgh

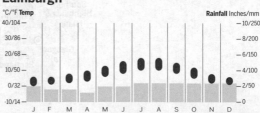

May Good weather (usually), flowers and cherry blossom everywhere and (gasp!) no crowds.

Aug Festival time! Crowded and mad but irresistible.

Dec Christmas decorations, cosy pubs with open fires, ice skating in Princes Street Gardens.

Edinburgh Highlights

❶ Taking in the views from the battlements of **Edinburgh Castle** (p45)

❷ Enjoying the finest of Scottish seafood at **Ondine** (p82) or **Fishers Bistro** (p84)

❸ Nosing around the Queen's private quarters on the former **Royal Yacht Britannia** (p64) at Leith

❹ Listening to live folk music at **Sandy Bell's** (p88)

❺ Trying to decipher the Da Vinci Code at mysterious **Rosslyn Chapel** (p95)

❻ Exploring Edinburgh's subterranean history in the haunted vaults of **South Bridge** (p78) and **Real Mary King's Close** (p53)

❼ Climbing to the summit of the city's miniature mountain, **Arthur's Seat** (p56)

EDINBURGH IN...

Two Days

A two-day trip to Edinburgh should start at **Edinburgh Castle**, followed by a stroll down the **Royal Mile** to the **Scottish Parliament Building** and the **Palace of Holyroodhouse**. You can work up an appetite by climbing **Arthur's Seat**, then satisfy your hunger with dinner at **Ondine** or **Castle Terrace**. On day two spend the morning in the **National Museum of Scotland**, then catch the bus to **Leith** for a visit to the **Royal Yacht Britannia**. In the evening, have dinner at one of Leith's many excellent restaurants, or scare yourself silly on a guided **ghost tour**.

Four Days

Two more days will give you time for a morning stroll around the **Royal Botanic Garden**, followed by a trip to the enigmatic and beautiful **Rosslyn Chapel**, or a relaxing afternoon visit to the seaside village of **Cramond** – bring binoculars (for birdwatching and yacht-spotting) and a book (to read in the sun). Dinner at **Gardener's Cottage** could be before or after your sunset walk to the summit of **Calton Hill**. On day four head out to the pretty harbour village of **Queensferry**, nestled beneath the **Forth Bridges**, and take a cruise to **Inchcolm** island.

History

Edinburgh owes its existence to the Castle Rock, the glacier-worn stump of a long-extinct volcano that provided a near-perfect defensive position guarding the coastal route from northeast England into central Scotland.

In the 7th century the Castle Rock was called Dun Eiden (meaning 'Fort on the Hill Slope'). When it was captured by invaders from the kingdom of Northumbria in northeast England in 638, they took the existing Gaelic name 'Eiden' and tacked it onto their own Old English word for fort, 'burh', to create the name Edinburgh.

Originally a purely defensive site, Edinburgh began to expand in the 12th century when King David I held court at the castle and founded the abbey at Holyrood. The royal court came to prefer Edinburgh to Dunfermline and, as parliament followed the king, Edinburgh became Scotland's capital. The city's first effective town wall was constructed around 1450, enclosing the Old Town as far east as Netherbow and south to the Grassmarket. This overcrowded area – by then the most populous town in Scotland – became a medieval Manhattan, forcing its densely packed inhabitants to build upwards instead of outwards, creating tenements five and six storeys high.

The capital played an important role in the Reformation (1560–1690), led by the Calvinist firebrand John Knox. Mary, Queen of Scots held court in the Palace of Holyroodhouse for six brief years, but when her son James VI succeeded to the English throne in 1603 he moved his court to London. The Act of Union in 1707 further reduced Edinburgh's importance, but its cultural and intellectual life flourished.

In the second half of the 18th century a planned new town was created across the valley to the north of the Old Town. During the Scottish Enlightenment (c 1740–1830), Edinburgh became known as 'a hotbed of genius', inhabited by leading scientists and philosophers such as David Hume and Adam Smith.

In the 19th century the population quadrupled to 400,000, not much less than today's population, and the Old Town's tenements were taken over by refugees from the Highland clearances and the Irish famines. A new ring of crescents and circuses was built to the north of New Town, and grey Victorian terraces spread south of the Old Town.

In the 1920s the city's borders expanded again to encompass Leith in the north, Cramond in the west and the Pentland Hills in the south. Following WWII the city's cultural life blossomed, stimulated by the Edinburgh International Festival and its fellow traveller, the Fringe, both held for the first time in 1947 and now recognised as world-class arts festivals.

Edinburgh entered a new era following the 1997 referendum vote in favour of a devolved Scottish parliament, which first convened in 1999 in a controversial modern building at the foot of the Royal Mile. The 2014 independence referendum saw Scots vote to remain part of the United Kingdom.

◎ Sights

Edinburgh's main attractions are concentrated in the city centre – on and around the Old Town's Royal Mile between the castle and Holyrood, and in the New Town. A major exception is the Royal Yacht Britannia, which is in the redeveloped docklands district of Leith, two miles northeast of the centre.

If you tire of sightseeing, good areas for aimless wandering include the posh suburbs of Stockbridge and Morningside, the pretty riverside village of Cramond and the winding footpaths of Calton Hill and Arthur's Seat.

◎ Old Town

Edinburgh's Old Town (Map p52) stretches along a ridge to the east of the castle, and tumbles down Victoria St to the broad expanse of the Grassmarket. It's a jagged and jumbled maze of masonry riddled with closes (alleys) and wynds, stairs and vaults, and cleft along its spine by the cobbled ravine of the Royal Mile.

Until the founding of the New Town in the 18th century, old Edinburgh was an overcrowded and insanitary hive of humanity squeezed between the boggy ground of the Nor' Loch (North Loch, now drained and occupied by Princes Street Gardens) to the north and the city walls to the south and east. The only way for the town to expand was upwards, and the five- and six-storey tenements that were raised along the Royal Mile in the 16th and 17th centuries were the skyscrapers of their day, remarked upon with wonder by visiting writers such as Daniel Defoe. All classes of society, from beggars to magistrates, lived cheek by jowl in these urban ant nests, the wealthy occupying the middle floors – high enough to be above the noise and stink of the streets, but not so high that climbing the stairs would be too tiring – while the poor squeezed into attics, basements, cellars and vaults amid rats, rubbish and raw sewage.

The renovated Old Town tenements still support a thriving city-centre community, and today the street level is crammed with cafes, restaurants, bars, backpacker hostels and tacky souvenir shops. Few visitors wander beyond the main drag of the Royal Mile,

but it's worth taking time to explore the countless closes that lead into quiet courtyards, often with unexpected views of city, sea and hills.

◎ The Royal Mile

This mile-long street earned its regal nickname in the 16th century when it was used by the king to travel between the castle and the Palace of Holyroodhouse. There are five sections (the Castle Esplanade, Castlehill, Lawnmarket, High St and Canongate), the names of which reflect their historical origins.

★**Edinburgh Castle**   CASTLE
(Map p52; www.edinburghcastle.gov.uk; adult/child incl audioguide £16/9.60; ⊗9.30am-6pm Apr-Sep, to 5pm Oct-Mar, last admission 45min before closing; 🚍23, 27, 41, 42) Edinburgh Castle has played a pivotal role in Scottish history, both as a royal residence – King Malcolm Canmore (r 1058–93) and Queen Margaret first made their home here in the 11th century – and as a military stronghold. The castle last saw military action in 1745; from then until the 1920s it served as the British army's main base in Scotland. Today it is one of Scotland's most atmospheric and popular tourist attractions.

The brooding, black crags of Castle Rock, rising above the western end of Princes St, are the very reason for Edinburgh's existence. This rocky hill was the most easily defended hilltop on the invasion route between England and central Scotland, a route followed by countless armies from the Roman legions of the 1st and 2nd centuries AD to the Jacobite troops of Bonnie Prince Charlie in 1745.

The **Entrance Gateway**, flanked by statues of Robert the Bruce and William Wallace, opens to a cobbled lane that leads up

---

DON'T MISS

CASTLE HIT LIST

If you're pushed for time, here are the top things to see at Edinburgh Castle:

➡ Views from Argyle Battery

➡ One O'Clock Gun

➡ Great Hall

➡ Honours of Scotland

➡ Prisons of War

Edinburgh

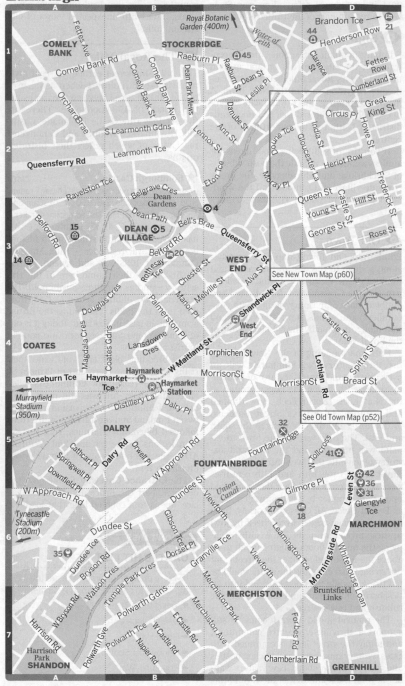

Royal Botanic Garden (400m)

Water of Leith

Brandon Tce
44
Henderson Row 21

COMELY BANK
STOCKBRIDGE
Raeburn Pl 45

Fettes Ave
Comely Bank Rd
Comely Bank Ave
Comely Bank St
Dean Park Mews
Raeburn St
Dean St
Leslie Pl
Danube St
Ann St
Clarence St
Fettes Row
Cumberland St

Circus Pl
Great King St
Howe St
India St
Gloucester La
Heriot Row

S Learmonth Gdns
Learmonth Tce
Lennox St
Eton Tce
Doune Tce
Moray Pl

Queensferry Rd
Queen St
Young St
Castle St
Hill St
Frederick St

Ravelston Tce
Belgrave Cres
Dean Gardens
Dean Path
Bell's Brae
4

George St
Rose St

Belford Rd
15
DEAN VILLAGE 5
Belford Rd
20
Queensferry St

See New Town Map (p60)

14

Rothesay Tce
Chester St
Melville St
WEST END
Alva St
Shandwick Pl

Douglas Cres
Magdala Cres
Coates Gdns
Palmerston Pl
Manor Pl
West End

Castle Tce

COATES
Lansdowne Cres
W Maitland St
Torphichen St
MorrisonSt

Lothian Rd
Spittal St
Bread St

Roseburn Tce
Haymarket
Haymarket Tce
Haymarket Station
MorrisonSt

Murrayfield Stadium (950m)
Distillery La
Dalry Pl

See Old Town Map (p52)

DALRY
Dalry Rd
Orwell Pl
W Approach Rd
Fountainbridge
32

Cathcart Pl
Springwell Pl
Downfield Pl
W Approach Rd
FOUNTAINBRIDGE
Dundee St
W Tollcross
41

Tynecastle Stadium (200m)
Viewforth
Gilmore Pl
27
18
Leven St
42
36
31
Glengyle Tce

35
Dundee St
Dundee Tce
Bryson Rd
Watson Cres
Gibson Tce
Dorset Pl
Granville Tce
Viewforth
Leamington Tce
Morningside Rd
Whitehouse Loan
MARCHMONT

W Bryson Rd
Temple Park Cres
Polwarth Gdns
Merchiston Park
Merchiston Ave
Bruntsfield Links

Harrison Rd
Harrison Park
SHANDON
Polwarth Gve
Polwarth Tce
W Castle Rd
Napier Rd
E Castle Rd
MERCHISTON
Forbes Rd
Chamberlain Rd
GREENHILL

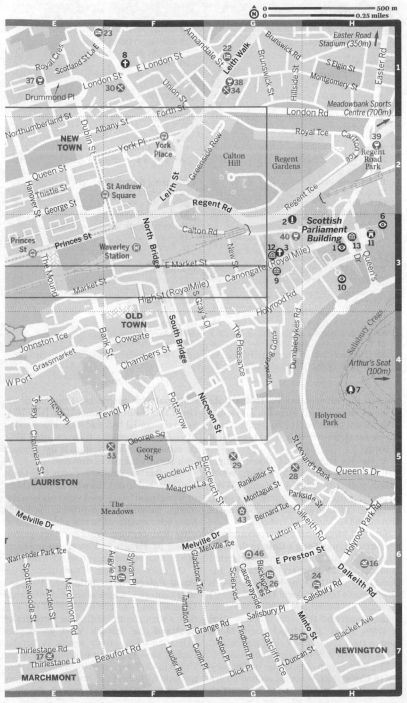

N

0 ___ 500 m
0 ___ 0.25 miles

Easter Road
Stadium (350m)

Royal Cres
Scotland St La E
23
London St
8
E London St
37
Drummond Pl
30
London St
Annandale St
22
Leith Walk
Brunswick Rd
S Elgin St
Hillside St
Brunswick St
Montgomery St
Easter Rd
Union St
Forth St
38
34
London Rd
Meadowbank Sports
Centre (700m)

Northumberland St
Dublin St
Albany St
NEW
TOWN
York Pl
Greenside Row
Calton
Hill
Regent
Gardens
Royal Tce
Carlton Tce
39
Regent
Road
Park

Queen St
Hanover St
Thistle St
George St
York Place
St Andrew
Square
Leith St
Regent Rd
Regent Tce

Princes
St
Princes St
The Mound
Waverley
Station
North Bridge
Calton Rd
New St
E Market St
Canongate (Royal Mile)
40
Scottish
Parliament
Building
1
13
6
11
12
3
9
10

Market St
High St (Royal Mile)
OLD
TOWN
Bank St
Cowgate
Chambers St
South Bridge
S Gray's Cl
The Pleasance
Holyrood Rd
Viewcraig Gdns
Dumbiedykes Rd
Salisbury Crags
Arthur's Seat
(100m)
7

Johnston Tce
Grassmarket
W Port
Key
Hevot Pl
Teviol Pl
Potterrow
Nicolson St
Holyrood
Park
Queen's Dr

Chalmers St
LAURISTON
33
George Sq
George Sq
Buccleuch Pl
Buccleuch St
Meadow La
29
Rankeillor St
Montague St
28
St Leonard's Bank
Parkside St

Melville Dr
The
Meadows
Melville Dr
Melville Tce
Bernard Tce
Dalkeith Rd
Lutton Pl
43
Holyrood Park Rd

Warrender Park Tce
Spottiswoode St
Arden St
Marchmont Rd
Argyle Pl
Sylvan Pl
19
Gladstone Tce
Sciennes
Causewayside
Tantallon Pl
46
Blackwood Cres
26
E Preston St
24
Salisbury Rd
Dalkeith Rd
16
Minto St

Thirlestane Rd
17
Thirlestane La
MARCHMONT
Beaufort Rd
Lauder Rd
Grange Rd
Findhorn Pl
Seton Pl
Cumin Pl
Dick Pl
Salisbury Pl
Ratcliffe Tce
25
Duncan St
NEWINGTON

Edinburgh

beneath the 16th-century **Portcullis Gate** to the cannons ranged along the Argyle and Mills Mount batteries. The battlements here have great views over New Town to the Firth of Forth.

At the far end of Mills Mount Battery is the famous **One O'Clock Gun**, where crowds gather to watch a gleaming WWII 25-pounder fire an ear-splitting time signal at exactly 1pm (every day except Sunday, Christmas Day and Good Friday).

South of Mills Mount, the road curls up leftwards through **Foog's Gate** to the highest part of Castle Rock, crowned by the tiny, Romanesque **St Margaret's Chapel**, the oldest surviving building in Edinburgh. It was probably built by David I or Alexander I in memory of their mother, Queen Margaret, sometime around 1130 (she was canonised in 1250). Beside the chapel stands **Mons Meg**, a giant 15th-century siege gun built at Mons (in what is now Belgium) in 1449.

The main group of buildings on the summit of Castle Rock is ranged around Crown Sq, dominated by the shrine of the **Scottish National War Memorial**. Opposite is the Great Hall, built for James IV (r 1488–1513) as a ceremonial hall and used as a meeting place for the Scottish parliament until 1639. Its most remarkable feature is the original, 16th-century hammer-beam roof.

The **Castle Vaults** beneath the Great Hall (entered from Crown Sq via the Prisons of War exhibit) were used variously as storerooms, bakeries and a prison. The vaults have been renovated to resemble 18th- and early 19th-century prisons, where graffiti carved by French and American prisoners can be seen on the ancient wooden doors.

On the eastern side of the square is the **Royal Palace**, built during the 15th and 16th centuries, where a series of historical tableaux leads to the highlight of the castle – a strongroom housing the **Honours of Scotland** (the Scottish crown jewels), the oldest surviving crown jewels in Europe. Locked away in a chest following the Act of Union in 1707, the crown (made in 1540 from the gold of Robert the Bruce's 14th-century coronet), sword and sceptre lay forgotten until they were unearthed at the instigation of the novelist Sir Walter Scott in 1818. Also on display here is the **Stone of Destiny**.

Among the neighbouring **Royal Apartments** is the bedchamber where Mary, Queen of Scots gave birth to her son James VI, who was to unite the crowns of Scotland and England in 1603.

National War Museum of Scotland MUSEUM

(Map p52; www.nms.ac.uk; admission incl in Edinburgh Castle ticket; ☉9.45am-5.45pm Apr-Oct, to 4.45pm Nov-Mar; 🚍23, 27, 41, 42) At the western end of the castle, to the left of the castle tearooms, a road leads down to the National War Museum of Scotland, which brings Scotland's military history vividly to life. The exhibits have been personalised by telling the stories of the original owners of the objects on display, making it easier to empathise with the experiences of war than any dry display of dusty weaponry ever could.

Scotch Whisky Experience EXHIBITION

(Map p52; www.scotchwhiskyexperience.co.uk; 354 Castlehill; adult/child incl tour & tasting £13.50/6.75; ☉10am-6.30pm Jun-Aug, to 6pm Sep-May; 🚍2, 23, 27, 41, 42, 45) A former school houses this multimedia centre explaining the making of whisky from barley to bottle in a series of exhibits, demonstrations and tours that combine sight, sound and smell, including the world's largest collection of malt whiskies; look out for Peat the distillery cat! More expensive tours include more extensive whisky tastings and samples of Scottish cuisine. There's also a restaurant (p81) that serves traditional Scottish dishes with, where possible, a dash of whisky thrown in.

Camera Obscura EXHIBITION

(Map p52; www.camera-obscura.co.uk; Castlehill; adult/child £12.95/9.50; ☉9.30am-9pm Jul & Aug, to 7pm Apr-Jun & Sep-Oct, 10am-6pm Nov-Mar; 🚍2, 23, 27, 42) Edinburgh's camera obscura is a curious 19th-century device – in constant use since 1853 – that uses lenses and mirrors to throw a live image of the city onto a large horizontal screen. The accompanying commentary is entertaining and the whole experience has a quirky charm, complemented by an intriguing exhibition dedicated to illusions of all kinds. Stairs lead up through various displays to the **Outlook Tower**, which offers great views over the city.

Gladstone's Land HISTORIC BUILDING

(Map p52; NTS; www.nts.org.uk; 477 Lawnmarket; adult/child £6.50/5; ☉10am-6.30pm Jul & Aug, to 5pm Apr-Jun & Sep-Oct; 🚍23, 27, 41, 42) One of Edinburgh's most prominent 17th-century merchants was Thomas Gledstanes, who in 1617 purchased the tenement later known as Gladstone's Land. It contains fine painted ceilings, walls and beams, and some splendid furniture from the 17th and 18th centuries. The volunteer guides provide a wealth of anecdotes and a detailed history.

Writers' Museum MUSEUM

(Map p52; www.edinburghmuseums.org.uk; Lady Stair's Close, Lawnmarket; ☉10am-5pm Mon-Sat year-round, noon-5pm Sun Aug; 🚍23, 27, 41, 42) **FREE** Tucked down a close between the Royal Mile and the Mound you'll find Lady Stair's House (1622), home to this museum that contains manuscripts and memorabilia belonging to three of Scotland's most

---

CASTLE TO CANONGATE

➡ **Castle Esplanade** Open area outside the castle gates; originally a parade ground, it forms the stage for the Military Tattoo during festival time.

➡ **Castlehill** The short slope connecting the Castle Esplanade to the Lawnmarket.

➡ **Lawnmarket** A corruption of 'Landmarket', a market selling goods from land outside the city. Takes its name from the large cloth market that flourished here until the 18th century. This was the poshest part of the Old Town, where many of its most distinguished citizens made their homes.

➡ **High St** Stretches from George IV Bridge down to the Netherbow at St Mary's St. It's the heart and soul of the Old Town, home to the city's main church, the law courts, the city council and – until 1707 – the Scottish parliament.

➡ **Canongate** The stretch of the Royal Mile from Netherbow to Holyrood takes its name from the Augustinian canons (monks) of Holyrood Abbey. From the 16th century it was home to aristocrats attracted to the Palace of Holyroodhouse. Originally governed by the monks, Canongate was an independent burgh separate from Edinburgh until 1856.

Royal Mile

A GRAND DAY OUT

Planning your own procession along the Royal Mile involves some tough decisions – it would be impossible to see everything in a single day, so it's wise to decide in advance what you don't want to miss and shape your visit around that. Remember to leave time for lunch, for exploring some of the Mile's countless side alleys and, during festival time, for enjoying the street theatre that is bound to be happening in High St.

The most pleasant way to reach the Castle Esplanade at the start of the Royal Mile is to hike up the zigzag path from the footbridge behind the Ross Bandstand in Princes Street Gardens (in springtime you'll be knee-deep in daffodils). Starting at **Edinburgh Castle** ❶ means that the rest of your walk is downhill. For a superb view up and down the length of the Mile, climb the **Camera Obscura's Outlook Tower** ❷ before visiting **Gladstone's**

ROYAL VISITS TO THE ROYAL MILE

1561: Mary, Queen of Scots arrives from France and holds an audience with John Knox.
1745: Bonnie Prince Charlie fails to capture Edinburgh Castle, and instead sets up court in Holyroodhouse.
2004: Queen Elizabeth II officially opens the Scottish Parliament building.

Edinburgh Castle
If you're pushed for time, visit the Great Hall, the Honours of Scotland and the Prisons of War exhibit. Head for the Half Moon Battery for a photo looking down the length of the Royal Mile.

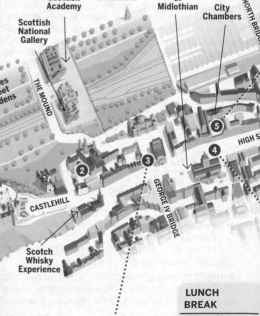

Royal Scottish Academy

Scott Monument

Heart of Midlothian

City Chambers

NORTH BRIDGE

Scottish National Gallery

Princes Street Gardens

THE MOUND

HIGH ST

GEORGE IV BRIDGE

CASTLEHILL

Scotch Whisky Experience

Gladstone's Land
The 1st floor houses a faithful recreation of how a wealthy Edinburgh merchant lived in the 17th century. Check out the beautiful Painted Bedchamber, with its ornately decorated walls and wooden ceilings.

LUNCH BREAK

Burger and a beer at **Holyrood 9A**; steak and chips at **Maxie's Bistro**; slap-up seafood at **Ondine**.

Land **3** and **St Giles Cathedral** **4**. If history's your thing, you'll want to add **Real Mary King's Close** **5**, **John Knox House** **6** and the **Museum of Edinburgh** **7** to your must-see list.

At the foot of the mile, choose between modern and ancient seats of power – the **Scottish Parliament** **8** or the **Palace of Holyroodhouse** **9**. Round off the day with an evening ascent of Arthur's Seat or, slightly less strenuously, Calton Hill. Both make great sunset viewpoints.

TAKING YOUR TIME

Minimum time needed for each attraction:

» **Edinburgh Castle**: two hours
» **Gladstone's Land**: 45 minutes
» **St Giles Cathedral**: 30 minutes
» **Real Mary King's Close**: one hour (tour)
» **Scottish Parliament**: one hour (tour)
» **Palace of Holyroodhouse**: one hour

Real Mary King's Close
The guided tour is heavy on ghost stories, but a highlight is standing in an original 17th-century room with tufts of horsehair poking from the crumbling plaster, and breathing in the ancient scent of stone, dust and history.

Canongate Kirk

CANONGATE

ST MARY'S ST

SOUTH BRIDGE

Our Dynamic Earth

Scottish Parliament
Don't have time for the guided tour? Pick up a 'Discover the Scottish Parliament Building' leaflet from reception and take a self-guided tour of the exterior, then hike up to Salisbury Crags for a great view of the complex.

Palace of Holyroodhouse
Find the secret staircase joining Mary, Queen of Scots' bedchamber with that of her husband, Lord Darnley, who restrained the queen while his henchmen stabbed to death her secretary (and possible lover), David Rizzio.

St Giles Cathedral
Look out for the Burne-Jones stained-glass window (1873) at the west end, showing the crossing of the River Jordan, and the bronze memorial to Robert Louis Stevenson in the Moray Aisle.

RICK LEWIS/GETTY IMAGES © ARCHITECT: ENRIC MIRALLES

RIEGER BERTRAND/GETTY IMAGES ©

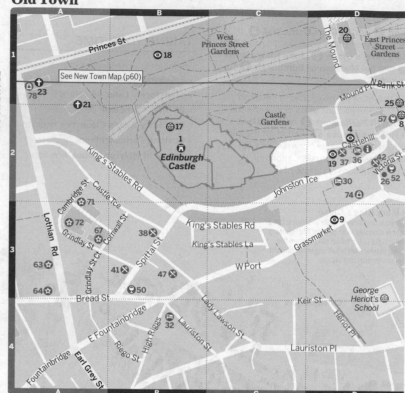

famous writers: Robert Burns, Sir Walter Scott and Robert Louis Stevenson.

St Giles Cathedral

CHURCH

(Map p52; www.stgilescathedral.org.uk; High St; suggested donation £3; ⊙9am-7pm Mon-Fri, to 5pm Sat, 1-5pm Sun May-Sep, 9am-5pm Mon-Sat, 1-5pm Sun Oct-Apr; ☐23, 27, 41, 42) The great grey bulk of St Giles Cathedral dominates Edinburgh's High St. Properly called the High Kirk of Edinburgh (it was only a true cathedral – the seat of a bishop – from 1633 to 1638 and from 1661 to 1689), the church was named after the patron saint of cripples and beggars. The present building dates largely from the 15th century – the beautiful crown spire was completed in 1495 – but much of it was restored in the 19th century.

The interior lacks grandeur but is rich in history: a Norman-style church was built here in 1126 but was destroyed by English invaders in 1385 (the only substantial remains are the central piers that support the tower).

St Giles was at the heart of the Scottish Reformation, and John Knox served as minister here from 1559 to 1572. One of the most interesting corners of the kirk is the **Thistle Chapel**, built in 1911 for the Knights of the Most Ancient & Most Noble Order of the Thistle. The elaborately carved Gothic-style stalls have canopies topped with the helms and arms of the 16 knights – look out for the bagpipe-playing angel amid the vaulting.

By the side of the street, outside the western door of St Giles, is the **Heart of Midlothian**, set into the cobblestone paving. This marks the site of the Tolbooth. Built in the 15th century and demolished in the early 19th century, the Tolbooth served variously as a meeting place for parliament, the town council and the General Assembly of the Reformed Kirk, before becoming law courts and, finally, a notorious prison and place of execution. Passers-by traditionally spit on the heart for luck (don't stand downwind!).

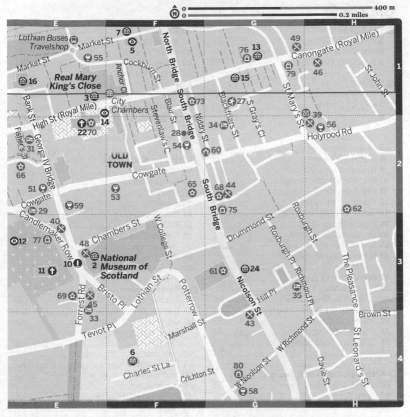

At the other end of St Giles is the **Mercat Cross**, a 19th-century copy of the 1365 original, where merchants and traders met to transact business and royal proclamations were read.

★**Real Mary King's Close** HISTORIC BUILDING
(Map p52; ☏0845 070 6244; www.realmarykings-close.com; 2 Warriston's Close, High St; adult/child £12.95/7.45; ⏱10am-9pm daily Apr-Oct, to 11pm Aug, 10am-5pm Sun-Thu & 10am-9pm Fri & Sat Nov-Mar; 🚌23, 27, 41, 42) Edinburgh's 18th-century City Chambers were built over the sealed-off remains of Mary King's Close, and the lower levels of this medieval Old Town alley have survived almost unchanged amid the foundations for 250 years. Now open to the public, this spooky, subterranean labyrinth gives a fascinating insight into the everyday life of 17th-century Edinburgh. Costumed characters lead tours through a 16th-century town house and the plague-stricken home of a 17th-century gravedigger. Advance booking recommended.

The scripted tour, complete with ghostly tales and gruesome tableaux, can seem a little naff, milking the scary and scatological aspects of the close's history for all they're worth. But there are many things of genuine interest to see; there's something about the crumbling 17th-century **tenement room** that makes the hairs rise on the back of your neck, with tufts of horsehair poking from the collapsing lath-and-plaster walls, the ghost of a pattern on the walls, and the ancient smell of stone and dust thick in your nostrils.

In one of the former bedrooms off the close, a psychic once claimed to have been approached by the ghost of a little girl called Annie. It's hard to tell what's more frightening – the story of the ghostly child, or the bizarre heap of tiny dolls and teddies left in a corner by sympathetic visitors.

Old Town

Museum of Childhood   MUSEUM

(Map p52; www.edinburghmuseums.org.uk; 42 High
St; ⊙10am-5pm Mon-Sat, noon-5pm Sun; 🚌35)
FREE Halfway down the Royal Mile is 'the
noisiest museum in the world'. Often filled
with the chatter of excited children, it covers
serious issues related to childhood – health,
education, upbringing etc – but also has an
enormous collection of toys, dolls, games
and books, recordings of school lessons from
the 1930s, and film of kids playing street
games in 1950s Edinburgh.

John Knox House   HISTORIC BUILDING

(Map p52; www.scottishstorytellingcentre.co.uk;
43-45 High St; adult/child £5/1; ⊙10am-6pm Mon-

Sat year-round, noon-6pm Sun Jul & Aug; (🏛35) The Royal Mile narrows at the foot of High St beside the jutting facade of John Knox House. This is the oldest surviving tenement in Edinburgh, dating from around 1490. John Knox, an influential church reformer and leader of the Protestant Reformation in Scotland, is thought to have lived here from 1561 to 1572. The labyrinthine interior has some beautiful painted-timber ceilings and an interesting display on Knox's life.

People's Story MUSEUM

(Map p46; www.edinburghmuseums.org.uk; 163 Canongate; ⊙10am-5pm Mon-Sat year-round, noon-5pm Sun Aug; 🏛35) FREE One of the surviving symbols of the Canongate district's former independence is the **Canongate Tolbooth**. Built in 1591 it served successively as a collection point for tolls (taxes), a council house, a courtroom and a jail. With picturesque turrets and a projecting clock, it's an interesting example of 16th-century architecture. It now houses a fascinating museum called the People's Story, which covers the life, work and pastimes of ordinary Edinburgh folk from the 18th century to today.

Museum of Edinburgh MUSEUM

(Map p46; www.edinburghmuseums.org.uk; 142 Canongate; ⊙10am-5pm Mon-Sat year-round, noon-5pm Sun Aug; 🏛35) FREE You can't miss the colourful facade of Huntly House, brightly renovated in red and yellow ochre, opposite the Tolbooth clock on the Royal Mile. Built in 1570, it houses a museum covering Edinburgh from its prehistory to the present. Exhibits of national importance include an original copy of the National Covenant of 1638, but the big crowd-pleaser is the dog collar and feeding bowl that once belonged to Greyfriars Bobby, the city's most famous canine citizen.

Canongate Kirk CHURCH

(Map p46; canongatekirk.org.uk; Canongate; 🏛35) The attractive curved gable of the Canongate Kirk, built in 1688, overlooks a kirkyard that contains the graves of several famous people, including the economist **Adam Smith**, author of *The Wealth of Nations*; Mrs Agnes MacLehose (the 'Clarinda' of Robert Burns' love poems); and poet **Robert Fergusson** (1750–74; there's a statue of him on the street outside the church). An information board just inside the gate lists famous graves and their locations.

Fergusson was much admired by Robert Burns, who paid for his gravestone and penned the epitaph – take a look at the inscription on the back.

◎ Holyrood

Palace of Holyroodhouse PALACE

(Map p46; www.royalcollection.org.uk; Horse Wynd; adult/child £11.30/6.80; ⊙9.30am-6pm Apr-Oct, to 4.30pm Nov-Mar; 🏛35, 36) This palace is the royal family's official residence in Scotland, but is more famous as the 16th-century home of the ill-fated Mary, Queen of Scots. The highlight of the tour is **Mary's Bed Chamber**, home to the unfortunate queen from 1561 to 1567. It was here that her jealous first husband, Lord Darnley, restrained the pregnant queen while his henchmen murdered her secretary – and favourite – Rizzio. A plaque in the neighbouring room marks the spot where he bled to death.

The palace developed from a guest house, attached to Holyrood Abbey, which was extended by King James IV in 1501. The oldest surviving part of the building, the northwestern tower, was built in 1529 as a royal apartment for James V and his wife, Mary of Guise. Mary, Queen of Scots spent six turbulent years here, during which time she debated with John Knox, married both her first and second husbands, and witnessed the murder of her secretary David Rizzio.

The self-guided audio tour leads you through a series of impressive royal apartments, culminating in the **Great Gallery**. The 89 portraits of Scottish kings were commissioned by Charles II and supposedly record his unbroken lineage from Scota, the Egyptian pharaoh's daughter who discovered the infant Moses in a reed basket on the banks of the Nile. The tour continues to the oldest part of the palace, which contains Mary's Bed Chamber, connected by a secret stairway to her husband's bedroom, and ends with the ruins of Holyrood Abbey.

Holyrood Abbey ABBEY

(Map p46; admission incl in Palace of Holyroodhouse ticket; ⊙9.30am-6pm Apr-Oct, to 4.30pm Nov-Mar; 🏛35, 36) King David I founded the abbey here in the shadow of Salisbury Crags in 1128. It was probably named after a fragment of the True Cross (*rood* is an old Scots word for cross), said to have been brought to Scotland by his mother, St Margaret. Most of the surviving ruins date from the 12th and 13th centuries, although a doorway in the far southeastern corner has survived from the original Norman church.

Queen's Gallery   GALLERY
(Map p46; www.royalcollection.org.uk; Horse Wynd; adult/child £6.50/3.25, combined admission to gallery & Holyroodhouse £16/9; ⊙9.30am-6pm Apr-Oct, to 4.30pm Nov-Mar; 🚌35, 36) This stunning modern gallery, which occupies the shell of a former church and school, was opened in 2002 as a showcase for exhibitions of art from the Royal Collections. The exhibitions change every six months or so.

Our Dynamic Earth   EXHIBITION
(Map p46; www.dynamicearth.co.uk; Holyrood Rd; adult/child £11.50/7.50; ⊙10am-6pm daily Jul & Aug, to 5.30pm Apr-Jun, Sep & Oct, 10am-5.30pm Wed-Sun Nov-Mar, last admission 90min before closing; ♿; 🚌35, 36) Housed in a modernistic white marquee, Our Dynamic Earth is billed as an interactive, multimedia journey of discovery through Earth's history from the Big Bang to the present day. Hugely popular with kids of all ages, it's a slick extravaganza of whiz-bang special effects and 3D movies cleverly designed to fire up young minds with curiosity about all things geological and environmental. Its true purpose, of course, is to disgorge you into a gift shop where you can buy model dinosaurs and souvenir T-shirts.

★**Arthur's Seat**   LANDMARK
(Map p46; Holyrood Park) The rocky peak of Arthur's Seat (251m), carved by ice sheets from the deeply eroded stump of a long-extinct volcano, is a distinctive feature of Edinburgh's skyline. The view from the summit is well worth the walk, extending from the Forth Bridges in the west to the distant conical hill of North Berwick Law in the east, with the Ochil Hills and the Highlands on the northwestern horizon. The hike from Holyrood to the top takes about 45 minutes.

Holyrood Park   PARK
(Map p46; 🚌35, 36) In Holyrood Park Edinburgh is blessed with a little bit of wilderness in the heart of the city. The former hunting ground of Scottish monarchs, the

---

SCOTTISH PARLIAMENT BUILDING

The **Scottish Parliament Building** (Map p46; ☎0131-348 5200; www.scottish.parliament. uk; Horse Wynd; ⊙9am-6.30pm Tue-Thu, 10am-5.30pm Mon, Fri & Sat in session, 10am-6pm Mon-Sat in recess; 🚌35, 36) FREE, built on the site of a former brewery close to the Palace of Holyroodhouse, was officially opened by HM the Queen in October 2005.

The public areas of the building – the Main Hall, where there is an exhibition, shop and cafe; and the **public gallery** in the Debating Chamber – are open to visitors (tickets, although free, are needed for public gallery – see website for details). You can also take a free, one-hour **guided tour** (advance booking recommended) that includes a visit to the Debating Chamber, a committee room, the Garden Lobby and, when possible, the office of an MSP (Member of the Scottish Parliament). If you want to see the parliament in session, check the website for sitting times – business days are normally Tuesday to Thursday year-round.

Enric Miralles (1955–2000), the architect who conceived the Scottish Parliament Building, believed that a building could be a work of art. However, this weird concrete confection at the foot of Salisbury Crags has left the good people of Edinburgh staring and scratching their heads in confusion. What does it all mean? The strange forms of the exterior are all symbolic in some way, from the oddly shaped windows on the west wall (inspired by the silhouette of the *Reverend Robert Walker Skating on Duddingston Loch*, one of Scotland's most famous paintings), to the ground plan of the whole complex, which represents a 'flower of democracy rooted in Scottish soil' (best seen looking down from Salisbury Crags).

The **Main Hall**, inside the public entrance, has a low, triple-arched ceiling of polished concrete, like a cave, or cellar, or castle vault. It is a dimly lit space, the starting point for a metaphorical journey from this relative darkness up to the **Debating Chamber** (sitting directly above the Main Hall), which is, in contrast, a palace of light – the light of democracy. This magnificent chamber is the centrepiece of the parliament, designed not to glorify but to humble the politicians who sit within it. The windows face Calton Hill, allowing MSPs to look up to its monuments (reminders of the Scottish Enlightenment), while the massive, pointed oak beams of the roof are suspended by steel threads above the MSPs' heads like so many Damoclean swords.

park covers 263 hectares of varied landscape, including crags, moorland and loch, and the 251m summit of Arthur's Seat (p56). Holyrood Park can be circumnavigated by car or bike along Queen's Dr.

◎ North of Royal Mile

Fruitmarket Gallery GALLERY
(Map p52; www.fruitmarket.co.uk; 45 Market St; ☺11am-6pm Mon-Sat, noon-5pm Sun; ☐36) **FREE** One of Edinburgh's most innovative and popular galleries, the Fruitmarket showcases contemporary Scottish and international artists, and also has an excellent arts bookshop and cafe.

City Art Centre ART CENTRE
(Map p52; www.edinburghmuseums.org.uk; 2 Market St; fee for temporary exhibitions; ☺10am-5pm Mon-Sat, noon-5pm Sun; ☐36) **FREE** This art centre comprises six floors of exhibitions with a variety of themes, including an extensive collection of Scottish art.

◎ South of the Royal Mile

★National Museum of Scotland MUSEUM
(Map p52; www.nms.ac.uk; Chambers St; fee for special exhibitions; ☺10am-5pm; ☐2, 23, 27, 35, 41, 42, 45) **FREE** Broad, elegant Chambers St is dominated by the long facade of the National Museum of Scotland. Its extensive collections are spread between two buildings, one modern, one Victorian – the golden stone and striking modern architecture of the new building, opened in 1998, is one of the city's most distinctive landmarks. The five floors of the museum trace the history of Scotland from geological beginnings to the 1990s, with many imaginative and stimulating exhibits – audioguides are available in several languages.

The new building connects with the original Victorian museum, dating from 1861, the stolid, grey exterior of which gives way to a beautifully bright and airy, glass-roofed exhibition hall. The old building houses an eclectic collection covering natural history, archaeology, scientific and industrial technology, and the decorative arts of ancient Egypt, Islam, China, Japan, Korea and the West.

Greyfriars Kirk & Kirkyard CHURCH
(Map p52; www.greyfriarskirk.com; Candlemaker Row; ☺10.30am-4.30pm Mon-Fri & 11am-2pm Sat Apr-Oct, closed Nov-Mar; ☐2, 23, 27, 41, 42, 45) **FREE** One of Edinburgh's most famous churches, Greyfriars Kirk was built on the site of a Franciscan friary and opened for worship on Christmas Day 1620. Surrounding the church, Greyfriars Kirkyard is one of Edinburgh's most evocative cemeteries, a peaceful green oasis dotted with elaborate monuments. Many famous Edinburgh names are buried here, including the poet Allan Ramsay (1686–1758), architect William Adam (1689–1748) and William Smellie (1740–95), the editor of the first edition of the *Encyclopedia Britannica*.

In 1638 the **National Covenant** was signed in the kirk, rejecting Charles I's attempts to impose episcopacy and a new English prayer book on the Scots, and affirming the independence of the Scottish Church. Many who signed were later executed at the Grassmarket and, in 1679, 1200 Covenanters were held prisoner in terrible conditions in the southwestern corner of the kirkyard. There's a small exhibition inside the church.

If you want to experience the graveyard at its scariest – inside a burial vault, in the dark, at night – go on one of the City of the Dead (p69) guided tours.

Greyfriars Bobby Statue MONUMENT
(Map p52; cnr George IV Bridge & Candlemaker Row; ☐2, 23, 27, 35, 41, 42, 45) Probably the most popular photo opportunity in Edinburgh, the life-size statue of Greyfriars Bobby, a Skye terrier who captured the hearts of the British public, stands outside Greyfriars Kirkyard. From 1858 to 1872, the wee dog maintained a vigil over the grave of his master, an Edinburgh police officer. The story was immortalised in a novel by Eleanor Atkinson in 1912, and in 1963 was made into a movie by – who else? – Walt Disney.

The statue is always surrounded by crowds of visitors taking photos of themselves posing beside the little dog. Bobby's own grave, marked by a small, pink granite stone, is just inside the entrance to Greyfriars Kirkyard, behind the monument, and you can see his original collar and bowl in the Museum of Edinburgh (p55).

Grassmarket STREET
(Map p52; ☐2) The site of a cattle market from the 15th century until the start of the 20th century, the Grassmarket has always been a focal point of the Old Town. It was once the city's main place of execution, and more than 100 martyred Covenanters are commemorated by a monument at the eastern end, where the gallows used to

NATIONAL MUSEUM OF SCOTLAND: HIGHLIGHTS

Begin at the main entrance in the middle of Chambers St, rather than the modern tower at the west end of the street. This opens into an atmospheric **entrance hall** occupying what used to be the museum cellars where you'll find an information desk with museum maps and leaflets, a cloakroom, toilets and a cafe-restaurant. Stairs lead up into the light of the **Grand Gallery**, a spectacular glass-roofed atrium lined with cast-iron pillars and balconies that is the centrepiece of the original Victorian museum.

This half of the building is devoted to the natural world, art and design, and world cultures. A door at the east end of the gallery leads into **Animal World**, one of the most impressive of the museum's new exhibits. No dusty, static regiments of stuffed creatures here, but a beautiful and dynamic display of animals apparently caught in the act of bounding, leaping or pouncing, arranged in groups that illustrate different means of locomotion, methods of feeding and modes of reproduction. Extinct creatures mingle with the living, including a full-size skeleton of *Tyrannosaurus rex*.

Take some time to explore the exhibits ranged around the balconies of the Grand Gallery, billed as a **Window on the World** that showcases more than 800 items from the museum's collections, ranging from the world's largest scrimshaw carving, occupying two full-size sperm whale jawbones, to a four-seat racing bicycle dating from 1898.

Return to the ground floor of the Grand Gallery and go through the Connect exhibit at the western end – where **Dolly the Sheep**, the world's first mammal cloned from an adult cell, is on display. Emerge into Hawthornden Court, the soaring central atrium of the modern half of the museum, graced by the **Formula 1 racing car** driven by Sir Jackie Stewart in the 1970s. This half of the building is devoted to Scottish history and culture.

Stairs at the far end lead down to the Early Peoples galleries on level 0, decorated with intriguing humanoid sculptures by Sir Eduardo Paolozzi. Look for the **Cramond Lioness**, a Roman sculpture of a lion gripping a human head in her jaws that was discovered in the River Almond in 1997, and the 20kg of 5th-century silver that makes up the **Traprain Treasure**.

From here, you work your way upwards through the history of Scotland. Highlights of the medieval Kingdom of the Scots galleries, on levels 1 and 2, include the **Monymusk Reliquary**, a tiny silver casket dating from AD 750, which is said to have been carried into battle with Robert the Bruce at Bannockburn in 1314; and the famous **Lewis Chessmen**, a set of charming 12th-century chess pieces carved from walrus ivory, that was discovered on Uig beach on the Isle of Lewis.

Continue up through levels 3 and 4, which follow Scotland's progress through the Industrial Revolution, potently symbolised by the towering **Newcomen atmospheric engine** that once pumped water from flooded Ayrshire coal mines. The Ways of Death exhibit on level 5 – a Goth's paradise of jet jewellery and mourning bracelets made from human hair – contains several fascinating objects, including the tiny and mysterious **Arthur's Seat coffins** that were discovered in Holyrood Park in 1836, and which featured in Ian Rankin's Inspector Rebus novel *The Falls*.

Level 6 is given over to the 20th century, with galleries devoted to war and industry, and a particularly affecting exhibition called **Leaving Scotland**, containing stories of the Scottish diaspora that emigrated to begin new lives in Canada, Australia, the USA and other places.

Finally, find the elevator in the corner near the war gallery and go up to the **Roof Terrace** to enjoy a fantastic view across the city to the castle.

stand. The notorious murderers Burke and Hare operated from a now-vanished close off the western end.

Nowadays the broad, open square, lined by tall tenements and dominated by the looming castle, has many lively pubs and restaurants, including the **White Hart Inn**, which was once patronised by Robert Burns. Claiming to be the city's oldest pub in continuous use (since 1516), it also hosted William Wordsworth in 1803. **Cowgate** – the long, dark ravine leading eastwards from the Grassmarket – was once the road along which cattle were driven from the pastures around Arthur's Seat to the safety of the city walls. Today it is the heart of Edinburgh's nightlife, with around two dozen clubs and bars within five minutes' walk of each other.

◉ New Town

Edinburgh's New Town (Map p60) lies north of the Old Town, on a ridge running parallel to the Royal Mile and separated from it by the valley of Princes Street Gardens. Its regular grid of elegant Georgian terraces is a complete contrast to the chaotic tangle of tenements and wynds that characterise the Old Town.

Between the end of the 14th century and the start of the 18th, the population of Edinburgh – still confined within the walls of the Old Town – increased from 2000 to 50,000. The tottering tenements were unsafe and occasionally collapsed, fire was an ever-present danger, and the overcrowding and squalor became unbearable.

When the Act of Union in 1707 brought the prospect of long-term stability, the upper classes were keen to find healthier, more spacious living quarters, and in 1766 an architectural competition was held to design an extension to the city. It was won by an unknown 23-year-old, James Craig, a self-taught architect whose simple and elegant plan envisaged a main axis along George St, with grand squares at either end, and with building restricted to one side only of Princes and Queen Sts so that the houses enjoyed views over the Firth of Forth to the north and to the castle and Old Town to the south.

During the 18th and 19th centuries, the New Town continued to sprout squares, circuses, parks and terraces, with some of its finest neoclassical architecture designed by Robert Adam. Today Edinburgh's New Town remains the world's most complete and unspoilt example of Georgian architecture and town planning. Along with the Old Town, it was declared a Unesco World Heritage Site in 1995.

◉ Princes Street

Princes St is one of the world's most spectacular shopping streets. Built up on the north side only, it catches the sun in summer and allows expansive views across Princes Street Gardens to the castle and the crowded skyline of the Old Town.

The western end of Princes St is dominated by the red-sandstone edifice of the Caledonian Hilton Hotel and the tower of **St John's Church** (Map p52), worth visiting for its fine Gothic Revival interior. It overlooks **St Cuthbert's Parish Church** (Map p52), built in the 1890s on a site of great antiquity – there has been a church here since at least the 12th century, and perhaps since the 7th century. There is a circular **watchtower** in the graveyard – a reminder of the Burke and Hare days when graves had to be guarded against robbers.

At the eastern end is the prominent clock tower – traditionally three minutes fast so you don't miss your train – of the **Balmoral Hotel** (Map p60; www.thebalmoralhotel.com; 1 Princes St) (originally the North British Hotel, built by the railway company of the same name in 1902) and the beautiful 1788 **Register House** (Map p60), designed by Robert Adam, with a statue of the Duke of Wellington in front. It houses the National Archives of Scotland and the ScotlandsPeople genealogical research centre.

Princes Street Gardens (Map p52; Princes St; ☉dawn-dusk; ▣all Princes St buses) **FREE** lie in a valley that was once occupied by the Nor' Loch, a boggy depression that was drained in the early 19th century. The gardens are split in the middle by **The Mound**, which was created from around two million cartloads of earth excavated from the foundations of the New Town and dumped here to provide a road link across the valley to the Old Town. It was completed in 1830.

Scott Monument   MONUMENT
(Map p60; www.edinburghmuseums.org.uk; East Princes Street Gardens; admission £4; ☉10am-7pm Apr-Sep, 10am-4pm Oct-Mar; ▣all Princes St buses) The eastern half of Princes Street Gardens is dominated by the massive Gothic spire of the Scott Monument, built by public subscription in memory of the novelist Sir Walter Scott after his death in 1832. The exterior is decorated with carvings of characters from his novels; inside you can see an exhibition on Scott's life, and climb the 287 steps to the top for a superb view of the city.

Scottish National Gallery   GALLERY
(Map p52; www.nationalgalleries.org; The Mound; fee for special exhibitions; ☉10am-5pm Fri-Wed, to 7pm Thu; ▣all Princes St buses) **FREE** Designed by William Playfair, this imposing classical building with its Ionic porticoes dates from the 1850s. Its octagonal rooms, lit by

New Town

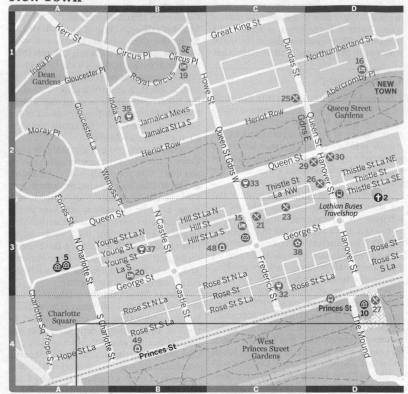

skylights, have been restored to their original Victorian decor of deep-green carpets and dark-red walls. The gallery houses an important collection of European art from the Renaissance to post-Impressionism, with works by Verrocchio (Leonardo da Vinci's teacher), Tintoretto, Titian, Holbein, Rubens, Van Dyck, Vermeer, El Greco, Rembrandt, Gainsborough, Turner, Constable, Monet, Pissarro, Gauguin and Cézanne.

The upstairs galleries house portraits by Sir Joshua Reynolds and Sir Henry Raeburn, and a clutch of Impressionist paintings, including Monet's luminous *Haystacks,* Van Gogh's demonic *Olive Trees* and Gauguin's hallucinatory *Vision After the Sermon.* But the painting that really catches your eye is the gorgeous portrait of Lady Agnew of Lochnaw by John Singer Sargent.

The basement galleries dedicated to Scottish art include glowing portraits by Allan Ramsay and Sir Henry Raeburn, rural scenes by Sir David Wilkie and Impressionistic landscapes by William MacTaggart. Look out for Raeburn's iconic *Reverend Robert Walker Skating on Duddingston Loch,* and Sir George Harvey's hugely entertaining *A Schule Skailin* (A School Emptying) – a stern dominie (teacher) looks on as the boys stampede for the classroom door, one reaching for a confiscated spinning top. Kids will love the fantasy paintings of Sir Joseph Noel Paton in room B5; the incredibly detailed canvases are crammed with hundreds of tiny fairies, goblins and elves.

Each January the gallery exhibits its collection of Turner watercolours, bequeathed by Henry Vaughan in 1900. Room X is graced by Antonio Canova's white marble sculpture, 'The Three Graces'; it is owned jointly with London's Victoria & Albert Museum.

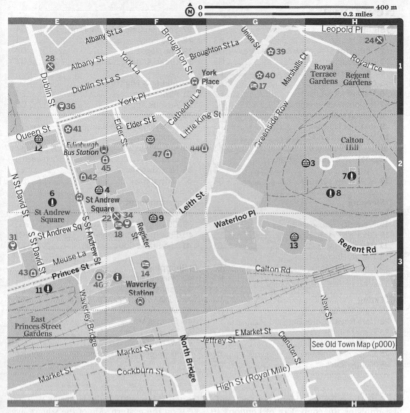

Royal Scottish Academy   GALLERY

(Map p60; www.royalscottishacademy.org; The Mound; fee for special exhibitions; ⏰10am-5pm Mon-Sat, 2-5pm Sun; 🚌all Princes St buses) **FREE**
The distinguished Greek Doric temple at the corner of The Mound and Princes St, crowned by a seated figure of Queen Victoria, is the home of the Royal Scottish Academy. Designed by William Playfair and built between 1823 and 1836, it was originally called the Royal Institution; the RSA took over the building in 1910. The galleries display a collection of paintings, sculptures and architectural drawings by academy members dating from 1831, and they also host temporary exhibitions throughout the year.

The RSA and the Scottish National Gallery (p59) are linked via an underground mall – the Weston Link – which gives them twice the temporary exhibition space of the Prado in Madrid and three times that of the Royal Academy in London, as well as housing cloakrooms, a lecture theatre and a restaurant.

⊙ George Street & Charlotte Square

Until the 1990s George St – the major axis of the New Town – was the centre of Edinburgh's financial industry and Scotland's equivalent of Wall St. Today the big financial firms have moved to premises in the new Exchange office district west of Lothian Rd, and George St's former banks and offices house upmarket shops, pubs and restaurants.

At the western end of George St is Charlotte Sq, the architectural jewel of the New Town, designed by Robert Adam shortly before his death in 1791. The northern side of the square is Adam's masterpiece and one of the finest examples of Georgian architecture anywhere. **Bute House**, in the centre at

New Town

◎ Sights
1	Bute House	A3
2	Church of St Andrew & St George	D2
3	City Observatory	H2
4	Dundas House	E2
5	Georgian House	A3
6	Melville Monument	E2
7	National Monument	H2
8	Nelson Monument	H2
9	Register House	F3
10	Royal Scottish Academy	D4
11	Scott Monument	E3
12	Scottish National Portrait Gallery	E2
13	St Andrew's House	G3

🛏 Sleeping
14	Balmoral Hotel	F3
15	Frederick House Hotel	C3
16	Gerald's Place	D1
17	Glasshouse	G1
18	Haggis Hostel	F3
19	One Royal Circus	B1
20	Tigerlily	B3

✖ Eating
21	Café Marlayne	C3
22	Café Royal Oyster Bar	F3
23	Fishers in the City	C3
24	Gardener's Cottage	H1
25	Glass & Thompson	C1
26	Henderson's	D2
27	Scottish Cafe & Restaurant	D4
28	Stac Polly	E1
29	The Dogs	D2
30	Urban Angel	D2

🍷 Drinking & Nightlife
31	Abbotsford	E3
32	Amicus Apple	C3
33	Bramble	C2
	Café Royal Circle Bar	(see 22)
34	Guildford Arms	F3
35	Kay's Bar	B2
	Lulu	(see 20)
36	Newtown Bar	E1
37	Oxford Bar	B3

✪ Entertainment
38	Assembly	C3
39	CC Blooms	G1
40	Edinburgh Playhouse	G1
41	The Stand Comedy Club	E2

🛍 Shopping
42	Harvey Nichols	E2
43	Jenners	E3
44	John Lewis	F2
45	Multrees Walk	E2
46	Princes Mall	E3
47	St James Centre	F2
48	Waterstone's George St	C3
49	Waterstone's West End	B4

No 6, is the official residence of Scotland's first minister, the equivalent of London's 10 Downing St.

Georgian House HISTORIC BUILDING
(Map p60; NTS; www.nts.org.uk; 7 Charlotte Sq; adult/child £6.50/5; ⊙10am-6pm Jul & Aug, 10am-5pm Apr-Jun & Sep-Oct, 11am-4pm Mar, 11am-3pm Nov; ▣47) The National Trust for Scotland's Georgian House has been beautifully restored and furnished to show how Edinburgh's wealthy elite lived at the end of the 18th century. The walls are decorated with paintings by Allan Ramsay, Sir Henry Raeburn and Sir Joshua Reynolds.

◉ St Andrew Square

St Andrew Sq is dominated by the fluted column of the **Melville Monument** (Map p60), commemorating Henry Dundas, 1st Viscount Melville (1742–1811). Dundas was the most powerful Scottish politician of his time, often referred to when alive as 'Harry IX, the Uncrowned King of Scotland'. The impressive Palladian mansion of **Dundas House** (Map p60), built between 1772 and 1774, on the eastern side of the square, was built for Sir Laurence Dundas (1712–81; no relation to Viscount Melville). It has been the head office of the Royal Bank of Scotland since 1825 and has a spectacular domed banking hall dating from 1857 (you can nip inside for a look).

A short distance along George St is the **Church of St Andrew & St George** (Map p60), built in 1784 with an unusual oval nave. It was the scene of the Disruption of 1843, when 451 dissenting ministers left the Church of Scotland to form the Free Church.

Scottish National Portrait Gallery GALLERY
(Map p60; www.nationalgalleries.org; 1 Queen St; ⊙10am-5pm Fri-Wed, to 7pm Thu) FREE The Venetian Gothic palace of the Scottish National Portrait Gallery reopened its doors in 2011 after a two-year renovation, emerging as one of the city's top attractions. Its galleries illustrate Scottish history through paintings, photographs and sculptures, putting faces to famous names from Scotland's

past and present, from Robert Burns, Mary, Queen of Scots and Bonnie Prince Charlie to Sean Connery, Billy Connolly and Jackie Kay.

The gallery's interior is decorated in Arts and Crafts style, and nowhere more splendidly than in the **Great Hall**. Above the gothic colonnade a processional frieze painted by William Hole in 1898 serves as a 'visual encyclopedia' of famous Scots, shown in chronological order from Calgacus (the chieftain who led the Caledonian tribes into battle against the Romans) to writer and philosopher Thomas Carlyle (1795–1881). The murals on the first-floor balcony depict scenes from Scottish history, while the ceiling is painted with the constellations of the night sky. The gallery's selection of 'trails' leaflets adds a bit of background information while leading you around the various exhibits; the Hidden Histories trail is particularly interesting.

◉ Calton Hill

Calton Hill (100m), rising dramatically above the eastern end of Princes St, is Edinburgh's acropolis, its summit scattered with grandiose memorials dating mostly from the first half of the 19th century. It is also one of the best viewpoints in the city, with a panorama that takes in the castle, Holyrood, Arthur's Seat, the Firth of Forth, New Town and the full length of Princes St

On the southern side of the hill, on Regent Rd, is the modernist facade of **St Andrew's House** (Map p60), built between 1936 and 1939 and housing the Westminster government's Scottish Office until they were moved to the new Scottish Executive building in Leith in 1996.

Just beyond St Andrew's House, and on the opposite side of the road, is the imposing **Royal High School** building, dating from 1829 and modelled on the Temple of Theseus in Athens. Former pupils include Robert Adam, Alexander Graham Bell and Sir Walter Scott. It now stands empty. To its east, on the other side of Regent Rd, is the 1830 **Burns Monument** (Map p46), a Greek-style memorial to Robert Burns.

You can reach the summit of Calton Hill via the road beside the Royal High School or by the stairs at the eastern end of Waterloo Pl. The largest structure on the summit is the **National Monument** (Map p60; Calton Hill), an overambitious attempt to replicate the Parthenon in Athens and intended to honour Scotland's dead in the Napoleonic

Wars. Construction – paid for by public subscription – began in 1822, but funds ran dry when only 12 columns had been completed.

Looking a bit like an upturned telescope – the similarity is intentional – and offering even better views, the **Nelson Monument** (Map p60; www.edinburghmuseums.org.uk; Calton Hill; admission £4; ⊘10am-7pm Mon-Sat & noon-5pm Sun Apr-Sep, 10am-3pm Mon-Sat Oct-Mar; ⌑all Leith St buses) was built to commemorate Nelson's victory at Trafalgar in 1805.

The design of the **City Observatory**, (Map p60) built in 1818, was based on the ancient Greek Temple of the Winds in Athens. Its original function was to provide a precise, astronomical time-keeping service for marine navigators, but smoke from Waverley train station forced the astronomers to move to Blackford Hill in the south of Edinburgh in 1895.

◉ Dean Village

If you follow Queensferry St northwards from the western end of Princes St, you come to **Dean Bridge** (Map p46; ⌑19, 36, 37, 41, 47), designed by Thomas Telford and built between 1829 and 1832. Down in the valley, just west of the bridge, is **Dean Village** (Map p46; ⌑19, 36, 37, 41, 47) (from 'dene', a Scots word for valley). It was founded as a milling community by the canons of Holyrood Abbey in the 12th century and by 1700 there were 11 watermills here operated by the Incorporation of Baxters (the bakers' trade guild). One of the old mill buildings has been converted into flats, and the village is now an attractive residential area

Scottish National Gallery of Modern Art   GALLERY
(Map p46; www.nationalgalleries.org; 75 Belford Rd; fee for special exhibitions; ⊘10am-5pm; ⌑13) **FREE** Edinburgh's gallery of modern art is split between two impressive neoclassical buildings surrounded by landscaped grounds some 500m west of Dean Village. As well as showcasing a stunning collection of paintings by the popular, post-Impressionist Scottish Colourists – in *Reflections, Balloch,* Leslie Hunter pulls off the improbable trick of making Scotland look like the south of France – the gallery is the starting point for a walk along the Water of Leith, following a trail of sculptures by Anthony Gormley.

The main collection, known as **Modern One**, concentrates on 20th-century art, with various European movements represented by the likes of Matisse, Picasso, Kirchner, Magritte, Miró, Mondrian and Giacometti. American and English artists are also represented, but most space is given to Scottish painters – from the Scottish colourists of the early 20th century to contemporary artists such as Peter Howson and Ken Currie.

There's an excellent cafe downstairs, and the surrounding park features sculptures by Henry Moore, Rachel Whiteread and Barbara Hepworth, among others, as well as a 'landform artwork' by Charles Jencks.

A footpath and stairs at the rear of the gallery lead down to the **Water of Leith Walkway**, which you can follow along the river for 4 miles to Leith. This takes you past **6 Times**, a sculptural project by Antony Gormley consisting of six human figures standing at various points along the river. (The statues are designed to fall over in flood conditions, so some of them may not be visible after heavy rain.)

Directly across Belford Rd from Modern One, another neoclassical mansion (formerly an orphanage) houses its annexe, **Modern Two** (Map p46; ⊘10am-5pm), which is home to a large collection of sculpture and graphic art created by the Edinburgh-born artist Sir Eduardo Paolozzi. One of the 1st-floor rooms houses a re-creation of Paolozzi's studio, while the rest of the building stages temporary exhibitions of modern art.

◉ Leith

Two miles northeast of the city centre, Leith has been Edinburgh's seaport since the 14th century and remained an independent burgh with its own town council until it was incorporated by the city in the 1920s. Like many of Britain's dockland areas, it fell into decay in the decades following WWII but has been undergoing a revival since the late 1980s. Old warehouses have been turned into luxury flats, and a lush crop of trendy bars and restaurants has sprouted along the waterfront. The area was given an additional boost in the late 1990s when the Scottish Executive (a government department) moved to a new building on Leith docks.

The city council has formulated a major redevelopment plan for the entire Edinburgh waterfront from Leith to Granton, the first phase of which is Ocean Terminal (p90), a shopping and leisure complex that includes the former Royal Yacht Britannia and a berth for visiting cruise liners. Parts of Leith are still a bit rough but it's a distinctive corner of the city and well worth a bit of exploring.

★**Royal Yacht Britannia**   SHIP
(www.royalyachtbritannia.co.uk; Ocean Terminal; adult/child £12.75/7.75; ⊘9.30am-6pm Jul-Sep, to 5.30pm Apr-Jun & Oct, 10am-5pm Nov-Mar, last admission 90min before closing; ⊡11, 22, 34, 35, 36)
Built on Clydeside, the former Royal Yacht Britannia was the British royal family's floating holiday home during their foreign travels from the time of her launch in 1953 until her decommissioning in 1997, and is now moored permanently in front of Ocean Terminal. The tour, which you take at your own pace with an audioguide (included in admission fee and available in 20 languages), lifts the curtain on the everyday lives of the royals, and gives an intriguing insight into the Queen's private tastes.

Britannia is a monument to 1950s decor, and the accommodation reveals Her Majesty's preference for simple, unfussy surroundings. There was nothing simple or unfussy, however, about the running of the ship. When the Queen travelled, with her went 45 members of the royal household, five tons of luggage and a Rolls-Royce that was carefully squeezed into a specially built garage on the deck. The ship's company consisted of an admiral, 20 officers and 220 yachtsmen.

The decks (of Burmese teak) were scrubbed daily, but all work near the royal accommodation was carried out in complete silence and had to be finished by 8am. A thermometer was kept in the Queen's bathroom to make sure the water was the correct temperature, and when in harbour one yachtsman was charged with ensuring that the angle of the gangway never exceeded 12 degrees. Note the mahogany windbreak that was added to the balcony deck in front of the bridge. It was put there to stop wayward breezes from blowing up skirts and inadvertently revealing the royal undies.

Britannia was joined in 2010 by the 1930s **racing yacht Bloodhound**, which was owned by the Queen in the 1960s. She is moored alongside Britannia (except in July and August, when she is away cruising) as part of an exhibition about the Royal family's love of all things nautical.

The Majestic Tour (p68) bus runs from Waverley Bridge to Britannia during opening times.

◎ Greater Edinburgh

Edinburgh Zoo   ZOO
(www.edinburghzoo.org.uk; 134 Corstorphine Rd; adult/child £16.50/12; ☺9am-6pm Apr-Sep, to 5pm Oct & Mar, to 4.30pm Nov-Feb) Opened in 1913, Edinburgh Zoo is one of the world's leading conservation zoos. Edinburgh's captive breeding program has helped save many endangered species, including Siberian tigers, pygmy hippos and red pandas. The main attractions are the two giant pandas, Tian Tian and Yang Guang, who arrived in December 2011; the penguin parade (the zoo's penguins go for a walk every day at 2.15pm), and the sea lion training session (daily at 11.15am).

The zoo is 2.5 miles west of the city centre; take Lothian Bus 12, 26 or 31, First Bus 16, 18, 80 or 86, or the Airlink Bus 100 westbound from Princes St.

Royal Botanic Garden   GARDENS
(www.rbge.org.uk; Arboretum Pl; ☺10am-6pm Mar-Sep, to 5pm Feb & Oct, to 4pm Nov-Jan; ⛟8, 23, 27) **FREE** Edinburgh's Royal Botanic Garden is the second oldest institution of its kind in Britain (after Oxford), and one of the most respected in the world. Founded near Holyrood in 1670 and moved to its present location in 1823, its 70 beautifully landscaped acres include splendid Victorian glass houses, colourful swathes of rhododendron and azalea, and a world-famous rock garden. The garden's new visitor centre, the John Hope Gateway, is housed in a striking, environmentally-friendly building overlooking the main entrance on Arboretum Place.

The centre has exhibitions on biodiversity, climate change and sustainable development, as well as displays of rare plants from the institution's collection and a specially created biodiversity garden. Take Lothian Bus 8, 23 or 27 to the East Gate, or the Majestic Tour (p68) bus to the main entrance.

Cramond   NEIGHBOURHOOD
With its moored yachts, stately swans and whitewashed houses spilling down the hillside at the mouth of the River Almond, Cramond is the most picturesque corner of Edinburgh. It is also rich in history. The Romans built a fort here in the 2nd century AD, but recent archaeological excavations have revealed evidence of a Bronze Age settlement dating from 8500 BC, the oldest-known site in Scotland.

Cramond, which was originally a mill village, has a historic 17th-century church and a 15th-century tower house, as well as some rather unimpressive Roman remains, but most people come to enjoy the walks along the river to the ruined mills and to stroll along the seafront. On the riverside, opposite the cottage on the far bank, is the **Maltings** (☑0131-336 2124; www.cramondassociation.org.uk; Riverside, Cramond; ☺2-5pm Sat & Sun Apr-Sep, daily during Edinburgh Festival) **FREE**, which hosts an interesting exhibition on Cramond's history.

Cramond is 5 miles northwest of the city centre; take bus 41 from George St (westbound) or Queensferry St to Cramond Glebe Rd, then walk north for 400m.

Craigmillar Castle   CASTLE
(HS; Craigmillar Castle Rd; adult/child £5.50/3.30; ☺9.30am-5.30pm Apr-Sep, to 4.30pm Oct-Mar) If you want to explore a Scottish fortress away from the crowds that throng Edinburgh Castle, try Craigmillar. Dating from the 15th century, the tower house rises above two sets of machicolated curtain walls. Mary, Queen of Scots took refuge here after the murder of Rizzio; it was here too that plans to murder her husband Darnley were laid. Look for the prison cell complete with built-in sanitation, something some 'modern' British prisons only finally managed in 1996.

The castle is 2.5 miles southeast of the city centre. Take bus 33 (eastbound) from Princes St to Old Dalkeith Rd and walk 500m up Craigmillar Castle Rd.

◎ Quirky Edinburgh

Edinburgh is full of unusual attractions and out-of-the-way corners that most visitors never see – even though they may be standing just a few metres away. Here are a few of the city's less-mainstream attractions.

Surgeons' Hall Museum   MUSEUM
(Map p52; www.museum.rcsed.ac.uk; Nicolson St; adult/child £5/3; ☺10am-5pm daily Apr-Oct, noon-4pm Mon-Fri Nov-Mar; ⛟all South Bridge buses) Housed in a grand Ionic temple designed by William Playfair in 1832, the History of Surgery display provides a fascinating look at surgery in Scotland from the 15th century – when barbers supplemented their income with bloodletting, amputations and other surgical procedures – to the present day. The highlight is the exhibit on Burke and Hare, which includes Burke's death mask and a

THE RESURRECTION MEN

In 1505, Edinburgh's newly founded Royal College of Surgeons was officially allocated the corpse of one executed criminal per year for the purposes of dissection. But this was not nearly enough to satisfy the curiosity of the city's anatomists, and in the following centuries an illegal trade in dead bodies emerged, which reached its culmination in the early 19th century when the anatomy classes of famous surgeons such as Professor Robert Knox drew audiences of up to 500.

The readiest supply of corpses was to be found in the city's graveyards, especially Greyfriars. Grave robbers – who came to be known as 'resurrection men' – plundered newly buried coffins and sold the cadavers to the anatomists, who turned a blind eye to the source of their research material.

This gruesome trade led to a series of countermeasures, including the mort-safe – a metal cage that was placed over a coffin until the corpse had begun to decompose; you can see examples in Greyfriars Kirkyard (p57) and on level 5 of the National Museum of Scotland (p57). Watchtowers, where a sexton, or relatives of the deceased, would keep watch over new graves, survive in St Cuthbert's and Duddingston kirkyards.

The notorious William Burke and William Hare, who kept a lodging house in Tanner's Close at the west end of the Grassmarket, took the body-snatching business a step further. When an elderly lodger died without paying his rent, Burke and Hare stole his body from the coffin and sold it to the famous Professor Knox. Seeing a lucrative business opportunity, they figured that rather than waiting for someone else to die, they could create their own supply of fresh cadavers by resorting to murder.

Burke and Hare preyed on the poor and weak of Edinburgh's Grassmarket, luring them back to Hare's lodging house, plying them with drink and then suffocating their victims. Between December 1827 and October 1828, they murdered at least 16 people, selling their bodies to Professor Knox. When the law finally caught up with them, Hare turned King's evidence and testified against Burke.

Burke was hanged outside St Giles Cathedral in January 1829 and, in an ironic twist, his body was given to the anatomy school for public dissection. His skeleton, and a wallet made from his flayed skin, are still on display in Surgeons' Hall Museums (p65).

It was as a result of the Burke and Hare case that the Anatomy Act of 1832 – regulating the supply of cadavers for dissection, and still in force today – was passed.

pocketbook bound in his skin. The museum will be closed for redevelopment until summer 2015.

The adjacent Dental Collection, with its wince-inducing collections of extraction tools, covers the history of dentistry, while the Pathology Museum houses a gruesome but compelling 19th-century collection of diseased organs and massive tumours pickled in formaldehyde.

Gilmerton Cove　　　　　　HISTORIC SITE
(www.gilmertoncove.org.uk; 16 Drum St; adult/child £7.50/4; ◷10am-4pm) While ghost tours of Edinburgh's underground vaults and haunted graveyards have become a mainstream attraction, Gilmerton Cove remains an off-the-beaten-track gem. Hidden in the southern suburbs, the mysterious 'cove' is a series of manmade subterranean caverns hacked out of the rock, their origin and function unknown. Advance booking essential through

Rosslyn Tours (☑0845 894 5295; www.rosslyntours.co.uk).

Mansfield Place Church　　　　　CHURCH
(Map p46; www.mansfieldtraquair.org.uk; Mansfield Pl; ◷1-4pm 2nd Sun of the month, 11am-1pm most days during Edinburgh Festival Fringe; 🚌8) FREE In complete contrast to the austerity of most of Edinburgh's religious buildings, this 19th-century, neo-Romanesque church at the foot of Broughton St contains a remarkable series of Renaissance-style frescos painted in the 1890s by Irish-born artist Phoebe Anna Traquair (1852–1936). The murals have been restored and are on view to the public (check the website for any changes to viewing times).

Museum on the Mound　　　　　MUSEUM
(Map p52; www.museumonthemound.com; The Mound; ◷10am-5pm Tue-Fri, 1-5pm Sat & Sun; 🚌23, 27, 41, 42) FREE Housed in the Bank of Scotland's splendid Georgian HQ, this

museum is a treasure trove of gold coins, bullion chests, safes, banknotes, forgeries, cartoons and lots of fascinating old documents and photographs charting the history of Scotland's oldest bank.

Edinburgh University Collection of Historic Musical Instruments   MUSEUM
(Map p52; www.music.ed.ac.uk/euchmi; Reid Concert Hall, Teviot Pl; ⊙3-5pm Wed, 10am-1pm Sat year-round, 2-5pm Mon-Fri during Edinburgh Festival) FREE Musicians will enjoy this collection, which contains more than 1000 instruments, ranging from a 400-year-old lute to a 1959 synthesiser.

Burry Man   CULTURAL
If you're in Edinburgh on the first Friday of August, head to the village of Queensferry to see the bizarre Burry Man. As part of the village gala day, a local man roams the streets wearing a woolly suit, which has been laboriously covered in prickly burrs. One glance at his costume – he looks like a child's drawing of a Martian, with added prickles – would make you think he's suffering a medieval punishment, but it's actually a great honour to be selected.

🏃 Activities

Walking
Edinburgh is lucky to have several good walking areas within the city boundary, including Arthur's Seat, Calton Hill, Blackford Hill, Hermitage of Braid, Corstorphine Hill and the coast and river at Cramond. The Pentland Hills, which rise to over 500m, stretch southwest from the city for 15 miles, offering excellent high- and low-level walking.

You can follow the Water of Leith Walkway from the city centre to Balerno (8 miles), and continue across the Pentlands to Silverburn (6.5 miles) or Carlops (8 miles), and return to Edinburgh by bus. Another good walk is along the Union Canal towpath, which begins in Fountainbridge and runs all the way to Falkirk (31 miles). You can return to Edinburgh by bus at Ratho (8.5 miles) or Broxburn (12 miles), and by bus or train from Linlithgow (21 miles).

Cycling
Edinburgh and its surroundings offer many excellent opportunities for cycling (see www.cyclingedinburgh.info and www.cycling-edinburgh.org.uk). The main off-road routes from the city centre out to the countryside follow the Union Canal towpath then the Water of Leith Walkway from Tollcross southwestwards to Balerno (7.5 miles) on the edge of the Pentland Hills, and the Innocent Railway Cycle Path from the southern side of Arthur's Seat eastwards to Musselburgh (5 miles) and on to Ormiston and Pencaitland.

There are several routes through the Pentland Hills that are suitable for mountain bikes. For details ask at any bike shop or check out the Pentland Hills Regional Park (www.pentlandhills.org) website. The Spokes *Edinburgh Cycle Map* (www.spokes.org.uk; available from cycle shops for £6) shows all the city's cycle routes.

Cycle Scotland   BICYCLE RENTAL
(Map p52; ☑0131-556 5560; www.cyclescotland.co.uk; 29 Blackfriars St; per day £15-20, per week £70-90; ⊙10am-6pm Mon-Sat) The friendly and helpful folk here rent out top-quality bikes; rates include helmet, lock and repair kit. You can hire tents and touring equipment too. The company also organises cycle tours in Edinburgh and all over Scotland – check the website for details.

Golf
There are no fewer than 19 golf courses in Edinburgh – the following are two of the best city courses.

Braid Hills Public Golf Course   GOLF
(www.edinburghleisuregolf.co.uk; Braid Hills Approach; green fees weekday/weekend £22/24.75) A scenic but challenging course to the south of the city centre.

Duddingston Golf Course   GOLF
(www.duddingstongolfclub.co.uk; Duddingston Rd West; green fees weekday/weekend £44/50) Enjoys a picturesque setting at the foot of Arthur's Seat.

Swimming
The Firth of Forth is a bit on the chilly side for enjoyable swimming, but there are indoor alternatives.

Royal Commonwealth Pool   SWIMMING
(Map p46; www.thecommiepool.co.uk; 21 Dalkeith Rd; adult/child £5.90/3; ⊙5.30am-10pm Mon-Fri, to 8pm Sat, 7.30am-8pm Sun) Edinburgh's main facility – built for the 1970 Commonwealth Games, and which served again as a venue for the 2014 Glasgow games – is affectionately known as the 'Commie Pool'. Recently refurbished, it has a 50m eight-lane pool,

diving pool, teaching/children's pool, fitness centre and kids' soft play area.

Warrender Swim Centre SWIMMING
(Map p46; www.edinburghleisure.co.uk; Thirlestane Rd; adult/child £4.20/2.10; ⊗7am-10pm Mon-Fri, 9am-6pm Sat & Sun) Beautiful Victorian-era 25-yard (23m) pool, with gym and sauna.

☞ Tours

Bus Tours
Open-topped buses leave from Waverley Bridge, outside the main train station, and offer hop-on, hop-off tours of the main sights, taking in New Town, the Grassmarket and the Royal Mile. They're a good way to get your bearings, although with a bus map and a Day Saver bus ticket (£3.50) you could do much the same thing (but without the commentary).

Tickets for the following three tours are valid for 24 hours.

Majestic Tour BUS TOUR
(www.edinburghtour.com; adult/child £13/6; ⊗daily year-round except 25 Dec) Hop on–hop off tour departing every 15 to 20 minutes from Waverley Bridge to the Royal Yacht Britannia at Ocean Terminal via the New Town, Royal Botanic Garden and Newhaven, returning via Leith Walk, Holyrood and the Royal Mile.

City Sightseeing BUS TOUR
(www.edinburghtour.com; adult/child £13/6; ⊗daily year-round except 25 Dec) Bright-red, open-top buses depart every 20 minutes from Waverley Bridge.

EDINBURGH FOR CHILDREN

Edinburgh has a multitude of attractions for children, and most things to see and do are child-friendly. During the Edinburgh and Fringe Festivals there's lots of street theatre for kids, especially on High St and at the foot of The Mound, and in December there's a ferris wheel, an open-air ice rink and fairground rides in Princes Street Gardens.

The Edinburgh Tourist Office (p92) has lots of info on children's events, and the handy guidebook **Edinburgh for Under Fives** (www.edinburghforunderfives.co.uk) can be found in most bookshops. The List (p92) magazine has a special kids' section listing children's activities and events in and around Edinburgh. The week-long Imaginate Festival of children's theatre, dance and puppetry takes place each year in late May/early June.

There are good, safe playgrounds in most Edinburgh parks, including Princes Street Gardens West, Inverleith Park (opposite the Royal Botanic Garden), George V Park (New Town), the Meadows and Bruntsfield Links.

Some more ideas for outdoor activities include exploring the Royal Botanic Garden (p65), going to see the animals at Edinburgh Zoo (p65), visiting the statue of Greyfriars Bobby (p57) and feeding the swans and playing on the beach at Cramond (p65).

If it's raining, you can visit the Discovery Centre, a hands-on activity zone on level 3 of the National Museum of Scotland (p57), play on the flumes at the Royal Commonwealth Pool (p67), try out the earthquake simulator at Our Dynamic Earth (p56), or take a tour of the haunted Real Mary King's Close (p53).

You should be aware that the majority of Scottish pubs, even those that serve bar meals, are forbidden by law to admit children under the age of 14. Even in the family-friendly pubs (ie those in possession of a Children's Certificate), under-14s are only admitted between the hours of 11am and 8pm for a meal, and only when accompanied by an adult. Sixteen- and 17-year-olds can buy and drink beer and wine with a meal in a restaurant.

Childminding Services
For information on government-approved childminding services, contact **Edinburgh Childcare Information Service** (☑0800 032 0323; childcareinformation@edinburgh.gov.uk). The following are reliable Edinburgh agencies that charge from £8 an hour for babysitting:

➡ **Super Mums** (☑0131-225 1744; www.supermums.co.uk)

➡ **Panda's Nanny Agency** (☑0131-663 3967; www.pandasnannyagency.co.uk)

MacTours   BUS TOUR
(www.edinburghtour.com; adult/child £14/6; ☺ Apr-Oct) A quick tour around the highlights of the Old and New Towns, from the castle to Calton Hill, aboard an open-topped vintage bus.

Walking Tours
There are plenty of organised walks around Edinburgh, many of them related to ghosts, murders and witches. For starting times of individual walks, check the websites.

City of the Dead Tours   WALKING TOUR
(www.cityofthedeadtours.com; adult/concession £10/8) This tour of Greyfriars Kirkyard is probably the scariest of Edinburgh's 'ghost' tours. Many people have reported encounters with the 'Mackenzie Poltergeist', the ghost of a 17th-century judge who persecuted the Covenanters, and now haunts their former prison in a corner of the kirkyard. Not suitable for young children.

Cadies & Witchery Tours   WALKING TOUR
(Map p52; www.witcherytours.com; adult/child £8.50/6) The becloaked and pasty-faced Adam Lyal (deceased) leads a 'Murder & Mystery' tour of the Old Town's darker corners. These tours are famous for their 'jumper-ooters' – costumed actors who 'jump oot' when you least expect it.

Edinburgh Literary Pub Tour   WALKING TOUR
(www.edinburghliterarypubtour.co.uk; adult/student £14/10) An enlightening two-hour trawl through Edinburgh's literary history – and its associated howffs (pubs) – in the entertaining company of Messrs Clart and McBrain. One of the city's best walking tours.

Mercat Tours   WALKING TOUR
(Map p52; www.mercattours.com; adult/child £10/5) Mercat offers a wide range of fascinating history walks and 'Ghosts & Ghouls' tours, but its most famous is a visit to the hidden, haunted, underground vaults beneath South Bridge.

Rebus Tours   WALKING TOUR
(www.rebustours.com; adult/student £10/9) A two-hour guided tour of the 'hidden Edinburgh' frequented by novelist Ian Rankin's fictional detective, John Rebus. Not recommended for children under 10.

Trainspotting Tours   WALKING TOUR
(www.leithwalks.co.uk; per person £8) A tour of locations from Irvine Welsh's notorious 1993 novel *Trainspotting*, delivered with wit and enthusiasm. Not suitable for kids.

🎭 Festivals & Events

Edinburgh hosts an amazing number of festivals throughout the year, notably the Edinburgh International Festival, the Edinburgh Festival Fringe and the Military Tattoo. Hogmanay, Scotland's New Year's celebrations, is also a peak party time.

April
**Edinburgh International
Science Festival**   SCIENCE FESTIVAL
(www.sciencefestival.co.uk) First held in 1987, it hosts a wide range of events, including talks, lectures, exhibitions, demonstrations, guided tours and interactive experiments designed to stimulate, inspire and challenge. From dinosaurs to ghosts to alien life forms, there's something to interest everyone. The festival runs over two weeks in April.

May
Imagine Festival   ARTS FESTIVAL
(www.imaginate.org.uk) This is Britain's biggest festival of performing arts for children, with events suitable for kids from three to 12. Groups from around the world perform classic tales such as *Hansel and Gretel*, as well as new material written specially for children. The one-week festival takes place annually in May.

June
Royal Highland Show   AGRICULTURAL SHOW
(www.royalhighlandshow.org; Royal Highland Centre, Ingliston) Scotland's hugely popular national agricultural show is a four-day feast of all things rural, with everything from showjumping and tractor driving to sheep shearing and falconry. Countless pens are filled with coiffed show cattle and pedicured prize ewes. The show is held over a long weekend (Thursday to Sunday) in late June.

**Edinburgh International Film
Festival**   FILM FESTIVAL
(www.edfilmfest.org.uk) One of the original Edinburgh Festival trinity, having first been staged in 1947 along with the International Festival and the Fringe, the two-week June film festival is a major international event, serving as a showcase for new British and European films, and staging the European premieres of one or two Hollywood blockbusters.

1. Balmoral Hotel, Princes Street & the Scott Monument, Edinburgh
The clock on the Balmoral Hotel is traditionally three minutes fast so you don't miss your train.

2. View of Edinburgh from Arthur's Seat (p56)
Expansive views of the city and beyond are the reward for climbing to the summit of Arthur's Seat.

3. National Museum of Scotland, Edinburgh (p57)
Exhibits tracing the history of Scotland are divided between a striking modern new museum building, and a fine example of Victorian architecture.

4. Edinburgh Castle (p45)
Used as a royal residence, a prison and an army base, the castle now houses the Scottish crown jewels and the Stone of Destiny.

FESTIVAL CITY

August in Edinburgh sees a frenzy of festivals, with several world-class events running at the same time.

Edinburgh Festival Fringe

When the first Edinburgh Festival was held in 1947, there were eight theatre companies who didn't make it onto the main program. Undeterred, they grouped together and held their own mini-festival – on the fringe – and an Edinburgh institution was born. Today the **Edinburgh Festival Fringe** (☑ 0131-226 0026; www.edfringe.com) is the biggest festival of the performing arts anywhere in the world.

Since 1990 the Fringe has been dominated by stand-up comedy, but the sheer variety of shows on offer is staggering – everything from chainsaw juggling to performance poetry to Tibetan yak-milk gargling. So how do you decide what to see? There are daily reviews in the *Scotsman* newspaper – one good *Scotsman* review and a show sells out in hours – but the best recommendation is word of mouth. If you have the time, go to at least one unknown show – it may be crap, but at least you'll have your obligatory 'worst show I ever saw' story.

The big names play at megavenues organised by big agencies such as **Assembly** (www.assemblyfestival.com) and the **Gilded Balloon** (www.gildedballoon.co.uk), and charge megaprices (£15 a ticket and up, with some famous comedians notoriously charging more than £30), but there are plenty of good shows in the £5 to £10 range and, best of all, lots of free stuff. **Fringe Sunday** – usually the second Sunday – is a smorgasbord of free performances, staged in the Meadows park to the south of the city centre.

The Fringe takes place over 3½ weeks, the last two weeks overlapping with the first two of the Edinburgh International Festival.

Edinburgh International Festival

First held in 1947 to mark a return to peace after the ordeal of WWII, the **Edinburgh International Festival** (☑ 0131-473 2099; www.eif.co.uk) is festooned with superlatives – the

---

Scottish Real Ale Festival FOOD & DRINK FESTIVAL
(www.scottishbeerfestival.org.uk) A celebration of all things fermented and yeasty, Scotland's biggest beer-fest gives you the opportunity to sample a wide range of traditionally brewed beers from Scotland and around the world. Froth-topped bliss. The festival is held over a weekend in June or July.

July

Edinburgh International Jazz & Blues Festival MUSIC FESTIVAL
(www.edinburghjazzfestival.com) Held annually since 1978, the Jazz & Blues Festival pulls in top talent from all over the world. It runs for nine days, beginning on a Friday, a week before the Fringe and Tattoo begin. The first weekend sees a carnival parade on Princes St and an afternoon of free, open-air music in Princes Street Gardens.

August

The Edinburgh International Festival, the Edinburgh Festival Fringe, the Edinburgh International Book Festival and the Military Tattoo are all held around the same time in August.

December

Edinburgh's Hogmanay is the biggest winter festival in Europe (see p90).

Edinburgh's Christmas FESTIVAL
(www.edinburghschristmas.com) The youngest of the Scottish capital's festivals, first held in 2000, the Christmas bash runs from late November to early January and includes a big street parade, a Christmas market, a fairground and Ferris wheel, and an open-air ice rink in Princes Street Gardens.

🛌 Sleeping

Despite a boom in hotel building in the early 2000s, you can still guarantee the city will be packed to the gills during the festival period (August) and over Hogmanay (New Year). If you want a room during these periods, book as far in advance as possible – a year ahead if possible. In general, it's best to book at least a few months ahead for accommodation at Easter and from mid-May to mid-September.

oldest, the biggest, the most famous, the best in the world. The original was a modest affair, but today hundreds of the world's top musicians and performers congregate in Edinburgh for three weeks of diverse and inspirational music, opera, theatre and dance.

The festival takes place over the three weeks ending on the first Saturday in September; the program is usually available from April. Tickets for popular events – especially music and opera – sell out quickly, so it's best to book as far in advance as possible. You can buy tickets in person at the **Hub** (☑ 0131-473 2015; www.thehub-edinburgh.com; Castlehill; admission free; ☺ ticket centre 10am-5pm Mon-Sat), or by phone or internet.

Edinburgh Military Tattoo

August in Edinburgh kicks off with the **Edinburgh Military Tattoo** (☑ 0131-225 1188; www.edintattoo.co.uk), a spectacular display of military marching bands, massed pipes and drums, acrobats, cheerleaders and motorcycle display teams, all played out in front of the magnificent backdrop of the floodlit castle. Each show traditionally finishes with a lone piper, dramatically lit, playing a lament on the battlements. The Tattoo takes place over the first three weeks of August (from a Friday to a Saturday); there's one show at 9pm Monday to Friday and two (at 7.30pm and 10.30pm) on Saturday, but no performance on Sunday.

Edinburgh International Book Festival

Held in a little village of marquees in the middle of Charlotte Sq, the **Edinburgh International Book Festival** (☑ 0845 373 5888; www.edbookfest.co.uk) is a fun fortnight of talks, readings, debates, lectures, book signings and meet-the-author events, with a cafe-bar and tented bookshop thrown in. The festival lasts for two weeks (usually the first two weeks of the Edinburgh International Festival).

Hotels and hostels are found throughout the Old and New Towns; midrange B&Bs and guest houses are concentrated outside the centre in the suburbs of Tollcross, Bruntsfield, Newington and Pilrig.

Edinburgh accommodation is slightly more expensive than the rest of Scotland, so the price breakdown here is as follows: budget is less than £60, midrange £60 to £150, and top end is more than £150, based on the cost of a double room with bed and breakfast.

🛏 Old Town

Most of the interesting accommodation in the Old Town is either backpacker hostels or expensive hotels. For midrange options you'll have to resort to chain hotels – check the websites of Travelodge, Ibis etc.

★ **Malone's Old Town Hostel**   HOSTEL £
(Map p52; ☑ 0131-226 7648; www.maloneshostel.com; 14 Forrest Rd; dm £16-25; @ ☺) No fancy decor or style credentials here, but they've got the basics right: it's clean, comfortable and friendly, and set upstairs from an Irish pub where guests get discounts on food and drink. It's in a superbly central location, an easy walk from the Royal Mile, the castle, the Grassmarket and Princes St.

Castle Rock Hostel   HOSTEL £
(Map p52; ☑ 0131-225-9666; www.scotlands-top-hostels.com; 15 Johnston Tce; dm £14-24, tr £54-60; @ ☺) With its bright, spacious, single-sex dorms, superb views and friendly staff, the 200-bed Castle Rock has lots to like. It has a great location – the only way to get closer to the castle would be to pitch a tent on the esplanade – a games room, reading lounge and big-screen video nights.

Smart City Hostel   HOSTEL £
(Map p52; ☑ 0131-524 1989; www.smartcityhostels.com; 50 Blackfriars St; dm £24-28, tr £99; @ ☺) A big, modern hostel, with a convivial cafe where you can buy breakfast, and mod cons such as keycard access and charging stations for mobile phones, MP3 players and laptops. Lockers in every room, a huge bar and a central location just off the Royal Mile make this a favourite among the young, party-mad crowd – don't expect a quiet night!

Budget Backpackers   HOSTEL £

(Map p52; ☑ 0131-226 6351; www.budgetbackpack-ers.com; 9 Cowgate; dm£13-18, tw from £48; @ 🛜) This fun spot piles on the extras, with bike storage, pool tables, laundry and a colourful chill-out lounge. You'll pay a little more for four-bunk dorms, but larger dorms are great value. The only downside is that prices increase at weekends, but otherwise a brilliant spot to doss.

Ten Hill Place   HOTEL ££

(Map p52; ☑ 0131-662 2080; www.tenhillplace.com; 10 Hill Pl; r from £113; P 🛜) 🅿 This attractive modern hotel offers good-value accommodation close to the city centre. The standard bedrooms are comfortable and stylish with a sober but sophisticated colour scheme in rich browns, purples and tweedy greens, and appealing modern bathrooms. For a special weekend, ask for one of the four 'skyline' rooms on the top floor, with panoramic views of Salisbury Crags.

★ Witchery by the Castle   B&B £££

(Map p52; ☑ 0131-225 5613; www.thewitchery.com; Castlehill, Royal Mile; ste £325-360) Set in a 16th-century Old Town house in the shadow of Edinburgh Castle, the Witchery's nine lavish Gothic suites are extravagantly furnished with antiques, oak panelling, tapestries, open fires, four-poster beds and roll-top baths, and supplied with flowers, chocolates and complimentary champagne. Overwhelmingly popular – you'll have to book several months in advance to be sure of getting a room.

Hotel Missoni   BOUTIQUE HOTEL £££

(Map p52; ☑ 0131-220 6666; www.hotelmissoni.com; 1 George IV Bridge; r £125-290; 🛜) The Italian fashion house has established a style icon in the heart of the medieval Old Town with this bold statement of a hotel – modernistic architecture, black-and-white decor with well-judged splashes of colour, impeccably mannered staff and, most importantly, very comfortable bedrooms and bathrooms with lots of nice little touches, from fresh milk in the minibar to plush bathrobes.

Knight Residence   APARTMENTS £££

(Map p52; ☑ 0131-622 8120; www.theknightresidence.co.uk; 12 Lauriston St; 1-/2-bedroom apt from £150/200; P 🛜) Works by contemporary artists adorn these modern one- and two-bedroom apartments (available by the night; the latter sleep up to four adults and one child), each with fully equipped kitchen

---

🏃 City Walk
Old Town Alleys

START CASTLE ESPLANADE
FINISH COCKBURN ST
DISTANCE ONE MILE
DURATION 1–2 HOURS

This walk explores the alleys and side streets around the Royal Mile, and involves a bit of climbing up and down steep stairs.

Begin on the ❶ **Castle Esplanade**, which provides a grandstand view south over the Grassmarket; the prominent quadrangular building with all the turrets is George Heriot's School, which you'll be passing later on. Head towards Castlehill and the start of the Royal Mile.

The 17th-century house on the right is known as ❷ **Cannonball House** because of the iron ball lodged in the wall (look between, and slightly below, the two largest windows on the wall facing the castle). It was not fired in anger, but marks the gravitation height to which water would flow naturally from the city's first piped water supply.

The low, rectangular building across the street (now a touristy tartan-weaving mill) was originally the reservoir that held the Old Town's water supply. On its west wall is the ❸ **Witches Well**, where a bronze fountain commemorates around 4000 people (mostly women) who were executed between 1479 and 1722 on suspicion of witchcraft.

Go past the reservoir and turn left down Ramsay Lane. Take a look at ❹ **Ramsay Garden** – one of Edinburgh's most desirable addresses – where late-19th-century apartments were built around the octagonal Ramsay Lodge, once home to poet Allan Ramsay. The cobbled street continues around to the right below student residences, to the towers of the ❺ **New College**, home to Edinburgh University's Faculty of Divinity. Nip into the courtyard to see the statue of John Knox (a firebrand preacher who led the Protestant Reformation in Scotland, and was instrumental in the creation of the Church of Scotland in 1560).

Just past New College turn right and climb the stairs into Milne's Court, a student residence belonging to Edinburgh University. Exit into Lawnmarket, cross the

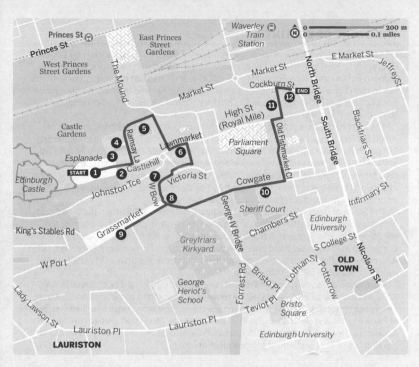

street (bearing slightly left) and duck into
6 Riddell's Court, a typical Old Town close
at No 322–8. You'll find yourself in a small
courtyard, but the house in front of you (built in
1590) was originally the edge of the street (the
building you just walked under was added in
1726 – look for the inscription in the doorway
on the right). The arch with the inscription
Vivendo discimus (we live and learn) leads into
the original 16th-century courtyard.

Go back into the street, turn right and right
again down Fisher's Close, which leads to
the delightful Victoria Terrace, strung above
the cobbled curve of shop-lined Victoria St.
Wander right, enjoying the view – **7 Maxie's
Bistro** (p81), at the far end of the terrace, is a
great place to stop for a drink – then descend
the stairs at the foot of Upper Bow and continue downhill to the Grassmarket. At the east
end, outside Maggie Dickson's pub, is the **8
Covenanters Monument**, which marks the
site of the gallows where more than 100 Covenanters were martyred in the 17th century.

If you're feeling peckish, the Grassmarket
has several good places to eat and a couple
of good pubs – Robert Burns once stayed at
the **9 White Hart Inn**. Head east along the
gloomy defile of the Cowgate, passing under

the arch of George IV Bridge – the buildings to
your right are the new law courts, while high up
to the left you can see the complex of buildings
behind Parliament Sq. Past the courts, on the
right, is **10 Tailors Hall** (built 1621, extended
1757), now a hotel and bar but formerly the
meeting place of the Companie of Tailzeours
(Tailors' Guild).

Turn left and climb up Old Fishmarket
Close, a typical cobbled Old Town wynd, and
emerge once more onto the Royal Mile. Across
the street and slightly downhill is **11 Anchor
Close**, named for a tavern that once stood
there. It hosted the Crochallan Fencibles, an
18th-century drinking club that provided its
patrons with an agreeable blend of intellectual
debate and intoxicating liquor. The club was
founded by William Smellie, editor of the first
edition of the *Encyclopedia Brittanica;* its best-
known member was the poet Robert Burns.

Go down Anchor Close, to finish the walk
on **12 Cockburn St**, one of the city's coolest
shopping streets, lined with record shops and
clothing boutiques. The street was cut through
Old Town tenements in the 1850s to provide an
easy route between Waverley Station and the
Royal Mile.

THE STONE OF DESTINY

On St Andrew's Day 1996 a block of sandstone – 26.5 inches by 16.5 inches by 11 inches in size, with rusted iron hoops at either end – was installed with much pomp and ceremony in Edinburgh Castle. For the previous 700 years it had lain in London, beneath the Coronation Chair in Westminster Abbey. Almost all English, and later British, monarchs from Edward II in 1307 to Elizabeth II in 1953 have parked their backsides firmly over this stone during their coronation ceremony.

The legendary Stone of Destiny – said to have originated in the Holy Land, and on which Scottish kings placed their feet during their coronation (not their bums; the English got that bit wrong) – was stolen from Scone Abbey near Perth by King Edward I of England in 1296. It was taken to London and there it remained for seven centuries – except for a brief removal to Gloucester during WWII air raids, and a three-month sojourn in Scotland after it was stolen by Scottish Nationalist students at Christmas in 1950 – as an enduring symbol of Scotland's subjugation by England.

The Stone of Destiny returned to the political limelight in 1996, when the then Scottish Secretary and Conservative Party MP Michael Forsyth arranged for the return of the sandstone block to Scotland. A blatant attempt to boost the flagging popularity of the Conservative Party in Scotland prior to a general election, Forsyth's publicity stunt failed miserably. The Scots said thanks very much for the stone and then, in May 1997, voted every Conservative MP in Scotland into oblivion.

Many people, however, believe Edward I was fobbed off with a shoddy imitation in 1296 and that the true Stone of Destiny remains safely hidden somewhere in Scotland. This is not impossible – some descriptions of the original stone state that it was made of black marble and decorated with elaborate carvings. Interested parties should read *Scotland's Stone of Destiny* by Nick Aitchinson, which details the history and cultural significance of Scotland's most famous lump of rock.

and comfortable lounge with cable TV, video and stereo. It has a good central location in a quiet street only a few minutes' walk from the Grassmarket.

New Town & Around

Haggis Hostel HOSTEL £
(Map p60; ☑0131-557 0036; www.haggishostels. co.uk; 3 West Register St; dm £18-30; @🖤) The Haggis is a small, clean and relatively quiet hostel, with pine-wood bunks and comfy mattresses in four-, eight- and 10-bed dorms. There's a small kitchen and recreation area, and a laundry. The location is great, off the east end of Princes St and just two minutes' walk from train and bus stations.

★ **Sheridan Guest House** B&B ££
(☑0131-554 4107; www.sheridanedinburgh.co.uk; 1 Bonnington Tce, Newhaven Rd; s/d from £55/70; 🖤) Flowerpots filled with colourful blooms line the steps of this little haven hidden away to the north of the New Town. The eight bedrooms (all en suite) blend crisp colours with contemporary furniture, stylish lighting and colourful paintings, which complement the house's clean-cut Georgian lines, while the

breakfast menu adds omelettes, pancakes with maple syrup, and scrambled eggs with smoked salmon to the usual offerings. Take bus 11 from the city centre.

B+B Edinburgh HOTEL ££
(Map p46; ☑0131-225 5084; www.bb-edinburgh. com; 3 Rothesay Tce; d/ste from £110/170; 🖤) Built in 1883 as a grand home for the proprietor of the *Scotsman* newspaper, this Victorian extravaganza of carved oak, parquet floors, stained glass and elaborate fireplaces was given a designer makeover in 2011 to create a striking contemporary hotel. Rooms on the 2nd floor are the most spacious, but the smaller top-floor rooms enjoy the finest views.

Gerald's Place B&B ££
(Map p60; ☑0131-558 7017; www.geraldsplace. com; 21b Abercromby Pl; d £119-169; @🖤) Gerald is an unfailingly charming and helpful host, and his lovely Georgian garden flat (just two guest bedrooms) has a great location across from a peaceful park, an easy stroll from the city centre. There may be a minimum three-night stay in peak season.

Mingalar Guest House B&B ££
(Map p46; ☎ 0131-556 7000; www.mingalar.eu; 2 East Claremont St; s/d £75/90; @; ☐ 8, 17) This townhouse has been beautifully refurbished to highlight its elegant Georgian lines, retaining many original features including ceiling cornices, marble fireplaces and stained-glass front door. There are eight bright, high-ceilinged bedrooms, all with en suite bathrooms (showers only), including two family rooms. Breakfast is a cheerful affair and well above average, with eggs and bacon freshly cooked to order.

Dene Guest House B&B ££
(Map p46; ☎ 0131-556 2700; www.deneguesthouse. com; 7 Eyre Pl; per person £25-50; ☎) The Dene is a friendly and informal place, set in a charming Georgian town house, with a welcoming owner and spacious bedrooms. The inexpensive single rooms make it ideal for solo travellers; children under 10 staying in their parents' room pay half price.

Frederick House Hotel HOTEL ££
(Map p 60; ☎ 0131-226 1999; www.frederickhouse-hotel.com; 42 Frederick St; s/d £120/150; ☎) This well-positioned, good-value hotel has roomy double beds and large baths to soak away the day's walking aches. It's also one of few options in this price range that has a lift, which is ideal is you've got lots of baggage. Breakfast is served in the cafe across the street.

One Royal Circus B&B £££
(Map p60; ☎ 0131-625 6669; www.oneroyalcircus. com; 1 Royal Circus; r £180-260; ☎) Live the New Town dream at this incredibly chic Georgian mansion where genuine antiques and parquet floors sit comfortably alongside slate bathrooms and Philippe Starck furniture. Bedrooms are kitted out with Egyptian cotton sheets, iPod docks and Arran Aromatics toiletries, and there are foosball and pool tables in the drawing room.

Tigerlily BOUTIQUE HOTEL £££
(Map p 60; ☎ 0131-225 5005; www.tigerlilyedinburgh.co.uk; 125 George St; r from £210; ☎) Georgian meets gorgeous at this glamorous, glittering boutique hotel (complete with its own nightclub) decked out in mirror mosaics, beaded curtains, swirling Timorous Beasties textiles and wall coverings, and atmospheric pink uplighting. Book the Georgian Suite (from £410) for a truly special romantic getaway.

Glasshouse HOTEL £££
(Map p60; ☎ 0131-525 8200; www.theglasshouse-hotel.co.uk; 2 Greenside Pl; r from £156; P☎) A palace of cutting-edge design perched atop the Omni Centre at the foot of Calton Hill, and entered through the preserved facade of a 19th-century church, the Glasshouse sports luxury rooms with floor-to-ceiling windows, leather sofas, marble bathrooms and a rooftop garden.

🛏 South Edinburgh

There are lots of guest houses in the South Edinburgh suburbs of Tollcross, Morningside, Marchmont and Newington, especially on and around Minto St and Mayfield Gardens (the continuation of North Bridge and Nicolson St) in Newington. This is the main traffic artery from the south and a key bus route into the city centre.

Argyle Backpackers HOSTEL £
(Map p46; ☎ 0131-667 9991; www.argyle-backpackers.co.uk; 14 Argyle Pl; dm £18-22, s/tw £56/58; @☎) The Argyle, spread across three adjacent terraced houses, is a quiet and relaxed hostel offering single, double and twin rooms as well as four- to 10-bed dorms (mixed sex). There is a comfortable TV lounge, an attractive little conservatory and a pleasant walled garden at the back where you can sit outside in summer.

★Southside Guest House B&B ££
(Map p46; ☎ 0131-668 4422; www.southsideg-uesthouse.co.uk; 8 Newington Rd; s/d £75/95; ☎) Though set in a typical Victorian terrace, the Southside transcends the traditional guesthouse category and feels more like a modern boutique hotel. Its eight stylish rooms ooze interior design, standing out from other

ACCOMMODATION AGENCIES

If you arrive in Edinburgh without a room, the Edinburgh Tourist Office (p92) booking service will try to find a room to suit you (and will charge a £5 fee if successful). If you have the time, pick up the tourist office's accommodation brochure and ring around yourself.

You can also try VisitScotland's **booking hotline** (☎ 0845 859 1006), which has a £3 surcharge; or search for accommodation on the VisitScotland Edinburgh & Lothians (p92) website.

Newington B&Bs through the clever use of bold colours and modern furniture. Breakfast is an event, with Bucks fizz (champagne mixed with orange juice) on offer to smooth the rough edges off your hangover!

No 45 B&B ££
(☎ 0131-667 3536; www.edinburghbedbreakfast.com; 45 Gilmour Rd; s/d £70/140; ☎) A peaceful setting, large garden and friendly owners contribute to the appeal of this Victorian terraced house, which overlooks the local bowling green. The decor is a blend of 19th- and 20th-century, with bold Victorian reds, pine floors and period fireplace in the lounge, a rocking horse and art-nouveau lamp in the hallway, and a 1930s vibe in the three spacious bedrooms. It's two miles south of the city.

Aonach Mor Guest House B&B ££
(☎ 0131-667 8694; www.aonachmor.com; 14 Kilmaurs Tce; r £50-125; @ ☎) This elegant Victorian terraced house is located on a quiet back street and has seven bedrooms, beautifully decorated, with many original period features. Our favourite is the four-poster bedroom with polished mahogany furniture and period fireplace. Located one mile southeast of the city centre.

Sherwood Guest House B&B ££
(Map p46; ☎ 0131-667 1200; www.sherwood-edinburgh.com; 42 Minto St; d £55-100; P ☎) One of the most attractive guest houses on Minto St's B&B strip, the Sherwood is a refurbished Georgian terraced house decked out with hanging baskets and shrubs. Inside are six en suite rooms that combine Regency-style

UNDERGROUND EDINBURGH

As Edinburgh expanded in the late 18th and early 19th centuries, many old tenements were demolished and new bridges were built to link the Old Town to the newly built areas to its north and south. South Bridge (built between 1785 and 1788) and George IV Bridge (built between 1829 and 1834) lead south from the Royal Mile over the deep valley of Cowgate, but so many buildings have been constructed around them you can hardly tell they are bridges – George IV Bridge has a total of nine arches but only two are visible; South Bridge has no less than 18 hidden arches.

These subterranean vaults were originally used as storerooms, workshops and drinking dens. But as Edinburgh's population swelled in the early 19th century with an influx of penniless Highlanders cleared from their lands, and Irish refugees from the potato famine, the dark, dripping chambers were given over to slum accommodation and abandoned to poverty, filth and crime.

The vaults were eventually cleared in the late 19th century, then lay forgotten until 1994 when the **South Bridge vaults** were opened to guided tours. Certain chambers are said to be haunted and one particular vault was investigated by paranormal researchers in 2001.

Nevertheless, the most ghoulish aspect of Edinburgh's hidden history dates from much earlier – from the plague that struck the city in 1645. Legend has it that the disease-ridden inhabitants of **Mary King's Close** (a lane on the northern side of the Royal Mile, on the site of the City Chambers – you can still see its blocked-off northern end from Cockburn St) were walled up in their houses and left to perish. When the lifeless bodies were eventually cleared from the houses, they were so stiff that workmen had to hack off limbs to get them through the small doorways and narrow, twisting stairs.

From that day on, the close was said to be haunted by the spirits of the plague victims. The few people who were prepared to live there reported seeing apparitions of severed heads and limbs, and the largely abandoned close fell into ruin. When the Royal Exchange (now the City Chambers) was constructed between 1753 and 1761, it was built over the lower levels of Mary King's Close, which were left intact and sealed off beneath the building.

Interest in the close revived in the 20th century when Edinburgh's city council began to allow occasional guided tours to enter. Visitors have reported many supernatural experiences – the most famous ghost is 'Sarah', a little girl whose sad tale has prompted people to leave gifts of dolls in a corner of one of the rooms. In 2003 the close was opened to the public as the Real Mary King's Close (p53).

striped wallpaper with modern fabrics and pine furniture.

Town House
B&B ££

(Map p46; ☑ 0131-229 1985; www.thetownhouse.com; 65 Gilmore Pl; per person £45-62; P ⚡) The five-room Town House is a plush little B&B, offering the sort of quality and comfort you might expect from a much larger and more expensive place. It's an elegant Victorian terraced house with big bay windows, spacious bedrooms (all en suite) and a breakfast menu that includes salmon fishcakes and kippers alongside the more usual offerings.

Amaryllis Guest House
B&B ££

(Map p46; ☑ 0131-229 3293; www.amaryllisguesthouse.com; 21 Upper Gilmore Pl; s/d/f £60/80/100; ⚡) The Amaryllis is a cute little Georgian town house on a quiet back street. There are five bedrooms, including a spacious family room that can take two adults and up to four kids. Princes St is only 10 minutes' walk.

Salisbury Hotel
HOTEL ££

(Map p46; ☑ 0131-667 1264; www.the-salisbury.co.uk; 45 Salisbury Rd; s/d/f from £75/90/145; P ⚡) Boutique-style guest house in a comfortable Georgian villa with large garden.

Kenvie Guest House
B&B ££

(☑ 0131-668 1964; www.kenvie.co.uk; 16 Kilmaurs Rd; r per person £30-45; ⚡) Top value, warm welcome. Situated in a quiet side street but close to a main bus route, about two miles from the city.

★ Prestonfield House Hotel
BOUTIQUE HOTEL £££

(☑ 0131-668 3346; www.prestonfield.com; Priestfield Rd; r/ste from £295/375; P ⚡) If the blonde wood and brushed steel of modern boutique hotels leave you cold, then this is the place for you. A 17th-century mansion set in 8 hectares of parkland (complete with peacocks and Highland cattle), Prestonfield House is draped in damask and packed with antiques – look out for original tapestries, 17th-century embossed-leather panels, and £500-a-roll hand-painted wallpaper. The sumptuous bedrooms are supplied with all mod cons, including Bose sound systems and DVD players. The hotel is southeast of the city centre, east of Dalkeith Rd.

🛏 Leith Walk & Pilrig St

Northeast of the New Town, the area around Leith Walk and Pilrig St has lots of guest houses, all within about a mile of the centre. To get to Pilrig St you'll need to take bus 11 from Princes St.

Edinburgh Central Youth Hostel
HOSTEL £

(SYHA; ☑ 0131-524 2090; www.edinburghcentral.org; 9 Haddington Pl, Leith Walk; dm/s/tw £25/49/74; @ ⚡) This modern, purpose-built hostel, about a half-mile north of Waverley train station, is a big (300 beds), flashy, five-star establishment with its own cafe-bistro as well as self-catering kitchen, smart and comfortable eight-bed dorms and private rooms, and mod cons including keycard entry and plasma-screen TVs.

★ Wallace's Arthouse
B&B ££

(☑ 0131-538 3320; www.wallacesarthousescotland.com; 41/4 Constitution St; s/d £100/110; ⚡) This Georgian flat, housed in the neoclassical Leith Assembly Rooms (a grade A listed building), offers B&B in two beautifully nostalgic bedrooms, styled by former fashion designer Wallace, who comes as part of the package – your charming host and breakfast chef is an unfailing source of colourful anecdotes and local knowledge.

Sandaig Guest House
B&B ££

(☑ 0131-554 7357; www.sandaigguesthouse.co.uk; 5 East Hermitage Pl, Leith Links; s/d from £70/90; ⚡) From the welcoming tot of whisky liqueur to the cheerful goodbye wave, the owners of the Sandaig know a thing or two about hospitality. There are plenty of things that make staying here a pleasure, from the boldly coloured decor to the crisp cotton sheets, big fluffy towels and refreshing power showers, and a breakfast menu that includes porridge with cream and maple syrup.

Millers 64
B&B ££

(☑ 0131-454 3666; www.millers64.com; 64 Pilrig St; s from £80, d £90-150; ⚡) Luxury textiles, colourful cushions, stylish bathrooms and fresh flowers added to a warm Edinburgh welcome make this Victorian town house a highly desirable address. There are just two bedrooms (and a minimum three-night stay during festival periods), so book well in advance.

Ardmor House
B&B ££

(☑ 0131-554 4944; www.ardmorhouse.com; 74 Pilrig St; s £60-85, d £85-170; ⚡) The 'gay-owned, straight-friendly' Ardmor is a stylishly renovated Victorian house with five en suite bedrooms, and all those little touches that make a place special – an open fire, thick towels, crisp white bed linen and free newspapers at breakfast.

Balmoral Guest House

B&B ££

(☑0131-554 1857; www.balmoralguesthouse.co.uk; 32 Pilrig St; s/d £80/100; 🛜) A deservedly popular B&B set in an elegant, flower-bedecked, Victorian terraced house dating from 1856. The owners have a good eye for antiques (including, unusually, antique radios) and period furniture gives the bedrooms a pleasantly retro atmosphere.

🛏 Outside the Centre

Mortonhall Caravan Park

CAMPGROUND £

(☑0131-664 1533; www.meadowhead.co.uk; 38 Mortonhall Gate, Frogston Rd East; tent site incl 1 car & 2 people £21-27; 🛜) Located in attractive parkland 5 miles southeast of the centre, Mortonhall has an on-site shop, bar and restaurant. Note: the one-person, no car tent rate (£13) is not available during the Edinburgh International Festival. Take bus 11 from Princes St (westbound).

✖ Eating

Edinburgh has more restaurants per head of population than any other UK city. Eating out has become a commonplace event rather than something reserved for special occasions, and the choice of eateries ranges from stylish but inexpensive bistros and cafes to Michelin-starred gourmet restaurants.

In addition most pubs also serve food, offering either bar meals or a more formal restaurant or both, but be aware that pubs without a Children's Certificate are not allowed to serve children under the age of 14.

If you want more listings than we can provide here, the excellent *Edinburgh & Glasgow Eating & Drinking Guide* (http://food.list.co.uk), published annually by *The List* magazine, contains reviews of around 800 restaurants, cafes and bars.

✖ Old Town & Around

★Mums

CAFE £

(Map p52; www.monstermashcafe.co.uk; 4a Forrest Rd; mains £6-9; ☺9am-10pm Mon-Sat, 10am-10pm Sun; 🚌23, 27, 41, 42) 🍃 This nostalgia-fuelled cafe serves up classic British comfort food that wouldn't look out of place on a 1950s menu – bacon and eggs, bangers and mash, shepherd's pie, fish and chips. But there's a twist – the food is all top-quality nosh freshly prepared from local produce, including Crombie's gourmet sausages. There's even a wine list, though we prefer the real ales and Scottish-brewed cider.

Elephant House

CAFE £

(Map p52; www.elephanthouse.biz; 21 George IV Bridge; mains £6-9; ☺8am-10pm Mon-Thu, to 11pm Fri & Sat, 9am-10pm Sun; 🛜) Here you'll find counters at the front, tables and views of the castle at the back (where JK Rowling famously wrote in the days before Harry Potter was published), and little effigies and images of elephants everywhere. Excellent coffee and tasty, homemade food – pizzas, quiches, pies, sandwiches and cakes – at reasonable prices.

★Timberyard

SCOTTISH ££

(Map p52; ☑0131-221 1222; www.timberyard.co; 10 Lady Lawson St; mains £16-21; ☺noon-9.30pm Tue-Sat; 🛜; 🚌2, 35) 🍃 Ancient, worn floorboards, cast-iron pillars, exposed joists and tables made from slabs of old mahogany create a rustic, retro atmosphere in this slow-food restaurant where the accent is on locally sourced produce from artisan growers and foragers. Typical dishes include seared scallop with apple, jerusalem artichoke and sorrel; and juniper-smoked pigeon with wild garlic flowers and beetroot.

Leven's

THAI, FUSION ££

(Map p46; ☑0131-229 8988; www.levensrestaurant.net; 30-32 Leven St; mains £11-19; ☺noon-2.30pm & 5-11.30pm Mon-Thu, noon-11.30pm Fri & Sat, 1-11.30pm Sun; 🖐; 🚌11, 15, 16, 23, 45) From the spectacular chandeliers and slowly pulsing blue/purple mood lighting to the designer colour palette and Villeroy and Boch tableware, everything about this restaurant oozes style. The food lives up to the surroundings, with clever and unexpected combinations of Scottish produce and Thai flavours, colours and textures in dishes such as grilled beef sirloin with tamarind sauce.

Kanpai Sushi

JAPANESE ££

(Map p 52; ☑0131-228 1602; www.kanpaisushi.co.uk; 8-10 Grindlay St; mains £9-15, sushi per piece £4-10; ☺noon-2.30pm & 5-10.30pm Tue-Sun; 🚌all Lothian Rd buses) What is probably Edinburgh's best sushi restaurant impresses with its minimalist interior, fresh, top-quality fish and elegantly presented dishes – the squid tempura comes in a delicate woven basket, while the sashimi combo is presented as a flower arrangement in an ice-filled stoneware bowl.

TOP VEGETARIAN RESTAURANTS

Many Edinburgh restaurants offer vegetarian options on the menu, some good, some bad, some indifferent. The places listed here are all 100% veggie and fall into the 'good' category.

David Bann (Map p 52; ☑ 0131-556 5888; www.davidbann.com; 56-58 St Mary's St; mains £9-13; ⊙ noon-10pm Mon-Fri, 11am-10pm Sat & Sun; ☑; ☑ 35) If you want to convince a carnivorous friend that cuisine à la veg can be as tasty and inventive as a meat-muncher's menu, take them to David Bann's stylish restaurant – dishes such as parsnip and blue cheese pudding, and spiced aduki bean and cashew pie are guaranteed to win converts.

Kalpna (Map p46; ☑ 667 9890; www.kalpnarestaurant.com; 2-3 St Patrick Sq; mains £6-11; ⊙ noon 2pm & 5.30-9.30pm Mon-Sat year-round, plus 6-10.30pm Sun May-Sep; ☑; ☑ all Newington buses) A long-standing Edinburgh favourite, Kalpna is one of the best Indian restaurants in the country, vegetarian or otherwise. The cuisine is mostly Gujarati, with a smattering of dishes from other parts of India. The all-you-can-eat lunch buffet (£8) is superb value.

Engine Shed (Map p46; www.theengineshed.org; 19 St Leonard's Lane; mains £4-7; ⊙ 10am-4pm Mon-Sat; ☑☑☑; ☑ 14) This fair-trade, organic vegetarian cafe is an ideal spot for a healthy lunch, or a cuppa and a bakery-fresh scone after climbing Arthur's Seat. It's been set up to provide employment and training for special-needs adults, and as well as having its own bakery it also makes its own tofu, which is used in its tasty curries.

Henderson's (Map p60; ☑ 0131-225 2131; www.hendersonsofedinburgh.co.uk; 94 Hanover St; mains £6-9; ⊙ 8am-10pm Mon-Wed, 8am-11pm Thu-Sat year-round, 11am-4pm Sun Aug & Dec; ☑) Established in 1962, Henderson's is the grandmother of Edinburgh's vegetarian restaurants. The food is mostly organic, guaranteed GM-free, and special dietary requirements can be catered for. The place still has a 1970s feel to it (in a good way), and the daily salads and hot dishes are as popular as ever.

Mosque Kitchen (Map p52; www.mosquekitchen.com; 31 Nicolson Sq; mains £3-6; ⊙ 11.30am-11pm, closed 12.50-1.50pm Fri; ☑; ☑ all South Bridge buses) Sophisticated it ain't – expect shared tables and disposable plates – but this is the place to go for cheap, authentic and delicious homemade curries, kebabs, pakoras and naan bread, all washed down with lassi or mango juice. Caters to Edinburgh's Central Mosque, but welcomes all – local students have taken to it big time. No alcohol.

Maxie's Bistro   BISTRO ££
(Map p52; ☑ 0131-226 7770; www.maxiesbistro.com; 5b Johnston Tce; mains £10-22; ⊙ 11am-11pm; ☑ 23, 27, 41, 42) Maxie's candlelit bistro, with its cushion-lined nooks set amid stone walls and wooden beams, is a pleasant setting for a cosy dinner, but at lunchtime in summer people queue for the outdoor tables on the terrace overlooking Victoria St. The food is dependable, ranging from pastas, steaks and stir-fries to seafood platters and daily specials. Best to book, especially in summer.

Mother India's Cafe   INDIAN ££
(Map p52; ☑ 0131-524 9801; www.motherindia.co.uk; 3-5 Infirmary St; tapas £4-6; ⊙ noon-2pm & 5-10.30pm Mon-Thu, noon-10pm Fri-Sun; ☑ all South Bridge buses) A simple concept pioneered in Glasgow has captured hearts and minds – and stomachs – in Edinburgh: Indian food served in tapas-size portions, so that you can sample a greater variety of different dishes without busting your gut. Hugely popular, so book a table.

Pancho Villa's   MEXICAN ££
(Map p52; ☑ 0131-557 4416; www.panchovillas.co.uk; 240 Canongate; mains £10-15; ⊙ noon-10pm Mon-Sat, 5-10pm Sun; ☑☑) With a Mexican-born owner and lots of Latin American and Spanish staff, it's not surprising that this colourful and lively restaurant is one of the most authentic-feeling Mexican places in town. The dinner menu includes delicious steak fajitas and great vegetarian spinach enchiladas. It's often busy, so book ahead.

Amber   SCOTTISH ££
(Map p52; ☑ 0131-477 8477; www.amber-restaurant.co.uk; 354 Castlehill; mains £12-20; ⊙ 10am-7.30pm Sun-Thu, to 9pm Fri & Sat; ☑ 23, 27, 41, 42) You've got to love a place where the waiter greets you with the words, 'My name is

Craig, and I'll be your whisky adviser for this evening'. Located in the Scotch Whisky Experience (p49), this whisky-themed restaurant manages to avoid the tourist clichés and creates genuinely interesting and flavoursome dishes blending top Scottish produce with whisky-inspired sauces.

★**Castle Terrace**　　　SCOTTISH £££
(Map p52; ☑ 0131-229 1222; www.castleterracerestaurant.com; 33-35 Castle Tce; mains £25-42, 3-course lunch £28.50; ⊗ noon-2pm & 6.30-10pm Tue-Sat; ☐ 2) ✔ It was little more than a year after opening in 2010 that Castle Terrace was awarded a Michelin star under chef-patron Dominic Jack. The menu is seasonal and applies sharply whetted Parisian skills to the finest of local produce, be it Ayrshire pork, Aberdeenshire lamb or Newhaven crab – even the cheese in the sauces is Scottish.

Wedgwood　　　SCOTTISH £££
(Map p52; ☑ 0131-558 8737; www.wedgwoodtherestaurant.co.uk; 267 Canongate; mains £16-27, 2-/3-course lunch £13/17; ⊗ noon-3pm & 6-10pm; ☐ 35) ✔ Fine food without the fuss is the motto at this friendly and unpretentious restaurant. Scottish produce is served with an inventive flair in dishes such as wild venison with its own haggis, herbed barley and a truffled jus, while the menu includes foraged wild salad leaves collected by the chef.

★**Ondine**　　　SEAFOOD £££
(Map p52; ☑ 0131-226 1888; www.ondinerestaurant.co.uk; 2 George IV Bridge; mains £14-39, 2-/3-course lunch £22/25; ⊗ noon-3pm & 5.30-10pm Mon-Sat; ☐ 23, 27, 41, 42) Ondine is one of Edinburgh's finest seafood restaurants, with a menu based on sustainably sourced fish. Take a seat at the curved Oyster Bar and tuck into oysters Kilpatrick, lobster thermidor, a roast shellfish platter or just good old haddock and chips (with minted pea purée, just to keep things posh).

Tower　　　SCOTTISH £££
(Map p52; ☑ 0131-225 3003; www.tower-restaurant.com; National Museum of Scotland, Chambers St; mains £18-39, 2-course lunch & pretheatre menu £19, afternoon tea £19; ⊗ 10am-11pm; ☐ 23, 27, 41, 42) Chic and sleek, with a great view of the castle, Tower is perched in a turret atop the National Museum of Scotland building. A star-studded guest list of celebrities has enjoyed its menu of quality Scottish food, simply prepared – try half a dozen oysters followed by roast loin of venison. Afternoon tea (£18) is served from 2.30pm to 5.30pm.

✖ **New Town**

★**Gardener's Cottage**　　　SCOTTISH ££
(Map p60; ☑ 0131-558 1221; www.thegardenerscottage.co; 1 Royal Terrace Gardens, London Rd; lunch mains £16-17, dinner set menu £30; ⊗ noon-2.30pm & 5-10pm Thu-Mon, 10am-2pm Sat & Sun; ☐ all London Rd buses) ✔ This country cottage in the heart of the city, bedecked with flowers and fairy lights, offers one of Edinburgh's most interesting dining experiences – two tiny rooms with communal tables made of salvaged timber, and a set menu based on fresh local produce (most of the vegetables and fruit are grown in an organic garden in the city suburbs). Booking essential.

The Dogs　　　BRITISH ££
(Map p60; ☑ 0131-220 1208; www.thedogsonline.co.uk; 110 Hanover St; mains £10-15; ⊗ noon-4pm & 5-10pm; ☐ 23, 27) ✔ One of the coolest tables in town, this bistro-style place uses cheaper cuts of meat and less-well-known, more-sustainable species of fish to create hearty, no-nonsense dishes such as lamb sweetbreads on toast, baked coley with *skirlie* (fried oatmeal and onion), and devilled liver with bacon and onions.

Urban Angel　　　CAFE ££
(Map p60; ☑ 0131-225 6215; www.urban-angel.co.uk; 121 Hanover St; mains £5-13; ⊗ 8am-5pm Mon-Fri, 9am-5pm Sat & Sun; ☑ 🖮; ☐ 23, 27) ✔ A wholesome deli that puts the emphasis on fair-trade, organic and locally sourced produce, Urban Angel is also a delightfully informal cafe-bistro that serves all-day brunch, tapas and a wide range of light, snacky meals.

Café Marlayne　　　FRENCH ££
(Map p60; ☑ 0131-226 2230; www.cafemarlayne.com; 76 Thistle St; mains £12-15; ⊗ noon-10pm; ☐ 24, 29, 42) All weathered wood and candlelit tables, Café Marlayne is a cosy nook offering French farmhouse cooking – *brandade de morue* (salt cod) with green salad, slow-roast rack of lamb, *boudin noir* (black pudding) with scallops and sautéed potato – at very reasonable prices. Booking recommended.

L'Escargot Bleu　　　FRENCH ££
(Map p46; ☑ 0131-556 1600; www.lescargotbleu.co.uk; 56 Broughton St; mains £13-18; ⊗ noon-2.30pm & 5.30-10pm Mon-Thu, noon-3pm & 5.30-10.30pm Fri & Sat; ☐ 8) As with its sister restaurant, l'Escargot Blanc on Queensferry St, this cute little bistro is as Gallic as

garlic but makes fine use of quality Scottish produce – the French-speaking staff will lead you through a menu that includes authentic Savoyard *tartiflette*, *quenelle* of pike with lobster sauce, and pigs' cheeks braised in red wine with roast winter vegetables.

Fishers in the City
SEAFOOD ££

(Map p60; ☎ 0131-225 5109; www.fishersbistros. co.uk; 58 Thistle St; mains £15-21; ⊙ noon-10.30pm; ☎ ✉; ▢ 13, 19, 37, 41) This more sophisticated version of the famous Fishers Bistro in Leith, with its granite topped tables, warm yellow walls and a nautical theme, specialises in superior Scottish seafood – the knowledgeable staff serve up plump and succulent oysters, meltingly sweet scallops, and sea bass that's been grilled to perfection.

Scottish Cafe & Restaurant
SCOTTISH ££

(Map p60; ☎ 0131-226 6524; www.thescottish-cafeandrestaurant.com; The Mound; mains £15; ⊙ 9am-5pm Mon-Wed, Fri & Sat, to 7pm Thu, 10am-5pm Sun; ☎) ✎ This appealing modern restaurant (part of the Scottish National Gallery complex) has picture windows providing a view along Princes Street Gardens, and offers the chance to try traditional Scottish dishes such as Cullen skink (smoked haddock soup), haggis, smoked salmon and venison, made with seasonal, sustainably sourced produce.

Café Royal Oyster Bar
SEAFOOD £££

(Map p60; ☎ 0131-556 4124; www.caferoyaledinburgh.co.uk; 17a West Register St; mains £13-22; ⊙ noon-9.30pm Mon-Sat, 12.30-9.30pm Sun) Pass through the revolving doors on the corner of West Register St and you're transported back to Victorian times – a palace of glinting mahogany, polished brass, marble floors, stained glass, Doulton tiles, gilded cornices and starched table linen so thick it creaks

---

TOP FIVE EDINBURGH CAFES

Cafe culture is firmly ensconced in Edinburgh, and it is as easy to get your daily caffeine fix here as it is in New York or Paris. Most cafes offer some kind of food, from cakes and sandwiches to full-on meals.

Loudon's Café & Bakery (Map p46; www.loudons-cafe.co.uk; 94b Fountainbridge; mains £4-8; ⊙ 8am-6pm Mon-Fri, 9am-6pm Sat & Sun; ☎ ✉) A cafe that bakes its own organic bread and cakes on the premises, ethically sourced coffee, daily and weekend newspapers scattered about, even some outdoor tables – what's not to like? All-day brunch (9am to 3pm) served at weekends includes eggs Benedict, warm spiced quinoa with dried fruit, and specials such as blueberry pancakes with fruit salad.

Glass & Thompson (Map p60; 2 Dundas St; mains £7-11; ⊙ 8am-6pm Mon-Sat, 10.30am-4.30pm Sun) Grab a table in this spick-and-span New Town deli and sip a double espresso as you ogle the cheeses in the cold counter or watch the world go by through the floor-to-ceiling windows (the cafe is featured in the novels of Alexander McCall Smith). Munchies include tasty platters such as dolmati and falafel, or Parma ham and parmesan.

Circle Cafe (www.thecirclecafe.com; 1 Brandon Tce; mains £5-10; ⊙ 8.30am-4.30pm Mon-Thu, to 10pm Fri & Sat, 9am-4.30pm Sun) A great place for breakfast or a good-value lunch, Circle is a bustling neighbourhood cafe serving great coffee and cakes, and fresh, tasty lunch dishes ranging from chunky, home-baked quiches to smoked haddock fishcakes.

Valvona & Crolla Caffé Bar (Map p46; www.valvonacrolla.co.uk; 19 Elm Row, Leith Walk; mains £10-16; ⊙ 8.30am-5.30pm Mon-Thu, 8am-6pm Fri & Sat, 10.30am-3.30pm Sun; ☎) Try breakfast (served till 11.30am) with an Italian flavour – full *paesano* (meat) or *verdure* (veggie) fry-ups, or deliciously light and crisp *panettone* in *carrozza* (sweet brioche dipped in egg and fried) – or choose from almond croissants, muesli, yogurt and fruit, freshly squeezed orange juice and perfect Italian coffee. There's also a tasty lunch menu (noon to 3.30pm) of classic Italian dishes.

Peter's Yard (Map p46; www.petersyard.com; 27 Simpson Loan; mains £5-8; ⊙ 7.30am-7pm Mon-Fri, 9am-7pm Sat & Sun; ✎; ▢ 23, 27, 35, 45, 47) This Swedish-style coffee house produces its own home-baked breads, from sourdough to focaccia, which form the basis for lunchtime sandwiches with fillings such as roast beef with beetroot and caper salad, and roast butternut squash with sunblush tomato pesto. Breakfast (served till noon) can be a basket of breads with conserves and cheeses, or yoghurt with granola and fruit.

when you fold it. The menu is mostly classic seafood, from oysters on ice to lobster with Cafe Royal sauce.

Stac Polly
SCOTTISH £££

(Map p60; ☎0131-556 2231; www.stacpolly.com; 29-33 Dublin St; mains £18-27; ☺noon-2pm Mon-Sat, 6-10pm daily) Named after a mountain in northwestern Scotland, this rustic cellar restaurant (recently joined by a chic modern brasserie section) adds sophisticated twists to fresh Highland produce. Dishes such as haggis in filo parcels with plum sauce might have Robert Burns spinning in his grave, but keep satisfied customers coming back for more. Orkney Brewery beers available.

✖ Leith

Chop Chop
CHINESE £

(☎0131-553 1818; www.chop-chop.co.uk; 76 Commercial St; mains £7-11; ☺noon-2pm & 6-10pm Mon & Wed-Fri, noon-2pm & 5-10pm Sat, 12.30-2pm & 5-10pm Sun) A Chinese restaurant with a difference, in that it serves dishes popular in China rather than Britain – as its slogan says, 'Can a billion people be wrong?'. No sweet-and-sour pork here, but a range of delicious dumplings filled with pork and coriander, beef and chilli, or lamb and leek, and unusual vegetarian dishes such as aubergine fried with garlic and Chinese spices.

★ Fishers Bistro
SEAFOOD ££

(☎0131-554 5666; www.fishersbistros.co.uk; 1 The Shore; mains £11-23; ☺noon-10.30pm Mon-Sat, 12.30-10.30pm Sun; 🕑🖉🖟; 🚌16, 22, 35, 36) This cosy little restaurant, tucked beneath a 17th-century signal tower, is one of the city's best seafood places. The menu ranges widely in price, from cheaper dishes such as classic fishcakes with lemon and chive mayonnaise, to more expensive delights such as North Berwick lobster thermidor.

Diner 7
STEAK ££

(www.diner7.co.uk; 7 Commercial St; mains £8-13; ☺4-11pm Mon-Sat, 11am-11pm Sun; 🚌16, 22, 35, 36) A neat local eatery with rust-coloured leather booths and banquettes, black and copper tables, and local art on the walls, this diner has a menu of succulent Aberdeen Angus steaks and homemade burgers, but also offers more unusual fare such as chicken and chorizo kebabs, or smoked haddock with black-pudding stovies.

★ The Kitchin
SCOTTISH £££

(☎0131-555 1755; www.thekitchin.com; 78 Commercial Quay; mains £33-38, 3-course lunch £28.50; ☺12.15-2.30pm & 6.30-10pm Tue-Thu, to 10.30pm Fri & Sat; 🖉; 🚌16, 22, 35, 36) Fresh, seasonal, locally sourced Scottish produce is the philosophy that has won a Michelin star for this elegant but unpretentious restaurant. The menu moves with the seasons, of course, so expect fresh salads in summer and game in winter, and shellfish dishes such as seared scallops with endive *tarte tatin* when there's an 'r' in the month.

Plumed Horse
SCOTTISH £££

(☎0131-554 5556; www.plumedhorse.co.uk; 50-54 Henderson St; 3-course dinner £55; ☺12.30-1.30pm Tue-Sat, 7-9pm Tue-Thu, 6.30-9pm Fri & Sat) Smartly suited and booted staff welcome you to this quiet corner of understated elegance, where the muted decor of pale blues and greens, cream leather chairs and crisp white linen places the focus firmly on the exquisitely prepared and presented food. Eight-course tasting menu £69, plus £48 for matching wines.

🍷 Drinking & Nightlife

Edinburgh has more than 700 bars, which are as varied as the population – everything from Victorian palaces to rough-and-ready drinking dens, and from bearded, real-ale howffs to trendy cocktail bars.

The city's club scene has some fine DJ talent and is well worth exploring; there are club-night listings in The List. Most of the venues are concentrated in and around the twin sumps of Cowgate and Calton Rd – so it's downhill all the way...

🍷 Old Town

The pubs in the Grassmarket have outdoor tables on sunny summer afternoons, but in the evenings are favoured by boozed-up lads on the pull, so steer clear if that's not your thing. The Cowgate – the Grassmarket's extension to the east – is Edinburgh's clubland.

★ Bow Bar
PUB

(Map p52; 80 West Bow; 🚌23, 27, 41, 42) One of the city's best traditional-style pubs (it's not as old as it looks), serving a range of excellent real ales and a vast selection of malt whiskies, the Bow Bar often has standing-room only on Friday and Saturday evenings.

TOP FIVE TRADITIONAL PUBS

Edinburgh is blessed with a large number of traditional 19th- and early 20th-century pubs, which have preserved much of their original Victorian or Edwardian decoration and serve cask-conditioned real ales and a staggering range of malt whiskies.

Bennet's Bar (Map p 46; www.bennetsbar.co.uk; 8 Leven St; all Tollcross buses) Situated beside the King's Theatre, Bennet's has managed to hang on to almost all of its beautiful Victorian fittings, from the leaded stained-glass windows and ornate mirrors to the wooden gantry and the brass water taps on the bar (for your whisky – there are more than 100 malts from which to choose).

Café Royal Circle Bar (Map p 60; www.caferoyaledinburgh.co.uk; 17 West Register St; all Princes St buses) Perhaps *the* classic Edinburgh pub, the Cafe Royal's main claims to fame are its magnificent oval bar and its Doulton tile portraits of famous Victorian inventors. Sit at the bar or claim one of the cosy leather booths beneath the stained-glass windows, and choose from the seven real ales on tap.

Athletic Arms (Map p46; Diggers; 1-3 Angle Park Tce; 1, 34, 35) Nicknamed for the cemetery across the street – gravediggers used to nip in and slake their thirst here – the Diggers dates from the 1890s. It's still staunchly traditional – the decor has barely changed in 100 years – and is a real-ale drinker's mecca, serving locally brewed 80-shilling ale. Packed to the gills with football and rugby fans on match days.

Abbotsford (Map p60; www.theabbotsford.com; 3 Rose St) One of the few pubs in Rose St that has retained its Edwardian splendour, the Abbotsford has long been a hang-out for writers, actors, journalists and media people, and has many loyal regulars. Dating from 1902, and named after Sir Walter Scott's country house, the pub's centrepiece is a splendid mahogany island bar. Good selection of real ales.

Sheep Heid Inn (www.thesheepheidedinburgh.co.uk; 43-45 The Causeway; ; 42) Possibly the oldest inn in Edinburgh (with a licence dating back to 1360) the Sheep Heid feels more like a country pub than an Edinburgh bar. Set in the semirural shadow of Arthur's Seat, it's famous for its 19th-century skittles alley and the lovely little beer garden.

⭐ **Cabaret Voltaire** CLUB
(Map p52; www.thecabaretvoltaire.com; 36-38 Blair St; all South Bridge buses) An atmospheric warren of stone-lined vaults houses this self-consciously 'alternative' club, which eschews huge dance floors and egotistical DJ worship in favour of a 'creative crucible' hosting an eclectic mix of DJs, live acts, comedy, theatre, visual arts and the spoken word. Well worth a look.

Jolly Judge PUB
(Map p52; www.jollyjudge.co.uk; 7a James Ct; ; 2, 23, 27, 41, 42, 45) A snug little howff tucked away down a close, the Judge exudes a cosy 17th-century atmosphere (low, timber-beamed painted ceilings) and has the added attraction of a cheering open fire in cold weather. No music or gaming machines, just the buzz of conversation.

BrewDog BAR
(Map p52; www.brewdog.com; 143 Cowgate; ; 36) The Edinburgh outpost of Scotland's self-styled 'punk brewery', BrewDog stands out among the grimy, sticky-floored dives that line the Cowgate, with its cool, industrial-chic designer look. As well as its own highly rated beers, there's also a choice of four guest real ales.

Bongo Club CLUB
(Map p52; www.thebongoclub.co.uk; 66 Cowgate; , 2) Owned by a local arts charity, the weird and wonderful Bongo Club boasts a long history of hosting everything from wild club nights to local bands to performance art to kids' comedy shows, and is open as a cafe and exhibition space during the day.

Ecco Vino WINE BAR
(Map p52; www.eccovinoedinburgh.com; 19 Cockburn St; ; 36, 41) With outdoor tables on sunny afternoons, and cosy candlelit intimacy in the evenings, this comfortably cramped Tuscan-style wine bar offers a tempting range of Italian wines, though not all are available by the glass – best to share a bottle.

Villager

BAR

(Map p52; www.villagerbar.com; 49-50 George IV Bridge; 🛜; 🚇23, 27, 41, 42) A cross between a traditional pub and a pre-club bar, Villager has a comfortable, laid-back vibe. It can be standing-room only in the main bar in the evenings (the cocktails are excellent), but the side room, with its brown leather sofas and pot plants, comes into its own for a lazy Sunday afternoon with the papers.

Blue Blazer

PUB

(Map p52; 📞0131-229 5030; 2 Spittal St; 🛜; 🚇2, 35) With its bare wooden floors, cosy fireplace and efficient bar staff, the Blue Blazer is a down-to-earth antidote to the designer excess of modern style bars, catering to a loyal clientele of real-ale enthusiasts, pie eaters and Saturday horse-racing fans.

Holyrood 9A

PUB

(Map p52; www.fullerthomson.com; 9a Holyrood Rd; 🛜; 🚇36) Candlelight flickering off hectares of polished wood creates an atmospheric setting for this superb real-ale bar, with no fewer than 20 taps pouring craft beers from all corners of the country. If you're peckish, it serves excellent gourmet burgers, too.

Pear Tree House

PUB

(Map p52; www.pear-tree-house.co.uk; 38 West Nicolson St; 🛜; 🚇2, 41, 42, 47) Set in an 18th-century house with cobbled courtyard, the Pear Tree is a student favourite with an open fire in winter, comfy sofas and board games inside, plus the city's biggest and most popular beer garden in summer.

Studio 24

CLUB

(Map p46; www.facebook.com/studio24edinburgh; 24 Calton Rd; 🚇35, 36) This is the dark heart of Edinburgh's underground music scene, with a program that covers all bases, from house to nu metal via punk, ska, reggae, crossover, tribal, electro, techno and dance.

🍸 New Town

The New Town has everything from grand Victorian pubs and quiet, old-fashioned drinking dens to cutting edge cocktail bars. Avoid the tourist crowds on Rose St and seek out the side streets off George St and Queen St to find the latest 'in' places to drink.

Oxford Bar

PUB

(Map p60; www.oxfordbar.co.uk; 8 Young St; 🚇19, 36, 37, 41, 47) The Oxford is that rarest of things: a real pub for real people, with no 'theme', no music, no frills and no pretensions. 'The Ox' has been immortalised by Ian Rankin, author of the Inspector Rebus novels, whose fictional detective is a regular.

Joseph Pearce's

PUB

(Map p46; 📞556 4140; www.bodabar.com; 23 Elm Row; 🚻; 🚇all Leith Walk buses) A traditional Victorian pub that has been remodelled and given a new lease of life by Swedish owners, Pearce's has become a real hub of the local community, with good food (very family friendly before 5pm), a relaxed atmosphere, and events such as Monday night Scrabble games and August crayfish parties.

Cumberland Bar

PUB

(Map p46; www.cumberlandbar.co.uk; 1-3 Cumberland St; 🛜; 🚇23, 27) Immortalised as the stereotypical New Town pub in Alexander McCall Smith's serialised novel *44 Scotland Street*, the Cumberland has an authentic, traditional wood-brass-and-mirrors look (despite being relatively new) and serves well-looked-after, cask-conditioned ales and a wide range of malt whiskies. There's also a pleasant little beer garden outside.

Guildford Arms

PUB

(Map p60; www.guildfordarms.com; 1 West Register St; 🚇all Princes St buses) Located next door to the Cafe Royal Circle Bar, the Guildford is another classic Victorian pub full of polished mahogany, brass and ornate cornices. The range of real ales is excellent – try to get a table in the unusual upstairs gallery, with a view over the sea of drinkers below.

Bramble

COCKTAIL BAR

(Map p60; www.bramblebar.co.uk; 16a Queen St; 🚇23, 27) One of those places that easily earns the sobriquet 'best-kept secret', Bramble is an unmarked cellar bar where a maze of stone and brick hideaways conceals the city's best cocktail venue. No beer taps, no fuss, just expertly mixed drinks.

Lulu

CLUB

(Map p60; www.luluedinburgh.co.uk; 125 George St; 🚇19, 36, 37, 41, 47) Lush leather sofas, red satin cushions, fetishistic steel-mesh curtains and dim red lighting all help to create a decadent atmosphere in this drop-dead-gorgeous club venue beneath the Tigerlily boutique hotel. Resident and guest DJs show a bit more originality than your average club.

Kay's Bar

PUB

(www.kaysbar.co.uk; 39 Jamaica St; 🚇24, 29, 42) Housed in a former wine merchant's office, tiny Kay's Bar is a cosy haven with a coal fire

GAY & LESBIAN EDINBURGH

Edinburgh has a small – but perfectly formed – gay and lesbian scene, centred on the area around Broughton St (known affectionately as the 'Pink Triangle') at the eastern end of New Town.

Scotsgay (www.scotsgay.co.uk) is the local monthly magazine covering gay and lesbian issues, with listings of gay-friendly pubs and clubs. See also www.edinburghgay-scene.com for online listings.

Useful contacts include **Edinburgh LGBT Centre** (www.lgbthealth.org.uk; 9 Howe St) and **Lothian LGBT Helpline** (☏ 0300 123 2523; www.lgbt-helpline-scotland.org.uk; ⊗ noon-9pm Tue & Wed)

Pubs & Clubs

CC Blooms (Map p60; ccbloomsedinburgh.com; 23 Greenside Pl; ⊗ 11am-3am Mon-Sat, 12.30pm-3am Sun) New owners have given the raddled old queen of Edinburgh's gay scene a shot in the arm, with two floors of deafening dance and disco every night. It's overcrowded and the drinks are a bit overpriced but it's worth a visit – go early, or sample the wild karaoke on Sunday nights.

Regent (Map p46; 2 Montrose Tce; ⊗ noon-1am Mon-Sat, 12.30pm-1am Sun) This is a pleasant gay local with a relaxed atmosphere (no loud music), serving coffee and croissants as well as excellent real ales, including Deuchars IPA and Caledonian 80/. Meeting place for the Lesbian and Gay Real Ale Drinkers club (first Monday of month, 9pm).

Newtown Bar (Map p60; www.newtownbar.co.uk; 26b Dublin St; ⊗ noon-1am Mon-Thu, to 2am Fri & Sat, 12.30pm-1am Sun) Stylish modern bar serving good food and drink, and basement club with resident DJ that hosts regular men-only events.

and a fine range of real ales. Good food is served in the back room at lunchtime, but you'll have to book a table – Kay's is a popular spot.

Amicus Apple　　　　　COCKTAIL BAR
(Map p60; www.amicusapple.com; 15 Frederick St; ☏; ☐ all Princes St buses) This laid-back cocktail lounge is the hippest hang-out in the New Town. The drinks menu ranges from retro classics such as bloody Marys and mojitos, to original and unusual concoctions such as the Cuillin martini (Tanqueray No 10 gin, Talisker malt whisky and smoked rosemary).

🍴 Leith

⭐ Roseleaf　　　　　CAFE, BAR
(☏ 476 5268; www.roseleaf.co.uk; 23-24 Sandport Pl; ⊗ 10am-1am; ☏ ♿; ☐ 16, 22, 35, 36) Cute and quaint and verging on chintzy, the Roseleaf could hardly be further from the average Leith bar. Decked out in flowered wallpaper, old furniture and rose-patterned china (cocktails are served in teapots), the real ales and bottled beers are complemented by a range of speciality teas, coffees and

fruit drinks (including rose lemonade) and well-above-average pub grub (served 10am to 10pm).

Teuchters Landing　　　　　PUB
(www.aroomin.co.uk; 1 Dock Pl; ☏; ☐ 16, 22, 35 or 36) A cosy warren of timber-lined nooks and crannies housed in a single-storey red-brick building (once a waiting room for ferries across the Firth of Forth), this real-ale and malt-whisky bar also has outdoor tables on a floating terrace in the dock.

Port O'Leith　　　　　PUB
(www.portoleithpub.com; 58 Constitution St; ☐ 16, 22, 35, 36) This is a good, old-fashioned, friendly local boozer, swathed with flags and cap bands left behind by visiting sailors – Leith docks are just down the road. Pop in for a pint and you'll probably stay until closing time.

Sofi's　　　　　BAR
(☏ 555 7019; www.bodabar.com; 65 Henderson St; ☏; ☐ 22, 36) Sofi's brings a little bit of Swedish sophistication to this former Leith pub, feeling more like a bohemian cafe with its mismatched furniture, candlelit tables, fresh flowers and colourful art. It's

a real community place too, hosting film screenings, book clubs, open-mic music nights, and even a knitting club!

☆ Entertainment

Edinburgh has a number of fine theatres and concert halls, and there are independent art-house cinemas as well as mainstream movie theatres. Many pubs offer entertainment ranging from live Scottish folk music to pop, rock and jazz as well as karaoke and quiz nights, while a range of stylish modern bars purvey house, dance and hip-hop to the preclubbing crowd.

The comprehensive source for what's-on info is The List (www.list.co.uk), an excellent listings magazine covering both Edinburgh and Glasgow. It's available from most newsagents, and is published fortnightly on a Thursday.

Live Music

The capital is a great place to hear traditional Scottish (and Irish) folk music, with a mix of regular spots and impromptu sessions. The Gig Guide (www.gigguide.co.uk) is a free email newsletter and listing website covering live music in Edinburgh and Scotland.

★ **Sandy Bell's**   FOLK
(Map p52; www.sandybellsedinburgh.co.uk; 25 Forrest Rd) This unassuming pub is a stalwart of the traditional music scene (the founder's wife sang with The Corries). There's music almost every evening at 9pm, and from 3pm Saturday and Sunday, plus lots of impromptu sessions.

Bannerman's   ROCK
(Map p52; www.bannermanslive.co.uk; 212 Cowgate) A long-established favourite – it seems like every Edinburgh student for the last four decades spent half their youth here – Bannerman's straggles through a warren of old vaults beneath South Bridge. It pulls in crowds of students, locals and backpackers alike with live rock, punk and indie bands.

Royal Oak   FOLK
(Map p52; www.royal-oak-folk.com; 1 Infirmary St; ☐ all South Bridge buses) This popular folk pub is tiny, so get there early (9pm start weekdays, 2.30pm Saturday) if you want to be sure of a place. Sundays from 4pm to 7pm is open session – bring your own instruments (or a good singing voice).

Henry's Cellar Bar   ROCK, BLUES
(Map p52; www.henryscellarbar.com; 16 Morrison St; admission free-£5) One of Edinburgh's most eclectic live-music venues, Henry's has something going on most nights of the week, from rock and indie to 'Balkan-inspired folk', funk to hip-hop to hardcore, staging both local bands and acts from around the world. Open till 3am at weekends.

Whistle Binkie's   ROCK
(Map p52; www.facebook.com/WhistleBinkiesEdinburgh; 4-6 South Bridge; admission free; ☐ all South Bridge buses) This crowded cellar bar, just off the Royal Mile, has live music every night till 3am, from rock and blues to folk and jazz. Open-mic night on Monday and breaking bands on Tuesday are showcases for new talent.

Jazz Bar   JAZZ, BLUES
(Map p52; www.thejazzbar.co.uk; 1a Chambers St; admission £3-7; ☎) This atmospheric cellar bar, with its polished parquet floors, bare stone walls, candlelit tables and stylish steel-framed chairs, is owned and operated by jazz musicians. There's live music every night from 9pm to 3am, and on Saturday from 3pm; as well as jazz, expect bands playing blues, funk, soul and fusion.

Liquid Room   ROCK, CLUB
(Map p52; www.liquidroom.com; 9c Victoria St; admission free-£10) Set in a subterranean vault deep beneath Victoria St, the Liquid Room is a superb club venue with a thundering sound system. There are regular club nights Wednesday to Saturday as well as live bands.

Edinburgh Folk Club   FOLK
(Map p52; www.edinburghfolkclub.co.uk; Pleasance Courtyard, 60 The Pleasance; admission £9; ☐ 36) The Pleasance Cabaret Bar is the home venue of the Edinburgh Folk Club, which runs a program of visiting bands and singers at 8pm on Wednesday nights.

Cinemas

Film buffs will find plenty to keep them happy in Edinburgh's art-house cinemas, while popcorn munchers can choose from a range of multiplexes.

Filmhouse   CINEMA
(Map p52; www.filmhousecinema.com; 88 Lothian Rd; ☎; ☐ all Lothian Rd buses) The Filmhouse is the main venue for the annual Edinburgh International Film Festival and screens a full program of art-house, classic, foreign and second-run films, with lots of themes,

retrospectives and 70mm screenings. It has wheelchair access to all three screens.

Cameo
CINEMA
(Map p46; www.picturehouses.co.uk; 38 Home St; 🚇 all Tollcross buses) The three-screen, independently owned Cameo is a good, old-fashioned cinema showing+ an imaginative mix of mainstream and art-house movies. There is a good program of late-night movies and Sunday matinees, and the seats in screen 1 are big enough to get lost in.

Classical Music, Opera & Ballet
The following are the main venues for classical music.

Edinburgh Festival Theatre
BALLET, OPERA
(Map p52; www.edtheatres.com/festival; 13-29 Nicolson St; ⊙ box office 10am-6pm Mon-Sat, to 8pm show nights, 4pm-showtime Sun; 🚇 all South Bridge buses) A beautifully restored art-deco theatre with a modern frontage, the Festival is the city's main venue for opera, dance and ballet, but also stages musicals, concerts, drama and children's shows.

Usher Hall
CLASSICAL MUSIC
(Map p52; www.usherhall.co.uk; Lothian Rd; ⊙ box office 10.30am-5.30pm, to 8pm show nights) The architecturally impressive Usher Hall hosts concerts by the Royal Scottish National Orchestra (RSNO) and performances of popular music.

Queen's Hall
CLASSICAL MUSIC
(Map p46; www.thequeenshall.net; Clerk St; ⊙ box office 10am-5.30pm Mon-Sat, or till 15min after show begins) The home of the Scottish Chamber Orchestra also stages jazz, blues, folk, rock and comedy.

St Giles Cathedral
CLASSICAL MUSIC
(Map p52; www.stgilescathedral.org.uk; High St) The big kirk on the Royal Mile plays host to a regular and varied program of classical music, including popular lunchtime and evening concerts and organ recitals. The cathedral choir sings at the 10am and 11.30am Sunday services.

Theatre, Musicals & Comedy
Royal Lyceum Theatre
THEATRE, MUSIC
(Map p52; www.lyceum.org.uk; 30b Grindlay St; ⊙ box office 10am-6pm Mon-Sat, to 8pm show nights; ♿) A grand Victorian theatre located beside the Usher Hall, the Lyceum stages drama, concerts, musicals and ballet.

Traverse Theatre
THEATRE, DANCE
(Map p52; www.traverse.co.uk; 10 Cambridge St; ⊙ box office 10am-6pm Mon-Sat, to 8pm show nights) The Traverse is the main focus for new Scottish writing and stages an adventurous program of contemporary drama and dance. The box office is only open on Sunday (from 4pm) when there's a show on.

King's Theatre
DRAMA, MUSICALS
(Map p46; www.edtheatres.com/kings; 2 Leven St; ⊙ box office open 1hr before show; 🚇 all Tollcross buses) King's is a traditional theatre with a program of musicals, drama, comedy and its famous Christmas pantomimes.

Edinburgh Playhouse
MUSIC
(Map p60; www.edinburgh-playhouse.co.uk; 18-22 Greenside Pl; ⊙ box office 10am-6pm Mon-Sat, to 8pm show nights; 🚇 all Leith Walk buses) This restored theatre at the top of Leith Walk stages Broadway musicals, dance shows, opera and popular-music concerts.

The Stand Comedy Club
COMEDY
(Map p60; www.thestand.co.uk; 5 York Pl; ⊙ from 7.30pm Mon-Sat, from 12.30pm Sun; 🚇 all York Pl buses) The Stand, founded in 1995, is Edinburgh's main independent comedy venue. It's an intimate cabaret bar with performances every night and a free Sunday lunchtime show.

Sport
Edinburgh is home to two rival **football** teams playing in the Scottish Premier League: **Heart of Midlothian** (aka Hearts) and **Hibernian** (aka Hibs). The domestic football season lasts from August to May, and most matches are played at 3pm on Saturday or 7.30pm on Tuesday or Wednesday.

Hearts has its home ground at **Tynecastle Stadium** (www.heartsfc.co.uk; Gorgie Rd), southwest of the city centre in Gorgie. Hibernian's home ground is northeast of the city centre at **Easter Road Stadium** (www.hibernianfc.co.uk; 12 Albion Pl).

Each year, from January to March, Scotland's national **rugby** team takes part in the Six Nations Rugby Union Championship. The most important fixture is the clash against England for the Calcutta Cup. At club level the season runs from September to May. **Murrayfield Stadium** (www.scottishrugby.org; 112 Roseburn St), about 1.5 miles west of the city centre, is the venue for international matches.

Other **sporting events**, including athletics and cycling, are held at **Meadowbank**

EDINBURGH'S HOGMANAY

Traditionally, the New Year has always been a more important celebration for Scots than Christmas. In towns, cities and villages all over the country, people fill the streets at midnight on 31 December to wish each other a Guid New Year and, yes, to knock back a dram or six to keep the cold at bay.

In 1993 Edinburgh's city council had the excellent idea of spicing up Hogmanay by organising some events, laying on some live music in Princes St and issuing an open invitation to the rest of the world. Most of them turned up, or so it seemed, and had such a good time that they told all their pals and came back again the next year.

Now Edinburgh's Hogmanay is the biggest winter festival in Europe. Events run from 29 December to 1 January, and include a torchlight procession, huge street party and the famous 'Loony Dook', a chilly sea-swimming event on New Year's Day. To get into the main party area in the city centre after 8pm on 31 December you'll need a ticket – book well in advance.

Sports Centre (www.edinburghleisure.co.uk; 139 London Rd), Scotland's main sports arena.

Horse-racing fans head 6 miles east to **Musselburgh Racecourse** (www.musselburgh-racecourse.co.uk; Linkfield Rd), Scotland's oldest racecourse (founded 1816), where meetings are held throughout the year.

🔒 Shopping

Princes St is Edinburgh's principal shopping street, lined with all the big high-street stores, and smaller shops along pedestrianised Rose St, and more expensive designer boutiques on George St and Thistle St. There are also two big shopping centres in the New Town – **Princes Mall**, at the eastern end of Princes St, and the nearby **St James Centre** at the top of Leith St, plus **Multrees Walk**, a designer shopping complex with a flagship Harvey Nichols store on the eastern side of St Andrew Sq. The huge **Ocean Terminal** (☎ 0131-555 8888; www.oceanterminal. com; Ocean Dr; ◉10am-8pm Mon-Fri, to 7pm Sat, 11am-6pm Sun; 🚇11, 22, 34, 35, 36) in Leith is the biggest shopping centre in the city.

Woollen textiles and knitwear are one of Scotland's classic exports. Scottish cashmere – a fine, soft wool from young goats and lambs – provides the most luxurious and expensive knitwear and has been seen gracing the torsos of pop star Robbie Williams and England footballer David Beckham. There are dozens of shops along the Royal Mile and Princes St where you can buy kilts and tartan goods.

For more off-beat shopping – including fashion, music, crafts, gifts and jewellery – head for the cobbled lanes of Cockburn, Victoria and St Mary's Sts, all near the Royal Mile in the Old Town; William St in the western part of the New Town; and the Stockbridge district, north of the New Town.

🔒 Old Town

Geoffrey (Tailor) Inc FASHION
(Map p52; www.geoffreykilts.co.uk; 57-59 High St; ◉10am-5.30pm Mon-Sat, 11am-5pm Sun; 🚇35) Can fit you out in traditional Highland dress, or run up a kilt in your own clan tartan. Its offshoot, **21st Century Kilts** (www.21stcenturykilts.co.uk; 57-59 High St; ◉9am-5.30pm Mon-Wed, Fri & Sat, 9am-7pm Thu, 10am-5pm Sun; 🚇35), offers modern fashion kilts in a variety of fabrics.

Bill Baber FASHION
(Map p52; ☎ 225 3249; www.billbaber.com; 66 Grassmarket; ◉9am-5.30pm Mon-Sat; 🚇2) This family-run designer knitwear studio has been in the business for more than 30 years, producing stylish and colourful creations using linen, merino wool, silk and cotton.

Ragamuffin FASHION
(Map p52; 278 Canongate; ◉10am-6pm Mon-Sat, noon-5pm Sun) Quality Scottish knitwear and fabrics including cashmere from Johnstons of Elgin, Fair Isle sweaters and Harris Tweed.

Joyce Forsyth Designer Knitwear FASHION
(Map p52; ☎ 220 4112; www.joyceforsyth.co.uk; 42 Candlemaker Row; ◉10am-5.30pm Tue-Sat) Colourful designs that will drag your ideas about woollens firmly into the 21st century.

🔒 New Town

Jenners DEPARTMENT STORE
(Map p60; www.houseoffraser.co.uk; 48 Princes St; ◉9.30am-6.30pm Mon-Wed, 9.30am-8pm Thu, 8am-9pm Fri, 9am-7pm Sat, 11am-6pm Sun; 🚇all Princes St buses) Founded in 1838, and acquired by House of Fraser in 2005, Jenners

is the *grande dame* of Scottish department stores. It stocks a wide range of quality goods, both classic and contemporary.

Galerie Mirages   JEWELLERY
(Map p46; www.galeriemirages.co.uk; 46a Raeburn Pl; ⊙10.30am-5.30pm Mon-Sat, 1-5pm Sun; □24, 29, 42) An Aladdin's cave packed with jewellery, textiles and handicrafts from all over the world, best known for its silver, amber and gemstone jewellery in both ethnic and contemporary designs.

Harvey Nichols   DEPARTMENT STORE
(Map p60; www.harveynichols.com; 30-34 St Andrew Sq; ⊙10am-6pm Mon-Wed, 10am-8pm Thu, 10am-7pm Fri & Sat, 11am-6pm Sun) The jewel in the crown of Edinburgh's shopping scene has four floors of designer labels and eye-popping price tags.

Waterstone's   BOOKS
(www.waterstones.com) George St (Map p60; 83 George St; ⊙9.30am-7pm Mon-Fri, to 6pm Sat, 11am-6pm Sun); West End (Map p60; 128 Princes St; ⊙9am-7pm Mon-Wed & Fri-Sat, 9am-8pm Thu, 10.30am-6pm Sun; □all Princes St buses) The West End branch has an in-store cafe with great views.

John Lewis   DEPARTMENT STORE
(Map p60; www.johnlewis.com; St James Centre, Leith St; ⊙9am-6pm Mon-Wed & Fri, 9am-8pm Thu, 9am-6.30pm Sat, 10am-6pm Sun) The place to go for good-value clothes and household goods.

Adam Pottery   HANDICRAFTS
(Map p46; www.adampottery.co.uk; 76 Henderson Row; ⊙11am-6pm Mon-Sat, to 5pm Jan-Mar; □24, 29, 32) Produces its own ceramics, mostly decorative, in a wide range of styles.

One World Shop   HANDICRAFTS
(Map p52; www.oneworldshop.co.uk; St John's Church, Princes St; ⊙10am-5.30pm Mon-Sat, 11am-5.30pm Sun; □all Princes St buses) Stocks a wide range of handmade crafts from developing countries, including paper goods, rugs, textiles, jewellery, ceramics, accessories, food and drink, all from accredited fairtrade suppliers. During the festival period (when the shop stays open till 6pm) there's a crafts fair in the churchyard outside.

South Edinburgh

Word Power   BOOKS
(Map p52; www.word-power.co.uk; 43 West Nicolson St; ⊙10am-6pm Mon-Sat, noon-5pm Sun; □41,

42) Radical, independent bookshop with wide range of political, gay and feminist literature.

Meadows Pottery   HANDICRAFTS
(Map p46; www.themeadowspottery.com; 11a Summerhall Pl; ⊙10.30am-7.30pm Mon-Tue, to 6pm Wed-Sat; □2, 41, 42, 47) Sells colourful stoneware, all hand-thrown on the premises.

Blackwell's Bookshop   BOOKS
(Map p52; www.blackwell.co.uk; 53-62 South Bridge; ⊙9am-8pm Mon & Wed-Fri, 9.30am-8pm Tue, 9am-6pm Sat, noon-6pm Sun) The city's principal bookstore; big selection of academic books.

Leith

Kinloch Anderson   FASHION
(www.kinlochanderson.com; 4 Dock St; ⊙9am-5.30pm Mon-Sat; □16, 22, 35, 36) One of the best, this was founded in 1868 and is still family run. Kinloch Anderson is a supplier of kilts and Highland dress to the royal family.

Information

EMERGENCY
In an emergency, dial 999 or 112 (free from public payphones) and ask for police, ambulance, fire brigade or coastguard.

Edinburgh Rape Crisis Centre (☑08088 01 03 02; www.rapecrisisscotland.org.uk)

Police Information Centre (☑0131-226 6966; 188 High St; ⊙10am-1pm & 2-5.30pm, to 9.30pm during Fringe Festival) Report a crime, ask a question or make lost-property inquiries here.

Police Scotland (☑non-emergency 101; www.scotland.police.uk; 3-5 Torphichen Pl)

INTERNET ACCESS
There are internet-enabled telephone boxes scattered around the city centre, and countless wi-fi hot spots. Internet cafes are spread around the city. Some convenient ones:

Coffee Home (www.coffeehome.co.uk; 28 Crighton Pl, Leith Walk; per 20min 60p; ⊙10am-9pm Mon-Fri, 10am-8pm Sat, noon-8pm Sun)

e-corner (www.e-corner.co.uk; 54 Blackfriars St; per 20min £1; ⊙10am-7pm Mon-Sat, noon-7pm Sun; 🛜)

G-Tec (www.grassmarket-technologies.com; 67 Grassmarket; per 20min £1; ⊙10am-5.30pm Mon-Fri, to 4pm Sat)

MEDIA
Edinburgh's home-grown daily newspapers include the *Scotsman* (www.scotsman.com), a quality daily covering Scottish, UK and

---

❶ CITY MAPS

For coverage of the whole city in detail, the best maps are Nicolson's *Edinburgh Citymap* and the Ordnance Survey's (OS) *Edinburgh Street Atlas*. You can buy these at the Edinburgh Tourist Office (p92), bookshops and newsagents. Note that long streets may be known by different names along their length. For example, the southern end of Leith Walk is variously called Union Pl and Antigua St on one side, and Elm Row and Greenside Pl on the other.

The OS's 1:50,000 Landranger map *Edinburgh, Penicuik & North Berwick* (sheet No 66) covers the city and the surrounding region to the south and east at a scale of 1.25 inches to 1 mile; it's useful for walking in the Pentland Hills and exploring Edinburgh's fringes and East Lothian.

---

international news, sport and current affairs; and the *Edinburgh Evening News* (www.edinburghnews.com), covering news and entertainment in the city and its environs. *Scotland on Sunday* is the weekend newspaper from the same publisher.

MEDICAL SERVICES

For urgent medical advice you can call the **NHS 24 Helpline** (☑ 08454 24 24 24; www.nhs24.com). Chemists (pharmacists) can advise you on minor ailments. At least one local chemist remains open round the clock – its location will be displayed in the windows of other chemists.

For urgent dental treatment, you can visit the walk-in **Chalmers Street Dental Clinic** (3 Chalmers St; ⊙9am-4.45pm Mon-Thu, to 4.15pm Fri; ▯23, 27, 35, 45, 47). In the case of a dental emergency in the evenings or at weekends, call **Lothian Dental Advice Line** (☑ 0131-536 4800; ⊙5-10pm Mon-Fri, 9am-10pm Sat & Sun).

Boots (48 Shandwick Pl; ⊙7.30am-8pm Mon-Fri, 9am-6pm Sat, 10.30am-5pm Sun) Chemist open longer hours than most.

Royal Hospital for Sick Children (☑ 0131-536 0000; www.nhslothian.scot.nhs.uk; 9 Sciennes Rd; ⊙24hrs) Casualty department for children aged under 13 years; located in Marchmont (moving to a new location near Royal Infirmary in 2017).

Royal Infirmary of Edinburgh (☑ 0131-536 1000; www.nhslothian.scot.nhs.uk; 51 Little France Cres, Old Dalkeith Rd; ⊙24hrs) Edinburgh's main general hospital; has 24-hour accident and emergency department.

Western General Hospital (☑ 0131-537 1330; www.nhslothian.scot.nhs.uk; Crewe Rd South; ⊙8am-9pm) For non-life-threatening injuries and ailments, you can attend the Minor Injuries Clinic here without having to make an appointment.

POST

Main Post Office (St James Shopping Centre, Leith St; ⊙9am-5.30pm Mon-Sat) Hidden away inside a shopping centre.

TOURIST INFORMATION

Edinburgh Airport Information Centre (☑ 0131-344 3120; main concourse, Edinburgh Airport; ⊙7.30am-9pm)

Edinburgh Tourist Office (☑ 0131-473 3868; www.edinburgh.org; Princes Mall, 3 Princes St; ⊙9am-9pm Mon-Sat, 10am-8pm Sun Jul & Aug, 9am-7pm Mon-Sat, 10am-7pm Sun May-Jun & Sep, 9am-5pm Mon-Wed, to 6pm Thu-Sun Oct-Apr) Includes an accommodation booking service, currency exchange, gift and bookshop, internet access and counters selling tickets for Edinburgh city tours and Scottish Citylink bus services.

USEFUL WEBSITES

Edinburgh Architecture (www.edinburgharchitecture.co.uk) Informative site dedicated to the city's modern architecture.

Edinburgh Festival Guide (www.edinburghfestivals.co.uk) Everything you need to know about Edinburgh's many festivals.

Events Edinburgh (www.eventsedinburgh.org.uk) The city council's official events guide.

The List (www.list.co.uk) Listings of restaurants, pubs, clubs and nightlife.

VisitScotland Edinburgh & Lothians (www.edinburgh.org) Official tourist-board site, with listings of accommodation, sights, activities and events.

❶ Getting There & Away

AIR

Edinburgh Airport (☑ 0844 448 8833; www.edinburghairport.com) Edinburgh Airport, 8 miles west of the city, has numerous flights to other parts of Scotland and the UK, Ireland and mainland Europe. FlyBe/Loganair (☑ 0871 700 2000; www.loganair.co.uk) operates daily flights to Inverness, Wick, Orkney, Shetland and Stornoway.

BUS

Edinburgh bus station (left luggage lockers per 24hr £3-10; ⊙4.30am-midnight Sun-Thu, 4.30am-12.30am Fri & Sat) is at the northeast corner of St Andrew Sq, with pedestrian entrances from the square and from Elder St. For timetable information, call **Traveline** (☑ 0871 200 22 33; www.travelinescotland.com).

ℹ BUS INFO ON YOUR PHONE

Lothian Buses has created free smartphone apps that provide route maps, timetables and live waiting times for city buses. Search for EdinBus (iPhone), My Bus Edinburgh (Android) or BusTracker Edinburgh (Windows Phone).

Scottish Citylink (☏ 0871 266 3333; www.citylink.co.uk) buses connect Edinburgh with all of Scotland's cities and major towns. The following are sample one-way fares departing from Edinburgh.

Destination	Fare
Aberdeen	£30
Dundee	£16
Fort William	£34
Glasgow	£7.30
Inverness	£30
Portree	£54
Stirling	£8

It's also worth checking with **Megabus** (☏ 0900 1600 900; www.megabus.com) for cheap intercity bus fares (from as little as £5) from Edinburgh to Aberdeen, Dundee, Glasgow, Inverness and Perth.

There are various buses to Edinburgh from London and the rest of the UK.

CAR & MOTORCYCLE

Arriving in or leaving Edinburgh by car during the morning and evening rush hours (7.30am to 9.30am and 4.30pm to 6.30pm Monday to Friday) is an experience you can live without. Try to time your journey to avoid these periods.

TRAIN

The main terminus in Edinburgh is **Waverley train station**, located in the heart of the city. Trains arriving from, and departing for, the west also stop at Haymarket station, which is more convenient for the West End.

You can buy tickets, make reservations and get travel information at the **Edinburgh Rail Travel Centre** (◷ 4.45am-12.30am Mon-Sat, 7am-12.30am Sun) in Waverley station. For fare and timetable information, phone the **National Rail Enquiry Service** (☏ 08457 48 49 50; www.nationalrail.co.uk) or use the journey planner on the website.

First ScotRail (☏ 08457 55 00 33; www.scotrail.co.uk) operates a regular shuttle service between Edinburgh and Glasgow (£13.20, 50 minutes, every 15 minutes), and frequent daily services to all Scottish cities, including Aberdeen (£34, 2½ hours), Dundee (£17.30, 1¼ hours) and Inverness (£72, 3½ hours).

ℹ Getting Around

TO/FROM THE AIRPORT

The Lothian Buses **Airlink** (www.flybybus.com) service 100 runs from Waverley Bridge, outside the train station, to the airport (£4/7 one way/return, 30 minutes, every 10 minutes, 4am to midnight) via the West End and Haymarket.

Edinburgh Trams run from the airport to the city centre (£4.50/7.50 one way/return, 33 minutes, every six to eight minutes, 6am to midnight).

An airport taxi to the city centre costs around £20 and takes about 20 to 30 minutes. Trams, buses and taxis all depart from outside the arrivals hall; go out through the main doors and turn left.

BICYCLE

Thanks to the efforts of local cycling campaign group Spokes and a bike-friendly city council, Edinburgh is well equipped with bike lanes and dedicated cycle tracks. You can buy a map of the city's cycle routes from most bike shops.

Biketrax (☏ 0131-228 6633; www.biketrax.co.uk; 11 Lochrin Pl; ◷ 9.30am-6pm Mon-Fri, to 5.30pm Sat, noon-5pm Sun; 🚌 all Tollcross buses) rents out hybrid bikes, road bikes and Brompton folding bikes (no mountain bikes, though). A hybrid bike costs £17 for 24 hours, £13 for extra days, and £75 for one week. You'll need a £100 cash or credit-card deposit and photographic ID.

CAR & MOTORCYCLE

Though useful for day trips beyond the city, a car in central Edinburgh is more of a liability than a convenience. There is restricted access on Princes St, George St and Charlotte Sq, many streets are one-way, and finding a parking place in the city centre is like striking gold. Queen's Dr around Holyrood Park is closed to motorised traffic on Sunday.

Car Rental

All the big, international car-rental agencies have offices in Edinburgh.

There are many smaller, local agencies that offer better rates. **Arnold Clark** (☏ 0141-237 4374; www.arnoldclarkrental.co.uk) charges from £30 a day, or £180 a week for a small car, including VAT and insurance.

Parking

There's no parking on main roads into the city from 7.30am to 6.30pm Monday to Saturday. Also, parking in the city centre can be a nightmare. **On-street parking** is controlled by self-service ticket machines from 8.30am to 6.30pm Monday to Saturday, and costs £1 to £2 per hour, with a 30-minute to four-hour maximum. If you break the rules, you'll get a fine, often within minutes of your ticket expiring – Edinburgh's parking wardens are both numerous and notorious. The fine is £60, reduced to £30 if you pay up within 14 days. Cars parked illegally will be towed away. There are large, long-stay car parks at the St James Centre, Greenside Pl, New St, Castle Tce and Morrison St. Motorcycles can be parked free at designated areas in the city centre.

PUBLIC TRANSPORT

Edinburgh's public transport system consists of an extensive bus network and a single tram line that runs from the airport via Haymarket and Princes St to York Pl at the east end of the city centre. The main operators are **Edinburgh Trams** (www.edinburghtrams.com), **Lothian Buses** (www.lothianbuses.com) and **First** (☎ 0131-663 9233; www.firstedinburgh.co.uk); for timetable information contact Traveline.

Bus and tram timetables, route maps and fare guides are posted at all main bus and tram stops, and you can pick up a copy of the free *Lothian Buses Route Map* from **Lothian Buses Travelshops**.

Adult **fares** within the city are £1.50 on both bus and tram; purchase from the bus driver, or from machines at tram stops. Children aged under five travel free and those aged five to 15 pay a flat fare of 70p.

On Lothian Buses you must pay the driver the exact fare, but First buses will give change. Lothian Bus drivers also sell a **day ticket** (£3.50) that gives unlimited travel (on Lothian buses and trams) for a day; a **family day ticket** (up to two adults and three children) costs £7.50. **Night-service buses**, which run hourly between midnight and 5am, charge a flat fare of £3.

You can also buy a **Ridacard** (from Travelshops; not available from bus drivers) that gives unlimited travel for one week for £17.

The Lothian Buses lost-property office is in the Hanover St Travelshop.

Lothian Buses Travelshop (31 Waverley Bridge; ⊙9am-6pm Mon-Fri, 10am-6pm Sat, 10am-5.15pm Sun)

Lothian Buses Travelshop (27 Hanover St; ⊙8am-8pm Mon-Fri, 9am-5.30pm Sat, 10am-5.30pm Sun)

TAXI

Edinburgh's black taxis can be hailed in the street, ordered by phone (extra 80p charge), or picked up at one of the many central ranks. The minimum charge is £2.10 (£3.10 at night) for the first 450m, then 25p for every subsequent 188m – a typical 2-mile trip across the city centre will cost around £6 to £7. Tipping is up to you – because of the high fares local people rarely tip on short journeys, but occasionally round up to the nearest 50p on longer ones. Some taxi companies:

Central Taxis (☎0131-229 2468; www.taxis-edinburgh.co.uk)

City Cabs (☎0131-228 1211; www.citycabs.co.uk)

ComCab (☎0131-272 8000; www.comcab-edinburgh.co.uk)

AROUND EDINBURGH

Edinburgh is small enough that, when you need a break from the city, the beautiful surrounding countryside isn't far away and is easily accessible by public transport, or even by bike. The old counties around Edinburgh are called Midlothian, West Lothian and East Lothian, often referred to collectively as 'the Lothians'.

Midlothian

Queensferry

Queensferry is at the narrowest part of the Firth of Forth, where ferries have crossed to Fife from the earliest times. The village takes its name from Queen Margaret (1046–93), who gave pilgrims free passage across the firth on their way to St Andrews. Ferries continued to operate until 1964 when the graceful Forth Road Bridge was opened. Construction work is underway on a second road bridge, the Queensferry Crossing, scheduled to open in 2016.

Predating the road bridge by 74 years, the magnificent Forth Bridge – only outsiders ever call it the Forth Rail Bridge – is one of the finest engineering achievements of the 19th century. Completed in 1890 after seven years' work, its three huge cantilevers span 1447m and took 59,000 tonnes of steel, eight million rivets and the lives of 58 men to build.

In the pretty, terraced High St in Queensferry is the small Queensferry Museum (www.edinburghmuseums.org.uk; 53 High St; ⊙10am-1pm & 2.15-5pm Mon & Thu-Sat, noon-5pm Sun) FREE. It contains some interesting background information on the bridges, and a fascinating exhibit on the Burry Man (p67), part of the village's summer gala festivities.

There are several good places to eat and drink along the High St, including the stylish **Orocco Pier** (www.oroccopier.co.uk; 17 High St, Queensferry; mains £15-24; ☺9am-10pm; 🔊), which has a modern dining area and outdoor terrace with a stunning view of the Forth Bridge.

The atmospheric **Hawes Inn** (📞0131-331 1990; www.vintageinn.co.uk; Newhalls Rd, Queensferry; mains £8-18; ☺food served noon-10pm; 🚊First Edinburgh 43), famously mentioned in Robert Louis Stevenson's novel *Kidnapped*, serves excellent pub grub; it's opposite the Inchcolm ferry, right beside the railway bridge.

❶ Getting There & Away

Queensferry lies on the southern bank of the Firth of Forth, 8 miles west of Edinburgh city centre. To get there, take First bus 43 or Stagecoach bus 40 (£2.70, 30 to 40 minutes, four to six hourly) from Edinburgh Bus Station. It's a 10-minute walk from the bus stop to the Hawes Inn and the Inchcolm ferry.

Trains go from Edinburgh's Waverley and Haymarket stations to Dalmeny station (£4.30, 15 minutes, two to four hourly). From the station exit, the Hawes Inn is five minutes' walk along a footpath (across the road, behind the bus stop) that leads north beside the railway and then downhill under the Forth Bridge.

Inchcolm

Known as the 'Iona of the East', the island of Inchcolm (meaning 'St Columba's Island') lies east of the Forth bridges, less than a mile off the coast of Fife. Only 800m long, it is home to the ruins of **Inchcolm Abbey** (HS; adult/child £5.50/3.30; ☺9.30am-5.30pm Apr-Sep, 9.30am-4.30pm Oct), one of Scotland's best-preserved medieval abbeys, founded by Augustinian priors in 1123.

The ferry boat **Maid of the Forth** (www.maidoftheforth.co.uk) sails to Inchcolm from Hawes Pier in Queensferry. There are one to four sailings most days from April to October. The return fare is £17.50/8.30 per adult/child, including admission to the abbey. It's a half-hour sail to Inchcolm and you get 1½ hours ashore. As well as the abbey, the trip gives you the chance to see the island's grey seals, puffins and other seabirds.

Hopetoun House

One of Scotland's finest stately homes, **Hopetoun House** (www.hopetoun.co.uk; house & ground adult/child £9.20/4.90, grounds only £4.25/2.50; ☺10.30am-5pm Easter-Sep, last ad-

ROSSLYN CHAPEL

The success of Dan Brown's novel *The Da Vinci Code* and the subsequent Hollywood film has seen a flood of visitors descend on Scotland's most beautiful and enigmatic church: **Rosslyn Chapel** (Collegiate Church of St Matthew; www.rosslynchapel.org.uk; Chapel Loan, Roslin; adult/child £9/free; ☺9.30am-5pm Mon-Sat, noon-4.45pm Sun). The chapel was built in the mid-15th century for William St Clair, third earl of Orkney, and the ornately carved interior – at odds with the architectural fashion of its time – is a monument to the mason's art, rich in symbolic imagery. As well as flowers, vines, angels and biblical figures, the carved stones include many examples of the pagan 'Green Man'; other figures are associated with Freemasonry and the Knights Templar. Intriguingly, there are also carvings of plants from the Americas that predate Columbus' voyage of discovery. The symbolism of these images has led some researchers to conclude that Rosslyn is some kind of secret Templar repository, and it has been claimed that hidden vaults beneath the chapel could conceal anything from the Holy Grail or the head of John the Baptist to the body of Christ himself. The chapel is owned by the Episcopal Church of Scotland and services are still held here on Sunday mornings.

The chapel is on the eastern edge of the village of Roslin, 7 miles south of Edinburgh's centre. Lothian Bus 15 (not 15A) runs from the west end of Princes St in Edinburgh to Roslin (£1.50, 30 minutes, every 30 minutes) via Penicuik (it may be faster to catch any bus to Penicuik, then the 15 to Roslin).

mission 4pm) has a superb location in lovely grounds beside the Firth of Forth. There are two parts – the older built to Sir William Bruce's plans between 1699 and 1702 and dominated by a splendid stairwell with (modern) trompe l'oeil paintings; and the newer, designed between 1720 and 1750 by three members of the Adam family, William and sons Robert and John. The highlights are the red and yellow Adam drawing

Rosslyn Chapel

DECIPHERING ROSSLYN

Rosslyn Chapel is a small building, but the density of decoration inside can be overwhelming. It's well worth buying the official guidebook by the Earl of Rosslyn first; find a bench in the gardens and have a skim through before going into the chapel – the background information will make your visit all the more interesting. The book also offers a useful self-guided tour of the chapel, and explains the legend of the Master Mason and the Apprentice.

Entrance is through the **north door** ①. Take a pew and sit for a while to allow your eyes to adjust to the dim interior; then look up at the ceiling vault, decorated with engraved roses, lilies and stars, (Can you spot the sun and the moon?). Walk left along the north aisle to reach the Lady Chapel, separated from the rest of the church by the **Mason's Pillar** ② and the **Apprentice Pillar** ③.
Here you'll find carvings of **Lucifer** ④, the Fallen Angel, and the **Green Man** ⑤. Nearby are **carvings** ⑥ that appear to resemble Indian corn (maize). Finally, go to the western end and look up at the wall – in the left corner is the head of the **Apprentice** ⑦; to the right is the (rather worn) head of the **Master Mason** ⑧.

ROSSLYN CHAPEL & THE DA VINCI CODE

Dan Brown was referencing Rosslyn Chapel's alleged links to the Knights Templar and the Freemasons – unusual symbols found among the carvings, and the fact that a descendant of its founder, William St Clair, was a Grand Master Mason – when he chose it as the setting for his novel's denouement. Rosslyn is indeed a coded work, written in stone, but its meaning depends on your point of view. See The Rosslyn Hoax? by Robert LD Cooper for an alternative interpretation of the chapel's symbolism.

EXPLORE SOME MORE

After visiting the chapel, head downhill to see the spectacularly sited ruins of Roslin Castle, then take a walk along leafy Roslin Glen.

SANDRO VANNINI/CORBIS ©

Lucifer, the Fallen Angel
At head height, to the left of the second window from the left, is an upside-down angel bound with rope, a symbol often associated with Freemasonry. The arch above is decorated with the Dance of Death.

The Apprentice
High in the corner, beneath an empty statue niche, is the head of the murdered Apprentice, with a deep wound in his forehead above the right eye. Legend says the Apprentice was murdered in a jealous rage by the Master Mason. The worn head on the side wall to the left of the Apprentice is that of his mother.

The Master Mason ⑧

Baptistery

PRACTICAL TIPS

Buy your tickets in advance through the chapel's website (except in August, when no bookings are taken). No photography is allowed inside the chapel.

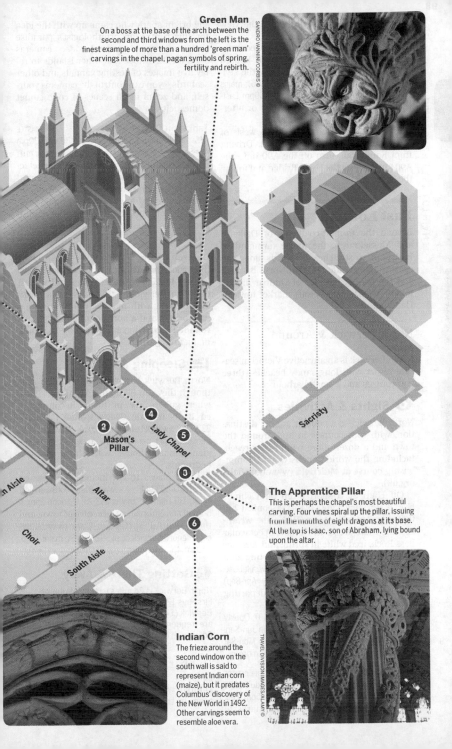

Green Man
On a boss at the base of the arch between the second and third windows from the left is the finest example of more than a hundred 'green man' carvings in the chapel, pagan symbols of spring, fertility and rebirth.

SANDRO VANNINI/CORBIS ©

Green Man
② **Mason's Pillar**
④
Lady Chapel
⑤
③
Sacristy

Choir
Altar
South Aisle
n Aisle

The Apprentice Pillar
This is perhaps the chapel's most beautiful carving. Four vines spiral up the pillar, issuing from the mouths of eight dragons at its base. At the top is Isaac, son of Abraham, lying bound upon the altar.

⑥

Indian Corn
The frieze around the second window on the south wall is said to represent Indian corn (maize), but it predates Columbus' discovery of the New World in 1492. Other carvings seem to resemble aloe vera.

TRAVEL DIVISION IMAGES/ALAMY ©

rooms, lined in silk damask, and the view from the roof terrace.

Britain's most elegant equine accommodation – where the marquis once housed his pampered racehorses – is now the stylish **Stables Tearoom** (☑0131-331 3661; mains £6-8, afternoon tea £12.75; ☺11am-4.30pm Easter-Sep), a delightful spot for lunch or afternoon tea.

Hopetoun House is 2 miles west of Queensferry along the coast road. Driving from Edinburgh, turn off the A90 onto the A904 just before the Forth Bridge and follow the signs.

East Lothian

Beyond the former coalfields of Dalkeith and Musselburgh, the fertile farmland of East Lothian stretches eastwards along the coast to the seaside resort of North Berwick and the fishing harbour of Dunbar. In the middle lies the prosperous market town of Haddington.

North Berwick & Around

POP 6600

North Berwick is an attractive Victorian seaside resort with long sandy beaches, three golf courses and a small harbour.

◉ Sights & Activities

North Berwick is a popular golfing destination, with four courses in and around the town and a dozen more within easy reach, including the world-famous Open Championship course at **Muirfield** (www.muirfield. org.uk).

Off High St, a short steep path climbs **North Berwick Law** (184m), a conical hill that dominates the town. When the weather's fine there are great views to spectacular Bass Rock, iced white in spring and summer with guano from thousands of nesting gannets. **Sula II** (☑01620-880770; www.sulaboat-trips.co.uk; adult/child £14/8; ☺daily Apr-Sep) runs boat trips around Bass Rock, departing from North Berwick's harbour.

The **tourist office** (☑01620-892197; Quality St; ☺9am-6pm Mon-Sat, 11am-4pm Sun Jun-Sep, 9am-6pm Mon-Sat Apr & May, 9am-5pm Mon-Sat Oct) is two blocks inland from the harbour.

Scottish Seabird Centre   WILDLIFE CENTRE (www.seabird.org; The Harbour; adult/child £8.95/4.95; ☺10am-6pm Apr-Aug, to 5pm Feb, Mar, Sep & Oct, to 4pm Nov-Jan) Top marks to the bright spark who came up with the idea for this centre, an ornithologist's paradise that uses remote-control video cameras sited on Bass Rock and other islands to relay live images of nesting gannets and other seabirds – you can control the cameras yourself, and zoom in on scenes of cosy gannet domesticity.

Tantallon Castle   CASTLE (HS; adult/child £5.50/3.30; ☺9.30am-5.30pm Apr-Sep, to 4.30pm Oct-Mar) Perched on a cliff 3 miles east of North Berwick is the spectacular ruin of Tantallon Castle. Built around 1350, it was the fortress residence of the Douglas earls of Angus (the Red Douglases), defended on one side by a series of ditches and on the other by an almost sheer drop into the sea.

Dirleton Castle   CASTLE (HS; adult/child £5.50/3.30; ☺9.30am-5.30pm Apr-Sep, to 4.30pm Oct-Mar) Two miles west of North Berwick is this impressive medieval fortress with massive round towers, a drawbridge and a horrific pit dungeon, surrounded rather incongruously by beautiful, manicured gardens.

🛏 Sleeping & Eating

North Berwick has plenty of places to stay, though they can fill up quickly at weekends, when golfers are in town. Recommended B&Bs include **Glebe House** (☑01620-892608; www.glebehouse-nb.co.uk; Law Rd, North Berwick; r per person £60), a beautiful Georgian country house with three spacious bedrooms.

Good places to eat include the **Grange** (☑01620-893344; www.grangenorthberwick. co.uk; 35 High St; mains £13-25; ☺noon-2pm & 6-9pm) steakhouse in the centre of town, and the delightful **Buttercup Cafe** (www.butter-cupcafenorthberwick.co.uk; 92 High St; mains £3-5; ☺9am-4pm Mon-Wed, Fri & Sat, 10am-4pm Sun).

❶ Getting There & Away

North Berwick is 24 miles east of Edinburgh. First bus 124 runs between Edinburgh and North Berwick (£4, 1¼ hours, every 30 minutes). There are frequent trains between North Berwick and Edinburgh (£6.10, 35 minutes, hourly).

Dunbar

POP 8500

Dunbar was an important Scottish fortress town in the Middle Ages, but little remains of its past, save for the tottering ruins of **Dunbar Castle** overlooking the harbour. Today the town survives as a fishing port and seaside resort, famed in the USA as the birthplace of **John Muir** (1838–1914), pioneer conservationist and father of the US national park system. The town centre is home to **John Muir House** (www.jmbt.org. uk; 126 High St; ☺10am-5pm Mon-Sat, 1-5pm Sun, closed Mon & Tue Oct-Mar) **FREE**, the birthplace and childhood home of the great man himself. The nearby **Dunbar Town House Museum** (www.eastlothianmuseums.org; High St; ☺1-5pm Apr-Sep) **FREE** provides an introduction to local history and archaeology.

From the castle, a scenic 2-mile clifftop trail follows the coastline west to Belhaven Bay and **John Muir Country Park**.

First bus X6 (£5.80, one hour, hourly) runs between Edinburgh and Dunbar. Trains from Edinburgh's Waverley train station serve Dunbar (£7.60, 20 minutes) every hour or so.

West Lothian

Linlithgow

POP 13,500

This ancient royal burgh is one of Scotland's oldest towns, though much of it 'only' dates from the 15th to 17th centuries. Its centre retains a certain charm, despite some ugly modern buildings and occasional traffic congestion, and the town makes an excellent day trip from Edinburgh.

The **tourist office** (☎01506-282720; Burgh Halls, The Cross; ☺9am-6pm Mon-Sat, 11am-5pm Sun) is close to the palace entrance.

⊙ Sights & Activities

Linlithgow Palace HISTORIC BUILDING
(HS; Church Peel; adult/child £5.50/3.30; ☺9.30am-5.30pm Apr-Sep, to 4.30pm Oct-Mar) The building of this magnificent palace, begun by James I in 1425, continued for more than a century and it became a favourite royal residence. James V was born here in 1512, as was his daughter Mary (later Queen of Scots) in 1542, and Bonnie Prince Charlie visited briefly in 1745. The elaborately carved **King's Fountain**, the centrepiece of the palace courtyard, flowed with wine during Charlie's stay; commissioned by James V in 1537, it is the oldest in Britain.

St Michael's Church CHURCH
(www.stmichaelsparish.org.uk; Church Peel; ☺10.30am-4pm May-Sep, 10.30am-1pm Oct-Apr) **FREE** Built between the 1420s and 1530s, the Gothic St Michael's Church is topped by a controversial aluminium spire that was added in 1964. The church is said to be haunted by a ghost that foretold King James IV of his impending defeat at Flodden in 1513.

Linlithgow Canal Centre MUSEUM
(www.lucs.org.uk; Manse Rd; ☺1.30-5pm Sat & Sun Easter-Sep, 2-5pm Mon-Fri Jul–mid-Aug) **FREE** Just 150m south of the town centre lies the Union Canal and this pretty little museum that records the history of the canal. The centre runs three-hour canal-boat trips (adult/child £8/5) west to the Avon Aqueduct, departing at 2pm Saturday and Sunday, Easter to September, and occasionally to the Falkirk Wheel (£20). Shorter 20-minute cruises (adult/child £4/2) leave every half hour during the centre's opening times.

✗ Eating & Drinking

Four Marys PUB FOOD ££
(www.thefourmarys.co.uk; 65-76 High St; mains £7-15; ☺food served noon-2.30pm & 6-9pm Mon-Fri, noon-9pm Sat, 12.30-8.30pm Sun) The Four Marys is an attractive traditional pub (opposite the palace entrance) that serves real ales and excellent pub grub, including haggis, neeps and tatties (haggis, mashed turnip and mashed potato).

Champany Inn SCOTTISH £££
(☎01506-834532; www.champany.com; 3-course lunch/dinner £26/43; ☺12.30-2pm Mon-Fri, 7-10pm Mon-Sat) This rustic inn is a trencherman's delight, famous for its excellent Aberdeen Angus steaks and Scottish lobsters (booking essential). The neighbouring **Chop & Ale House** (mains £12-25; ☺noon-2.30pm & 6.30-10pm Mon-Thu, noon-10pm Fri & Sat, 12.30-10pm Sun) is a less-expensive alternative to the main dining room, offering delicious homemade burgers and steaks. The inn is 2 miles northeast of Linlithgow, on the A803/A904 road towards Bo'ness and Queensferry.

❶ Getting There & Away

Linlithgow is 15 miles west of Edinburgh, and is served by frequent trains from the capital (£5, 20 minutes, four every hour); the train station is 250m east of the town centre.

You can also cycle from Edinburgh to Linlithgow along the Union Canal towpath (21 miles); allow two hours.

SPENCER BOWMAN / GETTY IMAGES ©

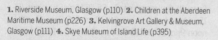

1. Riverside Museum, Glasgow (p110) **2.** Children at the Aberdeen Maritime Museum (p226) **3.** Kelvingrove Art Gallery & Museum, Glasgow (p111) **4.** Skye Museum of Island Life (p395)

VISIT BRITAIN / NATALIE PECHT / GETTY IMAGES ©

Scotland's Museums

Scotland's rich culture and history are celebrated in countless museums, from internationally important collections to specialist exhibits such as the Grampian Transport Museum in Alford, and tiny museums such as Groam House Museum in Rosemarkie, with its carved Pictish stones.

National Museums

The National Museum of Scotland is complemented by several other nationally important collections, including Glasgow's Kelvingrove Museum and the Riverside Museum, a modern masterpiece celebrating transport, with a tall ship moored alongside. There are more things nautical at Dundee's Discovery Point, a shrine to polar exploration, and Aberdeen's superb Maritime Museum.

Folk Museums

The culture and traditions of Scottish rural life come to the fore in places such as the Highland Folk Museum in Kingussie, where a farming township is recreated with historic buildings and demonstrations of traditional crafts. Other, smaller folk museums include the Angus Folk Museum at Glamis, Glencoe Folk Museum, and Kildonan Museum (South Uist).

Island Museums

Each Scottish island has its own culture and identity. The hardy lifestyle of Hebridean crofters is told in the Arnol Blackhouse Museum in Lewis, and in the Skye Museum of Island Life in Trotternish, while the Norse influences of the Northern Isles is explored in the Stromness Museum and the Shetland Museum.

Offbeat Museums

The Museum of Lead Mining in Wanlockhead is one of the country's more unusual museums, offering fascinating insights into a little-known subject. Similar places include the Surgeons' Hall Museum in Edinburgh (pathology), the British Golf Museum in St Andrews and the Scottish Lighthouse Museum in Fraserburgh.

Glasgow

POP 595,100

Best Places to Stay

➜ Malmaison (p120)

➜ Blythswood Square (p120)

➜ Hotel du Vin (p121)

➜ Alamo Guest House (p121)

➜ Grasshoppers (p118)

Best Places to Eat

➜ Ubiquitous Chip (p127)

➜ Stravaigin (p126)

➜ Mother India (p127)

➜ Loon Fung (p125)

➜ Saramago Café Bar (p124)

Why Go?

Disarmingly blending sophistication and earthiness, Scotland's biggest city has evolved over the last couple of decades to become one of Britain's most intriguing metropolises.

At first glance, the soberly handsome Victorian buildings, legacies of wealth generated from manufacturing and trade, suggest a staid sort of place. Very wrong. They are packed with stylish bars, top-notch restaurants, hedonistic clubs and one of Britain's best live-music scenes. The sheer vitality is gloriously infectious: the combination of edgy urbanity and the residents' legendary friendliness is captivating.

Glasgow also offers plenty by day. Its shopping – whether you're looking for Italian fashion or pre-loved denim – is famous and there are top-drawer museums and galleries. Charles Rennie Mackintosh's sublime designs dot the city, which also innovatively displays its industrial heritage. The River Clyde, traditionally associated with Glasgow's earthier side, is now a symbol of the city's renaissance.

When to Go
Glasgow

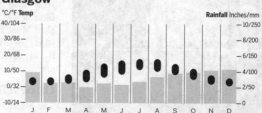

Feb The drizzle won't lift? Maroon yourself in one of Glasgow's fabulous pubs or clubs.

Jun The West End Festival and the Glasgow Jazz Festival make the city music heaven.

Aug Glasgow is friendly at any time, but when the sun is shining there's no happier city in Britain.

History

Glasgow grew around the cathedral founded by St Kertigan, later to become St Mungo, in the 6th century. Unfortunately, with the exception of the cathedral, virtually nothing of the medieval city remains. It was swept away by the energies of a new age – the age of capitalism, the Industrial Revolution and the British Empire.

In the 18th century, much of the tobacco trade between Europe and the USA was routed through Glasgow, providing a great source of wealth. Even after the tobacco trade declined in the 19th century, the city continued to prosper as a centre of textile manufacturing, shipbuilding and the coal and steel industries. The outward appearance of prosperity, however, was tempered by the dire working conditions in the factories.

In the first half of the 20th century Glasgow was the centre of Britain's munitions industry, supplying arms and ships for the two world wars, in the second of which the city was carpet-bombed. Post-war, however, the port and heavy industries began to dwindle, and by the early 1970s the city looked doomed. Glasgow became synonymous with unemployment, economic depression and urban violence, centred around high-rise housing schemes such as the infamous Gorbals. More recently, urban development and a booming cultural sector have injected style and confidence into the city; though the standard of living remains low for Britain and life continues to be tough for many, the ongoing regeneration process gives grounds for optimism. The successful hosting of the 2014 Commonwealth Games highlighted this regeneration to a wide global audience.

⊙ Sights

Glasgow's major sights are fairly evenly dispersed, with many found along the Clyde (the focus of a long-term regeneration program). Many museums are free.

⊙ City Centre

The grid layout and pedestrian streets of the city centre make it easy to get around, and there are numerous cafes and pubs that make good pit stops between attractions.

★ **Glasgow School of Art**   HISTORIC BUILDING
(Map p106; ☑0141-353 4526; www.gsa.ac.uk/tours; 167 Renfrew St; adult/child £9.75/4.75; ⊙9.30am-6.30pm Mar-Oct, 10am-5pm Nov-Feb) Charles Rennie Mackintosh's greatest building – extensively damaged by fire in 2014, so access may be limited by renovation works – still fulfils its original function, so just follow the steady stream of eclectically dressed students up the hill to find it. It's one of Glasgow's architectural showpieces and has now been joined by Steven Holl's spectacular glacial, green School of Design (the Reid Building) right opposite. A risqué combination, but it works.

Visits are by excellent hour-long guided tours (roughly hourly in summer; 11am, 1pm and 3pm in winter, multilingual translations available) run by architecture students. These leave from the new building; book online or by phone at busy times.

Particularly impressive is the thoroughness of the design; the architect's pencil seems to have shaped everything inside and outside the building. The interior is strikingly austere, with simple colour combinations (often just black and cream) and the uncomfortable-looking high-backed chairs for which Mackintosh is famous. The library, designed as an addition in 1907, is a masterpiece.

There's a Mackintosh shop at the end of the tour. If you liked the visit, the same folk run recommended architecturally-minded walking tours of central Glasgow: see the website for details.

Willow Tearooms   HISTORIC BUILDING
(Map p106; www.willowtearooms.co.uk; 217 Sauchiehall St; ⊙9am-5pm Mon-Sat, 11am-5pm Sun) FREE Admirers of the great Charles Rennie Mackintosh will love the Willow Tearooms, an authentic reconstruction of tearooms Mackintosh designed and furnished in the early 20th century for restaurateur Kate Cranston. You can relive the original splendour of this unique tearoom while admiring the architect's distinctive touch in just about every element; he had a free rein and even the teaspoons were given his attention. Reconstruction took two years and the Willow reopened as a tearoom in 1980 (having been closed since 1926).

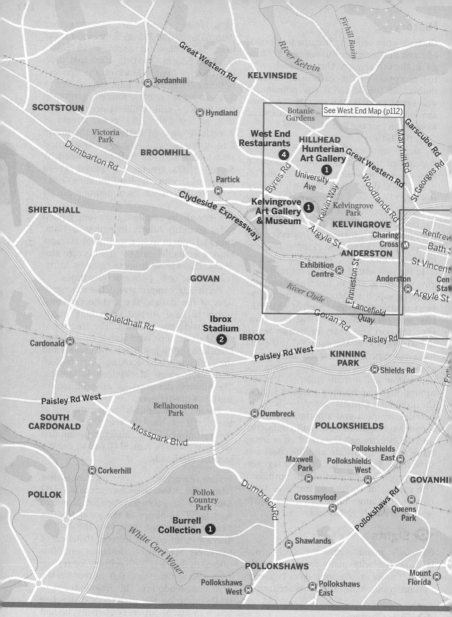

Glasgow Highlights

❶ Gazing at the city's fabulous paintings in the **Burrell Collection** (p114), the **Kelvingrove Art Gallery** (p111) and the **Hunterian Art Gallery** (p113)

❷ Catching a match in one of **Celtic** (p132) or **Rangers'** (p132) massive cauldrons of football

❸ Showing your latest dance moves in Glasgow's

nightclubs (p128) where the best DJs strut their stuff

❹ Deciding which one of the West End's excellent **restaurants** (p126) you are going to dine at next

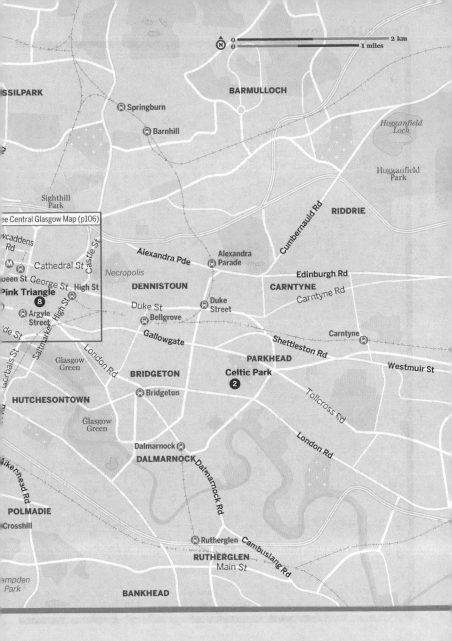

See Central Glasgow Map (p106)

5 Discovering the work of **Charles Rennie Mackintosh** (p119) – 'genius' is an overused word, but few would argue with it here

6 Plunging into the legendary and diverse **live music scene** (p131) in one of the city's iconic pubs

7 Grabbing a bike for a leisurely exploration of Glasgow's industrial heritage and green surroundings on one of the great **cycle routes** (p116)

8 Immersing yourself in Glasgow's friendly gay culture in one of the bars of the **Pink Triangle** (p131)

Central Glasgow

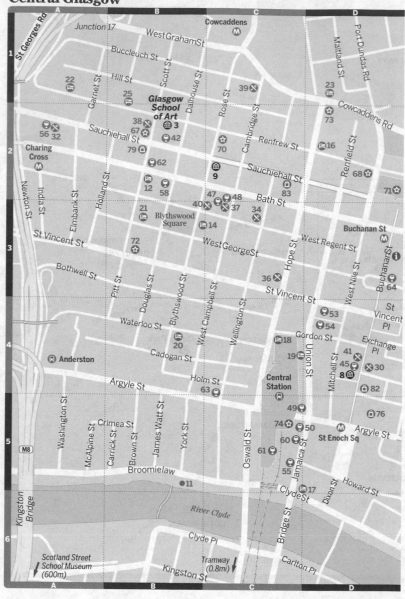

★ **City Chambers**   TOWN HALL
(Map p106; www.glasgow.gov.uk; George Sq;
⊙9am-5pm Mon-Fri) The seat of local government was built in the 1880s. The interior is even more extravagant than the exterior, and the chambers have sometimes been used as a movie location to represent the Kremlin or the Vatican. You can have a look at the opulent ground floor during opening hours: to see more, free guided tours are held at 10.30am and 2.30pm Monday to Friday; it's worth prebooking at busy times.

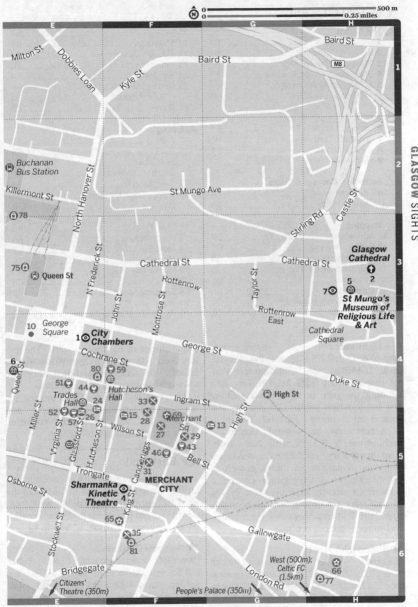

Gallery of Modern Art   GALLERY
(GoMA; Map p106; www.glasgowmuseums.com;
Royal Exchange Sq; ⊙10am-5pm Mon-Wed &
Sat, 10am-8pm Thu, 11am-5pm Fri & Sun) FREE
Scotland's most popular contemporary art
gallery features modern works from international artists, housed in a graceful neoclassical building. The original interior is used to
make a daring, inventive art display. Social
issues are a focal point of the museum but
it's not all heavy going: there's a big effort
made to keep the kids entertained.

Central Glasgow

◎ Top Sights

◎ Sights

⊕ Activities, Courses & Tours

⊜ Sleeping

⊗ Eating

The Lighthouse   HISTORIC BUILDING
(Map p106; ☎0141-276 5365; www.thelighthouse.
co.uk; 11 Mitchell Lane; ⊗10.30am-5pm Mon-
Sat, noon-5pm Sun) FREE Mackintosh's first
building, designed in 1893, was a striking
new headquarters for the *Glasgow Herald*.
Tucked up a narrow lane off Buchanan
St, it now serves as Scotland's Centre for
Architecture & Design, with fairly tech-
nical temporary exhibitions (sometimes
admission is payable for these), as well as
the Mackintosh Interpretation Centre, a
detailed (if slightly dry) overview of his
life and work. On the top floor of the 'lighthouse', drink in great views over the rooftops
and spires of the city centre.

**★Sharmanka Kinetic
Theatre**   MECHANICAL THEATRE
(Map p106; ☎0141-552 7080; www.sharmanka.
com; 103 Trongate; adult/child £5/free; ⊗45-min
shows 3pm Wed-Sun, 70-min shows 7pm Thu &
Sun) This extraordinary mechanical theatre
is located at the Trongate 103 arts centre.
The amazing creativity of Eduard Bersud-
sky, a Russian sculptor and mechanic, now
resident in Scotland, has created a series of
large, wondrous figures sculpted from bits of
scrap and elaborate carvings. Set to haunting
music, the figures perform humorous and

tragic stories of the human spirit. The gallery is open from 1pm to 3pm Wednesday to
Sunday – the sculptures and their stories are
fascinating even when not in motion.

It's great for kids and very moving for
adults: inspirational one moment and
macabre the next, but always colourful,
clever and thought-provoking.

◉ East End

The oldest part of the city is concentrated
around Glasgow Cathedral, to the east of the
modern centre. It's a 15-minute walk from
George Sq, but numerous buses pass nearby,
including buses 11, 12, 36, 37, 38 and 42.

★Glasgow Cathedral   CHURCH
(Map p106; www.historic-scotland.gov.uk; Cathedral Sq; ⊗9.30am-5.30pm Mon-Sat & 1-5pm Sun
Apr-Sep, closes 4.30pm Oct-Mar) FREE Glasgow Cathedral has a rare timelessness. The
dark, imposing interior conjures up medieval might and can send a shiver down
the spine. It's a shining example of Gothic
architecture, and, unlike nearly all of Scotland's cathedrals, survived the turmoil of
the Reformation mobs almost intact. Most
of the current building dates from the 15th
century.

Entry is through a side door into the nave, hung with regimental colours. The wooden roof has been restored many times since its original construction, but some of the timber dates from the 14th century; note the impressive shields. Many of the cathedral's stunning, narrow stained-glass windows are modern; to your left is Francis Spear's 1958 work *The Creation*, which fills the west window.

The cathedral, divided by a late-15th-century stone choir screen, is decorated with seven pairs of figures representing the seven deadly sins. The four stained-glass panels of the east window, depicting the Apostles (also by Francis Spear) are particularly evocative. At the northeastern corner is the entrance to the 15th-century upper chapter house, where Glasgow University was founded. It's now used as a sacristy.

The most interesting part of the cathedral, the lower church, is reached by a stairway. Its forest of pillars creates a powerful atmosphere around St Mungo's tomb (St Mungo founded a monastic community here in the 5th century), the focus of a famous medieval pilgrimage that was believed to be as meritorious as a visit to Rome.

Behind the cathedral, the **necropolis** stretches picturesquely up and over a green hill. The elaborate Victorian tombs of the city's wealthy industrialists make for an intriguing stroll, great views and a vague Gothic thrill.

★**St Mungo's Museum of Religious Life & Art** MUSEUM
(Map p106; www.glasgowmuseums.com; 2 Castle St; ⊙10am-5pm Tue-Thu & Sat, 11am-5pm Fri & Sun) **FREE** Set in a reconstruction of the bishop's palace that once stood in the cathedral forecourt, this museum audaciously attempts to capture the world's major religions in an artistic nutshell. A startling achievement, it presents the similarities and differences of how various religions approach common themes such as birth, marriage and death. The attraction is twofold: firstly, impressive art that blurs the lines between religion and culture; and secondly, the opportunity to delve into different faiths, as deep or shallow as you wish.

Provand's Lordship HISTORIC HOUSE
(Map p106; www.glasgowmuseums.com; 3 Castle St; ⊙10am-5pm Tue-Thu & Sat, 11am-5pm Fri & Sun) **FREE** Near the cathedral is Provand's Lordship, the oldest house in Glasgow. A

VISITING KELVINGROVE ART GALLERY & MUSEUM

There are over a million objects in the museum's collection, but fortunately they've pared things down so you won't feel overwhelmed. Enter from either side and first admire the building's interior, with its high central hall, elaborate lamps and organ (recitals at 1pm).

The museum is divided into two wings, one focusing on Life (history, archaeology and natural history) and the other on Expression (art). Follow the itinerary below (duration: three hours) to check out the highlights.

First Floor

Start with the art: upstairs in the hall with the hanging heads. The Dutch room has Rembrandt's magnificent *A Man in Armour*, with chiaroscuro techniques learned from Caravaggio. Hit the interactive screen and decide whom you think the painting represents.

The next-but-one French gallery holds a fine Renoir portrait of his pupil Valentine Fray, and an early Van Gogh depicting his Glaswegian flatmate Alexander Reid. Nearby, Monet's *Vétheuil* offers a quintessential representation of both Impressionism and the French countryside; contrast it with the less ethereal landscape by Cézanne located alongside. Dufy's famous canvas of *The Jetty at Trouville-Deauville* also inhabits this room, as do works by many other masters.

The Scottish landscape gallery has some jaw-dropping depictions of Highland scenes. Standing in front of Gustave Doré's *Glen Massan* you can almost feel the drizzle and smell the heather. David Wilkie's *The Cottar's Saturday Night* is based on the poem by Robert Burns, which you can listen to alongside.

While you're up here, don't miss the paintings around the arcade. The collection's highlight, however, sits upstairs in the central atrium. Based on dreams, Salvador Dalí's *Christ of St John of the Cross* is arguably his greatest work. Forget ridiculous moustaches and Surre-

rare example of 15th-century domestic Scottish architecture, it was built in 1471 as a manse. The ceilings and doorways are low, and the rooms are sparsely furnished with period artefacts, except for an upstairs room which has been furnished to reflect the living space of an early-16th-century chaplain. The building's biggest draw is its authentic feel – if you ignore the tacky imitation-stone linoleum covering the ground floor.

People's Palace　　　　　　　　　　MUSEUM
(www.glasgowmuseums.com; Glasgow Green; ◷10am-5pm Tue-Thu & Sat, 11am-5pm Fri & Sun) **FREE** Set in the city's oldest park, Glasgow Green, is the solid orange stone People's Palace. It is an impressive museum of social history, telling the story of Glasgow from 1750 to the present through creative, inventive family-friendly displays. The palace was built in the late 19th century as a cultural centre for Glasgow's East End. The attached greenhouse, the **Winter Gardens** (10am to 5pm daily), has tropical plants and is a nice spot for a coffee.

◉ The Clyde

Once a thriving shipbuilding area, the Clyde sank into dereliction during the post-war

era but is slowly being rejuvenated. To find out more, see www.clydewaterfront.com.

There are several good attractions along the Clyde, but the walk along its banks still isn't all that it could be; it can feel bleak and impersonal, with oversized buildings dwarfing the humble pedestrian.

★ Riverside Museum　　　　　　　MUSEUM
(www.glasgowmuseums.com; 100 Pointhouse Pl; ◷10am-5pm Mon-Thu & Sat, 11am-5pm Fri & Sun; ♿) **FREE** This visually impressive modern museum at Glasgow Harbour (west of the centre – get bus 100 from the north side of George Sq, or the Clyde Cruises boat service) owes its striking curved forms to British-Iraqi architect Zaha Hadid. A transport museum forms the main part of the collection, featuring a fascinating series of cars made in Scotland, plus assorted railway locos, trams, bikes (including the world's first pedal-powered bicycle from 1847) and model Clyde-built ships.

An atmospheric recreation of a Glasgow shopping street from the early 20th century puts the vintage vehicles into a social context. The museum also has a cafe.

alist frippery: this is a serious, awesomely powerful painting. A sinewy man-god looks down through an infinity of sky and darkness to a simple fishing boat in Galilee (or Catalonia in this case). You could spend a while in front of this.

Ground Floor

Downstairs, check out the **Art Discovery Centre**, aimed at kids but well worth a stroll, then head for the large room devoted to the Glasgow Boys. Inspired by Whistler, these artists broke with romanticism to pioneer a more modern style. Compare William Kennedy's grounded *Stirling Station* or the realism of James Guthrie's *A Funeral Service in the Highlands* with those misty Scottish landscapes upstairs. Also noteworthy in this space are John Lavery's famous theatrical portrait of Anna Pavlova, and EA Hornel's much-reproduced *The Coming of Spring*.

You've seen most of the paintings now, but there's plenty left to discover if you're not worn out. Try the room dedicated to the interiors and designs of art deco and the Glasgow style. 'Margaret has genius, I have only talent', said Charles Rennie Mackintosh of his wife, and there's a good display of her work here, as well as that of her sister, Frances Macdonald.

The other side of the museum, dominated by a hanging Spitfire, has two floors of rooms including impressive prehistoric and Viking-era carved stones, Egyptian grave goods and other archaeological finds. Suits of armour are cleverly placed in an exhibition about the human consequences of war, and there are some fine social history displays. The taxidermy animals downstairs are a reminder of the museum's Victorian past. Don't miss John Fulton's elaborate orrery, a working model of the solar system: you'll find it near the much-loved elephant (who is called Sir Roger, if you'd like to be introduced).

Glenlee   SHIP
(www.thetallship.com; Riverside Museum; ⊙10am-5pm; 🚸) **FREE** The magnificent three-masted *Glenlee*, launched in 1896, is berthed alongside the museum. On board are family-friendly displays about the ship's history, restoration and shipboard life during its heyday. Upkeep costs are high, so do donate something or have a coffee below decks.

★ Glasgow Science Centre   MUSEUM
(Map p112; 📞0141 420 5000; www.glasgowsciencecentre.org; 50 Pacific Quay; adult/child £10.50/8.50, IMAX, tower or planetarium extra £2.50; ⊙10am-5pm Wed-Sun Nov-Mar, 10am-5pm daily Apr-Oct; 🚸) This ultramodern science museum will keep the kids entertained for hours (that's middle-aged kids, too!). It brings science and technology alive through hundreds of interactive exhibits on four floors: a bounty of discovery for inquisitive minds. There's also an **IMAX theatre** (see www.cineworld.com for current screenings), a rotating 127m high **observation tower**; a **planetarium**, and a **Science Theatre**, with live science demonstrations. To get here, take bus 89 or 90 from Union St.

◉ West End

With its appealing student buzz, trendy bars and cafes and nonchalant swagger, the West End is probably the most engaging area of Glasgow – it's great for people-watching, and is as close as Glasgow gets to bohemian. From the centre, buses 9, 16 and 23 run towards Kelvingrove, buses 8, 11, and 16 to the university, and buses 20, 44 and 66 to Byres Rd (among others).

★ Kelvingrove Art Gallery & Museum   GALLERY, MUSEUM
(Map p112; www.glasgowmuseums.com; Argyle St; ⊙10am-5pm Mon-Thu & Sat, 11am-5pm Fri & Sun) **FREE** A magnificent stone building, this grand Victorian cathedral of culture is a fascinating and unusual museum, with a bewildering variety of exhibits. You'll find fine art alongside stuffed animals, and Micronesian shark-tooth swords alongside a Spitfire plane, but it's not mix 'n' match: rooms are carefully and thoughtfully themed, and the collection is a manageable size. There's an excellent room of Scottish art, a room of fine French Impressionist works, and quality Renaissance paintings from Italy and Flanders (for more detail, see the boxed text above).

West End

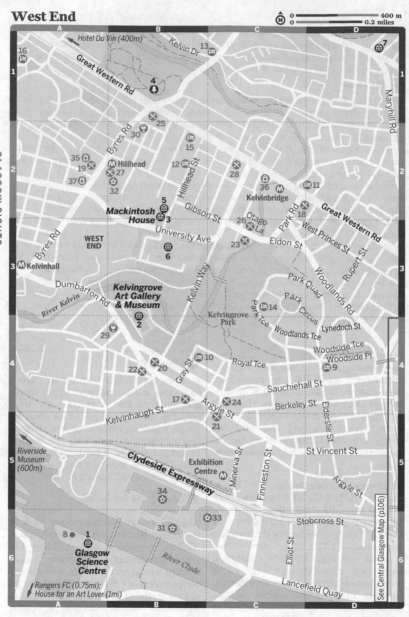

Salvador Dalí's superb *Christ of St John of the Cross* is also here. Best of all, nearly everything, including the paintings, has an easy-reading paragraph of interpretation. You can learn a lot about art here, and it's excellent for children, with plenty to do and displays aimed at a variety of ages. Free hour-long guided tours begin at 11am and 2.30pm. Bus 17, among many others, runs here from Renfield St.

West End

Hunterian Museum   MUSEUM

(Map p112; www.hunterian.gla.ac.uk; University Ave; ⊙10am-5pm Tue-Sat, 11am-4pm Sun) FREE Housed in the glorious sandstone university building, which is in itself reason enough to pay a visit, this quirky museum contains the collection of renowned one-time student of the university, William Hunter (1718–83). Hunter was primarily an anatomist and physician but, as one of those gloriously well-rounded Enlightenment figures, he interested himself in everything the world had to offer. Pickled organs in glass jars take their place alongside geological phenomena, potsherds gleaned from ancient brochs, dinosaur skeletons and a creepy case of deformed animals. The main halls of the exhibition, with their high vaulted roofs, are magnificent in themselves. A highlight is the 1674 Chinese *Map of the Whole World* in the World Culture section.

Hunterian Art Gallery   GALLERY

(Map p112; www.hunterian.gla.ac.uk; 82 Hillhead St; ⊙10am-5pm Tue-Sat, 11am-4pm Sun) FREE Across the road from the Hunterian Museum, and part of the same bequest, the bold tones of the Scottish Colourists (Samuel Peploe, Francis Cadell, JD Fergusson and Leslie Hunter) are well represented in this gallery. There are William MacTaggart's Impressionistic Scottish landscapes and a gem by Thomas Millie Dow. There's also a special collection of James McNeill Whistler's limpid prints, drawings and paintings. Upstairs, in a section devoted to late-19th-century Scottish art, you can see works by several of the Glasgow Boys.

★Mackintosh House   HISTORIC BUILDING

(Map p112; www.hunterian.gla.ac.uk; 82 Hillhead St; ⊙10am-5pm Tue-Sat, 11am-4pm Sun) FREE Attached to the Hunterian Art Gallery, this is a reconstruction of the first home that Charles Rennie Mackintosh bought with his wife, noted designer/artist Margaret Macdonald. It's fair to say that interior decoration was one of their strong points; Mackintosh House is startling even today. The quiet elegance of the hall and dining room on the ground floor give way to a stunning drawing room.

There's something otherworldly about the very mannered style of the beaten silver panels, the long-backed chairs and the surface decorations echoing Celtic manuscript illuminations. You wouldn't have wanted to be the guest that spilled a glass of red on this carpet. Visits are by free guided tour on the half hour.

Botanic Gardens
PARK

(Map p112; 730 Great Western Rd; ☉7am-dusk, glasshouse 10am-6pm summer, to 4.15pm winter) A marvellous thing about walking in here is the way the noise of Great Western Rd suddenly recedes into the background. The wooded gardens follow the riverbank of the River Kelvin and there are plenty of tropical species to discover. Kibble Palace, an impressive Victorian iron and glass structure dating from 1873, is one of the largest glasshouses in Britain; check out the herb garden, too, with its medicinal species.

The gorgeous hilly grounds make the perfect place for a picnic lunch. There are also organised walks and concerts in summer – have a look at the noticeboard near the entrance to see what's on.

◉ South Side

The south side is a tangled web of busy roads with a few oases giving relief from the urban congestion. It does, however, contain some excellent attractions.

★ Burrell Collection
GALLERY

(www.glasgowmuseums.com; Pollok Country Park; ☉10am-5pm Mon-Thu & Sat, 11am-5pm Fri & Sun) FREE One of Glasgow's top attractions was amassed by wealthy industrialist Sir William Burrell then donated to the city and is housed in an outstanding museum, in a park 3 miles south of the city centre. Burrell collected all manner of art, from his teens to his death at 97, and this idiosyncratic collection of treasure includes everything from Chinese porcelain and medieval furniture to paintings by Degas and Cézanne. It's not so big as to be overwhelming, and the stamp of the collector lends an intriguing coherence.

Visitors will find their own favourite part of this museum, but the exquisite tapestry galleries are outstanding. Intricate stories capturing life in Europe are woven into staggering wall-size pieces dating from the 13th to 16th centuries.

Within the spectacular interior, carved-stone Romanesque doorways are incorporated into the structure so you actually walk through them. Floor-to-ceiling windows

admit a flood of light. In springtime, it's worth spending a full day of your trip here and making some time to wander in the beautiful flower-studded park. If you're not heading further north, here's the place to see shaggy Highland cattle, as well as heavy horses.

Many buses pass the park gates (including buses 45, 47, 48 and 57), and there's a twice-hourly bus service between the gallery and the gates (a pleasant 10-minute walk). Alternatively catch a train to Pollokshaws West from Central station (four per hour; second station on the line for East Kilbride or Kilmarnock).

Scotland Street School Museum
NOTABLE BUILDING

(www.glasgowmuseums.com; 225 Scotland St; ☉10am-5pm Tue-Thu & Sat, 11am-5pm Fri & Sun) FREE Mackintosh's Scotland Street School seems a bit forlorn these days, on a wind-swept industrial street with no babble of young voices filling its corridors. Nevertheless it's worth a visit for its stunning facade and interesting museum of education that occupies the interior. Reconstructions of classrooms from various points in the school's lifetime, combined with grumbling headmaster and cleaner, will have older visitors recalling their own schooldays. It's right opposite Shields Rd subway station and there's also an OK cafe.

House for an Art Lover
NOTABLE BUILDING

(☏0141-353 4770; www.houseforanartlover.co.uk; Bellahouston Park, Dumbreck Rd; adult/child £4.50/3; ☉10am-4pm Mon-Wed, to 12.30pm Thu-Sun) Although designed in 1901 as an entry in a competition run by a German magazine, the House for an Art Lover was not built until the 1990s. Mackintosh worked closely with his wife on the design and her influence is evident, especially in the rose motif. The overall effect of this brilliant architect's design is one of space and light. Buses 3, 9, 54, 55 and 56 all run here from the centre; check the website before making the journey, as it's regularly booked for events.

Holmwood House
HISTORIC HOUSE

(www.nts.org.uk; 61-63 Netherlee Rd; adult/child £6.50/5; ☉noon-5pm Thu-Mon Apr-Oct) An interesting building designed by Alexander 'Greek' Thomson, Holmwood House dates from 1857. Despite ongoing renovations, it's well worth a visit. Look for sun symbols downstairs and stars upstairs in this attractive house with its adaptation of classical

VISITING THE BURRELL COLLECTION

The Burrell collection is of a manageable size, but the surrounding parkland is so lovely, you should come equipped for strolling and, if it's a fine day, bring a picnic. Follow this guide to check out the highlights (duration: two hours). In the museum itself, start in the luminous main courtyard, which is dotted with Rodin bronzes, including an 1880 version of *The Thinker*, the fabulous *Eve After the Fall* and *The Age of Bronze*. Next, pass through the ornate portal; this 16th-century work was originally part of Hornby Castle in Yorkshire and is appropriate preparation for the eclectic nature of the collection.

As you pass through the portal, you are thrown back millennia in time to ancient Egypt. Admire the fine carvings and the delicate faience *shawabtiu* – mummylike figures that accompanied the deceased to the afterlife. Attic black- and red-figure vases are next; continuing along the windows you jump forward via Chinese porcelain to religious sculpture; look for the noteworthy *Lamentation over the Crucified Christ*, an early-16th-century German work by that most versatile and prolific of artists, Anonymous.

Also on the ground floor are recreated interiors of Hutton Castle, a small section on Islamic art, and the Burrell's superb collection of tapestries, which are rotated regularly.

Retrace your steps to the Greek vases, and head up the stairs to the small suite of rooms that make this gallery a must-see for art lovers. First up are some wonderful 15th- and 16th-century Flemish paintings, mostly on wood, and beautifully restored. *Rest on the Flight into Egypt* stands out here, the title belied by the very European landscape in the background.

The rest of this assemblage of art is French. Burrell was an important patron of Edgar Degas, whose series of ballet paintings, snapshotlike *Woman With a Parasol*, and masterful portrait of his friend Edmond Duranty are highlights. A series of Manets showcases the artist's versatility, while Géricault's horses are also to be admired. You can feel the French summer sun in Alfred Sisley's *Church at Noisy-le-Roi*; compare it to the more dreamlike landscape of Cézanne's almost tropical *Château de Médan*.

Pleasingly, there's good information provided on each painting and, downstairs, computers where you can browse the database of the collection.

Greek architecture. Cathcart is 4 miles south of the centre; get a train via Queen's Park or Neilston. Otherwise, take bus 44, 44A, 44D or 66 from the city centre. Follow Rhannan Rd for about 800m to find the house.

Scottish Football Museum   MUSEUM
(The Hampden Experience; www.scottishfootballmuseum.org.uk; Hampden Park, adult/child £7/3; ⊙10am-5pm Mon-Sat, 11am-5pm Sun) This museum features exhibits on the history of the game in Scotland and the influence of Scots on the world game. Football inspires an incredible passion in Scotland and the museum is crammed full of impressive memorabilia, including a cap and match ticket from the very first international football game ever played, held in Glasgow in 1872. You can also take a tour of the stadium (adult/child £8/3.50; combined ticket with museum £11/5), home ground of the national football side and of lower league outfit Queens Park.

The museum is at Hampden Park, off Aikenhead Rd. Take a train to Mount Florida station or take bus 5, 31, 37 or 75 from Stockwell St.

◎ North Side

Mackintosh Church   HISTORIC BUILDING
(Queen's Cross Church; Map p112; www.crmsociety.com; 870 Garscube Rd; adult/child £4/free; ⊙10am 5pm Mon, Wed & Fri Apr-Oct, to 4pm Nov-Mar) Now headquarters of the Charles Rennie Mackintosh Society, this is the only one of Mackintosh's church designs to be built. It has an excellent stained glass window and exquisite relief carvings. The wonderful simplicity and grace of the barrel-shaped design is particularly inspiring. The luminous church hall is arguably even finer. There's a good gift shop, and a detailed Mackintosh DVD playing. Garscube Rd is the northern extension of Rose St in the city centre.

🏃 Activities

There are numerous green spaces within the city. **Pollok Country Park** surrounds the Burrell Collection and has several woodland trails. Nearer the centre of the city, the Kelvin Walkway follows the River Kelvin through Kelvingrove Park, the Botanic Gardens and on to Dawsholm Park.

Walking & Cycling

The Clyde Walkway extends from Glasgow upriver to the Falls of Clyde near New Lanark, some 40 miles away. The tourist office (p134) has a good leaflet pack detailing different sections of this walk. The 10-mile section through Glasgow has interesting parts, though modern buildings have replaced most of the old shipyards.

The well-trodden, long-distance footpath the West Highland Way begins in Milngavie, 8 miles north of Glasgow (you can walk to Milngavie from Glasgow along the River Kelvin), and runs for 95 spectacular miles to Fort William.

There are several long-distance pedestrian/cycle routes that begin in Glasgow and follow off-road routes for most of the way. Check www.sustrans.org.uk for more details.

The Clyde–Loch Lomond route traverses residential and industrial areas in a 20-mile ride from Bell's Bridge to Loch Lomond. This route continues to Inverness; it's part of the Lochs and Glens National Cycle Route.

The Clyde to Forth cycle route runs through Glasgow. One way takes you to Edinburgh via Bathgate, the other takes you via Paisley to Greenock and Gourock, the first section partly on roads. Another branch heads down to Irvine and Ardrossan, for the ferry to Arran. An extension via Ayr, Maybole and Glentrool leads to the Solway coast and Carlisle.

☞ Tours

City Sightseeing   BUS TOUR
(Map p106; ☎0141-204 0444; www.citysightseeingglasgow.co.uk; adult/child £14/7; ☼late-Mar–Sep) These double-decker, hop-on, hop-off tourist buses run a circuit along the main sightseeing routes, starting on George Sq. You get on and off as you wish. A ticket, bought from the driver, online or in the tourist office, is valid for two consecutive days. All buses have wheelchair access and multilingual commentary.

Glasgow Taxis City Tour   TAXI TOUR
(☎0141-429 7070; www.glasgowtaxis.co.uk) If you're confident you can understand the driver's accent, a taxi tour is a good way to get a feel of the city and its sights. The 60-minute tour takes you around all the centre's important landmarks, with commentary. The standard tour costs £35 for up to five people.

Seaforce   BOAT TOUR
(☎0141-221 1070; www.seaforce.co.uk; Riverside Museum) Departing from the Riverside Museum, Seaforce offers speedy all-weather powerboat jaunts along the Clyde. There's a variety of trips, including a half-hour ride around central Glasgow (adult/child £12/6), an hour-long trip to the Erskine Bridge (adult/child £15/10) or four-hour rides to local wildlife hot spots (adult/child £50/35).

Clyde Cruises   BOAT TRIP
(Map p106; ☎01475-721281; www.clydecruises.com; adult/child £15/8; ☼late Jun–mid-Sep) Cruises on the Clyde in summer, with hop-on, hop-off service to the Science Centre and Riverside Museum. Check the website for departure times.

Waverley   BOAT TRIP
(Map p112; ☎0845-130 4647; www.waverleyexcursions.co.uk; ☼Apr-Oct) The world's last ocean-going paddle steamer (built in 1947) cruises Scotland's west coast in summer, with many different routes; the website details days of departure. It serves several towns and the islands of Bute, Great Cumbrae and Arran, among others. Its Glasgow departures are from the Glasgow Science Centre, while it also has frequent departures from other spots, including Largs and Ayr.

☆☆ Festivals & Events

Celtic Connections   MUSIC
(☎0141-353 8000; www.celticconnections.com) Two-week music festival held in January.

Glasgow Film Festival   FILM
(www.glasgowfilm.org) Ten-day film festival in February with screenings in various locations across the city.

Glasgow International Festival of Visual Art   VISUAL ART
(☎0141-276 8384; www.glasgowinternational.org) Held in late April in even years, this festival features a range of innovative installations, performances and exhibitions around town.

Glasgow Jazz Festival   JAZZ
(www.jazzfest.co.uk) Excellent festival held in June.

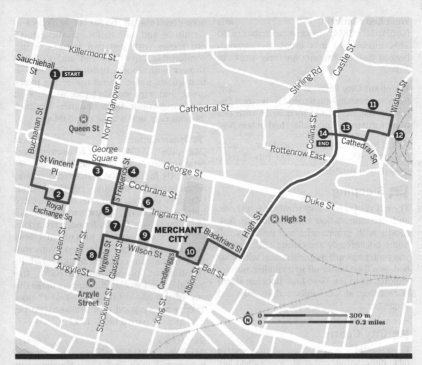

🏃 Walking Tour
Glasgow

START BUCHANAN ST
FINISH GLASGOW CATHEDRAL
DISTANCE 1¾ MILES
DURATION 1½ HOURS

This stroll takes you to Glasgow Cathedral through trendy Merchant City.

Start at the junction of Sauchiehall and Buchanan Streets, overseen by a bronze **1** **statue of Donald Dewar**, Scotland's inaugural First Minister. Stroll down pedestrian Buchanan St, then left through one of the handsome gateways into Merchant City. Here, the strikingly colonnaded **2** **Gallery of Modern Art** (p107) was once the Royal Exchange and now hosts some of the country's best contemporary art displays. Turn left up Queen St to **3** **George Square**, surrounded by imposing Victorian architecture: including the grandiose **4** **City Chambers** (p106). Walk down South Frederick St. Ahead of you, the former Court House cells now house the **5** **Corinthian Club** (p128); drop into the bar for a glimpse of the extravagant interior, then continue to

6 **Hutcheson's Hall**. This was built in 1805 as a hospital and school for the poor. Retrace your steps one block and continue south down Glassford St past **7** **Trades Hall**, designed by Robert Adam in 1791 to house the trades guild. Turn right into Wilson St and left along Virginia St, lined with the old warehouses of the Tobacco Lords. The **8** **Tobacco Exchange** is flanked by pretty Virginia Court. Sugar and tobacco were traded here in the 18th and 19th centuries. Back on Wilson St, the **9** **Old Sheriff Court** fills a whole block and has been both Glasgow's town hall and main lawcourt. Continue east on Wilson St past Ingram Sq to **10** **Merchant Square**, a covered courtyard that was once the city's fruit market but now bustles with cafes and bars. Head up Albion St, then right into Blackfriars St. Emerging onto High St, turn left and follow it up to the **11** **cathedral** (p108). Behind the cathedral wind your way up through the **12** **Necropolis**, which offers great city views. Lastly, check out **13** **St Mungo's Museum of Religious Life & Art** (p109) and **14** **Provand's Lordship** (p109).

West End Festival
ARTS

(☎0141-341 0844; www.westendfestival.co.uk) This music and arts event is Glasgow's biggest festival, running for three weeks in June.

Merchant City Festival
ARTS

(www.merchantcityfestival.com) Lively street festival in the Merchant City quarter, with lots of performances and stalls. Held in late July.

World Pipe Band Championships
MUSIC

(www.theworlds.co.uk) Over 200 pipe bands; held in mid-August.

🛏 Sleeping

The city centre gets very rowdy at weekends, and accommodation options fill up fast, mostly with groups who will probably roll home boisterously some time after 3am. If you prefer an earlier appointment with your bed, you'll be better off in a smaller, quieter lodging, or in the West End. Booking ahead is essential at weekends and in July and August.

🛏 City Centre

Euro Hostel
HOSTEL £

(Map p106; ☎0141-222 2828; www.euro-hostels.co.uk; 318 Clyde St; dm £14-22, s £22-60, d £44-80; @🛜) With hundreds of beds, this mammoth hostel is handily central. While it feels a bit institutional and businesslike, and is often booked out by rowdy groups, it has lots of facilities, including en-suite dorms with lockers, internet access, a compact kitchen, breakfast, on-site public bar, games room and a laundry. Dorms range in size from four to 14 beds, and price varies on a daily basis. Renovations are ongoing.

McLay's Guesthouse
GUESTHOUSE £

(Map p106; ☎0141-332 4796; www.mclays.com; 264 Renfrew St; s/d £42/56, without bathroom £35/48; 🛜) The string of cheapish guesthouses along the western end of Renfrew St are a mixed bag offering no luxury but a tempting location right by the Sauchiehall nightlife and College of Art. This is among the best of them; a solid choice with decent warm rooms and fair prices. There's a big variety of rooms and rates. Wi-fi doesn't reach the rooms.

★ Citizen M
HOTEL ££

(Map p106; ☎0141-404 9485; www.citizenm.com; 60 Renfrew St; r £75-105; @🛜) This modern chain does away with some normal hotel accoutrements in favour of self-check-in terminals and minimalist, plasticky modern rooms with just two features: a big, comfortable king-sized bed and a decent shower with mood lighting. The idea is that guests make liberal use of the public areas, and why wouldn't you, with upbeat and super-comfortable designer furniture, 24-hour cafe, and a table full of iMacs.

★ Grasshoppers
HOTEL ££

(Map p106; ☎0141-222 2666; www.grasshoppersglasgow.com; 87 Union St; r £85-115; 🛜) Discreetly hidden atop a timeworn railway administration building right alongside Glasgow Central, this small, well-priced hotel is a modern, upbeat surprise. Rooms are compact – a few larger ones are available – but well-appointed, with unusual views over the station roof's glass sea. Numerous nice touches are on offer: friendly staff, interesting art, proper in-room coffee, free cupcakes, and weeknight suppers make this one of the city centre's homeliest choices. There's a very good deal available (£6 per day) at a car park a block away.

Rab Ha's
INN ££

(Map p106; ☎0141-572 0400; www.rabhas.com; 83 Hutcheson St; r £69-89; 🛜) This Merchant City favourite is an atmospheric pub-restaurant with four stylish rooms upstairs. They are all quite distinct and colourful. Room 1 is the best and largest, but all are comfortable, and the location is great. The personal touches such as fresh flowers, iPod docks, a big welcome and any-time breakfast make you feel special.

Pipers Tryst Hotel
HOTEL ££

(Map p106; ☎0141-353 5551; www.thepipingcentre.co.uk; 30-34 McPhater St; s/d £65/80; 🛜) The name is no tartan-tourist-trap; this intimate, cosy hotel in a noble building is actually run by the adjacent bagpiping centre, and profits go towards maintaining it. Cheery staff, great value and a prime city-centre location make this a wise choice. You won't have far to migrate after a night of Celtic music and fine single malts in the snug bar-restaurant downstairs.

Grand Central Hotel
HOTEL ££

(Map p106; ☎0141-240 3700; www.thegrandcentralhotel.com; 99 Gordon St; r £100-130; @🛜) This handsome Victorian hotel, which retains its former glory, is part of the central railway station: some rooms overlook the platforms. High ceilings, vast corridors stretching into the distance and a fabulous ballroom are the highlights of this throwback to the golden age of rail. Decent modern bathrooms and spacious rooms – the executives are worth the upgrade – make this a far more comfortable trainspotting base than a level crossing in the drizzle.

Indigo
HOTEL **££**
(Map p106; ☏ 0141-226 7700; www.hotelindigoglasgow.com; 75 Waterloo St; r £110-180; @ 🛜)
Once the power station for the first trams, this boutique-chain conversion of an elegant building has resulted in a satisfying, surprisingly quiet option in the heart of things. Rooms have mural-style artwork, great beds and a free minibar (with better stuff in it as you go up the room grades). Space is good, and bathrooms have rainfall showers. Prices vary; there are usually good online deals.

Brunswick Hotel
HOTEL **££**
(Map p106; ☏ 0141-552 0001; www.brunswick-hotel.co.uk; 106 Brunswick St; d £50-105; 🛜)
Especially suiting people wanting a base for nightlife, this is a pleasing Merchant City option. The rooms are all stylish with a mixture of minimalism and rich colours. Compact and standard doubles are small but will do if you're here for a night out, but king-size rooms are well worth the upgrade. There's a good restaurant downstairs and various events on in the basement space.

Babbity Bowster
INN **££**
(Map p106; ☏ 0141-552 5055; www.babbitybowster.com; 16-18 Blackfriars St; s/d £50/65; P 🛜)
Smack bang in the heart of the trendy Merchant City, this lively, pleasant pub has simple rooms with sleek furnishings and a minimalist design (no 3 is a good one). Staying here is an excellent Glaswegian experience – the building's design is attributed to Robert Adam. Unusually, room rates do not include breakfast – but that helps keep prices down.

Spires
APARTMENTS **££**
(Map p106; ☏ 0845-270 0090; www.thespires.co.uk; 77 Glassford St; apt £85-191; P 🛜) This range of smart serviced apartments offer a modern, polished stay in a very appealing Merchant City location. They come in various sizes and sleep up to six, some with a roof terrace. Space is very generous and staff are helpful, but wi-fi is expensive and there are a few glitches. Reception closes at 7pm and doesn't open Sundays, so make sure

THE GENIUS OF CHARLES RENNIE MACKINTOSH

Great cities have great artists, designers and architects contributing to their urban environment while expressing its soul and individuality. Charles Rennie Mackintosh was all of these and his quirky, linear and geometric designs have had an enormous influence on Glasgow. Many of the buildings Mackintosh designed are open to the public, and you'll see his tall, thin, art nouveau typeface repeatedly reproduced.

Born in 1868, Mackintosh studied at the Glasgow School of Art. It was there that he met the also influential artist and designer Margaret Macdonald, whom he married; they collaborated on many projects and were major influences on each other's work. In 1896, aged only 27, he won a competition for his design of the School of Art's new building, Mackintosh's supreme architectural achievement. The first section was opened in 1899 and is considered to be the earliest example of art nouveau in Britain. This building demonstrates his skill in combining function and style.

Although Mackintosh's genius was quickly recognised on the Continent, he did not receive the same encouragement in Scotland. His architectural career here lasted only until 1914, when he moved to England to concentrate on furniture design. He died in 1928, and it is only since the last decades of the 20th century that Mackintosh's genius has been widely recognised. For more about the man and his work, contact the **Charles Rennie Mackintosh Society** (☏ 0141-946 6600; www.crmsociety.com; 870 Garscube Rd, Mackintosh Church). Check its website for special events.

Another of Mackintosh's finest works is **Hill House** (☏ 0844 493-2208; www.nts.org.uk; Upper Colquhoun St; adult/child £10.50/7.50; ⊙ 1.30-5.30pm Apr-Oct), in Helensburgh. If you're planning to visit some of the farther-flung attractions, the **Mackintosh Trail ticket** (£10), available at the tourist office (p134) or any Mackintosh building, gives you a day's admission to Hill House, the Mackintosh Church (p115) and House for an Art Lover (p114), as well as unlimited bus and subway travel.

they know if you'll be arriving outside reception hours.

Adelaide's
GUESTHOUSE ££

(Map p106; ☑0141-248 4970; www.adelaides.co.uk; 209 Bath St; s/d £55/75, s without bathroom £37; ☎) Quiet and cordial, this is ideal for folk who want location at a reasonable price. It's an unusual place – a simple, friendly guesthouse on prestigious Bath St set in a historic church conversion and still Baptist-run, though there's not a hint of preachiness in the air. Tariffs include a continental breakfast, with cooked available for extra – and families are very welcome. Aim for the back to minimise weekend noise.

Rennie Mackintosh Art School Hotel
GUESTHOUSE ££

(Map p106; ☑0141-333 9992; www.rmghotels.com; 218 Renfrew St; s £40-75, d £55-83; ☎) If you can book this place at one of its regularly discounted prices, it represents a good deal, as it's a block above Sauchiehall St and a shortish walk to the museums of the West End too. The rooms are more stylish and comfortable than the rest of the string of guesthouses on this street and it feels better looked-after. Wi-fi doesn't reach all the rooms. Room-only rates also available.

Malmaison
HOTEL £££

(Map p106; ☑0141-572 1000; www.malmaison.com; 278 West George St; r/ste £160/210; ☎) A former church, this is a longtime favourite for its decadent decor and plush lines. Stylish rooms with mood lighting have a dark, brooding tone and opulent furnishings. It's a hedonistic sort of place so can be cheerfully boisterous at weekends. It's best to book online, as it's cheaper, and various suite offers can be mighty tempting.

Blythswood Square
HOTEL £££

(Map p106; ☑0141-248 8888; www.blythswoodsquare.com; 11 Blythswood Sq; r £145-249; @☎☎☎) In a gorgeous Georgian terrace, this elegant five-star hotel offers plenty of inner-city luxury, with grey and cerise tweeds providing casual soft-toned style throughout. Grades of rooms range from standard to penthouse with corresponding increases in comfort; it's hard to resist the traditional 'classic' ones with windows onto the delightful square, but at weekends you'll have a quieter sleep in the new wing at the back. There's an excellent bar and superb restaurant, as well as a very handsome floor-boarded and colonnaded salon space on the 1st floor that functions as an evening spot for cocktails. Other facilities include valet parking and a seductive spa complex.

🛏 West End

Glasgow SYHA
HOSTEL £

(Map p112; ☑0141-332 3004; www.syha.org.uk; 8 Park Tce; dm/tw £22/64; @☎) Perched on a hill overlooking Kelvingrove Park in a charming town house, this place is one of Scotland's best official hostels. Dorms are mostly four to six beds with padlock lockers and all have their own en suite. The common rooms are spacious, plush and good for lounging about. There's no curfew, a good kitchen, and meals are available. The prices listed reflect maximums and are usually cheaper.

Heritage Hotel
HOTEL £

(Map p112; ☑0141-339 6955; www.theheritage-hotel.net; 4 Alfred Tce, Great Western Rd; s/d £40/60; P☎☎) A stone's throw from all the action of the West End, this friendly hotel has an open, airy feel despite the rather

---

GLASGOW FOR CHILDREN

Although Glasgow is a bigger, busier city than Edinburgh, it's easy to explore with children due to its extensive public transport system and friendly locals. The city boasts excellent family attractions, including the Glasgow Science Centre (p111) and Sharmanka Kinetic Theatre (p108), which both vie for the title of Glasgow's top child-friendly attraction. The Riverside Museum (p110) and People's Palace (p110) are also recommended.

For suggestions for short-term child-care agencies, get in touch with the council-run **Glasgow Childcare Information Service** (☑0141-287 5223; www.scottishfamilies.co.uk; 100 Morrison St). The **KidsGlasgow website** (www.kidsglasgow.com) lists upcoming events for children, as well as soft play areas and other recommendations.

Most parks in Glasgow have playgrounds for children. In the centre of town, the major shopping complexes are handy stops, with baby-changing facilities and shops and activities designed to keep the kids occupied for an hour or two.

dilapidated raised terrace it's located on. Generally, the rooms on the 1st and 2nd floors are a bit more spacious (no 21 is best of the doubles) and have a better outlook. The location, parking option and very fair prices mark it out.

Bunkum Backpackers
HOSTEL £

(Map p112; ☑ 0141-581 4481; www.bunkumglasgow. co.uk; 26 Hillhead St; dm/tw £14/36; P 🛜) A tempting budget headquarters for assaults on the eateries and pubs of the West End, kind and casual Bunkum Backpackers occupies a noble old Victorian terrace on a quiet street. The dorms are spacious – one exaggeratedly so – and the common room and kitchen are also large. There's no curfew but it's not a party hostel. The place isn't well signposted; it's slightly cheaper midweek.

Craigendmuir Caravan & Camping
CAMPSITE £

(☑ 0141-779 4159; www.craigendmuir.co.uk; Campsie View; sites for 1/2 people £14.50/17.25; P) The nearest camping ground to town, Craigendmuir Park is about 800m from Stepps station. It has sites for caravans and tents and there are a few well-equipped chalets and holiday homes for weekly rental.

★Alamo Guest House
B&B ££

(Map p112; ☑ 0141-339 2395; www.alamoguesthouse.com; 46 Gray St; d/superior d £89/149, without bathroom s/d £49/59; @ 🛜) The Alamo may not sound a peaceful spot, but that's exactly what this great place is. Opposite Kelvingrove Park, it feels miles from the city's hustle, but several of the best museums and restaurants in town are very close by. The decor is an enchanting mixture of antique furnishings and modern design, with excellent bathrooms, and the owners will make you very welcome. The front superior room is a sumptuous sight to behold. Breakfast is abundant but there's no full-Scottish option.

Amadeus Guest House
B&B ££

(Map p112; ☑ 0141-339 8257; www.amadeusguesthouse.co.uk; 411 North Woodside Rd; s £40 60, d £72-88; 🛜) Just off the bustle of Great Western Rd, a minute's walk from the subway but on a quiet street by the riverside pathway, this B&B has compact, bright rooms with cheerful cushions on the comfortable beds. There's a variety of room types, but prices are very good for all of them and come down substantially midweek. Breakfast is continental.

Embassy Apartments
APARTMENTS ££

(Map p112; ☑ 0141-946 6698; www.glasgowhotelsandapartments.co.uk; 8 Kelvin Dr; 1-/2-/4-person flat per night £60/80/99; P 🛜) This elegant self-catering place offers both facilities and location. Situated on a quiet, exclusive street right on the edge of the Botanical Gardens, the studio-style apartments sleep one to seven, have fully-equipped kitchens and are sparkling clean. They're a particularly good option for couples and families with older kids. Available by the day, but prices drop for longer rentals and vary extensively by demand.

Acorn Hotel
HOTEL ££

(Map p112; ☑ 0141-332 6556; www.glasgowhotelsandapartments.co.uk; 140 Elderslie St; s/d £60/90; @ 🛜) Enjoying a peaceful location by a park, yet just a block from Sauchiehall St, this smart little place has rooms that are compact but boast stylish colours and comfortable beds. A few niggles detract from the experience but it's good value nevertheless. Room-only rates are available.

Kirklee Hotel
B&B ££

(Map p112; ☑ 0141-334 5555; www.kirkleehotel. co.uk; 11 Kensington Gate; s/d £68/85; 🛜) In a leafy West End neighbourhood, Kirklee is a quiet little gem that offers a warm welcome in an elegant Edwardian terraced house. This could be the city's most beautiful street. The rooms are furnished in comfortable classical style and mostly look onto lush gardens; bathrooms are appropriately veteran. For families, there is an excellent downstairs room with enormous en suite. Breakfast is served in the room. You can park free on the street outside.

Hotel du Vin
HOTEL £££

(One Devonshire Gardens; ☑ 0141-339 2001; www. hotelduvin.com; 1 Devonshire Gardens; r/ste from £180/440; P @ 🛜 🐾) This is traditionally Glasgow's favoured hotel of the rich and famous, and the patriarch of sophistication and comfort. A study in elegance, it's sumptuously decorated and occupies three classical sandstone terrace houses. There's a bewildering array of room types, all different in style and size. The hospitality is old-school courteous, and there's an excellent restaurant on site with a wine selection exceeding 600 options. Breakfast is extra.

1. Gallery of Modern Art (p107), Glasgow

Black Elegy by Toby Paterson (2004 © Toby Paterson), one of the works on display at Scotland's most popular contemporary art gallery.

2. Glasgow Cathedral (p108)

A fine example of Gothic architecture with some roof timbers dating from the 14th century.

3. Botanic Gardens (p114), Glasgow

The gardens house one of the largest glasshouses in Britain, built in 1873.

✕ Eating

Glasgow is the best place to eat in Scotland, with an excellent range of eateries. The West End is the culinary centre, with Merchant City also boasting a high concentration of quality restaurants and cafes. Many Glasgow restaurants post offers on the internet (changing daily) at 5pm.co.uk. Pubs and bars mentioned in Drinking & Nightlife (p128) are often good lunchtime options.

✕ City Centre

★ Saramago Café Bar   CAFE £
(Map p106; www.facebook.com/saramagocafebar; 350 Sauchiehall St; light meals £3-9; ⊙food 10am-10pm Mon-Wed, 10am-11.30pm Thu-Sat, noon-11.30pm Sun; ☎⦿) In the airy atmosphere of the Centre for Contemporary Arts, this place does a great line in eclectic vegan fusion food, with a range of top flavour combinations from around the globe. The upstairs bar has a great deck on steep Scott St and packs out inside with a friendly hipster crowd enjoying the eclectic DJ sets and quality tap beers.

Brutti Ma Buoni   MEDITERRANEAN £
(Map p106; ☎0141-552 0001; www.brunswickhotel.co.uk; 106 Brunswick St; mains £8-12; ⊙11am-10pm Sun-Thu, to 11pm Fri & Sat; ☎⦿) If you like dining in a place that has a sense of fun, Brutti delivers – it's the antithesis of some of the pretentious places around the Merchant City. With dishes such as 'ugly but good' pizza and 'angry or peaceful' prawns, Brutti's menu draws a smile for its quirkiness and its prices. Italian and Spanish influences give rise to tapas-like servings or full-blown meals, which are imaginative, fresh and frankly delicious.

Wee Curry Shop   INDIAN £
(Map p106; ☎0141-353 0777; www.weecurryshop. co.uk; 7 Buccleuch St; 2-course lunch £5.50, dinner mains £6-8; ⊙noon-2pm & 5.30-10.30pm Mon-Sat, 5-10pm Sun; ☎⦿) Great home-cooked curries. It's wise to book – it's a snug place with a big reputation, a limited menu and a sensational-value two-course lunch.

Lunch@Lily's   CAFE, CHINESE £
(Map p106; 103 Ingram St; mains £3-6; ⊙9.30am-4pm Mon-Sat) Don't be put off by the slightly sterile feel: Lily's is a top lunch spot fusing a creative blend of East and West with made-to-order Chinese food (such as dumpling buns and mandarin-duck wraps) and standards including tarted-up burgers and baked potatoes. The Chinese food is particularly outstanding – fresh, lively and served with fruits and salad.

Where the Monkey Sleeps   CAFE £
(Map p106; www.monkeysleeps.com; 182 West Regent St; dishes £3-7; ⊙7am-4pm Mon-Fri; ☎) This funky little number in the middle of the business district is a perfect escape from the ubiquitous coffee chains. Laid-back and a little hippy, the bagels and panini – with names like Witchfynder or Meathammer –

GLASGOW IN...

Two Days
On your first day, hit the East End for Glasgow Cathedral (p108), St Mungo's Museum (p109) and a wander through the hillside necropolis. Later, take in one of the city's top museums: either the Burrell Collection (p114) or the Kelvingrove (p111). As evening falls, head to trendy Merchant City for a stroll and dinner; try Café Gandolfi (p125) maybe. Check out Artá (p128) for a pre- or post-meal drink. The next day, visit whichever museum you missed yesterday, and then it's Mackintosh time. Glasgow School of Art (p103) is his finest work: if you like his style, head to the West End for Mackintosh House (p113). Hungry? Thirsty? Some of the city's best restaurants and bars are up this end of town, so you could make a night of it. Make sure to check out one of the numerous excellent music venues around the city.

Four Days
A four-day stay gives better scope to get to grips with Glasgow. Spend a day along the Clyde visiting the Riverside Museum (p110) and the Glasgow Science Centre (p111). Plan your weekend around a night out at Arches (p128) or the legendary Sub Club (p129), and a day strolling the stylish city-centre clothing emporia or a football game. Don't miss trying at least one of the city's classic curry houses.

are highlights, as are some very inventive dishes, such as the 'nuclear' beans, dripping with cayenne and Tabasco.

Chippy Doon the Lane   FISH & CHIPS £

(Map p106; www.thechippyglasgow.com; McCormick Lane, 84 Buchanan St; meals £6-10; ⊙noon-9.30pm; 🖘) ✒ Don't be put off by its location in a down-at-heel alleyway off the shopping precinct: this is a cut above your average chip shop. Sustainable seafood is served in a chic space, all old-time brick, metal archways and jazz. Otherwise, chow down on your takeaway at the wooden tables in the lane or out on Buchanan St itself.

Bar 91   PUB FOOD £

(Map p106; www.bar91.co.uk; 91 Candleriggs; mains £6-9; ⊙meals noon-9pm Mon-Thu, to 5pm Fri-Sun; 🖘) By day this happy, buzzy bar serves excellent meals, far better than your average pub food. Salads, pasta and burgers are among the many tasty offerings, and in summer tables spill out onto the sidewalk – ideal for some people-watching.

Mono   VEGETARIAN £

(Map p106; www.monocafebar.com; 12 Kings Ct, King St; mains £3-8; ⊙noon-9pm; 🖘✒) Combining vegetarian food with music, Mono is one of Glasgow's best vegetarian and vegan eateries. There is an indie record shop, Monorail, on the premises, so you can browse while your food is prepared. The all-day bar menu serves classics such as a breakfast fry-up, while the main menu has a touch of flair and a Mediterranean influence. The lasagne is well worth ploughing through. Mono also makes a relaxing place for a coffee or a beer.

Willow Tearooms   CAFE £

(www.willowtearooms.co.uk; light meals £3-9; ⊙9am-5pm Mon-Sat, 10.30am-5pm Sun; 🖘) There are two separate locations for these famous tearooms, one on Buchanan St (Map p106; 97 Buchanan St) and one on Sauchiehall St (Map p106; 217 Sauchiehall St). Both are re-creations of the tearooms designed by Charles Rennie Mackintosh in 1904. They back up their wonderful design elements with good teas and reasonable bagels, pastries or, more splendidly, afternoon teas with (at Buchanan Street) champagne. At busy times the queues for a table can be long.

★Loon Fung   CHINESE ££

(Map p106; ☑0141-332 1240; www.loonfung-glasgow.co.uk; 417 Sauchiehall St; mains £9-15; ⊙noon-4am; 🖘✒) Accessed down the side of a travel agent, this elegant Cantonese oasis is one of Scotland's most authentic Chinese restaurants; indeed, it's quite a surprise after a spot of late-night dining to emerge to boisterous Sauchiehall rather than Hong Kong. The dim-sum choices are very toothsome, and the seafood – try the sea bass – really excellent. The ultra-late opening hours make it a very flexible option.

Café Gandolfi   CAFE, BISTRO ££

(Map p106; ☑0141-552 6813; 64 Albion St; mains £9-15; ⊙8am-11.30pm Mon-Sat, 9am-11.30pm Sun; 🖘) In Merchant City, this cafe was once part of the old cheese market. It's been pulling in the punters for years and attracts an interesting mix of die-hard Gandolfers, the upwardly mobile and tourists. It covers all the bases with excellent breakfasts and coffee, an enticing upstairs bar, and top-notch bistro food, covering Scottish and Continental dishes in an atmospheric medieval-like setting. There's an expansion, specialising in fish, next door, with a takeaway outlet.

Red Onion   BISTRO ££

(Map p106; ☑0141-221 6000; www.red-onion.co.uk; 257 West Campbell St; mains £11-20; ⊙noon-10pm; 🖘♿) This comfortable split-level bistro buzzes with contented chatter. French, Mediterranean and Asian touches add intrigue to the predominantly British menu, and a good-value fixed-price deal is available at lunch and dinnertime daily, though only for early diners at weekends.

Mussel Inn   SEAFOOD ££

(Map p106; ☑0141-572 1405; www.mussel-inn.com; 157 Hope St; mains £10-19; ⊙noon-2.30pm & 5-10pm Mon-Fri, noon-10pm Sat, 12.30-10pm Sun; 🖘) ✒ Airy and easygoing, this two-level eatery specialises in sustainable scallops, oysters, and mussels at affordable prices, served with a smile. There's a good deal for mussels with chips and a drink at lunchtime for around eight quid.

Dakhin   INDIAN ££

(Map p106; ☑0141-553 2585; www.dakhin.com; 89 Candleriggs; mains £10-19; ⊙noon-2pm & 5-11pm Mon-Fri, 1-11pm Sat & Sun; 🖘✒) This south Indian restaurant breathes some fresh air into the city's curry scene. Dishes are from all over the south, and include dosas (thin rice-based crêpes) and a yummy variety of fragrant coconut-based curries. If you're really hungry, try a thali: an assortment of Indian dishes.

Bar Soba

ASIAN FUSION ££

(Map p106; ☑0141-204 2404; www.barsoba.co.uk; 11 Mitchell Lane; mains £10-13; ☺noon-10pm; ☜) With candles flickering in windows there's a certain sense of intimacy in stylish Bar Soba where industrial meets plush. You can eat in the bar or downstairs restaurant. The food is Asian fusion and the laksas go down a treat. Background beats are perfect for chilling with a cocktail and it's a good stop in the heart of the shopping zone for lunch.

Meat Bar

AMERICAN ££

(Map p106; ☑0141-204 3605; www.themeatbar. co.uk; 142 West Regent St; mains £8-14; ☺food noon-10pm; ☜) Like a mafia film speakeasy where some minor henchman gets whacked, this spot has underworld atmosphere and carries it off with style. As the name suggests, it's all about meat here: it even makes its way into some of the cocktails. Daily cuts of prime Scottish beef (£23 to £35) accompany a range of American-style slow-smoked meats. Tasty and atmospheric, it also has a range of interesting beers.

Guy's

SCOTTISH ££

(Map p106; ☑0141-552 1114; www.guysrestaurant. co.uk; 24 Candleriggs; mains £14-28; ☺noon-10.30pm Mon-Thu, noon-11.30pm Fri & Sat, 12.30-9.30pm Sun) This Merchant City restaurant offers a very authentic Glasgow blend of style and friendly informality, and has a long list of devoted regulars. The buzzing atmosphere and decor – from gilt mirrors to porcelain plates – actually slightly outdo the food, which is tasty but unremarkable. Drinks are way overpriced and the service, though willing, is painfully slow. But the experience is a worthwhile one.

Arisaig

SCOTTISH ££

(Map p106; ☑0141-553 1010; www.arisaigrestaurant.co.uk; 1 Merchant Sq; mains £12-20; ☺5-10pm Mon, noon-3pm & 5-10pm Tue-Sun; ☜) Located in the Merchant Square building, a historical location converted into an echoing food court, Arisaig offers a good chance to try well-prepared Scottish cuisine at a fair price, with friendly service to boot. Candlelight and crisp linen make for atmosphere despite the artificial situation, with both terrace and indoor seating on two levels.

✖ West End

There are numerous excellent restaurants in the West End. They cluster along Byres Rd and just off it, on Ashton Lane and Ruthven Lane. Gibson St and Great Western Rd also have plenty to offer, while the Argyle Rd strip in Finnieston has lots of interesting new options.

Bay Tree Café

CAFE £

(Map p112; www.thebaytreewestend.co.uk; 403 Great Western Rd; mains £7-11; ☺9am-10.30pm Mon-Sat, 9am-9.30pm Sun; ☜☑) There are many good cafes in the two or three blocks around here, but the Bay Tree is still a solid choice. With lots of vegan and vegetarian options, it has smiling staff, filling mains (mostly Middle Eastern and Greek), generous salads and a good range of hot drinks. The cafe is famous for its all-day breakfasts.

Wudon

ASIAN FUSION £

(Map p112; www.wudon-noodlebar.co.uk; 535 Great Western Rd; dishes £8-11; ☺noon-11pm Mon-Sat, 12.30-10pm Sun) Tasty sushi, fried noodles, and ramen soups among other Asian dishes in a clean, contemporary setting. It's a friendly spot with helpful service.

78 Cafe Bar

CAFE, VEGETARIAN £

(Map p112; www.the78cafebar.com; 10 Kelvinhaugh St; mains £5-8; ☺noon-9pm; ☜☑) More a comfortable lounge than your typical veggie restaurant, this cafe offers cosy couch seating and reassuringly solid wooden tables, as well as an inviting range of ales. The low-priced vegan food includes hearty stews and curries, and there's regular live music in a very welcoming atmosphere.

Hanoi Bike Shop

VIETNAMESE £

(Map p112; www.thehanoibikeshop.co.uk; 8 Ruthven Lane; mains £8-11; ☺noon-11pm Mon-Wed, noon-12.30am Thu & Fri, 11am-12.30am Sat, 11am-11pm Sun; ☜) ✿ Tucked away just off Byres Rd, this upbeat spot offers creative takes on Vietnamese food, using fresh ingredients and home-made tofu. The various pho dishes are delicious.

★ Stravaigin

SCOTTISH ££

(Map p112; ☑0141-334 2665; www.stravaigin.co.uk; 28 Gibson St; mains £10-18; ☺9am-11pm; ☜) Stravaigin is a serious foodie's delight, with a menu constantly pushing the boundaries of originality and offering creative culinary excellence. The cool contemporary dining space in the basement has booth seating, and helpful, laid-back waiting-staff to assist in deciphering the audacious menu. Entry-level has a buzzing two-level bar; you can also eat here. There are always plenty of menu deals and special culinary nights.

★ Mother India
INDIAN ££

(Map p112; ☑ 0141-221 1663; www.motherindia. co.uk; 28 Westminster Tce, Sauchiehall St; mains £9-15; ⊙ 5.30-10.30pm Mon-Thu, noon-11pm Fri, 1-11pm Sat, 1-10pm Sun; ⊜ ☑ ⊞) Glasgow curry buffs forever debate the merits of the city's numerous excellent South Asian restaurants; this restaurant features in every discussion. It may lack the trendiness of some of the up-and-comers but it's been a stalwart for years, and the quality and innovation on show is superb. The three separate dining areas are all attractive and they make an effort for kids, with a separate menu. There are various other innovative, distinct sister restaurants around town.

Left Bank
BISTRO ££

(Map p112; ☑ 0141-339 5969; www.theleftbank. co.uk; 33 Gibson St; mains £8-15; ⊙ 9am-10pm Mon-Fri, 10am-10pm Sat & Sun; ⊜ ☑ ⊞) ✔ Huge windows fronting the street greet patrons to this outstanding eatery specialising in gastronomic delights and lazy afternoons. There are lots of little spaces filled with couches and chunky tables, reflecting a sense of intimacy. The large starter-menu can be treated like tapas, making it good for sharing. Lots of delightful creations use seasonal and local produce, with an eclectic variety of influences. Breakfasts and brunches are another highlight.

Finnieston
SEAFOOD, PUB ££

(Map p112; www.thefinniestonbar.com; 1125 Argyle St; mains £13-19; ⊙ noon-10pm Mon-Sat, noon-9pm Sun; ⊜) ✔ A flagship of this increasingly vibrant strip, this gastropub recalls the area's sailing heritage with a cosily romantic below-decks atmosphere and artfully placed nautical motifs. It's been well thought-through, with excellent mixed drinks and cocktails accompanying a short menu of really high-quality upmarket pub fare focusing on sustainable Scottish seafood.

Òran Mór Brasserie
SCOTTISH ££

(Map p112; ☑ 0141-357 6226; www.oran-mor.co.uk; 731 Great Western Rd; mains £10-18; ⊙ noon-9pm Tue-Thu, noon-10pm Fri & Sat, noon-8pm Sun; ⊜) This temple to Scottish dining and drinking is a superb venue in an old church. Giving new meaning to the word 'conversion', the brasserie pumps out high-quality meals in a dark, Mackintosh-inspired space. The menu runs from burgers to more elaborate mains and offers some great-value two-course specials in the evenings.

Firebird
BISTRO ££

(Map p112; www.firebirdglasgow.com; 1321 Argyle St; mains £10-14; ⊙ noon-10pm; ⊜) A combined bar and bistro with a cheery feel, Firebird has zany artwork on its bright walls and, more importantly, quality nosh whisked under the noses of its patrons. Local flavours and Mediterranean highlights (mainly North African, Italian and Spanish) are evident and organic produce is used wherever possible. Taste sensations range from wood-fired pizzas to Moroccan-influenced salads.

Bothy
SCOTTISH ££

(Map p112; ☑ 0141-334 4040; www.g1group.co.uk; 11 Ruthven Lane; mains £10-19; ⊜) This West End player, boasting a combo of modern design and comfy retro furnishings, blows apart the myth that Scottish food is stodgy and uninteresting. The Bothy dishes out traditional home-style fare with a modern twist. It's filling, but leave room for dessert. Lunch deals are cheaper.

★ Ubiquitous Chip
SCOTTISH £££

(Map p112; ☑ 0141-334 5007; www.ubiquitous-chip.co.uk; 12 Ashton Lane; 2-/3-course lunch £16/20, mains £23-27, brasserie mains £9-14; ⊙ noon-2.30pm & 5-11pm; ⊜) ✔ The original champion of Scottish produce, this place is legendary for its unparalleled Scottish cuisine and lengthy wine list. Named to poke fun at Scotland's culinary reputation, it offers a French touch but resolutely Scottish ingredients, carefully selected and following sustainable principles. The elegant courtyard space offers some of Glasgow's highest-quality dining, while the cheaper brasserie menu offers exceptional value for money.

The cute 'Wee Pub' down the side alley offers plenty of drinking pleasure. There's always something going on at the Chip – check the website for upcoming events.

Butchershop Bar & Grill
STEAK £££

(Map p112; ☑ 0141-339 2999; www.butchershop-glasgow.com; 1055 Sauchiehall St; steaks £18-32; ⊙ noon-10pm; ⊜) Offering several different cuts of traceably sourced, properly aged beef, this is just about the best spot in Glasgow for a tasty, served-as-you-want-it steak; it's a perfect lunch venue after the Kelvingrove museum. There are seats out the front if the weather happens to be fine. There's also a little seafood on the menu, and decently mixed cocktails.

Drinking & Nightlife

Some of Britain's best nightlife is found in the din and sometimes roar of Glasgow's pubs and bars. There are as many different styles of bar as there are punters to guzzle in them. Some pubs and especially clubs have begun to enforce a 21-year-old minimum age.

Glasgow has one of Britain's biggest and best clubbing scenes, attracting devotees from afar. Glaswegians usually hit clubs after the pubs have closed, so many clubs offer discounted admission and cheaper drinks if you go early. Entry costs £5 to £10 (up to £25 for big events), although bars often hand out free passes. By law, clubs shut at 3am, so keep your ear to the ground to find out where the after parties are at.

City Centre

★ Artà
BAR, CLUB

(Map p106; www.arta.co.uk; 62 Albion St; ⊙5pm-3am Thu-Sat; 🕾) This extraordinary place is so baroque that when you hear a Mozart concerto over the sound system, it wouldn't surprise you to see the man himself at the other end of the bar. Set in a former cheese market, it really does have to be seen to be believed. Despite the luxury, it's got a relaxed, chilled vibe. The big cocktails are great.

Babbity Bowster
PUB

(Map p106; www.babbitybowster.com; 16-18 Blackfriars St; ⊙11am-midnight Mon-Sat, 12.30pm-midnight Sun; 🕾) In a quiet corner of Merchant City, this handsome spot is perfect for a tranquil daytime drink, particularly in the adjoining beer garden. Service is attentive, and the smell of sausages may tempt you to lunch; it also offers accommodation (see p119). This is one of the city centre's most charming pubs, in one of its noblest buildings.

Corinthian Club
BAR

(Map p106; www.thecorinthianclub.co.uk; 191 Ingram St; ⊙11am-6am Mon-Sat, noon-6am Sun; 🕾) A breathtaking domed ceiling and majestic chandeliers make this casino a special space. Originally a bank and later Glasgow's High Court, this regal building's main bar, Teller's, has to be seen to be believed. Cosy wrap-around seating and space to spare are complemented by a snug wine bar and a plush club downstairs in old court cells.

MacSorley's
BAR

(Map p106; www.macsorleys.com; 42 Jamaica St; ⊙11am-midnight Mon-Sat, 12.30pm-midnight Sun; 🕾) There's nothing better than a good horseshoe-shaped bar in Glasgow, and here the elegantly moulded windows and ceiling add a touch of class to this happy place, which offers live music every night and some excellent, inventive pub food. There's live music and good DJs at weekends – check the schedule on the website.

Butterfly & The Pig
PUB

(Map p106; www.thebutterflyandthepig.com; 153 Bath St; ⊙11am-1am Mon-Thu, 11am-3am Fri & Sat, 12.30pm-midnight Sun; 🕾) A breath of fresh air, the piggery is a little offbeat and makes you feel comfortable as soon as you plunge into its basement depths. The decor is eclectic with a retro feel and this adds to its familiarity. There's regular live jazz or similar, a sizable menu – if you can decipher it – of pub grub, and a rather wonderful tearoom upstairs, great for breakfast before the pub opens.

Arches
CAFE, BAR

(Map p106; www.thearches.co.uk; 253 Argyle St; ⊙11am-midnight Mon-Sat; 🕾) A one-stop culture-entertainment fix, Arches is cafe, bar, nightclub and theatre showing contemporary, avant-garde productions. The hotel-like entrance belies the deep interior, which makes you feel as though you've discovered Hades' bohemian underworld. The crowd is mixed – hiking boots are as welcome as Versace. It also does a more-than-acceptable line in pub food.

West
BREWERY

(www.westbeer.com; Binnie Pl; ⊙11am-11pm Sun-Thu, 11am-midnight Fri & Sat; 🕾) Something a bit different, this welcoming, spacious brewpub on the edge of Glasgow Green churns out beers brewed to the traditional German purity laws (which basically means they're bloody good) in a bizarrely ornate former carpet factory opposite the People's Palace. German dishes such as sausages and pork knuckle can accompany the amber fluid. There's a great grassy beer garden outside.

Horse Shoe
PUB

(Map p106; www.horseshoebar.co.uk; 17 Drury St; ⊙10am-midnight Mon-Sat, 11am-midnight Sun) This legendary city pub and popular meeting place dates from the late 19th century and is largely unchanged. It's a picturesque spot, with the longest continuous bar in the UK, but its main attraction is what's served over it – real ale and good cheer. Upstairs in the lounge is some of the best value pub food (three-course lunch £4.50) in town.

Bar 10
BAR

(Map p106; www.navantaverns.com; 10 Mitchell Lane; ☺11am-midnight Mon-Sat, 12.30pm-midnight Sun; ☎) This tiny city treasure will cause the canny Glasgow drinker to give you a knowing glance if you mention its name. As laid-back as you could ask, a hip city bar to be, the friendly, tuned-in staff complete the happy picture. It transforms from a quiet daytime bar to a happening weekend pub on Friday and Saturday nights. It also does decent cheap panini, salads and the like during the day.

Blackfriars
PUB

(Map p106; www.blackfriarsglasgow.com; 36 Bell St; ☺11am-midnight Mon-Sat, 12.30pm-midnight Sun; ☎) One of Merchant City's most relaxed and atmospheric pubs, and far less posh than the rest on this square, Blackfriars' friendly staff and chilled-out house make it special. They take their cask ales seriously here, and there's a seating area with large windows that are great for people-watching. Buzzy and inclusive.

Slouch Bar
BAR

(Map p106; www.slouch-bar.co.uk; 203 Bath St; ☺11am-2am or 3am, ☎) There's a basement bar for all types on Bath St, with subversive hideaways under brokers' offices and a range of vibes. This is low-lit and casual but handsomely designed, with a southern US feel to the decor, drinks and rock soundtrack. It's got an intriguing spirits selection, more-than-acceptable comfort food and regular live music.

Drum & Monkey
PUB

(Map p106; www.nicholsonspubs.co.uk; 93-95 St Vincent St; ☺11am-midnight Mon-Sat, 12.30-11pm Sun; ☎) Dark wood and marble columns frame this attractive drinking emporium, peppered with church pews and leather lounge chairs. Its cosy and relaxing vibe makes you want to curl up in an armchair with a pint for the afternoon. Its central location makes it popular with business folk after work. The food is mediocre.

Nice 'n' Sleazy
BAR, CLUB

(Map p106; www.nicensleazy.com; 421 Sauchiehall St; ☺noon-3am; ☎) On the rowdy Sauchie-

hall strip, students from the nearby School of Art make the buzz here reliably friendly. If you're over 35 you'll feel like a professor not a punter, but retro decor, a big selection of tap and bottled beers, 3am closing, and nightly alternative live music downstairs followed by a club at weekends make this a winner. There's also popular, cheap Tex-Mex food (dishes £6 to £9).

Tiki Bar & Kitsch Inn
BAR

(Map p106; www.tikibarglasgow.com; 214 Bath St; ☎) Hawaiian shirts, palms and leis provide an appropriate backdrop to colourful cocktails in the hedonistic and amiable basement Tiki bar. Upstairs, Kitsch plays the relative straight man, though MAD magazine covers mean it's not all poker-faces. It also does a good line in Thai food. Order top-shelf spirits to watch the bar staff negotiate the ladder.

Waxy O'Connors
PUB

(Map p106; www.waxyoconnors.co.uk; 46 West George St; ☺noon-midnight Mon-Sat, 12.30-11pm Sun; ☎) This lager labyrinth with its fantasy-realm elven-treehouse feel could be an Escher sketch brought to life, and it's a cut above most Irish theme pubs.

Sub Club
CLUB

(Map p106; www.subclub.co.uk; 22 Jamaica St; ☺11pm-3am Tue-Sun) Saturdays at the Sub Club are one of Glasgow's legendary nights, offering serious clubbing with a sound system that aficionados usually rate as the city's best. The claustrophobic, last-one-in vibe is not for those faint of heart.

The Arches
CLUB

(Map p106; www.thearches.co.uk; 30 Midland St; ☺to 3am Thu-Sun, opening time varies) The Godfather of Glaswegian clubs, this has a design based around hundreds of arches slammed together, and has a range of different club nights; it's a must for funk and hip-hop freaks. It is one of the city's biggest clubs pulling top DJs, and you'll also hear some of the UK's up-and-coming turntable spinners. The dingy road under the railway adds atmosphere.

Classic Grand
CLUB

(Map p106; www.classicgrand.com; 18 Jamaica St; ☺11pm-3am Thu-Sat) Rock, industrial, electronic, and powerpop grace the stage and the turntables at this unpretentious central venue. It doesn't take itself too seriously, drinks are cheap and the locals are welcoming.

Cathouse
CLUB

(Map p106; www.cathouse.co.uk; 15 Union St; ⏱10.30pm-3am Thu-Sun) It's mostly rock, alternative and metal with a touch of goth and post-punk at this long-standing indie venue. There are two dance floors: upstairs is pretty intense with lots of metal and hard rock, downstairs is a little more tranquil.

ABC
CLUB

(O2 ABC; Map p106; www.o2abcglasgow.co.uk; 300 Sauchiehall St; ⏱opening hours vary) Both nightclub and venue, this star of Sauchiehall has two large concert spaces and several attractive bars. It's a good all-rounder, with a variety of DJs playing every Thursday to Saturday. Punters scrub up fairly well here.

Buff Club
CLUB

(Map p106; www.thebuffclub.com; 142 Bath Lane; ⏱11pm-3am) Tucked away in a laneway behind the Bath St bar strip, this club is open nightly and presents eclectic, honest music without dress pretensions. The sounds vary substantially depending on the night, and can range from hip-hop to disco via electronica. It's more down-to-earth than many Glasgow venues, and has seriously cheap drinks midweek.

☕ West End

Brewdog
PUB

(Map p112; www.brewdog.com; 1397 Argyle St; ⏱noon-midnight; 📶) Perfect for a pint after visiting the Kelvingrove Museum, this is a great small spot offering the delicious range of artisanal beers from the brewery of the same name. Punk IPA is refreshingly hoppy and fruity, more so than the formidable WattDickie, which comes in at a whisky-like 35%. Tasting flights mean you can try several, while burgers and dogs are on hand to soak it up.

Hillhead Bookclub
BAR

(Map p112; www.hillheadbookclub.com; 17 Vinicombe St; ⏱11am-midnight Mon-Fri, 10am-midnight Sat & Sun; 📶) Atmosphere in spades is the call sign of this easygoing West End bar. An ornate wooden ceiling overlooks two levels of well-mixed cocktails, seriously cheap drinks, comfort food and numerous intriguing decorative touches. There's even a ping-pong table in a cage.

Òran Mór
BAR, CLUB

(Map p112; www.oran-mor.co.uk; 731 Great Western Rd; ⏱9am-3am Mon-Sat, 12.30pm-3am Sun; 📶) Now some may be a little uncomfortable with the thought of drinking in a church. But we say: the Lord giveth. This sizeable converted church is now a bar, restaurant, club and theatre venue. Look out for the "A Play, a Pie and a Pint" deals. There's an excellent array of whiskies.

Brel
BAR

(Map p112; www.brelbar.com; 39 Ashton Lane; ⏱11am-midnight Mon-Sat, 12.30pm-midnight Sun; 📶) Perhaps the best bar on Ashton Lane, Brel can seem tightly packed, but there's a conservatory for eating out the back so you can pretend you're sitting outside when it's raining, and when the sun does peek through, there's a beer garden. It's got a huge range of Belgian beers, and also does mussels and langoustines among other tasty fare.

Jinty McGuinty's
PUB

(Map p112; www.jintys.com; 23 Ashton Lane; ⏱11am-midnight Mon-Sat, 12.30pm-midnight Sun; 📶) There's something rather authentically Irish about this place, which has an aged wooden floor, unusual booth seating, a literary hall of fame and a beer garden alongside. There's live music most nights.

Vodka Wodka
BAR

(Map p112; www.vodkawodka.co.uk; 31 Ashton Lane; ⏱noon-midnight) Every vodka drinker's dream, Vodka Wodka has more varieties of the stealthy poison than you could possibly conquer in one sitting. Its brushed metal bar dishes out the liquid fire straight and in cocktails to students during the day and groups of mid-20s in the evening.

☆ Entertainment

Glasgow is Scotland's entertainment city, from classical music, fine theatres and ballet to an amazing range of live music venues. To tap into the scene, check out *The List* (www.list.co.uk), an invaluable events guide released every four weeks and available at newsagents and bookshops.

For theatre tickets, book directly with the venue. For concerts, a useful booking centre is **Tickets Scotland** (Map p106; ☎0141-204 5151; www.tickets-scotland.com; 237 Argyle St; ⏱9am-6pm Mon-Wed, Fri & Sat, 9am-7pm Thu, noon-5pm Sun).

Live Music

Glasgow is the king of Scotland's live-music scene. Year after year, touring musicians and travellers alike name Glasgow one of their favourite cities in the world to enjoy live music. Much of Glasgow's character is encapsulated in the soul and humour of its inhabitants, and the main reason for the city's musical success lies within its audience and the musical community it has bred and nurtured for years.

There are so many venues it's impossible to keep track of them all. Pick up a copy or check the website of the Gig Guide (www.gig-guide.co.uk), available free in most pubs and venues, for the latest listings.

One of the city's premier live-music pub venues, the excellent **King Tut's Wah Wah Hut** (Map p106; ☏0141-221 5279; www.kingtuts.

co.uk; 272a St Vincent St; ☺noon-midnight) hosts bands every night of the week. Oasis were signed after playing here.

Several of the bars mentioned under Drinking & Nightlife are great for live music, including Classic Grand (p129), MacSorley's (p128) and Nice 'n' Sleazy (p129). The ABC is also a popular venue.

13th Note Café VENUE, CAFE
(Map p106; www.13thnote.co.uk; 50-60 King St; ☺noon-midnight) Cosy basement venue with small independent bands as well as weekend DJs and regular comedy and theatre performances. At street level the cafe does decent vegetarian and vegan food.

Barrowland VENUE
(Map p106; www.glasgow-barrowland.com; 244 Gallowgate) A down-at-heel but exceptional

---

GAY & LESBIAN GLASGOW

Glasgow has a vibrant gay scene, with the gay quarter found in and around the Merchant City (particularly Virginia, Wilson and Glassford Sts). The city's gay community has a reputation for being very friendly.

To tap into the scene, check out *The List* (www.list.co.uk) and the free *Scots Gay* (www.scotsgay.co.uk) magazine and website. If you're in Glasgow in autumn check out **Glasgay** (☏0141-552 7575; www.glasgay.co.uk), a gay performing arts festival held around October/November each year.

Many straight clubs and bars have gay and lesbian nights. The following are just a selection of gay and lesbian pubs and clubs in the city:

AXM (Map p106; www.axmgroup.co.uk; 80 Glassford St; ☺11pm-3am Wed & Thu, 10pm-3am Fri-Sun) This popular Manchester club's Glasgow branch is a cheery spot, not too scene-y, with all welcome.

Delmonica's (Map p106; ☏0141-552 4803; www.delmonicas.co.uk; 68 Virginia St; ☺noon-midnight) In the heart of the Pink Triangle, this is a popular bar with a bit of a feeling of people on the pull. It's packed on weekday evenings but a pleasant spot for a quiet drink during the day. Drop in here before heading to the adjacent Polo Lounge, as it often gives out free passes.

FHQ (Map p106; www.fhqbar.co.uk; 10 John St; ☺10pm-3am Fri & Sat) Fashionable women-only location in the heart of the Pink Triangle.

Polo Lounge (Map p106; www.pologlasgow.co.uk; 84 Wilson St; ☺11pm-3am Sun-Thu, 10pm-3am Fri, 9pm-3am Sat) This place doesn't have the friendliest of staff, but it still attracts talent. The downstairs Polo Club and Club X areas pack out on weekends; just the main bars open on other nights.

Underground (Map p106; www.underground-glasgow.com; 6a John St; ☺noon-midnight Mon-Sat, 1pm-midnight Sun) Downstairs on cosmopolitan John St, this bar sports a relaxed crowd and, crucially, a free jukebox. You'll be listening to indie rather than Abba here.

Speakeasy (Map p106; www.speakeasyglasgow.co.uk; 10 John St; ☺5pm-1am Thu, 5pm-3am Fri & Sat) Relaxed and friendly bar that starts out pub-like and gets louder with gay anthem DJs as the night progresses. Serves food too.

Waterloo Bar (Map p106; 306 Argyle St; ☺noon-midnight) This traditional pub is Scotland's oldest gay bar. It attracts punters of all ages. It's very friendly and, with a large group of regulars, a good place to meet people away from the scene.

old dancehall catering for some of the larger acts that visit the city.

Hydro
AUDITORIUM

(Map p112; ☑ 0141-248 3000; www.thessehydro.com; Finnieston Quay) A spectacular modern building keeping the adjacent 'Armadillo' (Clyde Auditorium) company, the Hydro amphitheatre is a phenomenally popular venue for big-name concerts and shows, and also hosted gymnastics and netball in the Commonwealth Games.

Clyde Auditorium
AUDITORIUM

(Map p112; ☑ 0844 395 4000; www.secc.co.uk; Finnieston Quay) Also known as the Armadillo because of its bizarre shape, the Clyde adjoins the SECC auditorium and caters for big national and international acts.

SECC
AUDITORIUM

(Map p112; ☑ 0844 395 4000; www.secc.co.uk; Finnieston Quay) The headquarters of the complex that includes the Clyde Auditorium and Hydro hosts major national and international acts.

Cinemas

Glasgow Film Theatre
CINEMA

(Map p106; ☑ 0141-332 6535; www.glasgowfilm.org; 12 Rose St; adult/child £8/5) This much-loved three-screener off Sauchiehall St shows art-house cinema and classics.

Cineworld
CINEMA

(Map p106; ☑ 0871-200 2000; www.cineworld.co.uk; 7 Renfrew St; adult £7.70-9.50) Shows mainstream films. Tuesdays are cheaper.

Grosvenor Cinema
CINEMA

(Map p112; ☑ 0845-166 6002; www.grosvenorcafe.co.uk; Ashton Lane) Puts you in the heart of West End eating and nightlife for post-show debriefings.

Theatres & Concert Halls

Theatre Royal
OPERA HOUSE

(Map p106; ☑ 0844 871 7627; www.atgtickets.com; 282 Hope St) Proudly sporting an eyecatching modern facelift, Glasgow's oldest theatre is the home of Scottish Opera and Scottish Ballet.

City Halls
CONCERT HALL

(Map p106; ☑ 0141-353 8000; www.glasgowconcerthalls.com; Candleriggs) In the heart of Merchant City, there are regular performances here by the Scottish Chamber Orchestra and the Scottish Symphony Orchestra. The adjacent Old Fruitmarket venue also has concerts.

Glasgow Royal Concert Hall
CONCERT VENUE

(Map p106; ☑ 0141-353 8000; www.glasgowconcerthalls.com; 2 Sauchiehall St) A feast of classical music is showcased at this concert hall, the modern home of the Royal Scottish National Orchestra.

Citizens' Theatre
THEATRE

(☑ 0141-429 0022; www.citz.co.uk; 119 Gorbals St) This is one of the top theatres in Scotland and it's well worth trying to catch a performance here.

Centre for Contemporary Arts
ARTS SPACE

(Map p106; www.cca-glasgow.com; 350 Sauchiehall St; ⊙ 10am-midnight Mon-Thu, 10am-1am Fri & Sat, noon-midnight Sun) This is a chic venue making terrific use of space and light. It showcases the visual and performing arts, including movies, talks and galleries. There's a good cafe-bar here too.

Tramway
ARTS SPACE

(☑ 0845-330 3501; www.tramway.org; 25 Albert Dr) Attracts cutting-edge theatrical groups, the visual and performing arts, and a varied range of artistic exhibitions. It's very close to Pollokshields East train station.

Sport

Two football clubs – Rangers and Celtic – dominate the sporting scene in Scotland, having vastly more resources than other clubs and a long history (and rivalry). This runs along partisan lines, with Rangers representing Protestant supporters, and Celtic, Catholic. It's worth going to a game; both play in magnificent arenas with great atmosphere. Games between the two (four a year when in the same division) are fiercely contested, but tickets aren't sold to the general public; you'll need to know a season-ticket holder. Rangers have had to work their way back up the divisions after a financial meltdown.

Celtic FC
FOOTBALL

(☑ 0871 226 1888; www.celticfc.net; Celtic Park, Parkhead) There are daily stadium tours (adult/child £8.50/5.50). Catch bus 61 or 62 from outside St Enoch centre.

Rangers FC
FOOTBALL

(☑ 0871 702 1972; www.rangers.co.uk; Ibrox Stadium, 150 Edmiston Dr) Tours of the stadium and trophy room run Friday to Sunday (adult/

child £8/5.50). Take the subway to Ibrox station.

 Shopping

Boasting the UK's largest retail phalanx outside London, Glasgow is a shopaholic's paradise. The 'Style Mile' around Buchanan St, Argyle St and Merchant City (particularly upmarket Ingram St) is a fashion hub, while the West End has quirkier, more bohemian shopping options: Byres Rd is great for vintage clothing.

Barras   FLEA MARKET
(Map p106; www.glasgow-barrowland.com; btwn Gallowgate & London Rd; ⊙10am-5pm Sat & Sun) At Glasgow's legendary weekend flea market, the Barras on Gallowgate, cheap tat rules the roost these days but it's still an intriguing stroll, as much for the assortment of local characters as what's on offer. People come here just for a wander, and it's got a real feel of a nearly-vanished Britain of whelk stalls and rag-and-bone merchants. Watch your wallet.

Italian Centre   FASHION
(Map p106; 7 John St; ⊙10am-6pm Mon-Fri, 10am-7pm Sat, noon-6pm Sun) Fashion junkies can procure relief at Emporio Armani among other boutiques here.

Buchanan Galleries   SHOPPING CENTRE
(Map p106; www.buchanangalleries.co.uk; Royal Exchange Sq; ⊙10am-7pm, to 8pm Thu, to 6pm Sun; 🕾) Huge number of contemporary clothing retailers.

Princes Square   FASHION
(Map p106, www.princessquare.co.uk; 48 Buchanan St; ⊙10am-7pm Mon-Fri, 9am-6pm Sat, 11am-5pm Sun) Set in a magnificent 1841 renovated square with an exuberant metal leaf facade. Beauty and fashion outlets including Vivienne Westwood.

Argyll Arcade   JEWELLERY
(Map p106; www.argyll-arcade.com; Buchanan St; ⊙10am-5.30pm Mon-Sat, noon-5pm Sun) Splendid, jewellery-laden arcade doglegging between Buchanan and Argyle Sts.

Geoffrey (Tailor) Kiltmaker   KILTS
(Map p106; www.geoffreykilts.co.uk; 309 Sauchiehall St; ⊙10am-5pm Mon-Sat) The place to head if you want to take some tartan home.

Adventure 1   OUTDOOR
(Map p106; ☑0141-353 3788; www.adventure1.co.uk; 38 Dundas St; ⊙9am-5.30pm Mon-Sat) An

DON'T MISS

VINTAGE CLOTHING – GLASGOW'S BEST

Snag a bargain and bring out the hipster in you with Glasgow's fabulous range of retro rag stores.

Vintage Guru (Map p112; www.vintage guru.co.uk; 195 Byres Rd; ⊙10am-6pm Mon-Sat, 11am-6pm Sun) You might have to elbow your way into this tightly-packed West End favourite, but it's worth it for the always-intriguing and frequently-updated selection and fair prices.

Mr Ben (Map p106; www.mrbenretro clothing.com; 101 King St; ⊙10.30am-5.30pm Mon-Sat, 1-5pm Sun) This cute place is one of Glasgow's best destinations for vintage clothing, with a great selection of brands such as Fred Perry, as well as more glam choices, on offer.

Circa Vintage (Map p112; www.circa vintage.co.uk; 37 Ruthven Lane; ⊙11.30am-5.30pm Mon-Sat, 1-5pm Sun) Tucked away off Byres Road in a little market of second-hand and quirky shops, Circa Vintage offers online shopping as well as a fab range of in-store jewellery and well-kept clothes.

Glasgow Vintage Company (Map p112; www.glasgowvintage.co.uk; 453 Great Western Rd; ⊙11am-5.30pm Mon-Sat, noon-5pm Sun) With a little more breathing room than some, this offers more relaxed browsing.

excellent place to buy hiking boots, backpacks and military surplus gear.

Waterstone's   BOOKS
(Map p106; ☑0141-332 9105; www.waterstones.com; 153 Sauchiehall St; ⊙8.30am-7pm Mon-Fri, to 8pm Thu, 9am-7pm Sat, 10am-6pm Sun) A major bookshop, which also sells guidebooks and street maps of Glasgow.

ℹ Information

The List (www.list.co.uk; £2.50), available from newsagents, is Glasgow and Edinburgh's invaluable guide to films, theatre, cabaret, music and clubs, released every four weeks. The excellent *Eating & Drinking Guide* (£5.95), published by *the List* every second April, covers both Glasgow and Edinburgh.

INTERNET ACCESS

Gallery of Modern Art (0141-229 1996; Royal Exchange Sq; 10am-5pm Mon-Wed & Sat, 10am-8pm Thu, 11am-5pm Fri & Sun;) Basement library; free internet access. Bookings recommended.

Hillhead Library (348 Byres Rd; 10am-8pm Mon-Tue & Thu, 10am-5pm Wed, 9am-5pm Fri & Sat, noon-5pm Sun;) Free internet terminals.

iCafe (www.icafe.uk.com; 250 Woodlands Rd; per hr £2.50; 8.30am-10.30pm;) Sip a coffee and munch on a pastry while you check your emails on super-fast connections. Wi-fi too. It's actually a very good cafe in its own right. There are other branches, including one on Sauchiehall St (www.icafe.uk.com; 315 Sauchiehall St; 7am-11pm Mon-Sat, 8am-11pm Sun;).

Mitchell Library (0141-287 2999; www.glasgowlife.org.uk; North St; 9am-8pm Mon-Thu, 9am-5pm Fri & Sat) Free internet access; bookings recommended.

MEDICAL SERVICES

Glasgow Dental Hospital (0141-211 9600; www.nhsggc.org.uk; 378 Sauchiehall St)

Glasgow Royal Infirmary (0141-211 4000; www.nhsggc.org.uk; 84 Castle St) Medical emergencies and outpatient facilities.

POST

There are post offices in some supermarkets; some of these are open Sunday as well.

Glassford St Post Office (Map p106; www.postoffice.co.uk; 59 Glassford St; 8.30am-5.30pm Mon-Sat) The most central post office.

TOURIST INFORMATION

Glasgow Tourist Officee (Map p106; 0845-225 5121; www.visitscotland.com; 170 Buchanan St; 9am-6pm Mon-Sat, noon-4pm or 10am-5pm Sun;) In the heart of the shopping area.

Airport Tourist Office (0141-848 4440; Glasgow International Airport; 7.30am-5pm Mon-Sat, 8am-3.30pm Sun)

🛈 Getting There & Away

AIR

Ten miles west of the city, **Glasgow International Airport** (GLA; 0844 481-5555; www.glasgowairport.com) handles international and domestic flights. **Prestwick Airport** (PIK; 0871 223-0700; www.glasgowprestwick.com), 30 miles southwest of Glasgow, is used by **Ryanair** (www.ryanair.com) and some other budget airlines, with connections to the rest of Britain and Europe.

BUS

All long-distance buses arrive at and depart from **Buchanan bus station** (Map p106; 0141-333 3708; www.spt.co.uk; Killermont St), which has lockers (small/large £5/7), ATMs, and a cafe with wi-fi.

Your first port of call if you're looking for the cheapest fare should be **Megabus** (www.megabus.com), which offers very cheap demand-dependent prices on many major bus routes, including to Edinburgh and London.

Scottish Citylink (0871 266 3333; www.citylink.co.uk) has buses to Edinburgh (£7.30, 1¼ hours, every 15 minutes) and most major towns in Scotland. National Express also runs daily to several English cities.

CAR & MOTORCYLE

There are numerous car-rental companies; both big names and discount operators have airport offices. Companies include the following:

Arnold Clark (0141-423 9559; www.arnoldclarkrental.com; 43 Allison St)

Avis (0844 544 6064; www.avis.co.uk; 70 Lancefield St)

Europcar (0844 384 8471; www.europcar.co.uk; 76 Lancefield Quay)

TRAIN

As a general rule, **Glasgow Central station** serves southern Scotland, England and Wales, and **Queen St station** serves the north and east. Buses run between the two stations every 10 minutes. There are direct trains to London's Euston station (advance purchase single £56, full fare off-peak/peak £130/176, 4½ hours, more than hourly); they're much quicker and more comfortable than the bus.

Scotrail (08457 55 00 33; www.scotrail.co.uk) runs Scottish trains. Destinations include: Edinburgh (£12.50, 50 minutes, every 15 minutes), Oban (£23.10, three hours, three to six daily), Fort William (£28.20, 3¾ hours, four to five daily), Dundee (£21.30, 1½ hours, hourly), Aberdeen (£38.20, 2½ hours, hourly) and Inverness (£84.70, 3½ hours, 10 daily, four on Sunday).

🛈 Getting Around

TO/FROM THE AIRPORT

There are buses every 10 or 15 minutes from Glasgow International Airport to Buchanan bus station via Central and Queen St stations (single/return £6/8.50, 25 minutes). This is a 24-hour service. Another bus, the 747, covers the same route via Finnieston and Kelvingrove, taking longer. A taxi costs £24. There are also buses from Buchanan bus station direct to/from Edinburgh Airport (£11, one hour, half-hourly).

BIKE
There are several places to hire a bike; the tourist office (p134) has a full list.

Alpine Bikes (www.alpinebikes.com; 6 St Georges Pl; per day £20; ⊙9.30am-6pm Mon-Sat, 11am-5pm Sun, 9.30am-7pm Thu) Hardtail and roadbikes available.

Gear Bikes (☑0141-339 1179; www.gearbikes.com; 19 Gibson St; half-/1/2 days £15/20/35; ⊙10am-6pm Mon-Sat, noon-5pm Sun) Decent hybrids rented in the summer months.

CAR & MOTORCYCLE
The most difficult thing about driving in Glasgow is the confusing one-way system. For short-term parking (up to two hours), you've got a decent chance of finding something on the street, paying at the meters, which cost up to £3.60 per hour. Otherwise, multistorey car parks are probably your best bet. Ask your hotel in advance if they offer parking discounts.

PUBLIC TRANSPORT

Bus City bus services, mostly run by **First Glasgow** (☑0141-423 6600; www.firstglasgow.com), are frequent. You can buy tickets when you board buses but on most you must have the exact change. Short journeys in town cost £1.20 or £1.95; a day ticket (£4.10) is good value and is valid until 1am, when a night network starts. A weekly ticket is £16.50. The tourist office (p134) hands out the highly complicated SPT Bus Map, detailing all routes in and around the city.

Train & Underground There's an extensive suburban network of trains in and around Glasgow; tickets should be bought before travel if the station is staffed, or from the conductor if it isn't. There's also an underground line, the Subway, that serves 15 stations in the centre, west and south of the city (single £1.60). The train network connects with the Subway at Buchanan St station. The Discovery Ticket (£4) gives you unlimited travel on the Subway for a day, while the Roundabout ticket gives a day's unlimited train and Subway travel for £6.30. The Subway annoyingly shuts down at around 6pm on a Sunday.

Combined Ticket The Daytripper ticket gives you a day's unlimited travel on buses, the Subway, rail and some ferries in the Glasgow region. It costs £11.20 for one person or £19.80 for two. Two kids per adult are included free.

TAXI
There's no shortage of taxis and fares are very reasonable – you can get across the centre for around a fiver, and there's no surcharge for calling a taxi. You can pay by credit card with **Glasgow Taxis** (☑0141-429 7070; www.glasgowtaxis.co.uk) if you order by phone; most of its taxis are wheelchair accessible. Download its app to make booking easy.

AROUND GLASGOW
Good transport connections mean it's easy to plan day trips out of Glasgow. There are some excellent sights along the southern shore of the Clyde, where the ghosts of shipbuilding haunt places like Greenock, and Paisley's magnificent abbey tells a tale of nobler architectural times.

Inverclyde
The ghostly remains of once-great shipyards still line the banks of the Clyde west of Glasgow. The places most worth a stop along the coast west of the city are Greenock and Gourock, although there are a couple of items of interest in the otherwise unprepossessing town of Port Glasgow.

Port Glasgow
The fine 16th-century **Newark Castle** (www.historic-scotland.gov.uk; adult/child £4.50/2.70; ⊙9.30am-5.30pm Apr-Sep) is still largely intact and has a spectacular position on the shores of the Clyde. Once a far grimmer fortified tower, it was converted to a Renaissance mansion in the 1590s by its rogue owner Patrick Maxwell. The hall boasts a magnificent fireplace, and you can climb a claustrophobic spiral stair to great views from the ramparts.

Greenock & Gourock
POP 54,900
The towns of Gourock and Greenock were always warming sights to a Glasgow mariner's heart as their ships rounded the point from the Firth of Clyde into the river proper and thence to home. Gourock's firthside views are spectacular, and Greenock's historical buildings – despite the scrappy shopping complexes in its centre – invite a stop. Before the Clyde was dredged, larger ships couldn't progress further than Greenock, which raked in considerable customs dues from the fact. In summer and on fine days, these become little resort towns for Glasgow families looking for a day out.

The **McLean Museum & Art Gallery** (☑01475 715624; www.inverclyde.gov.uk; 15 Kelly St; ⊙10am-5pm Mon-Sat) FREE in the historic

WORTH A TRIP

PAISLEY

Once a proud weaving town, but these days effectively a southwestern suburb of Glasgow, Paisley gave its name to the funky patterned fabric. Though flanked by green countryside, it's not an engaging place, but it has an ace up its sleeve in the shape of the magnificent **Paisley Abbey** (www.paisleyabbey.org.uk; Abbey Close; ⏲10am-3.30pm Mon-Sat) FREE, which is well worth the short trip from Glasgow. This majestic Gothic building was founded in 1163 by Walter Fitzalan, the first high steward of Scotland and ancestor of the Stuart dynasty. A monastery for Cluny monks, it was damaged by fire during the Wars of Independence in 1306 but rebuilt soon after. Most of the nave is 14th or 15th century. The building was mostly a ruin from the 16th century until the 19th-century restoration, completed in 1928. Apart from the magnificent perspective down the nave, points of interest include royal tombs, some excellent 19th- and 20th-century stained glass, including three windows by Edward Burne-Jones, and the 10th-century Celtic **Barochan Cross**. A window commemorates the fact that William Wallace was educated by monks from this monastery.

At the western end of the High St, worthwhile **Paisley Museum** (www.renfrewshire.gov.uk/museums; High St; ⏲11am-4pm Tue-Sat, 2-5pm Sun) FREE is housed in an elegant Victorian Grecian edifice and has a decent collection of 19th century Scottish art, as well as a bit of everything else, from dinosaur footprints to a stuffed terrier, and plenty of information on the town's textile history, including looms, and the famous Paisley pattern's origins in ancient Mesopotamia.

Trains run from Glasgow's Central station to Paisley (10 minutes, eight per hour).

centre of Greenock is well worth checking out. There's quite an extensive collection, with displays charting the history of steam power and Clyde shipping. The art gallery has some fine pieces, and several canvases give you an idea of just how busy Greenock's harbour once was. There's also a pictorial history of Greenock through the ages, while upstairs are small displays from China, Japan and Egypt. The natural history section highlights the sad reality of species' extinction in the modern world. There are free internet terminals here.

Greenock was the birthplace of James Watt, the inventor whose work on the steam engine was one of the key developments of the Industrial Revolution. A statue marks his birthplace; behind this looms the spectacular Italian-style **Victoria Tower** on the municipal buildings, constructed in 1886.

Sleeping & Eating

Tontine Hotel HOTEL ££
(☎01475-723316; www.tontinehotel.co.uk; 6 Ardgowan Sq; s/d £65/75, superior s/d £85/95; P 📶) This noble hotel in the nicest part of Greenock has recently refurbished rooms that provide comfort alongside the building's older features. Superior rooms in the old part of the building are more spacious. There's an old fashioned lounge bar and decent restaurant here, and staff are very welcoming. Book ahead in summer.

Spinnaker Hotel HOTEL ££
(☎01475-633107; www.spinnakerhotel.co.uk; 121 Albert Rd; s/d £48/80; 📶) The Spinnaker is a friendly pub looking out on Gourock's great view across the firth to Dunoon. The modern rooms upstairs are very decent value, especially if you grab one at the front with a view. Downstairs, the comfy bar, popular with an older crowd enjoying the vistas, is laid-back and has ales on tap. Pub grub (mains £8 to £11) is also on offer.

Getting There & Away

Greenock is 27 miles west of Glasgow, and Gourock is 3 miles further west. The Glasgow–Greenock–Gourock leg of the Clyde to Forth pedestrian and cycle route follows an old train track for 10 miles. Trains from Glasgow Central station (£6, 30 to 40 minutes, two to three per hour) and hourly buses stop in both towns.

Gourock is an important ferry hub. **Argyll Ferries** (☎01475-650338; www.argyllferries.co.uk) has a passenger service for Dunoon (£4.40, 25 minutes, half-hourly Monday to Saturday, hourly Sunday) on Argyll's Cowal peninsula. Gourock's train station is next to the CalMac terminal.

There's a passenger-only **ferry service** (☎0871-705 0888; www.kilcregganferry.com) service to Kilcreggan (£2.50, 15 minutes, 12 to 13 daily Monday to Saturday year-round, three Sunday April to October); buy tickets on board.

Western Ferries ([J] 01369-704452; www.
western-ferries.co.uk) also has a service
(passenger/car £4.30/12.20, 20 minutes, two
to three hourly) to Dunoon from McInroy's Point,
2 miles from the train station on the Irvine road;
Scottish Citylink buses run to here.

Wemyss Bay

POP 2600

Eight miles south of Gourock is Wemyss Bay
(pronounced 'weemz'), where you can jump
off a train and onto a ferry for Rothesay
on the Isle of Bute. There are trains from
Glasgow (£6.90, one hour, hourly). **CalMac**
([J] 0800 066 5000; www.calmac.co.uk) ferries
to Rothesay connect with trains and cost
£5.05/19.85 per passenger/car.

Blantyre

POP 17,200

Though technically part of Lanarkshire,
Blantyre, birthplace of David Livingstone, is
an outlying suburb of Glasgow these days.
Livingstone, a zealous and pious doctor,
missionary and explorer was raised in a
one-room tenement and worked in a cotton
mill by day from the age of 10, going to the
local school at night. Amazingly for a time in
which most mill-workers were barely able to
write their names, he managed to get himself into university to study medicine. The
David Livingstone Centre (NTS; www.nts.
org.uk; adult/child £6.50/5; ☺ 10am-5pm Mon-Sat,
12.30-5pm Sun Apr-late Dec) tells the story of his
life from his early days in Blantyre to the 30
years he spent in Africa, where he named
the Victoria Falls on one of his numerous
journeys. It's a good display and brings to
life the incredible hardships of his missionary existence, his battles against slavery, and
his famous meeting with Stanley. There's a
child-friendly African wildlife feature and
the grassy park the museum is set in makes
a perfect picnic spot.

It's a 30-minute walk along the river to
Bothwell Castle (www.historic-scotland.gov.
uk; adult/child £4.50/2.70; ☺ 9.30am-5.30pm
daily Apr-Sep, 9.30am-4.30pm Sat-Wed Oct-Mar),
regarded as the finest 13th-century castle in
Scotland. The stark, roofless, red-sandstone
ruins are substantial and, largely due to
their beautiful green setting, romantic.

Trains run from Glasgow Central station
to Blantyre (20 minutes, three hourly). Head
straight down the hill from the station to
reach the museum.

The Campsies &
Strathblane

The beautiful Campsies reach an altitude of
nearly 600m and lie just 10 miles north of
Glasgow. The plain of the River Forth lies to
the north; Strathblane and Loch Lomond are
to the west. One of several villages around
the Campsies, attractive **Killearn** is known
for its 31m-high obelisk, raised in honour of
George Buchanan, James VI's tutor. Eight
miles to the east, **Fintry** has carved itself a
gorgeous spot deep in the Campsies on the
banks of Endrick Water, which has an impressive 28m waterfall, the **Loup of Fintry**.

🏃 Activities

Glengoyne Distillery   DISTILLERY
([J] 01360-550254; www.glengoyne.com; A81, nr
Killearn; tours from £7.50; ☺ 10am-5pm Mar-Nov,
10am-4pm Dec-Feb, last tour 1hr before closing)
About 2 miles south of Killearn, this traditional place is run by genuine people in
lovely surrounds. There are various tours:
the basic ones run on the hour and are reliably excellent. One of the best walks in the
area is the ascent of spectacular Dumgoyne
hill (427m) from the distillery: allow at least
one hour for the 1.5 mile climb. It's another
1.5 miles (one hour) to Earl's Seat, and three
miles (1½ hours) to return from there to the
distillery. From Drymen, the **Rob Roy Way**
(www.robroyway.com) is a great week's walk (77
miles or 94 miles, depending on the route)
through Central Scotland's most beautiful
lochlands to Pitlochry.

🛏 Sleeping & Eating

Culcreuch Castle   HOTEL **££**
([J] 01360-860555; www.culcreuch.com; Fintry;
s/d from £83/116; [P][❄][🐾]) Fancy a night in
a 700-year-old castle? Parts of Culcreuch
date to 1296 and the whole is a remarkably
well-preserved historic building. The rooms
vary substantially in size, price and comfort,
and most look out onto the collage of greenery engulfing the surrounding estate. A little
dowdy perhaps and popular with groups, but
this place, with its period furnishings, has
real character. There are also self-catering
lodges a little removed from the castle itself,
great for families; one is pet-friendly.

ℹ Getting There & Away

First bus 10 runs from Glasgow to Killearn
(£5.20, one hour) regularly.

Southern Scotland

Includes ➡

Best Places to Eat

➡ Coltman's (p142)

➡ Cobbles (p150)

➡ Campbell's (p177)

Best Places to Stay

➡ Corsewall Lighthouse Hotel (p177)

➡ Churches Hotel (p152)

➡ Cornhill House (p156)

➡ Knockinaam Lodge (p177)

➡ 26 The Crescent (p160)

➡ Old Bank House (p143)

Why Go?

Though wise folk are well aware of its charms, for many southern Scotland is just something to drive through on the way to northern Scotland. Big mistake. But it does mean there's breathing room here in summer, and peaceful corners.

Proximity to England brought raiding and strife; grim borderland fortifications saw skirmishes aplenty. There was loot to be had in the Borders, where large prosperous abbeys ruled over agricultural communities. Regularly ransacked before their destruction in the Reformation, the ruins of these churches, linked by cycling and walking paths, are among Scotland's most atmospheric historic sites.

The rolling west enjoys extensive forest cover between bustling market towns. The hills cascade down to sandy stretches of coastline blessed with Scotland's sunniest weather. It's the land of Robert Burns, whose verse reflected his earthy attitudes and active social life.

When to Go

Ayr

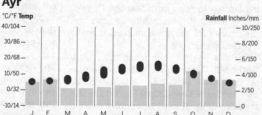

May Take a fortnight to cross the whole region, hiking the gorgeous Southern Upland Way.

Jun The perfect time to visit the region's numerous stately homes, with spectacular gardens in bloom.

Oct Hit Galloway's forests to see red deer battling it out in the rutting season.

BORDERS REGION

The Borders has had a rough history: centuries of war and plunder have left a battle-scarred landscape, encapsulated by the magnificent ruins of the Border abbeys. Their wealth was an irresistible magnet during cross-frontier wars, and they were destroyed and rebuilt numerous times. Today these massive stone shells are the region's finest attraction. And don't miss Hermitage Castle; nothing encapsulates the region's turbulent history like this spooky stronghold.

But the Borders is also genteel. Welcoming villages with ancient traditions pepper the countryside and grandiose mansions await exploration. It's fine walking and cycling country too, the hills lush with an artist's palette of shades of green. Offshore is some of Europe's best cold-water diving.

Peebles

POP 8400

With a picturesque main street set on a ridge between the River Tweed and the Eddleston Water, Peebles is one of the most handsome of the Border towns. Though it lacks a major sight, the agreeable atmosphere and good walking options in the rolling, wooded hills thereabouts will entice you to linger for a couple of days. There are some excellent eating choices.

◉ Sights & Activities

The riverside walk along the River Tweed has plenty of grassed areas ideal for a picnic, and there's a children's playground (near the main road bridge). A mile west of the town centre, **Neidpath Castle** is a tower house perched on a bluff above the river; it's closed but worth a look from the riverbank.

Two miles east of town off the A72, in **Glentress forest**, is the busiest of the **7stanes mountain-biking hubs** (www.7 stanesmountainbiking.com), as well as osprey viewing and marked walking trails. The **shop** (☑01721-724522; www.alpinebikes.com; ◷9am-5pm Mon-Fri, to 5.30pm Sat & Sun) here hires rigs and will put you on the right trail for your ability. These are some of Britain's best biking routes. **Go Ape** (www.goape.co.uk) also has swing and zip line forest routes and there are camping huts available (see www.glentressforestlodges.co.uk). In town, you can hire bikes to explore the region from **Glentress Bikes** (☑01721-729756; 20a Northgate; day hire £22).

There are further mountain-biking trails at Innerleithen, 7 miles east of Peebles.

🛏 Sleeping

Rosetta Holiday Park   CAMPSITE £
(☑01721-720770; www.rosettaholidaypark.co.uk; Rosetta Rd; sites for 1/2 £12/18; ◷Apr-Oct; P🐕🛜🌳) This camping ground, about 800m north of the town centre, has a likeably green setting with lots of trees and grass. There are plenty of amusements for the kids, such as a bowling green and a games room.

Tontine Hotel   HOTEL ££
(☑01721-720892; www.tontinehotel.com; High St; s £55, d £110-120; P🐕🛜) Right in the heart of things, this is a bastion of Borders hospitality. Refurbished rooms have high comfort levels, modish colours and top-notch bathrooms, while service couldn't be more helpful. There's a small supplement for rooms with four-poster beds and/or river views. There's a good restaurant and bar here: it's the heart of town.

Rowanbrae   B&B ££
(☑01721-721630; www.aboutscotland.co.uk/peebles/rowanbrae.html; 103 Northgate; s/d £42/65; 🛜) In a quiet cul-de-sac but not far from the main street, this hospitable spot treats its guests like family friends. It's pleasantly and comfortably old-fashioned; there are three upstairs bedrooms, two en suite, and a commodious guest lounge for relaxation.

Cringletie House   HOTEL £££
(☑01721-725750; www.cringletie.com; r £135-260; P🛜🌳) Luxury without snobbery is this hotel's hallmark, and more power to it. To call it a house is being coy; it's an elegant baronial mansion, 2 miles north of Peebles on the A703, set in lush, wooded grounds. Rooms are plush and feature genteel elegance and linen so soft you could wrap a newborn in it. There's an excellent restaurant (dinner £37.50) on-site.

✖ Eating

Cocoa Black   CAFE £
(www.cocoablack.com; 1 Cuddy Bridge; sweets £1.50-3; ◷9.30am-5pm Mon-Fri, 9am-5pm Sat, 11am-4pm Sun; 🛜) Chocaholics should make a beeline for this friendly cafe, where exquisite cakes and other patisserie offerings will satisfy any cacao-focused cravings. It also runs a school where you can learn to make them yourself.

Southern Scotland Highlights

1 Exploring the evocative ruins of the **Border Abbeys**

2 Admiring 18th-century architectural genius at **Culzean Castle** (p162), perched on wild sea cliffs

3 Pondering the tough life on the England–Scotland frontier at desolate **Hermitage Castle** (p148)

4 Exploring charming, **Kirkcudbright** (p170), and

marvelling at the creative flair of its inhabitants

5 Learning some Lallans words at the **Robert Burns Birthplace Museum** (p160) in Alloway

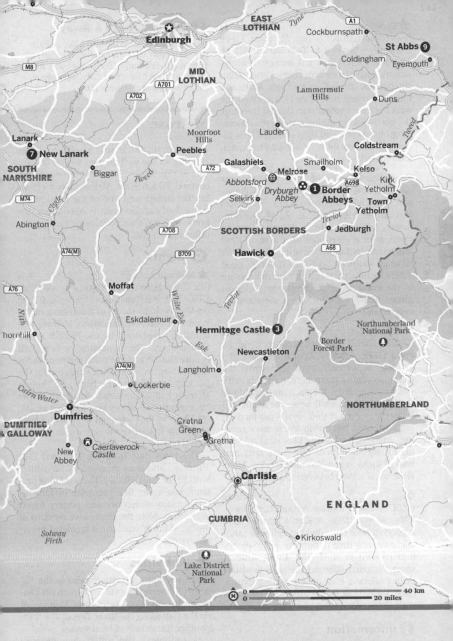

Whooshing down forest trails at the **7stanes mountain-biking hubs** near Glentrool and across the region (p173)

Marvelling at the radical social reform instituted in the handsome mill community of **New Lanark** (p154)

Hiking or cycling one of the grand **long-distance routes** (p150)

Plunging the deeps off the picturesque fishing village of **St Abbs** (p153), a top-notch coldwater diving site

★ **Coltman's** BISTRO, DELI ££

(www.coltmans.co.uk; 71 High St; mains £11-19; ⊙10am-5pm Sun-Wed, to 10pm Thu-Sat; 🐾) 🍴 This main street deli has numerous temptations, such as excellent cheeses and Italian smallgoods, as well as perhaps Scotland's tastiest sausage roll – buy two to avoid the walk back for another one. Behind the shop, the good-looking dining area serves up confident bistro fare and light snacks with a variety of culinary influences, using top-notch local ingredients.

Sunflower Restaurant FUSION ££

(☑ 01721-722420; www.thesunflower.net; 4 Bridgegate; lunch £6-9, dinner mains £12-16; ⊙noon-3pm Mon-Sat, plus 6-9pm Fri & Sat; 🍴) 🍴 The Sunflower, with its warmly decorated dining room, is in a quiet spot off the main drag and has a reputation that brings diners from all over southern Scotland. It serves good salads for lunch and has an admirable menu in the evenings, with creative and elegant dishes that always include some standout vegetarian fare.

Tontine Hotel SCOTTISH ££

(☑ 01721-720892; www.tontinehotel.com; High St; mains £11-19; ⊙noon-2.30pm & 6-8.45pm; 🐾) Glorious is the only word to describe the Georgian dining room here, complete with musicians' gallery, fireplace, and windows the like of which we'll never see again. It'd be worth it even if they served cat food on mouldy bread, but luckily the meals – ranging from pub classics like steak-and-ale pie to more ambitious fare – are tasty and backed up by very welcoming service. Afternoon tea is served between meal times.

Osso BISTRO ££

(☑ 01721-724477; www.ossorestaurant.com; Innerleithen Rd; mains £9-19; ⊙10am-4.30pm & 6-9pm) A good stop for home baking, coffee or sandwiches at any time of day, this bistro comes into its own at lunch and dinner time. A short, regularly-changed menu of delicious dishes offers a high-quality dining experience. Everything is prepared with patience, with slow-cooked meats a highlight.

ℹ Information

Peebles Tourist Office (☑ 01721-723159; www.visitscottishborders.com; High St; ⊙9am-5pm Mon-Sat, 11am-4pm Sun) Closed Sundays from January to March. Open until 5.30pm July and August.

ℹ Getting There & Away

The bus stop is beside the post office on Eastgate. Bus 62A/X62 runs half-hourly (hourly on Sundays) to Edinburgh (£5.10, one hour). In the other direction it heads for Galashiels, where you can change for Melrose (£6).

Melrose

POP 2300

Tiny, charming Melrose is a polished village running on the well-greased wheels of tourism. Sitting at the feet of the three heathercovered Eildon Hills, Melrose has a classic market square and one of the great abbey ruins. Just outside town is Abbotsford, the home of Sir Walter Scott, which makes another superb visit.

◉ Sights

★ **Melrose Abbey** RUIN

(HS; www.historic-scotland.gov.uk; adult/child £5.50/3.30; ⊙9.30am-5.30pm Apr-Sep, to 4.30pm Oct-Mar) Perhaps the most interesting of the Border abbeys, red-sandstone Melrose was repeatedly destroyed by the English in the 14th century. The remaining broken shell is pure Gothic and the ruins are famous for their decorative stonework – look out for the pig gargoyle playing the bagpipes. Though Melrose had a monastery way back in the 7th century, this abbey was founded by David I in 1136 for Cistercian monks, and later rebuilt by Robert the Bruce, whose heart is buried here.

The ruins date from the 14th and 15th centuries, and were repaired by Sir Walter Scott in the 19th century. The adjoining museum has many fine examples of 12th- to 15th-century stonework and pottery found in the area. Note the impressive remains of the 'great drain' outside – a medieval sewerage system.

⚡ Activities

There are many attractive walks in the Eildon Hills, accessible via a footpath off Dingleton Rd (the B6359) south of Melrose, or via the trail along the River Tweed. The tourist office has details of local walks.

St Cuthbert's Way (p150) long-distance walking path starts in Melrose, while the coast-to-coast Southern Upland Way (p150) passes through town. You can do a day's walk along St Cuthbert's Way as far as Harestanes (16 miles), on the A68 near Jedburgh, and return to Melrose on the hourly

TRAQUAIR HOUSE

One of Scotland's great country houses, **Traquair House** (www.traquair.co.uk; adult/child/family £8.50/4.25/23; ⏰11am-5pm Easter-Sep, 11am-4pm Oct, 11am-3pm Sat & Sun Nov) has a powerful, ethereal beauty, and exploring it is like time travel. Odd, sloping floors and a musty odour bestow a genuine feel, and parts of the building are believed to have been constructed long before the first official record of its existence in 1107. The massive tower house was gradually expanded over the next 500 years but has remained virtually unchanged since the 17th century. Traquair is 1.5 miles south of Innerleithen, about 6 miles southeast of Peebles.

Since the 15th century, the house has belonged to various branches of the Stuart family, and the family's unwavering Catholicism and loyalty to the Stuart cause led to famous visitors like Mary, Queen of Scots and Bonnie Prince Charlie, but also to numerous problems after the deposal of James II of England in 1688. The family's estate, wealth and influence were gradually whittled away, as life as a Jacobite became a furtive, clandestine affair.

One of Traquair's most interesting places is the concealed room where priests secretly lived and performed Mass – up until 1829 when the Catholic Emancipation Act was finally passed. Other beautiful, time-worn rooms hold fascinating relics, including the cradle used by Mary for her son, James VI of Scotland (who also became James I of England), and fascinating letters from the Jacobite earls of Traquair and their families, including one particularly moving one written from death row in the Tower of London. The main gates to the house were locked by one earl in the 18th century until the day a Stuart king reclaims the throne in London, so meanwhile you'll have to enter by a side gate.

In addition to the house, there's a garden maze, a small brewery producing the tasty Bear Ale, and a series of craft workshops.

Bus 62 runs from Edinburgh via Peebles to Innerleithen and on to Galashiels and Melrose.

Jedburgh–Galashiels bus. The Tweed Cycle Way also passes through Melrose.

🎪 Festivals & Events

Melrose Rugby Sevens RUGBY
(www.melrose7s.com) In mid-April rugby followers fill the town to see the week-long competition.

Borders Book Festival BOOKS
(www.bordersbookfestival.org) Runs over four days in late June.

🛏 Sleeping

⭐ **Old Bank House** B&B ££
(☏01896-823712; www.oldbankhousemelrose.co.uk; 27 Buccleuch St; s/d £45/70; 🖥🐾) Right in the middle of town, this is a superb B&B in a charming old building. The owner's artistic touch is evident throughout, from walls covered with paintings, some his own, a house full of curios and tasteful art nouveau features, and a sumptuous breakfast room. Rooms are spacious with comfortable furniture and top modern bathrooms; they are complemented by a generous can-do attitude. They go the extra mile here and that makes it a great Borders base.

Braidwood B&B ££
(☏01896-822488; www.braidwoodmelrose.co.uk; Buccleuch St; s £40-45, d £60-69; 🐾🖥) This popular option near the abbey is solid and comfortable. The bright rooms have a well-cared-for feel, and the twin room has great views. Breakfast features fresh fruit salad. The owners are courteous and generally leave you to your own devices. No singles are available in summer.

⭐ **Townhouse** HOTEL £££
(☏01896-822645; www.thetownhousemelrose.co.uk; Market Sq; s/d £95/130; 🅿🖥) The classy Townhouse exudes warmth and professionalism, and has some of the best rooms in town, tastefully furnished with attention to detail. There are superior rooms (£147) that are enormous in size with lavish furnishings and excellent en suites, some with jacuzzi. Standard rooms are a fair bit smaller but recently refurbished and very comfortable. It's well worth the price.

SOUTHERN SCOTLAND MELROSE

Burts Hotel
HOTEL £££

(☑ 01896-822285; www.burtshotel.co.uk; Market Sq; s/d/superior d £74/136/145; [P][🛜][🐾]) Set in an early-18th-century house, and with a solid reputation, Burts retains much of its period charm and has been run by the same couple for over 30 years. Rooms vary – the renovated ones with modern plaid fabrics are very smart, and the superiors are extra-spacious. It's got an air of friendly formality that makes it a favourite with older visitors. Appealing food is served too.

🍴 Eating

Russell's
CAFE £

(Market Sq; light meals £6-10; ⏱ 9.30am-5pm Tue-Sat) Solid wooden furniture and big windows looking out over the centre of Melrose make this stylish little tearoom a popular option. There's a large range of snacks and some more substantial lunch offerings, with daily specials. It's famous throughout the Borders for its excellent scones.

Cellar
CAFE £

(Abbey Fine Wines, Rhymer's Fayre; www.abbeyfinewines.co.uk; 17 Market Sq; mains £5-8; ⏱ 9.30am-4.30pm Mon-Sat) Drop into the Cellar for a caffeine hit. It's also a good spot for a glass of wine on the town square, as well as food platters and speciality cheeses. Out front is a more-than-decent wine-and-whisky shop.

Townhouse
SCOTTISH ££

(☑ 01896-822645; www.thetownhousemelrose.co.uk; Market Sq; mains £10-16; ⏱ noon-2pm & 6-9pm Mon-Thu, noon-2pm & 6-9.30pm Fri & Sat, noon-2.30pm & 6-9pm Sun; 🛜) The brasserie and restaurant here turn out just about the best gourmet cuisine in town and offer decent value. There's some rich, elaborate, beautifully presented fare here, with plenty of venison and other game choices, but for a lighter feed you can always opt for the range of creative lunchtime sandwiches.

Marmion's Brasserie
SCOTTISH ££

(☑ 01896-822245; www.marmionsbrasserie.co.uk; 5 Buccleuch St; mains £11-17; ⏱ noon-3pm & 6-9pm Mon-Sat; 🛜🖊) This atmospheric, oak-panelled niche serves snacks all day, but the lunch and dinner menus include modern Scottish bistro classics: expect duck breast, chicken stuffed with haggis, smoked salmon and the like, but also several more-than-token offerings for vegetarians.

ℹ️ Information

Melrose Tourist Office (☑ 01896-822283; www.visitscottishborders.com; Abbey St; ⏱ 10am-4pm Mon-Sat, noon-4pm Sun Apr-Oct) Located by the abbey.

ℹ️ Getting There & Away

Buses run to/from nearby Galashiels, with connections for Edinburgh (£7.20, two hours, hourly) and other Borders destinations.

Around Melrose

In the vicinity of Melrose are a couple of excellent attractions intimately connected with Sir Walter Scott.

⊙ Sights

★ Abbotsford
HISTORIC BUILDING

(www.scottsabbotsford.co.uk; visitor centre free, house adult/child £8.75/4.50; ⏱ 10am-5pm Apr-Sep, to 4pm Oct-Mar) Just outside Melrose, this is where to discover the life and works of Sir Walter Scott (see p146), to whom we arguably owe both the modern novel and our mind's-eye view of Scotland. The whimsical, fabulous house where he lived – and which ruined him when his publishers went bust – really brings this 19th-century writer to life. The grounds on the banks of the Tweed are lovely, and Scott drew much inspiration from the surrounding countryside.

A modern visitors centre displays memorabilia and gives an intriguing overview of the man, before a swish audioguide system – with one designed for kids – shows you round the house. In the house are some gloriously over-the-top features, with elaborate carvings, enough swords and dirks to equip a small army, a Chinese drawing room and a lovely study and library.

Abbotsford is 2 miles west of Melrose; buses between Galashiels and Melrose will drop you at the nearby Tweedbank roundabout. You can also walk from Melrose in under an hour along the southern bank of the Tweed. There's a cafe-restaurant atop the visitor centre.

★ Dryburgh Abbey
RUIN

(HS; www.historic-scotland.gov.uk; adult/child £5/3; ⏱ 9.30am-5.30pm Apr-Sep, to 4.30pm Oct-Mar) This is the most beautiful and complete of the Border abbeys, partly because the neighbouring town of Dryburgh no longer exists (another victim of the wars) and partly for its lovely site by the Tweed in a sheltered

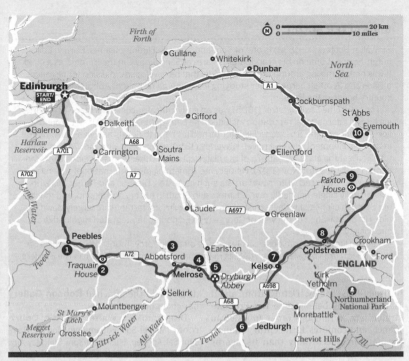

Driving Tour
Historic Sights of the Borders

START EDINBURGH
FINISH EDINBURGH
DISTANCE 155 MILES
DURATION 1–3 DAYS

You could do this drive in a long day, but to give yourself time to explore better take two or three.

Starting in Edinburgh, head south on the A701 to ❶ **Peebles**; Rosslyn Chapel is an easy detour along the way. Stroll around Peebles, a typically attractive Borders town, then head east along the A72, deviating at Innerleithen to historic ❷ **Traquair House** (p143), offering 10 centuries of history and great insights into the Jacobite cause and rebellions. Continue eastwards on the A72 pausing at excellent ❸ **Abbotsford**, Sir Walter Scott's one-time home. The pretty bijou village of ❹ **Melrose**, with its fabulous abbey, is a must-see and a good meal- or overnight-stop. Head east again, then turn south down the A68 to ❺ **Dryburgh Abbey**, perhaps the most evocative of the great Borders ruins.

Head on via the A68 to attractive ❻ **Jedburgh**, dominated by the skeleton of the third of the abbeys. The turbulent history of these once-powerful communities tells of the constant strife in these frontier lands.

From Jedburgh, take the A698 northeast to ❼ **Kelso**, an historic market town and the location of grandiose Floors Castle, the last and least intact of the abbey ruins. There are several other historic buildings within easy striking distance: the classical elegance of Mellerstain House and the contrastingly grim Smailholm Tower are particularly worthwhile. Beyond Kelso, the A698 takes you along to ❽ **Coldstream**, which gives its name to the famous regiment once based here. Head north and take the left turn to the magnificent 18th-century ❾ **Paxton House** (p153). Continue north to ❿ **Eyemouth**, with a fascinating maritime history. Here, Gunsgreen House is an elegant 18th-century mansion with an intriguing smuggling past. From here, it's an easy drive up the A1 through East Lothian and back to Edinburgh.

SIR WALTER SCOTT

Sir Walter Scott (1771–1832) is one of Scotland's greatest literary figures. Born in Edinburgh, he spent time on his grandparents' farm at Sandyknowe in the Borders as a child. It was here, rambling around the countryside, that he developed a passion for historical ballads and Scottish heroes. After studying in Edinburgh he bought Abbotsford (p144), a country house in the Borders.

The Lay of the Last Minstrel (1805) was an early critical success. Further works earning him an international reputation included *The Lady of the Lake* (1810), set around Loch Katrine and the Trossachs. He later turned his hand to novels and was instrumental in their development. His first novel, *Waverley* (1814), which dealt with the 1745 Jacobite rebellion, set the classical pattern of the historical novel. Other works included *Guy Mannering* (1815) and *Rob Roy* (1817). He became something of an international superstar, and heavily influenced writers and artists such as Austen, Dickens and Turner. His writings virtually single-handedly revived interest in Scottish history and legend, and much of our Scottish cliches of today – misty glens, fierce warriors, tartan – are largely down to him. His organisation of the visit of George IV to Edinburgh reintegrated Highland dress into society.

Later in life Scott wrote obsessively to stave off bankruptcy. Tourist offices stock a *Sir Walter Scott Trail* booklet, which details many places associated with him in the Borders.

birdsong-filled valley. Dating from about 1150, the abbey belonged to the Premonstratensians, a religious order founded in France, and conjures 12th-century monastic life more successfully than its nearby counterparts. The pink-hued stone ruins are the burial place of Sir Walter Scott.

The abbey is 5 miles southeast of Melrose on the B6404, which passes the famous Scott's View outlook. Hike there along the southern bank of the River Tweed, or take a bus to the nearby village of Newtown St Boswells.

Selkirk

POP 5800

While the noisy throb of machinery once filled the valleys below Selkirk, a prosperous mill town in the early 19th century, today it sits placid and pretty – apart from busy traffic through the centre – atop its steep ridge. Naughty millworkers who fell foul of the law would have come face to face in court with Sir Walter Scott, sheriff here for three decades.

The helpful **tourist office** (☑01750-20054; www.visitscottishborders.com; Halliwell's Close; ⊙11am-4pm Mon-Sat, noon-3pm Sun Apr-Oct) is tucked away off Market Sq inside **Halliwell's House Museum** (⊙11am-4pm Mon-Sat, noon-3pm Sun Apr-Oct) FREE, the oldest building (1712) in Selkirk. The museum charts local history with an engrossing

display, and the attached **Robson Gallery** has changing exhibitions.

Drop into **Sir Walter Scott's Courtroom** (Market Sq; ⊙10am-4pm Mon-Fri, 11am-3pm Sat Apr-Sep, plus 11am-3pm Sun May-Aug, noon-3pm Mon-Sat Oct) FREE, where there's an exhibition on his life and writings, plus a fascinating account of the courageous explorer Mungo Park (born near Selkirk) and his search for the River Niger.

🛏 Sleeping

Philipburn House Hotel HOTEL ££
(☑01750-720747; www.bw-philipburnhousehotel.co.uk; s/d £100/130, luxury s/d £140/175; P🐾🛜🐕) On the edge of town, this former dower house has a jazzy 21st-century look that hasn't ruined its historic features, as well as appealing renovated rooms and a snug bar and restaurant. The luxury rooms are particularly great – some have a jacuzzi, while another is a split-level affair with a double balcony. There are usually cheaper deals online. Self-catering facilities are on offer in the separate lodges, where pets are also welcome.

County Hotel INN ££
(☑01750-721233; www.countyhotelselkirk.co.uk; 1 High St; s/d/executive d £49/96/110; P🐾🛜🐕) Located in the centre of town, this is a former coaching inn with the odd Norwegian touch that has comfortable, modernised rooms that vary in size. Executive rooms are super-spacious and handsome. There's

a stylish restaurant and lounge with original art and upmarket bar meals (£10 to £16; food noon to 9pm). Room-only rates are also available for £7.50 less per person.

Place
BISTRO ££

(☑01750-778174; www.simplytheplace.co.uk; 73 High St; 2-/3-course dinner £19/23; ⊙6-11pm Thu-Sat) Offering high-quality fare on the main street, this place combines carefully selected, tasty ingredients with a home-cooking approach. Expect lots of stews and other heartwarming fare. Try the venison if it is on the menu as it is delicious.

❶ Getting There & Away

First buses 95 and X95 run at least hourly between Hawick, Selkirk, Galashiels and Edinburgh (£7.20, two hours).

Hawick

POP 14,300

Straddling the River Teviot, Hawick (pronounced 'hoik') is one of the largest towns in the Borders and has long been a major production centre for knitwear. There are several large outlets to buy jumpers and other woollens around town. Hawick is famous for rugby; the local club has produced dozens of Scotland internationals.

◉ Sights

Heart of Hawick
VISITOR CENTRE

(www.heartofhawick.co.uk; Kirkstile) Three buildings form the 'heart' of Hawick. A former mill holds the tourist office (☑01450-373993; www.visitscottishborders.com; ⊙10am-5.30pm Mon & Wed, 10am-6.15pm Tue & Thu, 10am-7.15pm Fri & Sat, noon-2.45pm Sun; ☏) and a cinema. Opposite, historic **Drumlanrig's Tower**, once a major seat of the Douglas clan, now houses the **Borders Textile Towerhouse** (⊙10am-4.30pm Mon-Sat, noon-3pm Sun Apr-Oct, 10am-4pm Mon & Wed-Sat Nov-Mar). This tells the story of the town's knitwear-producing history. Behind the tourist office, the **Heritage Hub** (☑01450-360699; ⊙9.30am-12.45pm & 1.15-4.45pm Mon, Wed & Fri, to 7pm Tue & Thu, 10am-2pm Sat) is a state-of-the-art facility open to anyone wishing to trace their Scottish heritage or explore other local archives.

Hawick Museum & Art Gallery
MUSEUM, GALLERY

(☑01450-373457; Wilton Lodge Park; ⊙10am-noon & 1-5pm Mon-Fri, 2-5pm Sat & Sun Apr-Sep, noon-3pm Mon-Fri, 1-3pm Sun Oct-Mar) **FREE** Across the river, this museum has an interesting collection of mostly 19th-century manufacturing and domestic memorabilia as well as details on a tragic pair of local motorcycling legends. There are usually a couple of temporary exhibitions on as well.

⌖ Sleeping & Eating

Bank Guest House
B&B ££

(☑01450-363760; www.thebankno12highst.com; 12 High St; d £65-75; P ☏) This posh boutique B&B in the centre of Hawick brings out the best in this solid 19th-century building with modish wallpapers and designer furniture and fabrics. Modern comforts like iPod docks and fully-functioning wi-fi, as well as numerous thoughtful extras, make this a great place to stay.

Damascus Drum
CAFE £

(www.damascusdrum.co.uk; 2 Silver St; light meals £4-8; ⊙10am-5pm Mon-Sat; ☏☝) The Middle East meets the Borders in this enticing cafe behind the tourist office. Patterned rugs and a secondhand bookshop make for a relaxing environment to enjoy breakfasts, bagels, burgers, and tasty Turkish-style meze options.

Sergio's
ITALIAN ££

(www.sergiosofhawick.co.uk; Sandbed; pizza & pasta £6-10, mains £16-18; ⊙noon-2.30pm & 6-10pm Tue-Sun) This well-established Italian restaurant near the river is a fine choice for pizza and pasta dishes or elaborate, if a little overpriced, mains. Go for the blackboard specials, which always include beautifully prepared fish dishes.

❶ Getting Around

Half-hourly First buses 95 and X95 connect Hawick with Galashiels, Selkirk and Edinburgh (£7.20, two hours).

Jedburgh

POP 4000

Attractive Jedburgh, where many old buildings and wynds (narrow alleys) have been intelligently restored, invites exploration by foot. It's centred on the noble skeleton of its ruined abbey.

WORTH A TRIP

HERMITAGE CASTLE

The 'guardhouse of the bloodiest valley in Britain', **Hermitage Castle** (HS; www.historic-scotland.gov.uk; adult/child £4.50/2.70; ⏲ 9.30am-5.30pm Apr-Sep) embodies the brutal history of the Scottish Borders. Desolate but proud with its massive squared stone walls, it looks more like a lair for orc raiding parties than a home for Scottish nobility, and is one of the bleakest and most stirring of Scottish ruins.

Strategically crucial, the castle was the scene of many a dark deed and dirty deal with the English invaders, all of which rebounded heavily on the perfidious Scottish lord in question. Here, in 1338, Sir William Douglas imprisoned his enemy Sir Alexander Ramsay and deliberately starved him to death. Ramsay survived for 17 days by eating grain that trickled into his pit (which can still be seen) from the granary above. In 1566, Mary, Queen of Scots famously visited the wounded tenant of the castle, Lord Bothwell, here. Fortified, he recovered to (probably) murder her husband, marry her himself, then abandon her months later and flee into exile.

The castle is about 12 miles south of Hawick on the B6357.

⊙ Sights

★ **Jedburgh Abbey**　　　RUIN
(HS; www.historic-scotland.gov.uk; Abbey Rd; adult/child £5.50/3.30; ⏲ 9.30am-5.30pm Apr-Sep, to 4.30pm Oct-Mar) Dominating the town skyline, this was the first of the great Border abbeys to be passed into state care, and it shows – audio and visual presentations telling the abbey's story are scattered throughout the carefully preserved ruins (good for the kids). The red-sandstone ruins are roofless but relatively intact, and the ingenuity of the master mason can be seen in some of the rich (if somewhat faded) stone carvings in the nave. The abbey was founded in 1138 by David I as a priory for Augustinian canons.

Mary, Queen of
Scots House　　　HISTORIC BUILDING
(Queen St; ⏲ 9.30am-4.30pm Mon-Sat, 10.30am-4pm Sun early Mar-Nov) **FREE** Mary stayed at this beautiful 16th-century tower house in 1566 after her famous ride to visit the injured earl of Bothwell, her future husband, at Hermitage Castle. The interesting exhibition evokes the sad saga of Mary's life and death. Various objects associated with her – including a lock of her hair – are on display.

🏃 Activities

The tourist office has handy booklets for walks around the town, including sections of the Southern Upland Way (p150) or Borders Abbeys Way (p150).

🎊 Festivals & Events

Jethart Callant's Festival　　　CULTURAL
(www.jethartcallantsfestival.com) For two weeks from late June, this cavalcade recalls the perilous time when people rode out on horseback checking for English incursions.

🛏 Sleeping

Maplebank　　　B&B £
(☏ 01835-862051; maplebank3@btinternet.com; 3 Smiths Wynd; s/d £30/50; ℗ 🐾) It's very pleasing to come across places like this, where it really feels like you're staying in someone's home. In this case, that someone is a bit like your favourite aunt: friendly, chaotic and generous. There's lots of clutter and it's very informal. The rooms are comfortable and large, and share a good bathroom. Breakfast (particularly if you like fruit, yoghurts, homemade jams and a selection of everything) is much better than you get at most posher places.

Willow Court　　　B&B ££
(☏ 01835-863702; www.willowcourtjedburgh. co.uk; The Friars; d £80-86; ℗ 🛜) It seems inadequate to call this impressive option a B&B; it's more like a boutique hotel. Three impeccable rooms with elegant wallpaper, showroom bathrooms and great beds are complemented by a courteous professional welcome. Breakfast can include a grapefruit medley or smoked salmon, and you could spend hours in the conservatory lounge admiring the views over the garden and town.

Glenbank House Hotel　　　HOTEL ££
(☏ 01835-862258; www.jedburgh-hotel.com; Castlegate; s/d/superior d £55/75/90; ℗ 🛜) This lovely old building has modern, comfortable rooms – some of which are rather compact – shiny modern bathrooms and nice views over the town and hills. It's a likeable place, with a bar and decent food, as well as a

very friendly owner who is great value for a breakfast-time chat.

Eating

Clock Tower
BISTRO ££

(☑ 01835-869788; www.clocktowerbistro.co.uk; Abbey Pl; mains £9-15; ⊙ 10am-4pm & 6-9pm Tue-Sat; ☞) Opposite the skeleton of the abbey, this place will put meat on your bones with its eclectic menu of upmarket bistro fare, drizzling truffle oil or Rioja jus over ingredients like tuna steaks, duck confit or west coast scallops. Prices are good for this level of food, though some of the flavours could be more adventurous.

Carters Rest
PUB ££

(Abbey Pl; mains £9-12; ⊙ 10am-8pm; ☞) Right opposite the abbey, here you'll find upmarket pub grub in an attractive lounge bar. The standard fare is fleshed out with an evening dinner menu featuring local lamb and other goodies. Portions are generous and served with a smile.

❶ Information

There's a free wi-fi zone around the centre, strongest around the tourist office.

Jedburgh Library (www.scotborders.gov.uk; Castlegate; ⊙ 10am-1pm & 2-5pm Mon & Thu, 2-7pm Tue, 10am-3pm Fri, 9.30am-12.30pm Sat) Free internet.

Jedburgh Tourist Office (☑ 01835-863170; jedburgh@visitscotland.com; Murray's Green; ⊙ 9.15am-5pm Mon-Sat, 10am-4pm Sun Apr-Oct, 10am-4pm Mon-Sat Nov-Mar; ☞) Head tourist office for the Borders region. Very helpful.

❶ Getting There & Away

Jedburgh has good bus connections to Hawick, Melrose and Kelso (all around 25 minutes, roughly hourly, two-hourly on Sunday). Buses also run to Edinburgh (£7.20, two hours, hourly Monday to Saturday, five Sunday).

Kelso

POP 5600

Kelso, a prosperous market town with a broad, cobbled square flanked by Georgian buildings, has a cheery feel and historic appeal. During the day it's a busy little place, but after 8pm you'll have the streets to yourself. The town has a lovely site at the junction of the Tweed and Teviot, and is one of the most enjoyable places in the Borders.

◉ Sights

Floors Castle
CASTLE

(www.floorscastle.com; adult/child £8.50/4.50; ⊙ 10.30am-5pm mid-Apr–mid-Oct) Grandiose Floors Castle is Scotland's largest inhabited mansion, home to the Duke of Roxburghe, and overlooks the Tweed about a mile west of Kelso. Built by William Adam in the 1720s, the original Georgian simplicity was 'improved' in the 1840s with the addition of rather ridiculous battlements and turrets. Inside, view the vivid colours of the 17th-century Brussels tapestries in the drawing room and the intricate oak carvings in the ornate ballroom.

Kelso Abbey
RUIN

(HS; www.historic-scotland.gov.uk; Bridge St; ⊙ 9.30am-6.30pm Apr-Sep, 9.30am-4.30pm Sat-Wed Oct-Mar) **FREE** Once one of the richest abbeys in southern Scotland, Kelso Abbey was built by the Tironensians, an order founded in Picardy and brought to the Borders around 1113 by David I. English raids in the 16th century reduced it to ruins, though what little remains today is some of the finest surviving Romanesque architecture in Scotland.

⚑ Activities

The Kelso–Jedburgh section (12 miles) of the Borders Abbeys Way (p150) is a fairly easy walk, largely following the River Teviot. The tourist office has a free leaflet with map and route description.

For a shorter ramble, leave the Square by Roxburgh St and take the signposted alley to **Cobby Riverside Walk**, a pleasant stroll along the river to Floors Castle (rejoin Roxburgh St to gain admission to the castle).

🛏 Sleeping

Central Guest House
B&B £

(☑ 01890-883664; www.thecentralguesthouse-kelso.co.uk; s/d/f £35/50/90; ☞) A bargain in sometimes pricey Kelso and just on the central square. The owners live off-site, so call ahead first. The rooms are fine: spacious, with firm beds, carpets and good bathrooms. Rates are room-only, but you get a fridge, toaster and microwave so you can create your own breakfast.

★ Old Priory
B&B ££

(☑ 01573-223030; www.theoldpriorykelso.com; 33 Woodmarket St; s/d £55/85; P ☞) Fantastic rooms here are allied with numerous personal details – they turn down the beds at night and make you feel very welcome. Doubles are top-notch and the family room has to be seen to be believed. The good news extends to the garden – perfect for a coffee in the morning – and a comfortable sitting room and conservatory lounge. The huge windows flood the rooms with natural light.

★ **Edenbank House** B&B ££

(☎01573-226734; www.edenbank.co.uk; Stichill Rd; s/d £45/80; P🖥) Half a mile down the road to Stichill, this grand Victorian house sits in spacious grounds where only the bleating of lambs in the green fields and birds in the garden break the silence. It's a fabulous place, with huge opulent rooms, lovely views over the fields, and incredibly warm, generous hospitality. Breakfast features homemade produce, and a laissez-faire attitude makes for an utterly relaxing stay. Don't just show up: call ahead.

Ednam House Hotel HOTEL £££

(☎01573-224168; www.ednamhouse.com; Bridge St; P🖥📺) The genteel, Georgian Ednam House, touched with a quiet dignity, contains many of its original features, with fine gardens overlooking the river. We've not included prices, for at time of writing a new owner planned to gradually convert it into a luxury country-house hotel, keeping it open all the while. During salmon season, from the end of August until November, the hotel is very busy. Some of the rooms have lovely river views.

✗ Eating & Drinking

★ **Cobbles** PUB FOOD ££

(☎01573-223548; www.thecobblesinn.co.uk; 7 Bowmont St; mains £10-17; ⊙noon-2.30pm & 5.45-9pm; 🖥) We've included the phone number for a reason: this inn off the main square is so popular you will need to book a table at weekends. It's cheery, very welcoming, warm, and serves excellent upmarket pub food in generous portions. Pick and mix from bar menu, blackboard specials and upmarket options. Leave room for cheese and/or dessert. The bar's own microbrewed ales are really excellent. A cracking place.

Oscar's BISTRO ££

(☎01573-224008; www.oscars-kelso.com; 33 Horsemarket; mains £10-17; ⊙6-9.30pm Mon & Wed-Sat; 🖥📺) Posh comfort food and the work of local artists sit side by side in this likeable bar-restaurant-gallery in the centre of town. A list of excellent daily specials complements the more standard permanent selection. A wide choice of wines is availa-

---

WALKING & CYCLING IN SOUTHERN SCOTLAND

Walking

The region's most famous walk is challenging 212-mile **Southern Upland Way** (www.southernuplandway.gov.uk). If you want a sample, one of the best bits is the three- to four-day section from Dalry to Beattock. Another long-distance walk is 62-mile **St Cuthbert's Way** (www.stcuthbertsway.info), inspired by the travels of St Cuthbert, a 7th-century saint who lived at the first Melrose monastery. It crosses some superb scenery between Melrose and Lindisfarne (in England). In Galloway, the **Pilgrims Way** follows a 25-mile trail from Glenluce Abbey to the Isle of Whithorn.

The **Borders Abbeys Way** (www.bordersabbeysway.com) links all the great Border abbeys in a 65-mile circuit. For shorter walks and especially circular loops in the hills, the towns of Melrose, Jedburgh and Kelso all make ideal bases. For baggage transfer on these walks, contact **Walking Support** (☎01896-822079; www.walkingsupport.co.uk). In early September look out for the **Scottish Borders Walking Festival** (www.borders walking.com), with a week of walks for all abilities and an instant social scene.

Cycling

With the exception of the main A-roads, traffic is sparse, which, along with the beauty of the countryside, makes this ideal cycling country. The **Tweed Cycle Route** is 95 waymarked miles along the beautiful Tweed Valley, following minor roads from Biggar to Peebles (22 miles), Melrose (25 miles), Coldstream (28 miles) and Berwick-upon-Tweed (19 miles). The **4 Abbeys Cycle Route** is a 55-mile circuit of the Border abbeys. Local tourist offices have route maps; these and other routes are also detailed at www.cycle scottishborders.com.

ble, and you can browse the exhibition space downstairs while you wait for your meal.

❶ Information

Kelso Library (Bowmont St; ⊘10am-5pm Mon & Thu, 1-7pm Tue, 10am-2pm Wed, 10am-4pm Fri, 9.30am-12.30pm Sat; 🛜 🖥) Free internet access.

Kelso Tourist Office (📞01573-228055; www. visitscottishborders.com; The Square; ⊘10am-4pm Mon-Sat Apr-Oct, to 5pm Jul & Aug plus 10am-2pm Sun Jul & Aug)

❶ Getting There & Away

There are frequent services to Edinburgh (£7.20, two hours), other Borders towns and Berwick-upon-Tweed.

Around Kelso

The area around Kelso has two starkly contrasting historic buildings to visit, and the twin walkers' villages of Town and Kirk Yetholm.

◉ Sights

Smailholm Tower   TOWER
(HS; www.historic-scotland.gov.uk; adult/child £4.50/2.70; ⊘9.30am-5.30pm Apr-Sep) Perched on a rocky knoll above a small lake, this narrow stone tower provides one of the most evocative sights in the Borders and keeps its bloody history alive. Although displays inside are sparse, the panoramic view from the top is worth the climb. The tower is 6 miles west of Kelso, a mile south of Smailholm village on the B6397. First bus 66 between Kelso and Galashiels stops in Smailholm village.

The nearby privately owned farm, **Sandyknowe**, was owned by Sir Walter Scott's grandfather. As Scott himself recognised, his imagination was fired by the ballads and stories he heard as a child at Sandyknowe, and by the ruined tower a stone's throw away.

Mellerstain House   HISTORIC BUILDING
(www.mellerstain.com; adult/child £8.50/4; ⊘12.30-5pm Fri-Mon Easter & May-Sep) Finished in 1778, this is considered to be Scotland's finest Robert Adam–designed mansion. It is famous for its classic elegance, ornate interiors and plaster ceilings; the library in particular is outstanding. The upstairs bedrooms are less attractive, but have a peek at the bizarre puppet-and-doll collection in the gallery.

It's about 6 miles northwest of Kelso, near Gordon. First bus 66 between Kelso and Galashiels passes about a mile from Mellerstain House.

Town Yetholm & Kirk Yetholm

The twin villages of Town Yetholm and Kirk Yetholm, separated by Bowmont Water, are close to the English border, about 6 miles southeast of Kelso. Hill-walking centres, they lie at the northern end of the **Pennine Way** and on St Cuthbert's Way. There are several places to stay, including the excellent **Border Hotel** (📞01573-420237; www.theborderhotel.com; The Green, Kirk Yetholm; s £50-60, d £80-100; 🅿🛜🐾), the bar of which is welcome after a long trek, and **Friends of Nature House** (📞01573-420234; www.thefriendsofnature.org.uk; Kirk Yetholm; dm/tw £19/42; ⊘mid-Mar–early Nov; 🅿🛜) 🐾, a compact but sociable walkers' hostel.

Bus 81 from Kelso runs up to seven times a day Monday to Saturday.

Coldstream

POP 1900
On a sweeping bend of the River Tweed, which forms the border with England, Coldstream is small and relatively hidden from the well-trodden Borders tourist beat.

◉ Sights

Coldstream Museum   MUSEUM
(12 Market Sq; ⊘10am-4pm Mon-Sat, 2-4pm Sun Apr-Sep, 1-4pm Mon-Sat Oct) **FREE** The proud history of the Coldstream Guards is covered here. Formed as part of Oliver Cromwell's New Model Army in 1650, the guards played a significant part in the restoration of the monarchy in 1660 and saw service at Waterloo, in Crimea, in the Boer War, at the Somme and Ypres in WWI, and at Dunkirk and Tobruk in WWII. It remains the oldest regiment in continuous existence in the British army.

Walk This Way   MUSEUM
(www.walkthisway.co.uk; 80 High St; ⊘9.30am-5pm Tue-Fri, to 12.30pm Sat) Pop into this army-surplus store on the main road to see the small but atmospheric basement collection of WWII memorabilia.

🛏 Sleeping & Eating

Calico House   B&B **££**
(☑0845-873 3100; www.bedandbreakfast-luxury.
co.uk; 44 High St; d/ste £75/110; P 🐨) Set above
a high-quality interior-design shop, this is a
superb option with sumptuous rooms blessed with great views and attention to detail;
expect lovely fabrics and furnishings. Privacy from your hosts and value for money are
two very strong points in this classy accommodation option. There's also an apartment,
which can be self-catering or B&B. They prefer stays of more than one night.

Eastbraes B&B   B&B **££**
(☑01890-883949; www.eastbraes.co.uk; 100c
High St; d £45/70) Trundling down the main
street in Coldstream, you simply don't expect the view you get out the back of this
welcoming place; an idyllic vista over a
grassy garden and a picture-book bend in
the Tweed beyond with good birdwatching
opportunities. A double and twin share a
bathroom and there's one en suite double,
which is simply enormous and comes with a
separate sitting area.

❶ Getting There & Away

Coldstream is on the busy A697 linking Newcas-
tle with Edinburgh. There are nine buses daily
Monday to Saturday (four on Sunday) between
Kelso (20 minutes) and Berwick-upon-Tweed (20
to 40 minutes) via here.

Eyemouth

POP 3500

Eyemouth is a busy fishing port and popular
domestic holiday destination. The harbour
itself is very atmospheric – you may even
spot seals frolicking in the water, as well as
tourists frolicking around the boats, snapping pics of old fishing nets accompanied by
the cry of seagulls.

The community here suffered its greatest
catastrophe in October 1881, when a terrible
storm destroyed the coastal fishing fleet,
killing 189 fishermen, 129 of whom were locals. Peter Aitchison's *Black Friday* is a good
book about the disaster.

◉ Sights

Eyemouth Maritime Centre   MUSEUM
(www.worldofboats.org; Harbour Rd; adult/child
£3/2; ⊙10am-5pm Apr-Nov) Situated right on
Eyemouth's working fishing harbour, what
was once the fish market has been decked

out to resemble an 18th-century man o' war.
A changing yearly exhibition occupies most
of the interior, drawing on the museum's
large collection of well-loved wooden coastal craft. The friendly museum guides are
happy to provide extra information

Gunsgreen House   MUSEUM
(www.gunsgreenhouse.org; adult/child £6/3.50;
⊙11am-5pm Thu-Mon Apr-Oct) Standing proud
and four-square across the harbour, this elegant 18th-century John Adam mansion was
built on the profits of smuggling: Eyemouth
was an important landing point for illegal
cargoes from northern Europe and the Baltic. The house has been beautifully restored
to reflect this and other aspects of its varied past. Both the house and the adjacent
tower-like dovecote can be hired out as self-
catering accommodation.

Eyemouth Museum   MUSEUM
(www.eyemouthmuseum.org; Manse Rd; adult/
child £3.50/free; ⊙10am-4pm Tue-Sat, noon-4pm
Sun Apr-Oct) Has intriguing local history displays, particularly relating to the town's fishing heritage. Its centrepiece is the tapestry
commemorating the 1881 fishing disaster.

🛏 Sleeping & Eating

★**Churches Hotel**   HOTEL **££**
(☑01890-750401; www.churcheshotel.com; Albert
Rd; s £75-85, d £95-120; ⊙Easter-Oct; P 🐨) This
is a very stylish place in an 18th-century
building, with rooms exuding a cool and
classic demeanour. Each room has a different theme but No 4, with its four-poster bed,
and No 6, with huge windows overlooking
the harbour, are our favourites. Little conveniences like bottled water, a DVD library
and iPod docks are complemented by excellent personal service from the owners. The
restaurant is likely to be only open to guests
in future: expect delicious fresh seafood.

Bantry   B&B **££**
(Mackays; ☑01890-751900; www.mackay-
sofeyemouth.co.uk; 20 High St; s without bathroom
£35, d with/without bathroom £75/65; P 🐨)
Plonked on top of the restaurant of the same
name on the main drag, this B&B has redec-
orated and refurbished rooms with muted
tones and a luxurious, modern feel and is
positioned right on the waterfront. Try to get
room No 3 if you're after a double, as it's the
only one with sea views. There's a fabulous
deck with loungers and a summer hot tub,

PAXTON HOUSE

Five miles west of Berwick along the B6461, **Paxton House** (www.paxton-house.com; adult/child £7.60/free; ⊙10am-5pm Easter-Oct, grounds 10am-sunset) is beside the River Tweed and surrounded by parkland and gardens. It was built in 1758 by Patrick Home for his intended wife, the daughter of Prussia's Frederick the Great. Unfortunately, she stood him up, but it was her loss; designed by the Adam family – brothers John, James and Robert – Paxton House is acknowledged as one of the finest 18th-century Palladian houses in Britain. It contains a large collection of Chippendale and Regency furniture, and houses paintings from the national galleries of Scotland. The nursery is a feature designed to provide insight into an 18th-century child's life. In the grounds are walking trails, an adventure playground, a campsite and a riverside museum on salmon fishing. There's plenty to keep the kids entertained here.

overlooking the lapping waves. No-breakfast rates available too.

Oblò   BISTRO ££
(www.oblobar.com; 20 Harbour St; mains £8-14; ⊙food 10am-8pm Mon & Tue, to 9pm Wed-Sat, to 7pm Sun; 🛜🌱) For a meal pretty much anytime, find your way upstairs to this modern Mediterranean-fusion bar-bistro with comfy seating and a modish interior. It's just down from the tourist office, and it's got a great deck to lap up the sunshine. Try the local seafood.

ℹ Information

Eyemouth Tourist Office (☎018907 50678; www.visiteyemouth.com; Manse Rd; ⊙10am-4pm Tue-Sat, noon-4pm Sun Apr-Oct) Very helpful; inside Eyemouth Museum near the harbour.

ℹ Getting There & Away

Eyemouth is 5 miles north of the Scotland–England border. Buses go to Berwick-up-on-Tweed (£2.90, 15 minutes, frequent), which has a train station, and to Edinburgh (£10.50, 1¾ hours, seven daily Monday to Saturday, three Sunday).

Coldingham & St Abbs

This picturesque area is fantastic for those who love the great outdoors. There's some of the UK's best diving here, as well as great cycling, walking, angling, and birdwatching. From the village of Coldingham, with its twisting streets, take the B6438 downhill to the small fishing village of St Abbs, a gorgeous, peaceful little community with a picture-perfect harbour below the cliffs.

◉ Sights & Activities

St Abbs Visitor Centre   MUSEUM
(www.stabbsvisitorcentre.co.uk; ⊙10am-5pm daily Apr-Oct, 11am-4pm Fri-Sun Nov) **FREE** This modern exhibition in St Abbs has interesting interactive displays on the often-stormy history of this harbour village. Spoken reminiscences from locals like a fisherman and lighthouse keeper are the highlight.

**St Abb's Head National
Nature Reserve**   NATURE RESERVE
(www.nts.org.uk) North of St Abbs, this 78-hectare reserve is an ornithologist's wonderland, with large colonies of guillemots, kittiwakes, herring gulls, fulmars, razorbills and some puffins. You get to the reserve by following the 2-mile circular trail that begins beside the Northfield Farm car park (£2) on the road just west of St Abbs. The clifftop walks here are spectacular, especially on sunny days. There's a good little **nature exhibition** (⊙11am-4pm Apr-Oct) **FREE** in the Old Smiddy complex alongside.

Coldingham Bay   BEACH, SURFING
In Coldingham, a signposted turn-off to the east leads just under a mile down to away-from-it-all Coldingham Bay, which has a sandy beach and a clifftop walking trail to Eyemouth (3 miles). At **St Vedas Surf Shop** (☎018907-71679; www.stvedas.co.uk; ⊙9am-dusk) you can hire surfboards (£11 per hour), sea kayaks and snorkelling gear; there's a hotel here that serves cheap food. Surfing lessons (£35) are also available.

Diving

The clear clean waters around St Abbs form part of the **St Abbs & Eyemouth Voluntary Marine Reserve** (☎018907-71443; www.marine-reserve.co.uk), one of the best cold-water diving sites in Europe. The reserve is home to a variety of marine life, including grey seals, porpoises, and wolf-fish. Visibility is about 7m to 8m but has been recorded at

24m. Beds of brown kelp form a hypnotically undulating forest on the seabed.

Four dive boats operate out of St Abbs, run by **Paul Crowe** (☎01890-771945, 07710-961050; www.divestabbs.info), **Paul O'Callaghan** (☎07780-980179, 018907-71525; www.stabbsdiving.com), **Graeme Crowe** (☎018907-71766, 07803-608050; www.stingrayboatcharters.co.uk) and **Peter Gibson** (☎018907-71681; www.stabbs.org/selkie.html). You can charter them whole, or phone to book a spot on a boat; these cost around £35 per person for two dives.

To hire diving equipment and for tips on the best dive sites, drop by the excellent **Scoutscroft** (☎01890-771338; www.scoutscroft.co.uk) dive shop in Coldingham on the road to St Abbs. You can also hire equipment here and organise a boat dive. This professional set-up can kit you up with nitrox tanks and do a full range of IANTD courses. The St Abbs Visitor Centre can also provide diving advice. A guide to local dive sites costs £7.50.

🛏 Sleeping

Rock House   HOSTEL, B&B **££**
(☎01890-771945; www.divestabbs.com; dm/s/d £22/32/64) Right by the harbour in St Abbs, this is run by a friendly dive skipper; you can almost roll out of bed onto the boat. There's a bunkhouse which is normally booked up by groups at the weekend, and a sweet B&B room that can sleep up to three. There's also a self-catering cottage.

❶ Getting There & Away

Bus 253 (seven daily Monday to Saturday, three Sunday) between Edinburgh (£10.50) and Berwick-upon-Tweed (£3.70) stops in Coldingham (some go to St Abbs on request). Bus 235 runs at least hourly to both from Eyemouth (£2.10).

SOUTH LANARKSHIRE

South Lanarkshire combines a highly urbanised area south of Glasgow with scenically gorgeous country around the Falls of Clyde and the World Heritage–listed area of New Lanark, by far the biggest drawcard of the region.

Lanark & New Lanark

POP 8900

Below the market town of Lanark, in an attractive gorge by the River Clyde, is the World Heritage Site of New Lanark – an intriguing collection of restored mill buildings and warehouses.

Once Britain's largest cotton-spinning complex, it is better known for the pioneering social experiments of Robert Owen, who managed the mill from 1800. New Lanark is really a memorial to this enlightened capitalist. He provided his workers with housing, a cooperative store (the inspiration for the modern cooperative movement), the world's first nursery school, adult-education classes, a sick-pay fund for workers and a social centre he called the New Institute for the Formation of Character. You'll need at least half a day to explore this site, as there's plenty to see, and appealing walks along the riverside. What must once have been a thriving, noisy, industrial village, pumping out enough cotton to wrap the planet, is now a peaceful oasis with only the swishing of trees and the rushing of the River Clyde to be heard.

◉ Sights & Activities

★**New Lanark Visitor Centre**   MUSEUM
(www.newlanark.org; adult/child/family £8.50/6/25; ◷10am-5pm Apr-Oct, to 4pm Nov-Mar) The main attractions of this World Heritage mill town are accessed via a single ticket. These include a huge working spinning mule, producing woollen yarn, and the **Historic Schoolhouse**, which contains an innovative, high-tech journey to New Lanark's past via a 3D hologram of the spirit of Annie McLeod, a 10-year-old mill girl who describes life here in 1820. The kids will love it as it's very realistic, although the 'do good for all mankind' theme is a little overbearing.

Included in your admission is entrance to a millworker's house, Robert Owen's home and exhibitions on 'saving New Lanark'. There's also a 1920s-style village store.

Falls of Clyde Wildlife Centre   NATURE DISPLAY
(www.scottishwildlifetrust.co.uk; New Lanark; adult/child £3/1; ◷10am-4pm) The wildlife centre is by the river in New Lanark and features child-friendly displays focused on badgers, bats, peregrine falcons and other prominent species. In season (April to July), there's a live video feed of peregrines nesting nearby. Entry is a pound cheaper if you buy it together with the New Lanark Visitor Centre entrance. The centre also organises various activities in summer, including badger-watching.

From the centre, you can walk through the beautiful nature reserve up to Corra Linn (¾ mile, 30 minutes) and Bonnington Linn (1½ miles, one hour), two of the Falls of Clyde that inspired Turner and Wordsworth. You could return via the muddier path on the opposite bank, pass New Lanark, and cross the river a little further downstream to make a circular walk of it (3 miles, three hours).

Craignethan Castle
CASTLE

(HS; www.historic-scotland.gov.uk; adult/child £4.50/2.70; ☉9.30am-5.30pm Apr-Sep) With a commanding position in a stunning, tranquil spot above the River Nethan, this extensive ruin includes a virtually intact tower house and a caponier – a small gun emplacement. The chilly chambers under the tower house are eerie. You'll feel miles from anywhere, so bring a picnic and make a day of it.

Craignethan is 5 miles northwest of Lanark. Without a car, take an hourly Lanark–Hamilton bus to Crossford, then follow the footpath along the northern bank of the River Nethan (20 minutes).

🛏 Sleeping & Eating

New Lanark makes a very relaxing, attractive place to stay.

New Lanark SYHA
HOSTEL £

(☎01555-666710; www.syha.org.uk; dm/tw £17/45; ☉mid-Mar–mid-Oct; P@🛜) This hostel has a great location in an old mill building by the River Clyde, in the heart of the New Lanark complex. It has comfortable en suite dormitories and a really good downstairs common area. It does breakfasts and dinners and will also make a packed lunch. Closed between 10am and 4pm.

New Lanark Mill Hotel
HOTEL ££

(☎01555-667200; www.newlanarkmillhotel.co.uk; r £99-119; P@🛜🐾🐾) Cleverly converted from an 18th-century mill, this hotel is full of character and is a stone's throw from the major attractions. It has luxury rooms (only a little extra for a spacious superior room), with contemporary art on the walls and views of the churning Clyde below, as well as self-catering accommodation in charming cottages (£89 to £109). There are good facilities for the disabled here. The hotel also serves good meals (bar meals £5 to £11, restaurant mains £14 to £16).

La Vigna
ITALIAN ££

(☎01555-664320; www.lavigna.co.uk; 40 Wellgate; 3-course lunch/dinner £14/24; ☉noon-2.30pm & 5-10pm Mon-Sat, noon-3pm & 5-9.30pm Sun) This well-established local favourite is a great spot, seemingly plucked from some bygone age with its quietly efficient service and, charmingly, a separate menu for ladies – without prices. The food is distinctly Italian, albeit using Scottish venison, beef and fish, and there are also vegetarian options. The set-price meals are great value.

ℹ Information

Lanark Tourist Office (☎01555-661661; lanark@visitscotland.com; Ladyacre Rd; ☉10am-5pm) Close to the bus and train stations. Closed Sundays October to March.

ℹ Getting There & Around

Lanark is 25 miles southeast of Glasgow. Express bus 240X runs hourly Monday to Saturday (£6, one hour); trains from Glasgow Central also run (£6.60, 55 minutes, every 30 minutes, hourly on Sundays).

It's a pleasant walk to New Lanark, but there's also a half-hourly bus service from the train station (daily). If you need a taxi, call **Clydewide** (☎0800-050 9264; www.clydewidetaxis.co.uk).

Biggar
POP 2300

Biggar is an attractive town in a rural setting dominated by Tinto Hill (712m). On the high street, the new museum should become a very worthwhile attraction. Biggar is also known for the nationalist, leftist poet Hugh MacDiarmid, who lived near here for nearly 30 years until his death in 1978.

◉ Sights & Activities

Museum of Biggar and Upper Clydesdale
MUSEUM

(www.biggarmuseumtrust.co.uk; High St) This new museum, opening in 2015, has been a major community project and incorporates the contents of several smaller museums that were dotted around the town. A highlight is Gladstone Court, a reconstructed street with historic Victorian-era nook-and-cranny shops that you can pop into to steal a glimpse of the past. Other displays cover archaeology, geography and history of the area, with a good feature on the Covenanters.

Biggar Puppet Theatre
THEATRE

(☑ 01899-220631; www.purvespuppets.com; Broughton Rd; seats £8; ⊙ Easter-Sep) A well-loved local institution that runs matinee shows every couple of days throughout the summer using miniature Victorian puppets and bizarre glow-in-the-dark modern ones over 1m high. Different shows are suitable for varying age groups, so inquire before you take along the kids. Check the website for performance times.

Tinto Hill
HIKING

The hill dominates town. It is a straightforward ascent by the northern ridge from the car park, just off the A73 by Thankerton Crossroads. Look out for the Stone Age **fort** on your way up. Allow two hours for the return trip (4½ miles).

🛏 Sleeping & Eating

★ Cornhill House
HOTEL ££

(☑ 01899-220001; www.cornhillhousehotel.com; s/d/superior d £85/115/125; P 🛜) Just off the A72 a couple of miles west of Biggar, this is a fabulous country hotel in a striking chateau-style building that offers artistic, opulent decor with not a hint of tartan. There are nine rooms and they are huge, with loads of character and appealing furniture, like leather sofas or four-poster beds. There's also a good on-site restaurant (three-course meals £21).

Elmsleigh
B&B ££

(☑ 01899-229429; www.elmsleighguestlodge.co.uk; 11 Broughton Rd; s £74-79, d £84-89; P 🛜) 🌿 The purpose-built extension out the back of this typically Victorian house offers the modern comforts of a good hotel along with the personal touch of a top B&B. Hosts have the knack of being attentive – and the number of thoughtful details is impressive – and simultaneously allowing privacy. Breakfast is great. An excellent package.

Barony
BRITISH ££

(☑ 01899-221159; www.barony-biggar.co.uk; 55 High St; mains £13; ⊙ noon-2.30pm & 5-9pm Wed-Sat, noon-3pm & 5-8pm Sun; 🛜) A classier option than Biggar's decent pubs, this well-run restaurant features a handsome dining area with exposed stone, candlelight, posh glassware and inviting chairs. The short menu covers upmarket comfort food and a few more ambitious creations. There are good lunch specials. Book at weekends.

Elphinstone Hotel
PUB FOOD ££

(www.elphinstonehotel.co.uk; 145 High St; mains £8-16; ⊙ noon-2.30pm & 5-9pm, to 10pm Sat; 🛜) Attentive and cordial, this main-street pub has a long menu of everything from bar classics to Asian-influenced seafood dishes. Interesting daily specials add still more choice. Reliably decent.

ℹ Getting There & Away

Biggar is 33 miles southeast of Glasgow. There are hourly buses (four on Sunday) to/from Edinburgh (£4.40, 1¼ hours). For Glasgow, change at Lanark (30 minutes). Other buses run to Peebles.

AYRSHIRE

Ayrshire is synonymous with golf and Robert Burns – and there's plenty on offer here to satisfy both of these pursuits. Troon has six golf courses for starters, and there's enough Burns memorabilia in the region to satisfy even his most fanatical admirers.

The best way to appreciate the Ayrshire coastline is on foot: the **Ayrshire Coastal Path** (www.ayrshirecoastalpath.org) offers 100 miles of spectacular waterside walking.

North Ayrshire

Largs
POP 11,300

On a sunny day, there are few places in southern Scotland more beautiful than Largs, where green grass meets the sparkling water of the Firth of Clyde. It's a resort-style waterfront town that harks back to seaside days in times of gentler pleasures, and the minigolf, amusements, old-fashioned eateries and bouncy castle mean you should get into the spirit, buy an ice cream, and stroll around this slice of retro Scotland.

◉ Sights

Vikingar!
MUSEUM

(☑ 01475-689777; www.kaleisure.com; Greenock Rd; adult/child £4.50/3.50; ⊙ 10am-2.30pm Apr-Jun & Sep-Oct, 10.30am-3.30pm Mon-Fri & 11.30am-3.30pm Sat & Sun Jul-Aug, 11.30am-2.30pm Sat & Sun Feb & Nov, 11.30am-1.30pm Mar; 🚼) The town's main attraction is a multimedia exhibition describing Viking influence in Scotland until its demise at the Battle of Largs in

1263. It's got a slightly downbeat municipal feel these days but tours with staff in Viking outfits run every hour; ring ahead to check though. There's also a swimming pool and leisure centre. It's on the waterfront road just north of the centre. You can't miss it, as it's the only place with a longship outside.

☞ Tours

In summer the *Waverley*, the last ocean-going paddle steamer ever built, runs spectacular coastal voyages. There are several departures a week from Largs; book online (www.waverleyexcursions.co.uk) or at the information office.

✿ Festivals

Viking Festival   HISTORIC
(www.largsvikingfestival.com) During the first week of September, this festival celebrates the Battle of Largs and the end of Viking political domination in Scotland.

⨋ Sleeping & Eating

Brisbane House Hotel   HOTEL ££
(☑ 01475-687200; www.brisbanehousehotel.com; 14 Greenock Rd; s/d £70/105, with sea view d/ste £125/145; ℗ 🐾) We're not sure about the modern facade on this genteel old building, but the rooms are quite luxurious, and some – it's aimed at wedding parties and is always booked out at weekends – have Jacuzzis and huge beds. It's on the waterfront, so paying extra for a sea view will reward in fine weather, as the sun sets over Great Cumbrae opposite. There's a decent bar and restaurant downstairs and a comfortable contemporary feel.

Glendarroch   B&B ££
(☑ 01475-676305; www.glendarrochlargs.com; 24 Irvine Rd; s £40, d £60-70; ℗ 🐾) This B&B on the main road through town has warm and friendly owners who keep their prices fair and their lovely rooms very shipshape. All are en suite and the kingsize double is particularly desirable.

St Leonards Guest House   B&B ££
(☑ 01475-673318; www.stleonardsguesthouse.com; 9 Irvine Rd; s £35-68, d £60-75; ℗ 🐾) On the main road through town, but excellently soundproofed, this spot offers a cordial welcome and spotless, well-decorated rooms, some of which share a top-notch modern bathroom. Breakfast is a pleasure.

Lounge   BISTRO ££
(www.loungeatlargs.com; 33 Main St; mains £10-14; ☺ noon-3.30pm & 5-9.30pm Mon-Fri, noon-4pm & 5-9.30pm Sat & Sun; 🐾) Tucked away above the Royal Bank of Scotland on the main road, this stunningly attractive bar and bistro comes as quite a surprise. Eating is done in an elegant tearoom space, with hardwood floor, ceramic fireplace and leather seats. Service is willing, and there's a nice range of classic Scottish pub fare alongside tasty seafood and a few fusion dishes.

Nardini's   CAFE, BISTRO ££
(www.nardinis.co.uk; 2 Greenock Rd; mains £9-15; ☺ 9am-10pm; 🐾) Nothing typifies the old-time feel of Largs more than this giant art deco gelateria: these guys have been making the stuff for a century and a quarter. The ice creams are decadently delicious, with rich flavours that'll have parents licking more than their fair share from the kids'. There's also a cafe with outdoor seating, and a franchise restaurant which does decent pizzas, pastas, and some more elaborate fare like duck breast and sardines on toast.

ℹ Information

Largs & Millport Tourist Office (☑ 01475-676182; www.largsinformation.co.uk; 88 Main St; ☺ 10am-4pm Mon-Sat, 1-4pm Sun Apr-Oct, 11am-3pm Mon-Sat, 1-3pm Sun Nov-Mar) By the train station. Covers Great Cumbrae too. Volunteers opened this office when the official one closed due to cuts; pop in for a friendly chat.

ℹ Getting There & Away

Largs is 32 miles west of Glasgow by road. There are trains from Glasgow Central (£7.70, one hour, hourly). Buses run the route more slowly via Greenock and Gourock. Buses also run once or twice hourly to Ayr (1¼ hours) via Ardrossan and Irvine. You can also reach these by rail, some with a change at Kilwinning.

ℹ ARDROSSAN

An otherwise unremarkable coastal town, Ardrossan is the main ferry port for Arran. Trains leave Glasgow Central station (£7.20, 40 to 50 minutes, half-hourly) to connect with ferries. From May to September there are also services to Campbeltown on the Kintyre peninsula.

WORTH A TRIP

IRVINE

Boat lovers should check out the **Scottish Maritime Museum** (☑ 01294-278283; www.scottishmaritimemuseum.org; Gottries Rd; adult/child £7/free; ⊙ 10am-5pm Mar-Dec) by the train station in Irvine, which long ago was west Scotland's busiest port. In the massive **Linthouse Engine Shop** – an old hangar with a cast-iron framework – is an absorbing collection of boats and machinery. Displays cover ropeworking, the age of steam, and the Clyde's shipbuilding industry. Every boat here has a story, some tragic. Free guided tours take you down to the dock where you can clamber over various ships, and visitors can also see a shipyard worker's restored flat.

Further along the harbour road, make sure to drop into the wonderful **Ship Inn** (www.theshipinnirvine.co.uk; 120 Harbour St; mains £7-9; ⊙ noon-9pm Mon-Thu, noon-9.30pm Fri, noon-10pm Sat, 12.30-9pm Sun; 🛜). It's the oldest pub in Irvine (1597), serves tasty bar meals (noon to 9pm) and has bucketloads of character.

Irvine is 26 miles from Glasgow. There are frequent buses from Ayr (30 minutes) and Largs (45 minutes). Trains run to/from Glasgow Central station (£7, 35 minutes, half-hourly); the other way they go to Ayr (£3.90, 20 minutes, half-hourly).

Isle of Great Cumbrae

POP 1400

Walking or cycling is the best way to explore this accessible, hilly island (it's only 4 miles long), ideal for a day trip from Largs. **Millport** is the only town, strung out around the bay overlooking neighbouring Little Cumbrae. The town boasts Britain's smallest cathedral, the lovely **Cathedral of the Isles** (☑ 01475-530353; College St; ⊙ daylight hours). Inside it's quite ornate, with a lattice woodwork ceiling and fragments of early Christian carved stones.

The island's minor roads have well-marked walking and cycling routes. Take the **Inner Circle route** up to the island's highest point, **Glaid Stone**, where you get good views of Arran and Largs, and even as far as the Paps of Jura on a clear day. You can walk between

the ferry and the town via here in about an hour. There are several bike-hire places in Millport.

If you're staying overnight there are several choices. Try the unusual **College of the Holy Spirit** (☑ 01475-530353; www.island-retreats.org; College St; d £80, s/d without bathroom £40/70; 🅿 🛜), next to the cathedral; there's a refectory-style dining room and a library. **Dancing Midge** (www.thedancingmidge.com; 24 Glasgow St; light meals £3-8; ⊙ 9am-5pm Mon-Sat, 10am-5pm Sun; 🛜) is a cheerful seafront cafe providing healthy, tasty alternatives to the chippies in town.

A very frequent **CalMac ferry** (www.calmac.co.uk) links Largs with Great Cumbrae (passenger/car return £5.55/23.85; 15 minutes). Buses meet the ferries for the 3.5-mile journey to Millport.

East Ayrshire

Kilmarnock

In Kilmarnock, where Johnnie Walker whisky was blended from 1820 to 2012, is **Dean Castle** (☑ 01563-522702; www.deancastle.com; Dean Rd; ⊙ 11am-5pm daily Apr-Sep, 10am-4pm Wed-Sun Oct-Mar; 🛗) FREE, a 15-minute walk from the bus and train stations. The castle, restored in the first half of the 20th century, has a virtually windowless keep (dating from 1350) and an adjacent palace (1468) with a superb collection of medieval arms, armour, tapestries and musical instruments. The huge grounds are a good place for a stroll or a picnic, or you can eat at the visitor centre's tearoom. From Ayr there are frequent buses to Kilmarnock throughout the day.

South Ayrshire

Ayr

POP 46,800

Ayr's long sandy beach has made it a popular family seaside resort since Victorian times, but it has struggled in the recent economic climate. Parts of the centre have a neglected air, though there are many fine Georgian and Victorian buildings, and it makes a convenient base for this section of coast. The huge drawcard is Alloway, three miles south, with its Robert Burns heritage.

◎ Sights

The biggest draws are in Alloway just to the south. Most things to see in Ayr are also Robert Burns–related. The bard was baptised in the **Auld Kirk** (Old Church; ⏱1-2pm

Ayr

Tue Feb-Jun & Sep-Nov, 10.30am-12.30pm Sat Jul & Aug) off High St. The atmospheric cemetery here overlooks the river and is good for a stroll, offering an escape from the bustle of High St. Several of Burns' poems are set in Ayr; in 'Twa Brigs', Ayr's old and new bridges argue with one another. The **Auld Brig** (Old Bridge) was built in 1491 and spans the river just north of the church.

St John's Tower (Eglinton Tce) is the only remnant of a church where a parliament was held in 1315, the year after the celebrated victory at Bannockburn. John Knox's son-in-law was the minister here, and Mary, Queen of Scots, stayed overnight in 1563.

⭐ Festivals & Events

Burns an' a' That   CULTURAL
(www.burnsfestival.com) Held in Ayr in late May, this festival has a bit of everything, from wine tasting to horse racing to concerts, some of it Burns-related.

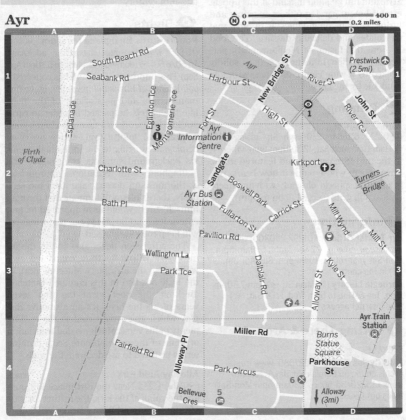

Ayr

SOUTHERN SCOTLAND SOUTH AYRSHIRE

🛏 Sleeping & Eating

Guesthouses and hotels are numerous, with several clustering along Miller Road.

Look out for the famous locally made Mancini's ice cream around town, often cited as Scotland's best.

★ 26 The Crescent B&B **££**
(☑ 01292-287329; www.26crescent.co.uk; 26 Bellevue Cres; s £53, d £75-97; 🛜) When the blossom's out, this is Ayr's prettiest street, with an excellent place to stay on it. The rooms are impeccable – an upgrade to the spacious four-poster room is a sound investment – but it's the warm welcome given by the hosts that makes this special. Numerous little extras, like iPod docks, Arran toiletries, bottled water, and silver cutlery at breakfast make this B&B at its best.

Beresford BISTRO **££**
(☑ 01292-280820; www.theberesfordayr.co.uk; 22 Beresford Tce; mains £10-13; ⊘ food 9am-9pm; 🛜) Style and fun go hand in hand at this upbeat establishment serving offbeat martinis and luring church-going ladies with artisanal chocolates and delicious desserts. The food is a creative fusion of Mediterranean, particularly Italian influences, and is solidly backed by a wide choice of wines, with lots available by the glass.

🍸 Drinking

Tam O'Shanter PUB
(☑ 01292 611684; 230 High St; mains £7-9; ⊘ 11am-11pm Mon-Sat, 12.30-11pm Sun) Opened in the mid-18th century and featured in the Burns poem whose name it now bears, this is an atmospheric old pub with mediocre typical pub grub (served noon to 9pm).

ℹ Information

Ayr Tourist Office (☑ 01292-290300; www.ayrshire-arran.com; 22 Sandgate; ⊘ 9am-5pm Mon-Sat year-round, 10am-5pm Sun Apr-Sep; 🖱) In the centre.

Carnegie Library (12 Main St; ⊘ 10am-7.30pm Mon, Tue & Thu, to 5pm Wed, Fri & Sat; 🛜) Free internet access.

ℹ Getting There & Around

BICYCLE
AMG Cycles (☑ 01292-287580; www.irvinecycles.co.uk; 55 Dalblair Rd; day/weekend/week £15/20/35-50; ⊘ 9.30am-5pm Mon-Sat) Hires out bikes.

BUS
Ayr is 33 miles from Glasgow and is Ayrshire's major transport hub. There are very frequent express services to Glasgow (£5.90, one hour) via Prestwick Airport, as well as services to Stranraer (£8.20, two hours, four to eight a day), other Ayrshire destinations, and Dumfries (£6.60, 2¼ hours, five to seven a day).

TRAIN
There are at least two trains an hour that run between Ayr and Glasgow Central station (£8, 50 minutes), and some trains continue south from Ayr to Stranraer (£10.50, 1½ hours).

Alloway

The pretty, lush village of Alloway (3 miles south of Ayr) should be on the itinerary of every Robert Burns fan – he was born here on 25 January 1759. Even if you haven't been seduced by Burnsmania, it's still well worth a visit, as the Burns-related exhibitions give a good impression of life in Ayrshire in the late 18th century.

⊙ Sights

Robert Burns Birthplace Museum MUSEUM
(NTS; www.burnsmuseum.org.uk; adult/child £8.50/6.50; ⊘ 10am-5pm Oct-Mar, to 5.30pm Apr-Sep) This impressive museum has collected a solid range of Burns memorabilia, including manuscripts and possessions of the poet, like the pistols he packed in order to carry out his daily work as a taxman. There's good biographical information, and a series of displays that bring to life individual poems via background snippets, translations and audiophones with recitations. Appropriately, the museum doesn't take itself too seriously: there's plenty of humour that the man himself surely would have approved of, and entertaining audio and visual performances will keep the kids amused.

The admission ticket also covers the atmospheric **Burns Cottage**, connected via a walkway to the Birthplace Museum. Born in the little box-bed in this cramped thatched dwelling, the poet spent the first seven years of his life here. It's an attractive display which gives you a context for reading plenty of his verse. Much-needed translation of some of the more obscure Scots farming terms he loved to use decorate the walls.

Alloway Auld Kirk CHURCH
(⊘ 24hr) FREE Near the Birthplace Museum are the ruins of the kirk, the setting for part of 'Tam o' Shanter'. Burns' father, William, is

THE SCOTTISH BARD

I see her in the dewy flowers,
I see her sweet and fair:
I hear her in the tunefu' birds,
I hear her charm the air:
There's not a bonnie flower that springs
By fountain, shaw, or green;
There's not a bonnie bird that sings,
But minds me o' my Jean.

Robert Burns, 'Of a' the Airts', 1788

Best remembered for penning the words of 'Auld Lang Syne', Robert Burns (1759–96) is Scotland's most famous poet and a popular hero; his birthday (25 January) is celebrated as Burns Night by Scots around the world.

Burns was born in 1759 in Alloway to a poor family, who scraped a living gardening and farming. At school he soon showed an aptitude for literature and a fondness for the folk song. He later began writing his own songs and satires. When the problems of his arduous farming life were compounded by the threat of prosecution from the father of Jean Armour, with whom he'd had an affair, he decided to emigrate to Jamaica. He gave up his share of the family farm and published his poems to raise money for the journey.

The poems were so well reviewed in Edinburgh that Burns decided to remain in Scotland and devote himself to writing. He went to Edinburgh in 1787 to publish a 2nd edition, but the financial rewards were not enough to live on and he had to take a job as an excise man in Dumfriesshire. Though he worked well, he wasn't a taxman by nature, and described his job as 'the execrable office of whip-person to the blood-hounds of justice'. He contributed many songs to collections, and a 3rd edition of his poems was published in 1793. A prodigious writer, Burns composed more than 28,000 lines of verse over 22 years. He died (probably of heart disease) in Dumfries in 1796, aged 37, having fathered more than a dozen children to several different women. Generous-spirited Jean bore nine of them and took in another, remarking 'Oor Robbie should hae had twa wives'.

Many of the local landmarks mentioned in the verse-tale 'Tam o' Shanter' can still be visited. Farmer Tam, riding home after a hard night's drinking in a pub in Ayr, sees witches dancing in Alloway churchyard. He calls out to the one pretty witch, but is pursued by them, and has to reach the other side of the River Doon to be safe. He just manages to cross the Brig o' Doon, but his mare loses her tail to the witches.

The Burns connection in southern Scotland is milked for all it's worth and tourist offices have a *Burns Heritage Trail* leaflet leading you to every place that can claim some link with the bard. Burns fans should have a look at www.robertburns.org.

buried in the kirkyard; read the poem on the back of the gravestone.

Burns Monument & Gardens GARDENS
The monument was built in 1823; the gardens afford a view of the 13th-century Brig o' Doon.

🛏 Sleeping

Brig O' Doon House HOTEL **££**
(☏ 01292-442466; www.brigodoonhouse.com; High Maybole Rd; s/d £85/120, 3-course dinner £25; ☏) On the main road right by the monument and bridge, a charming ivy-covered facade conceals this romantic, rather luxurious hotel, which will appeal greatly to Burns fans. The heavyish decor of plaid carpets is relieved by slate-floored bathrooms; rooms are spacious and very comfortable, and there's a decent restaurant, but the place is often booked up by wedding parties at weekends.

Across the road, there are further bedrooms in Doonbrae, blessed with a lovely garden, and a couple of cottages – Rose, traditionally decorated, and Gables, more contemporary.

ℹ Getting There & Away

Bus 361 runs hourly between Alloway and Ayr (7 minutes). Otherwise, walk or rent a bike and cycle here.

Troon

POP 14,800

Troon, a major sailing centre on the coast 7 miles north of Ayr, has excellent sandy beaches and six golf courses. The demanding championship Old Course at **Royal Troon** (☑ 01292-311555; www.royaltroon.com; Craigend Rd; ☺ mid-Apr–mid-Oct) is a classic of links golf. There are offers on its website; the standard green fee is £190, which includes a complimentary round at the Portland course. Troon hosts the Open in July 2016.

Four miles northeast, **Dundonald Castle** (HS; www.dundonaldcastle.org.uk; adult/child £4.50/2.70; ☺ 10am-5pm Apr-Oct) commands impressive views and, in its main hall, has one of the finest preserved barrel-vaulted ceilings in Scotland. It was the first home of the Stuart kings, built by Robert II in 1371, and reckoned to be the third most important castle in Scotland in its time, after Edinburgh and Stirling. The visitor centre below the castle has good information on prior settlements, and scale models of the castle and its predecessors. Buses running between Troon and Kilmarnock stop in Dundonald village.

 Getting There & Away

FERRY

P&O (☑ 08716 64 20 20; www.poferries.com) sails twice daily to Larne in Northern Ireland (around £28/96 per person/car; two hours) between late March and early September.

TRAIN

There are half-hourly trains to Ayr (£3.10, 10 minutes) and Glasgow (£7.40, 40 minutes).

Culzean Castle

The Scottish National Trust's flagship property, magnificent **Culzean Castle** (NTS; ☑ 01655-884400; www.culzeanexperience.org; castle adult/child/family £15.50/11.50/38; ☺ castle 10.30am-5pm Apr-Oct, last entry 4pm, park 9.30am-sunset year-round) (pronounced kull-*ane*) is one of the most impressive of Scotland's great stately homes. The entrance is an unusual viaduct, and on approach the castle appears like a mirage, floating into view. Designed by Robert Adam, who was encouraged to exercise his romantic genius, this 18th-century mansion is perched dramatically on the edge of the cliffs. Adam was the most influential architect of his time,

renowned for his meticulous attention to detail and the elegant classical embellishments with which he decorated his ceilings and fireplaces. The beautiful oval staircase here is regarded as one of his finest achievements. On the 1st floor, the opulence of the circular saloon contrasts violently with the views of the wild sea below. Lord Cassillis' bedroom is said to be haunted by a lady in green, mourning for a lost baby. Even the bathrooms are palatial.

There are also two ice houses, a swan pond, a pagoda, a re-creation of a Victorian vinery, an orangery, a deer park and an aviary. Wildlife in the area includes otters. It's worth dropping by the visitor centre first, to take in the background DVD; there are activities for kids here too.

If you really want to experience the magic of this place, it's possible to stay in the castle (☑ 01655-884455; culzean@nts.org.uk; s/d from £150/225, Eisenhower ste s/d £250/375; ☺ Apr-Oct; P ☎), which has a magnificent suite used by Eisenhower, and several other plush chambers. There's also a **Camping & Caravanning Club** (☑ 01655-760627; www.campingandcaravanningclub.co.uk; sites per adult/child from £10.30/5.15, plus £7.20 per site for nonmembers; ☺ Apr-late Oct; P ☎ ☎) at the entrance to the park, offering grassy pitches with great views. Non-UK residents can grab a three-month temporary membership for £20.

Culzean is 12 miles south of Ayr; buses (£4.20, 30 minutes, 11 daily Monday to Saturday) pass the park gates, from where it's a 20-minute walk through the grounds to the castle.

Turnberry

Turnberry's **Ailsa golf course** (☑ 01655-331000; www.turnberry.co.uk; Maidens Rd, Turnberry) is on the Open circuit and is one of Scotland's most prestigious links, with spectacular views of Ailsa Craig offshore. You don't need a handicap certificate to play, just plenty of pounds – the standard green fee is £250. In summer though, you can take advantage of the after-3pm 'sunset' rate and go round for £99 a head: a great deal.

Opposite the course, superluxurious **Turnberry Resort** (☑ 01655-331000; www.turnberryresort.co.uk; r standard/deluxe £345/395; P @ ☎ ☎ ☎) offers everything you can think of, including kilted staff, an airstrip and a helipad. As well as the luxurious rooms and excellent restaurant, there's a series of self-contained lodges. Rooms with sea views cost somewhat more.

Kirkoswald

Just 2 miles east of Kirkoswald, by the A77, **Crossraguel Abbey** (HS; www.historic-scotland.gov.uk; adult/child £4.50/2.70; ⊙ 9.30am-5.30pm Apr-Sep) is a substantial ruin dating back to the 13th century that's good fun to explore. The renovated 16th-century gatehouse is the best part – you'll find decorative stonework and superb views from the top. Inside, if you have the place to yourself, you'll hear only the whistling wind – an apt reflection of the abbey's long-departed monastic tradition. Don't miss the echo in the chilly sacristy.

Stagecoach Western runs Ayr–Girvan buses via Crossraguel Abbey and Kirkoswald (35 minutes, hourly Monday to Saturday, every two hours Sunday).

Ailsa Craig

The curiously shaped island of Ailsa Craig can be seen from much of southern Ayrshire. While its unusual blue-tinted granite – famous for making the best curling stones – has been used by geologists to trace the movements of the great Ice Age ice sheet, birdwatchers know Ailsa Craig as the world's second-largest gannet colony – around 10,000 pairs breed annually on the island's sheer cliffs.

To see the island close up, take a cruise from Girvan on the **MV Glorious** (☑ 07773-794358, 01465-713219; www.ailsacraig.org.uk; 7 Harbour St). It's possible to land if the sea is reasonably calm; a tour-hour trip costs £20/15 per adult/child (£25 per person if you want three hours ashore).

Trains going to Girvan run approximately hourly (with only three trains on Sundays) from Ayr (30 minutes).

DUMFRIES & GALLOWAY

Some of the region's finest attractions lie in the gentle hills and lush valleys of Dumfries & Galloway. It's an ideal destination for families, as there's plenty on offer for the kids. Galloway Forest, with its sublime views, mountain-biking and walking trails, red deer, kites and other wildlife, is a highlight, as are the dreamlike ruins of Caerlaverock Castle. Adding to the appeal of this entic-

WORTH A TRIP

DUMFRIES HOUSE

A Palladian mansion designed in the 1750s by the Adam brothers, **Dumfries House** (☑ 01290-421742; www.dumfries-house.org.uk; adult/child £9/4; ⊙ 11am-3.30pm Sun-Fri and sometimes Sat Mar-Oct, 11am-1.45pm Sat & Sun Nov-Feb) is an architectural jewel: such is its preservation that Prince Charles personally intervened to ensure its protection. It contains an extraordinarily well-preserved collection of Chippendale furniture and numerous objets d'art. Visits are by guided tour; book ahead by phone or internet. There's a discount for Historic Scotland members. The once-daily **Grand Tour** (adult/child £12.50/4) also takes you to the bedrooms upstairs and the grounds. There's a cafe here.

The house is located 13 miles east of Ayr, near Cumnock. Bus it from Ayr or Dumfries to Cumnock and walk or cab it the 2 miles to the house; you can also get a train from Glasgow to Auchinleck.

ing region is a string of southern Scotland's most idyllic towns, charming when the sun shines. And shine it does. Warmed by the Gulf Stream, this is the mildest region in Scotland, a phenomenon that has allowed the development of some famous gardens.

Dumfries

POP 32,900

Lovely, red-hued sandstone bridges crisscross pleasant Dumfries, bisected by the wide River Nith, with grassy banks. Historically, Dumfries held a strategic position in the path of vengeful English armies; consequently, although it has existed since Roman times, the oldest standing building dates from the 17th century. Plenty of famous names have passed through: Robert Burns lived here and worked as a tax collector; JM Barrie, creator of Peter Pan, was schooled here; and former racing driver David Coulthard also hails from the town.

⊙ Sights

The red-sandstone bridges arching over the River Nith are the most attractive feature of the town: **Devorgilla Bridge** (1431) is one

Dumfries

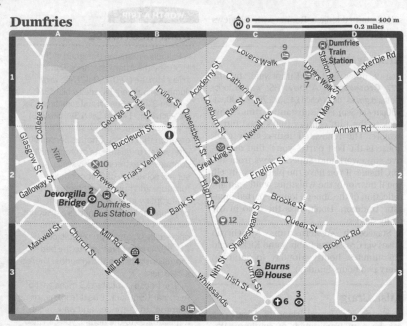

of the oldest bridges in Scotland. You can download a multilingual MP3 audio tour of the town at www.dumgal.gov.uk/audiotour.

There are more Burns-related sights scattered throughout town; you'll find Robert Burns' **mausoleum** in the graveyard at **St Michael's Kirk** it's in the far left corner as you go in. His wife is also buried here. At the top of High St is a **statue** of the bard.

★ Burns House   MUSEUM
(www.dumgal.gov.uk/museums; Burns St; ⊙10am-5pm Mon-Sat, 2-5pm Sun Apr-Sep, 10am-1pm & 2-5pm Tue-Sat Oct-Mar) **FREE** This is a place of pilgrimage for Burns enthusiasts. It's here that the poet spent the last years of his life, and there are various possessions of his in glass cases, as well as manuscripts and, entertainingly, letters: make sure you have a read.

Robert Burns Centre   MUSEUM
(www.dumgal.gov.uk/museums; Mill Rd; audiovisual presentation £2.25; ⊙10am-5pm Mon-Sat, 2-5pm Sun Apr-Sep, 10am-1pm, 2-5pm Tue-Sat Oct-Mar) **FREE** A worthwhile Burns exhibition in an old mill on the banks of the River Nith. It tells the story of the poet and Dumfries in the 1790s. The optional audiovisual presentations give more background on Dumfries, and explain the exhibition's contents.

Ellisland Farm   MUSEUM
(www.ellislandfarm.co.uk; adult/child £4/free; ⊙10am-1pm & 2-5pm Mon-Sat, 2-5pm Sun Apr-Sep, 10am-1pm & 2-5pm Tue-Sat Oct-Mar) If you're not Burnsed out, you can head 6 miles northwest of town and visit the farm he leased. It still preserves some original features from when he and his family lived here, and there's a small exhibition. It's signposted off the A76 to Kilmarnock.

🛏 Sleeping

Hotels in central Dumfries are mundane, but luckily there are some excellent B&Bs in town.

Merlin   B&B £
(☑01387-261002; www.themerlin.webeden.co.uk/; 2 Kenmure Tce; s/d without bathroom £35/56; 🛜) Beautifully located on the riverbank across a pedestrian bridge from the centre, this is a top place to hole up in Dumfries. So much work goes on behind the scenes here that it seems effortless: numerous small details and a friendly welcome make this a very impressive set-up. Rooms share a bathroom, and have supercomfy beds; the breakfast table is also quite a sight.

Dumfries

Ferintosh Guest House　　　　B&B ££
(✆ 01387-252262; www.ferintosh.net; 30 Lovers Walk; s £35, d £60-66; ☎ 🐕) A Victorian villa opposite the train station, Ferintosh is a good-humoured place with excellent rooms and a warm welcome. These people have the right attitude towards hospitality, with comfortable plush beds, a free dram on arrival, and plenty of good chat on distilleries and kilts. The showers sound like light aircraft taking off but deliver impressive results. The owner's original artwork complements the decor and cyclists are welcomed with a shed and bike-washing facilities.

Torbay Lodge　　　　　　　　B&B ££
(✆ 01387-253922; www.torbaylodge.co.uk; 31 Lovers Walk; s £30-45, d/f £66/75; 🅿 ☎) This high-quality guesthouse has beautifully presented bedrooms with big windows, elegant bedsteads and generously sized en suites (and a single without); the good vibe is topped off by an excellent breakfast. It's handy for the station and there's a laundry service.

✖ Eating & Drinking

Cavens Arms　　　　　　　　PUB £
(20 Buccleuch St; mains £8-14; ⊙ 11.30am-9pm Tue-Sat, 12.30-8.30pm Sun; ☎) Engaging staff, 10 real ales on tap and a warm contented buzz make this a legendary Dumfries pub. Generous portions of typical pub nosh backed up by a long list of more adventur-ous daily specials make it one of the town's most enjoyable places to eat too. It gets packed at weekends but they still try and find a table for all. If you were going to move to Dumfries, you'd make sure you were within a block or two of here. There's no food on Monday but the pub's still open.

Kings　　　　　　　　　　　　CAFE £
(www.kings-online.co.uk; 12 Queensberry St; snacks £2-6; ⊙ 8am-5.30pm Mon-Sat, noon-4pm Sun) This buzzy cafe in the centre of town doubles as a bookshop. It does tasty fair-trade coffee, has big windows for observing Dumfries life passing by, and serves toothsome sweet things, breakfasts and filled rolls.

Hullabaloo　　　　　　CAFE, BISTRO ££
(✆ 01387-259679; www.hullabaloorestaurant.co.uk; Mill Rd; mains £9-17; ⊙ noon-3pm Mon, noon-3pm & 5.30-8.30pm Tue-Sat, noon-3pm Sun; ✎) The best eating option in Dumfries is this cosy space upstairs at the Robert Burns Centre. For lunch there's wraps, melts and ciabattas, but come dinner time it's inventive angles and interesting cuts and combinations. There's a distinct Mediterranean flavour to the regularly changing specials, including expertly prepared fish dishes and appetizing vegetarian choices. There's a vegan and a gluten-free menu. Closed Sundays from October to Easter.

Globe Inn　　　　　　　　　　PUB
(www.globeinndumfries.co.uk; 56 High St; ⊙ 10am-11pm Mon-Wed, to midnight Thu, to 1am Fri & Sat, 12.30-11pm Sun) A traditional, rickety old nook-and-cranny pub down a narrow wynd off the main pedestrian drag, this was reputedly Burns' favourite watering hole, and scene of one of his numerous seductions. It's not an upmarket place, but can have good atmosphere created more by its welcoming locals and staff than the numerous pictures of the 'ploughman poet' himself.

ⓘ Information

Dumfries Tourist Office (Map p164; ✆ 01387-253862; www.visitdumfriesandgalloway.co.uk; 64 Whitesands; ⊙ 9.30am-4pm Mon-Sat Nov-Mar, to 5pm Apr-Jun & Sep-Oct, to 5.30pm Jul-Aug, plus 11am-4pm Sun Jul-Sep) Offers plenty of information on the region.

Ewart Library (✆ 01387-253820; Catherine St; ⊙ 8am-4pm Mon, 9am-5pm Tue & Fri, 9am-7pm Wed & Thu, 10am-4pm Sat; ☎) Free internet access.

SOUTHERN SCOTLAND DUMFRIES

🛈 BUS PASS

A Megarider ticket costs £22 and gives you unlimited travel on Stagecoach buses within Dumfries & Galloway for a week – not a bad deal.

🛈 Getting There & Away

BUS

Buses run to towns along the A75 to Stranraer (£7, 2¼ hours, eight daily Monday to Saturday, three on Sunday) as well as to Castle Douglas and Kirkcudbright. Bus 100/101 runs to/from Edinburgh (£8.80, 2¾ hours, four to seven daily), via Moffat and Biggar.

TRAIN

There are trains between Carlisle and Dumfries (£10.40, 35 minutes, every hour or two), and direct trains between Dumfries and Glasgow (£15.60, 1¾ hours, eight daily Monday to Saturday). Services are reduced on Sundays.

South of Dumfries

Caerlaverock

Caerlaverock Castle   CASTLE
(HS; www.historic-scotland.gov.uk; adult/child £5.50/3.30; ⊘9.30am-5.30pm Apr-Sep, to 4.30pm Oct-Mar) The ruins of this castle by Glencaple on a beautiful stretch of the Solway coast, are among the loveliest in Britain. Surrounded by a moat, lawns and stands of trees, the unusual pink-stoned triangular castle looks impregnable. In fact, it fell several times, most famously when it was attacked in 1300 by Edward I: the siege became the subject of an epic poem, 'The Siege of Caerlaverock'. The current castle dates from the late 13th century but, once defensive purposes were no longer a design necessity, it was refitted as a luxurious Scottish Renaissance mansion house in 1634. Ironically, the rampaging Covenanter militia sacked it a few years later. With nooks and crannies to explore, passageways and remnants of fireplaces, this castle is great for the whole family.

Caerlaverock Wetland Centre   WILDLIFE RESERVE
(www.wwt.org.uk/caerlaverock; adult/child £7.05/3.45, free for WWT members; ⊘10am-5pm), The Caerlaverock Wetland Centre protects 546 hectares of salt marsh and mud flats, the habitat for numerous birds, including barnacle geese. There are various activities, including badger-watching, dawn goose flights, and child-focused events, a good nature-watching bookshop and a coffee shop that serves organic food. It also offers accommodation in private rooms with a shared kitchen (£30 to £35 per person). It's one mile east of the castle.

From Dumfries, bus 6A runs several times a day (twice on Sunday) to Caerlaverock Castle. If you're travelling by car, take the B725 south.

Ruthwell

Just off the B724, east of Caerlaverock, **Ruthwell Church** (⊘daylight hours) **FREE** holds one of Europe's most important early Christian monuments. The 6m-high, 7th-century **Ruthwell Cross** is carved top to bottom in New Testament scenes and is inscribed with a poem called 'The Dream of the Rood'; written in a Saxon runic alphabet, it's considered one of the earliest examples of English-language literature.

Bus 79 running between Dumfries and Carlisle stops in Ruthwell on request.

New Abbey

The small, picturesque whitewashed village of New Abbey lies 7 miles south of Dumfries and has several worthwhile things to see and do.

⊙ Sights & Activities

Sweetheart Abbey   RUIN
(HS; www.historic-scotland.gov.uk; adult/child £4.50/2.70; ⊘9.30am-5.30pm Apr-Sep, 9.30am-4.30pm Sat-Wed Oct-Mar) The shattered, red-sandstone remnants of this 13th-century Cistercian abbey stand in stark contrast to the manicured lawns surrounding them. The abbey, the last of the major monasteries to be established in Scotland, was founded by Devorgilla of Galloway in 1273 in honour of her dead husband John Balliol (with whom she had founded Balliol College, Oxford). On his death, she had his heart embalmed and carried it with her until she died 22 years later. She and the heart were buried by the altar – hence the name.

WANLOCKHEAD

Even the phrase 'lead mining' has a sort of dulling effect on the brain, so you'd think it'd be a tough ask to make the subject interesting. But at the fabulous Hidden Treasures **Museum of Lead Mining** (www.leadminingmuseum.co.uk; Wanlockhead; adult/child £7.75/5.70; ⊙11am-4.30pm Apr-Sep) at little Wanlockhead, signposted 10 miles off the motorway northwest of Moffat, they pull it off. It's apparently Scotland's highest village, set amidst a striking landscape of treeless hills and burbling streams. The place is fascinating, and family friendly, taking in a tour of a real mine, re-created miners' cottages, a remarkable 18th-century library, and a display on lead mining and other minerals. In summer it also runs gold-panning activities. The palpable enthusiasm and personableness of the staff bring the social history of the place alive. It's really rather special, and is one of our favourite museums in Scotland.

Buses running between Ayr and Dumfries stop in Sanquhar, from where there's a bus to Wanlockhead five times daily Monday to Saturday. Wanlockhead is also a stop on the Southern Upland Way walking route.

Mabie Farm Park   FARM, (www.mabiefarmpark.co.uk; adult/child/family £7.50/7/28; ⊙10am-5pm daily Apr-Oct, Sat & Sun Mar; 🚼) If your kids are complaining about all the historic sights and Robert Burns, pack up the clan and get down to this spot, between Dumfries and New Abbey off the A710. It's a brilliantly run complex with plenty of animals and activities, including petting-and-feeding sessions, donkey rides, go-karting, slides, a soft play area, picnic spots...the list goes on. Put a full day aside.

Mabie Forest Park   MOUNTAIN BIKING (☑01387-270275; www.7stanesmountainbiking. com) **FREE** Mabie Forest Park is one of southern Scotland's 7stanes mountain-biking hubs, set among forested hills a couple of miles north of New Abbey. There are nearly 40 miles of trails for all levels, the closest bike hire is in Dumfries. It's very close to the Mabie Farm Park, handy if you've got kids of different ages.

🛏 Sleeping

Mabie House Hotel   HOTEL **££** (☑01387-263188; www.mabiehousehotel.co.uk; s/d/ste £45/80/150; **P 🛜 🐾**) Four miles north of New Abbey, this welcoming country-house hotel is a great base, especially if you've got kids, as the farm park and mountain-biking trails are on the doorstep. The rooms are stylish and luxurious, offering excellent comfort at a very fair price. In the garden are three cosy mini-huts which sleep four (£40), a good budget option for bikers or to give the younger generation some independence.

ℹ Getting There & Away

To get to New Abbey, take Bus 372 from Dumfries (15 minutes).

Annandale & Eskdale

These valleys, in Dumfries & Galloway's east, form part of two major routes that cut across Scotland's south. Away from the highways, the roads are quiet and there are some interesting places to visit, especially if you're looking to break up a road trip.

Gretna & Gretna Green

POP 3100

Firmly on the coach-tour circuit for its romantic associations, Gretna Green is on the outskirts of the town of Gretna, just across the river from Cumbria in England. Historically famous as a destination for eloping couples to get married, it's still one of Britain's most popular wedding venues.

The centre of the village is the **Old Blacksmith's Shop** (www.gretnagreen.com; exhibition adult/child £3.50/free; ⊙9am-5pm Oct-Mar, to 5.30pm Apr-May, to 6pm Jun-Sep) complex, with tourist shops and eateries as well as quite an entertaining multilingual exhibition on Gretna Green's history, with tales of intrigues, elopements, scoundrels, and angry parents arriving minutes too late. There's a recreation of a blacksmith's forge, a collection of handsome carriages, and a few marriage rooms: you may well run into a modern-day wedding as you walk through.

Across the road, **Smith's at Gretna Green** (☑01461-337007; www.smithsgretnagreen.com; s/d £145/155; **P 🛜**) is a large

TYING THE KNOT IN GRETNA GREEN

The Marriage Act passed in England in 1754 suddenly required couples that did not have their parents' consent to be 21 years of age before they could marry. But cunning teenage sweethearts soon realized that the law didn't apply in Scotland, where a simple declaration in front of a pair of witnesses would suffice. As the first village in Scotland, Gretna Green's border location made it the most popular venue for eloping couples to get hitched.

Locals competed for the incoming trade, and marriages were performed by just about anyone who could round up a couple of witnesses from the nearest pub. One legendary Gretna vow-taker was the local blacksmith, who became known as the 'Anvil Priest'. In 1856 eloping was made more difficult when a law was passed obliging couples to have spent at least three weeks in Scotland prior to tying the knot, but Gretna Green remained popular. And it still is: some 5000 couples annually take or reaffirm their marriage vows in the village. If you want to get married over the famous anvil in the Old Blacksmith's Shop at Gretna Green, check out www.gretnagreen.com or www.gretnaweddings.co.uk.

contemporary hotel with a decent restaurant (mains £16-21; ⊗noon-9pm). Though the blocky exterior won't delight everybody, the interior is much more stylish. The rooms are decorated in a chic, restrained style with king-sized beds. Various grades are available; you'll get much cheaper rates booking online. There's a little noise from the adjacent motorway.

A mile away in Gretna's shopping centre, the very helpful **tourist office** (☎01461-337834; gretnatic@visitscotland.com; Gretna Gateway; ⊗10am-6pm Apr-Oct, 10am-4.30pm Mon-Sat, 10am-4pm Sun Nov-Mar) is a good first stop for information on Scotland if you're driving across from England.

Bus 79 between Dumfries (one hour) and Carlisle (35 minutes) stops in Gretna and Gretna Green (hourly Monday to Saturday, every two hours Sunday). Trains also run from Gretna Green to Dumfries and Carlisle.

Moffat

POP 2600

Moffat lies in wild, hilly country near the upper reaches of Annandale. It's really enjoyed by the older brigade and is a popular tourist-coach spot. The former spa town is a centre for the local wool industry, symbolised by the bronze ram statue on High St.

At **Moffat Mill** (☎01683-220134; www.ewm-store.co.uk; ⊗9am-5pm) **FREE**, near the tourist office, there's a moribund weaving exhibition within a sizeable retail outlet selling woollens and other Scottish souvenirs. There's tourist information too.

Flower-decked **Buchan Guest House** (☎01683-220378; www.buchanguesthouse.co.uk; Beechgrove; s/d £38/65; P⊗) is in a quiet central street. There's a lovely garden, family rooms, and a pleasant lounge overlooking the bowling green opposite. It's cyclist-friendly, with a bike garage out the back. The **Moffat House Hotel** (☎01683-220039; www.moffathouse.co.uk; High St; s/d £75/109; P⊗⊗) is a noble creeper-covered 18th-century mansion in the centre of town, offering comfortable beds in spacious rooms in the main building or an annexe in one of the wings. The modernised four-poster rooms are best, but cost a bit more.

There are several buses daily to Edinburgh, Glasgow and Dumfries.

Langholm

POP 2200

The waters of three rivers – the Esk, Ewes and Wauchope – meet at Langholm, a gracious old town at the centre of Scotland's tweed industry. Most people come for fishing and walking in the surrounding moors and woodlands; check out the Langholm Walks website (www.langholmwalks.co.uk) for details.

Hugh MacDiarmid, poet, communist and seminal figure in 20th-century Scottish nationalism was born Christopher Grieve here in Langholm in 1892.

Border House (☎013873-80376; www.border-house.co.uk; High St; s £40, d £70-80; P⊗⊗), on the main road, is an excellent central accommodation option with large rooms, a lovely hostess and big sink-in-and-smile beds. They run a chocolate shop a few doors along so you may get a wee sample. Chocolate-making workshops are also available through the year. The garden runs right down to the river.

Buses between Edinburgh and Carlisle pass through Langholm. There are frequent services to Lockerbie, where you can change to other routes.

Eskdalemuir

Surrounded by wooded hills, Eskdalemuir is a remote settlement 13 miles northwest of Langholm. About 1.5 miles further north is the **Samye Ling Tibetan Centre** (☎01387-373232; www.samyeling.org; camping/dm/s/d incl full board £17.50/26/41/62; **P**), the first Tibetan Buddhist monastery built in the West (1968). The colourful prayer flags and the red and gold of the temple itself are a striking contrast to the stark grey and green landscape. You can visit the centre during the day (donation suggested, cafe on site) or stay overnight in simple accommodation which includes full vegetarian board. There are also meditation courses and weekend workshops available. Reserve accommodation online, not by phone.

Bus 112 or 124 from Langholm/Lockerbie stops at the centre Monday to Saturday.

Castle Douglas & Around

POP 4200

Castle Douglas attracts a lot of day trippers but hasn't been 'spruced up' for tourism. It's an open, attractive, well-cared-for town, with some remarkably beautiful areas close to the centre, such as the small Carlingwark Loch. The town was laid out in the 18th century by Sir William Douglas, who had made a fortune in the Americas.

◎ Sights & Activities

Threave Castle   CASTLE
(HS; www.historic-scotland.gov.uk; adult/child incl ferry £4.50/2.70; ⊙10am-5pm Apr-Sep, to 4pm Oct) Two miles west of Castle Douglas, this impressive tower sits on a small river island. Built in the late 14th century, it became a principal stronghold of the Black Douglases, including the excellently named Archibald the Grim. It's now basically a shell, having been badly damaged by the Covenanters in the 1640s, but it's a romantic ruin nonetheless. It's a 15-minute walk from the car park to the ferry landing, where you ring a bell for the custodian to take you across.

Also from the car park, where there's a small nature exhibition, a 1.5-mile circular nature path gives you the chance to spot deer and ospreys, as well as waterbirds from hides. At dusk it's good for bat-watching.

Loch Ken   LAKE
Stretching for 9 miles northwest of Castle Douglas between the A713 and A762, Loch Ken is a popular outdoor recreational area. The range of water sports includes windsurfing, sailing, canoeing, power-boating and kayaking. There are also walking trails and a rich variety of bird life. The Royal Society for the Protection of Birds (RSPB) has a **nature reserve** (www.rspb.org.uk) on the western bank, north of Glenlochar.

Sulwath Brewery   BREWERY
(☎01556-504525; www.sulwathbrewers.co.uk; 209 King St; adult/child £3.50/free; ⊙10am-6pm Mon-Sat) You can see traditional brewing processes at this main-street alemaker's. Tours, which include a pint, only run twice a week, at 1pm on Monday and Friday (ring ahead), but the brewery functions as a sort of speakeasy where you can try the beers. Recommended is the Criffel, an India pale ale, and Knockendoch, a dark brew with a delicious taste of roasted malt.

★ **Galloway
Activity Centre**   WATER SPORTS, MOUNTAIN BIKING
(☎01556-502011; www.lochken.co.uk; ⊙10am-5pm; 🚲) On the eastern bank of Loch Ken north of Parton, this excellent set-up runs a wide range of activities, and also provides equipment and a variety of camping and hostel accommodation. Activities run in sessions of 1½ hours; one session costs £20 each for two, and the price reduces substantially for further sessions. Best to book in advance.

🛏 Sleeping & Eating

Camping options around nearby Loch Ken are appealing.

Castle Douglas bills itself as a food town, and the main street is bristling with high-quality delis, butchers and cafes. Decent restaurants are scarcer however.

**Lochside Caravan & Camping
Site**   CAMPSITE £
(☎01556-502949; www.dumgal.gov.uk/caravanandcamping; Lochside Park; unpowered/powered sites £18.50/22; ⊙Apr-Oct; **P**🐕) Very central campsite attractively situated beside Carlingwark Loch; there's plenty of grass and fine trees providing shade.

Douglas House
B&B ££

([☑] 01556-503262; www.douglas-house.com; 63 Queen St; s £39-41, d £78-82; [📶][🐾]) Set in a beautiful 200-year-old stone house, this has big, beautiful bathrooms that complement the light, stylish chambers, which include flatscreen digital TVs with inbuilt DVD players. The two upstairs doubles are the best, although the downstairs double is huge and has a superking-size bed – you could sleep four in it! Breakfast is reader-recommended, with locally sourced produce.

Craig
B&B ££

([☑] 01556-504840; www.thecraigcastledouglas. co.uk; 44 Abercromby Rd; s/d £38/60; [⊙] Feb-Oct; [P][📶]) This solid old property is a fine B&B with a conscientious owner, large rooms and fresh fruit served up for breakfast. It's old-fashioned hospitality – genuine and very comfortable. Would suit older visitors. It's on the edge of town on the road to New Galloway.

Blackwater Bistro
GREEK ££

(www.blackwaterproduce.co.uk; 139 King St; mains £14-17; [⊙] 11am-3pm & 6-9pm Mon-Sat; [📶]) It's quite a surprise to find authentic Greek food here in provincial Castle Douglas. The charismatic, welcoming host prepares delicious, authentic mezze and mains, and a variety of cheaper lunchtime specials (£5 to £7). It's on the main street.

King Street Sandwich Bar & Deli
TAKEAWAY £

(173 King St; baguettes £3-4; [⊙] 8am-4pm Mon-Sat) For a truly awesome baguette or ciabatta drop into this deli, which also does a nice line in olives and cheeses. We recommend 'the Godfather'. Sandwiches tend to run out by around 2pm, so get in quick.

ℹ Information

Castle Douglas Library ([☑] 01556-502643; King St; [⊙] 10am-7.30pm Mon-Wed & Fri, 10am-5pm Thu & Sat; [📶]) Free internet access.

Castle Douglas Tourist Office ([☑] 01556-502611; King St; [⊙] 10am-5pm Mon-Sat Apr-Jun & Sep-Oct, 9.30am-6pm Mon-Sat, 10am-3.30pm Sun Jul & Aug) Located in a small park behind the library.

ℹ Getting There & Away

Buses run roughly hourly from Castle Douglas to Dumfries (45 minutes); there are also services to Kirkcudbright (20 minutes), Stranraer, New Galloway and Ayr.

Kirkcudbright

POP 3400

Kirkcudbright (kirk-*coo*-bree), with its dignified streets of 17th- and 18th-century merchants' houses and appealing harbour, is the ideal base from which to explore the south coast. Look out for the nook-and-cranny wynds in the elbow of beautifully restored High St. With its architecture and setting, it's easy to see why Kirkcudbright has been an artists' colony since the late 19th century.

◉ Sights & Activities

Broughton House
GALLERY

(NTS; www.nts.org.uk; 12 High St; adult/child £6.50/5; [⊙] noon-5pm Apr-Oct) The 18th-century Broughton House displays paintings by EA Hornel (he lived and worked here), one of the Glasgow Boys. The library, with its wood panelling and stone carvings, is probably the most impressive room. Behind the house is a lovely Japanese-style garden (also open 11am to 4pm Monday to Friday in February and March).

MacLellan's Castle
CASTLE

(HS; www.historic-scotland.gov.uk; Castle St; adult/child £4.50/2.70; [⊙] 9.30am-1pm & 2-5.30pm Apr-Sep) Near the harbour, this is a large, atmospheric ruin built in 1577 by Thomas MacLellan, then provost of Kirkcudbright, as his town residence. Inside look for the 'laird's lug', a 16th-century hidey-hole designed for the laird to eavesdrop on his guests.

Tolbooth Art Centre
EXHIBITION, GALLERY

(www.dumgal.gov.uk; High St; [⊙] 10am-4pm Mon-Sat, 1-4pm Sun mid-Apr–Sep, 11am-4pm Mon-Sat Oct–mid-Apr) [FREE] As well as catering for today's local artists, this centre has an exhibition on the history of the town's artistic development. The place is as interesting for the building itself as for the artistic works on display; it's one of the oldest and best-preserved tollbooths in Scotland, and there are interpretative signboards to explain its past.

Stewartry Museum
MUSEUM

(St Mary St; [⊙] 11am-4pm Mon-Sat) [FREE] There's a certain charm to this higgledy-piggledy old-fashioned local history museum. There's everything from coronation teacups to lumps of local granite to stuffed fish. Reduced hours in winter, sometimes opens Sundays in summer.

Galloway Wildlife Conservation Park ZOO
(www.gallowaywildlife.co.uk; Lochfergus Plantation; adult/child £7.50/5; ⊙10am-dusk Feb-Nov) A mile from Kirkcudbright on the B727, this park is an easy walk from town, and you'll see red pandas, wolves, meerkats, monkeys, kangaroos, Scottish wildcats and many more creatures in a peaceful rural setting. An important role of the park is the conservation of rare and threatened species. It could do with a bit of a facelift but funds are tight.

✦ Festivals

Thursdays in high summer are Scottish theme nights, with music, dancing and more in the centre of town.

Kirkcudbright Jazz Festival MUSIC
(www.kirkcudbrightjazzfestival.co.uk) This is four days of swing, trad, and dixie, in June.

Wickerman Festival MUSIC
(www.thewickermanfestival.co.uk) A diverse two-day music festival held in July on farmland a few miles southeast of town. From punk to reggae via indie rock, there's something for everyone. The festival climaxes with the burning of an enormous wickerman; much of the 1973 cult movie of the same name was filmed around this area.

🛏 Sleeping & Eating

Kirkcudbright has a swath of good B&Bs, though single rooms are scarce.

Silvercraigs Caravan & Camping Site CAMPSITE £
(☎01557-330123; www.dumgal.gov.uk/caravanandcamping; Silvercraigs Rd; unpowered/powered site £18.50/22; ⊙Apr Oct; P🐾) There are brilliant views from this camping ground; you feel like you're sleeping on top of the town. It's great for stargazing on clear nights, and there are good facilities, including a laundry.

★ Selkirk Arms Hotel HOTEL ££
(☎01557-330402; www.selkirkarmshotel.co.uk; High St; s/d/ superior d £84/110/130; P@🛜) What a haven of good hospitality this is. All the rooms have been recently refurbished, and are looking good with a stylish purply finish and slate-floored bathrooms. Superior rooms are excellent – wood furnishings and views over the back garden give them a rustic appeal. Staff are happy to be there, and you will be too.

Baytree House B&B ££
(☎01557-330824; www.baytreekirkcudbright.co.uk; 110 High St; s/d £65/82; @🛜) This is a very high-standard B&B, but always directed towards the guest's comfort: it never feels too posh. Rooms are of a very good size and feature plush, comfortable beds and lots of little extras like a sherry decanter, earplugs (not that you need them) and fresh milk. A great lounge space has DVDs and reading material. There's a self-catering flat too.

Kirkcudbright Bay Hotel PUB ££
(☎01557-339544; www.kirkcudbrightbay.com; 25 St Cuthbert St; s/d £55/75; 🛜) Enthusiastic new owners have given this central pub a much-needed fillip and it's now a very pleasant place to lay your head, with comfortable modernised en suite rooms and an attractive downstairs bar.

Anchorlee B&B ££
(☎01557-330197; www.anchorlee.co.uk; 95 St Mary St; s £55, d £75-80; P🛜🐾) This elegant residence on the main road is a comfortable haven of classic B&B style. Welcoming hosts, cheerfully flowery rooms and a solid breakfast make staying here a pleasure.

Greengate B&B ££
(☎01557-331895; www.thegreengate.co.uk; 46 High St; s/d £60/80; 🛜) The artistically inclined should snap up the one double room in this lovely place, which has both historic and current painterly connections.

Selkirk Arms Hotel BISTRO ££
(www.selkirkarmshotel.co.uk; High St; mains £11-19; ⊙noon-2pm & 6-9pm; P🛜♿) Cheery servers and a wide-ranging menu of well-presented dishes give you plenty of options here, where you can sit in the more formal restaurant area or the more casual bar zone. Local scallops are a highlight, and some fairly elaborate mains can round out the meal, but you can also chow down on 'posh fish 'n' chips'. All positive.

Castle Street Bistro BISTRO ££
(☎01557-330569; www.facebook.com/castlestbistro; 5 Castle St; mains £8-12; ⊙5.30-9pm Mon & Tue, 11.30am-2pm & 5.30-9pm Wed-Sun; 🛜♿) This bright and breezy spot opposite the picturesque castle offers creative takes on uncomplicated dishes like pasta or mussels. Wednesdays are pizza nights.

ℹ Information

Check out www.kirkcudbright.co.uk and www.artiststown.org.uk for heaps of information on the town.

Kirkcudbright Tourist Office (☎ 01557-330494; www.visitdumfriesandgalloway.co.uk; Harbour Sq; ☺10am-5pm Mon-Sat & 11am-3pm Sun Apr-Jun & Sep-Oct, 9.30am-6pm Mon-Sat & 10am-5pm Sun Jul & Aug, 11am-4pm Mon-Sat Nov-Mar) Handy office with useful brochures detailing walks and road tours in the surrounding district.

ℹ Getting There & Away

Kirkcudbright is 28 miles southwest of Dumfries. Buses run to Dumfries (one hour) via either Castle Douglas or changing in Dalbeattie. Change at Gatehouse of Fleet for Stranraer.

Gatehouse of Fleet

POP 1000

Gatehouse of Fleet is an attractive little town stretched along a sloping main street, in the middle of which sits an unusual castellated clock tower. The town lies on the banks of the Water of Fleet, off the beaten track, and is surrounded by partly wooded hills.

◉ Sights

Mill on the Fleet   EXHIBITION
(www.millonthefleet.co.uk; High St; ☺10am-5pm Apr-Oct) FREE In the centre of town, in a converted 18th-century cotton mill, this centre has an exhibition on the history of the local industry and environment. The town was originally planned as millworkers' accommodation. There's also tourist information, a cafe, gallery and likeably chaotic second-hand bookshop here.

Cardoness Castle   CASTLE
(HS; www.historic-scotland.gov.uk; adult/child £4.50/2.70; ☺9.30am-5.30pm Apr-Sep) One mile southwest on the A75, this well-preserved stronghold was the home of the McCulloch clan. It's a classic 15th-century tower house with great views from the top.

⌂ Sleeping

Bobbin Guest House   B&B £
(☎ 01557-814229; www.bobbinguesthouse.co.uk; 36 High St; s/d £35/65; �) Situated right in the middle of town, this is a real home-from-home with a variety of spacious, well-appointed rooms with good en suite bathrooms. The welcome is exceptional.

Cally Palace Hotel   HOTEL ££
(☎ 01557-814341; www.mcmillanhotels.co.uk; s/d from £90/100; ⓟⓡⓢⓦ) On the edge of town, accessed through a wood and sitting in substantial grounds that include a rather decent private golf course, this 18th-century mansion is a comfortable, upmarket hotel with various grades of old-fashioned but commodious rooms and numerous facilities including tennis court, gym, heated indoor pool and restaurant. It's a curious mixture of old-style luxury and ugly '80s details.

ℹ Getting There & Away

Buses X75 and 500 between Dumfries (one hour) and Stranraer (1¼ hours) stop here eight times daily (three on Sunday). They also stop in Castle Douglas and Newton Stewart. Further buses run to Kirkcudbright.

Around Gatehouse

Ideal for families, **Cream o' Galloway** (☎ 01557-815222; www.creamogalloway.co.uk; adults free, child all-inclusive £5-12.50; ☺10am-5pm mid-Mar-Oct, to 6pm Jul & Aug) is the home of that delicious ice cream you'll see all around the region, and offers a plethora of activities and events. There are 4 miles of nature trails, an ultra-popular bouncy net, an adventure playground for all ages, a 3D maze, wildlife-watching, a farm to explore and plenty of ice cream to taste. There are also regular events and special happenings. It's about 4 miles from Gatehouse off the A75 – signposted all the way. You can hire bikes from here in summer.

Galloway Forest Park

South and northwest of the small town of New Galloway is 300-sq-mile Galloway Forest Park, with numerous lochs and great whale-backed, heather- and pine-covered mountains. The highest point is **Merrick** (843m). The park is criss-crossed by off-road bike routes and some superb signposted walking trails, from gentle strolls to long-distance paths, including the Southern Upland Way (p150). The park is very family focused; look out for the booklet of annual events in tourist offices.

The park is also great for stargazing; it's been named a Dark Sky Park by the International Dark-Sky Association (www.darksky.org).

The scenic 19-mile A712 (Queen's Way) between New Galloway and Newton Stewart slices through the southern section of the park.

On the shore of **Clatteringshaws Loch**, 6 miles west of New Galloway, is **Clatteringshaws Visitor Centre** (☏01671-402420; www.forestry.gov.uk/scotland; ⊙10am-4pm, to 5pm Jul & Aug), which is basically a cafe but has the odd display panel. Pick up a copy of the *Galloway Kite Trail* leaflet here, which details a circular route through impressive scenery that offers a good chance to spot one of the majestic reintroduced red kites. From the visitor centre you can walk to a replica of a Romano-British homestead (½ mile), and to **Bruce's Stone** (1 mile), where Robert the Bruce is said to have rested after defeating the English at the Battle of Rapploch Moss in 1307.

About a mile west of Clatteringshaws, **Raiders Rd** is a 10-mile drive through the forest with various picnic spots, child-friendly activities, and short walks marked along the way. It costs £2 per vehicle; drive slowly as there's plenty of wildlife about.

Further west is the **Galloway Red Deer Range** where you can observe Britain's largest land-based beast. During rutting season in autumn it's a bit like watching a bullfight as snorting, charging stags compete for the harem. From April to September there are guided **ranger-led visits** (adult/child £5/3) to see these impressive beasts.

Walkers and cyclists should head for **Glentrool** in the park's west, accessed by the forest road east from Bargrennan off the A714, north of Newton Stewart. Located just over a mile from Bargrennan is the **Glentrool Visitor Centre** (⊙10am-4pm, to 5pm Jul & Aug), which has a cafe and information on activities, including mountain biking. The road then winds and climbs up to **Loch Trool**, where there are magnificent views.

Dalry

St John's Town of Dalry, to give it its full name, is a charming village, hugging the hillside about 3 miles north of New Galloway on the A713. It's on the Water of Ken and gives access to the Southern Upland Way. It's also a good base for Galloway Forest Park.

In the heart of the village, the **Clachan Inn** (☏01644-430241; www.theclachaninn.co.uk; 8 Main St; s/d £40/70; P♠) is an atmos-

MOUNTAIN BIKING HEAVEN

A brilliant way to experience southern Scotland's forests is by pedal power. The **7stanes** (stones) are seven mountain-biking centres around the region, featuring trails through some of the finest forest scenery you'll find in the country.

Glentrool is one of these centres; the **Blue Route** here is 5.6 miles in length and is a lovely ride climbing up to Green Torr Ridge overlooking Loch Trool. If you've more serious intentions, the **Big Country Route** is 36 miles of challenging ascents and descents that afford magnificent views of the Galloway Forest. It takes a full day and is not for wimps.

Another of the trailheads is at **Kirroughtree Visitor Centre**, 3 miles southeast of Newton Stewart. This centre offers plenty of singletrack at four different skill levels. You can hire also bikes here (www.thebreakpad.com). For more information on routes see www.7stanesmountainbiking.com.

pheric pub with a fireplace and real ales. It serves a more-original-than-usual bar menu (£9 to £12, food served noon to 2pm and 6pm to 9pm) and has luminous renovated rooms with light wood furniture and new mattresses.

Bus 521 runs twice daily (except Sunday) to Dumfries (55 minutes). Bus 520 connects Dalry with Castle Douglas (30 minutes, 11 daily Monday to Saturday); two services continue north to Ayr (1½ hours).

Newton Stewart

POP 4100

On the banks of the sparkling River Cree, Newton Stewart is at the heart of some beautiful countryside, and is popular with hikers and anglers. On the eastern bank, across the bridge, is the older and smaller settlement of **Minnigaff**. With excellent accommodation and eating options, this makes a tempting base for exploring the Galloway Forest Park.

This is great angling country. For fishing gear and permits, as well as advice on landing the big one, drop into **Galloway Angling Centre** (☏01671-401333; www.gallowayangling.co.uk; 1 Queen St; ⊙9am-

5pm Mon-Sat). You can also check out the very useful website www.fishgalloway.co.uk.

🛏 Sleeping & Eating

Minnigaff SYHA   HOSTEL £
(SYHA; ☑01671-402211; www.syha.org.uk; dm £16; ⊙Easter–mid-Sep; ℗) This converted school is now a somewhat rundown hostel with eight-bed dorms. It's in a tranquil spot 800m north of the bridge, on the eastern bank. Although it's popular with outdoor enthusiasts, you may just about have the place to yourself. Expect a lockout until 5pm.

Creebridge House Hotel   HOTEL ££
(☑01671-402121; www.creebridge.co.uk; s/d/superior d £65/116/130; ℗🛜🐾) This is a magnificent refurbished 18th-century mansion built for the Earl of Galloway. A maze inside, it has tastefully decorated refurbished rooms with a classical style and plenty of character. Bathrooms are OK but don't quite have the same wow factor. Try to get a room overlooking the garden (No 7 is a good one). There's also good food here (mains £11 to £18).

Flowerbank Guest House   B&B ££
(☑01671-402629; www.flowerbankgh.com; Millcroft Rd; s/d £42/62; ⊙Apr-Oct; ℗🛜🐾) This dignified 18th-century house is set in a magnificent landscaped garden in Minnigaff on the banks of the River Cree. The two elegantly furnished rooms at the front of the house are slightly more expensive (£68), but are spacious and have lovely garden and river views. It's a quiet, peaceful stop.

Galloway Arms Hotel   HOTEL, PUB ££
(☑01671-402653; www.gallowayarmshotel.com; 54 Victoria St; s/d £43/99; ℗🛜🐾) There are attractive renovated rooms at this historic main-street pub; the best ones are upstairs, with plenty of space. The hotel is walker- and cyclist-friendly, with bike storage and a drying room, while the bar and restaurant churn out excellent local fare.

Galloway Arms Hotel   PUB ££
(www.gallowayarmshotel.com; 54 Victoria St; mains £7-16; ⊙noon-2pm & 5-9pm; ℗🛜🐾) This high-street pub is characterful and very cosy, with a fireplace. It does a wide range of good grub, with a nice line in burgers – try the pork and apple one.

ℹ Information

Belted Galloway Visitor Centre (www.thebeltedgalloway.co.uk; ⊙10am-5pm Mon-Sat Sep-May, 10am-5pm Jun, 10am-7pm Jul & Aug; 🛜) Named after the striped local breed of cow, this visitor centre just off the main street offers a good licensed cafe, giftshop selling books and maps, and displays on local history and attractions. It's the best spot for information on the many walks to be done in the Newton Stewart area. Good disabled access.

Newton Stewart Tourist Office (☑01671-402431; www.visitdumfriesandgalloway.com; Dashwood Sq; ⊙10am-4pm Tue-Sat Apr-Oct) Off the main street.

ℹ Getting There & Away

Buses stop in Newton Stewart (Dashwood Sq) on their way to Stranraer (45 minutes) and Dumfries (1½ hours); both run several times daily. There are also connections to Ayr and Glasgow via Girvan. Frequent buses run south to the Machars.

The Machars

South of Newton Stewart, the Galloway Hills give way to the softly rolling pastures of the triangular peninsula known as the Machars. The south has many early Christian sites and the 25-mile Pilgrims Way walk.

Bus 415 runs every hour or so between Newton Stewart and Isle of Whithorn (one hour) via Wigtown (15 minutes) and Whithorn.

Wigtown
POP 900

Little Wigtown, officially Scotland's National Book Town, has more than a dozen bookshops offering an astonishingly wide selection of volumes, giving book enthusiasts the opportunity to get lost here for days. A major **book festival** (www.wigtownbookfestival.com) is held here in late September.

⊙ Sights & Activities

Wigtown County Buildings   NATURE DISPLAY
(Market Sq; ⊙10am-5pm) **FREE** Folk in this town love their resident ospreys. It's a good conversation starter and if you'd like to learn a bit more about the majestic birds, and see a live CCTV link to a nearby nest, drop by the top floor of the Wigtown County Buildings.

Bladnoch Distillery DISTILLERY
(01988-402605; www.bladnoch.co.uk) Browsing books can be thirsty work, so it's fortunate that Bladnoch Distillery is just a couple of miles away from Wigtown, in the village of Bladnoch. Ring for opening hours, as it was closed down when we last passed by.

Torhouse Stone Circle RUIN
Four miles west of Wigtown, off the B733, this well-preserved ruin dates from the 2nd millennium BC.

🛏 Sleeping & Eating

Hillcrest House B&B ££
(01988-402018; www.hillcrest-wigtown.co.uk; Station Rd; s £40-45, d £70-78; P 🛜 🐾) A noble stone building in a quiet part of town, this offers a genuine welcome and a lovely interior featuring high ceilings and huge windows. Spend the extra for one of the superior rooms, which have stupendous views overlooking rolling green hills and the sea beyond. This is all complemented by a ripper breakfast involving fresh local produce.

ReadingLasses Bookshop Café CAFE £
(www.reading-lasses.com; 17 South Main St; mains £7-8; 10am-5pm Mon-Sat, plus 11am-4pm Sun May-Oct; 🛜 🐾) This bookshop is set around a brilliantly welcoming cafe serving decent coffee to prolong your reading time and a toothsome range of home cooking prepared with care and offering several vegetarian/vegan options. It specialises in books on the social sciences and women's studies.

🔒 Shopping

The Bookshop BOOKS
(www.the-bookshop.com; 17 North Main St; 9am-5pm Mon-Sat) This claims to be Scotland's largest secondhand bookshop, and has a great collection of Scottish and regional titles.

Whithorn
POP 800
Whithorn has a broad, attractive main street which is virtually closed at both ends (it was designed to enclose a medieval market). There are few facilities in town, but it's worth visiting because of its fascinating history.

In 397, while the Romans were still in Britain, St Ninian established the first Christian mission beyond Hadrian's Wall in Whithorn (pre-dating St Columba on Iona by 166 years). After his death, **Whithorn Priory**, the earliest recorded church in Scotland, was built to house his remains, and Whithorn became the focus of an important medieval pilgrimage.

Today the ruined priory is part of the excellent **Whithorn Trust Discovery Centre** (www.whithorn.com; 45 George St; adult/child £4.50/2.25, 20% Historic Scotland discount; 10.30am-5pm Apr-Oct), which introduces you to the history of the town through a very informative audiovisual exhibition. Outside, you can see the site of earlier churches. There's also a museum with some fascinating early Christian stone sculptures, including the **Latinus Stone** (c 450), reputedly Scotland's oldest Christian artefact. Learn about the influences their carvers drew on, from around the British Isles and beyond.

Isle of Whithorn
POP 400
The Isle of Whithorn, once an island but now linked to the mainland by a causeway, is a curious place with an attractive natural harbour and colourful houses. The roofless 13th-century **St Ninian's Chapel**, probably built for pilgrims who landed nearby, sits on the windswept, evocative rocky headland. Around Burrow Head, to the southwest but accessed off the A747 before you enter the Isle of Whithorn, is **St Ninian's Cave**, where the saint went to pray.

The quayside **Steam Packet Inn** (01988-500334; www.steampacketinn.biz; Harbour Row; r per person £45, without bathroom £40; food noon 2pm & 6.30 9pm; 🛜 🐾) is a popular pub with great real ales, scrumptious bar meals (mains £7 to £11) and comfy lodgings. Try to get a room at the front of the building as they have lovely views over the little harbour (No 2 is a good one).

Stranraer
POP 10,600
The friendly but somewhat ramshackle port of Stranraer has seen its tourist mainstay, the ferry traffic to Northern Ireland, move up the road to Cairnryan. The town's still wondering what to do with itself, but there's lots to explore in the surrounding area.

◉ Sights

Castle Kennedy Gardens   GARDENS, CASTLE
(www.castlekennedygardens.co.uk;   adult/child
£5/1.50; ⊙ 10am-5pm daily Apr-Oct, Sat & Sun only
Feb-Mar) Three miles east of Stranraer, these
magnificent gardens are among Scotland's
most renowned. They cover 30 hectares and
are set on an isthmus between two lochs
and two castles. The landscaping was undertaken in 1730 by the Earl of Stair, who
used unoccupied soldiers to do the work.
Buses heading east from Stranraer stop at
the gate on the main road; it's a pleasant
20-minute stroll from here to the entrance
to the gardens.

St John's Castle   CASTLE
(George St; ⊙ 10am-1pm & 1.30-4.30pm Tue-Sat
Jun-Sep) FREE Worth a quick visit, St John's
Castle is a tower built in 1510 by the Adairs
of Kilhilt, a powerful local family. The old
stone cells carry a distinctly musty smell.
There are displays and a couple of videos
that trace its history and, from the top of the
castle, superb views of Loch Ryan.

Stranraer Museum   MUSEUM
(55 George St; ⊙ 10am-5pm Mon-Fri, 10am-1pm &
1.30-4.30pm Sat) FREE This museum houses exhibits on local history and you can
learn about Stranraer's polar explorers.
The highlight is the carved stone pipe from
Madagascar.

🛏 Sleeping & Eating

Purgatory must look something like Stranraer at dinner time. Several pubs and cafes
do mediocre standards in big portions, so
you won't go hungry.

Ivy House   B&B £
(☏ 01776-704176; www.ivyhouse-ferrylink.co.uk;
3 Ivy Pl; s/d £30/50, s without bathroom £25; 🖘)
This is a great guesthouse that does Scottish
hospitality proud, with excellent facilities,
tidy en suite rooms and a smashing breakfast. Nothing is too much trouble for the genial host, who always has a smile. The room
at the back overlooking the churchyard is
particularly light and quiet.

Balyett Farm   B&B ££
(☏ 01776-703395; www.balyettbb.co.uk; Cairnryan
Rd; s £55, d £65-75; 🅿🖘) A mile north of town
on the A77, Balyett has top relaxing rooms
in a tranquil setting; they are light, bright,
clean as a whistle and boast lovely views
over the surrounding country. Ring ahead,

as they might be further up the road in
Cairnryan by the time you read this.

North West Castle Hotel   HOTEL ££
(☏ 01776-704413; www.mcmillanhotels.com; s/d
£80/120; 🅿🖘🕿🏊) Showing its age but still
an enjoyable time-warp experience, this was
formerly the home of Arctic explorer Sir
John Ross. Rooms are comfortable enough,
with a quaint feel: try for sea views. Despite
too much family propaganda about the owners, service is excellent. It was the first hotel
in the world to have an indoor curling rink.
The bar's a great place to sit and watch those
unusual ice antics when there's a match on.

ℹ Information

Stranraer Library (North Strand St; ⊙ 9am-
7pm Mon, 9am-5pm Tue & Wed, noon-8pm Thu,
8am-4pm Fri, 10am-1pm Sat; 🖘) Free internet
access.

Stranraer Tourist Office (☏ 01776-702595;
28 Harbour St; ⊙ 10am-4pm Mon-Sat Sep-Jun,
9am-5pm Mon-Sat Jul & Aug, 11am-3pm Sun
Jul) Efficient and friendly.

ℹ Getting There & Away

Stranraer is 6 miles south of Cairnryan, which is
on the eastern side of Loch Ryan. Bus 358 runs
frequently between Stranraer and Ayr stopping
in Cairnryan. For a taxi to Cairnryan (around
£8), contact **McLean's Taxis** (☏ 01776-703343;
21 North Strand St; ⊙ 24hr), just up from the
tourist office.

BOAT

P&O (☏ 08716 64 20 20; www.poferries.com)
Runs six to eight fast ferries a day from Cairnryan to Larne (Northern Ireland). The crossing
takes two hours.

Stena Line (☏ 08447 70 70 70; www.stenaline.
co.uk; passenger £20-29, driver plus car £99-
150) Runs five to six ferries from Cairnryan to
Belfast (2¾ hours).

BUS

Scottish Citylink buses run to Glasgow (£18.50,
2½ hours, three daily) and Edinburgh (£21.50,
four hours, three daily).

There are also several daily local buses to
Kirkcudbright and the towns along the A75, such
as Newton Stewart (45 minutes, at least hourly)
and Dumfries (£7, 2¼ hours, nine daily Monday
to Saturday, three on Sunday).

TRAIN

First Scotrail runs to/from Glasgow (£12.40, 2¼
hours, two to seven trains daily); it may be necessary to change at Ayr.

Portpatrick

POP 500

Portpatrick is a charming harbour village on the rugged west coast of the Rhinns of Galloway peninsula. It is a good base from which to explore the south of the peninsula, and it's the starting or finishing point for the Southern Upland Way (p150). You can follow part of the way to Stranraer (9 miles). It's a clifftop walk, with sections of farmland and heather moor.

🛏 Sleeping & Eating

Harbour House Hotel   INN ££

(☑ 01776-810456; www.theharbourhousehotel. co.uk; 53 Main St; s/d £60/100; 🛜🐕) Formerly the customs house, this is now a popular, old pub. Some of the recently refurbished rooms have brilliant views over the harbour. The hotel is also a warm nook for a traditional bar meal (mains £8 to £10).

★ Knockinaam Lodge   HOTEL £££

(☑ 01776-810471; www.knockinaamlodge.com; dinner, bed & breakfast s £200-310, d £320-420; 🅿🛜🐕) For a real dose of luxury, head 3 miles southeast to this former hunting lodge in a secluded location with grassy lawns rolling down to a sandy cove. It's where Churchill plotted the endgame of WWII – you can stay in his suite – and it's a very romantic place to get away from it all. The excellent French-influenced cuisine (lunch/dinner £40/65) is backed up by a great range of wines and single malts.

★ Campbell's   SEAFOOD ££

(☑ 01776-810314; www.campbellsrestaurant.co.uk; 1 South Crescent; mains £11 18; ⊙noon-2pm & 5.30-9pm Tue-Sun) Fresh local seafood is the stock-in-trade of this unprepossessing local favourite, and it is done very well. Ask for whatever is good that day and enjoy the flavour burst of locally caught fish or shellfish.

❶ Getting There & Away

Bus 367 runs to Stranraer (20 minutes, hourly Monday to Saturday, three Sunday).

South of Portpatrick

From Portpatrick, the road south to the Mull of Galloway passes coastal scenery that includes rugged cliffs, tiny harbours and sandy beaches. Dairy cattle graze on the greenest grass you've ever seen, and the warm waters

CORSEWALL LIGHTHOUSE HOTEL

It's just you and the cruel sea out here at this fabulously romantic 200-year-old **lighthouse** (☑ 01776-853220; www. lighthousehotel.co.uk; s/d from £170/190; 🅿🛜), right at the tip of the peninsula, 13 miles northwest of Stranraer. On a sunny day, the water shimmers with light, and you can see Ireland, Kintyre, Arran and Ailsa Craig. But when the wind and rain beat in, it's just great to be cosily holed up in the bar-restaurant or snuggling under the covers in your room. Rooms in the lighthouse building itself are attractive if necessarily compact; chalets are also available.

of the Gulf Stream give the peninsula the mildest climate in Scotland. This mildness is demonstrated at **Logan Botanic Garden** (www.rbge.org.uk/logan; adult/child £6/free; ⊙10am-4pm Sun Feb, 10am-5pm daily mid-Mar–Oct), a mile north of Port Logan, where subtropical flora include tree ferns and cabbage palms. The garden is an outpost of the Royal Botanic Garden in Edinburgh. **Port Logan** itself is a sleepy place with a decent pub and an excellent sandy beach.

Further south, **Drummore** is a fishing village on the east coast. From here it's another 5 miles to the **Mull of Galloway**, Scotland's most southerly point. It's a spectacular spot, with views of Scotland, England, the Isle of Man and Northern Ireland. The **lighthouse** (adult/child £2.50/1; ⊙10am-4pm Sat & Sun Easter-Oct, plus Mon-Wed Jul & Aug) here was built by Robert Stevenson, grandfather of the writer, in 1826. You can learn more about the Stevenson clan of lighthouse builders in the small **exhibition** (www.mull-of-galloway.co.uk; adult/child £2.50/1; ⊙10am-4pm Easter-Oct) at the lighthouse's base. The Mull of Galloway RSPB nature reserve, home to thousands of seabirds, is also important for its wildflowers. It has a **visitor centre** (www.rspb.org.uk; ⊙10am-5pm Apr-Oct) with plenty of information on local species and camera feeds from nesting birds on the cliff-face. There are guided walks on Tuesdays and Thursdays at 1pm. At the entrance to the reserve is a cafe (open 10am to 5.30pm April to October) with great views. The former homes of the lightkeepers are available to stay in; check out www.lighthouseholidaycottages.co.uk.

Central Scotland

Includes ➡

Best Seafood Restaurants

➡ Cellar Restaurant (p200)

➡ Craig Millar @ 16 West End (p201)

➡ Seafood Restaurant (p197)

Best Places to Stay

➡ Forth View Hotel (p191)

➡ Gleneagles Hotel (p204)

➡ Gilmore House (p208)

Why Go?

The country's historic roots are deeply embedded in central Scotland. Significant ruins and castles from the region's history pepper the landscape; key battles around Stirling shaped Scotland's fortunes; and Perth, the former capital, is where kings were crowned on the Stone of Destiny.

Arriving from Glasgow and Edinburgh, visitors begin to get a sense of the country further north as the Lowland belt gives way to Highland splendour. It is here that the majesty of Scotland's landscape unfolds in deep, dark, steely-blue lochs that reflect the silhouettes of soaring, sentinel-like craggy peaks on still days.

Whether in the softly wooded country of lowland Perthshire, or the green Fife coastline dotted with fishing villages, opportunities to enjoy the landscape abound: walking, cycling and angling are all easy possibilities. The region also has some of the country's best pubs and eateries, which greet weary visitors at day's end.

When to Go
Stirling

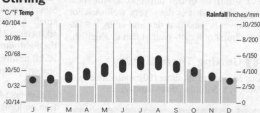

May A magical time to explore before summer crowds arrive, and to enjoy the Perth Arts Festival.

Jul–Aug Summer is best for seafood feasts in Fife, and fresh raspberries in Blairgowrie.

Oct–Nov Autumn colours enliven walks in the Perthshire woods around Crieff and Blairgowrie.

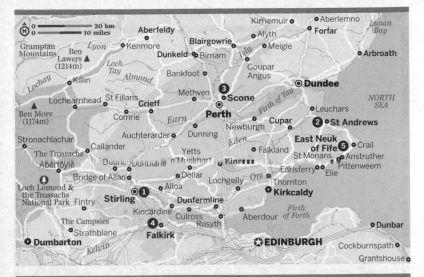

Central Scotland Highlights

1 Admiring the views from magnificent **Stirling Castle** (p179), across ancient independence battlefields

2 Pacing through the historic birthplace of golf, **St Andrews** (p192), to play the famous Old Course

3 Strutting with peacocks at noble **Scone Palace** (p202), where Scottish kings were once crowned

4 Taking a canal-boat trip through the engineering marvel that is the **Falkirk Wheel** (p188)

5 Feasting on local seafood in the picturesque fishing villages of the **East Neuk of Fife** (p198)

STIRLING REGION

Covering Scotland's wasplike waist, this region has always been a crucial strategic point dividing the Lowlands from the Highlands. Scotland's two most important independence battles were fought here, within sight of Stirling's hilltop stronghold. William Wallace's victory over the English at Stirling Bridge in 1297, followed by Robert Bruce's triumph at Bannockburn in 1314, established Scottish nationhood. The region remains a focus of much national pride.

Stirling

POP 36,150

With an utterly impregnable position atop a mighty wooded crag (the plug of an extinct volcano), Stirling's beautifully preserved Old Town is a treasure trove of historic buildings and cobbled streets winding up to the ramparts of its dominant castle, which offer views for miles around. Clearly visible is

the brooding Wallace Monument, a strange Victorian Gothic creation honouring the legendary freedom fighter of *Braveheart* fame. Nearby is Bannockburn, scene of Robert the Bruce's pivotal triumph over the English.

The castle makes a fascinating visit, but make sure you also spend time exploring the Old Town and the picturesque path that encircles it. Below the Old Town, retail-minded modern Stirling doesn't offer the same appeal; stick to the high ground as much as possible and you'll love the place.

◎ Sights

★ **Stirling Castle** CASTLE
(HS;www.stirlingcastle.gov.uk; adult/child £14/7.50; ◎9.30am-6pm Apr-Sep, to 5pm Oct-Mar) Hold Stirling and you control Scotland. This maxim has ensured that a fortress of some kind has existed here since prehistoric times. You cannot help drawing parallels with Edinburgh Castle, but many find Stirling's fortress more atmospheric – the location, architecture, historical significance and com-

Stirling

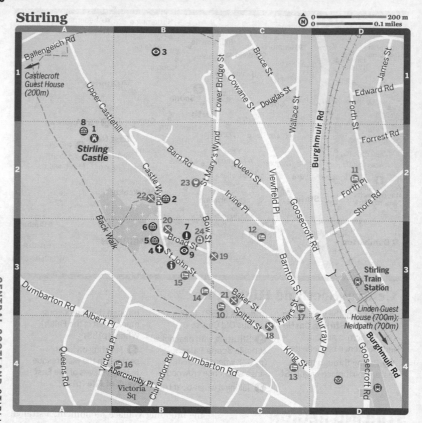

manding views combine to make it a grand and memorable sight. It's best to visit in the afternoon; many tourists come on day trips, so you may have the castle almost to yourself by about 4pm.

The current castle dates from the late 14th to the 16th century, when it was a residence of the Stuart monarchs. The undisputed highlight of a visit is the fabulous, recently restored **Royal Palace**. The idea was that it should look brand new, just as when it was constructed by French masons under the orders of James V in the mid-16th century with the aim of impressing his new (also French) bride and other crowned heads of Europe. The suite of six rooms – three for the king, three for the queen – is a sumptuous riot of colour. Particularly notable are the fine fireplaces, the **Stirling Heads** – modern reproductions of painted oak discs in the ceiling of the king's audience chamber – and the fabulous series of tapestries that have been

painstakingly woven over many years. Based on originals in New York's Metropolitan Museum, they depict the hunting of a unicorn – an event ripe with Christian metaphor – and are breathtakingly beautiful. Don't miss the palace exterior, studded with beautiful sculptures, or the **Stirling Heads Gallery** above the royal chambers. This displays the original carved oak roundels that decorated the king's audience chamber – a real rogue's gallery of royals, courtiers and classical personalities. In the vaults beneath the palace is a kid-friendly exhibition on various aspects of castle life.

The other buildings surrounding the main castle courtyard are the vast **Great Hall**, built by James IV; the **Royal Chapel**, remodelled in the early 17th century by James VI and with the colourful original mural painting intact; and the King's Old Building. This is now home to the **Museum of the Argyll & Sutherland Highlanders**

Stirling

(donations encouraged), which traces the history of this famous regiment from 1794, including its famous defensive action in the Battle of Balaclava in 1854. Make sure you read the moving letters from the world wars.

Other displays include the **Great Kitchens**, bringing to life the bustle and scale of the enterprise of cooking for the king and, near the entrance, the **Castle Exhibition**, which gives good background information on the Stuart kings and updates on current archaeological investigations. The magnificent vistas from the ramparts are stirring.

Admission includes an audioguide, and free guided tours leave regularly from near the entrance. Tours also run to **Argyll's Lodging** (Castle Wynd), at the top of Castle Wynd. Complete with turrets, this spectacular lodge is Scotland's most impressive 17th-century town house. It's the former home of William Alexander, Earl of Stirling and noted literary figure. It has been tastefully restored and gives an insight into lavish, 17th-century aristocratic life. There are four or five tours daily (you can't enter by other means).

Old Town   HISTORIC DISTRICT
Sloping steeply down from Stirling Castle, the Old Town has a remarkably different feel to modern Stirling, its cobblestone streets packed with 15th- to 17th-century architectural gems, and surrounded by Scotland's best-surviving town wall. Its growth began when Stirling became a royal burgh (about 1124), and in the 15th and 16th centuries rich merchants built their houses here.

Stirling's town wall was built around 1547 when Henry VIII of England began the 'Rough Wooing' – attacking the town in order to force Mary, Queen of Scots to marry his son so the two kingdoms could be united. The wall can be explored on the **Back Walk**, which follows the line of the wall from Dumbarton Rd to the castle. You pass the town cemeteries (check out the **Star Pyramid**, an outsized affirmation of Reformation values dating from 1863), then continue around the back of the castle to Gowan Hill, where you can see the **Beheading Stone**, now encased in iron bars to prevent contemporary use.

Mar's Wark, on Castle Wynd at the head of the Old Town, is the ornate facade of a Renaissance town house commissioned in 1569 by the wealthy Earl of Mar, regent of Scotland during James VI's minority.

The **Church of the Holy Rude** (www.holyrude.org; St John St; suggested donation £2; ⊙11am-4pm Easter & May-Sep) **FREE** has been the town's parish church for 600 years and James VI was crowned here in 1567. The nave and tower date from 1456, and the church has one of the few surviving medieval open-timber roofs. Stunning stained-glass windows and huge stone pillars create a powerful effect.

Behind the church is **Cowane's Hospital** (www.cowanes.org.uk; 49 St John St; ⊙10.30am-4.30pm May-Oct, 10.30am-5pm Tue-Sun Nov-Apr) **FREE**, built as an almshouse in 1637 by the merchant John Cowane. The high vaulted hall was much modified in the 19th century.

The **Mercat Cross**, in Broad St, is topped with a unicorn (known as 'The Puggie') and

Stirling Castle

PLANNING YOUR ATTACK

Stirling's a sizeable fortress, but not so huge that you'll have to decide what to leave out – there's time to see it all. Unless you've got a working knowledge of Scottish monarchs, head to the **Castle Exhibition ❶** first: it'll help you sort one James from another. That done, take on the sights at leisure. First, stop and look around you from the **ramparts ❷**; the views high over this flat valley, a key strategic point in Scotland's history, are magnificent.

Track back towards the citadel's heart, stopping for a quick tour through the **Great Kitchens ❸**; looking at all that fake food might make you seriously hungry, though. Then enter the main courtyard. Around you are the principal castle buildings. During summer there are events (such as Renaissance dancing) in the **Great Hall ❹** – get details at the entrance. The **Museum of the Argyll & Sutherland Highlanders ❺** is a treasure trove if you're interested in regimental history, but missable if you're not. Leave the best for last – crowds thin in the afternoon – and enter the sumptuous **Royal Palace ❻**.

Take time to admire the beautiful **Stirling Tapestries ❼**, skillfully woven by hand on-site between 2001-2014.

THE WAY UP & DOWN

If you have time, take the atmospheric Back Walk, a peaceful, shady stroll around the Old Town's fortifications and up to the castle's imposing crag-top position. Afterwards, wander down through the Old Town to admire its facades.

TOP TIPS

» **Admission** Entrance is free for Historic Scotland members. If you'll be visiting several Historic Scotland sites a membership will save you plenty.

» **Vital Statistics** First constructed: before 1110; number of sieges: at least nine; last besieger: Bonnie Prince Charlie (unsuccessful); money spent refurbishing the Royal Palace: £12 million.

DAVID ROBERTSON/ALAMY ©

Museum of the Argyll & Sutherland Highlanders
The history of one of Scotland's legendary regiments – now subsumed into the Royal Regiment of Scotland – is on display here, featuring memorabilia, weapons and uniforms.

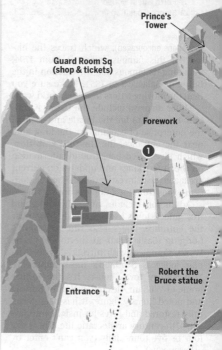

Prince's Tower

Guard Room Sq (shop & tickets)

Forework

❶

Robert the Bruce statue

Entrance

Castle Exhibition
A great overview of the Stewart dynasty here will get your facts straight, and also offers the latest archaeological titbits from the ongoing excavations under the citadel. Analysis of skeletons has revealed surprising amounts of biographical data.

Royal Palace
The impressive new highlight of a visit to the castle is this recreation of the royal lodgings originally built by James V. The finely worked ceiling, ornate furniture and sumptuous unicorn tapestries dazzle.

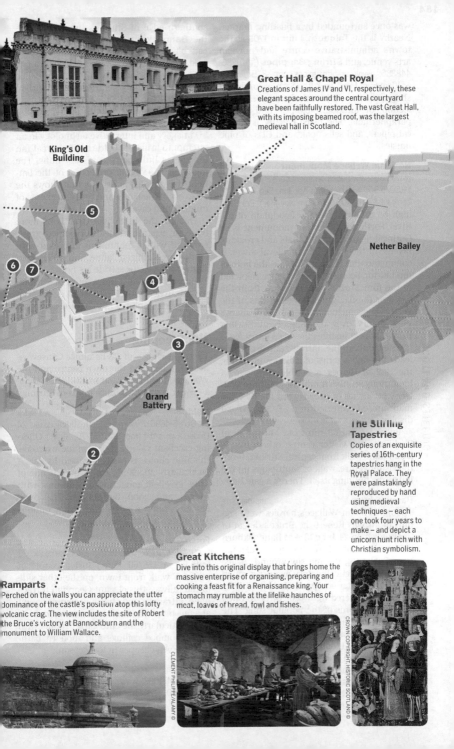

Great Hall & Chapel Royal

Creations of James IV and VI, respectively, these elegant spaces around the central courtyard have been faithfully restored. The vast Great Hall, with its imposing beamed roof, was the largest medieval hall in Scotland.

King's Old Building

⑤

⑥ ⑦

④

③

Nether Bailey

Grand Battery

② ②

The Stirling Tapestries

Copies of an exquisite series of 16th-century tapestries hang in the Royal Palace. They were painstakingly reproduced by hand using medieval techniques – each one took four years to make – and depict a unicorn hunt rich with Christian symbolism.

Great Kitchens

Dive into this original display that brings home the massive enterprise of organising, preparing and cooking a feast fit for a Renaissance king. Your stomach may rumble at the lifelike haunches of meat, loaves of bread, fowl and fishes.

Ramparts

Perched on the walls you can appreciate the utter dominance of the castle's position atop this lofty volcanic crag. The view includes the site of Robert the Bruce's victory at Bannockburn and the monument to William Wallace.

CLEMENT PHILIPPE/ALAMY ©

CROWN COPYRIGHT, HISTORIC SCOTLAND ©

was once surrounded by a bustling market. Nearby is the **Tolbooth**, built in 1705 as the town's administrative centre and now an arts venue, and **Stirling Bagpipes** (☑01786-448886; www.stirlingbagpipes.com; 8 Broad St; ◷10am-6pm Mon, Tue & Thu-Sat), a combined shop and workshop that also houses a collection of antique bagpipes and piping paraphernalia. The place is a focus for local pipers, and sells books and CDs of pipe music.

National Wallace Monument   MONUMENT
(www.nationalwallacemonument.com; adult/child £9.50/5.90; ◷10am-5pm Apr-Jun, Sep & Oct, to 6pm Jul & Aug, 10.30am-4pm Nov-Mar) Perched high on a crag above the floodplain of the River Forth, this Victorian monument is so Gothic it deserves circling bats and croaking ravens. In the shape of a medieval tower, it commemorates William Wallace, the hero of the bid for Scottish independence depicted in the film *Braveheart*. The view from the top over the flat, green gorgeousness of the Forth Valley, including the site of Wallace's 1297 victory over the English at Stirling Bridge, almost justifies the steep entry fee.

The climb up the narrow staircase inside leads through a series of galleries including the Hall of Heroes, a marble pantheon of lugubrious Scottish luminaries. Admire Wallace's 66 inches of broadsword and see the man himself recreated in a 3D audiovisual display.

Buses 62 and 63 run from Murray Pl in Stirling to the visitor centre; otherwise it's a half-hour walk from central Stirling. From the visitor centre, walk or shuttle-bus up the hill to the building itself. There's a cafe here.

Bannockburn   HISTORIC SITE
Though William Wallace's heroics were significant, it was Robert the Bruce's defeat of the English on 24 June 1314 at Bannockburn that finally established a lasting Scottish nation. Exploiting the marshy ground, Bruce won a great tactical victory against a much larger and better-equipped force (the Scots were outnumbered by two or three to one), and, in the words of the popular song 'The Flower of Scotland', sent Edward II 'homeward, tae think again' (Roy Williamson, The Corries (Music) Ltd, by permission).

The problem with 700-year-old battlefields is that there isn't much left to see today. There has been much debate over exactly where the main battle took place, but it was somewhere on what is now the southern edge of Stirling's urban sprawl – the **Bannockburn Heritage Centre** (NTS; battleofbannockburn.com; Glasgow Rd; adult/child/family £11/8/30; ◷10am-5.30pm Mar-Oct, to 5pm Nov-Feb) looks for all the world like a 1970s community centre set in suburban parkland. Reopened after a major refurbishment in time for the 700th anniversary of the battle, the centre uses animated films, 3D imagery and interactive technology in an attempt to bring the battle to life – great fun for kids, a little naff for history buffs. The highlight is a digital projection of the battlefield onto a 3D landscape that shows the progress of the battle and the movements of infantry and cavalry.

Outside, the 'battlefield' itself is no more than an expanse of neatly trimmed grass, crowned with a monument inscribed with a poem by Kathleen Jamie, and a Victorian statue of the victor astride his horse.

Bannockburn is 2 miles south of Stirling; you can reach it on First bus 24 or 54 from Stirling bus station (£1.80, 10 minutes, three per hour).

🛏 Sleeping

There's a choice of B&Bs along Causewayhead Rd, between the town centre and the Wallace Monument, and in Bridge of Allan, a former spa town 3 miles north of Stirling.

Neidpath   B&B £
(☑01786-469017; www.neidpath-stirling.co.uk; 24 Linden Ave; s/d/f from £40/60/70; ℗🖤) Offering excellent value and a genuine welcome, this fine choice is easily accessed by car. A particularly appealing front room is one of three excellent modernised bedrooms with fridges and good bathrooms. The owners also run various self-catering options around town; details via the website.

Forth Guest House   B&B £
(☑01786-471020; www.forthguesthouse.co.uk; 23 Forth Pl; s/d £55/60; ℗🖤) Just a couple of minutes' walk from town, on the other side of the railway, this elegant Georgian terrace offers attractive and stylish accommodation at a fair price. The rooms are very commodious, particularly the cute garret rooms with their coombed ceilings and modern bathrooms. Even cheaper in low season.

Sruighlea   B&B £
(☑01786-471082; www.sruighlea.com; 27 King St; s/d £45/60; 🖤) This place feels like a secret hideaway – there's no sign – but it's conven-

WILLIAM WALLACE, SCOTTISH PATRIOT

William Wallace is one of Scotland's best-known historical figures, a patriot whose exploits set the scene for Scotland's wars of independence. Born in 1270, he was cata-pulted into fame and a place in history as a highly successful guerrilla commander who harassed the English invaders for many years.

In the wake of his victory over the English at Stirling Bridge in 1297, Wallace was knighted by Robert the Bruce and proclaimed Guardian of Scotland. However, it was only a short time before English military superiority and the fickle loyalties of the Scots nobili-ty turned against the defender of Scottish independence.

Disaster struck in July 1298 when King Edward's forces defeated the Scots at the Battle of Falkirk. Wallace went into hiding and travelled throughout Europe to drum up support for the Scottish cause. But many Scottish nobles were prepared to side with Edward, and Wallace was betrayed after his return to Scotland in 1305; he was found guilty of treason at Westminster and hanged, beheaded and disembowelled at Smith-field, London.

iently located smack bang in the centre of town. You'll feel like a local staying here, and there are eating and drinking places practically on the doorstep. It's a B&B that welcomes guests with the kind of warmth that keeps them returning.

Cairns Guest House B&B £
(☑ 01786-479228; www.cairnsguesthouse.co.uk; 12 Princes St; s/tw £35/60; ☎) This central guest-house gives decent value for simple comfort. The friendly, flexible, easygoing owners will offer discounts for stays of more than one night, or if you don't want breakfast.

Munro Guesthouse B&B £
(☑ 01786-472685; www.munroguesthouse.co.uk; 14 Princes St; s/d/f from £34/58/85; ☎) Cosy and cheery, Munro Guesthouse is right in the centre of town but located on a quiet side street. Things are done with a smile here, and the smallish rooms are most in-viting, particularly the cute attic ones. The breakfast is also better than the norm, with fruit salad on hand. There's easy (pay) park-ing opposite.

Willy Wallace Backpackers Hostel HOSTEL £
(☑ 01786-446773;www.willywallacehostel.com; 77 Murray Pl; dm/tw £18/38; @☎) This highly convenient central hostel is friendly, roomy and sociable. The colourful, spacious dorms are clean and light, and it has free tea and coffee, a good kitchen and a laissez-faire at-mosphere. Other amenities include bicycle hire, laundry service and free internet and wi-fi.

Stirling SYHA HOSTEL £
(☑ 01786-473442; www.syha.org.uk; St John St; dm/tw £21/55; P@☎) This hostel has an

unbeatable location and great facilities. Though its facade is that of a former church, the interior is modern and efficient. The dorms are compact but comfortable, with lockers and en suite bathrooms; other high-lights include a pool table, a bike shed and, at busy times, cheap meals on offer. Lack of atmosphere can be the only problem.

Witches Craig Caravan Park CAMPSITE £
(☑ 01786-474947; www.witchescraig.co.uk; tent site for 1/2/2 plus car £10/12.50/19.50; ☉ Apr-Oct; P☎) In a brilliant spot right at the foot of the Ochil Hills, which are just begging to be walked, Witches Craig is 3 miles east of Stir-ling by the A91.

Castlecroft Guest House B&B ££
(☑ 01786-474933; www.castlecroft-uk.com; Bal-lengeich Rd; s/d £50/65; P@☎) Nestling into the hillside under the back of the castle, this great hideaway feels like a rural retreat but is a short, spectacular walk from the heart of Stirling. The lounge and deck area enjoy views over green fields to the nearby hills, the rooms have excellent modern bathrooms and the welcome couldn't be more hospita-ble. Breakfast features homemade bread, among other delights.

Victoria Square Guesthouse B&B ££
(☑ 01786-473920; www.victoriasquareguesthouse. com; 12 Victoria Sq; s/d £70/105; ☎) Though close to the centre of town, Victoria Sq is a quiet oasis with elegant Victorian buildings surrounding a verdant swath of lawn. This luxury guesthouse's huge rooms, bay win-dows and period features make it a winner – there's a great four-poster room for romantic

getaways, and some bedrooms have views to the castle towering above. No children.

Linden Guest House
B&B ££

(☑ 01786-448850; www.lindenguesthouse.co.uk; 22 Linden Ave; d £65-80, f £90-150; P @ 🛜) The warm welcome and easy parking here offer understandable appeal. The rooms, two of which are great for families, have fridges and posh TVs with DVD and iPod dock, and the gleaming bathrooms could feature in ads for cleaning products. Breakfast features fresh fruit and kippers, among other choices.

Stirling Highland Hotel
HOTEL £££

(☑ 01786-272727; www.pumahotels.co.uk; Spittal St; r from £130; P @ 🛜 ⛳) A sympathetic refurbishment of the old high school, the Stirling Highland has something of the atmosphere of an Edwardian gentleman's club but has great facilities that include pool, spa, gym, sauna and squash courts. It's convenient for the castle and Old Town and service is helpful, though the comfortably modernised rooms vary considerably in size.

Premium rooms offer the best views but aren't really worth the £30 to £50 upgrade; internet bookings can be cheaper than the prices listed here.

Colessio Hotel
HOTEL £££

(☑ 01786-448880; www.hotelcolessio.com; 33 Spittal St; r from £160; 🛜) Opened in July 2014, this new luxury hotel and spa occupies a landmark neoclassical building (a former hospital) in the heart of the Old Town. The luxury conversion includes sumptuous rooms and suites with a touch of designer decadence, and a sophisticated cocktail bar and restaurant.

🍴 Eating & Drinking

Darnley Coffee House
CAFE £

(☑ 01786-474468; www.facebook.com/DarnleyCoffeeHouse; 18 Bow St; mains £3-5; ⊙ 11am-4pm Mon-Sat, noon-4pm Sun) Just down the hill from Stirling Castle, this is a good pit stop for home baking, soup and speciality coffees during a walk around the Old Town. The cafe is in the vaulted cellars of a 16th-century house where Darnley, lover and later husband of Mary, Queen of Scots, once stayed while visiting her.

Breá
CAFE ££

(www.breastirling.com; 5 Baker St; mains £9-18; ⊙ 10am-9.30pm Tue-Sun; 🖬) 🌱 Bringing a bohemian touch to central Stirling, this busy bistro has pared-back contemporary decor and a short menu showcasing carefully sourced Scottish produce, including Brewdog beers. Best in show is perhaps the pork burger with apple and black pudding – a huge thing served with homemade bread.

Hermann's
AUSTRIAN, SCOTTISH ££

(☑ 01786-450632; www.hermanns.co.uk; 58 Broad St; 3-course lunch/dinner £13/22, mains £12-23; ⊙ noon-3pm & 6-10pm; 🍴) This elegant Scottish-Austrian restaurant is a reliable and popular choice. The solid, conservative decor is oddly offset by magazine-spread skiing photos, but the food doesn't miss a beat and ranges from Scottish favourites to gourmet schnitzel and *spätzle* noodles. Vegetarian options are good, and quality Austrian wines provide an out-of-the-ordinary accompaniment.

Mamma Mia
ITALIAN ££

(www.mammamiastirling.co.uk; 52 Spittal St; mains £10-17; ⊙ noon-3pm Tue-Sat, 5-10pm Mon-Sat) This Old Town split-level favourite has a short menu of southern Italian cuisine augmented by weekly specials, which are definitely worth going for. It shows a sure touch with sea bass and Scottish steaks alike, though it's hard not to feel the pasta dishes are a mite overpriced.

Portcullis
PUB FOOD ££

(☑ 01786-472290; www.theportcullishotel.com; Castle Wynd; bar meals £9-13; ⊙ food served noon-3.30pm & 5.30-9pm; 🛜) Built in stone as solid as the castle that it stands below, this former school is just the spot for a pint and a pub lunch after your castle visit. With bar meals that would have had even William Wallace loosening his belt a couple of notches, a little beer garden and a cosy buzz indoors, it's well worth a visit.

Settle Inn
PUB

(☑ 01786-474609; 91 St Mary's Wynd; ⊙ 11am-11pm; 🛜) A warm welcome is guaranteed at Stirling's oldest pub (1733), a spot redolent with atmosphere, what with its log fire, vaulted back room and low-slung ceilings. Guest ales, atmospheric nooks for settling in for the night and a blend of local characters make it a classic of its kind.

ℹ️ Information

Stirling Community Hospital (☑ 01786-434000; www.nhsforthvalley.com; Livilands Rd) South of the town centre; has a minor injuries unit. Nearest emergency department is

Forth Valley Royal Hospital in Larbert, 9 miles southeast of Stirling.

Stirling Library (Corn Exchange Rd; ⊘9.30am-5.30pm Mon, Wed & Fri, to 7pm Tue & Thu, to 5pm Sat) Free internet access.

Stirling Tourist Office (⊡01786-475019; www.visitstirling.org; Old Town Jail, St John St; ⊘10am-5pm) Accommodation booking, internet access.

❶ Getting There & Away

BUS

The **bus station** is on Goosecroft Rd. **Citylink** (⊡0871 266 33 33; www.citylink.co.uk) offers a number of services to/from Stirling:

Dundee £14, 1¾ hours, hourly

Edinburgh £8, one hour, hourly

Glasgow £7.50, 40 minutes, hourly

Perth £9, 50 minutes, at least hourly

Some buses continue to Aberdeen, Inverness and Fort William; more frequently a change will be required.

TRAIN

First ScotRail (www.scotrail.co.uk) has services to/from a number of destinations, including the following:

Aberdeen £32, 2¼ hours, hourly weekdays, every two hours Sunday

Dundee £14, one hour, hourly weekdays, every two hours Sunday

Edinburgh £8.30, one hour, twice hourly Monday to Saturday, hourly Sunday

Glasgow £8.60, 50 minutes, twice hourly Monday to Saturday, hourly Sunday

Perth £12.60, 30 minutes, hourly weekdays, every two hours Sunday

Around Stirling

Dunblane

POP 8800

Dunblane, 5 miles northwest of Stirling, is a pretty town with a notable cathedral. It's difficult not to remember the horrific massacre that took place in the primary school in 1996, but happier headlines have come the town's way more recently when Dunblane-born tennis star Andy Murray won Wimbledon in 2013 – a gold-painted letterbox near the cathedral commemorates his 2012 Olympic gold medal.

Fabulous **Dunblane Cathedral** (HS; www.dunblanecathedral.org.uk; Cathedral Sq; ⊘9.30am-12.30pm & 1.30-5pm Mon-Sat 2-5pm Sun Apr-Sep, 9.30am-4pm Mon-Sat 2-4pm Sun

Oct-Mar) **FREE** is well worth a detour. It's a superb, elegant Gothic sandstone building. The lower parts of the walls date from Norman times, the rest mainly from the 13th to 15th centuries, though the bell tower stood alongside an earlier 12th-century structure. A 10th-century carved Celtic stone is at the nave's head, and a standing stone commemorates the town's slain children.

Just down from the cathedral, the musty old **Leighton Library** (61 High St; ⊘11am-1pm Mon-Sat May-Sep) **FREE**, dating from 1684, is the oldest private library in Scotland, with 4500 books in 90 languages.

There are frequent buses and trains from Stirling to Dunblane.

Doune

POP 1630

Doune is not far beyond Dunblane, on the road to Callander. Stop here to visit magnificent **Doune Castle** (HS; www.historic-scotland.gov.uk; adult/child £5.50/3.30; ⊘9.30am-5.30pm Apr-Sep, to 4.30pm Oct-Mar, closed Thu-Fri Nov-Mar), one of the best-preserved 14th-century castles in Scotland. It was a favourite royal hunting lodge, but was also of great strategic importance because it controlled the route between the Lowlands and Highlands. Mary, Queen of Scots, stayed here, as did Bonnie Prince Charlie, who used it to imprison government troops. There are great views from the castle walls, and the lofty gatehouse is very impressive, rising nearly 30m. Some may recognise the castle from *Monty Python and the Holy Grail*.

Doune is 8 miles northwest of Stirling. **First** (www.firstgroup.com) buses run every hour or two (£3.80, 30 minutes), less frequently on Sunday.

Dollar

Castle Campbell   CASTLE
(HS; www.historic-scotland.gov.uk; adult/child £5.50/3.30; ⊘9.30am-5.30pm Apr-Sep, to 4.30pm Oct, to 4.30pm Sat-Wed Nov-Mar) Castle Campbell is a 20-minute walk up Dollar Glen, into the wooded hills above the charming village of Dollar. It's a spooky old stronghold of the Dukes of Argyll and stands between two ravines; you can clearly see why it was known as 'Castle Gloom'.

There's been a fortress of some kind on this site from the 11th century, but the present structure dates from the 15th century. The castle was sacked by Cromwell in 1654,

WORTH A TRIP

THE FALKIRK WHEEL & THE KELPIES

Scotland's canals were once vital avenues for goods transport, but the railway age left them to fall into dereliction. A millennium project restored two of Scotland's major canals, the Union and the Forth & Clyde, which were once linked by an arduous series of 11 locks covering the difference in level of 115ft. The construction of the unique Falkirk Wheel changed all that. Its rotating arms literally scoop boats up and lift them to the higher waterway.

Falkirk is a large town about 10 miles southeast of Stirling. Regular buses and trains link the two, and also connect Falkirk with Glasgow and Edinburgh.

Falkirk Wheel (www.thefalkirkwheel.co.uk; visitor centre free, boat trips per adult/child £8.95/4.95; ☺10am-5.30pm daily Mar-Oct, 11am-4pm Wed-Sun Nov-Feb; P) The Falkirk Wheel is a modern engineering marvel, a rotating boat lift that raises vessels 115ft from the Forth and Clyde Canal to the Union Canal. Boat trips depart from the lower basin every 40 minutes (hourly in winter) and travel into the wheel, which delivers you to the Union Canal high above.

Boats then go through Roughcastle Tunnel before the return descent on the wheel. Anyone with an interest in engineering should not miss this boat ride – it's great for kids, too. There's also a cafe and a visitor centre which explains the workings of the mighty wheel – it only takes the power of about eight toasters for a full rotation!

The Kelpies (01324-506850; www.thehelix.co.uk; The Helix; guided tours adult/child £4.95/3; ☺tours 10am-3.30pm) The Kelpies, a pair of stunning equine statues gracing the eastern entrance to the Forth & Clyde Canal, are named after mythical Scottish water-horses. The two 30m-tall horse's heads are fashioned out of stainless steel, and are a tribute to the working horses that once hauled barges along the canal. They are clearly visible from the M9 motorway between Edinburgh and Stirling.

but the tower is well preserved. From the little car park near the castle there's a great ramble with sweeping views over Castle Campbell and the surrounding country.

Dollar is about 11 miles east of Stirling and is served by a regular bus service.

FIFE

Protruding like a serpent's head from Scotland's east coast, Fife (www.visitfife.com) is a tongue of land between the Firths of Forth and Tay. An atmosphere distinct from the rest of Scotland and a place in royal history have seen the region style itself as 'The Kingdom of Fife'.

Though overdeveloped southern Fife is commuter-belt territory, the eastern part's rolling green farmland and quaint fishing villages are prime turf for exploration, and the fresh sea air feels like it's doing a power of good. Fife's biggest attraction, St Andrews, has Scotland's most venerable university and a wealth of historic buildings. It's also, of course, the home of golf and draws professionals and keen amateurs alike to

take on the Old Course – the classic links experience.

🏃 Activities

The **Fife Coastal Path** (www.fifecoastalpath. co.uk) runs more than 80 miles, following the entire Fife coastline from the Forth Road Bridge to the Tay Bridge and beyond. It's well waymarked, picturesque and not too rigorous, though winds can buffet. It's easily accessed for shorter sections or day walks, and long stretches of it can also be tackled on a mountain bike.

ℹ️ Getting Around

The main bus operator here is **Stagecoach Fife** (0871 200 2233; www.stagecoachbus.com). For £8 you can buy a Fife Dayrider ticket, which gives one day's unlimited travel around Fife on Stagecoach buses.

If you are driving from the Forth Road Bridge to St Andrews, a slower but much more scenic route than the M90/A91 is along the signposted **Fife Coastal Tourist Route**.

Culross

POP 400

An enchanting little town, Culross (*koo-ross*) is Scotland's best-preserved example of a 17th-century Scottish burgh: the National Trust for Scotland (NTS) owns 20 of the town's buildings, including the palace. Small, red-tiled, whitewashed buildings line the cobbled streets, and the winding Back Causeway to the abbey is lined with whimsical stone cottages.

As the birthplace of St Mungo, Glasgow's patron saint, Culross was an important religious centre from the 6th century. The burgh developed, under laird George Bruce, by mining coal through extraordinary underwater tunnels. When mining was ended by flooding of the tunnels, the town switched to making linen and shoes.

Culross Palace (NTS; www.nts.org.uk; adult/child £10.50/7.50; ⊙noon-5pm Thu-Mon Apr-May & Sep, noon-5pm daily Jun-Aug, noon-4pm Thu-Mon Oct) is more a large house than a palace, and features extraordinary decorative painted woodwork, barrel-vaulted ceilings and an interior largely unchanged since the early 17th century. The Town House (tourist office downstairs) and the Study, completed in the early 17th century, are also open to the public (via guided tour included in palace admission), but the other NTS properties can only be viewed from the outside.

Ruined Culross Abbey (HS; www.historic-scotland.gov.uk; ⊙9.30am-4pm Mon-Sat, 2-7pm Sun Apr-Sep, 9.30am-4pm Mon-Sat, 2-4pm Sun Oct-Mar) **FREE**, founded by the Cistercians in 1217, is on a hill in a lovely peaceful spot with vistas of the firth. Part of the ruins were converted into the parish church in the 16th century; it's worth a peek inside for the stained glass and the Gothic Argyll tomb.

Above a pottery workshop near the palace, Biscuit Café (www.culrosspottery.com; mains £3-6; ⊙10am-5pm) has a tranquil little garden and sells coffee, tempting organic cakes and scones, and tasty light meals.

Culross is 12 miles west of the Forth Road Bridge. Stagecoach (www.stagecoachbus.com) bus 78 runs from Dunfermline (£2.75, 25 minutes, hourly) via Culross to Stirling (£4.70, 50 minutes, hourly Monday to Saturday).

Dunfermline

POP 49,700

Dunfermline is a large and unlovely town, sprawling eastwards through once-distinct villages. Its history is centred on evocative Dunfermline Abbey (HS; www.historic-scotland.gov.uk; St Margaret St; adult/child £4.50/2.70; ⊙9.30am-5.30pm daily Apr-Sep, to 4.30pm Oct, 9.30am-4.30pm Sat-Wed Nov-Mar), founded by David I in the 12th century as a Benedictine monastery. Dunfermline was already favoured by religious royals; Malcolm III married the exiled Saxon princess Margaret here in the 11th century, and both chose to be interred here. There were many more royal burials, none more notable than Robert the Bruce, whose remains were interred here in 1329.

What's left of the abbey are the ruins of the impressive three-tiered refectory building, and the atmosphere-laden nave of the old church, endowed with geometrically patterned columns and fine Romanesque and Gothic windows. It adjoins the 19th-century church (⊙10am-4.30pm Mon-Sat, 2-4.30pm Sun Apr-Oct) **FREE** where Robert the Bruce lies under the ornate pulpit.

Next to the refectory (and included in your abbey admission price) is Dunfermline Palace. Once the abbey guesthouse, it was converted for James VI, whose son, the ill-fated Charles I, was born here in 1600. Below stretches the leafy, strollable Pittencrieff Park.

The distinctive Abbot House Heritage Centre (www.abbothouse.co.uk; Maygate; adult/child £4/free, ⊙9.30am-5pm Mon Sat, 10am-5pm

---

WORTH A TRIP

DEEP SEA WORLD

If the kids are tiring of historic buildings, a trip to Deep Sea World (www.deepseaworld.com; North Queensferry; adult/child £13.50/9.50; ⊙10am-6pm) might make them feel more kindly towards Fife. Situated at North Queensferry, just by the Forth bridges, this is a blockbuster aquarium with all those 'respect' species like sharks and piranhas, as well as seals and touch pools with rays and other sea creatures. You can even arrange guided dives with sharks. It's a little cheaper if you pre-purchase tickets online.

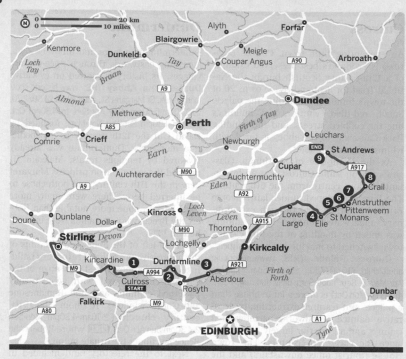

Driving Tour
The Fife Coast

START STIRLING
FINISH ST ANDREWS
DISTANCE 76 MILES
DURATION ONE DAY

Head south from Stirling on the M9 and at Junction 7 turn east towards Kincardine Bridge. As you approach the bridge, follow signs for Kincardine and Kirkcaldy then, once across the Firth of Forth, follow the Fife Coastal Tourist Route signposts to the historic village of **❶ Culross**. Spend an hour or so exploring the medieval buildings of Culross before continuing via the A994 to **❷ Dunfermline**, for a look at its fine abbey and palace ruins.

From Dunfermline take the M90 towards the Forth Road Bridge, but leave at Junction 1 (signposted A921 Dalgety Bay) and continue to the attractive seaside village of **❸ Aberdour** for lunch at the Aberdour Inn or the Room with a View restaurant. Stay on the A921 as far as Kirkcaldy, then take the faster A915 (signposted St Andrews) as far as Up-

per Largo where you follow the A917 towards Elie; from here on, you will be following the brown Fife Coastal Tourist Route signs.

❹ Elie, with its sandy beaches and coastal footpaths, is a great place to stretch your legs and take in some bracing sea air before driving just a couple of miles further on to explore the neighbouring fishing villages of **❺ St Monans** and **❻ Pittenweem**. Just 1 mile beyond Pittenweem, **❼ Anstruther** deserves a slightly longer stop for a visit to the Scottish Fisheries Museum, a stroll by the harbour and an ice cream. If time allows, you may want to detour inland a couple of miles to visit Kellie Castle or Scotland's Secret Bunker.

The final stop before St Andrews is the pretty fishing village of **❽ Crail**, where the late afternoon or early evening light will provide ideal conditions for capturing one of Scotland's most photographed harbours. A brisk hike along the coastal path towards Fife Ness, keeping an eye out for seals and seabirds, will round off the day before driving the last 10 miles into **❾ St Andrews**.

Sun Apr-Oct, 10am-4pm Mon-Sat Nov-Mar) near the abbey dates from the 15th century. History buffs could get lost for hours among the absorbing displays about the history of Scotland, the abbey and Dunfermline; entry includes a guided tour. There's a good cafe here, which serves beers brewed in the neighbouring 17th-century-style brewhouse.

There are frequent buses between Dunfermline and Edinburgh (£5.30, 50 minutes), Stirling (£4.70, 1¼ hours) and St Andrews (£10.45, 1¼ hours), and trains to/from Edinburgh (£5.10, 40 minutes).

Aberdour

POP 1630

It's worth stopping in this popular seaside town to ramble around impressive **Aberdour Castle** (HS; www.historic-scotland.gov. uk; adult/child £5.50/3.30; ☻9.30am-5.30pm Apr-Sep, to 4.30pm Oct, 9.30am-4.30pm Sat-Wed Nov-Mar). Long a residence of the Douglases of Morton, the stately structure exhibits several architectural phases; it's worth purchasing the guidebook to better comprehend what you see. Most charming of all is the elaborate *doocot* (dovecote) in the garden. Be sure to pop into the beautiful Romanesque **church of St Fillan's**, next door to the castle.

It's difficult to imagine a more enchanting setting than that enjoyed by the **Forth View Hotel** (☏01383-860402; www.forthviewhotel. co.uk; Hawkcraig Point; s £45-70, d £65-98; ☻Apr-Oct; P🛜), a friendly B&B right on the water in a secluded location. The front rooms offer utterly fabulous views through huge windows across the firth to Edinburgh and the hospitality is most welcoming. Happily, there's also an excellent little seafood restaurant, **Room with a View** (☏01383-860402; www.roomwithaviewrestaurant.co.uk; Hawkcraig Point; lunch mains £10-13, dinner mains £14-20; ☻noon-2pm Wed-Sun, 6-10pm Wed-Sat), in the front room. It's tough to find the place – part of its charm; follow signs for Silver Sands beach, go through the car park and down a steep narrow lane on the other side.

With real ales and good vegetarian choices on the menu, the family-run **Aberdour Hotel** (☏01383-860325; www.aberdourhotel. co.uk; 38 High St; s/d £70/93; P🛜🐾), on the main road through town, is not only a good place to stay, but also a tummy-warming meal stop with an emphasis on hearty, home-cooked food.

There are regular trains to Edinburgh (£5.80, 40 minutes) and Dundee (£13.60, 1¼ hours) from Aberdour, as well as buses to nearby Dunfermline (£4, 40 minutes).

Kirkcaldy

POP 49,700

Kirkcaldy (kir-*caw*-day) wins no prizes for prettiness, its slightly shabby promenade sprawling along the edge of the sea for several miles, with spectacular pounding surf on windy days. The town is famous as the birthplace of 18th-century Enlightenment philosopher and economist **Adam Smith** (the man who features on the English £20 note), but is only worth a stop for its excellent museum.

Kirkcaldy Museum & Art Gallery (www. kirkcaldygalleries.org.uk; War Memorial Gardens, Abbotshall Rd; ☻noon-7pm Mon, 9.30am-5pm Wed & Fri, 9.30am-7pm Tue & Thu, 9.30am-4pm Sat, noon-4pm Sun) FREE, recently reopened after extensive remodelling, houses an impressive collection of **Scottish paintings** from the 18th to the 20th century, including work from the Scottish Colourists and the Glasgow Boys. The kids will have a ball as there are plenty of hands-on attractions.

The **tourist office** (☏01592-267775; www. visitfife.com; 339 High St; ☻10am-5pm Mon-Sat Apr-Sep, 10am-4pm Mon-Sat Oct-Mar) is at the eastern end of the waterfront strip, and the museum is a short walk east from the train and bus stations.

Frequent buses run to St Andrews (£7.80, one hour), Anstruther (£6, 1¼ hours) and Edinburgh (£6.50, one hour). Two to four trains an hour run to Edinburgh (£7.60, 45 minutes) and Dundee (£11.30, 40 minutes).

Falkland

POP 1100

Below the soft ridges of the Lomond Hills in the centre of Fife lies the charming village of Falkland. Rising majestically out of the town centre is 16th-century **Falkland Palace** (NTS; www.nts.org.uk; adult/child £12.50/9; ☻11am-5pm Mon-Sat, noon-5pm Sun Mar-Oct), a country residence of the Stuart monarchs, where Mary, Queen of Scots is said to have spent the happiest days of her life 'playing the country girl in the woods and parks'. The palace was built between 1501 and 1541 to replace a castle dating from the 12th century; French and Scottish craftspeople were employed to create a masterpiece of Scottish Gothic architecture. The king's bedchamber and the chapel, with its beautiful painted ceiling, have both been restored. Don't miss the prodigious 17th-century Flemish hunting tapestries in the hall, and the oldest royal tennis court in Britain, built in 1539 for James V. It's in the grounds and still in use.

Falkland village is 11 miles north of Kirkcaldy. Stagecoach bus 64 links St Andrews to Falkland direct (£5.30, 1½ hours, hourly Monday to Saturday, five on Sunday). If travelling from Edinburgh (£11.70, hourly Monday to Saturday, five on Sunday), change buses at Glenrothes.

St Andrews

POP 16,900

For a small place, St Andrews has made a big name for itself. Firstly as a religious centre, then as Scotland's oldest university town (and third-oldest in Britain), but it is its status as the home of golf that has propelled it to even greater fame, and today's pilgrims mostly arrive with a set of clubs. Nevertheless, it's a lovely place to visit even if you've no interest in the game, with impressive medieval ruins, stately university buildings, idyllic white sands and excellent accommodation and eating options.

The Old Course, the world's most famous golf links, has a striking seaside location at the western end of town – it's a thrilling experience to stroll the hallowed turf.

History

St Andrews is said to have been founded by St Regulus (also known as St Rule), who arrived from Greece in the 4th century bringing with him the bones of St Andrew, Scotland's patron saint. The town soon grew into a major pilgrimage centre and St Andrews developed into the ecclesiastical capital of the country. The university, the first in Scotland, was founded in 1410.

Golf has been played at St Andrews for more than 600 years; the game's governing body was founded here in 1754 and the imposing Royal & Ancient clubhouse was built 100 years later.

⊙ Sights

St Andrews Cathedral RUIN
(HS; www.historic-scotland.gov.uk; The Pends; adult/child £4.50/2.70, incl castle £7.20/4.40; ⊙9.30am-5.30pm Apr-Sep, to 4.30pm Oct-Mar) The ruins of this cathedral are all that's left of one of Britain's most magnificent medieval buildings. You can appreciate the scale and majesty of the edifice from the small sections that remain standing. Although founded in 1160, it was not consecrated until 1318. It stood as the focus of this important pilgrimage centre until 1559, when it was pillaged during the Reformation.

St Andrew's supposed bones lie under the altar; until the cathedral was built, they had been enshrined in the nearby **Church of St Regulus** (or Rule). All that remains of this church is **St Rule's Tower**, worth the climb for the view across St Andrews. There's also a museum with a collection of Celtic crosses and gravestones found on the site. The entrance fee only applies for the tower and museum; you can wander freely around the atmospheric ruins, a fine picnic spot.

St Andrews Castle CASTLE
(HS; www.historic-scotland.gov.uk; The Scores; adult/child £5.50/3.30, incl cathedral £7.20/4.40; ⊙9.30am-5.30pm Apr-Sep, to 4.30pm Oct-Mar) The town's castle is mainly in ruins, but the site itself is evocative and has dramatic coastline views. It was founded around 1200 as a fortified home for the bishop of St Andrews. After the execution of Protestant reformers in 1545, other reformers retaliated by murdering Cardinal Beaton and taking over the castle. They spent almost a year holed up, during which they and their attackers dug a complex of siege tunnels; you can walk (or stoop) along their damp mossy lengths.

The visitor centre gives a good audiovisual introduction and has a small collection of Pictish stones.

British Golf Museum MUSEUM
(www.britishgolfmuseum.co.uk; Bruce Embankment; adult/child £6.50/3; ⊙9.30am-5pm Mon-Sat, 10am-5pm Sun Apr-Oct, 10am-4pm Sun Nov-Mar) This museum provides an extraordinarily comprehensive overview of the history and development of the game and the role of St Andrews in it. Favourite fact: bad players were formerly known as 'foozlers'. Interactive panels allow you to relive former British Opens (watch Paul Azinger snapping his putter in frustration), and there's a large

collection of memorabilia from Open winners both male and female.

Opposite the museum is the **Royal & Ancient Golf Club**, which stands proudly at the head of the Old Course (p196). Beside it stretches magnificent **West Sands** beach, made famous by the film *Chariots of Fire*.

Museum of the University of St Andrews
MUSEUM

(MUSA; www.st-andrews.ac.uk/musa; 7a The Scores; ☉10am-5pm Mon-Sat, noon-4pm Sun Apr-Oct, noon-4pm Thu-Sun Nov-Mar) **FREE** MUSA celebrates the history of Scotland's oldest university, and showcases treasures such as medieval silver maces, rare books and manuscripts, and 16th-century astronomical instruments.

St Andrews Aquarium
AQUARIUM

(www.standrewsaquarium.co.uk; adult/child £10/7; ☉10am-5pm Mon-Fri, to 6pm Sat & Sun; 🖐) As well as a seal sanctuary, rays and sharks from Scottish waters and exotic tropical favourites, St Andrews Aquarium has penguins, alligators and a cute family of meerkats.

St Andrews Museum
MUSEUM

(www.fifedirect.org.uk/museums; Doubledykes Rd; ☉10am-5pm Apr-Sep, 10.30am-4pm Oct-Mar) ✔**FREE** St Andrews Museum has interesting displays that chart the history of the town from its founding by St Regulus to its growth as an ecclesiastical, academic and sporting centre.

🏃 Activities

Apart from the obvious one – golf – the tourist office has a list of local walks and also sells OS maps. **Fergus Cook** (www.guidedtoursofstandrews.co.uk; adult/child £5/free; ☉twice daily Mon & Tue) offers guided walking tours of the town.

The Fife Coastal Path (p188) section between St Andrews and the East Neuk is fun, either on foot or mountain bike. Parts of the track can be covered by the tide, so check tide times before you go. The tourist office has a detailed map. All the East Neuk attractions are within easy cycling distance.

🎉 Festivals & Events

Open Championship
GOLF

(www.theopen.com; ☉Jul) One of international golf's four majors, this takes place in July. The tournament venue changes from year to year, and the Open only comes to St Andrews every five years (next in 2015) – check the website for future venues.

St Andrews Food & Drink Festival
FOOD & DRINK

(foodfest.visitstandrews.com; ☉Nov) Leading up to St Andrews Day (30 November), the feast day of Scotland's patron saint, this month-long festival celebrates Scottish food and drink; events include farmers markets, cookery demonstrations and a pipe-band parade on the 30th.

🛏 Sleeping

St Andrews' accommodation is overpriced and often heavily booked (especially in summer), so reserve in advance. Almost every house on super-central Murray Park and Murray Pl is a guesthouse.

St Andrews Tourist Hostel
HOSTEL £

(☎01334-479911; www.cowgatehostel.com/st-andrews; St Marys Pl; dm £11-13; 🖢) Laid-back and central, this hostel is the only backpacker accommodation in town. Occupying a stately old building, it has high corniced ceilings, especially in the huge lounge. There's a laissez-faire approach, which can verge on chaotic at times, but the staff and location can't be beat. Reception is closed between 2pm and 5pm.

Cairnsmill Caravan Park
CAMPSITE £

(☎01334-473604; www.cairnsmill.co.uk; Largo Rd; tent without/with car £10/18; dm £18; ☉Apr-Oct; 🅿🖢🐕🍽) About a mile west of St Andrews on the A915, this campsite has brilliant views over the town. Facilities are good, though it's very caravan-heavy. There's also a simple bunkhouse.

Five Pilmour Place
B&B ££

(☎01334-478665; www.5pilmourplace.com; 5 Pilmour Pl; s/d from £75/110; @🖢) Just around the corner from the Old Course, this luxurious and intimate spot offers stylish, compact rooms with an eclectic range of styles as well as modern conveniences such as flatscreen TV and DVD player. The king-size beds are especially comfortable, and the lounge area is a stylish treat.

Aslar House
B&B ££

(☎01334-473460; www.aslar.com; 120 North St; s/d/ste £55/100/110; ☉Feb-mid-Nov; 🖢) The rooms are so impeccable at this place that it's frightening to imagine how much work goes on behind the scenes. The modern comforts don't detract from the house's

St Andrews

0 — 200 m
0 — 0.1 miles

West Sands (200m)

Bruce Embankment

9

The Links

Old Course Hotel (350m); Leuchars Train Station (5m); Dundee (13m)

10

3

1

14

Golf Pl

Pilmour Pl

Hope St

15

17

Alexandra Pl

23

City Rd

Bus Station

Station Rd

Kinburn Park

7

Doubledykes Rd

Argyle St

David Russell Hall (700m)

St Andrews Bay

G

The Pends

8

6

5

19

North Castle St

28

South Castle St

22

35

Abbey St

South St

27

West Burn La

Queen's Gdns

26

32

i

College St

Church St

Mercat Cross

24

25

Church Sq

Holy Trinity Church

31

37

Market St

30

North St

The Scores

North Sea

2

4

29

Murray Park

16

13

12

20

18

36

Murray Pl

Playfair Tce

Greyfriars Gdn

Bell St

33

21

St Mary's Pl

West Port (Old Gate)

34

St Andrews

◉ Sights
1 British Golf Museum	B1
2 Museum of the University of St Andrews	E2
3 Royal & Ancient Golf Club	B1
4 St Andrews Aquarium	C1
5 St Andrews Castle	F2
6 St Andrews Cathedral	G3
7 St Andrews Museum	B4
8 St Rule's Tower	G3

◉ Activities, Courses & Tours
9 Caddie Pavilion	A1
10 St Andrews Old Course	B1

◉ Sleeping
11 Aslar House	D3
12 Burness House	C2
13 Cameron House	C2
14 Fairways of St Andrews	B2
15 Five Pilmour Place	B2
16 Lorimer House	C2
17 McIntosh Hall	B2
18 Ogstons on North Street	C2
19 Old Fishergate House	F3
20 Six Murray Park	C2
21 St Andrews Tourist Hostel	C3

◉ Eating
22 B Jannetta	F3
23 Balaka	B3
24 Café in the Square	D3
25 Doll's House	D3
26 Glass House	E3
27 Kerachers	E4
28 Northpoint Cafe	F3
29 Seafood Restaurant	C1
30 Tailend	D3
31 Vine Leaf	D4

◉ Drinking & Nightlife
32 Central Bar	E3
33 Vic	C3
34 West Port	C4

◉ Entertainment
35 Byre Theatre	F4
36 New Picture House	D2

◉ Shopping
37 IJ Mellis	D4

historical features (including a whimsical turret room) but certainly add value. The master suite is very spacious and a good small extra investment. No under-16s.

Old Fishergate House B&B ££
(☏01334-470874; www.oldfishergatehouse.co.uk; North Castle St; s/d £80/110; 🛜) This historic 17th-century town house, furnished with period pieces, is in a great location – the oldest part of town, close to the cathedral and castle. The two twin rooms are very spacious and even have their own sitting room. On a scale of one to 10 for quaintness, we'd rate it about a 9½. Cracking breakfast menu features fresh fish and pancakes.

Cameron House B&B ££
(☏01334-472306; www.cameronhouse-sta.co.uk; 11 Murray Park; s/d £50/90; 🛜) Beautifully decorated rooms and warm, cheerful hosts make this a real home away from home on this guesthouse-filled street. The two single rooms share a bathroom. Prices drop £10 per person outside peak season.

Six Murray Park B&B ££
(☏01334-473319; www.sixmurraypark.co.uk; 6 Murray Park; s/d from £65/100; 🛜) Enticing rooms with classy contemporary styling

make this a most appealing option on this street bristling with guesthouses.

University of St Andrews UNIVERSITY ACCOMMODATION ££
(☏01334-463000; www.discoverstandrews.com; ◷Jun-Aug; 🅿@🛜) ◢ During the university summer vacation, three student residences open up as visitor accommodation. There's the B&B-style **Agnes Blackadder Hall** (North Haugh; s/d £61/88); self-catering apartments sleeping up to six at **David Russell Hall** (Buchanan Gardens; s/d £77/131) (both on the main campus west of town); and cheaper rooms in the central **McIntosh Hall** (s/d £41/70). These prices are all good value for the standard of accommodation on offer.

Burness House B&B ££
(☏01334-474314; www.burnesshouse.com; 1 Murray Park; d per person £32-45; ◷Mar-Nov; 🛜) Rich, Asian-inspired fabrics, golf pictures and shiny new bathrooms.

Lorimer House B&B ££
(☏01334-476599; www.lorimerhouse.com; 19 Murray Park; s £45-75, d £70-120; @🛜) Smallish, sparklingly clean rooms with extra-comfy beds and a fab deluxe double on the top floor.

Fairways of St Andrews
B&B £££

(☑ 01334-479513; www.fairwaysofstandrews.co.uk; 8a Golf Pl; d £130-170; ☎) Just a few paces from golf's most famous 18th green, this is more of a boutique hotel than a B&B, despite its small size. There are just three super-stylish rooms; the best on the top floor is huge and has its own balcony with views over the Old Course.

Old Course Hotel
HOTEL £££

(☑ 01334-474371; www.oldcoursehotel.co.uk; Old Station Rd; d with/without view £480/370, ste from £780; ℙ@☎≋) A byword for golfing luxury, this hotel is right alongside the famous 17th hole and has huge rooms, excellent service and a raft of facilities, including a spa complex. Fork out the extra £50 or so for a view over the Old Course. You can usually find better deals online than the rack rates we list here.

Ogstons on North Street
HOTEL £££

(☑ 01334-473387; www.ogstonsonnorthst.com; 127 North St; r £120-180; ☎) If you want to eat, drink and sleep in the same stylish place, this classy inn could be for you. Rooms feature elegant contemporary styling and beautiful bathrooms, some with spa. There are also DVD players, iPod docks, crisp white linen and large windows that give the rooms an airy feel.

The Oak Rooms (serving lunch and dinner) is the place for meals and a read of the paper. The bar is perfect for a snug tipple, and the Lizard Lounge in the basement is a late-night bar that cranks up with live gigs and regular DJs.

Eating

St Andrews has a great range of eating options. Places compete heavily for the student custom, so there are good deals to be had everywhere. Two great options for self-catering or picnic fare are the fine fishmonger **Kerachers** (73 South St), and **IJ Mellis** (www.mellischeese.co.uk; 149 South St), with a wealth of cheeses you can smell halfway down the street.

PLAYING THE OLD COURSE

St Andrews Old Course (www.standrews.org.uk; Golf Pl) Golf has been played at St Andrews since the 15th century, and by 1457 it was apparently so popular that James II had to ban it because it was interfering with his troops' archery practice. Although it lies beside the exclusive, all-male Royal & Ancient Golf Club, the Old Course is a public course and is not owned by the club. The Open Championship has been played at St Andrews 29 times from 1873 to 2015, coming around every five years since 1990.

You'll need to book in advance to play via **St Andrews Links Trust** (☑ 01334-466666; www.standrews.org.uk). Reservations open on the first Wednesday in September the year before you wish to play. No bookings are taken for Saturdays or the month of September.

Unless you've booked months in advance, getting a tee-off time is literally a lottery; enter the ballot at the **caddie office** (☑ 01334-466666; West Sands Rd) before 2pm two days before you wish to play (there's no Sunday play). Be warned that applications by ballot are normally heavily oversubscribed, and green fees are £150 in summer. Singles are not accepted in the ballot and should start queuing as early as possible on the day – 5am is good – in the hope of joining a group. You'll need a handicap certificate (24/36 for men/women). If your number doesn't come up, there are six other public courses in the area (book up to seven days in advance on ☑ 01334-466718, no handicap required), including the prestigious Castle Course (£120). Other summer green fees: New £70, Jubilee £70, Eden £40, Strathtyrum £25 and Balgove (nine-holer for beginners and kids) £12. There are various multiple-day tickets available. A caddie for your round costs £45 plus tip. If you play on a windy day, expect those scores to balloon: Nick Faldo famously stated, 'When it blows here, even the seagulls walk'.

Guided walks (per person £3; ⊙ 11am & 2pm Tue-Sun Jul & Aug) of the Old Course run Tuesday to Sunday in July and August, and hit famous landmarks such as the Swilcan Bridge and the Road Hole bunker. They run from outside the shop by the 18th green at 11am and 1.30pm and last 50 minutes. On Sunday, a three-hour walk (£5) takes you around the whole course. You are free to walk over the course on Sunday, or follow the footpaths around the edge at any time.

Northpoint Cafe
CAFE £

(24 North St; mains £3-7; ☻8.30am-5pm Mon-Fri, 10am-5pm Sat; ☎) The cafe where Prince William famously met his future wife Kate Middleton while they were both students at St Andrews. It serves good coffee and a broad range of breakfast fare, from porridge topped with banana to toasted bagels, pancake stacks and classic fry-ups.

Café in the Square
CAFE £

(www.cafeinthesquare.co.uk; 4 Church Sq; mains £4-8; ☻11am-5pm Mon-Sat, plus Sun in summer) Hidden away down the side of the library, this upbeat wee coffee stop also makes a good venue for a light lunch, with sandwiches, panini and salads and a couple of secluded picnic tables out the back.

Tailend
FISH & CHIPS £

(130 Market St; takeaway £4-8; ☻11.30am-10pm) ✿ Delicious fresh fish sourced from Arbroath, just up the coast, puts this a class above most chippies. It fries to order and it's worth the wait. The array of exquisite smoked delicacies at the counter will have you planning a picnic or fighting for a table in the licensed cafe out the back.

B Jannetta
ICE CREAM £

(☎01334-473285; www.jannettas.co.uk; 31 South St; 2-scoop cone £2.25; ☻9am-9pm) Jannetta's is a St Andrews institution, offering 52 varieties of ice cream, from the weird (Irn-Bru sorbet) to the decadent (strawberries-and-champagne).

Doll's House
SCOTTISH ££

(☎01334-477122; www.dolls-house.co.uk; 3 Church Sq; mains £12-18; ☷) With its high-backed chairs, bright colours and creaky wooden floor, the Doll's House blends a Victorian child's bedroom with modern stylings. The result is a surprising warmth and no pretensions. The menu makes the most of local fish and other Scottish produce, and the £6.95 two-course lunch is unbeatable value. The early evening two-course deal for £11.95 isn't bad, either.

Glass House
ITALIAN, SCOTTISH ££

(www.glasshouse-restaurant.co.uk; 80 North St; mains £8-11; ☻noon-10.30pm) Casual but comfortable, this restaurant offers plenty of light in its split-level, open-kitchen dining area. The menu is basically Italian, with attractively presented pizzas and pastas popular with students. But a handful of daily specials

offer more Scottish meat and game choices of notable quality. Two-course lunch £7.

Balaka
BANGLADESHI ££

(www.balaka.com; 3 Alexandra Pl; mains £8-15; ☻noon-2.30pm & 5pm-midnight Mon-Thu, noon-12.30am Fri & Sat, 5pm-midnight Sun; ☷) ✿ Long-established Bangladeshi restaurant with both standard choices and more inspiring discoveries – all delicious and seasoned with herbs the owners grow themselves. There's an interesting selection of fish cooked in the tandoor, and various cheap lunch and early dining deals.

★ Vine Leaf
SCOTTISH £££

(☎01334-477497; www.vineleafstandrews.co.uk; 131 South St; 2-/3-course dinner £27/30; ☻6-10pm Tue-Sat; ☷) Classy, comfortable and well-established, the friendly Vine Leaf offers a changing menu of sumptuous Scottish seafood, game and vegetarian dishes. There's a huge selection within the set-price menu, all well presented, and an interesting, mostly old-world wine list. It's down a close off South St.

Seafood Restaurant
SEAFOOD £££

(☎01334-479475; www.theseafoodrestaurant.com; The Scores; mains £13-28; ☻noon-2.30pm Mon-Sat, 12.30-3pm Sun, 6-10pm daily) ✿ The Seafood Restaurant occupies a stylish glass-walled room, built out over the sea, with plush navy carpet, crisp white linen, an open kitchen and panoramic views of St Andrews Bay. It offers top-notch seafood and an excellent wine list; look out for its special winter deals.

🍷 Drinking

Central Bar
PUB

(www.taylor-walker.co.uk; 77 Market St; ☻11am-11.45pm Mon-Thu, to midnight Fri & Sat, 12.30-11.45pm Sun) Rather staid compared to some of the wilder student-driven drinking options, this likeable pub keeps it real with traditional features, an island bar, lots of Scottish beers, decent service and filling (if uninspiring) pub grub.

West Port
PUB

(www.thewestport.co.uk; 170 South St; ☻9am-11.30pm Sun-Thu, to 12.30am Fri & Sat; ☎) Just by the gateway of the same name, this sleek, modernised pub has several levels and a great beer garden out the back. Cheap cocktails rock the uni crowd, mixed drinks are above average and there's some OK bar food.

Vic BAR

(www.vicstandrews.co.uk; 1 St Mary's Pl; ⊙10am-2am) Warehouse chic meets medieval conviviality in this strikingly restored student favourite. Walls plastered with black-and-white pop culture give way to a handsome, high-ceilinged bar with sociable long tables down the middle and an eclectic assortment of seating. Other spaces include a more romantic bar, a dance floor and a smokers' deck. There are regular events.

☆ Entertainment

There's always something on in the pubs around town during university terms.

Byre Theatre THEATRE
(☎01334-475000; www.byretheatre.com; Abbey St) This theatre company started life in a converted cow byre in the 1930s, and now occupies a flashy premises making clever use of light and space.

New Picture House CINEMA
(www.nphcinema.co.uk; North St) Two-screen cinema showing current films.

ⓘ Information

J&G Innes (www.jg-innes.co.uk; 107 South St; ⊙9am-5.15pm Mon-Sat, 12.30-4.30pm Sun) Plenty of local-interest books, such as ones about Fife's history of burning witches.

Library (Church Sq; ⊙9.30am-5pm Mon, Fri & Sat, to 7pm Tue-Thu) Free internet access – drop-in only; no bookings.

St Andrews Community Hospital (☎01334-465656; www.nhsfife.org; Largo Rd) Has a minor injuries unit.

St Andrews Tourist Office (☎01334-472021; www.visitstandrews.com; 70 Market St; ⊙9.15am-6pm Mon-Sat, 10am-5pm Sun Jul & Aug, shorter hours rest of year) Helpful staff with good knowledge of St Andrews and Fife.

ⓘ Getting There & Away

BUS

All buses leave from the bus station on Station Rd. There are frequent services to the following:

Anstruther £3.20, 25 minutes, hourly

Crail £4, 25 minutes, hourly

Dundee £4.50, 30 minutes, half-hourly

Edinburgh £10.45, two hours, hourly

Glasgow £10.45, 2½ hours, hourly

Stirling £7.80, two hours, every two hours Monday to Saturday

TRAIN

There is no train station in St Andrews itself, but you can take a train from Edinburgh (grab a seat on the right-hand side of the carriage for great firth views) to Leuchars (£13.50, one hour, hourly), 5 miles to the northwest. From here, buses leave regularly for St Andrews (£2.75, 10 minutes).

ⓘ Getting Around

To order a cab, call **Golf City Taxis** (☎01334-477788; www.golfcitytaxis.co.uk). A taxi between Leuchars train station and the town centre costs around £12.

Spokes (☎01334-477835; www.spokescycles.com; 37 South St; per day/week £15/80; ⊙9am-5.30pm Mon-Sat) hires out mountain bikes.

East Neuk

This charming stretch of coast runs south from St Andrews to the headland at Fife Ness, then as far west as Earlsferry. Neuk is an old Scots word for corner, and it's certainly an appealing nook of the country to investigate, with picturesque fishing villages whose distinctive red pantiled roofs and crowstep gables are a legacy of trading links with the Low Countries; the Fife Coastal Path's most scenic stretches are in this area. It's easily visited from St Andrews, but also makes a very pleasant place to stay.

Crail

POP 1640

Pretty and peaceful, little Crail has a much-photographed stone-built harbour surrounded by wee cottages with red-tiled roofs. You can buy lobster and crab from a shed (34 Shoregate; mains £4-5; ⊙noon-4pm Sat & Sun) here – the benches in the nearby grassed area are perfectly placed for munching your alfresco crustaceans while admiring the view across to the Isle of May.

The village's history and involvement with the fishing industry is outlined in the Crail Museum (www.crailmuseum.org.uk; 62 Marketgate; ⊙11am-4pm Mon-Sat, 1-4pm Sun Jun-Sep, Sat & Sun only May) **FREE**, which also offers tourist information.

Eighteenth-century Selcraig House (☎01333-450697; www.selcraighouse.co.uk; 47 Nethergate; s/d £35/70; ☜☸) is a characterful, well-run place with a variety of rooms. Curiously shaped top-floor chambers will appeal to the quirky, while the fantastic four-poster rooms will charm those with a taste for luxury and beautiful furnishings. Across the road from the museum, a lot of work has gone into making **Hazelton Guest House** (☑ 01333-450250; www.thehazelton.co.uk; 29 Marketgate North; s £45-50, d £70-85; 🐾) what it is. Attractively remodelled rooms make full use of the abundant natural light in this lovely old building. The super front rooms boast glorious views across to the Isle of May. Walkers and cyclists are well catered for.

Crail is 10 miles southeast of St Andrews. Stagecoach bus 95 between Leven, Anstruther, Crail and St Andrews passes through Crail hourly every day (£4, 25 minutes to St Andrews).

Anstruther

POP 3450

Once among Scotland's busiest ports, cheery Anstruther (locals pronounce it *ens*-ter) has ridden the tribulations of the declining fishing industry better than some, and now has a very pleasant mixture of bobbing boats, historic streets and visitors ambling around the harbour grazing on fish and chips or contemplating a trip to the Isle of May.

○ Sights

The displays at the excellent **Scottish Fisheries Museum** (www.scotfishmuseum.org; adult/child £7/free; ☺10am-5.30pm Mon-Sat, 11am-5pm Sun Apr-Sep, 10am-4.30pm Mon-Sat, noon-4.30pm Sun Oct-Mar) include the **Zulu Gallery**, which houses the huge, partly restored hull of a traditional Zulu-class fishing boat, redolent with the scent of tar and timber. Afloat in the harbour outside the museum lies the **Reaper**, a fully restored Fifie-class fishing boat built in 1902.

The mile-long **Isle of May**, 6 miles southeast of Anstruther, is a spectacular nature reserve. Between April and July the island's cliffs are packed with breeding kittiwakes, razorbills, guillemots, shags and around 40,000 puffins. Inland are the remains of the 12th-century **St Adrian's Chapel**, dedicated to a monk who was murdered on the island by the Danes in 875.

The five-hour round trip to the island on the **May Princess** (☑ 01333-311808; www.isleofmayferry.com; adult/child £24/12), including two to three hours ashore, sails almost daily from April to September. Buy tickets at the harbour kiosk at least an hour before departure. Departure times vary depending on the tide – check times by phone or via the web-

THE PEAT INN

Peat Inn (☑ 01334-840206; www.thepeatinn.co.uk; 3-course lunch/dinner £19/45; ☺12.30-1.30pm & 7-9pm Tue-Sat) Six miles west of St Andrews in the village also called Peat Inn, this superb restaurant, backed by a commodious suite of bedrooms, makes an ideal gourmet break. The chef makes a great effort to source premium-quality Scottish produce and presents it in innovative ways that never feel pretentious or over-modern.

The split-level rooms (s/d £205/225; **P**🐾) look over the garden and fields beyond; breakfast is brought to your chamber to enjoy at your leisure. There are various all-inclusive offers available. To get there, head west from St Andrews on the A915 then turn right on the B940.

site. There's also a faster boat, the 12-seater rigid-hull inflatable **Osprey** (☑ 07473-631671; www.isleofmayboattrips.co.uk; adult/child £25/12; ☺Apr-Sep), which makes nonlanding circuits of the island as well as trips ashore.

🛏 Sleeping & Eating

★ **Spindrift** B&B ££

(☑01333-310573; www.thespindrift.co.uk; Pittenweem Rd; s/d £58/85; **P**🐾) Arriving from the west, there's no need to go further than Anstruther's first house on the left, a redoubt of Scottish cheer and warm hospitality. The rooms are elegant, classy and extremely comfortable – some have views across to Edinburgh and one is like a ship's cabin, courtesy of the sea captain who once owned the house.

There are DVD players and teddies for company, an honesty bar with characterful ales and malts and fine company from your hosts. Breakfast includes porridge once voted the best in the kingdom. Dinner (£24) is also available.

Bank INN ££

(☑01333-310189; www.thebank-anstruther.co.uk; 23 High St; per person £35-50; 🐾) Refitted rooms at this modernised central pub offer loads of space, big beds and great bathrooms. The building backs onto the river mouth, meaning pleasant views from many of the bedrooms. The bar is enticing, with tables out the back, though its proximity means you might be better off in the lower rooms (7 and 8) at weekends.

Crichton House
B&B ££

(🖉 01333-310219; www.crichtonhouse.com; High St W; d £70-80; P 🛜) You'll spot this B&B on the right as you approach the centre of town from the west. Sparklingly clean rooms with fresh fruit and slate-floored bathrooms are complemented by a cheery host and plenty of breakfast options. Enter via the wooden stairs at the side of the house.

Wee Chippy
FISH & CHIPS £

(4 Shore St; takeaway £4-6; ⏲ noon-10pm Apr-Sep, to 9pm Oct-Mar) 🌱 The Anstruther Fish Bar is one of Britain's best chippies, but we – and plenty of locals – reckon this one might be even better. The fish is of a very high quality and there's less of a queue too. Eat your catch by the water.

Dreel Tavern
PUB ££

(www.dreeltavern.com; 16 High St W; mains £8-12; ⏲ food served noon-2.30pm & 6-9pm Mon-Sat, 1-7.30pm Sun; 🖫) This charming old pub on the banks of the Dreel Burn has bucketloads of character and serves reliably tasty bar meals. Chow down in the outdoor beer garden in summer. There are also some top-quality cask ales.

★ Cellar Restaurant
SEAFOOD £££

(🖉 01333-310378; www.thecellaranstruther.co.uk; 24 East Green; 2-/3-course set dinner £35/40; ⏲ noon-1.30pm Thu-Sun, 6.30-9pm Wed-Sun) Tucked away in an alley behind the Scottish Fisheries Museum, the elegant and upmarket Cellar has been famous for its superb seafood and fine wines since 1982; recently under new management, it is as good as ever. Try the local crab, lobster or whatever delicacies have been brought in that day. Advance bookings are essential.

ℹ Information

Anstruther Tourist Office (🖉 01333-311073; www.visitfife.com; Harbourhead; ⏲ 10am-5pm Mon-Sat, 11am-4pm Sun Apr-Oct) The best tourist office in the East Neuk.

ℹ Getting There & Away

Stagecoach bus X60 runs hourly from Edinburgh to Anstruther (£10.45, 2¼ hours) and on to St Andrews (£3.20, 25 minutes). Bus 95 runs from Anstruther to Crail (£2.05, 12 minutes, hourly).

Around Anstruther

Kellie Castle
CASTLE

(NTS; www.nts.org.uk; adult/child £10.50/7.50; ⏲ castle 12.30-5pm Sat-Wed Apr-May & Sep-Oct, daily Jun-Aug, gardens year-round 9.30am-6pm or dusk) A magnificent example of Lowland Scottish domestic architecture, Kellie Castle has creaky floors, crooked little doorways and some marvellous works of art, giving it an air of authenticity. It's set in a beautiful garden, and many rooms contain superb plasterwork, the Vine room being the most exquisite. The original part of the building dates from 1360; it was enlarged to its present dimensions around 1606.

The castle is 3 miles northwest of Pittenweem on the B9171. Bus 95 from St Andrews gets you closest – about 1.5 miles away. You can get straight to the castle by booking a **Go-Flexi** (🖉 01334-840340; www.go-flexi.org; £2) 'taxibus' from Anstruther.

Scotland's Secret Bunker
MUSEUM

(www.secretbunker.co.uk; adult/child/family £11/7/32; ⏲ 10am-6pm Mar-Oct) This fascinating Cold War relic was designed to be one of Britain's underground command centres and a home for Scots leaders in the event of nuclear war. Hidden 30m underground and surrounded by nearly 5m of reinforced concrete are the austere operation rooms, communication centre and dormitories. It's very authentic and uses artefacts from the period, which make for an absorbing exploration. The Scottish Campaign for Nuclear Disarmament (CND) has an exhibit, bringing home the realities of Britain's current nuclear Trident policy. The bunker is 3 miles north of Anstruther, off the B9131 to St Andrews. To get there, book a **Go-Flexi** (🖉 01334-840340; www.go-flexi.org; £2) 'taxibus' from Anstruther, or it's a standard taxi (£15 to £18) from St Andrews. Alternatively, jump off an X60 bus from Anstruther to St Andrews at the Drumrack crossroads and walk east for about 1.5 miles along the B940.

Pittenweem

POP 1490

Just a short stroll from Anstruther, Pittenweem is now the main fishing port on the East Neuk coast, and there are lively morning fish sales at the harbour. The village name means 'place of the cave', referring to **St Fillan's Cave** (Cove Wynd; adult/child £1/free; ⏲ 10am-6pm), which was used as a chapel by a 7th-century missionary. The peaceful, atmospheric cave is protected by a locked gate, but a key is available from the chocolate shop at 9 High St, a great street to wander in itself, with galleries, cafes and craft shops.

Bus details for Pittenweem are as for Anstruther.

St Monans

POP 450

This ancient fishing village is just over a mile west of Pittenweem and is named after another cave-dwelling saint who was probably killed by pirates. Apart from a historic windmill overlooking the sea, its main sight is the picturesque parish church, built in 1362 on the orders of a grateful King David II, who was rescued by villagers from a shipwreck in the Firth of Forth. It was burned by the English in 1544 but restored. The church commands sweeping views of the firth, and the past echoes inside its whitewashed walls.

St Monans Heritage Collection (5 West Shore; ⊙11am-1pm & 2-4pm Tue, Thu, Sat & Sun May Oct) FREE, on the harbour, is a wonderful small gallery devoted to the history of the St Monans' fishing industry through a collection of 20th-century black-and-white photos and several artefacts. Most of the photos were taken by a local photographer and the collection changes regularly.

There are a couple of B&Bs in St Monans, but there are more options in nearby Anstruther. For eating, Craig Millar @ 16 West End (☑01333-730327; www.16westend.com; 16 West End; 3-course dinner £42; ⊙noon-2pm & 7-9pm Wed-Sun) is a comfortable but classy seafood stalwart on the harbour. The menu details the provenance of its sustainable produce, and changes with market and season – bouillabaisse, Dover sole, scallops – so just swim with the tide.

Stagecoach bus X60 runs daily from St Monans to St Andrews (£3.20, 35 minutes, hourly), via Anstruther.

Elie & Earlsferry

POP 680

These two attractive villages mark the southwestern end of the East Neuk. There are great sandy beaches and good walks along the coast – seek out the Chain Walk, an adventurous scramble along the rocky shoreline between the two villages, using chains and steel rungs cemented into the rock (allow two hours, and ask local advice about

---

T TIME

Scotland's biggest music festival, T in the Park (www.tinthepark.com), rocks this corner of the country over the second weekend in July. A major event, with six stages and top-name acts, it moves to a new location from 2015, in the grounds of Strathallan Castle near Auchterarder. It's a three-day affair, with camping available from the night before the kick-off. The site is 2.5 miles north of the A9, about halfway between Perth and Stirling.

---

tides before setting off). On a more relaxing note, there's nothing better than a lazy summer Sunday in Elie, watching the local team play cricket on the strand below.

Elie Watersports (☑01333-330962; www.eliewatersports.com; canoe hire per hr £14; ⊙May-Sep, ring ahead at other times), on the harbour at Elie, hires out windsurfers (per two hours £28), sailing dinghies (Lasers/Wayfarers per hour £20/25), canoes (per hour £12) and mountain bikes (per day £12), and provides instruction as well.

The Ship Inn (www.ship-elie.com; mains £8-12; ☑), down by Elie harbour, is a pleasant and popular place for a bar lunch. Seafood and Asian dishes feature on the menu, and on a sunny day you can tuck in at an outside table, overlooking the wide sweep of the bay.

LOWLAND PERTHSHIRE & KINROSS

For sheer scenic variety, Perthshire is the pick of Scotland's regions and a place where everyone will find a special, personal spot – the county straddles the Highland border (for Highland Perthshire, see p327), with the lowland part ranging from the sedate streets of Perth itself, a fine country town with a fabulous attraction in lavish Scone Palace, to the rural market towns of Crieff and Blairgowrie.

Perth

POP 46,970

Elegantly arranged along the banks of the Tay, this former capital of Scotland is a most liveable place with large tracts of enticing parkland surrounding an easily managed centre. On its outskirts lies Scone Palace, a country house of staggering luxury built alongside the ancient crowning place of Scotland's kings. The palace is a must-see, and the town itself – known as the Fair City – is endowed with fine galleries and excellent restaurants, and is within easy striking distance of both Edinburgh and Glasgow.

◎ Sights

★ Scone Palace
PALACE

(www.scone-palace.co.uk; adult/child/family £10.50/7.60/33; ⏱palace & grounds 9.30am-5pm Apr-Oct, grounds only 10am-4pm Fri-Sun Nov-Mar) 'So thanks to all at once and to each one, whom we invite to see us crowned at Scone.' This line from *Macbeth* indicates the importance of Scone (pronounced 'skoon') as the coronation place of Scottish monarchs. The original palace of 1580, built on a site intrinsic to Scottish history, was rebuilt in the early 19th century as a Georgian mansion of extreme elegance and luxury. The visit takes you through a succession of sumptuous rooms filled with fine French furniture and noble portraits.

Scone has belonged for centuries to the Murray family, Earls of Mansfield, and many of the objects have fascinating history attached to them (friendly guides are on hand to explain). Each room has comprehensive multilingual information; there are also panels relating histories of some of the Scottish kings crowned at Scone over the centuries. Outside, peacocks – each named after a monarch – strut around the magnificent grounds, which incorporate woods, a butterfly garden and a maze.

Ancient kings were crowned on **Moot Hill**, now topped by a chapel next to the palace. It's said that the hill was created by bootfuls of earth, brought by nobles attending the coronations as an acknowledgement of the king's rights over their lands, although it's more likely the site of an ancient motte-and-bailey castle. Here in 838, Kenneth MacAlpin became the first king of a united Scotland and brought to Scone the **Stone of Destiny**, on which Scottish kings were ceremonially invested. In 1296 Edward I of England carted this talisman off to Westminster Abbey, where it remained for 700 years before being returned to Scotland in 1997.

Scone Palace is 2 miles north of Perth; from the town centre, cross the bridge, turn left, and keep bearing left until you reach the gates of the estate. From here, it's another half-mile to the palace (about 30 minutes' walk). Various buses from town stop here; the tourist office has timetables.

Fergusson Gallery
GALLERY

(www.pkc.gov.uk; cnr Marshall Pl & Tay St; ⏱10am-5pm Mon-Sat, plus noon-4.30pm Sun May-Sep) **FREE** Beautifully set in a circular cast-iron building that was once a waterworks, this gallery exhibits an extensive collection of paintings by the Scottish Colourist JD Fergusson in a most impressive display. Fergusson spent time in Paris, and the influence of artists such as Matisse on his work is evident; his voluptuous female portraits against a tropical-looking Riviera background are memorable, as is the story of his lifelong relationship with noted Scottish dancer Margaret Morris.

Perth Museum & Art Gallery
MUSEUM

(www.pkc.gov.uk; cnr George & Charlotte Sts; ⏱10am-5pm Mon-Sat, plus 10am-5pm Sun Apr-Oct) **FREE** The city's main museum is worth wandering through for the elegant neoclassical interior alone. There's a varied range of exhibits, from portraits of dour lairds to interesting local social history. A geological room provides more entertainment for the young, while there are often excellent temporary exhibitions.

St John's Kirk
CHURCH

(www.st-johns-kirk.co.uk; St John's St; ⏱10am-4pm Mon-Sat May-Sep) **FREE** Daunting St John's Kirk, surrounded by cobbled streets, was founded in 1126 and is still the centrepiece of the town. In 1559 John Knox preached a powerful sermon here that helped begin the Reformation, inciting a frenzied destruction of Scone abbey and other religious sites. Perth used to be known as St John's Town after this church, and the local football team is still called St Johnstone.

Black Watch Museum
MUSEUM

(www.theblackwatch.co.uk; Hay St; adult/child £7.50/3.50; ⏱9.30am-5pm Mon-Sat, plus 10am-4pm Sun Apr-Oct) Housed in Balhousie Castle on the edge of North Inch, this museum honours what was once Scotland's foremost regiment. Formed in 1725 to combat rural banditry, the Black Watch fought in numerous campaigns, recreated here with paintings, memorabilia and anecdotes.

Perth

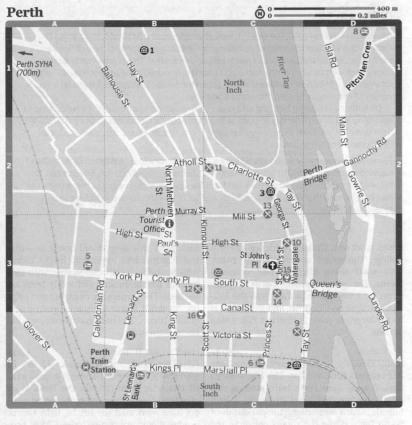

CENTRAL SCOTLAND PERTH

Perth

◎ Sights
1	Black Watch Museum	B1
2	Fergusson Gallery	C4
3	Perth Museum & Art Gallery	C2
4	St John's Kirk	C3

⬛ Sleeping
5	Heidl Guest House	A3
6	Kinnaird Guest House	C4
7	Parklands	B4
8	Pitcullen Guest House	D1

✕ Eating
9	63 Tay Street	C4
10	Breizh	C3
11	Deans@Let's Eat	C2
12	Kerachers	B3
13	Paco's	C2
14	Pig'Halle	C3

◯ Drinking & Nightlife
15	Greyfriars Bar	C3
16	Twa Tams	B4

Little attempt at perspective is evident: there's justifiable pride in the regiment's role in the gruelling trench warfare of WWI, where it suffered nearly 30,000 casualties, but no sheepishness about less glorious colonial engagements, such as against the 'Fuzzy Wuzzies' of Sudan. In 2006 the Black Watch was subsumed into the new Royal Regiment of Scotland.

🛏 Sleeping

Perth SYHA   HOSTEL £
(☎ 01738-877800; www.syha.org.uk; Crieff Rd; dm/tw £23/46; ☺ late Jun-late Aug) A 20-minute stroll from the centre, this summer-only

GLENEAGLES

Gleneagles Hotel (☑01764-662231; www.gleneagles.com; d £455-555; [P][@][☎][🏊]) Deep in rural Perthshire near the town of Auchterarder lies Gleneagles Hotel, one of Scotland's most famous lodgings. Not your typical bed-and-breakfast, this is a no-holds-barred luxury spot with three championship golf courses, Andrew Fairlie at Gleneagles – often referred to as Scotland's best restaurant (open for dinner Tuesday to Saturday) – and a variety of extravagantly elegant rooms and suites.

Despite the imposing building and kilted staff snapping to attention, it's welcoming to non-VIPs, and family-friendly to boot, with lots of activities available. There's Gleneagles train station if you wish to arrive sustainably; if not, limousine transfers are available. Check the website for deals.

Phoenix Falconry (☑01764-682823; www.scottishfalconry.co.uk; Easterton Farm, by Gleneagles; per person £30-180) If your interest in birdies and eagles extends beyond golf, this fascinating centre – just along the road from Gleneagles Hotel, near Auchterarder – offers experiences that range from one-hour falconry lessons, to bird-handling sessions, to all-day hunts with a harris hawk.

hostel is set in a student residence at Perth College. The rooms are all en suite twins, with good share kitchens and common rooms. For some reason, there's a price jump for a week in July. Turn into the Brahan entrance on Crieff Rd, and the hostel is by the large car park. Numerous buses stop outside.

Parklands HOTEL ££
(☑01738-622451; www.theparklandshotel.com; 2 St Leonard's Bank; s/d from £94/119; [P][@][☎]) Tucked away near Perth train station, this relaxing, renovated hotel sits amid a lush hillside garden overlooking the parklands of South Inch. While the rooms conserve the character of this beautiful building, formerly the residence of the town's mayors, they also offer modern conveniences and plenty of style. There's a great terrace and garden area to lap up the Perthshire sun.

Pitcullen Guest House B&B ££
(☑01738-626506; www.pitcullen.co.uk; 17 Pitcullen Cres; s/d £50/70; [P][☎]) This excellent place has a much more contemporary look than other guesthouses on this strip. Great-looking fabrics and modern styling give the rooms an upbeat feel. Lots of thought has gone into making your stay more comfortable, with things like fridges with free drinks in the rooms, plenty of plugs to make recharging easy and handy maps on the walls.

Kinnaird Guest House B&B ££
(☑01738-628021; www.kinnaird-guesthouse.co.uk; 5 Marshall Pl; s £45-65, d £60-80; [P][☎]) The best of the handful of guesthouses enjoying a privileged position opposite the lovely South

Inch park, this elegant old house has original features and appealing, bright rooms with big beds. It's all impeccable, with nice touches like bathrobes and teddy bears on the beds. The owners are engaging and helpful; breakfast features organic produce and quality bacon. The back rooms receive occasional train noise.

Heidl Guest House B&B ££
(☑01738-635031; www.heidl.co.uk; 43 York Pl; s/d/f £34/50/100; [P][☎]) Though it lacks a little character from outside, the Heidl is an excellent guesthouse, and enthusiastic owners have renovated the bright, light rooms, leaving them very spruce indeed. Most bedrooms come with excellent en suite bathrooms; those that don't have good private exterior bathrooms. Writer John Buchan (of *Thirty-Nine Steps* fame) was born in the house opposite.

✗ Eating & Drinking

Perth has an exceptionally good dining scene.

★ 63 Tay Street SCOTTISH ££
(☑01738-441451; www.63taystreet.com; 63 Tay St; lunch mains £13.50, 4-course dinner £42; ⊘noon-2pm Thu-Sat, 5.45-9pm Tue-Fri, 6.30-9pm Sat) Classy and warmly welcoming, this understated restaurant is Perth's best, featuring a lightly decorated dining area, excellent service and quality food. In a culinary Auld Alliance, French influence is applied to the best of Scottish produce to deliver memorable game, seafood, beef and vegetarian plates.

Breizh BISTRO ££

(☑ 01738-444427; www.cafebreizh.co.uk; 28 High St; mains £7-17; ☺ 9am-9pm Sun-Thu, to 9.30pm Fri & Sat) This funkily French bistro – the name is Breton for Brittany – is a treat. Dishes are served with real panache, and the salads, featuring all sorts of delicious ingredients, are a feast of colour, texture and subtle flavours. The blackboard specials offer great value and a real taste of northwest France, including traditional *galettes* (Breton buckwheat pancakes with savoury fillings).

Deans@Let's Eat SCOTTISH ££

(☑ 01738-643377; www.letseatperth.co.uk; 77 Kinnoull St; mains £14-20; ☺ noon-3pm & 6-9pm Tue-Sat) A Perth favourite for splashing out on a special meal, this busy corner restaurant has a can-do attitude and an excellent line in fresh Scottish produce. Juicy scallops, fine Orkney beef, local venison or lamb may feature, but you can't really go wrong. Recession-busting lunch and dinner set menus are a good way to graze here on a budget.

Pig'Halle FRENCH ££

(www.pighalle.co.uk; 38 South St; mains £10-19; ☺ noon-3pm & 5.30-9.30pm Tue-Sun) A spacious bistro that presents the very best of pork products through traditional regional French cuisine. The sample platter of charcuterie is fabulous value, there are succulent mains and there's a decent selection of Gallic wines to accompany them. There are other dishes on the menu if pig ain't your thing, and there's a cheap early dinner deal.

Kerachers SEAFOOD ££

(☑ 01738-449777; www.kerachers restaurant.co.uk; 168 South St; 2-/3-course dinner £22.50/27.50; ☺ 6-9pm Tue-Sat) This classic seafood restaurant keeps things simple, combining fresh seafood with ingredients that add hints of flavour to complement but not overpower the dishes – a recipe for success!

Paco's INTERNATIONAL ££

(www.pacos.co.uk; 3 Mill St; mains £8-14; ☺ noon-11pm; 🛗) Something of an institution, Paco's keeps Perthers coming back over and over, perhaps because it would take dozens of visits to even try half the menu. There's something for everyone: steaks, seafood, pizza, pasta and Mexican, all served in generous portions. The fountain-tinkled terrace is the place for a sunny day.

Twa Tams PUB

(www.twatams-perth.co.uk; 79 Scott St; ☺ 11am-11pm Mon-Wed, to 12.30am Thu-Sat, 12.30pm-midnight Sun) Perth's best pub has a strange outdoor space with windows peering out onto the street, an ornate entrance gate and a large, cosy interior. There are regular events, including live music every Friday and Saturday night; it has a sound reputation for attracting talented young bands.

Greyfriars Bar PUB

(www.greyfriarsbar.com; 15 South St; ☺ 11am-11pm Mon-Sat, 12.30-11pm Sun) The smallest and friendliest pub in Perth serves up live music, great fish and chips, and fine ales from the local Inveralmond Brewery – try a pint of Ossian, a golden ale with a fresh, zesty, hoppy flavour.

ℹ Information

AK Bell Library (York Pl; ☺ 9.30am-5pm Mon, Wed & Fri, to 8pm Tue & Thu, to 4pm Sat) Free internet; lots of terminals.

Perth Royal Infirmary (☑ 01738-623311; www.nhstayside.scot.nhs.uk; Taymount Tce) West of the town centre.

Perth Tourist Office (☑ 01738-450600; www.perthshire.co.uk; West Mill St; ☺ 9am-5pm daily Apr-Oct, Mon-Sat Nov-Mar) Efficiently run tourist office.

ℹ Getting There & Away

BUS

Citylink (www.citylink.co.uk) operates, from the **bus station** (Leonard St), services to/from these cities:

Dundee £7.50, 40 minutes, hourly
Edinburgh £12, 1¾ hours, hourly
Glasgow £12, 1½ hours, hourly
Inverness £21, three hours, at least five daily
Stirling £9, 55 minutes, hourly

FAIR CITY FESTIVAL

Perth Festival of the Arts (☑ 01738-621031; www.perthfestival.co.uk) If you're in Perth in the last two weeks of May, you'll come across this low-profile but high-quality arts festival. Various venues around town host a diverse range of cultural events; don't be surprised to see some big-name band of yesteryear or quality ballet troupe appearing at very reasonable prices.

Further buses run from the Broxden Park & Ride on Glasgow Rd; this is connected regularly with the bus station by shuttle bus. These include **Megabus** (www.megabus.com) discount services to Aberdeen, Edinburgh, Glasgow, Dundee and Inverness.

Stagecoach (www.stagecoachbus.com) buses serve Perthshire destinations regularly, with reduced Sunday service. A Tayside Megarider ticket gives you seven days travel in Perth & Kinross and Dundee & Angus for £26.

TRAIN

Trains run between Perth and various destinations, including the following:

Dundee £7.60, 20 to 30 minutes, twice hourly, fewer on Sunday

Edinburgh £15.60, 1¼ hours, at least hourly Monday to Saturday, every two hours Sunday

Glasgow £15.60, one hour, at least hourly Monday to Saturday, every two hours Sunday

Pitlochry £13.20, 30 minutes, two hourly, fewer on Sunday

Stirling £8, 30 minutes, one or two per hour

Kinross & Loch Leven

POP (KINROSS) 4890

Kinross, just off the M90, sits on the banks of pretty Loch Leven. Stretch your legs or take a bike on the **Loch Leven Heritage Trail** (www.lochlevenheritagetrail.co.uk), which runs 8 miles around three-quarters of the loch, with sightings of deer common, or take a ferry to the island in its centre to visit evocative **Lochleven Castle** (HS; www.historic-scotland.gov.uk; adult/child incl boat £5.50/3.30; ⏲10am-5.30pm Apr-Sep, last sailing 1hr before closing), which served as a fortress and prison from the late 14th century. Its most famous captive was Mary, Queen of Scots, who was incarcerated here in 1567. Her famous charms bewitched Willie Douglas, who managed to get hold of the cell keys to release her, then rowed her across to the shore. The Boathouse Bistro by the ferry dock, near the centre of Kinross, serves decent light meals and you can rent bikes here (£12.50 per day).

Nearby, on the main street, **Roxburghe Guest House** (☎01577-864521; www.roxburgheguesthouse.co.uk; 126 High St; s £45-65, d £65-75; P 📶) is a welcoming home away from home with a good attitude and lovely garden. The owner is a professional masseuse and acupuncturist if you need any creases ironed out. It's a fair bit cheaper outside high summer.

Citylink (www.citylink.co.uk) runs bus services between Perth (£7, 30 minutes, hourly) and Kinross. In the other direction buses go to Edinburgh (£9.40, 45 minutes, hourly).

Strathearn

West of Perth, the wide strath (valley) of the River Earn was once a great forest where medieval kings hunted. The whole area is known as Strathearn, a very attractive region of undulating farmland, hills and lochs. The Highlands officially begin in the western section of Strathearn.

Dunning

POP 940

If you think you've entered spooky country around here, you may just be right. On the way into Dunning, about a mile west of the town by the B8062, there's a strange **cross** on a pile of stones, etched with the words 'Maggie Wall burnt here 1657 as a witch'.

The village is dominated by the 12th-century Norman tower of **St Serfs Church** (HS; www.historic-scotland.gov.uk; ⏲9.30am-5.30pm Apr-Sep) FREE, but most of the building dates from 1810. The main reason to come is the magnificent 9th-century **Dupplin Cross**, the finest Pictish cross known. Originally located near Forteviot (3 miles from Dunning), it's now the regal centrepiece here. The fascinating symbolism and artistic influences are explained in superb detail by the warden. It's rare to get such detailed insight at these places, and you'll walk out feeling like you've learned something new.

Dunning is about 8 miles southwest of Perth. **Stagecoach** (☎01382-227201; www.stagecoachbus.com) bus 17 runs from Perth (£2.05, 40 minutes, eight Monday to Saturday, two Sunday).

Crieff

POP 7370

Elegant Crieff is an old resort-style town, as popular with tourists today as it was in Victorian times. It sits in a valley amid some glorious Perthshire countryside. With excellent eating and accommodation options, it's a fine base for exploring this part of the country.

◉ Sights

In the basement at the tourist office is a small but interesting free exhibition of the town stocks, the Drummond Cross (1400–1600) and a formidable 9th-century Pictish cross slab.

At old Glenturret Distillery, 1 mile north of town, the **Famous Grouse Experience** (www.thefamousgrouse.com; standard tour adult/child £9/8; ⊙9am-6pm, last tour 4.30pm Apr-Oct, 10am-5pm, last tour 3pm Nov-Mar) offers a better-than-average tour that details the making of malt whisky and the blending process that creates the Famous Grouse whisky. There's also a dizzying audiovisual that takes you on a grouse's flight around Scotland. Two tiny drams are included in the standard tour; more expensive tours offer more detailed tasting sessions.

⌂ Sleeping

Comrie Croft   HOSTEL, CAMPGROUND £
(☎01764-670140; www.comriecroft.com; campsites per person £9.50, dm/s/d £16/29/44; P@⊙☎) 🚲 A rustic, hospitable place with great facilities, Comrie Croft has a bit of everything: camping; a pleasant, airy hostel; and Sami-style tepees (£69 per night) with wood stove that sleep up to four. Activities include mountain biking (bike hire available), fishing, walking, lots of games for the kids and plenty of places to just laze about.

The Croft is 4 miles west of Crieff, on the A85 towards Comrie.

Yann's   B&B ££
(☎01764-650111; www.yannsatglenearnhouse.com; Perth Rd; s/d £65/90; ⊙dinner Wed-Sun, lunch Sat & Sun; P⊙☎) On the main road heading east out of town, this most welcoming establishment offers big light rooms with plenty of understated style. The excellent restaurant serves French comfort-food classics such as crêpes and coq au vin, with a contemporary flair. It was for sale at time of research, but should continue to function as a quality B&B.

Merlindale   B&B ££
(☎01764-655205; www.merlindale.co.uk; Perth Rd; s/d from £55/75; ⊙Mar-Nov; P☎) Georgian architecture meets generous hospitality at this excellent option at the eastern end of town. The four fabulous rooms all have individual character, and two have sumptuous bathrooms with free-standing tubs. Thoughtful touches abound.

THE LIBRARY OF INNERPEFFRAY

Innerpeffray Library (www.innerpeffraylibrary.co.uk; Innerpeffray; adult/child £6/free; ⊙10am-12.45pm & 2-4.45pm Wed-Sat, 2-4pm Sun Mar-Oct, by appointment only Nov-Feb) About 5 miles southeast of Crieff on the B8062 is Innerpeffray Library, Scotland's first lending library (founded in 1680). There's a huge collection of rare, interesting and ancient books here, some of them 500 years old.

Comely Bank Guest House   B&B ££
(☎01764-653409; www.comelybankguesthouse.co.uk; 32 Burrell St; s/d £49/74; @☎) Just down from Crieff's main street, Comely Bank is homelike and neat as a pin. The downstairs double is huge and could accommodate four at a pinch, while upstairs rooms are equally appealing and are still a good size.

Crieff Hydro   HOTEL £££
(☎01764-655555; www.crieffhydro.com; Ferntower Rd; r from £258; P@⊙☎) This enormous spa hotel is nearly 150 years old, but apart from its monumental exterior it looks very different from its mannered Victorian past. It's attractively functional and really does have everything for a family holiday, from a cinema and gym to restaurants, activities and pools. It's exceptionally child friendly, with free daily childcare.

Room rates vary substantially, so check the website: the above prices are a guide only. Its sister hotel, Murraypark, is just around the corner, and offers a quieter, cheaper stay in a smaller, more couple-focused establishment (and you can still access all the leisure facilities at the Hydro).

✗ Eating

★**Delivino**   CAFE, ITALIAN £
(www.delivino.net; 6 King St; mains £6-8, sharing platters £14; ⊙9am-6pm Mon-Thu, to 9pm Fri & Sat, noon-4pm Sun) Delivino is an elegant cafe just down from the square on the main street. It offers something for everyone, from Crieff ladies-who-lunch to travellers looking for a light bite. An extensive selection of antipasti allows you to graze several flavours at a time, while delicious bruschettas and pizzas, accompanied by a glass of Italian red, make this central Crieff's best lunch option.

★ **Barley Bree** SCOTTISH ££
(☎ 01764-681451; www.barleybree.com; 6 Willoughby St; mains lunch £10-15, dinner £18-20; ☻ noon-2pm & 6.45-9pm Wed-Sat, noon-5.30pm Sun, to 7.30pm Sun May-Sep; ⓐ) ✿ Set in the pretty village of Muthill (pronounced *mooth*-il), 3 miles south of Crieff, the Barley Bree is a delightfully rustic restaurant with rooms. Bare wooden floorboards, a stone fireplace, stacked logs and deer antlers set the scene for dishes of fine Scottish seafood, beef and game, prepared by French chef-patron Fabrice Bouteloup. Half a dozen luxurious bedrooms (double £110) tempt you to stay the night.

Lounge BISTRO ££
(www.loungeincrieff.co.uk; 1 West High St; mains £8-15; ☻ noon-9.30pm Mon-Sat; ☏) Enter the romantic interior of this stylish central lounge bar and bistro for anything from a cup of tea to good wines by the glass, to an interesting array of portions of Scottish seafood and other delights – notably Alsatian *tarte flambée*, a delicious French version of thin and crispy pizza.

Gallery BISTRO ££
(☎ 01764-653249; 13 Hill St; mains £11-18; ☻ 5-10pm Tue-Sat) An inclusive atmosphere and lack of pretension accompany decent dishes featuring salmon, lamb, venison and the like in this cosy (too cosy if your neighbours are loud) restaurant just uphill from the main street. True to its name, works of local artists of varying quality adorn the walls. Two-course early-bird menu £9.95.

ⓘ Information

Crieff Tourist Office (☎ 01764-652578; www.perthshire.co.uk; ☻ 9am-5pm daily Apr-Oct, Mon-Sat Nov-Mar) Most helpful. In a clock tower on the main street.

ⓘ Getting There & Away

Hourly **Stagecoach** (www.stagecoachbus.com) buses link Crieff with Perth (£2.75, 50 minutes), less frequently on Sunday; and Stirling (£3, 55 minutes, four to 10 daily).

Blairgowrie & Around

Blairgowrie is a compact market town on the banks of the River Ericht, famed for its salmon fishing. Formerly a flax spinning centre, the town today is the hub of Scotland's soft fruits industry – the fields for miles around are ripe with raspberries and strawberries, for sale in season from kiosks on the edge of town. From April to September, on the last Saturday of the month, a **farmers market** (www.strathmoreglens.org; Wellmeadow; ☻ 10am-3pm Sat) takes over the grassy square in the middle of town, with stalls selling books, crafts and secondhand goods as well as fresh local produce.

The town is the start and finish point for the **Cateran Trail** (www.caterantrail.org), a circular 64-mile waymarked path that leads you through the mountains around Glenshee on the southern fringe of the Cairngorms National Park. The first mile or so along the banks of the River Ericht as far as the waterfall at **Cargill's Leap** and the former flax mill at Keathbank makes an excellent short walk.

About 5 miles east of Blairgowrie, **Alyth** is a charming historic village clustered along the banks of the Alyth Burn, which is crisscrossed picturesquely by several stone and iron footbridges. Ask at Blairgowrie's tourist office for the *Walk Auld Alyth* leaflet. Perusing the displays on local history at **Alyth Museum** (www.pkc.gov.uk; Commercial St; ☻ 1-5pm Wed-Sun May-Sep) FREE is a fine way to pass an hour or so.

Off the A94 and 8 miles east of Blairgowrie, **Meigle** is well worth the trip for those with a fascination for Pictish sculptured stones. The tiny **Meigle Museum** (HS; www.historic-scotland.gov.uk; adult/child £4.50/2.70; ☻ 9.30am-5.30pm Apr-Sep) has 26 beautifully carved stones dating from the 7th to the 9th centuries, all found in the local area. Motifs range from propaganda for local strongmen to intricate geometric designs, biblical scenes and a whole menagerie of strange beasts. If the manager is there, she's a mine of information on the carvings and is happy to help you unravel some of the complex symbolism.

🛏 Sleeping

Gilmore House B&B ££
(☎ 01250-872791; www.gilmorehouse.co.uk; Perth Rd; d £69-80; ⓟ☏) ✿ Blairgowrie's prosperous past has left a legacy of spacious Victorian villas like Gilmore House. Many have been turned into B&Bs, but few as successfully as this welcoming haven with three gorgeously fitted-out en suite bedrooms, two guest lounges and a hearty breakfast built around seasonal local produce.

Alyth Hotel INN ££
(☎ 01828-632447; www.alythhotel.com; 6 Commercial St; s/d £50/80, mains £8-12; ℗) The Alyth Hotel is a classic rural coaching inn right in the middle of the village. The old-style rooms upstairs are better than the renovated ones, though, with a lot more space and a user-friendly design. Either way, try to get a room overlooking the river; Room 1 is a good choice.

The bar and restaurant is infinitely cosy with a low-slung roof, stone walls and all manner of clutter giving it a homey feel.

ℹ Information

Blairgowrie Tourist Office (☎ 01250-872960; www.perthshire.co.uk; 26 Wellmeadow; ⊙ 9am-5pm daily Apr-Oct & Dec, Mon-Sat Nov & Jan-Mar) On the central square in Blairgowrie; has plenty of information on walking, and skiing at Glenshee.

Kate Fleming Shooting & Fishing (☎ 01250 873990; www.kateflemings.co.uk; 26 Allan St) Tackle shop with knowledgeable staff – everything you need to know about local trout and salmon fishing. Sells fishing permits as well as a full range of tackle, outdoor clothing and equipment.

ℹ Getting There & Away

Stagecoach (www.stagecoachbus.com) buses run from Perth to Blairgowrie (£3.20, 50 minutes, three to eight daily). Buses also run from Dundee to Blairgowrie (£3.60, one hour, hourly, less frequent on Sunday).

Currently the only service north from Blairgowrie is Stagecoach bus 71, which runs twice on Wednesday and four times on Saturday to Spittal of Glenshee (£2.40, one hour).

1. Smailholm Tower (p151) 2. Glamis Castle (p221) 3. Hermitage Castle (p148) 4. Caerlaverock Castle (p166)

IZZET KERIBAR / GETTY IMAGES ©

Scottish Castles

Scotland is home to more than 1000 castles, ranging from meagre 12th-century ruins to magnificent Victorian mansions. They all began with one purpose: to serve as fortified homes for the landowning aristocracy. But as society became more settled and peaceful, defensive features gave way to ostentatious displays of wealth and status.

Curtain Wall Castles

Norman castles of the 12th century were mainly of the 'motte-and-bailey' type, consisting of earthwork mounds and timber palisades. The first wave of stonebuilt castles emerged in the 13th century, characterised by massive curtain walls up to 3m thick and 30m tall to withstand sieges, well seen at Dunstaffnage Castle and Caerlaverock Castle.

Tower Houses

The appearance of the tower house in the 14th century marks the beginning of the development of the castle as a residence. Clan feuds, cattle raiders and wars between Scotland and England meant that local lords built fortified stone towers in which to live, from diminutive Smailholm Tower in the Borders to impressive Doune Castle near Stirling.

Artillery Castles

The arrival of gunpowder and cannon in the 15th century transformed castle design, with features such as gun loops, round towers, bulwarks and bastions making an appearance. Forbidding Hermitage Castle is a prime example of a castle adapted for artillery defence.

Status Symbols

The Scottish Baronial style of castle architecture, characterised by a profusion of pointy turrets, crenellations and stepped gables, had its origins in 16th- and 17th-century castles such as Craigievar and Castle Fraser, and reached its apotheosis in the royal residences of Glamis and Balmoral.

Northeast Scotland

Best Castles

➡ Crathes Castle (p233)

➡ Craigievar Castle (p235)

➡ Fyvie Castle (p233)

➡ Kildrummy Castle (p235)

➡ Glamis Castle (p221)

Best Places to Eat

➡ Adelphi Kitchen (p230)

➡ Parlour Cafe (p218)

➡ Tolbooth Restaurant (p234)

➡ Café 52 (p230)

➡ Metro (p218)

Why Go?

Many visitors pass by this corner of the country in their headlong rush to the tourist honeypots of Loch Ness and Skye. But they're missing out on a part of Scotland that's just as beautiful and diverse as the more obvious attractions of the west.

Within its bounds you'll find two of Scotland's four largest cities – Dundee, the city of jute, jam and journalism, cradle of some of Britain's favourite comic characters, and home to Captain Scott's Antarctic research ship, the *Discovery;* and Aberdeen, the granite city, an economic powerhouse fuelled by the riches of North Sea oil.

Angus is a region of rich farmland and scenic glens dotted with the mysterious stones left behind by the ancient Picts, while Aberdeenshire and Moray are home to the greatest concentration of Scottish Baronial castles in the country, and dozens of distilleries along the River Spey.

When to Go
Aberdeen

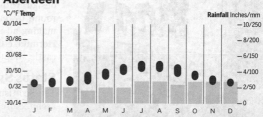

Jun/Jul Classic boats fill Portsoy harbour for the Scottish Traditional Boat Festival.

Sep Revellers gather for a whisky and music festival in Dufftown.

Dec Spectacular fireball ceremony in Stonehaven on Hogmanay (New Year's Eve).

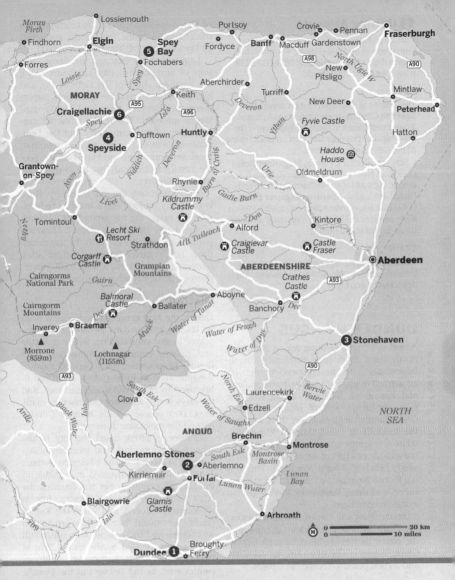

Northeast Scotland Highlights

1 Exploring below decks on board Captain Scott's famous polar exploration vessel **Discovery** (p215) in Dundee

2 Meditating on the meaning of the mysterious **Pictish stones** of Angus at Aberlemno (p224)

3 Tucking into the freshest of Scottish seafood at the **Tolbooth Restaurant** (p234) in Stonehaven

4 Being initiated into the mysteries of malt whisky on a Speyside **distillery tour** (p240)

5 Learning about the Moray Firth's bottlenose dolphins at the **Scottish Dolphin Centre** (p241) at Spey Bay

6 Sampling from 700-plus varieties of single malt in the Craigellachie Hotel's **Quaich Bar** (p239)

ℹ Getting Around

You can pick up a public transport map from tourist offices and bus stations. For timetable information, call **Traveline** (☏ 0871 200 2233; www.travelinescotland.com).

BUS

The Dundee to Aberdeen route is served by **Scottish Citylink** (www.citylink.co.uk) buses. **Stagecoach** (www.stagecoachbus.com) is the main regional bus operator, with services linking all the main towns and cities.

Stagecoach offers a **Moray Megarider ticket** (£29) that gives seven days unlimited bus travel around Elgin as far as Findhorn, Dufftown and Fochabers, and an **Aberdeen Explorer ticket** (£42) that allows seven days unlimited travel on all its services in Aberdeenshire, as far as Montrose, Braemar and Huntly.

TRAIN

The Dundee–Inverness railway line passes through Arbroath, Montrose, Stonehaven, Aberdeen, Huntly and Elgin.

DUNDEE & ANGUS

Angus is a fertile farming region stretching north from Dundee – Scotland's fourth-largest city – to the Highland border. It's an attractive area of broad straths (valleys) and low, green hills contrasting with the rich, red-brown soil of freshly ploughed fields. Romantic glens finger their way into the foothills of the Grampian Mountains, while the scenic coastline ranges from the red-sandstone cliffs of Arbroath to the long, sandy beaches around Montrose. This was the Pictish heartland of the 7th and 8th centuries, and many interesting Pictish symbol stones survive here.

Apart from the crowds visiting Discovery Point in newly confident Dundee and the coach parties shuffling through Glamis Castle, Angus is a bit of a tourism backwater and a good place to escape the crowds.

Dundee

POP 147,300

London's Trafalgar Sq has Nelson on his column, Edinburgh's Princes St has its monument to Sir Walter Scott and Belfast has a statue of Queen Victoria outside City Hall. Dundee's City Sq, on the other hand, is graced – rather endearingly – by the bronze figure of Desperate Dan. Familiar to generations of British school children, Dan is one of the best-loved cartoon characters from the children's comic the *Dandy*, published by Dundee firm DC Thomson since 1937.

Dundee enjoys perhaps the finest location of any Scottish city, spreading along the northern shore of the Firth of Tay, and boasts tourist attractions of national importance in Discovery Point and the Verdant Works museum. Add in the attractive seaside town of Broughty Ferry and the Dundonians themselves – among the friendliest, most welcoming and most entertaining people you'll meet – and Dundee is definitely worth a stopover.

The waterfront around Discovery Point is currently undergoing a massive redevelopment, preparing the ground for a branch of London's **Victoria & Albert Museum** (scheduled to open in 2016). In the meantime, be prepared for construction sites, temporary street layouts and traffic diversions on the approach to the Tay Bridge.

History

During the 19th century Dundee grew from its trading port origins to become a major player in the shipbuilding, whaling, textile and railway engineering industries. Dundonian firms owned and operated most of the jute mills in India (jute is a natural fibre used to make ropes and sacking), and the city's textile industry employed as many as 43,000 people – little wonder Dundee earned the nickname 'Juteopolis'.

Dundee is often called the city of the 'Three Js' – jute, jam and journalism. According to legend, it was a Dundee woman, Janet Keillor, who invented marmalade in the late 18th century; her son founded the city's famous Keillor jam factory. Jute is no longer produced, and when the Keillor factory was taken over in 1988, production was transferred to England. Journalism still thrives, however, led by the family firm of DC Thomson. Best known for children's comics such as the *Beano* and the *Dandy*, and regional newspapers including the *Press and Journal*, Thomson is now the city's largest employer.

In the late 19th and early 20th centuries Dundee was one of the richest cities in the country – there were more millionaires per head of population here than anywhere else in Britain – but the textile and engineering industries declined in the second half of the 20th century, leading to high unemployment and urban decay.

In the 1960s and '70s Dundee's cityscape was scarred by ugly blocks of flats, office buildings and shopping centres linked by unsightly concrete walkways and most visitors passed it by. Since the mid-1990s, however, Dundee has reinvented itself as a tourist destination, and a centre for banking, insurance and new industries, while its waterfront is currently undergoing a major redevelopment. It also has more university students – one in seven of the population – than any other town in Europe, except Heidelberg.

⊙ Sights

★ Discovery Point   MUSEUM

(www.rrsdiscovery.com; Discovery Quay; adult/child/family £8.75/5.25/25; ⊙10am-6pm Mon-Sat, 11am-6pm Sun Apr-Oct, to 5pm Nov-Mar) The three masts of Captain Robert Falcon Scott's famous polar expedition vessel the **RRS Discovery** dominate the riverside to the south of the city centre. Exhibitions and audio visual displays in the neighbouring visitor centre provide a fascinating history of both the ship and Antarctic exploration, but *Discovery* itself – afloat in a protected dock – is the star attraction. You can visit the bridge, the galley and the mahogany-panelled officers' wardroom, and poke your nose into the cabins used by Scott and his crew.

The ship was built in Dundee in 1900, with a wooden hull at least half a metre thick to survive the pack ice, and sailed for the Antarctic in 1901 where it spent two winters trapped in the ice. From 1931 on it was laid up in London where its condition steadily deteriorated, until it was rescued by the efforts of Peter Scott (Robert's son) and the Maritime Trust, and restored to its 1925 condition. In 1986 the ship was given a berth in its home port of Dundee, where it became a symbol of the city's regeneration.

A joint ticket that gives entry to both Discovery Point and the Verdant Works costs £15/8.50/40 per adult/child/family.

★ Verdant Works   MUSEUM

(www.verdantworks.com; West Henderson's Wynd; adult/child/familiy £8.75/5.25/25; ⊙10am-6pm Mon-Sat, 11am-6pm Sun Apr-Oct, 10:30am-4.30pm Wed-Sun Nov-Mar) One of the finest industrial museums in Europe, the Verdant Works explores the history of Dundee's jute industry. Housed in a restored jute mill, complete with original machinery still in working condition, the museum's interactive exhibits and computer displays follow the raw material from its origins in India through to the manufacture of a wide range of finished products, from sacking to rope to wagon covers for the pioneers of the American West.

The museum is 250m west of the city centre and is operating while undergoing a major renovation that will restore more buildings and double the size of the exhibition space.

McManus Galleries   MUSEUM

(www.mcmanus.co.uk; Albert Sq; ⊙10am-5pm Mon-Sat, 12.30-4.30pm Sun) **FREE** Housed in a solid Victorian Gothic building designed by Gilbert Scott in 1867, the McManus Galleries are a city museum on a human scale – you can see everything there is to see in a single visit, without feeling rushed or overwhelmed. The exhibits cover the history of the city from the Iron Age to the present day, including relics of the Tay Bridge Disaster and the Dundee whaling industry.

Computer geeks will enjoy the Sinclair ZX81 and Spectrum (pioneering personal computers with a whole 16K of memory!) which were made in Dundee in the early 1980s.

HM Frigate Unicorn   MUSEUM

(www.frigateunicorn.org; Victoria Dock; adult/child £5.25/3.25; ⊙10am-5pm Apr-Oct, noon-4pm Wed-Fri, 10am-4pm Sat & Sun Nov-Mar) Dundee's second floating tourist attraction – unlike the polished and much-restored *RRS Discovery* – retains the authentic atmosphere of a salty old sailing ship. Built in 1824, the 46-gun *Unicorn* is the oldest British-built ship still afloat – she was mothballed soon after launching and never saw action. Wandering around below deck gives you an excellent impression of what it must have been like for the crew forced to live in such cramped conditions.

By the mid-19th century sailing ships were outclassed by steam and the *Unicorn* served as a gunpowder store, then later as a training vessel. When it was proposed to break up the ship for scrap in the 1960s, a preservation society was formed. The ship is berthed in Victoria Dock, just northeast of the Tay Road Bridge. The entry price includes a self-guided tour (also available in French and German).

Dundee Contemporary Arts   ARTS CENTRE

(www.dca.org.uk; Nethergate; ⊙11am-6pm Tue, Wed & Fri-Sun, 11am-8pm Thu) **FREE** The focus

Dundee

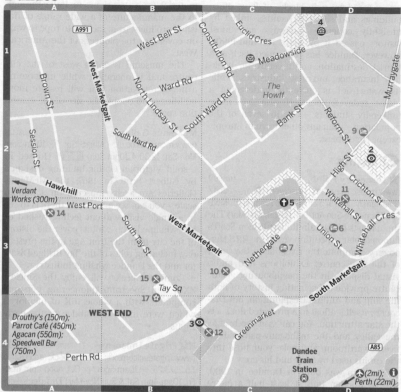

Dundee

◎ Top Sights
1 Discovery Point E4

◎ Sights
2 City Square D2
3 Dundee Contemporary Arts B4
4 McManus Galleries D1
5 St Mary's Church C3

🛏 Sleeping
6 Aabalree D3
7 Aauld Steeple Guest House C3
8 Apex City Quay Hotel F2

9 Dundee Backpackers D2

✕ Eating
10 Deep Sea C3
11 Fisher & Donaldson D2
12 Jute Café Bar C4
13 Metro F2
14 Parlour Cafe A3
15 Playwright B3

◉ Entertainment
16 Caird Hall E2
17 Dundee Rep Theatre B4

for the city's Cultural Quarter is Dundee Contemporary Arts, a centre for modern art, design and cinema. The galleries here exhibit work by contemporary UK and international artists, and there are printmakers' studios where you can watch artists at work, or even take part in craft demonstra-

tions and workshops. There's also the Jute Cafe-Bar (p218).

Dundee Law   PARK

It's worth making the climb up Dundee Law (174m) for great views of the city, the two Tay bridges, and across to Fife. The **Tay**

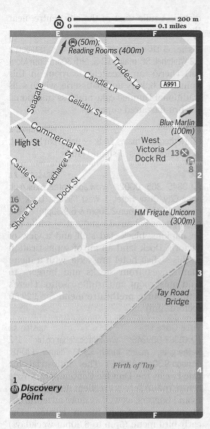

N
0 — 200 m
0 — 0.1 miles

(50m);
Reading Rooms (400m)

Trades La

Candle Ln

A991

Seagate

Gellatly St

Blue Marlin
(100m)

Commercial St

High St

West
Victoria
Dock Rd

13

8

Castle St

Exchange St

Dock St

16

Shore Tce

HM Frigate Unicorn
(300m)

3

Tay Road
Bridge

Firth of Tay

4

1
Discovery
Point

Rail Bridge – at just over 2 miles long, it was the world's longest when it was built – was completed in 1887. The 1.5-mile Tay Road Bridge was opened in 1966. Dundee Law is a short walk northwest of the city centre, along Constitution Rd.

The railway bridge replaced an earlier structure whose stumps can be seen alongside. The original bridge collapsed during a storm in 1879 less than two years after it was built, in the infamous Tay Bridge Disaster, taking a train and 75 lives along with it.

City Square
SQUARE

The heart of Dundee is City Sq, flanked to the south by the 1930s facade of Caird Hall, which was gifted to the city by a textile magnate and is now home to the City Chambers. A more recent addition to the square, unveiled in 2001, is a bronze statue of Desperate Dan, the lantern-jawed hero of children's comic the *Dandy* (he's clutching a copy in his right hand).

Pedestrianised High St leads west into Nethergate, flanked to the north by St Mary's Church. Most of the church dates from the 19th century, but the Old Steeple was built around 1460.

Festivals & Events

If you're around in late July, look out for the Dundee Blues Bonanza (www.dundee-bluesbonanza.co.uk), a two-day festival of free blues, boogie and roots music.

Sleeping

Most of Dundee's city-centre hotels are business oriented and offer lower rates on weekends. B&Bs are concentrated along Broughty Ferry Rd and Arbroath Rd east of the city centre, and on Perth Rd to the west. If you don't fancy a night in the city, consider staying at the nearby seaside town of Broughty Ferry.

Accommodation in Dundee is usually booked solid when the Open golf tournament is staged at Carnoustie or St Andrews – check www.theopen.com for future dates and venues (it'll be in St Andrews in 2015).

Dundee Backpackers   HOSTEL £
(☑ 01382-224646; www.hoppo.com/dundee; 71 High St; dm £16-18.50. s/tw from £25/40;@) Set in a beautifully converted historic building, with clean, modern kitchen, pool room, and an ideal location right in the city centre. Can get a bit noisy at night, but that's because it's close to pubs and nightlife.

Aabalree   B&B £
(☑ 01382-223867; www.aabalree.com; 20 Union St; s/d £26/44) This is a pretty basic B&B – there are no en suites – but the owners are welcoming (don't be put off by the dark entrance) and it couldn't be more central, close to both the train and bus stations. This makes it popular, so book ahead.

Auld Steeple Guest House   B&B £
(☑ 01382-200302; www.aauldsteepleguesthouse. co.uk; 94 Nethergate; s/d from £30/44;) Just as central as Aabalree but a bit more comfortable (if slightly old-fashioned), the Aauld Steeple has spacious double and family rooms, some with views of St Mary's Church. It can suffer a bit from street noise, though.

Balgowan House   B&B ££
(☑ 01382-200262; www.balgowanhouse.co.uk; 510 Perth Rd; s/d from £60/85;) Built in 1900 and perched in a prime location with stun-

ning views over the Firth of Tay, Balgowan is a wealthy merchant's mansion converted into a luxurious guesthouse with three sumptuous en suite bedrooms. It's 2 miles west of the city centre, overlooking the university botanic gardens.

Apex City Quay Hotel
HOTEL ££

(✆0845 365 0000; www.apexhotels.co.uk; 1 West Victoria Dock Rd; r from £77; P🕸🏐) Though it looks plain and boxy from the outside, the Apex sports the sort of stylish, spacious, sofa-equipped rooms that make you want to lounge around all evening munching chocolate in front of the TV. If you can drag yourself away from your room, there are spa treatments, saunas and Japanese hot tubs to enjoy.

The hotel is just east of the city centre, overlooking the city's redeveloping waterfront and close to the HM Frigate *Unicorn*.

Errolbank Guest House
B&B ££

(✆01382-462118; www.errolbank-guesthouse. com; 9 Dalgleish Rd; s/d £49/69; P) A mile east of the city centre, just north of the road to Broughty Ferry, Errolbank is a lovely Victorian family home with small but beautifully decorated en suite rooms set on a quiet street.

Shaftesbury Lodge
HOTEL ££

(✆01382-669216; www.shaftesburyhotel.net; 1 Hyndford St; s/d from £58/79;@🕸) The family-run, 12-room Shaftesbury is a Victorian mansion built for a jute baron and has many authentic period features, including a fine marble fireplace in the dining room. It's 1.5 miles west of the city centre, just off Perth Rd.

✗ Eating

★Parlour Cafe
CAFE £

(✆01382-203588; 58 West Port; mains £5-7;⊗8am-7pm Mon-Fri, to 5pm Sat, 10am-3pm Sun;🕸🍴) 🌱 Tiny but terrific, this friendly neighbourhood cafe is bursting with good things to eat including filled tortillas, savoury tarts, beanburgers, bagels and homemade soup, all freshly prepared using seasonal produce. Great coffee and cakes too, but be prepared to wait for a table or squeeze in among the locals.

Parrot Café
CAFE £

(91 Perth Rd; mains £3-8; ⊗ 10am-5pm Tue-Fri, 10am-4pm Sat;🍴) A cracking wee cafe with good coffee and tea, home baking like Mum used to make and a couple of hot lunch

dishes. A mile west of the city centre, near the university.

Fisher & Donaldson
TEAROOM £

(12 Whitehall St; mains £3-5; ⊗6.30am-5pm Mon-Sat) There's an excellent tearoom in this upmarket bakery and patisserie, which sells traditional Dundee cake and less traditional Irn-Bru-flavoured cupcakes.

Deep Sea
FISH & CHIPS £

(81 Nethergate; mains £4-8; ⊗9am-7pm Mon-Sat; 🍴) Dundee's best fish and chips.

★Metro
BRASSERIE ££

(✆0845 365 0002; www.apexhotels.co.uk/eat; Apex City Quay Hotel, 1 West Victoria Dock Rd; mains £11-27; ⊗noon-2.30pm & 6-9.30pm) Sleek, champagne-coloured banquettes, white linen napkins, black-clad staff and a view of Victoria Dock lend an air of sophistication to this stylish hotel brasserie, with a menu that ranges from steaks and burgers to wild mushroom and truffle risotto. There's a three-course pretheatre menu for £22.50 (before 7pm).

Jute Café Bar
BISTRO ££

(✆01382-909246; www.jutecafebar.co.uk; 152 Nethergate; mains lunch £9-13, dinner £10-18; ⊗noon-9.30pm; 🕸🍴) The industrial-chic cafe-bar in the Dundee Contemporary Arts centre (p215) serves excellent deli sandwiches and burgers, as well as more adventurous Mediterranean-Asian fusion cuisine. The early-bird menu (5pm to 6.30pm weekdays) offers a two-/three-course meal for £14/16. Tables spill out into the sunny courtyard in summer.

Agacán
TURKISH ££

(✆01382-644227; 113 Perth Rd; mains £11-18; ⊗5-10pm Tue-Sun; 🍴) With a charismatic owner, quirky decor and wonderfully aromatic Turkish specialities (İskender kebab is our favourite), it's no wonder that you have to book ahead at this colourful little restaurant, a 20-minute walk up Perth Rd from the centre. If you can't get a table, you can settle for takeaway.

Playwright
BISTRO £££

(✆01382-223113; www.theplaywright.co.uk; 11 Tay Sq; mains £24-26; ⊗noon-2.30pm & 6-9.30pm) 🌱 Next door to the Dundee Rep Theatre (p219), and decorated with photos of Scottish actors, this innovative bistro serves a set lunch (two course £13), pre-theatre menu (£17/20 for two/three courses, 5pm to

6.30pm) and a gourmet à la carte menu that concentrates on fine Scottish produce.

Blue Marlin
SEAFOOD £££

(☎ 01382-221397; www.thebluemarlin.co.uk; City Quay; mains £14-26; ⊗noon-2pm & 5.30-10pm Tue-Sat) The ongoing redevelopment of Dundee's former docks means that the setting for the city's best fish restaurant doesn't look too promising. But once inside, there is sleek and understated nautical-themed decor, and the chance to feast on the best of Scottish seafood. Two-course lunch and pretheatre menu £15.

Drinking

Dundee has many lively pubs, especially in the West End and along West Port.

Drouthy's
PUB

(www.drouthysdundee.co.uk; 142 Perth Rd; ⊗10am-midnight; 🛜) A perfectly unpretentious local pub, serving a wide range of Scottish and international craft beers and an all-day menu of tempting pub grub, including irresistible gourmet burgers. Live music in the basement club.

Speedwell Bar
PUB

(www.mennies.co.uk; 165-167 Perth Rd; ⊗11am-11pm Mon-Sat, 12.30pm-11pm Sun; 🛜) Known to generations of Dundonians as 'Mennie's', this university district pub, 1½ miles west of the city centre, is the city's best preserved Edwardian bar, complete with acres of polished mahogany, real ale on tap, and a choice of 150 malt whiskies.

☆ Entertainment

Dundee's nightlife may not be as hot as Glasgow's, but there are lots of places to go – pick up a free what's-on guide from the tourist office, or check out the What's On section of www.dundee.com. Tickets for most events are on sale at the Dundee Contemporary Arts centre.

Reading Rooms
CLUB, LIVE MUSIC

(www.readingroomsdundee.com; 57 Blackscroft; admission free-£8) Dundee's hippest venue is an arty, bohemian hang-out in a run-down former library that hosts some of Scotland's best indie club nights. Live gigs have ranged from island singer-songwriter Colin MacIntyre (aka Mull Historical Society) to Glasgow guitar band Franz Ferdinand and Ayrshire rockers Biffy Clyro.

Caird Hall
MUSIC, COMEDY

(www.cairdhall.co.uk; 6 City Sq; ⊗ box office 9am-4.30pm Mon-Fri, 9.30am-1.30pm Sat) The Caird Hall hosts regular concerts of classical music, as well as organ recitals, rock bands, dances, comedians, fetes and fairs. Check the website for details of coming events.

Dundee Rep Theatre
DRAMA

(www.dundeereptheatre.co.uk; Tay Sq; ⊗box office 10am-6pm or start of performance) Dundee's main venue for the performing arts, the Rep is home to Scotland's only full-time renertory company and to the Scottish Dance Theatre.

ⓘ Information

Dundee Tourist Office (☎ 01382-527527; www.angusanddundee.co.uk; Discovery Point; ⊗ 10am-5pm Mon-Sat, noon-4pm Sun Jun-Sep, 10am-4pm Mon-Sat Oct-May)

Ninewells Hospital (☎ 01382-660111; www.nhstayside.scot.nhs.uk; ⊗ casualty 24hr) At Menzieshill, west of the city centre.

ⓘ Getting There & Away

AIR

Two and a half miles west of the city centre, **Dundee Airport** (www.hial.co.uk) has daily scheduled services to London City airport, Birmingham and Belfast. A taxi from the city centre to the airport takes 10 minutes and costs around £4.

BUS

The bus station is northeast of the city centre. Some Aberdeen buses travel via Arbroath, others via Forfar.

Aberdeen £16.80, 1½ hours, hourly

Edinburgh £16.10, 1½ hours, hourly, some change at Perth

Glasgow £16.10, 1¾ hours, hourly

London £40, 11 hours; National Express, daily

Oban £35.50, 5½ hours, three daily

Perth £7.50, 35 minutes, hourly

TRAIN

Trains from Dundee to Aberdeen travel via Arbroath and Stonehaven.

Aberdeen £19.10, 1¼ hours, twice an hour

Edinburgh £17.30, 1¼ hours, at least hourly

Glasgow £21.30, 1½ hours, hourly

ⓘ Getting Around

The city centre is compact and is easy to get around on foot. For information on local public transport, contact **Dundee Travel Info** (www.dundeetravelinfo.com).

PICTISH SYMBOL STONES

The mysterious carved stones that dot the landscape of eastern Scotland are the legacy of the warrior tribes who inhabited these lands 2000 years ago. The Romans occupied the southern half of Britain from AD 43 to 410, but the region to the north of the firths of Forth and Clyde – known as Caledonia – was abandoned as being too dangerous, and sealed off behind the ramparts of the Antonine Wall and Hadrian's Wall.

Caledonia was the homeland of the Picts, a collection of tribes named by the Romans for their habit of painting or tattooing their bodies. In the 9th century they were culturally absorbed by the Scots, leaving behind only a few archaeological remains, a scattering of Pictish place names beginning with 'Pit', and hundreds of mysterious carved stones decorated with intricate symbols, mainly in northeast Scotland. The capital of the ancient Southern Pictish kingdom is said to have been at Forteviot in Strathearn; Pictish symbol stones are found throughout this area and all the way up the eastern coast of Scotland into Sutherland and Caithness.

It is thought that the stones were set up to record Pictish lineages and alliances, but noone is sure exactly how the system worked. They are decorated with unusual symbols, including z-rods (a lightning bolt?), circles (the sun?), double discs (a hand mirror?) and fantastical creatures, as well as figures of warriors on horseback, hunting scenes and (on the later stones) Christian symbols.

Local tourist offices provide a free leaflet titled the *Angus Pictish Trail*, which will guide you to the main sites, while Historic Scotland's **Pictish Stones** (www.pictishstones. org.uk) website details all the sites in Scotland. The finest assemblage of stones in their natural outdoor setting is at **Aberlemno** (p224), and there are excellent indoor collections at St Vigeans Museum (p222) and the Meigle Museum (p208). The Pictavia (p224) interpretive centre at Brechin provides a good introduction to the Picts and is worth a look before you visit the stones.

The Pictish Trail by Anthony Jackson lists 11 driving tours, while *The Symbol Stones of Scotland* by the same author provides more detail on the history and meaning of the Pictish stones.

BUS

City bus fares cost £1.35 to £2.25 depending on distance; buy your ticket from the driver (exact fare only – no change given).

CAR

Rental agencies include:

Arnold Clark (☑ 01382-225382; www.arnold-clarkrental.com; East Dock St)

National Car Rental (☑ 01382-224037; www.nationalcar.co.uk; 45-53 Gellatly St)

TAXI

Discovery Taxis (☑ 01382-732333)

Broughty Ferry

Dundee's attractive seaside suburb, known locally as 'The Ferry', lies 4 miles east of the city centre. It has a castle, a long, sandy beach and a number of good places to eat and drink. It's also handy for the golf courses at nearby Carnoustie.

⊙ Sights

Broughty Castle Museum MUSEUM
(www.leisureandculturedundee.com; Castle Green; ⊙10am-4pm Mon-Sat, 12.30-4pm Sun, closed Mon Oct-Mar) FREE A 16th-century tower that looms imposingly over the harbour, guarding the entrance to the Firth of Tay, houses a fascinating exhibit on Dundee's whaling industry, and the view from the top offers the chance of spotting seals and dolphins offshore.

🛏 Sleeping

Fisherman's Tavern B&B ££
(☑01382-775941; www.fishermanstavern.co.uk; 10-16 Fort St; s/d from £49/74; ☎) A delightful 17th-century terraced cottage just a few paces from the seafront, the Fisherman's was converted into a pub in 1827. It now has 12 stylishly modern rooms, most with en suite, and an atmospheric pub.

Hotel Broughty Ferry HOTEL ££
(☑01382-480027; www.hotelbroughtyferry.com; 16 W Queen St; s/d from £68/88; P🖙🖾) It may

not look like much from the outside, but this is the Ferry's swankiest place to stay, with 16 beautifully decorated bedrooms, a sauna, a solarium and a small heated pool. It's only a five-minute stroll from the waterfront.

Ashley House
B&B ££

(☎01382-776109; www.ashleyhousebroughtyferry.com; 15 Monifieth Rd; s/d £40/68; P🌐🏊) This spacious and comfortable guesthouse has long been one of Broughty Ferry's best. Its five cheerfully decorated bedrooms come equipped with hotel-grade beds and DVD players; one has a particularly grand bathroom.

🍴 Eating & Drinking

Ship Inn
PUB ££

(☎01382-779176; www.theshipinn-broughtyferry.co.uk; 121 Fisher St; mains £9-19; ⊘food served noon-2.30pm & 5-7pm) The Ship Inn is a snug, wood-panelled, 19th-century pub on the waterfront, which serves top-notch dishes ranging from gourmet haddock and chips to venison steaks; you can eat in the upstairs restaurant, or down in the bar (bar meals £7 to £9). It's always busy, so get there early to grab a seat.

Fisherman's Tavern
PUB £

(www.fishermanstavern-broughtyferry.co.uk; 10-16 Fort St; mains £6-13; ⊘food served noon-2.30pm & 5-7.30pm) The Fisherman's – a maze of cosy nooks and open fireplaces in a 17th-century cottage – is a lively little pub where you can wash down haddock and chips or steak and ale pie with a choice of Scottish ales.

Visocchi's
CAFE ££

(www.visocchis.co.uk; 40 Gray St; mains £9-11; ⊘9.30am-5pm Tue, 9.30am-8pm Wed, Thu & Sun, 9.30am-10pm Fri & Sat; 🍴) Visocchi's – a local institution since 1954 – is a traditional, family-run Italian cafe that sells delicious homemade ice cream, good coffee and a range of pizzas and pasta dishes.

ℹ Getting There & Away

City bus 5 and Stagecoach bus 73 run from Dundee High St to Broughty Ferry (£1.90, 20 minutes) several times an hour from Monday to Saturday, and hourly on Sunday.

There are five trains daily from Dundee (£1.30, five to 10 minutes).

Glamis Castle & Village

Looking every inch the Scottish Baronial castle, with its roofline sprouting a forest of pointed turrets and battlements, **Glamis Castle** (www.glamis-castle.co.uk; adult/child £10.90/8; ⊘10am-6pm Apr–Oct, last admission 4.30pm; P🐕) claims to be the legendary setting for Shakespeare's *Macbeth* . A royal residence since 1372, it is the family home of the earls of Strathmore and Kinghorne – the Queen Mother (born Elizabeth Bowes-Lyon; 1900–2002) spent her childhood at Glamis (pronounced 'glams') and Princess Margaret (the Queen's sister; 1930–2002) was born here.

The five-storey, L-shaped castle was given to the Lyon family in 1372, but was significantly altered in the 17th century. Inside, the most impressive room is the **drawing room**, with its vaulted plasterwork ceiling. There's a display of armour and weaponry in the haunted crypt and frescoes in the chapel (also haunted). **Duncan's Hall** is named for the murdered King Duncan from *Macbeth* (though the scene actually takes place in Macbeth's castle in Inverness). As with Cawdor Castle, the claimed Shakespeare connection is fictitious – the real Macbeth had nothing to do with either castle, and died long before either was built.

You can also look around the **royal apartments**, including the Queen Mother's bedroom. Hour-long guided tours (included in admission) depart every 15 minutes; the last tour is at 4.30pm.

The **Angus Folk Museum** (NTS; www.nts.org.uk; Kirkwynd; adult/child £6.50/5; ⊘10.30am-4.30pm Thu-Mon Jul & Aug, 11.30am-4.30pm Sat-Mon Apr-Jun, Sep & Oct; P), in a row of 18th-century cottages just off the flower-bedecked square in Glamis village, houses a fine collection of domestic and agricultural relics.

Glamis Castle is 12 miles north of Dundee. There are two to four buses a day from Dundee (£3.50, one hour) to Glamis; change at Forfar.

Arbroath

POP 23,900

Arbroath is an old-fashioned seaside resort and fishing harbour, home of the famous Arbroath smokie (a form of smoked haddock). The humble smokie achieved European Union 'Protected Geographical

Indication' status in 2004 – the term 'Arbroath smokie' can be only be used legally to describe haddock smoked in the traditional manner within an 8km radius of Arbroath. No visit is complete without buying a pair of smokies from one of the many fish shops and eating them with your fingers while sitting beside the harbour. Yum.

👁 Sights

Arbroath Abbey ABBEY
(HS; Abbey St; adult/child £5.50/3.30; ⊙9.30am-5.30pm Apr-Sep, to 4.30pm Oct-Mar) The magnificent, red-sandstone ruins of Arbroath Abbey, founded in 1178 by King William the Lion, dominate the town of Arbroath. It is thought that Bernard of Linton, the abbot here in the early 14th century, wrote the famous Declaration of Arbroath in 1320, asserting Scotland's right to independence from England. You can climb to the top of one of the towers for a grand view over the town.

St Vigeans Museum MUSEUM
(HS; ☎01241-878756; St Vigeans Lane; adult/child £4.50/2.70) About a mile north of Arbroath town centre, this cottage museum houses a superb collection of Pictish and medieval sculptured stones. The museum's masterpiece is the Drosten Stone, beautifully carved with animal figures and hunting scenes on one side, and an interlaced Celtic cross on the other (look for the devil perched in the top left corner). Phone ahead or ask at Arbroath Abbey to check current opening hours.

Signal House Museum MUSEUM
(Ladyloan; ⊙10am-5pm Tue-Sat) FREE This museum has displays dedicated to Arbroath's maritime heritage and the Bell Rock Lighthouse, which was built between 1807 and 1811 by the famous engineer Robert Stevenson (grandfather of writer Robert Louis Stevenson). It is housed in the elegant Signal Tower that was once used to communicate with the construction team working on the Bell Rock Lighthouse 12 miles offshore.

🏃 Activities

The coast northeast of Arbroath consists of dramatic red-sandstone cliffs riven by inlets, caves and natural arches. An excellent **clifftop walk** (pick up a leaflet from the tourist office) follows the coast for 3 miles to the quaint fishing village of Auchmithie, which claims to have invented the Arbroath smokie.

If you fancy catching your own fish, the **Marie Dawn** (☎07836-770609) and **Girl Katherine II** (☎07752-470621) offer three-hour sea-angling trips (usually from 2pm to 5pm) out of Arbroath harbour for £16 to £20 per person, including tackle and bait.

🛏 Sleeping

Harbour Nights Guest House B&B ££
(☎01241-434343; www.harbournights-scotland.com; 4 The Shore; s/d from £50/70; 🖲) With a superb location overlooking the harbour, four stylishly decorated bedrooms and a gourmet breakfast menu, Harbour Nights is our favourite place to stay in Arbroath. Rooms 2 and 3, with harbour views, are a bit more expensive (doubles £75 to £80), but well worth asking for when booking.

Old Vicarage B&B ££
(☎01241-430475; www.theoldvicaragebandb.co.uk; 2 Seaton Rd; s/d £60/85; 🖲) 🅿 The three five-star bedrooms in this attractive Victorian villa have a pleasantly old-fashioned atmosphere, and the extensive breakfast menu includes Arbroath smokies. The house is on a quiet street close to the start of the clifftop walk to Auchmithie.

🍴 Eating

Smithie's CAFE £
(16 Keptie St; mains £5-6; ⊙9.30am-4.30pm Mon-Fri, to 4pm Sat; 🖲) Housed in a former butcher's shop, with hand-painted tiles and meat hooks on the ceiling, Smithie's is a great little neighbourhood deli and cafe serving Fairtrade coffee, pancakes, wraps and freshly made pasta – butternut squash and sage

THE FORFAR BRIDIE

Forfar, the county town of Angus, is the home of Scotland's answer to the Cornish pasty: the famous Forfar bridie. A shortcrust pastry turnover filled with minced beef, onion and gravy, it was invented in Forfar in the early 19th century. If you fancy trying one, head for James McLaren & Son (☎01382-462762; 8 The Cross, Forfar; ⊙8am-4.30pm Mon-Wed, Fri & Sat, 8am-1pm Thu), a family bakery bang in the centre of Forfar, which has been selling tasty, home-baked bridies since 1893.

tortellini make a tasty change from macaroni cheese for a vegetarian lunch.

Sugar & Spice Tearoom   CAFE **£**
(www.sugarandspiceshop.co.uk; 9-13 High St; mains £6-12; ⊙10am-5pm Mon-Thu, 10am-9pm Fri & Sat, noon-7pm Sun, longer hours Jun-Sep; ⊕)
With its flounces, frills and black-and-white uniformed waitresses, this chintzy tearoom verges on the twee. However, the place is very child-friendly – there's an indoor play area and a play garden out the back – and the tea and scones are sublime. You can even try an Arbroath smokie, grilled with lemon butter.

But'n'Ben Restaurant   SCOTTISH **££**
(☑01241-877223; www.butnbenauchmithie.co.uk; 1 Auchmithie; mains lunch £8-11, dinner £12-22; ⊙noon-2pm Wed-Mon, 6-9pm Mon & Wed-Sat, 4-7pm Sun; ⊕) ⊘ Above the harbour in Auchmithie, this cosy cottage restaurant with open fireplace, rustic furniture and sea-themed art serves the best of local seafood – the Arbroath smokie pancakes are recommended – plus great homemade cakes and desserts, and high teas on Sunday (£14). Best to book.

Gordon's Restaurant   SCOTTISH **£££**
(☑01241-830364; www.gordonsrestaurant. co.uk; Main St, Inverkeillor; 3-course lunch £34, 4-course dinner £55; ⊙12.30-1.30pm Wed-Fri & Sun, 7-8.30pm Tue-Sun) ⊘ Six miles north of Arbroath, in the tiny and unpromising-looking village of Inverkeillor, lies this hidden gem – an intimate and rustic eatery serving gourmet-quality Scottish cuisine. There are five comfortable bedrooms (single/double from £85/110) for those who don't want to drive after dinner.

❶ Information

Visitor Centre & Tourist Office (☑01241-872609; Fishmarket Quay; ⊙9.30am-5.30pm Mon-Sat, 10am-3pm Sun Jun-Aug, 9am-5pm Mon-Fri, 10am-5pm Sat Apr, May & Sep, to 3pm Sat Oct-Mar) Beside the harbour.

❶ Getting There & Away

BUS

Bus 140 runs from Arbroath to Auchmithie (£1.90, 15 minutes, six daily Monday to Friday, three daily on Saturday and Sunday).

TRAIN

Trains from Dundee to Arbroath (£5.40, 20 minutes, two per hour) continue to Aberdeen (£18.70, 55 minutes) via Montrose and Stonehaven.

Kirriemuir

POP 6100

Known as the Wee Red Town because of its close-packed, red-sandstone houses, Kirriemuir is famed as the birthplace of JM Barrie (1860–1937), writer and creator of the much-loved *Peter Pan*. A bronze statue of the 'boy who wouldn't grow up' graces the intersection of Bank and High Sts.

The tourist office is in the Gateway to the Glens Museum.

◎ Sights

JM Barrie's Birthplace   MUSEUM
(NTS; 9 Brechin Rd; adult/child £6.50/5; ⊙11am-5pm Jul & Aug, noon-5pm Sat-Wed Apr-Jun, Sep & Oct) This is Kirriemuir's big attraction, a place of pilgrimage for Peter Pan fans from all over the world. The two-storey house where Barrie was born has been furnished in period style, and preserves Barrie's writing desk and the wash house at the back that served as his first 'theatre'. Your ticket also gives admission to the **Camera Obscura** (Camera Obscura only adult/child £3.50/2.50; ⊙noon-5pm Mon-Sat, 1-5pm Sun Jul-Sep, Sat & Sun only Easter-Jun) on the hilltop northeast of the town centre, given to the town by Barrie himself.

Gateway to the Glens Museum   MUSEUM
(32 High St; ⊙10am-5pm Tue-Sat) **FREE** The old Town House opposite the Peter Pan statue dates from 1604 and houses the Gateway to the Glens Museum, a useful introduction to local history, geology and wildlife for those planning to explore the Angus Glens.

✕ Eating

★88 Degrees   CAFE, DELI **£**
(☑07449 345089; 17 High St; mains £3-7; ⊙9.30am-5pm Wed-Fri, 9.30am-4pm Sat, 10am-4pm Sun) ⊘ This tiny deli serves the best cafe cuisine in the county – superb coffee (it's named for the ideal temperature of an espresso), delicious cakes and handmade chocolates. Breakfast (served till 10.30am) includes delicious omelettes made with free-range eggs.

🛍 Shopping

Star Rock Shop   CONFECTIONERY
(☑01575-572579; 27-29 Roods; ⊙9.30am-5pm Tue-Sat) For generations of local school kids, the big treat when visiting Kirriemuir was a trip to the Star Rock Shop. Established in

WORTH A TRIP

ABERLEMNO STONES

Five miles northeast of Forfar, on the B9134, are the mysterious **Aberlemno Stones**, some of Scotland's finest Pictish symbol stones.

By the roadside there are three 7th- to 9th-century slabs with various symbols, including the z-rod and double disc, and in the churchyard at the bottom of the hill there's a magnificent 8th-century stone displaying a Celtic cross, interlace decoration, entwined beasts and, on the reverse, scenes of the Battle of Nechtansmere (where the Picts vanquished the Northumbrians in 685). The stones are covered up from November to March; otherwise there's free access at all times.

1833, it still specialises in traditional Scottish 'sweeties', arranged in colourful jars along the walls – including humbugs, cola cubes, pear drops, and the original Star Rock candy, still made to an 1833 recipe.

❶ Getting There & Away

Stagecoach bus 20 runs from Dundee to Kirriemuir (£4.20, one hour, hourly Monday to Saturday, every two hours Sunday) via Forfar (25 minutes; change here for Glamis).

Edzell

POP 900

The picturesque village of Edzell, with its broad main street and grandiose monumental arch, dates from the early 19th century when Lord Panmure decided that the original medieval village, a mile to the west, spoiled the view from Edzell Castle. The old village was razed and the villagers moved to this pretty, planned settlement.

Lord Panmure's predecessors as owners of **Edzell Castle** (HS; adult/child £5.50/3.30; ⊙9.30am-5.30pm Apr-Sep) were the Lindsay earls of Crawford, who built this 16th-century L-plan tower house. Sir David Lindsay, a cultured and well-travelled man, laid out the castle's beautiful **pleasance** in 1604 as a place of contemplation and learning. Unique in all of Scotland, this Renaissance walled garden is lined with niches for nesting birds and sculptured plaques illustrating

the cardinal virtues, the arts and the planetary deities.

Two miles north of Edzell, the B966 to Fettercairn crosses the River North Esk at Gannochy Bridge. From the lay-by just over the bridge, a wooden door in the stone wall gives access to a delightful footpath that leads along the wooded river gorge for 1.5 miles to a scenic spot known as the **Rocks of Solitude**.

Stagecoach bus 21 or 21A from Brechin stops at Edzell (£.2.10, 10 to 15 minutes, seven daily Monday to Friday, five on Saturday).

Brechin

POP 7480

The name of the local football team, Brechin City, proclaims this diminutive town's main claim to fame – as the seat of **Brechin Cathedral** (now demoted to a parish church) it has the right to call itself a city, albeit the smallest one in Scotland. Adjacent to the cathedral is a 32m-high **round tower** built around 1000 as part of a Celtic monastery. It is of a type often seen in Ireland, but one of only three that survive in Scotland. Its elevated doorway, 2m above the ground, has carvings of animals, saints and a crucifix.

Housed nearby in the 18th-century former town hall, court room and prison, **Brechin Town House Museum** (St Ninian's Sq; ⊙10am-5pm Tue-Sat) FREE records the history of the round tower, cathedral and town.

The town's (OK, city's) picturesque Victorian train station dates from 1897 and is now the terminus of the restored **Caledonian Railway** (www.caledonianrailway. com; 2 Park Rd; adult/child £7/5), which runs heritage trains along a 3.5-mile stretch of track to Bridge of Dun. Steam trains run on Sundays from late May to August, and diesel trains on Saturdays in July and August; check the website for other dates. From Bridge of Dun station, it's a 15-minute signposted walk to the **House of Dun** (NTS; adult/child £10.50/7.50; ⊙11am-5pm Jul & Aug, noon-5pm Wed-Sun Apr-Jun, Sep & Oct), a beautiful Georgian country house built in 1730.

Adjoining Brechin Castle Centre (a gardening and horse-riding centre on the A90 just west of Brechin) is **Pictavia** (www. pictavia.org.uk; adult/child £3.25/2.25; ⊙9am-5pm Mon-Sat, 10am-5pm Sun Apr-Oct, Sat & Sun only Nov-Mar), an interpretive centre telling the story of the Picts and explaining current theories about the mysterious carved symbol stones they left behind. It's worth making a trip here before going to see the Pictish stones at Aberlemno (p224).

❶ Getting There & Away

Stagecoach bus 21 runs from Forfar to Brechin (£3.30, 30 minutes, hourly), via Aberlemno (£2, 15 minutes, six daily).

Bus 24 links Brechin and Stonehaven (£4.80, 55 minutes, at least three daily).

ABERDEENSHIRE & MORAY

Since medieval times Aberdeenshire and its northwestern neighbour Moray have been the richest and most fertile regions of the Highlands. Aberdeenshire is famed for its Aberdeen Angus beef cattle, its many fine castles and the prosperous 'granite city' of Aberdeen. Moray's main attractions are the Speyside whisky distilleries that line the valley of the River Spey and its tributaries.

Aberdeen

POP 195,000

Aberdeen is the powerhouse of the northeast, fuelled by the North Sea petroleum industry. Oil money has made the city as expensive as London and Edinburgh, and there are hotels, restaurants and clubs with prices to match the depth of oil-wealthy pockets. Fortunately, most of the cultural attractions, such as the excellent Maritime Museum and Aberdeen Art Gallery, are free.

Known throughout Scotland as the granite city, much of the town was built using silvery-grey granite hewn from the now abandoned Rubislaw Quarry, at one time the biggest artificial hole in the ground in Europe. On a sunny day the granite lends an attractive sparkle to the city, but when low, grey rain clouds scud in off the North Sea it can be hard to tell where the buildings stop and the sky begins.

Royal Deeside and the Cairngorms National Park are easily accessible to the west, Dunnottar Castle to the south, sandy beaches to the north and whisky country to the northwest.

History

Aberdeen was a prosperous trading and fishing port, centuries before oil became a valuable commodity. After the townspeople supported Robert the Bruce against the English at the Battle of Bannockburn in 1314, the king rewarded the town with land whose rental income was used to establish the Common Good Fund, to be spent on town amenities. The fund survives to this day: it helped to finance Marischal College, the Central Library, the art gallery and the hospital, and also pays for the colourful floral displays that have won the city numerous awards.

The name Aberdeen is a combination of two Pictish-Gaelic words, *aber* and *devana*, meaning 'the meeting of two waters' (the Rivers Dee and Don). The area was known to the Romans, and was raided by the Vikings when it was already an important port trading in wool, fish, hides and fur. By the 18th century paper and rope-making, whaling and textile manufacture were the main industries, and in the 19th century it became a major herring-fishing centre.

Since the 1970s Aberdeen has been the main focus of Scotland's offshore oil industry, home to oil company offices, engineering yards, a bustling harbour filled with supply ships, and the world's busiest civilian heliport. Unemployment rates, once among the highest in the country, are today among the lowest.

◉ Sights & Activities

◉ City Centre

Union Street is the city's main thoroughfare, lined with solid, Victorian granite buildings. The oldest area is Castlegate, at the eastern end, where the castle once stood. When it was captured from the English for Robert the Bruce, the password used by the townspeople was 'Bon Accord' (good fellowship), which is now the city's motto.

In the centre of Castle St stands the 17th-century Mercat Cross, bearing a sculpted frieze of portraits of Stuart monarchs. The baronial heap towering over the eastern end of Castle St is the Salvation Army Citadel, which was modelled on Balmoral Castle.

On the northern side of Union St, 200m west of Castlegate, is 17th-century Provost Skene's House (www.aagm.co.uk; ⊙10am-5pm

Aberdeen

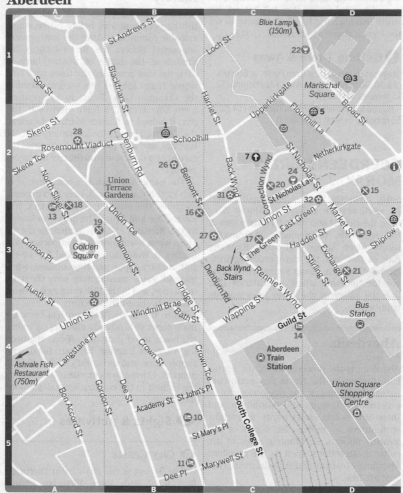

NORTHEAST SCOTLAND ABERDEEN

Mon-Sat) FREE, one of the city's oldest buildings (closed to the public until completion of the surrounding Marischal Square redevelopment). Another 100m to the west is **St Nicholas Church**, the so-called 'Mither Kirk' (Mother Church) of Aberdeen. The granite spire dates from the 19th century, but there has been a church on this site since the 12th century; the early-15th-century **St Mary's Chapel** survives in the eastern part of the church.

Aberdeen Maritime Museum　MUSEUM
(📋 01224-337700; www.aagm.co.uk; Shiprow; ⏱ 10am-5pm Tue-Sat, noon-3pm Sun) FREE Overlooking the nautical bustle of Aberdeen harbour is the Maritime Museum. Centred on a three-storey replica of a North Sea oil production platform, it explains all you ever wanted to know about the petroleum industry. Other galleries, some situated in **Provost Ross's House**, the oldest building in the city and part of the museum, cover the shipbuilding, whaling and fishing industries.

Sleek and speedy Aberdeen clippers were a 19th-century shipyard speciality, used by

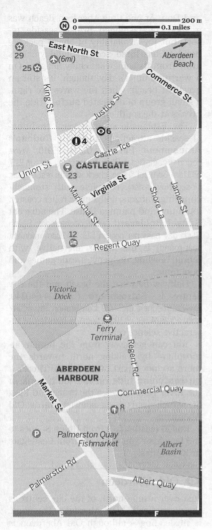

Aberdeen

British merchants for the importation of tea, wool and exotic goods (opium, for instance) to Britain, and, on the return journey, the transportation of emigrants to Australia.

Aberdeen Art Gallery GALLERY
(☎ 01224-523700; www.aagm.co.uk; Schoolhill; ⊙ 10am-5pm Tue-Sat, 2-5pm Sun) FREE Behind the grand facade of Aberdeen Art Gallery is a cool, marble-lined space exhibiting the work of contemporary Scottish and English painters, such as Gwen Hardie, Stephen Conroy, Trevor Sutton and Tim Ollivier. There are also several landscapes by Joan Eardley, who lived in a cottage on the cliffs near Stonehaven in the 1950s and '60s and painted tempestuous oils of the North Sea and poignant portraits of slum children.

Among the Pre-Raphaelite works upstairs, look out for the paintings by Aberdeen artist William Dyce (1806–64), ranging from religious works to rural scenes.

Marischal College HISTORIC BUILDING
(Broad St) Marischal College, founded in 1593 by the 5th Earl Marischal, merged with King's College (founded 1495) in 1860 to

create the modern University of Aberdeen. The college's huge and impressive facade overlooking Broad St, in Perpendicular Gothic style – unusual in having such elaborate masonry hewn from notoriously hard-to-work granite – dates from 1906 and is the world's second-largest granite structure (after L'Escorial near Madrid).

A recent renovation project saw the facade returned to its original silvery grey glory, and the building now houses Aberdeen City Council's new headquarters; the square outside is undergoing redevelopment into a pedestrian plaza, creating controversy over plans for modern architecture juxtaposed with the college's neo-Gothic facade.

Gordon Highlanders Museum   MUSEUM
(www.gordonhighlanders.com; St Lukes, Viewfield Rd; adult/child £6.50/3.50; ☺10am-4pm Tue-Sat Feb-Nov) This excellent museum records the history of one of the British Army's most famous fighting units, described by Winston Churchill as 'the finest regiment in the world'. Originally raised in the northeast of Scotland by the 4th Duke of Gordon in 1794, the regiment was amalgamated with the Seaforths and Camerons to form the Highlanders regiment in 1994. The museum is about a mile west of the western end of Union St – take bus 11 or X17 from Union St.

◉ Aberdeen Harbour

Aberdeen has a busy, working harbour crowded with survey vessels and supply ships servicing the offshore oil installations, and car ferries bound for Orkney and Shetland. Despite all this traffic, the waters outside the harbour are rich in marine life – in summer dolphins, porpoises and basking sharks can be seen from cruise boats or from the headland of Girdle Ness, south of the harbour entrance.

Clyde Cruises   BOAT TRIPS
(☑01475-721281; www.clydecruises.com; Aberdeen Harbour; adult/child from £16/8; ☺daily Jul-late Aug, Thu-Sun late Aug-mid Sep) Operates 45-minute cruises around Aberdeen's bustling commercial harbour, and 1¼-hour trips outside the harbour to look for dolphins and other marine wildlife.

◉ Aberdeen Beach

Just 800m east of Castlegate is a spectacular 2-mile sweep of clean, golden sand stretching between the mouths of the Rivers Dee

and Don. At one time Aberdeen Beach was a good, old-fashioned British seaside resort, but the availability of cheap package holidays has lured Scottish holidaymakers away from its somewhat chilly delights. On a warm summer's day, though, it's still an excellent beach; when the waves are right, a small group of dedicated surfers ride the breaks at the south end.

The Esplanade sports several traditional seaside attractions, including **Codona's Amusement Park** (☑01224-595910; www.codonas.com; Beach Blvd; day pass per person £13; ☺11am-6pm Jul & Aug, check website rest of year, closed Nov-Easter), complete with stomach-churning waltzers, dodgems, a roller coaster, log flume and haunted house. The adjacent **Sunset Boulevard** (www.codonas.com; Beach Blvd; day pass per person £13; ☺10am-midnight year-round) is the indoor alternative, with tenpin bowling, dodgems, arcade games and pool tables.

Halfway between the beach and the city centre is **Satrosphere** (☑01224-640340; www.satrosphere.net; 179 Constitution St; adult/child £5.75/4.50; ☺10am-5pm), a hands-on, interactive science centre.

You can get away from the funfair atmosphere by walking north towards the more secluded part of the beach. There's a **birdwatching hide** on the south bank of the River Don, between the beach and King St, which leads back south towards Old Aberdeen.

Bus 15 (eastbound) from Union St goes to the beach; or you can walk from Castlegate in 10 minutes.

◉ Old Aberdeen

Just over a mile north of the city centre is the district called Old Aberdeen. The name is misleading – although Old Aberdeen is certainly old, the area around Castlegate in the city centre is older still. This part of the city was originally called Aulton, from the Gaelic for 'village by the stream', and this was anglicised in the 17th century to Old Town.

Bus 20 from Littlejohn St (just north of Marischal College) runs to Old Aberdeen every 15 to 20 minutes.

King's College Chapel   HISTORIC BUILDING
(College Bounds; ☺10am-3.30pm Mon-Fri) **FREE** It was here that Bishop Elphinstone established King's College, Aberdeen's first university (and Scotland's third), in 1495.

The 16th-century college chapel is easily recognised by its crown spire; the interior is largely unchanged since it was first built, with impressive stained-glass windows and choir stalls.

Old Town House   HISTORICAL BUILDING
(☑ 01224-273650; www.abdn.ac.uk/oldtownhouse; High St; ⊙ 9am-5pm Mon-Sat) FREE At the north end of High St, the Old Town House now houses a visitor centre with information and exhibits on the history of Old Aberdeen. It also houses King's Museum with changing exhibits of items from the university's 18th-century collection.

St Machar's Cathedral   CATHEDRAL
(www.stmachar.com; The Chanonry; ⊙ 10am-4pm) FREE The 15th-century St Machar's Cathedral, with its massive twin towers, is a rare example of a fortified cathedral. According to legend, St Machar was ordered to establish a church where the river takes the shape of a bishop's crook, which it does just here. The cathedral is best known for its impressive heraldic ceiling, dating from 1520, which has 48 shields of kings, nobles, archbishops and bishops. Sunday services are held at 11am and 6pm.

🛏 Sleeping

There are clusters of B&Bs on Bon Accord St and Springbank Tce (both 400m southwest of the train station) and along Great Western Rd (the A93, a 25-minute walk southwest of the city centre). They're usually more expensive than the Scottish average and, with so many oil industry workers staying the night before flying offshore, single rooms are at a premium. Prices tend to be lower on weekends.

Aberdeen Youth Hostel   HOSTEL £
(SYHA; ☑ 01224-646988; 8 Queen's Rd; dm/q £22/100; @ �) This unexceptional but good-value hostel, set in a granite Victorian villa, is a mile west of the train station. Walk west along Union St and take the right fork along Albyn Pl until you reach a roundabout; Queen's Rd continues on the western side of the roundabout.

★ Globe Inn   B&B ££
(☑ 01224-624258; www.the-globe-inn.co.uk; 13-15 North Silver St; r £119) This popular pub has seven appealing and comfortable guest bedrooms upstairs, done out in dark wood with burgundy bedspreads. There's live music in the pub on weekends so it's not a place for early-to-bed types, but the price vs location factor can't be beaten. No dining room, so breakfast is continental, served on a tray in your room.

Butler's Guest House   B&B ££
(☑ 01224-212411; www.butlersguesthouse.com; 122 Crown St; s/d from £63/74; @ � annotated) Butler's is a cosy place with a big breakfast menu that includes fresh fruit salad, kippers and kedgeree as alternatives to the traditional fry-up (rates include a continental breakfast; cooked breakfast is £6.50 extra per person). There are cheaper rooms with shared bathrooms.

City Wharf Apartments   APARTMENT ££
(☑ 0845 094 2424; www.citywharfapartments.co.uk; 19-20 Regent Quay; d from £120; � annotated) You can watch the bustle of Aberdeen's commercial harbour as you eat breakfast in one of these luxury serviced apartments, complete with stylish, fully equipped kitchen, champagne-stocked minibar and daily cleaning service. Available by the night or the week, with discounts for longer stays.

Brentwood Villa   B&B ££
(☑ 01224-480633; www.brentwoodvillabandb.com; 560 King St; s/d £60/90; � annotated) Comfortable beds, spotless bathrooms and friendly and helpful owners tick all the right boxes in this homely B&B, attractively set opposite a park. The Brentwood is a mile north of the city centre (take bus 20) and close to Old Aberdeen and the university.

Brentwood Hotel   HOTEL ££
(☑ 01224-595440; www.brentwood-hotel.co.uk; 101 Crown St; s £45-104, d £59-114; P � annotated) The friendly and flower-bedecked Brentwood, set in a granite town house, is one of the most attractive hotels in the city centre. It's comfortable and conveniently located, but often busy during the week – weekend rates (Friday to Sunday) are much cheaper.

Dunrovin Guest House   B&B ££
(☑ 01224-586081; www.dunrovinguesthouse.co.uk; 168 Bon Accord St; s/d from £45/70; P � annotated) Dunrovin is a typical granite Victorian house with eight bedrooms; the upstairs rooms are bright and airy. The friendly owners will provide a veggie breakfast if you wish. Located 400m south of Union St.

Adelphi Guest House   B&B ££
(☑ 01224-583078; www.adelphiguesthouse.com; 8 Whinhill Rd; s/d from £45/70; � annotated) Basic but

comfortable and good value, located 400m south from western end of Union St.

Aberdeen Douglas Hotel
HOTEL £££

(📞 01224-582255; www.aberdeendouglas.com; 43-45 Market St; r Mon-Fri from £165, Sat & Sun from £145; 🛜) You can't miss the grand Victorian facade of this historic landmark, which first opened its doors as a hotel in 1853. Now renovated, it offers classy modern rooms with polished woodwork and crisp white bedlinen, and is barely a minute's walk from the train station.

Jurys Inn
HOTEL £££

(📞 01224-381200; www.jurysinns.com; Union Sq, Guild St; r from £129; 🛜) Stylish and comfortable hotel right next to the train station.

✗ Eating

Sand Dollar Café
CAFE £

(📞 01224-572288; www.sanddollarcafe.com; 2 Beach Esplanade; mains £6-12; ⊙7.30am-6pm Sun-Tue, to 7.30pm Wed, to 4pm Thu-Sat, also 6-9pm Thu-Sat) A cut above your usual seaside cafe – on sunny days you can sit at the wooden tables on the prom and share a bottle of chilled white wine, or choose from a menu that includes pancakes with maple syrup, homemade burgers and chocolate brownie with Orkney ice cream.

An evening bistro menu (mains £15 to £26) offers steak and seafood dishes; best to book for this. The cafe is on the esplanade, 800m northeast of the city centre.

Beautiful Mountain
CAFE £

(www.thebeautifulmountain.com; 11-13 Belmont St; mains £7-10; ⊙8am-3.30pm & 5.30-11pm Wed-Sat, 10.30am-2.45pm Sun; 🖋) This cosy cafe is squeezed into a couple of tiny rooms (seating upstairs), but serves all-day breakfasts and tasty sandwiches (smoked salmon, Thai chicken, pastrami) on sourdough, bagels, ciabatta and lots of other breads, along with exquisite espresso and consummate cappuccino. It's also open for dinner, when the menu switches to Spanish-style tapas.

Ashvale Fish Restaurant
FISH & CHIPS £

(www.theashvale.co.uk; 42-48 Great Western Rd; takeaway £5-9, sit-in £8-14; ⊙11.45am-10pm; 🖭) This is the flagship, 200-seat branch of the Ashvale, an award-winning fish-and-chip restaurant famed for its quality haddock. The Ashvale Whale – a 1lb fish fillet in batter (£12.25) – is a speciality; finish it off and you get a second one free (as if you'd want one

by then!). It's 300m southwest of the west end of Union St.

★ Café 52
BISTRO ££

(📞 01224-590094; www.cafe52.net; 52 The Green; mains £9-13; ⊙noon-midnight Mon-Sat, to 6pm Sun; 🛜) This little haven of laid-back industrial chic – a high, narrow space lined with bare stonework, rough plaster and exposed ventilation ducts – serves some of the finest and most inventive cuisine in the northeast. Try starters such as crisp black pudding with wine-poached pear, or mains like pan-fried herring with orange butter sauce.

★ Adelphi Kitchen
MODERN SCOTTISH ££

(📞 01224-211414; www.theadelphikitchen.co.uk; 28 Adelphi Ln, Union St; mains £12-28; ⊙noon-2.30pm & 5-10pm Tue-Sat; 🛜) 🖋 Cool and clever flavour combinations are the hallmark of this unsuspected little gem hidden down an alley off Union St, a small but sophisticated space decorated with weathered timber and muted natural colours. Charcoal grilling is a speciality, with aged Aberdeen Angus beef and pulled pork given the barbecue treatment alongside seafood treats such as west coast scallops and Shetland mussels.

Moonfish Café
MEDITERRANEAN ££

(📞 01224-644166; www.moonfishcafe.co.uk; 9 Correction Wynd; 2-/3-course dinner £27/32; ⊙noon-2pm & 6-9.30pm Tue-Sat) 🖋 The menu of this funky little eatery tucked away on a back street concentrates on good-quality Scottish produce that draws its influences from cuisines all around the world, from simple smoked haddock kedgeree to spiced monkfish with pickled carrot, mustard seed, yoghurt and coriander.

Musa Art Cafe
MODERN SCOTTISH ££

(📞 01224-571771; www.musaaberdeen.com; 33 Exchange St; mains lunch £10, dinner £13-29; ⊙noon-11pm Tue-Sat; 🛜 🖋) 🖋 The bright paintings on the walls match the vibrant furnishings and smart gastronomic creations at this great cafe-restaurant, set in a former church. As well as a menu that focuses on quality local produce cooked in a quirky way – think haggis-and-black pudding spring rolls with chilli jam – there are Brewdog beers from Fraserburgh, and interesting music, sometimes live.

Fusion
FUSION ££

(📞 01224-652959; www.fusionbarbistro.com; 10 North Silver St; lunch mains £10-15, 2-/3-course dinner £25/30; ⊙noon-10pm Tue-Sat; 🛜) 🖋 This chic and trendy bar-bistro in the upmarket Golden Square district has a menu that is true to its name, blending Scottish west-coast scallops with a ginger and chilli glaze, and giving braised shin of Scottish beef the French treatment by serving it with garlic risotto. The lunch menu is also served from 5pm to 6pm.

Granite Park   MODERN SCOTTISH ££
(📞 01224-478004; www.granitepark.co.uk; 8 Golden Sq; 2-/3-course lunch £15/20, dinner mains £18-29; ⏱ noon-2.30pm & 5-9.30pm) This smart and sophisticated restaurant and cocktail bar has become a local sensation, taking Scottish favourites such as venison, haddock and smoked salmon and giving them an Asian or Mediterranean twist. Best to book.

Silver Darling   SEAFOOD £££
(📞 01224-576229; www.thesilverdarling.co.uk; Pocra Quay, North Pier; 2-/3-course lunch £20/24, dinner mains £22-30; ⏱ noon-1.45pm Mon-Fri, 6.30-9.30pm Mon-Sat) The Silver Darling (an old Scottish nickname for herring) is the place for a special meal, housed in a former customs office at the entrance to Aberdeen harbour with picture windows overlooking the sea. Here you can enjoy fresh Scottish seafood prepared by a top French chef while you watch the porpoises playing in the harbour mouth. Bookings are recommended.

Drinking

Aberdeen is a great city for a pub crawl – it's more a question of knowing when to stop than where to start. There are lots of pre-club bars in and around Belmont St, with more traditional pubs scattered throughout the city centre.

Globe Inn   PUB
(www.the-globe-inn.co.uk; 13-15 North Silver St; ⏱ 11am-midnight, to 1am Fri & Sat) This lovely Edwardian-style pub with wood panelling, marble-topped tables and walls decorated with old musical instruments is a great place for a quiet lunchtime or afternoon drink. It serves good coffee as well as real ales and malt whiskies, and has live music (rock, blues, soul) Friday to Sunday. It's also got probably the poshest pub toilets in the country.

Prince of Wales   PUB
(www.princeofwales-aberdeen.co.uk; 7 St Nicholas Lane; ⏱ 10am-midnight Mon-Thu, to 1am Fri & Sat, 11am-midnight Sun; 🍴) Tucked down an alley off Union St, Aberdeen's best-known pub

boasts the longest bar in the city, a great range of real ales and good-value pub grub. Quiet in the afternoons, but standing-room only in the evenings.

Old Blackfriars   PUB
(www.oldblackfriars-aberdeen.co.uk; 52 Castlegate; ⏱ 11am-midnight Mon-Thu, 11am-1am Fri, 10am-1am Sat, 10am-11pm Sun; 🍴) One of the most attractive traditional pubs in the city, with a lovely stone and timber interior, stained-glass windows and a relaxed atmosphere – a great place for an afternoon pint. Live folk music on Thursday from 9pm.

Blue Lamp   PUB
(www.jazzatthebluelamp.com; 121 Gallowgate; ⏱ 11am-midnight Mon-Thu, to 1am Fri & Sat, 12.30-11pm Sun) A long-standing feature of the Aberdeen pub scene, the Blue Lamp is a favourite student hang-out – a cosy drinking den with good beer, good *craic* (lively conversation) and regular sessions of live jazz and standup comedy. The pub is 150m north of the city centre, along Broad St.

BrewDog   BAR
(www.brewdog.com/bars/aberdeen; 17 Gallowgate; ⏱ noon-midnight Mon-Thu, to 1am Fri & Sat, 12.30am-midnight Sun; 🍴) The flagship bar of northeast Scotland's most innovative craft brewery brings a bit of designer chic to Aberdeen's pub scene along with a vast range of guest beers from around the world.

☆ Entertainment

Cinemas

Belmont Filmhouse   CINEMA
(www.belmontfilmhouse.com, 49 Belmont St) The Belmont is a great little art-house cinema, with a lively programme of cult classics, director's seasons, foreign films and mainstream movies.

Clubs & Live Music

Cafe Drummond   LIVE MUSIC
(www.cafedrummond.com; 1 Belmont St) A long-established stalwart of Aberdeen's alternative music scene, Drummond is a crowded, grungy, student hang-out offering live gigs from up-and-coming local talent, and regular club nights extending into the wee hours of the night.

Tunnels   LIVE MUSIC
(www.thetunnels.co.uk; Carnegie's Brae) This cavernous, subterranean club – the entrance is in a road tunnel beneath Union St – is a great live music venue, with a packed programme

of up-and-coming Scottish bands. It also hosts regular DJ nights – check the website for the latest events.

O'Neill's
LIVE MUSIC

(www.oneills.co.uk; 9 Back Wynd) Upstairs at O'Neill's you're guaranteed a wild night of pounding, hardcore Irish rock, indie and alternative tunes Friday to Sunday; downstairs is a (slightly) quieter bar packed with rugby types downing large quantities of Murphy's stout.

Theatre & Concerts

You can book tickets for most concerts and other events at the **Aberdeen Box Office** (www.aberdeenperformingarts.com; ⏰ 9.30am-6pm Mon-Sat) next to the **Music Hall** (Union St), the main venue for classical music concerts.

Lemon Tree Theatre
PERFORMING ARTS

(www.aberdeenperformingarts.com; 5 West North St) Hosts an interesting program of dance, music and drama, and often has live rock, jazz and folk bands playing. There are also children's shows, ranging from comedy to drama to puppetry.

His Majesty's Theatre
BALLET, OPERA

(www.aberdeenperformingarts.com; Rosemount Viaduct) The main theatre in Aberdeen hosts everything from ballet and opera to pantomimes and musicals.

Aberdeen Arts Centre
THEATRE

(www.act-aberdeen.org.uk; King St) Stages regular drama productions in its theatre, and changing exhibitions in its gallery.

ⓘ Information

Aberdeen Royal Infirmary (☑ 0845 456 6000; www.nhsgrampian.org; Foresterhill) Medical services. About a mile northwest of the western end of Union St.

Aberdeen Tourist Office (☑ 01224-288828; www.aberdeen-grampian.com; 23 Union St; ⏰ 9am-6.30pm Mon-Sat, 10am-4pm Sun Jul & Aug, 9.30am-5pm Mon-Sat Sep-Jun) Handy for general information; has internet access (£1 per 20 minutes).

Books & Beans (www.booksandbeans.co.uk; 22 Belmont St; per 15min £1; ⏰ 8am-6pm) Internet access; also Fairtrade coffee and secondhand books.

Main Post Office (St Nicholas Shopping Centre, Upperkirkgate; ⏰ 9am-5.30pm Mon-Sat) In the WH Smith shop.

ⓘ Getting There & Away

AIR

Aberdeen Airport (ABZ; ☑ 0844 481 6666; www.aberdeenairport.com) is at Dyce, 6 miles northwest of the city centre. There are regular flights to numerous Scottish and UK destinations, including Orkney and Shetland, and international flights to the Netherlands, Norway, Denmark, Germany and France.

Stagecoach Jet bus 727 runs regularly from Aberdeen bus station to the airport (single £2.70, 35 minutes). A taxi from the airport to the city centre takes 25 minutes and costs £15.

BOAT

Car ferries from Aberdeen to Orkney and Shetland are run by **Northlink Ferries** (www.northlinkferries.co.uk). The **ferry terminal** is a short walk east of the train and bus stations.

BUS

The **bus station** (Guild St) is next to Jurys Inn, close to the train station.

Braemar £11, 2¼ hours, every two hours; via Ballater and Balmoral

Dundee £16.80, 1½ hours, hourly

Edinburgh £30, three hours, three daily direct, more frequent changing at Perth

Glasgow £30, three hours, at least hourly

Inverness £12.50, four hours, hourly; via Huntly, Keith, Fochabers, Elgin and Nairn

London £47, 12 hours, twice daily; National Express

Perth £23.50, two hours, hourly

TRAIN

The train station is south of the city centre, next to the massive Union Square shopping mall.

Dundee £19.10, 1¼ hours, twice an hour

Edinburgh £34, 2½ hours, hourly

Glasgow £34, 2¾ hours, hourly

Inverness £27, 2¼ hours, eight daily

London Kings Cross £110, eight to 11 hours, hourly; some direct, most change at Edinburgh

ⓘ Getting Around

BUS

The main city bus operator is **First Aberdeen** (www.firstaberdeen.com). Local fares cost from £1.20 to £2.50; pay the driver as you board the bus. A FirstDay ticket (adult/child £4.30/2.60) allows unlimited travel from the time of purchase until midnight on all First Aberdeen buses. Information, route maps and tickets are available from the **First Travel Centre** (47 Union St; ⏰ 8.45am-5.30pm Mon-Sat).

The most useful services for visitors are buses 15 and 19 from Union St to Great Western Rd (for B&Bs); bus 11 from Union St to Aberdeen Youth Hostel and the airport; and bus 20 from Marischal College to Old Aberdeen.

CAR

Car rental companies include:

Arnold Clark (☑ 01224-622714; www.arnold-clarkrental.com; Canal Rd)
Enterprise Car Hire (☑ 01224-642642; www.enterprise.co.uk; 80 Skene Sq)

TAXI

The main city-centre taxi ranks are at the train station and on Dask Wynd, off Union St. To order a taxi, phone **ComCab** (☑ 01224-353535; www.comcab-aberdeen.co.uk) or **Rainbow City Taxis** (☑ 01224-878787; www.rainbowcitytaxis.com).

Around Aberdeen

◉ Sights

Crathes Castle   CASTLE
(NTS; ☑ 01330-844525; adult/child £12.50/9; ☻ 10.30am-5pm Apr-Oct, 11am-4pm Sat & Sun Nov-Mar; ▥) The atmospheric, 16th-century Crathes Castle is famous for its Jacobean painted ceilings, magnificently carved canopied beds, and the 'Horn of Leys', presented to the Burnett family by Robert the Bruce in the 14th century. The beautiful formal gardens include 300-year-old yew hedges and colourful herbaceous borders. The castle is signposted off the A93; Stagecoach buses 201 and 202 from Aberdeen stop at the castle entrance (£4.80, 45 minutes, every 30 minutes).

Haddo House   HISTORIC BUILDING
(NTS; ☑ 0844 493 2179; adult/child £10.50/7.50; ☻ tours 11am, 1.30pm & 3.30pm daily Jul & Aug, Fri-Mon Apr-Jun, Sep & Oct) Designed in Georgian style by William Adam in 1732, Haddo House is best described as a classic English stately home transplanted to Scotland. Home to the Gordon family, it has sumptuous Victorian interiors with wood-panelled walls, Persian rug–scattered floors and a wealth of period antiques. The beautiful grounds and terraced gardens are open all year (9am to dusk); guided tours of the house are best booked in advance. Haddo is 19 miles north of Aberdeen, near Ellon.

Buses run hourly Monday to Saturday from Aberdeen to Tarves/Methlick (£5.80, one hour), stopping at the end of the Haddo House driveway; it's a one-mile walk from bus stop to house.

Fyvie Castle   CASTLE
(NTS; adult/child £12.50/9; ☻ 11am-5pm Jul & Aug, noon-5pm Sat-Wed Apr-Jun, Sep & Oct) Though a magnificent example of Scottish Baronial architecture, Fyvie Castle is probably more famous for its ghosts, including a phantom trumpeter and the mysterious Green Lady, and its art collection which displays portraits by Thomas Gainsborough and Sir Henry Raeburn. The grounds are open all year (9am to dusk).

The castle is 25 miles north of Aberdeen on the A947 towards Turriff. A bus runs hourly from Aberdeen to Banff and Elgin via Fyvie village (£7.50, 1½ hours), a mile from the castle.

Stonehaven

POP 11,430

Originally a small fishing village, Stonehaven has been the county town of Kincardineshire since 1600 and is now a thriving family-friendly seaside resort. There's a **tourist office** (☑ 01569-762806; 66 Allardice St; ☻ 10am-7pm Mon-Sat, 1-5.30pm Sun Jul & Aug, 10am-1pm & 2-5.30pm Mon-Sat Sep-Jun) near Market Sq in the town centre.

◉ Sights & Activities

From the lane beside the tourist office, a boardwalk leads south along the shoreline to the picturesque cliff-bound **harbour**, where you'll find a couple of appealing pubs and the town's oldest building, the **Tolbooth**, built about 1600 by the Earl Marischal. It now houses a small local history **museum** (www.stonehaventolbooth.co.uk; Old Quay; ☻ 1.30-4.30pm Wed-Mon Apr-Sep) FREE and a restaurant.

Dunnottar Castle   CASTLE
(☑ 01569 762173; www.dunnottarcastle.co.uk; adult/child £6/2; ☻ 9am-6pm Apr-Sep, 10am-5pm or dusk Oct-Mar) A pleasant, 15-minute walk along the clifftops south of Stonehaven harbour leads to the spectacular ruins of Dunnottar Castle, spread out across a grassy promontory 50m above the sea. As dramatic a film set as any director could wish for, it provided the backdrop for Franco Zeffirelli's *Hamlet* (1990), starring Mel Gibson. The original fortress was built in the 9th century; the keep is the most substantial remnant, but the drawing room (restored in 1926) is more interesting.

NORTHEAST SCOTLAND AROUND ABERDEEN

Open-Air Swimming Pool
SWIMMING

(☑ 01569-762134; www.stonehavenopenairpool.co.uk; adult/child £5/3; ☉ 10am-7.30pm Mon-Fri, to 6pm Sat & Sun Jul–mid-Aug, 1-7.30pm Mon-Fri, 10am-6pm Sat & Sun Jun & late Aug) This Olympic-size (50m), heated, sea-water pool was built in 1934 in art deco style, and sits on the seafront to the north of Stonehaven town centre. The pool is also open for 'midnight swims' from 10pm to midnight on Wednesday from the end of June to mid-August.

🎆 Festivals & Events

Fireball Ceremony
CULTURAL

(www.stonehavenfireballs.co.uk) Stonehaven's famous Fireball Ceremony takes place on Hogmanay (31 December), when people parade along the High St at midnight swinging blazing fireballs around their heads before throwing them into the harbour.

Stonehaven Real Ale Festival
FOOD & DRINK

(www.stonehavenrealalefestival.co.uk) Home to the Six Degrees North craft brewery and several excellent real ale pubs, Stonehaven makes a great setting for this convivial three-

---

SAND DUNES AND SAND TRAPS
....

Coastal sand dunes extend north from Aberdeen for more than 14 miles, one of the largest areas of dunes in the UK, and the least affected by human activity. **Forvie national nature reserve** (www.nnr-scotland.org.uk/forvie; ☉ 24hr) **FREE** has wildlife hides and waymarked trails through the dunes to an abandoned medieval village where only the ruins of the church survive. The dunes form an important nesting and feeding area for birds – don't wander off the trails during the nesting season (April to August).

American tycoon Donald Trump sparked off a major controversy when he opened **Trump International Golf Links** in 2012, amid a 'protected' area of sand dunes just four miles south of Forvie. In Trump's own words: 'I have never seen such an unspoiled and dramatic sea side landscape'. However, the development has split the community between those who welcome the potential economic benefits, and those worried about the environmental damage.

---

day celebration of artisan beers. Usually in November, but check website for dates.

Stonehaven Folk Festival
MUSIC

(www.stonehavenfolkfestival.co.uk) The town fills wth musicians for this lively four-day folk festival in mid-July.

🛏 Sleeping & Eating

★ 24 Shorehead
B&B ££

(☑ 01569-767750; www.twentyfourshorehead.co.uk; 24 Shorehead; s/d £60/80; @ 🛜) Location makes all the difference, and the location of this former cooperage offering peaceful and very stylish B&B accommodation can't be beaten – it's the last house at the end of the road, overlooking the harbour with lovely sea views. Using the binoculars provided, you can even spot seals from your bedroom. No credit cards.

Beachgate House
B&B ££

(☑ 01569-763155; www.beachgate.co.uk; Beachgate Lane; s/d £55/70; 🅿) This luxurious modern bungalow is right on the seafront, just a few paces from the tourist office; two of its five rooms have sea views, as does the lounge/dining room.

Marine Hotel
PUB, SEAFOOD ££

(☑ 01569-762155; www.marinehotelstonehaven.co.uk; 9-10 The Shore; mains £12-24; ☉ food noon-2.30pm & 6-9pm Mon-Sat, noon-9pm Sun) Bare timber, slate and dove-grey paintwork give this popular harbourside pub a boutique look; there are half a dozen real ales on tap, including beers from Stonehaven's own Six Degrees North craft brewery, and a bar-meals menu that includes fresh seafood specials.

Carron Restaurant
SCOTTISH ££

(☑ 01569-760460; www.carron-restaurant.co.uk; 20 Cameron St; mains £14-26; ☉ noon-2pm & 6-9.30pm Tue-Sat) This beautiful art deco restaurant is a remarkable survivor from the 1930s, complete with bow-fronted terrace, iron fanlights, deco mirrors, player piano and original ceramic-tiled toilets. The French- and Mediterranean-influenced menu makes the most of local produce, matching the elegance of the surroundings.

Tolbooth Restaurant
SEAFOOD £££

(☑ 01569-762287; www.tolbooth-restaurant.co.uk; Old Pier; mains £17-24; ☉ noon-2pm & 6-9.30pm Tue-Sat year-round, same hours Sun May-Sep) Set in the 17th-century Tolbooth building overlooking the harbour, and decorated with local art and crisp white linen, this is one of the best seafood restaurants in the region. Daily specials include dishes such as scallops with crispy bacon and pea purée. From Tuesday to Saturday you can get a two-/ three-course lunch for £16/20. Reservations recommended.

❶ Getting There & Away

Stonehaven is 15 miles south of Aberdeen and is served by frequent buses travelling between Aberdeen (£4.80, 45 minutes, hourly) and Dundee (1¾ hours). Trains to Dundee are faster (£14.60, 55 minutes, hourly) and offer a more scenic journey.

Strathdon

Strathdon – the valley of the River Don – is home to several of Aberdeenshire's finest castles, and stretches westward from Kintore, 13 miles northwest of Aberdeen, taking in the villages of Kemnay, Monymusk, Alford (ah-ford) and the tiny hamlet of Strathdon. The A944 parallels the lower valley; west of Alford, the A944, A97 and A939 follow the river's upper reaches.

Stagecoach bus X18 runs from Aberdeen to Alford (£8.50, 1¼ hours, six a day Monday to Friday, three on Saturday); bus 219 continues from Alford to Strathdon village (£4.20, 50 minutes, one to three daily Monday to Saturday) via Kildrummy.

◉ Sights

Grampian Transport Museum   MUSEUM
(📞 01975-562292; www.gtm.org.uk; Alford; adult/ child £9.50/free; ⊙ 10am-5pm Apr-Sep, 10am-4pm Oct) The Grampian Transport Museum in Alford houses a fascinating collection of vintage motorbikes, cars, buses and trams, including a Triumph Bonneville in excellent nick, a couple of Model T Fords (including one used by Drambuie), a Ferrari F40 and an Aston Martin V8 Mk II. More unusual exhibits include a 19th-century horse-drawn sleigh from Russia, a 1942 Mack snowplough and the Craigievar Express, a steam-powered tricycle built in 1895 by a local postman.

Next to the museum is the terminus of the narrow-gauge **Alford Valley Steam Railway** (📞 01975-562811; www.alfordvalleyrailway.org.uk; adult/child £4.50/3.50; ⊙ 12.30-4pm Jul & Aug, Sat & Sun only Apr-Jun & Sep), a heritage line that runs from here to Haughton Country Park.

Castle Fraser   CASTLE
(NTS; adult/child £10.50/7.50; ⊙ 11am-5pm Jul & Aug, noon-5pm Thu-Sun Apr-Jun, Sep & Oct) The impressive 16th- to 17th-century Castle Fraser, 16 miles west of Aberdeen, is the ancestral home of the Fraser family. The largely Victorian interior includes the great hall (with a hidden opening where the laird could eavesdrop on his guests), the library, various bedrooms and an ancient kitchen, plus a secret room for storing valuables. Fraser family relics on display include needlework hangings and a 19th-century artificial leg. The 'Woodland Secrets' area in the castle grounds is designed as an adventure playground for kids.

Buses from Aberdeen to Alford stop at the village of Kemnay, three miles north of the castle (a one-hour walk).

Craigievar Castle   CASTLE
(NTS; adult/child £12.50/9; ⊙ 11am-5.30pm daily Jul & Aug, Fri-Tue only Apr-Jun & Sep) A superb example of the original Scottish Baronial style, Craigievar has managed to survive pretty much unchanged since its completion in the 17th century. The lower half is a plain tower house, the upper half sprouts corbelled turrets, cupolas and battlements – an extravagant statement of its builder's wealth and status (last admission 4.45pm). It's 6 miles south of Alford.

Kildrummy Castle   CASTLE
(HS; 📞 01975-571331; adult/child £4.50/2.70; ⊙ 9.30am-5.30pm Apr-Sep) Nine miles west of Alford lie the extensive remains of this 13th-century castle, former seat of the Earl of Mar and once one of Scotland's most impressive fortresses. After the 1715 Jacobite rebellion the earl was exiled to France and his castle fell into ruin, but the curtain walls, round towers and the chapel are still standing.

Northern Aberdeenshire

North of Aberdeen, the Grampian Mountains fall away to rolling agricultural plains pocked with small, craggy volcanic hills. This fertile lowland corner of northeastern Scotland is known as Buchan, a region of traditional farming culture immortalised by Lewis Grassic Gibbon in his trilogy, A Scots Quair, based on the life of a farming community in the 1920s. The old Scots dialect called the Doric lives on in everyday use here – if you think the Glaswegian accent is

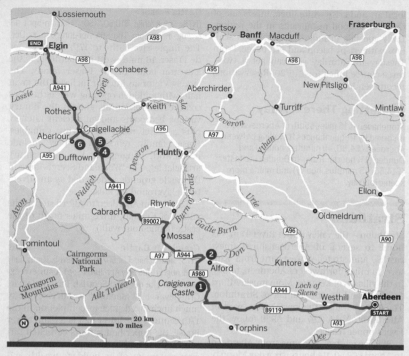

Driving Tour
Aberdeen to Elgin

START ABERDEEN
FINISH ELGIN
DISTANCE 80 MILES
DURATION 1 DAY

Head out of Aberdeen on the A944 and, just before Westhill, bear left on the B9119 towards Tarland. As you leave behind the fringes of the city you enter the sheep pastures, woods and barley fields of rural Aberdeenshire, with the foothills of the Cairngorm Mountains rising ahead.

Follow signs for Tarland for 18 miles, then turn right on the A980 towards Alford. A few miles along this road you'll see ❶ **Craigievar Castle** (p235) across the fields to your left; stop for an hour's visit (time your departure to arrive for opening time at 11am). Continue four miles north to the village of Alford where you can explore the ❷ **Grampian Transport Museum** (p235), and have lunch in one of the village's tearooms (there's one in the museum itself).

From Alford take the A944 and A97 west and north for 10 miles then turn left on the B9002 (signposted Craig and Cabrach). This minor road climbs across heather-clad hills to reach the A941; turn left towards Cabrach and Dufftown. This is remote country, but a few miles beyond the tiny hamlet of Cabrach you'll find the ❸ **Grouse Inn** (open Easter to October), a pub and tearoom famed for its whisky collection – there are more than 220 bottles behind the bar, all different.

Continue on the A941 as it climbs through a narrow pass in the hills and descends into the glen of the River Fiddich – the name tells you that you are now entering whisky country. Eight miles after the Grouse Inn you reach ❹ **Dufftown**, the whisky capital of Speyside. Visit the town's whisky museum or, better yet, take a tour of ❺ **Glenfiddich Distillery** (p240).

From Dufftown, head north on the A941 for four miles to Craigellachie, and detour west for a mile and a half on the A95 to ❻ **Aberlour** to round off your trip with a stroll along the banks of the River Spey, and perhaps a meal at the Mash Tun before driving the last 15 miles north to Elgin.

difficult to understand, just try listening in on a conversation in Fraserburgh.

The Buchan coast alternates between rugged cliffs and long, long stretches of sand, dotted with picturesque little fishing villages such as Pennan, where parts of the film *Local Hero* were shot.

Fraserburgh

POP 13,100

Fraserburgh, affectionately known to locals as the Broch, is Europe's largest shellfish port. The town's fortune was founded on the fishing industry and has suffered from its general decline, but the harbour is still fairly busy and is an interesting place to wander around; there are also good sandy beaches east of the town.

The fascinating **Scottish Lighthouse Museum** (☏01346-511022; www.lighthouse-museum.org.uk; Kinnaird Head; adult/child £6/3; ⊗10am-5pm Wed-Mon, noon-5pm Tue Mar-Oct, 11am-4pm Wed-Sun Nov-Feb) provides an insight into the network of lights that have safeguarded the Scottish coast for over 100 years, and the men and women who built and maintained them (plus a sobering fact – that *all* the world's lighthouses are to be decommissioned by 1 January 2080). A guided tour takes you to the top of the old Kinnaird Head lighthouse, built on top of a converted 16th-century castle; the engineering is so precise that the 4.5-ton light assembly can be rotated by pushing with a single finger. The anemometer here measured the strongest wind speed ever recorded in the UK, with a gust of 123 knots (142mph) on 13 February 1989.

Buses 67 and 68 run to Fraserburgh from Aberdeen (£9, 1½ hours, every 30 minutes Monday to Saturday, hourly on Sunday) via Ellon.

Moray

The old county of Moray (*murr*-ay), centred on the county town of Elgin, lies at the heart of an ancient Celtic earldom and is famed for its mild climate and rich farmland – the barley fields of the 19th century once provided the raw material for the Speyside whisky distilleries, one of the region's main attractions for present-day visitors.

Elgin

POP 23,130

Elgin has been the provincial capital of Moray for over eight centuries and was an important town in medieval times. Dominated by a hilltop monument to the 5th Duke of Gordon, Elgin's main attraction is its impressive ruined cathedral, where the tombs of the duke's ancestors lie.

◉ Sights

Elgin Cathedral   CATHEDRAL

(HS; King St; adult/child £5.50/3.30; ⊗9.30am-5.30pm daily Apr-Sep, 9.30am-4.30pm Sat-Wed Oct-Mar) Many people think that the ruins of Elgin Cathedral, known as the 'lantern of the north', are the most beautiful and evocative in Scotland; its octagonal chapter house is the finest in the country. Consecrated in 1224, the cathedral was burned down in 1390 by the infamous Wolf of Badenoch, the illegitimate son of Robert II, following his excommunication by the Bishop of Moray. Guided tours are available on weekdays.

🍽 Sleeping & Eating

Croft Guesthouse   B&B ££

(☏01343-546004; www.thecroftelgin.co.uk; 10 Institution Rd; s/d from £55/78; P🐾) The Croft offers a taste of Victorian high society, set in a spacious mansion built for a local lawyer back in 1848. The house is filled with period features – check out the cast-iron and tile fireplaces – and the three large bedrooms are equipped with easy chairs and crisp bedlinen.

Southbank Guest House   B&B ££

(☏01343-547132; www.southbankguesthouse.co.uk; 36 Academy St; s/d/f from £55/75/120; P) The family-run, 15-room Southbank is set in a large Georgian town house in a quiet street south of Elgin's centre, just five minutes' walk from the cathedral and other sights.

Johnstons Coffee Shop   CAFE £

(Newmill; mains £5-10; ⊗10am-5pm Mon-Sat, 11am-4.30pm Sun; P🐾) The coffee shop at Johnstons woollen mill is the best place to eat in town, serving breakfast till 11.45am, hot lunches noon to 3pm (crepes with a range of fillings, including smoked salmon with cream cheese and dill), and cream teas.

WORTH A TRIP

PENNAN

Pennan is a picturesque harbour village tucked beneath red-sandstone cliffs, 12 miles west of Fraserburgh. It featured in the 1983 film *Local Hero*, and fans of the film still come to make a call from the red telephone box that played a prominent part in the plot (the box in the film was just a prop, and it was only later that film buffs and locals successfully campaigned for a real one to be installed).

The interior of the village hotel, the **Pennan Inn**, also appeared in the film, though one of the houses further along the seafront to the east doubled for the exterior of the fictional hotel. The beach scenes were filmed on the other side of the country, at Camasdarach Beach in Arisaig.

🛍 Shopping

Gordon & MacPhail   FOOD & DRINK
(www.gordonandmacphail.com; 58-60 South St; ⏱8.30am-5pm Mon-Sat, alcohol on sale from 10am) Gordon & MacPhail is the world's largest specialist malt-whisky dealer. Over a century old and offering around 450 different varieties, its Elgin shop is a place of pilgrimage for whisky connoisseurs, as well as housing a mouth-watering delicatessen.

Johnstons of Elgin   FASHION
(☎01343-554009; www.johnstonscashmere.com; Newmill; ⏱9am-5.30pm Mon-Sat, 11am-5pm Sun) Founded in 1797, Johnstons is famous for its cashmere woollen clothing, and is the only UK woollen mill that still sees the manufacturing process through from raw fibre to finished garment. There's a retail outlet and coffee shop, and free guided tours of the works.

ℹ Information

Post Office (Batchen St; ⏱8.30am-6pm Mon-Fri, 8.30am-4pm Sat)

Tourist Office (☎01343-562608; Elgin Library, Cooper Park; ⏱10am-5pm Mon-Sat, 10am-4pm Sun) Internet access upstairs.

ℹ Getting There & Away

The bus station is a block north of the High St, and the train station is 900m south of the town centre.

BUS
Elgin is a stop on the hourly Stagecoach bus 10 service between Inverness (£10.20, 1½ hours) and Aberdeen (£12.50, 2½ hours). Bus 35 goes from Elgin to Banff and Macduff (£12.50, 1¾ hours, hourly), continuing to Aberdeen via Fyvie. Bus 36 goes to Dufftown (£5.60, 50 minutes, hourly Monday to Saturday).

TRAIN
There are five trains a day to Aberdeen (£18.20, 1½ hours) and Inverness (£11.90, 40 minutes).

Dufftown & Aberlour

Rome may be built on seven hills, but **Dufftown** is built on seven stills, say the locals. Founded in 1817 by James Duff, 4th Earl of Fife, Dufftown is 17 miles south of Elgin and lies at the heart of the Speyside whisky-distilling region. With seven working distilleries nearby, Dufftown has been dubbed Scotland's malt-whisky capital and is host to the biannual Spirit of Speyside (p240) whisky festival. Ask at the whisky museum about the **Malt Whisky Trail** (www.maltwhiskytrail.com), a self-guided tour around the local distilleries.

Five miles to the northwest, **Aberlour** (www.aboutaberlour.co.uk) – or Charlestown of Aberlour, to give it its full name – is prettier than Dufftown, straggling along the banks of the River Spey. It is famous as the home of Walkers Shortbread, and has Aberlour Distillery right on the main street. Attractions include salmon fishing, and some lovely walks along the Speyside Way.

⊙ Sights & Activities

Whisky Museum   MUSEUM
(☎01340-821097; www.dufftown.co.uk; 12 Conval St; ⏱1-4pm Mon-Fri May-Sep) FREE As well as housing a selection of distillery memorabilia (try saying that after a few drams), the Whisky Museum holds 'nosing and tasting evenings' in the Commercial Hotel where you can learn what to look for in a fine single malt (£10 per person; 8pm Wednesday in July and August).

You can then test your new-found skills at the nearby **Whisky Shop** (☎01340-821097; www.whiskyshopdufftown.co.uk; 1 Fife St; ⏱10am-6pm Mon-Sat, to 5pm Sun), which stocks hundreds of single malts.

Keith and Dufftown Railway HERITAGE RAILWAY
(☎01340-821181; www.keith-dufftown-railway.co.uk; Dufftown Station; adult/child return £10/5) A line running for 11 miles from Dufftown

to Keith sees trains hauled by 1950s diesel motor units running on weekends from May to September, plus Fridays in July and August. There are also two 1930s 'Brighton Belle' Pullman coaches, and a cafe housed in a 1957 British Railways cafeteria car.

🛏 Sleeping & Eating

Mash Tun B&B ££
(📞01340-881771; www.mashtun-aberlour.com; 8 Broomfield Sq; s/d from £65/100; 🛜) Housed in a curious stone building made for a sea captain in the shape of a ship, this luxurious B&B is famous for its whisky bar – a place of pilgrimage for whisky enthusiasts – which has a collection of old and rare single malts. There's also an excellent restaurant (mains £10-20, lunch and dinner daily) that specialises in modern Scottish cuisine.

Davaar B&B B&B ££
(📞01340-820464; www.davaardufftown.co.uk; 17 Church St; d/f £65/80) Davaar is a sturdy Victorian villa with three smallish but comfy rooms; the breakfast menu is superb, offering the option of Portsoy kippers as well as the traditional fry-up (which uses eggs from the owners' own chickens).

Craigellachie Hotel HOTEL £££
(📞01340-881204; www.craigellachiehotel.co.uk; Craigellachie; d from £120; 🅿🛜) The recently refurbished Craigellachie has a wonderfully old-fashioned, hunting-lodge atmosphere, from the wood-panelled lobby to the opulent drawing room where you can sink into a sofa in front of the log fire. But the big attraction for whisky connoisseurs is the Quaich Bar, a cosy nook filled with green leather armchairs and lined with almost 700 varieties of single malt whisky.

The hotel is a mile northeast of Aberlour, overlooking the River Spey.

La Faisanderie SCOTTISH £££
(📞01340-821273; The Square; mains £19-23; ⏰noon-1.30pm & 6-8.30pm, closed Mon-Thu Nov-Mar) 🍽 This is a great place to eat, run by a local chef who shoots much of his own game. The interior is decorated in French auberge style with a cheerful mural and pheasants hiding in every corner. The three-course early-bird dinner menu (£19.50, from 5.30pm to 7pm) won't disappoint, but you can order à la carte as well.

ℹ Getting There & Away

Buses link Elgin to Aberour (£5.30, 35 minutes) and Dufftown (£5.60, 50 minutes) hourly Monday to Saturday, continuing to Huntly, Aberdeen and Inverness.

On summer weekends, you can take a train from Aberdeen or Inverness to Keith (£16.40, one hour, five daily), and then ride the Keith and Dufftown Railway to Dufftown.

Banff & Macduff

POP COMBINED: 9100

The handsome Georgian town of Banff and the busy fishing port of Macduff lie on either side of Banff Bay, separated only by the mouth of the River Deveron. Banff Links – 800m of clean golden sand stretching to the west – and Macduff's impressive aquarium pull in the holiday crowds.

The tourist office (📞01261-812419; Collie Lodge, High St; ⏰10am-5pm Mon-Sat, noon-5pm Sun Apr-Sep) is beside St Mary's car park in Banff.

◎ Sights

Duff House GALLERY
(📞01261-818181; www.duffhouse.org.uk; adult/child £7.10/4.30; ⏰11am-5pm Apr-Oct, 11am-4pm Thu-Sun Nov-Mar) One of Scotland's hidden gems, Duff House is an art gallery that displays a superb collection of Scottish and European art, including important works by Raeburn and Gainsborough. The house is an impressive baroque mansion on the southern edge of Banff, built between 1735 and 1740 as the seat of the Earls of Fife. It was designed by William Adam and bears similarities to that Adam masterpiece, Hopetoun House (p95) near Edinburgh.

Macduff Marine Aquarium AQUARIUM
(www.macduff-aquarium.org.uk; 11 High Shore, Macduff; adult/child £6.35/3.25; ⏰10am-5pm Mon-Fri & 11am-5pm Sat & Sun Apr-Oct, 11am-4pm Sat-Wed Nov-Mar; ♿) The centrepiece of Macduff's aquarium is a 400,000L open-air tank, complete with kelp-coated reef and wave machine. Marine oddities on view include the brightly coloured cuckoo wrasse, the warty-skinned lumpsucker and the vicious-looking wolf fish.

🛏 Sleeping & Eating

Bryvard Guest House B&B ££
(📞01261-818090; www.bryvardguesthouse.co.uk; Seafield St; s/d from £45/75; 🛜) The Bryvard is an imposing Edwardian town

BLAZE YOUR OWN WHISKY TRAIL

Visiting a distillery can be memorable, but only hardcore malthounds will want to go to more than one or two. Some are great to visit; others are depressingly corporate. The following are some recommendations.

→ **Aberlour** (☑ 01340-881249; www.aberlour.com; tours from £14; ⊙ 10am & 2pm daily Apr-Oct, by appointment Mon-Fri Nov-Mar) Has an excellent, detailed tour with a proper tasting session. It's on the main street in Aberlour.

→ **Glenfarclas** (☑ 01807-500257; www.glenfarclas.co.uk; admission £5; ⊙ 10am-4pm Mon-Fri Oct-Mar, to 5pm Mon-Fri Apr-Sep, plus to 4pm Sat Jul-Sep) Small, friendly and independent, Glenfarclas is 5 miles south of Aberlour on the Grantown road. The last tour leaves 90 minutes before closing. The in-depth Connoisseur's Tour (Fridays only July to September) is £20.

→ **Glenfiddich** (www.glenfiddich.com; ⊙ 9.30am-4.30pm daily year-round, closed Christmas & New Year) **FREE** It's big and busy, but handiest for Dufftown and foreign languages are available. The standard tour starts with an overblown video, but it's fun, informative and free. An in-depth Connoisseur's Tour (£20) must be prebooked. Glenfiddich kept single malt alive during the dark years.

→ **Macallan** (☑ 01340-872280; www.themacallan.com; tours £15; ⊙ 9.30am-6pm Mon-Sat Easter-Oct, 9.30am-5pm Mon-Fri Nov-Mar) Excellent sherry-casked malt. Several small-group tours are available (last tour at 3.30pm), including an expert one (£20); all should be prebooked. Lovely location 2 miles northwest of Craigellachie.

→ **Speyside Cooperage** (☑ 01340-871108; www.speysidecooperage.co.uk; adult/child £3.50/2; ⊙ 9am-4pm Mon-Fri, closed mid Dec-early Jan) Here you can see the fascinating art of barrel-making in action. It's a mile from Craigellachie on the Dufftown road.

→ **Spirit of Speyside** (www.spiritofspeyside.com) This biannual whisky festival in Dufftown has a number of great events. It takes place in early May and late September; both accommodation and events should be booked well ahead.

house close to the town centre, with four beautiful period-furnished bedrooms (two with en suite). Go for the 'Moffat' room, which has a four-poster bed and a sea view.

County Hotel HOTEL **££**
(☑ 01261-815353; www.thecountyhotel.com; 32 High St; s/d from £60/95; 🅿) The County occupies an elegant Georgian mansion in the town centre, and is owned by a French chef – the hotel's bistro serves light meals (mains £6 to £10), while **Restaurant L'Auberge** offers the finest French cuisine (à la carte mains £29 to £35, three-course dinner £31).

❶ Getting There & Away

Bus 35 runs from Banff to Elgin (£12.50, 1¾ hours, hourly) and Aberdeen (£12.50, two hours), while bus 272 runs to Fraserburgh (£8.50, 55 minutes, three daily) on weekdays only.

Portsoy

POP 1750

The pretty fishing village of Portsoy has an atmospheric 17th-century harbour and a maze of narrow streets lined with picturesque cottages. An ornamental stone known as Portsoy marble – actually a beautifully patterned green-and-pale-pink serpentine – was quarried near Portsoy in the 17th and 18th centuries, and was reputedly used in the decoration of some rooms in the Palace of Versailles. Beside the harbour, the **Portsoy Pottery** (Shorehead; ⊙ 10am-5pm Apr-Oct) sells handmade stoneware and objects made from the local marble.

Each year on the last weekend in June or first weekend in July, Portsoy harbour is home to the **Scottish Traditional Boat Festival** (www.scottishtraditionalboatfestival. co.uk), a lively gathering of historic wooden sailing boats accompanied by sailing races, live folk music, crafts demonstrations, street theatre and a food festival.

The **Shore Inn** (☏01261-842831; 49 Church St; ⊙noon-11pm) is a characterful real-ale pub overlooking the harbour.

Portsoy is 8 miles west of Banff; the hourly bus between Banff (£4.80, 25 minutes) and Elgin stops here.

Fochabers & Around

POP 1730

Fochabers sits beside the last bridge over the River Spey before it enters the sea. The town has a pleasant square, with a church and clock tower dated 1798, and a handful of interesting antique shops.

West of the bridge over the Spey is **Baxters Highland Village** (www.baxters.com; admission free; ⊙10am-5pm; 🖶) **FREE**, which charts the history of the Baxter family and their well-known brand of quality Scottish foodstuffs, founded in 1868. There's a factory tour with cookery demonstrations on weekdays, and a coffee shop.

Four miles north of Fochabers, at the mouth of the River Spey, is the tiny village of **Spey Bay**, the starting point for the Speyside Way long-distance footpath. It's also home to the **Scottish Dolphin Centre** (☏01343-820339; www.whales.org/scottish dolphincentre; Tugnet Ice House, Spey Bay; admission free; ⊙10.30am-5pm Apr-Oct) **FREE**, one of the best land-based dolphin-spotting places in the country. Based in a historic ice house that was once used to store ice for preserving local salmon catches, the indoor attractions include feeds from nearby wildlife cameras, a 'dry dive' audiovisual experience that takes you beneath the waves of the Moray Firth, and a pleasant cafe. Outdoors, you can watch for dolphins, seals and other marine creatures at the mouth of the River Spey, or join a guided wildlife walk.

Fochabers is on the Aberdeen-to-Inverness bus route.

Findhorn

POP 900

The attractive village of Findhorn lies at the mouth of the River Findhorn, just east of the Findhorn Bay nature reserve. It's a great place for birdwatching, seal-spotting and coastal walks.

Findhorn Heritage Centre (www.find horn-heritage.co.uk; admission free; ⊙2-5pm daily Jun-Aug, 2-5pm Sat & Sun May & Sep) **FREE**,

CULBIN FOREST

On the western side of Findhorn Bay is **Culbin Forest** (www.culbin.org.uk), a vast swath of Scots and Corsican pine that was planted in the 1940s to stabilise the shifting sand dunes that buried the Culbin Estate in the 17th century. The forest is a unique wildlife habitat, supporting plants, birds and animals (such as the pine marten) that are normally found only in ancient natural pine woods.

The forest is criss-crossed by a maze of walking and cycling trails which lead to a fantastic beach near the mouth of Findhorn Bay, a great birdwatching spot. Check the website for more info, or pick up a leaflet from local tourist offices.

housed in a former salmon-fisher's bothy at the northern end of the village, records the history of the settlement. The beach is just over the dunes north of the heritage centre – at low tide, you can see seals hauled out on the sandbanks off the mouth of the River Findhorn.

Hippies old and new should check out the **Findhorn Foundation** (www.findhorn.org; guided tours per person £8; ⊙visitor centre 10am-5pm Mon-Fri year-round, plus 1-4pm Sat & Sun May-Sep), an international spiritual community founded in 1962. There's a permanent population of around 150, but the community receives thousands of visitors each year. Guided tours (£8) start from the visitor centre at 2pm on Monday, Wednesday and Friday from April to November, and on Saturday and Sunday as well from May to September, or you can take a self-guided tour with guidebook (£5).

There are two good places to eat: the **Bakehouse** (www.bakehousecafe.co.uk; mains £4-9; ⊙10am-4pm), an organic bakery and cafe in the village centre, and the **Blue Angel Cafe** (www.phoenixshop.co.uk; mains £3-9; ⊙10am-5pm Apr-Nov, to 4pm Dec-Mar; 🛜🖉), an organic and vegetarian eatery in the Findhorn Foundation's eco-village.

Bus 34 runs from Elgin to Findhorn (£4.80, 40 minutes, every two hours) from Monday to Saturday.

242

MICHAEL ROULAN - MGFOTOUK.COM / GETTY IMAGES ©

1. Puffin on Staffa (p295) **2.** Glenbrittle, Isle of Skye (p391)
3. Cliffs between Silwick and Westerwick, North Isles, Shetland
(p435) **4.** Iona Abbey (p293)

JOHN LAWSON, BELHAVEN / GETTY IMAGES ©

Scotland's Islands

Scotland's sweeping array of islands – 790 at last count, around a hundred of which are inhabited – defines the country's complex coastline. Ruins, from prehistoric religious centres to staunch castles, overlook landscapes where sheep crop lush grass, the scant remaining fisherfolk take on powerful seas, and urban professionals looking for a quieter life battle with unreliable wi-fi.

Geography & History

Though in the modern world these islands might seem remote outposts, Scotland's complex geography has meant that, from Celts through to Vikings and the Lords of the Isles, transport, trade and power are intimately tied to the sea. Today's lonely island stronghold was yesteryear's hub of connections spreading right across western and northern Britain and beyond.

Sights & Activities

For the visitor, there's bewildering scope. The once-Norse islands of Orkney and Shetland are Britain's northernmost parts, while the Hebrides guard the west coast like a storm shield against the mighty Atlantic. The choice is yours: for scenic splendour with hills to climb and memorable walks you might choose spectacular Skye, diverse Mull, accessible Arran or lonely Jura. Neolithic villages, standing stones, evocative prehistoric monuments? Head to far-flung Orkney, Shetland or the Outer Hebrides. Abbeys, castles or stately homes? Magical Iona, Bute, Coll, Barra or Westray. Beaches? Pick Harris or Tiree. Birdlife? Unst, the Uists, Fair Isle, Noss, North Ronaldsay or Staffa. Whisky? It's got to be Islay. A convivial pub, local seafood and a warm welcome? Take your pick of any and find yourself a snug cottage with a scent of the salty breeze and call it home for a day or three.

Southern Highlands & Islands

Best Places to Eat

- ➡ Callander Meadows (p257)
- ➡ Starfish (p266)
- ➡ Café Fish (p290)
- ➡ Seafood Temple (p284)
- ➡ Brodick Bar (p271)

Best Places to Stay

- ➡ Monachyle Mhor (p257)
- ➡ Lake of Menteith Hotel (p253)
- ➡ Calgary Farmhouse (p291)
- ➡ Iona Hostel (p294)
- ➡ Argyll Hotel (p294)

Why Go?

The impossibly complex coastline of Scotland's southwest harbours some of its most inspiring corners. Here, sea travel is as important as road and rail – dozens of ferries allow you to island-hop from the scenic splendour of Arran to majestic Mull or Tiree's lonely sands, via the whisky distilleries of Islay, the wild mountains of Jura, the scenic delights of diminutive Colonsay and Oban's sustainable-seafood scene.

On fresh water too, passenger ferries, vintage steamboats, canoes and kayaks ply the lochs of Loch Lomond and the Trossachs National Park, a memorable concentration of scenic splendour that's very accessible from Glasgow or Edinburgh but possessed of a wild beauty.

Wildlife experiences are a highlight here; from the rasping spout of a minke whale to the 'krek-krek' of a corncrake. You can spot otters tumbling in the kelp, watch sea eagles snatch fish from a lonely loch and thrill to the sight of dolphins riding the bow-wave of your boat.

When to Go
Oban

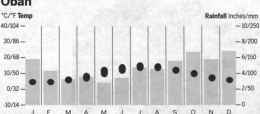

May Fèis Ìle (Islay Festival) celebrates traditional Scottish music and whisky.

Jun Roadsides and gardens become a blaze of colour with deep-pink rhododendron blooms.

Aug The best month of the year for whale-watching off the west coast.

Southern Highlands & Islands Highlights

1 Exploring the lovely lochscapes and accessible walking and cycling routes of the **Trossachs** (p252)

2 Visiting the smoky heavyweights of the whisky world on their peaty home turf of **Islay** (p276)

3 Blowing away the cobwebs on scenic, activity-packed **Isle of Arran** (p268)

4 Visiting the white waters of the **Corryvreckan whirlpool** (p279) of the north end of lonely Jura

5 Journeying through wildlife-rich **Mull** (p286) to reach the holy emerald isle of **Iona** (p293)

6 Hiking the **West Highland Way** (p246) along the eastern shore of Loch Lomond

7 Tucking into a platter of fresh local langoustines at the seafood restaurants in **Oban** (p284)

8 Teeing off on the great-value old and new courses at **Machrihanish** (p267) down the Kintyre peninsula

LOCH LOMOND & AROUND

The 'bonnie banks' and 'bonnie braes' of Loch Lomond have long been Glasgow's rural retreat – a scenic region of hills, lochs and healthy fresh air within easy reach of Scotland's largest city. Today the loch's popularity shows no sign of decreasing.

Loch Lomond

Loch Lomond is mainland Britain's largest lake and, after Loch Ness, the most famous of Scotland's lochs. Its proximity to Glasgow (20 miles away) means that the tourist honeypots of Balloch, Loch Lomond Shores and Luss get pretty crowded in summer. The eastern shore, which is followed by the West Highland Way long-distance footpath, is quieter and offers a better chance to appreciate the loch away from the busy main road.

Loch Lomond straddles the Highland border. The southern part is broad and island-studded, fringed by woods and Lowland meadows. However, north of Luss the loch narrows, occupying a deep trench gouged out by glaciers during the Ice Age, with 900m mountains crowding either side. The length of Loch Lomond means that access between the western part of the national park and the Trossachs is either in the far north of the region via Crianlarich or the far south via Drymen.

Activities

Walking

The **West Highland Way** (www.west-highland-way.co.uk) runs along the loch's eastern shore, while the **Rob Roy Way** (www.robroyway.com) heads from Drymen to Pitlochry via the Trossachs. The **Three Lochs Way** (www.threelochsway.co.uk) loops west from Balloch through Helensburgh and Arrochar before returning to Loch Lomond at Inveruglas. There are numerous shorter walks around: get further information from information centres.

Rowardennan is the starting point for ascents of **Ben Lomond** (974m), a popular and relatively straighforward (if strenuous) 7.5-mile round trip (five to six hours). The route starts at the car park just past the Rowardennan Hotel.

Other Activities

The mostly traffic-free **Clyde and Loch Lomond Cycle Way** links Glasgow to Balloch (20 miles), where it links with the **West Loch Lomond Cycle Path**, which continues along the loch shore to Tarbet (10 miles). The park website details some other local routes.

CanYou Experience CANOEING, CYCLING
(☑ 01389-756251; www.canyouexperience.com; Loch Lomond Shores, Balloch; ⏰ 9am-5.30pm Easter-Oct) Offers a huge range of activities on water and land from various bases around Loch Lomond. Hires mountain bikes (£13/17 per half-/full day), canoes and kayaks, and offers a full-day guided canoe safari (£50).

Loch Lomond Seaplanes SCENIC FLIGHTS
(Map p112; ☑ 01436-675030; www.lochlomond-seaplanes.com; flights from £129) Leaving from the Cameron House Hotel just north of Balloch, this company offers a variety of scenic flights over the loch and western Scotland.

Tours

Sweeney's Cruises BOAT TOURS
(☑ 01389-752376; www.sweeneyscruises.com; Balloch Rd, Balloch) Offers a range of trips including a one-hour cruise to Inchmurrin and back (adult/child £9.80/6.50, five times daily), and a two-hour cruise (£17/9.50, departs 12.30pm and 3pm May to September) around the islands. The quay is directly opposite Balloch train station, beside the tourist office. It also runs some trips from a dock at Loch Lomond Shores.

Cruise Loch Lomond BOAT TOURS
(☑ 01301-702356; www.cruiselochlomond.co.uk; Tarbet/Luss; ⏰ 8.30am-5.30pm early Apr-late Oct) With departures from Tarbet and Luss, this company offers short cruises and two-hour trips to Arklet Falls and Rob Roy's Cave (adult/child £15/8). You can also be dropped off at Rowardennan to climb Ben Lomond (£15/9), getting picked up in the afternoon, or get picked up at Inversnaid after a 9-mile hike along the West Highland Way (£15/9). It also hires out bikes at Tarbet.

Balmaha Boatyard BOAT TOURS
(☑ 01360-870214; www.balmahaboatyard.co.uk; Balmaha) Runs a lovely old wooden mailboat from Balmaha to loch islands, departing at 11.30am and returning at 2pm, with a one-hour stop on Inchmurrin (£10/5 per adult/child). Trips depart daily (except Tuesday and Sunday) in July and August; and on

Monday, Thursday and Saturday in May, June and September. There are also various other low-priced cruises in summer.

It also hires out rowing boats (£10/40 per hour/day) and motorboats (£20/60).

ⓘ Information

Balloch Tourist Office (☏ 01389-753533; Balloch Rd, Balloch; ◷ 9.30am-6pm Jun-Aug, 10am-5pm Sep-May) Opposite Balloch train station.

Balmaha National Park Centre (☏ 01389-722100; www.lochlomond-trossachs.org; Balmaha; ◷ 9.30am-4.30pm Apr-Sep, 9.30am-4pm Sat & Sun Oct-Mar) Has maps showing local walking routes.

National Park Gateway Centre (☏ 01389-751035; www.lochlomondshores.com; Loch Lomond Shores, Balloch; ◷ 10am-6pm Apr-Sep, 10am-5pm Oct-Mar; ☏) Crowded information desk with shop and cafe.

Tarbet Tourist Office (☏ 01301-702260; Tarbet; ◷ 10am-4pm Easter & May-Sep) At the junction of the A82 and the A83.

ⓘ Getting There & Away

BUS

First Glasgow (p135) bus 1A runs from Argyle St in central Glasgow to Balloch (£4.50, 1½ hours, at least two per hour) and bus C8 to Drymen (£5.20, 1¼ hours, two daily)

Scottish Citylink (☏ 0871 266-3333; www.citylink.co.uk) coaches from Glasgow stop at Luss (£8.50, 55 minutes, nine daily), Tarbet (£8.50, 65 minutes, nine daily) and Ardlui (£14.90, 1¼ hours, four daily).

TRAIN

Glasgow–Ardlui £14.90, 1½ hours, three or four daily, continuing to Oban and Fort William

Glasgow–Arrochar & Tarbet £11.40, 1¼ hours, three or four daily

Glasgow–Balloch £5.10, 45 minutes, every 30 minutes

ⓘ Getting Around

McGill's (☏ 08000-515651; www.mcgillsbuses.co.uk) bus 309 runs from Balloch to Drymen and Balmaha (£2.90, 25 minutes, nine to 10 daily). An **SPT Daytripper ticket** (www.spt.co.uk) gives a family group unlimited travel for a day on most bus and train services in the Glasgow, Loch Lomond and Helensburgh area. Buy the ticket (£11.20 for one adult and two children, £19.80 for two adults and up to four children) from any train station or Glasgow bus station.

Local buses run from Helensburgh to Arrochar via Luss and Tarbet thrice daily Monday to Saturday.

LOCH LOMOND'S ISLANDS

There are around 60 islands, large and small, in Loch Lomond. Most are privately owned, and only two (Inchcailloch and Inchmurrin) can be reached without your own boat or canoe. Four of the most interesting:

➡ **Inchcailloch** A nature reserve reached by passenger ferry from Balmaha or Luss. The most accessible island, with nature trails and a small bookable campsite. See www.lochlomond-trossachs.org.

➡ **Inchmurrin** Privately owned, reached by passenger ferry from Arden on the loch's western shore. Has walking trails, beaches, self-catering cottages and a restaurant that is open from Easter to October. See www.inchmurrin-lochlomond.com.

➡ **Inchconnachan** Privately owned. Only accessible by boat or canoe. Has an unlikely wallaby population; the rare capercaillie nests here too.

➡ **Island I Vow** Privately owned. Only accessible by boat or canoe. The loch's most northerly island is home to a ruined castle; Wordsworth visited in 1814 and found a hermit living in it, inspiring his poem The Brownie's Cell.

Western Shore

Balloch, straddling the River Leven at Loch Lomond's southern end, is the loch's main population centre and transport hub. A Victorian resort once thronged by day trippers transferring between the train station and the steamer quay, it is now a 'gateway centre' for Loch Lomond and the Trossachs National Park. Visitors still arrive in abundance.

⊙ Sights & Activities

Loch Lomond Shores (www.lochlomondshores.com; ◷ 9.30am-6pm), a major tourism development, sports a park information centre plus various family-friendly visitor attractions, outdoor activities and boat trips. In keeping with the times, the heart of the development is a large shopping mall. Also here is a birds-of-prey exhibition and **Loch Lomond Aquarium** (www.sealife.co.uk; adult £13.20, adult plus child £23.40;

☺ 10am-5pm), with an otter enclosure (housing short-clawed Asian otters, not Scottish ones), and a host of sea-life exhibits ranging from sharks to stingrays to turtles. Look for discount vouchers in *Loch Lomond Area Guide,* available in the visitor centre, before entering.

The vintage paddle steamer **Maid of the Loch** (www.maidoftheloch.com; ☺ 11am-5pm Easter-Oct) FREE is moored here as she is gradually restored to working order – nip aboard for a look around or stop for tea in the cafe.

Unless it's raining, give Loch Lomond Shores a miss and head for the picture-postcard village of **Luss**. Stroll among the pretty cottages, built by the local laird in the 19th century for his estate workers, and admire the lochside vistas.

Beyond Luss, **Tarbet** sits at the junction where you choose between Argyll and Kintyre or Oban and the Highlands. Following the shore brings you to **Ardlui** and thence Crianlarich.

🛏 Sleeping & Eating

Ardlui Hotel HOTEL ££
(☎ 01301-704243; www.ardlui.co.uk; Ardlui; s/d £55/110; 🅿 🛜 🐕) This plush pub and hotel has a great lochside location, and a view of Ben Lomond from the breakfast room. The rooms are decorated in fairly classical Scottish country-comfort style and there are self-catering cabins available too.

Glenview B&B ££
(☎ 01436-860606; www.bonniebank.com; Luss; s/d £70/90; 🅿 🛜) In the centre of things on the road through the village of Luss, this white house offers a genuine welcome and highly appealing rooms. Both are showroom-spotless, one is plush and cosy, the other contemporary and stylish, with a modish four-poster bed. Both have swish bathrooms and a sitting area.

★ **Drover's Inn** PUB ££
(☎ 01301-704234; www.thedroversinn.co.uk; Ardlui; bar meals £8-12; ☺ 11.30am-10pm Mon-Sat, to 9.30pm Sun; 🅿 🛜) This is one *howff* (drinking den) you shouldn't miss – a low-ceilinged place just north of Ardlui with smoke-blackened stone, barmen in kilts, and walls festooned with moth-eaten stags' heads and stuffed birds. The bar, where Rob Roy allegedly dropped by for pints, serves hearty hill-walking fuel and hosts live folk at weekends. We recommend this more as an atmospheric place to eat and drink than somewhere to stay.

Village Rest CAFE ££
(www.the-village-rest.co.uk; Pier Rd, Luss; mains £9-12; ☺ 10am-9pm; 🛜) Set in a typically cute Luss cottage, this spot offers appealing outdoor seating for when the sun shines, a sweet interior and tasty, well-proportioned if overpriced dishes that run from pastas and rolls to satisfying posh burgers.

Eastern Shore

The road along the loch's eastern shore runs from the walkers' hub of **Drymen** through attractive **Balmaha**, where you can hire boats or take a cruise. A short but steep climb from the car park leads up **Conic Hill** (361m), a superb viewpoint (2.5 miles round trip, allow two to three hours). The **Millennium Forest Path** is a 40-minute introduction to the area's tree and plant life.

There are several lochside picnic areas: **Millarochy Bay** (1.5 miles north of Balmaha) has a nice gravel beach and superb views across the loch to the Luss hills.

The road ends at **Rowardennan**, but the West Highland Way (p246) hiking trail continues north along the shore of the loch. It's 7 miles to **Inversnaid**, reachable by road from the Trossachs, and 15 miles to **Inverarnan** at the loch's northern end.

🛏 Sleeping & Eating

From March to October, wild camping is banned on the eastern shore of Loch Lomond between Drymen and Ptarmigan Lodge (just north of Rowardennan Youth Hostel). There are campsites at Millarochy, Cashel and Sallochy. See also the hostel at Inversnaid (p253).

★ **Rowardennan SYHA** HOSTEL £
(☎ 01360-870259; www.syha.org.uk; Rowardennan; dm/tw £18/42; ☺ late Mar-early Oct; 🅿 🛜)

Loch Lomond & the Trossachs NP

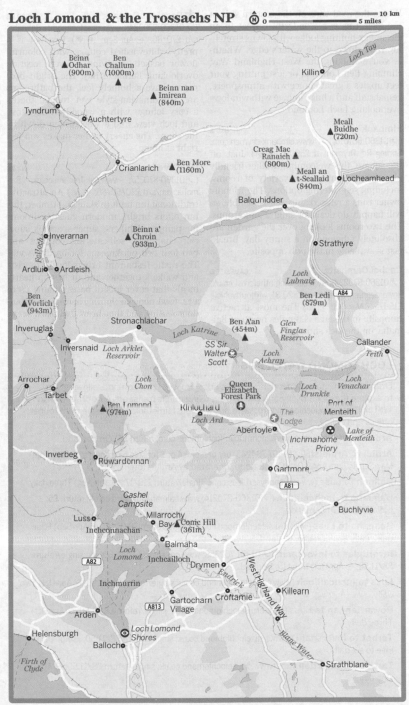

Where the road ends on the eastern side of the loch, this is a wonderful retreat in an elegant ex-hunting lodge with lawns stretching right down to the water's edge. Whether you're walking the West Highland Way, climbing Ben Lomond, or just putting your feet up, it's a great choice with atmosphere, genial staff and a huge lounge with windows overlooking Loch Lomond.

Elmbank
B&B £

(☎ 01360-661016; www.elmbank-drymen.com; Stirling Rd, Drymen; d £56-70; P ♠) Just off the square, this welcoming, walker-friendly place has an interesting variety of rooms, including self-catering options. The friendly owner runs a relaxed ship and is flexible, so will happily do deals for singles and groups. The two rooms looking over the garden are absolutely fabulous on a sunny day. Breakfast is available in the pub opposite.

Cashel Campsite
CAMPSITE £

(☎ 01360-870234; www.campingintheforest.co.uk; Rowardennan; sites incl car £20-31, without vehicle £15-17; ☺ Mar-Oct; P ☎) The most attractive campsite in the area is 3 miles north of Balmaha, on the loch shore.

★ Passfoot Cottage
B&B ££

(☎ 01360-870324; www.passfoot.com; Balmaha; s/d £70/80; ☺ Apr-Sep; P ♠) Passfoot is a pretty whitewashed cottage with colourful flower baskets, enjoying a lovely location overlooking Balmaha Bay. The bright bedrooms have a homely feel, the bathrooms are Scandinavian-style wet rooms, there's a cosy lounge with a wood-burning stove and loch view, and a wee garden down by the shore. The cheery owner makes you feel right at home.

Oak Tree Inn
INN ££

(☎ 01360-870357; www.oak-tree-inn.co.uk; Balmaha; dm/s/d £30/50/85; P ♠) An attractive traditional inn built in slate and timber, this inn offers bright, modern guest bedrooms for pampered hikers, super-spacious superior chambers, self-catering cottages and two four-bed bunkrooms for hardier souls. The rustic restaurant brings locals, tourists and walkers together and dishes up hearty meals that cover lots of bases (mains £9 to £12, food noon to 9pm). There's lots of outdoor seating and they brew their own beers.

LOCH LOMOND WATER BUS

From April to October a network of boats criss-crosses Loch Lomond, allowing you to explore the loch's hiking and biking trails using public transport. A **Loch Lomond Water Bus** (www.lochlomond-trossachs.org/waterbus) timetable is available from tourist offices and online.

Arden to Inchmurrin (www.inchmurrin-lochlomond.com; return £4) On demand.

Ardlui to Ardleish (☎ 01307-704243; per person £4 or £ for solo passengers; ☺ 9am-7pm May-Sep, to 6pm Apr & Oct) On demand; operated by Ardlui Hotel.

Balloch to Luss (www.sweeneyscruises.com; single/return £10/17; ☺ Jun-Aug) Three daily.

Balmaha to Inchcailloch (☎ 01360-870214; www.balmahaboatyard.co.uk; return £5; ☺ 9am-8pm) On demand.

Balmaha to Luss (www.cruiselochlomond.co.uk; single/return £8/11.50; ☺ Apr-Sep) Four daily, calls at Inchcailloch island.

Inveruglas to Inversnaid (☎ 01301-702356; www.cruiselochlomond.co.uk; single/return £8/11.50; ☺ Apr-Oct) Must be booked.

Luss to Inchcailloch (www.cruiselochlomond.co.uk; single/return £8/11.50; ☺ Apr-Oct) Two daily.

Rowardennan to Luss (www.cruiselochlomond.co.uk; single/return £8/11.50; ☺ Apr-Oct) Three daily.

Tarbet to Inversnaid (www.cruiselochlomond.co.uk; single/return £8/11.50; ☺ Apr-Oct) Five to six daily.

Tarbet to Rowardennan (www.cruiselochlomond.co.uk; single/return £8/11.50; ☺ Apr-Oct) One daily

Crianlarich & Tyndrum

POP 400

Surrounded by spectacular hillscapes at the northern edge of the Loch Lomond and the Trossachs National Park, these villages are popular pit stops on the main A82 road, for walkers on the West Highland Way and Munro-baggers. Crianlarich has a train station and more community atmosphere but Tyndrum (*tyne*-drum), 5 miles up the road, has two stations, a bus interchange, petrol station, late-opening motorists' cafes and **tourist office** (☑01838-400246; 6 Main St, Tyndrum; ⏰10am-5pm Apr-Oct) – a good spot for route information and maps for ascents of Munros **Cruach Ardrain** (1046m), **Ben More** (1174m) and magnificent **Ben Lui** (1130m).

🛏 Sleeping & Eating

Crianlarich makes a more appealing base than Tyndrum: vehicles slow down through town and the views are better.

Crianlarich SYHA HOSTEL £
(☑01838-300260; www.syha.org.uk; Station Rd, Crianlarich; dm £18; P@🛜) Well-run and comfortable, with a spacious kitchen, dining area and lounge, this is a real haven for walkers or anyone passing through. Dorms vary in size – there are some great en suite family rooms that should be prebooked – but all are clean and roomy.

Strathfillan Wigwams CAMPSITE CABIN £
(☑01838-400251; www.wigwamholidays.com; sites per adult/child £8/3, wigwam d small/large £38/44, lodge d from £60; P@🛜🐾) A working farm off the A82 between Crianlarich and Tyndrum, this has 16 heated 'wigwams' – wooden A-frame cabins with fridge and foam mattresses, that can sleep four at a pinch. More upmarket are the self-contained lodges with their own bathroom and kitchen facilities. There's also camping and decent facilities.

Tigh-na-Fraoch B&B ££
(☑01838-400354; www.tigh-na-fraoch.com; Lower Station Rd, Tyndrum; d £66; ⏰Jan-Oct; P🛜) The name means 'house of the heather' and Heather is the name of the owner – an alternative therapist offering kinesiology and head massages as well as three bright, clean and comfortable bedrooms, and a breakfast menu that includes (resident anglers' luck permitting) freshly caught trout as well as the usual bacon and eggs. Walker friendly.

Real Food Café CAFE £
(☑01838-400235; www.therealfoodcafe.com; Tyndrum; mains £7-10; ⏰11am-9.30pm Sun-Fri, 7.30am-9.30pm Sat, opens at 8.30am Sun-Fri Jul & Aug; 🛜🐾) 🍴 Hungry hill walkers throng the tables in this justifiably popular eatery. The menu looks familiar – with fish and chips, soups, salads and burgers – but the owners make an effort to source sustainably and locally, and the quality shines through. Hours are reduced in winter.

ℹ Getting There & Away

Scottish Citylink (www.citylink.co.uk) runs several buses daily to Edinburgh, Glasgow, Oban and Skye from both villages.

Trains run to Tyndrum and Crianlarich from Fort William (£19.30, 1¾ hours, four daily Monday to Saturday, two on Sunday), Oban (£11.70, 1¼ hours, three or four daily) and Glasgow (£18.20, 1¾ hours, three to five daily).

CLIMBING BEN LOMOND

Standing guard over the eastern shore of Loch Lomond is Ben Lomond (974m), Scotland's most southerly Munro. It's a popular climb: most follow the **Tourist Route** up and down from Rowardennan car park. It's a straightforward climb on a well-used and maintained path; allow five hours for the 7 mile (11km) round trip.

The **Ptarmigan Route** is less crowded and has better views, following a narrow but clearly defined path up the western flank, directly overlooking the loch, to a curving ridge leading to the summit. You can then descend via the tourist route, making a satisfying circuit.

To find the start of the Ptarmigan path, head north from Rowardennan car park 600m, past the youth hostel; cross the bridge after Ben Lomond Cottage and immediately turn right along a path through the trees. The route is then easy to follow.

Helensburgh

POP 14,200

With the coming of the railway in the mid-19th century, Helensburgh – named after the wife of Sir James Colquhoun of Luss – became a popular seaside retreat for wealthy Glaswegian families. Their spacious Victorian villas now populate the hillside above the Firth of Clyde, but none can compare with splendid **Hill House** (NTS; ☑0844 493-2208; www.nts.org.uk; Upper Colquhoun St; adult/child £10.50/7.50; ⊙1.30-5.30pm Apr-Oct). Built in 1902 for Glasgow publisher Walter Blackie, it is perhaps architect Charles Rennie Mackintosh's finest creation – its timeless elegance still feels chic today. Mackintosh was keen not to cast his pearls before swine: he once chided Mrs Blackie for putting the wrong-coloured flowers in a vase in the hall. You can stay here – check www.landmark trust.org.uk.

On the eastern side of town, peaceful **Braeholm** (☑01436-671880; www.braeholm. org.uk; 31 East Montrose St; s/d £40/60; P☎) ⌖ is a sizeable guesthouse run by a naval charity and managed by a friendly family. Rooms are great value, and on-site facilities include gym, sauna and laundry. Breakfast is very tasty.

Helensburgh has frequent trains to Glasgow (£6, 50 minutes, two per hour). Hill House is near Upper Helensburgh station, but not all trains stop there.

Arrochar

POP 700

The village of Arrochar has a wonderful location, looking across the head of Loch Long to the jagged peaks of the **Cobbler** (Ben Arthur; 884m). The mountain takes its name from the shape of its north peak (the one on the right, seen from Arrochar), which looks like a cobbler hunched over his bench. The village makes a picturesque overnight stop.

If you want to climb the Cobbler, start from the roadside car park at Succoth near the head of Loch Long. A steep uphill hike through woods is followed by an easier section heading into the valley below the triple peaks. Then it's steeply uphill again to the saddle between the north and central peaks. The central peak is higher, but it's awkward to get to – scramble through the hole and along the ledge to reach the airy summit. The north peak to the right is an easy walk. Allow five to six hours for the 5-mile round trip.

The black-and-white, 19th-century **Village Inn** (☑01301-702279; www.villageinnarrochar.co.uk; s/d from £55/85; mains £9-15; ⊙food

10am-9pm; P☎) is a gloriously convivial pub, which boasts a beer garden with a great view of the Cobbler. There are 14 lovely renovated chambers, some with loch views and most with decent bathrooms. Meals – bar standards supplemented by more ambitious blackboard specials – are somewhat overpriced but tasty enough.

Citylink (www.citylink.co.uk) buses from Glasgow to Inveraray and Campbeltown call at Arrochar (£8.50, 1¼ hours, seven daily). There are also three or four trains a day from Glasow to Arrochar & Tarbet station (£11.40, 1¼ hours), continuing to Oban or Fort William.

THE TROSSACHS

The Trossachs region has long been a favourite weekend getaway, offering outstanding natural beauty and excellent walking and cycling routes within easy reach of the southern population centres. With thickly forested hills, romantic lochs, national-park status and an interesting selection of places to stay and eat, its popularity is sure to continue.

The Trossachs first gained popularity in the early 19th century, when curious visitors came from across Britain, drawn by the romantic language of Walter Scott's poem *Lady of the Lake,* inspired by Loch Katrine, and *Rob Roy,* about the derring-do of the region's most famous son.

In summer the Trossachs can be overburdened with coach tours, but many of these are day trippers – peaceful, long evenings gazing at the reflections in the nearest loch are still possible. If you can, it's worth timing your visit not to coincide with a weekend.

Aberfoyle & Around

POP 800

Crawling with visitors on most weekends and dominated by a huge car park, little Aberfoyle is easily overwhelmed by day trippers. Callander or other Trossachs towns appeal more as places to stay, but Aberfoyle has lots to do close at hand and has great accommodation options nearby. It's also a stop on the Rob Roy Way.

⊙ Sights

There are also some good (and not too busy) walking trails in the woods south of Loch Ard, west of town.

Inchmahome Priory RUIN

(HS; www.historic-scotland.gov.uk; adult/child incl ferry £5.50/3.30; ⊙10am-5pm Apr-Sep, to 4pm Oct, last ferry to island 1hr before closing) From the **Lake of Menteith** (called lake not loch due to a mistranslation from Gaelic), 3 miles east of Aberfoyle, a ferry takes visitors to these substantial ruins. Mary, Queen of Scots, was kept safe here as a child during Henry VIII's 'Rough Wooing'. Henry attacked Stirling trying to force Mary to marry his son in order to unite the kingdoms.

The Lodge NATURE RESERVE

(David Marshall Lodge; www.forestry.gov.uk; car park £1-3; ⊙10am-4pm Nov-Mar, to 5pm Apr-Jun & Sep-Oct, to 6pm Jul & Aug) FREE Half a mile north of Aberfoyle, this nature centre has info about the many walks and cycle routes in and around the Queen Elizabeth Forest Park. There are live wildlife cameras offering a peek at osprey and barn owl nests among others. The centre is worth visiting solely for the views. Picturesque but busy waymarked trails start from here, ranging from a light 20-minute stroll to a nearby waterfall – with great interactive play options for kids – to a hilly 4-mile circuit.

The centre has a popular cafe. Also here, **Go Ape!** (☎0845 519 3023; www.goape.co.uk; adult/child £30/24; ⊙Sat & Sun Nov & Feb-Easter, Wed-Mon Easter-Oct) will bring out the monkey in you on its exhilarating adventure course of long zip lines, swings and rope bridges through the forest.

Activities

Cycling

An excellent 20-mile circular cycle route links with the boat at Loch Katrine. From Aberfoyle, join the Lochs & Glens Cycle Way on the forest trail, or take the A821 over Duke's Pass. Following the southern shore of Loch Achray, you reach the pier on Loch Katrine. The 10.30am boat (there's also a 2pm sailing in summer) can take you to Stronachlachar (one way with bike £15) on the western shore (or it's an extra 14 miles biking it along the northern shore), from where you can follow the beautiful B829 via Loch Ard back to Aberfoyle.

Sleeping & Eating

Inversnaid Bunkhouse HOSTEL £

(☎01877-386249; www.inversnaid.com; Inversnaid; tent site per person £8.50, dm £17.50-20.50, tw/d without bathroom £44/57; ⊙Apr-Sep; P🖥🐾) Fifteen miles from Aberfoyle by road, a ferry across Loch Lomond, or an 8-mile walk north from Rowardennan on the West Highland Way, this former church is now a remote welcoming hostel in a peaceful streamside location. It's very popular with walkers and offers simple accommodation in crowded dorms, decent twins, very pleasant doubles and grassy campsites (pre-pitched tents available). A hot tub is great for aching muscles.

It offers simple meals (noon to 4pm or 6pm to 8pm), packed lunches and decent beers in the cafe; you can also self-cater evening meals. It's a 15-minute uphill trudge from the lakeshore and trail, but there are free transfers. A modern self-catering cabin is also available.

Mayfield Guest House B&B ££

(☎01877-382962; www.mayfield-aberfoyle.co.uk; Main St, Aberfoyle; s £40, d £60-65; P🖥🐾) Nothing is too much trouble for the friendly hosts at this guest house right in the heart of Aberfoyle. It has three compact, comfortable ground-floor rooms, all painted in cheerful colours and very well kept. There's a sweet little conservatory lounge and it's bike and motorbike friendly, with a garage out back.

★ Lake of Menteith Hotel HOTEL £££

(☎01877-385258; www.lake-hotel.com; s £110, d £130-240; P🖥🐾) Soothingly situated on a lake (yes, it's the only non-loch in Scotland) 3 miles east of Aberfoyle, this makes a great romantic getaway. Though all rooms are excellent, with a handsome contemporary feel, it's worth the upgrade to the enormous 'lake heritage' ones with a view of the water: it really is a sensational outlook. Even if you're not staying, head down to the waterside bar-restaurant (mains £10 to £15; open noon to 2.30pm and 5.30pm to 9pm). Check the website for packages.

Duchray Castle B&B £££

(☎01877-389333; www.duchraycastle.com; Aberfoyle; d £130-185; P🖥) Splendidly set in secluded rural surrounds, all forest and stream but just three miles from Aberfoyle, this castle is a real treat, with four sumptuous rooms, a noble great hall, and a cosier lounge space with games, DVDs, CDs and books. It's good for a luxurious romantic break, but also for families – children will love the spiral stairs, castle atmosphere and acres to romp around in.

ⓘ TROSSACHS TRANSPORT

In a bid to cut public transport costs, 'Demand Responsive Transport' (DRT) now covers the Trossachs area. It sounds complex, but basically it means you get a taxi to where you want to go, for the price of a bus. There are various zones. Taxis should preferably be booked 24 hours in advance; call ☎ 01877-330496. A cab between Callander and Aberfoyle, for example, costs £5.

Breakfast is a treat, with quality produce served in an atmospheric stone-vaulted chamber. To get here, head across the stone bridge in Aberfoyle, take the third turning on the right (past a post box), and keep going.

Forth Inn   PUB £
(☎ 01877-382372; www.forthinn.com; Main St, Aberfoyle; mains £8-12; ☉ noon-5.30pm & 6-8.30pm; P 🛜 ♿ 🐶) In the middle of the village, locals and visitors alike queue up here for good, honest pub fare; the best bar meal in Aberfoyle. It's got a top selection of Scottish craft beers on tap and drinkers spilling outside into the sunny courtyard. Single (£60) and double (£80 to £90) rooms are available, but they can be noisy at weekends.

ⓘ Information

Aberfoyle Tourist Office (☎ 01877-382352; www.visitscottishheartlands.com; Main St, Aberfoyle; ☉ 10am-5pm Apr-Oct, to 4pm Nov-Mar; 🛜) Large office with good selection of walking information.

ⓘ Getting There & Away

First (www.firstgroup.com) has six daily buses (Monday to Saturday) from Stirling (£4.60, 40 minutes).

Lochs Katrine & Achray

This rugged area, 7 miles north of Aberfoyle and 10 miles west of Callander, is the heart of the Trossachs. From April to October, two **boats** (☎ 01877-376315; www.lochkatrine.com; Trossachs Pier; 1hr cruise adult/child £13/8; ☉ Easter-Oct) run cruises from Trossachs Pier at the eastern tip of Loch Katrine. One of these is the fabulous centenarian steamship *Sir Walter Scott*; check the website departures, as it's worth coinciding with this veteran if you can. There are various one-hour afternoon sailings, and at 10.30am (plus additional summer departures) there's a departure to Stronachlachar at the other end of the loch before returning (single/return adult £13/15.50, child £8/9.50, two hours return). From Stronachlachar (also accessible by car via a 12-mile road from Aberfoyle), you can reach the eastern shore of Loch Lomond at isolated Inversnaid. A tarmac path links Trossachs Pier with Stronachlachar, so you can take the boat out and walk/cycle back (14 miles). At Trossachs Pier, **Katrinewheelz** (☎ 01877-376366; www.katrinewheelz.co.uk; hire per half-/full day from £15/20; ☉ 9am-5pm Apr-Oct, 11am-3pm Sat & Sun Nov, Dec, Feb & Mar) hires out good bikes and even electric buggies. Bring a picnic; the cafe is mediocre.

Two good walks start from nearby Loch Achray. The path to the rocky cone called **Ben A'an** (460m) begins at a car park just east of the Loch Katrine turn-off. It's easy to follow and the return trip is just under 4 miles (allow 2½ hours). A tougher walk is up rugged **Ben Venue** (727m) – there's a path right to the summit. Start walking from the signed car park just south of the Loch Katrine turn-off. The return trip is 7.5 miles – allow around five to six hours.

Between here and Aberfoyle, the **Three Lochs Forest Drive** is a worthwhile 7.5-mile circuit (April to October, £2) through pine forest opening up to picturesque vistas. There are plenty of walks here to stretch your legs.

Callander

POP 3100

Callander, the principal Trossachs town, has been pulling in tourists for over 150 years, and has a laid-back ambience along its main thoroughfare that quickly lulls visitors into lazy pottering. There's an excellent array of accommodation options here, and some intriguing places to eat.

⊙ Sights & Activities

The **Hamilton Toy Collection** (☎ 01877-330004; www.thehamiltontoycollection.co.uk; 111 Main St; adult/child £3/1; ☉ 10am-4.30pm Mon-Sat, noon-4.30pm Sun Apr-Oct) is a powerhouse of 20th-century juvenile memorabilia, chock-full of dolls houses, puppets and toy soldiers. It's an amazing collection and a guaranteed nostalgia trip. Phone in winter as it opens some weekends.

Impressive **Bracklinn Falls** are reached by track and footpath from Bracklinn Rd (30 minutes each way from the car park). Also off Bracklinn Rd, a woodland trail leads up to **Callander Crags**, with great views over the surroundings; a return trip from the car park is about 4 miles.

The Trossachs is a lovely area to cycle around. On a cycle route, excellent **Wheels Cycling Centre** (☑01877-331100; www.wheelscyclingcentre.com; bike per hr/day/week from £8/20/90; ☺10am-6pm Mar-Oct) has a wide range of hire bikes. To get there, take Bridge St off Main St, turn right onto Invertrossachs Rd and continue for a mile.

🛏 Sleeping

White Shutters
B&B £

(☑01877-330442; www.incallander.co.uk/white-shutters.htm; 6 South Church St; s/d £26/46; ☎) A cute little house just off the main street, White Shutters offers pleasing rooms with shared bathroom and a friendly welcome. The large double is particularly appealing, but it's all clean and comfortable and offers exceptional value.

Callander Hostel
HOSTEL £

(☑01877-330141; www.callanderhostel.co.uk; 6 Bridgend; dm/d £23/70; ☑☎) ⚲ This hostel in a mock-Tudor building run by a youth project has well-furnished dorms and a welcoming and enthusiastic, if not wholly professional, attitude.

Arden House
B&B ££

(☑01877-339405; www.ardenhouse.org.uk; Bracklinn Rd; s from £70, d £85-100; ☺Mar-Oct; ☑☎) This elegant home has a fabulous hillside location with verdant garden and lovely vistas; close to the centre but far from the crowds. The commodious rooms are impeccable, with lots of natural light. They include large upstairs doubles with great views. Welcoming owners, noble architectural features – super bay windows – and a self-catering studio make this a top option.

Abbotsford Lodge
HOTEL ££

(☑01877-330066; www.abbotsfordlodge.com; Stirling Rd; s/d £65/85; ☺Mar-Nov; ☑☎) This friendly Victorian house offers something different to the norm, with tartan and florals consigned to the bonfire, replaced by stylish, comfortable contemporary design

that enhances the building's original features. There are fabulous, spacious superiors with modish grey fabrics (from £125) as well as cheaper top-floor rooms – shared bathroom – with lovably offbeat under-roof shapes. Room-only rates are available.

Callander Meadows
B&B ££

(☑01877-330181; www.callandermeadows.co.uk; 24 Main St; s £55, d £75-85; ☑☎☺) Upstairs at this recommended restaurant are some very appealing rooms, elegantly kitted out with solid furniture and good modern shower rooms. One, which can serve as a family room, has a four-poster bed. The owners are very welcoming.

Roslin Cottage
B&B ££

(☑01877-339787; www.roslincottage.co.uk; Stirling Rd; s £40, d £55-65; ☑☎) A characterful cottage that's a haven of good hospitality holds three snug en suite rooms that make an enticing Trossachs base. They all have charm: we love the Kirtle room with the original 17th-century wall exposed. Other delights include a lovely big back garden, a log fire in the lounge and sociable chef-cooked breakfasts. It's on the right as you enter Callander from the east, before the petrol station.

Highland Guest House
B&H ££

(☑01877-330269; www.thehighlandguesthouse.co.uk; 8 South Church St; s £39, d £65-70; ☎) The cheery welcome from the musical owner here makes up for a few minor quirks in the rooms. It offers solid comfort with a good central location, decent wi fi and maybe a blast on the bagpipes at breakfast time.

★ Roman Camp Hotel
HOTEL £££

(☑01877-330003; www.romancamphotel.co.uk; Main St; s/d/superior £110/160/210; ☑☎☺) Callander's best hotel is centrally located but feels rural, set by the river in beautiful grounds. Endearing features include a lounge with blazing fire and a library with a tiny secret chapel. It's an old-fashioned warren of a place with four grades of room; standards are certainly luxurious, but superiors are even more appealing, with period furniture, excellent bathrooms, armchairs and fireplace.

The upmarket restaurant is open to the public. Reassuringly, the name refers not to toga parties but to a ruin in the adjacent fields.

GAELIC & NORSE PLACE NAMES

Throughout the Highlands and islands of Scotland Gaelic place names are often intermixed with Old Norse names. The spelling is now Anglicised, but the meaning is still clear.

Gaelic Place Names

ach, auch – from *achadh* (field)

ard – from *ard* or *aird* (height, hill)

avon – from *abhainn* (river or stream)

bal – from *baile* (village or homestead)

ban – from *ban* (white, fair)

beg – from *beag* (small)

ben – from *beinn* (mountain)

buie – from *buidhe* (yellow)

dal – from *dail* (field or dale)

dow, dhu – from *dubh* (black)

drum – from *druim* (ridge or back)

dun – from *dun* or *duin* (fort or castle)

glen – from *gleann* (narrow valley)

gorm – from *gorm* (blue)

gower, gour – from *gabhar* (goat), eg Ardgour (height of the goats)

inch, insh – from *inis* (island, water-meadow or resting place for cattle)

inver – from *inbhir* (rivermouth or meeting of two rivers)

kil – from *cille* (church), eg Kilmartin (Church of St Martin)

kin, ken – from *ceann* (head), eg Kinlochleven (head of Loch Leven)

kyle, kyles – from *caol* or *caolas* (narrow sea channel)

more, vore – from *mor* or *mhor* (big), eg Ardmore (big height), Skerryvore (big reef)

strath – from *srath* (broad valley)

tarbert, tarbet – from *tairbeart* (portage), meaning a narrow neck of land between two bodies of water, across which a boat can be dragged

tay, ty – from *tigh* (house), eg Tyndrum (house on the ridge)

tober – from *tobar* (well), eg Tobermory (Mary's well)

tom – small hill

Norse Place Names

a, ay, ey – from *ey* (island)

bister, buster, bster – from *bolstaor* (dwelling place, homestead)

geo – from *gja* (chasm)

holm – from *holmr* (small island)

kirk – from *kirkja* (church)

pol, poll, bol – from *bol* (farm)

quoy – from *kvi* (sheep fold, cattle enclosure)

sker, skier, skerry – from *sker* (rocky reef)

ster, sett – from *setr* (house)

vig, vaig, wick – from *vik* (bay, creek)

voe, way – from *vagr* (bay, creek)

✗ Eating & Drinking

★ Callander Meadows
SCOTTISH ££

(☑ 01877-330181; www.callandermeadows.co.uk; 24 Main St; lunch £10, mains £12-16; ☺9am-9pm Thu-Sun; ☎) Informal but smart, this well-loved restaurant in the centre of Callander occupies the two front rooms of a house on the main street. There's a contemporary flair for presentation and unusual flavour combinations, but a solidly British base underpins the cuisine. There's a great beer/coffee garden out the back, where you can also eat. Opens daily from June to September.

Mhor Fish
SEAFOOD ££

(☑ 01877-330213; www.mhor.net; 75 Main St; mains £7-16; ☺noon-9pm Tue-Sun) 🖐 This simply decorated spot, with formica tables and a hodgepodge of chairs, sources brilliant sustainable seafood. Browse the fresh catch then eat it pan-seared in the dining area accompanied by a decent wine selection, or fried and wrapped in paper with chips to take away. It's all great – calamari and oysters are wonderfully toothsome starters.

Venachar Lochside
SEAFOOD ££

(Harbour Cafe; ☑ 01877-330011; www.venacharlochside.co.uk; Loch Venachar; mains £9-15; ☺lunch noon-3pm Jan-Nov, plus dinner 5.30-8.30pm Fri & Sat Jun-Sep; ☎) On lovely Loch Venachar, 4.5 miles west of Callander, this cafe-restaurant has a stunning waterside setting and does a nice line in delicious fresh seafood. It opens from 10am to 5pm daily for coffees, teas and baked goods. You can also hire boats here.

Poppies
SCOTTISH ££

(☑ 01877-330329; www.poppieshotel.com; Leny Rd; mains £10-19; ☺noon-2pm & 6-9pm, to 3pm Sun; ☎) This is the restaurant of a small main-road hotel, and offers high-class cuisine based on rigorously sourced quality Scottish meat and fish in an elegant dining space. It's a friendly place with an atmosphere that is more quiet clinks of cutlery than belches and belly laughs. There's a good-value early-dining special.

Lade Inn
PUB

(www.theladeinn.com; Kilmahog; ☺noon-11pm Mon-Thu, noon-1am Fri & Sat, 12.30-10.30pm Sun; ☎⚅) Callander's best pub isn't in Callander – it's a mile west of town. Staff pull a good pint (with their own real ales), and next door is a shop with a dazzling selection of Scottish beers. There's low-key live music here at weekends. The food (noon to 9pm, from 12.30pm Sunday; mains £9 to £12) at last visit was overpriced and mediocre.

ℹ Information

Callander Visitor Centre (☑ 01877-330342; www.lochlomond-trossachs.org; 52 Main St; ☺9.30am-5pm Apr-Oct, to 4pm Nov-Mar; ☎) Very helpful for information on the region and national park.

ℹ Getting There & Away

First (☑ 0871 200 2233; www.firstgroup.com) operates buses from Stirling (£5.20, 45 minutes, hourly Monday to Saturday, every two hours Sunday), while **Kingshouse** (☑ 01877-384768; www.kingshousetravel.com) buses run from Killin (£5.70, 45 minutes, five to six Monday to Saturday). For Aberfoyle, use DRT (see boxed text, p254) or get off a Stirling-bound bus at Blair Drummond safari park and cross the road. There are also **Citylink** (www.citylink.co.uk) buses via Callander from Edinburgh (£16.20, 1¾ hours, two daily mid-May to mid-October) to Oban (£21.30, 2¼ hours) or Fort William (£23.20, 2½ hours).

Balquhidder & Around

North of Callander, you'll skirt past the shores of gorgeous Loch Lubnaig. Not as famous as some of its cousins, it's still well worth a stop for its sublime views of forested hills. A campsite (£5 per person) with nine bookable lochside pitches plus motorhome bays is 4½ miles north of Callander. In the small village of Balquhidder (ball-whidder), 9 miles north of Callander off the A84, there's a churchyard with **Rob Roy's grave**. It's an appropriately beautiful spot in a deep, winding glen in big-sky country. In the church is the 8th-century **St Angus' stone**, probably a marker to the original tomb of St Angus, an 8th-century monk who built the first church here.

🛏 Sleeping

★ Monachyle Mhor
HOTEL £££

(☑ 01877-384622; www.mhor.net; d £195-265; ☺Feb-Dec; 🅿☎☎) 🖐 Monachyle Mhor is a luxury hideaway with a fantastically peaceful location overlooking two lochs. It's a great fusion of country Scotland and contemporary attitudes to design and food. The rooms are superb and feature quirkily original decor, particularly the fabulous 'feature rooms'; you might get your own steam room or a wonderful double bathtub. The restaurant serves soup-and-sandwich deals, delicious lunches and five-course dinners (£50), which are high in quality, sustainably sourced and deliciously innovative. Enchantment lies in its successful combination of top-class hospitality with a relaxed rural atmosphere; dogs and kids happily romp on the lawns, and no one looks askance if you come in flushed and muddy after a day's fishing or walking. It's 4 miles from Balquhidder.

Mhor 84 HOTEL ££
(☑ 01877-384646; www.mhor.net; A84, Kingshouse; r without breakfast £60-70; P 🖨) 🐾 At the A84 junction, this 18th-century inn has been given a modern-retro revamp and is now a great place with bags of facilities, simple, good-value rooms and a delicious menu of hearty, nourishing meals with the Mhor philosophy of local and sustainable. A great pit stop for drivers, walkers and cyclists.

❶ Getting There & Away

Local buses between Callander and Killin stop at the main road turn-off to Balquhidder, as do daily Citylink (www.citylink.co.uk) buses between Edinburgh and Oban/Fort William.

Killin

POP 800

A fine base for the Trossachs or Perthshire, this lovely village sits at the western end of Loch Tay and has a spread-out, relaxed feel, particularly around the scenic Falls of Dochart, which tumble through the centre. On a sunny day people sprawl over the rocks by the bridge, pint or picnic in hand. Killin offers fine walking around the town, and mighty mountains and glens close at hand.

🏃 Activities

Five miles northeast of Killin, Ben Lawers (1214m) rises above Loch Tay. Walking routes abound; one rewarding circular walk heads up into the Acharn forest south of town, emerging above the treeline to great views of Loch Tay and Ben Lawers. Killin Outdoor Centre offers walking advice.

Glen Lochay runs westwards from Killin into the hills of Mamlorn. You can take a mountain bike up the glen; the scenery is

impressive and the hills aren't too difficult. It's possible, on a nice summer day, to climb over the top of Ben Challum (1025m) and descend to Crianlarich, but it's hard work. A potholed road also connects Glen Lochay with Glen Lyon.

Killin is on the Lochs & Glens Cycle Way from Glasgow to Inverness. Hire bikes from helpful Killin Outdoor Centre (☑ 01567-820652; www.killinoutdoor.co.uk; Main St; bike per 24hr £25, kayak/canoe per 2hr £25/30; ⏰ 8.45am-5.45pm), which also has canoes and kayaks or, in winter, crampons and snowshoes.

🛏 Sleeping & Eating

High Creagan CAMPGROUND £
(☑ 01567-820449; www.highcreagan.co.uk; Aberfeldy Rd; per person tent/caravan site £5/8; ⏰ Apr-Oct; P 🐕) This place has a well-kept, sheltered campsite with plenty of grass set high on the slopes overlooking sparkling Loch Tay, 3 miles east of Killin. Kids under five aren't allowed in the tent area (for insurance reasons) as there's a stream running through it.

Old Smiddy B&B ££
(Riverview; ☑ 01567-820619; www.theoldsmiddy-killin.co.uk; Main St; s £38, d £65-70; ⏰ Apr-Oct; P 🖨) Three appealing rooms above a decent restaurant here are within hearing distance of the falls. All rooms have modern styling, are en suite and one can fit a family of four. The lively, friendly owner makes guests very welcome and breakfast is a pleasure.

Falls of Dochart Inn PUB ££
(☑ 01567-820270; www.falls-of-dochart-inn.co.uk; mains £11-14; ⏰ noon-3pm & 6-9pm Mon-Thu, to 9.30pm Fri, noon-9.30pm Sat, noon-8.30pm Sun; P 🖨) In a prime position overlooking the falls, this is a terrific pub, a snug, atmospheric space with a roaring fire, real ales, personable service and decent pub grub, with some Asian flavours adding a dimension to tasty staples and daily specials. The rooms (single/double from £60/80) are handsome but a few glitches like poor heating let some of them down. The outside tables are great spots on a sunny day.

❶ Information

Old Mill (☑ 07802-929796; Pier Rd; ⏰ 10am-4pm Mar-Oct; 🖨) This picturesque old mill building by the falls houses a thrift shop with volunteers who also give out tourist information.

ℹ Getting There & Away

Two daily **Citylink** (www.citylink.co.uk) buses between Edinburgh (£20.70, 2¼ hours) and Crianlarich/Oban/Fort William stop here; two buses from Dundee (£15.30, two hours) to Oban also pass through. Kingshouse (p257) runs five to six buses Monday to Saturday to Callander (£5.70, 45 minutes), where you can change for Stirling. A summer **bus** (www.breadalbane. org; ⊙Tue, Wed & Sun Jun–mid-Oct, plus Sat Jul-Aug) does a hop-on/hop-off Breadalbane circuit, running to Ben Lawers, Kenmore, Aberfeldy, Crieff and back.

SOUTH ARGYLL

Cowal

The remote and picturesque Cowal peninsula is cut off from the rest of the country by the lengthy fjords of Loch Long and Loch Fyne. It comprises rugged hills and narrow lochs, with only a few small villages and the old-fashioned holiday resort of Dunoon.

From Arrochar, the A83 to Inveraray loops around the head of Loch Long and climbs into spectacular Glen Croe. The pass at the head of the glen is called the Rest and Be Thankful. As you descend Glen Kinglas on the far side, the A815 forks to the left just before Cairndow, this is the main overland route into Cowal. From Glasgow, the most direct route is by ferry from Gourock to Dunoon.

Dunoon & Around

Like Rothesay on the Isle of Bute, Dunoon is a Victorian seaside resort that owes its existence to the steamers that once carried thousands of Glaswegians on pleasure trips 'doon the watter' in the 19th and 20th centuries. Fortunes declined when cheap foreign holidays stole the market and Dunoon is still a bit down in the dumps.

◉ Sights & Activities

The town's main attraction is still, as it was in the 1950s, strolling along the promenade, licking an ice-cream cone and watching the yachts at play in the Firth of Clyde.

Benmore Botanic Garden GARDENS
(www.rbge.org.uk; adult/child £6/free; ⊙10am-6pm Apr-Sep, to 5pm Mar & Oct) This garden, 7 miles north of Dunoon, has Scotland's finest collection of flowering trees and shrubs, including impressive displays of rhododendrons and azaleas, and is entered along a spectacular avenue of giant redwoods. A highlight is the Victorian fernery, nestled in an unlikely fold in the crags. The year-round cafe here appeals for lunch or coffee. Buses run between Dunoon and the gardens.

✦ Festivals & Events

Cowal Highland Gathering HIGHLAND GAMES
(www.cowalgathering.com) Held in Dunoon in late August. The finale features over a thousand bagpipers saluting the chieftain.

⫿ Sleeping & Eating

There are numerous guesthouses arrayed along the waterfront.

Dhailling Lodge B&B ££
(☑ 01369-701253; www.dhaillinglodge.com; 155 Alexandra Pde; s/d £45/85; ᴾ🔊☀) You can experience some of Dunoon's former elegance at this large Victorian villa with stirring views over the bay, pleasantly removed from the

ROB ROY

Nicknamed Red (*'ruadh'* in Gaelic, anglicised to 'roy') for his ginger locks, Robert MacGregor (1671–1734) was the wild leader of the wildest of Scotland's clans, outlawed by powerful neighbours, hence their sobriquet, Children of the Mist. Incognito, Rob became a prosperous livestock trader, before a dodgy deal led to a warrant for his arrest.

A legendary swordsman, the fugitive from justice then became notorious for daring raids into the Lowlands to carry off cattle and sheep. Forever hiding from potential captors, he was twice imprisoned, but escaped dramatically on both occasions. He finally turned himself in and received his liberty and a pardon from the king. He lies buried – perhaps – in the churchyard at Balquhidder; his uncompromising later epitaph reads 'MacGregor despite them'. His life has been glorified over the years due to Walter Scott's novel and the 1995 film. Many Scots see his life as a symbol of the struggle of the common folk against the inequitable ownership of vast tracts of the country by landed aristocrats.

shabby town centre but within a 10-minute walk. The owners are the essence of Scottish hospitality, and can provide excellent evening meals.

Chatters
SCOTTISH ££

(☑01369-706402; www.chattersdunoon.co.uk; 58 John St; mains lunch £5-9, dinner £15-22; ☺noon-3pm & 6-9.30pm Wed-Sat) This pretty little cottage restaurant has tartan sofas in the sitting room and a few tables in the tiny garden. It serves a mix of lunchtime snacks and more elaborate dinner dishes, and is famous for its open sandwiches and tempting homemade puddings. Booking recommended.

ℹ Information

The **tourist office** (☑01369-703785; www.visitcowal.co.uk; 7 Alexandra Pde; ☺10am-4pm Nov-Mar, 10am-5pm Apr–mid-Jun, Sep & Oct, 9am-5pm mid-Jun–Aug) is on the waterfront.

ℹ Getting There & Away

Dunoon is served by two competing ferry services from Gourock – Argyll Ferries is better if you are travelling on foot and want to arrive in the town centre.

McGill's (p247) runs buses from Glasgow to Dunoon (£9.50, 1¾ hours, six to nine daily). Buses around the Cowal Peninsula, to Inveraray (£3.90) and to Bute (£3.50) are operated by **West Coast Motors** (www.westcoastmotors.co.uk).

Tighnabruaich

POP 200

Sleepy little seaside Tighnabruaich (tinna-*broo*-ach) is one of the most attractive villages on the Firth of Clyde.

The village is home to **Royal an Lochan Hotel** (☑01700-811239; www.theroyalanlochan.co.uk; r £100-150; ☺food 12.30-2.30pm & 6.30-8.30pm; [P][⊚][❂][❄]), a local institution with a range of rooms that, typically for these venerable buildings, vary markedly in size. Sea views – most rooms have them – cost extra but are worth it. The restaurant serves fine seafoody fare and the cosy snug bar is a temple to the successes of the local shinty side, one of Scotland's finest.

A mile south, excellent **Kames Hotel** (☑01700-811489; www.kames-hotel.com; s £50, d £75-120; ☺food noon-2.30pm & 6-8.30pm; [❄]) has a variety of comfortable rooms, including cute low-bedded ones under the sloping roof on the top floor. The bar downstairs has great atmosphere and serves good-value bar meals (mains £7 to £15) with daily seafood specials.

For hearty homemade grub, go for local mussels and chips at central **Burnside Bistro** (www.burnsidebistro.co.uk; mains £7-13; ☺10am-5pm Sun-Thu, to 9pm Fri & Sat); the waterside tables are great for a sunny afternoon.

Isle of Bute

POP 6500

Bute lies pinched between the thumb and forefinger of the Cowal peninsula, separated from the mainland by a narrow, scenic strait. The Highland Boundary Fault cuts through the middle of the island so that, geologically speaking, the northern half is in the Highlands and the southern half is in the central Lowlands.

The **Isle of Bute Discovery Centre** (☑01700-502151; www.visitscottishheartlands.com; Victoria St, Rothesay; ☺9.30am-5.30pm Jul & Aug, 10am-5pm Apr-Jun & Sep, 10am-4pm Mon-Sat, 11am-3pm Sun Oct-Mar) is in Rothesay's restored Winter Gardens.

The five-day **Isle of Bute Jazz Festival** (www.butejazz.com) is held over the first weekend of May.

Rothesay

From the mid-19th century until the 1960s, Rothesay was one of Scotland's most popular holiday resorts, bustling with day trippers disembarking from numerous steamers crowded around the pier. Its hotels were filled with elderly holidaymakers and convalescents taking advantage of the famously mild climate.

Cheap foreign holidays saw Rothesay's fortunes decline, but a nostalgia-fuelled resurgence of interest has seen many Victorian buildings restored. The grassy, flowery waterfront and row of noble villas is a lovely place to be once again.

◉ Sights

Victorian Toilets
HISTORIC BUILDING

(Rothesay Pier; adult/child 30p/free; ☺9am-4.45pm daily Oct-Apr, 8am-5.45pm Tue-Thu, 8am-7.45pm Fri-Mon May-Sep) Dating from 1899, these are a monument to lavatorial luxury – a disinfectant-scented temple of green and black marbled stoneware, glistening white enamel, glass-sided cisterns and gleaming copper pipes. The attendant will escort

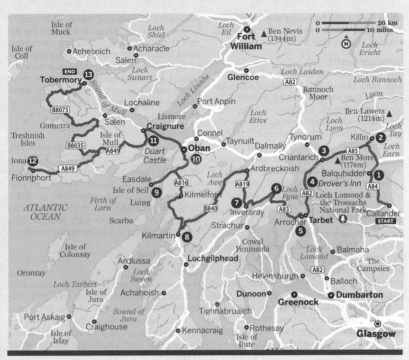

Driving Tour
The Trossachs to Mull

START CALLANDER
FINISH TOBERMORY
DISTANCE 240 MILES
DURATION 2–4 DAYS

Having explored the southern part of the Trossachs, head north out of Callander on the A84, following pretty Loch Lubnaig before optional detours of a few miles to see Rob Roy's grave at **1 Balquhidder** and the Falls of Dochart at pretty **2 Killin**. Continue on the A85 to **3 Crianlarich**, surrounded by Highland majesty, then turn left on the A82 to follow the western shore of Loch Lomond. Stop for a look and/or pint at the quirky **4 Drover's Inn** (p248), then deviate right at Tarbet onto the A83 – shortly thereafter, **5 Arrochar** makes a scenic lunch stop.

Head through scenic Glen Croe, over the pass and into Glen Kinglas, then follow the shore of **6 Loch Fyne** – stops at the brewery and/or oyster bar obligatory! – to picturesque **7 Inveraray**. Go right through

the arch here on the A819, then left onto the B840, a lonely road following stiletto-like Loch Awe. You'll eventually reach **8 Kilmartin**, with a great museum and evocative prehistoric sights. Follow the A816 north – you may want to deviate to see the **9 Isle of Seil** en-route: from here, great boat trips can take you out to the Corryvreckan whirlpool. Then on to **10 Oban** where good accommodation options, a handsome harbour and delicious seafood awaits you.

Catch a ferry from Oban to Mull and follow the A849 southwest via **11 Duart Castle** (p288) to the island's tip at Fionnphort, where you cross to the emerald jewel of **12 Iona** and can take a boat trip to the spectacular rock formations of Staffa. Retrace your steps, then follow Mull's winding west coast on the B8035 and B8073 via spectacular coastline and the beach at Calgary to arrive at the colourful shorefront houses of the main town, **13 Tobermory**.

women into the hallowed confines of the gents for a look around when unoccupied. You can shower here too.

Rothesay Castle
CASTLE

(HS; www.historic-scotland.gov.uk; King St; adult/child £4.50/2.70; ⊙9.30am-5.30pm Apr-Sep, to 4.30pm Sat-Wed Oct-Mar) Splendid ruined 13th-century Rothesay Castle, with seagulls and jackdaws nesting in the walls, was once a favourite residence of the Stuart kings. It is unique in Scotland in having a circular plan, with four stocky round towers. The landscaped moat, with manicured turf, flower gardens and lazily cruising ducks, makes a picturesque setting.

🛏 Sleeping

Bute Backpackers Hotel
HOSTEL £

(☑01700-501876; www.butebackpackers.co.uk; 36 Argyle St; r per person £20; P🗐) An appealing budget option on Rothesay's main thoroughfare, this large, well-equipped place offers private rooms of various sizes at a bargain price. Some are en suite, but shared bathrooms are modern and spotless, with power showers. The kitchen is huge, and there's a barbecue too.

Roseland Holiday Park
CAMPSITE, BUNGALOW £

(☑01700-501840; www.roselandlodgepark.co.uk; Roslin Rd; tent sites for two £10, pods s/d £25/30; ⊙Mar-Oct; P🗐🗐) A steep climb up the eccentric hairpins of Serpentine Rd, this campsite has a small but pleasant grassy area for tents amid the static caravans, and a handful of pitches for campervans. Adjacent, the holiday park section (open year-round) has bungalows, and cute little pods for glamping that sleep up to four.

Glendale Guest House
B&B ££

(☑01700-502329; www.glendalebute.com; 20 Battery Pl; s £40, d £64-90, f £120; P🗐) This noble Victorian waterfront villa, complete with turret, offers very commodious rooms with plush furniture and good family options. Front-facing bedrooms have superb sea views from large windows, as does the lavishly elegant lounge and the breakfast room, where you'll find homemade smoked haddock fish cakes on the menu among other interesting options. Genial hosts make for a pleasurable stay.

Boat House
B&B ££

(☑01700-502696; www.theboathouse-bute. co.uk; 15 Battery Pl; s/d from £38/65; 🗐) The Boat House brings a touch of class to Rothesay's guesthouse scene, with quality fabrics and furnishings and an eye for design that makes it feel a bit like a boutique hotel, without the expensive price tag. Other features include a garden, sea views, a central location and a ground-floor room kitted out for wheelchair users. The owners are helpful, with a great attitude to hospitality.

Moorings
B&B ££

(☑01700-502277; www.themoorings-bute.co.uk; 7 Mountstuart Rd; s/d/f £35/70/85; P🗐🗐) A delightful sandstone lodge with a great outlook over the water from huge windows: request a sea view when booking. All rooms are spacious, with a seating area; there's also an outdoor play area for kids and a high chair in the breakfast room.

🍴 Eating

★ Musicker
CAFE £

(www.musicker.co.uk; 11 High St; mains £3-7; ⊙10am-5pm Mon-Sat; 🗐) This cool little cafe serves Bute's best coffee, alongside a range of home baking and sandwiches with imaginative fillings. It also sells CDs, books and guitars and sports an old-fashioned jukebox.

Harry Haw's
BISTRO ££

(☑01700-505857; www.harryhaws.com; 23 High St; mains £8-12; ⊙11am-9pm; 🗐🗐) Great scenes at this welcoming modern bistro, where clement prices and a brilliant range of deli-style fare plus burgers, local roast meat and tasty pastas make it a standout. Staff are very friendly and so cheerful you wonder if there's something in the water.

Brechin's on Bridgend Street
BRASSERIE ££

(☑01700-502922; www.rothesaymusicshop. com; 2 Bridgend St; light meals £6-8; ⊙10.30am-2.30pm Tue-Sat, plus 7-9.30pm Fri & Sat; 🗐) A friendly neighbourhood eatery and music shop owned by jazz fan Tim, Brechin's serves unpretentious but delicious dinners (£35 for two people including a bottle of wine) at weekends, and light lunchtime fare like jacket potatoes and sandwiches. Hard to miss with its bright yellow-and-blue livery.

ℹ Information

The Isle of Bute's information centre (p260) is in the centre of Rothesay, in the Winter Gardens building, once an entertainment venue.

Around Rothesay

★ Mount Stuart
HISTORIC BUILDING

(☑01700-503877; www.mountstuart.com; adult/child £11.50/6.75; ⏲noon-4pm Apr-Oct, grounds 10am-6pm) The family seat of the Stuart Earls of Bute is one of Britain's more magnificent 19th-century stately homes, the first to have a telephone, underfloor heating and heated pool. Its eclectic interior, with a magnificent central hall and chapel in Italian marble, is heavily influenced by the third Marquess's interests in Greek mythology and astrology. The drawing room has paintings by Titian and Tintoretto among other masters.

Buy tickets at the visitor centre (last sale at 3pm), from where it's a 15-minute stroll through lovely grounds to the house. A shuttle bus runs the route. Private tours (£50) offer glimpses of the pool and more bedrooms.

Mount Stuart is 5 miles south of Rothesay; bus 490 runs hourly. Discounted ferry-plus-entrance tickets are available from Calmac.

Around Bute

In the southern part of the island you'll find the haunting 12th-century ruin of St Blane's Chapel and a sandy beach at Kilchattan Bay. There are more good beaches: Scalpsie Bay has a fantastic outlook to Arran, Ettrick Bay is bigger, and has a tearoom (ugly outside but great chat and snacks inside).

Cycling is excellent: you can hire a bike from the Bike Shed (☑01700-505515; david.thebikeshed@btinternet.com; 23-25 East Princes St; ⏲9.30am-5.30pm, closed Sun Oct-Mar) for £6/10 per half-/full day.

❶ Getting There & Away

BOAT

CalMac (www.calmac.co.uk) car ferries serve Bute from Wemyss Bay in Ayrshire and Colintraive in Cowal.

Colintraive to Rhubodach Passenger/car £1.60/9.90, five minutes, every 15 to 20 minutes

Wemyss Bay to Rothesay Passenger/car £5.05/19.85, 35 minutes, hourly

BUS

West Coast Motors (p260) buses run four or five times a week from Rothesay to Dunoon (£3.50, 1½ hours) via the ferry and Tighnabruaich. On Monday to Friday a bus goes from Rothesay to Portavadie (via the Rhubodach–Colintraive ferry), where there's another ferry to Tarbert in Kintyre.

Inveraray
POP 600

There's no fifty shades of grey around here: this historic planned village is all black and white – even logos of high-street shops conform. Spectacularly set on the shores of Loch Fyne, Inveraray was built by the Duke of Argyll in Georgian style when he revamped his nearby castle in the 18th century.

◉ Sights

Inveraray Castle
CASTLE

(☑01499-302203; www.inveraray-castle.com; adult/child £10/7, parking £2; ⏲10am-5.45pm Apr-Oct) This visually stunning castle has been the seat of the Dukes of Argyll – chiefs of Clan Campbell – since the 15th century. The 18th-century building, with its fairy tale turrets and fake battlements, houses an impressive armoury hall, its walls patterned with more than 1000 pole-arms, dirks, muskets and Lochaber axes. The castle is 500m north of town, entered from the A819 Dalmally road.

Inveraray Jail
MUSEUM

(☑01499-302381; www.inverarayjail.co.uk; Church Sq; adult/child £9.50/5.25; ⏲9.30am-6pm Apr-Oct, 10am-5pm Nov-Mar; ♿) At this entertaining interactive tourist attraction you can sit in on a trial, try out a cell and discover the harsh tortures that were meted out to unfortunate prisoners. The attention to detail – including a life-sized model of an inmate squatting on a 19th-century toilet – more than makes up for the sometimes tedious commentary.

🛏 Sleeping & Eating

Claonairigh House
B&B £

(☑01499-302160; www.inveraraybandb.co.uk; Bridge of Douglas; s £35-40, d £50-55; ⓟ@🛜) This attractive 18th-century house, built for the Duke of Argyll in 1745, is set in 3 hectares of grounds on the bank of a river complete with waterfall and salmon-fishing. There are three homely en suite rooms, one with a four-poster bed, others compact and cute with exposed stone and sloping ceiling. It's a cheerful country home with a resident menagerie of dogs, ducks and chickens, 4 miles south of town on the A83.

FYNE FOOD AND DRINK

Eight miles north of Inveraray, at the head of Loch Fyne, it pays to stop by two great local establishments.

Fyne Ales (☑01499-600120; www.fyneales.com; Achadunan, Cairndow; tours £5; ⊙10am-6pm) These friendly folk do a great range of craft beers and have recently upgraded to a shiny new brewery. There's a bar-cafe here where you can taste them all: the light, citrussy Jarl is a standout. Tours run at least twice daily – call for times. A range of walks tackle the pretty glen from a car park nearby.

Loch Fyne Oyster Bar (☑01499-600236; www.lochfyne.com; Clachan, Cairndow; mains £11-22; ⊙9am-7pm or 8pm; 🛜) The success of this cooperative is such that it now lends its name to dozens of restaurants throughout the UK. But the original's still the best, with salty oysters straight out of the lake, and fabulous salmon dishes. The atmosphere and decor is simple, friendly, and unpretentious; there's also a shop and deli.

Inveraray Hostel   HOSTEL £
(☑01499-302454; www.inverarayhostel.co.uk; Dalmally Rd; dm £17-18; ⊙Apr-Oct; 🅿🛜) To get to this hostel, housed in a comfortable, modern bungalow, go through the right hand one of the two arched entrances on the seafront. Metal bunk beds – rooms sleep only two or four – are comfortable, and there's a wee lounge and kitchen with plenty of stoves.

George Hotel   HOTEL ££
(☑01499-302111; www.thegeorgehotel.co.uk; Main St E; d £80-100; 🅿🛜🍽) The George boasts a magnificent choice of opulent, individual rooms complete with four-poster beds, period furniture, Victorian roll-top baths and private jacuzzis (superior rooms cost £145 to £170 per double). Some are in an annexe across the way. The cosy wood-panelled bar, with rough stone walls, flagstone floor and peat fires, is a delightful place for all-day bar meals (mains £9 to £16; noon to 9pm) and has a beer garden.

ⓘ Information

Inveraray Tourist Office (☑01499-302063; Front St; ⊙9am-5.30pm Jun-Aug, 10am-5pm

Apr, May, Sep & Oct, 10am-4pm Nov-Mar; 🛜) On the seafront.

ⓘ Getting There & Away

Scottish Citylink (www.citylink.co.uk) buses run from Glasgow to Inveraray (£11.90, 1¾ hours, seven daily). Five continue to Campbeltown (£13, 2½ hours); the others to Oban (£9.90, 1¼ hours, two daily). There are also buses to Dunoon (£3.90, 1¼ hours, three daily Monday to Saturday)

Crinan Canal

Completed in 1801, picturesque Crinan Canal runs for 9 miles from Ardrishaig to Crinan allowing seagoing vessels – mostly yachts, these days – to take a short cut from the Firth of Clyde and Loch Fyne to the west coast of Scotland, avoiding the long passage around the Mull of Kintyre. You can easily walk or cycle the canal towpath in an afternoon.

The Crinan end is overlooked by romantic **Crinan Hotel** (☑01546-830261; www.crinanhotel.com; Crinan; s/d from £110/180; 🅿🛜🍽), which boasts one of the west coast's most spectacular views. All the bright, light rooms enjoy wonderful perspectives, and the somewhat faded olde-worlde atmosphere is beguiling, with paintings throughout and a top-floor gallery. You're paying for the ambience and view here: don't expect five-star luxury. The hotel offers various eating options: **Westward** (set dinner £35; ⊙7-8.30pm) does posh set dinners, the cosy **Seafood Bar** (mains £11-20; ⊙noon-2.30pm & 6-8.30pm; 🛜) does great fresh food, including excellent local mussels with white wine, thyme and garlic, and the **coffee shop** (snacks £3-7; ⊙9am-6pm Apr-Oct) below the hotel has great home baking.

If you want to walk along the canal and take the bus back, buses 425/426 from Lochgilphead run along it Monday to Saturday.

Kilmartin Glen

This magical glen is the focus of one of the biggest concentrations of prehistoric sites in Scotland. Burial cairns, standing stones, stone circles, hill forts and cup-and-ring-marked rocks litter the countryside. Within a 6-mile radius of Kilmartin village there are 25 sites with standing stones and over 100 rock carvings.

In the 6th century, Irish settlers arrived in this part of Argyll and founded the kingdom of Dál Riata (Dalriada), which eventually united with the Picts in 843 to create the first Scottish kingdom. Their capital was the hill fort of Dunadd, on the plain to the south of Kilmartin.

Sights

Your first stop should be **Kilmartin House Museum** (☏01546-510278; www.kilmartin. org; Kilmartin; adult/child £5/2; ☉10am-5.30pm Mar-Oct, 11am-4pm Nov-23 Dec), in Kilmartin village. Its a fascinating interpretive centre that provides a context for the ancient monuments you can go on to explore, alongside displays of artefacts recovered from various sites. There's also an excellent **cafe** (☏01546-510278; mains £5-9; ☉10am-5pm Mar-Oct, 11am-4pm Nov-Christmas; ☎) and a shop with handcrafts and books on Scotland.

The oldest monuments at Kilmartin date from 5000 years ago and comprise a linear cemetery of **burial cairns** that runs south 1.5 miles from Kilmartin village. There are also two stone circles at **Temple Wood**, 0.75 miles southwest of Kilmartin.

Kilmartin Churchyard contains 10th-century Celtic crosses and medieval grave slabs with carved effigies of knights. Some researchers have surmised that these were the tombs of Knights Templar who fled persecution in France in the 14th century.

The hill fort of **Dunadd**, 3.5 miles south of Kilmartin village, was the seat of power of the first kings of Dál Riata, and may have been where the **Stone of Destiny** was originally located. Faint rock carvings of a boar and two footprints with an Ogham inscription may have been used in some kind of inauguration ceremony. The prominent little hill rises straight out of the boggy plain of **Moine Mhor Nature Reserve**. A slippery path leads to the summit where you can gaze out on much the same view that the kings of Dál Riata enjoyed 1300 years ago.

Getting There & Away

Bus 423 between Oban and Ardrishaig (three to five Monday to Friday, two on Saturday) stops at Kilmartin (£5.60, one hour).

You can walk or cycle along the Crinan Canal from Ardrishaig, then turn north at Bellanoch on the minor B8025 road to reach Kilmartin (12 miles one way).

RETURN OF THE BEAVER

Beavers have been extinct in Britain since the 16th century. But in 2009 they returned to Scotland, when a population of Norwegian beavers was released into the hill lochs of Knapdale, Argyll. After a broadly successful five-year trial, a mid-2015 decision will decide on the future of the beaver project.

Meanwhile, you can try and get a glimpse of them on the **Beaver Detective Trail**. It starts from the Barnluasgan forestry car park on the B8025 road to Tayvallich, about 1.5 miles south of the Crinan Canal. There's an information centre here. The trail is three miles but you might glimpse them at pretty Dubh Loch just half a mile down the track. Rangers offer **guided walks** (☏01546-603346; adult/child £2/1) in summer: phone to book.

Kintyre

The 40-mile long Kintyre peninsula is almost an island, with only a narrow isthmus at Tarbert connecting it to Knapdale. During the Norse occupation of the Western Isles, the Scottish king decreed that the Vikings could claim as their own any island they circumnavigated in a longship. So in 1098 the wily Magnus Barefoot stood at the helm while his men dragged their boat across this neck of land, validating his claim to Kintyre.

Tarbert
POP 1200

The attractive fishing village and yachting centre of Tarbert is the gateway to Kintyre, and the most scenic, with buildings strung around its excellent natural harbour. It's well worth a stopover.

Sights & Activities

The picturesque harbour is overlooked by the crumbling, ivy-covered ruins of **Tarbert Castle**, rebuilt by Robert the Bruce in the 14th century. You can hike up via a signposted footpath beside **Loch Fyne Gallery** (www. lochfynegallery.com; Harbour St; ☉10am-5pm Mon-Sat, 10.30am-5pm Sun), which showcases the work of local artists.

Tarbert is the starting point for the 100-mile Kintyre Way. The nine-mile first section to Skipness makes a pleasant day hike, climbing through forestry plantations to a high moorland plateau where you can soak up superb views to the Isle of Arran.

🍴 Sleeping & Eating

There are plenty of B&Bs and hotels, but book ahead in summer, as there are regular festivals and events in town.

Knap Guest House B&B **££**
(☑ 01880-820015; www.knapguesthouse.co.uk; Campbeltown Rd; s/d from £50/70; @ 🕾) A flight of stairs lit by Edwardian stained glass leads to this 1st-floor flat with three spacious en suite bedrooms sporting an attractive blend of Scottish and Far Eastern decor. The welcome is warm, and there are great harbour views from the lounge (leather sofas, log fire and a small library) and breakfast room.

Moorings B&B **££**
(☑ 01880-820756; www.themooringsbb.co.uk; Pier Rd; s £40, d £70-80; P 🕾) Follow the harbour just past the centre to this spot which is beautifully maintained and decorated by one man and his dogs, has great views over the water and an eclectic menagerie of ceramic and wooden animals and offbeat artwork.

Springside B&B B&B **££**
(☑ 01880-820413; www.scotland-info.co.uk/springside; Pier Rd; s/d £40/70; P 🕾 🐾) You can sit in front of this attractive fisherman's cottage, which overlooks the entrance to the harbour, and watch the yachts and fishing boats come and go. There are four comfy rooms, three with en suite, and the house is just five minutes' walk from the village centre. It's run with kind good humour by an older couple who know how to make guests feel welcome.

★ Starfish SEAFOOD **££**
(☑ 01880-820733; wwwstarfishtarbert.com; Castle St; mains £11-19; ☺ noon-2pm & 6-9pm Tue-Sun) Simple but stylish describes not only the decor in this friendly restaurant, but the seafood menu too. A great variety of specials – anything from classic French fish dishes to Thai curries – are prepared with whatever's fresh off the Tarbert boats that day. Best to book a table. Reduced hours in the low season.

ℹ Information

Tarbert Tourist Office (☑ 01880-820429; Harbour St; ☺ 10am-5pm Mon-Sat, 11am-5pm Sun Apr-Oct) Some years this opens in the winter months too.

ℹ Getting There & Away

BOAT

CalMac (☑ 0800 066-5000; www.calmac.co.uk) operates a car ferry from Tarbert to Portavadie on the Cowal peninsula (passenger/car £4.30/19, 25 minutes, hourly).

Ferries to Islay and Colonsay depart from Kennacraig ferry terminal, 5 miles southwest.

BUS

Tarbert is served by five daily **Scottish Citylink** (www.citylink.co.uk) coaches between Campbeltown (£7.70, one hour) and Glasgow (£16.20, three hours).

Skipness
POP 100

Tiny Skipness, 13 miles south of Tarbert, is pleasant and quiet with great views of Arran. Beyond the village rise the substantial remains of 13th-century **Skipness Castle** (HS; admission free; ☺ 24hr, tower Apr-Sep only), a former possession of the Lords of the Isles. It's strikingly composed of dark-green local stone trimmed with Arran red-brown sandstone. The tower house was added in the 16th century. From the top you can see roofless, 13th-century **St Brendan's Chapel** by the shore. The kirkyard contains some excellent carved grave slabs. In summer a cabin in the grounds of nearby Skipness House does cracking crab sandwiches.

Local bus 448 runs from Tarbert (£2.80, 35 minutes, two daily Monday to Saturday).

At Claonaig, 2 miles southwest, there's a ferry to Lochranza on Arran (passenger/car return £10.35/47, 30 minutes, seven to nine daily April to September).

Isle of Gigha
POP 160

Gigha (ghee-ah; www.gigha.org.uk) is a low-lying island, 6 miles long by about 1 mile wide, famous for sandy beaches, pristine turquoise water and mild climate – sub tropical plants thrive in **Achamore Gardens** (☑ 01583-505254; www.gigha.org.uk/gardens; Achamore House; adult/child £6/3; ☺ dawn-dusk). Other highlights include the ruined **church** at Kilchattan, the **bible garden** at the manse, and Gigha's picturesque northern end. The island was bought by its residents in 2002.

You can hire bikes, as well as sea kayaks and rowing boats from **Gigha Boats Activity Centre** (☑07876-506520; www.gighaboatsactivitycentre.co.uk; bike hire per half-/full day £8/12; ◔10am-6pm Easter-Oct) near the ferry slip.

There are several B&B and self-catering options; check the website. Communityowned **Gigha Hotel** (☑01583-505254; www.gigha.org.uk; s/d £50/90; ◔food noon-2pm & 6-8pm; [P][☎][🐾]) has a dozen rooms and serves bar meals. The friendly island shop, **Ardminish Stores** (☑01583-505251; www.facebook.com/ardminishstores; ◔shop 9am-6.30pm Mon-Sat, noon-5pm Sun; [P]), sells petrol, food and hires bikes. There is a bunkhouse with dorms and a family room planned to open by the time you read this. The **Boat House Café Bar** (☑01583-505123; mains £8-15; ◔10.30am-9pm; [☎]) does simple dishes as well as quality fresh local seafood. You can also camp here: there's no charge but space is limited, so call in advance.

CalMac (www.calmac.co.uk) runs from Tayinloan in Kintyre (passenger/car return £4.80/14.20, 20 minutes, roughly hourly).

Campbeltown

POP 4900

Blue-collar Campbeltown, set around a beautiful harbour, still suffers from the decline of its fishing and whisky industries and the closure of the nearby air-force base, but is rebounding on the back of golf tourism and a ferry link to Ayrshire. The spruced-up seafront backed by green hills lends the town a distinctly optimistic air.

The **Mull of Kintyre Music Festival** (☑01586-551053; www.mokfest.com), held in late August, is a popular event featuring traditional Scottish and Irish music.

◎ Sights & Activities

Springbank   DISTILLERY
(☑01586-552009; www.springbankwhisky.com; 85 Longrow; tours from £6.50; ◔tours 10am & 2pm Mon-Sat) There were once no fewer than 32 distilleries around Campbeltown, but most closed in the 1920s. Today this is one of only three operational. It is also one of the few around that distils, matures and bottles all its whisky on the one site, making for an interesting tour. It's a quality malt, one of Scotland's finest.

Davaar Cave   CAVE
An unusual sight awaits in this cave on the southern side of Davaar island, at the mouth of Campbeltown Loch. On the wall of the cave is an eerie painting of the Crucifixion by local artist Archibald MacKinnon, dating from 1887. You can walk to the island at low tide: check tide times with the tourist office.

Machrihanish Bay   BEACH, GOLF
Five miles northwest of Campbeltown, this bay has a 3-mile-long sandy beach popular with surfers and windsurfers. There are two great golf courses here, both very competitively priced compared to their more famous rivals: **Machrihanish Golf Club** (☑01586-810213; www.machgolf.com; green fee £65) is a classic links course, designed by Old Tom Morris. Much-newer **Machrihanish Dunes** (☑01586-810000; www.machrihanishdunes.com; Campbeltown; green fee around £70) offers another impressive seaside experience, commendably light on snobbery: the clubhouse is a convivial little hut, kids play free and there are always website offers.

◎ Tours

Mull of Kintyre Seatours   BOAT TOURS
(☑07785-542811; www.mull-of-kintyre.co.uk; ◔Apr-Sep) Operates high-speed boat trips out of Campbeltown harbour to the spectacular sea cliffs of the Mull of Kintyre, Arran, Ailsa Craig (£30; gannet colony and puffins), or Sanda Island (£25; seals, puffins and other seabirds) as well as whale-watching (£30, best late July to early September). Book in advance by phone or at the tourist office.

◎ Sleeping & Eating

Campbeltown Backpackers   HOSTEL £
(☑01586-551188; www.campbeltownbackpackers.co.uk; Big Kiln St; dm £20; [P][☎]) 🌱 This beautiful hostel occupies a central former school building: it's great, with a modern kitchen, disabled access, and state-of-the-art wooden bunks. Profits go to maintain the Heritage Centre that runs it. Rates are £2 cheaper if you prebook.

Redknowe   B&B ££

(☑ 01586-550374; www.redknowe.co.uk; Witch-burn Rd; s £35, d £60-70; P 🛜 🐕) An interesting Victorian home that's a short walk from the centre of town but feels rural with a lovely garden and an outlook over green fields. There's a fine welcome from the friendly couple that run it, a very decent breakfast, and comfortable rooms, a couple of which share an immaculate bathroom.

Royal Hotel   HOTEL £££

(☑ 01586-810000; www.machrihanishdunes.com; Main St; r £142-152; ⊙ food noon-9pm Sun-Thu, to 10pm Fri & Sat; P 🛜) Historically Campbeltown's best address, this hotel opposite the harbour is looking swish again. It caters mostly to yachties and golfers; though rack rates feel overpriced, there are often online specials and rooms are very spacious and attractive. The restaurant (mains £11 to £30) is the town's best, with fresh seafood and tasty grilled steaks the highlight.

ℹ️ Information

Campbeltown Tourist Office (☑ 01586-552056; www.visitscottishheartlands.com; The Pier; ⊙ 10am-4pm Mon-Fri Nov-Mar, 10am-5pm Mon-Sat Apr & Oct, 10am-5pm Mon-Sat & noon-4pm Sun May, Jun & Sep, 9am-6pm Mon-Sat & 11am-5pm Sun Jul & Aug) Beside the harbour. Very helpful.

ℹ️ Getting There & Away

AIR

Loganair/FlyBe (www.flybe.com) flies six days a week between Glasgow and Campbeltown's mighty runway.

BOAT

Kintyre Express (☑ 01586-555895; www.kintyreexpress.com) operates a small, high-speed passenger ferry from Campbeltown to Ballycastle in Northern Ireland (£35/60 one way/return, 1½ hours, daily May to August, four weekly April and September, two weekly October to March). You must book in advance.

Calmac (☑ 0800 066-5000; www.calmac. co.uk) runs thrice weekly May to September between Ardrossan in Ayrshire and Campbeltown (adult/car £9.80/60, 2¾ hours); the Saturday return service stops at Brodick on Arran.

BUS

Scottish Citylink (www.citylink.co.uk) runs from Campbeltown to Glasgow (£19.80, 4¼ hours, five daily) via Tarbert, Inveraray and Loch Lomond. Change at Inveraray for Oban.

Mull of Kintyre

A narrow winding road, 15 miles long, leads south from Campbeltown to the **Mull of Kintyre**, passing some good sandy beaches near Southend. This remote headland was immortalised in Paul McCartney's famous song – the former Beatle owns a farmhouse in the area. From where the road ends, a 30-minute steep downhill walk leads to a clifftop **lighthouse**, with Northern Ireland, only 12 miles away, visible across the channel. Don't leave the road when the frequent mists roll in as it's easy to become disoriented.

Isle of Arran

POP 4600

Enchanting Arran is a jewel in Scotland's scenic crown. The island is a visual feast, and boasts culinary delights, its own brewery and distillery and stacks of accommodation options. The variations in Scotland's dramatic landscape can all be experienced on this one island, best explored by pulling on the hiking boots or jumping on a bicycle. Arran offers some challenging walks in the mountainous north while the island's circular coastal road is deservedly popular with cyclists.

ℹ️ Information

Brodick Tourist Office (☑ 01770-303774; www.ayrshire-arran.com; Brodick; ⊙ 9am-5pm Mon-Sat) Efficient. Located by Brodick ferry pier; also open Sundays in summer. Slightly reduced hours in winter.

ℹ️ Getting There & Away

CalMac (☑ 0800 066-5000; www.calmac. co.uk) runs between Ardrossan and Brodick (passenger/car return £11.35/70, 55 minutes, four to 10 daily), and from April to late October also runs services between Claonaig on the Kintyre peninsula and Lochranza (passenger/car return £10.35/47, 30 minutes, seven to nine daily).

ℹ️ Getting Around

BICYCLE

Arran Adventure Company (☑ 01770-303479; www.arranadventure.com; Auchrannie Rd, Brodick; day/3 days £15/37) Good mountain bikes.

Arran Bike Hire (☑ 01770-302377; www. arranbikehire.com; The Shorehouse, Shore Rd, Brodick; half-day/full day/week £10/15/50)

On the water front in Brodick. Trail bikes and hybrids and can offer mountain-biking route advice.

CAR

Isle of Arran Car Hire ([📞] 01770-302839; The Pier, Brodick; car part-day/24hr £30/40) is at the service station by Brodick ferry pier.

PUBLIC TRANSPORT

Four to seven buses daily go from Brodick pier to Lochranza (£2.95, 45 minutes), and many head to Lamlash (£2.05) and Whiting Bay (£2.95, 30 minutes), then on to Kildonan and Blackwaterfoot. Pick up a timetable from the tourist office. An Arran Dayrider costs £5.40 from the driver, giving a day's travel.

Brodick & Around

Most visitors arrive in Brodick, the beating heart of the island, and congregate along the coastal road to admire the town's long curving bay. Main attractions are just out of town, off the Lochranza road.

⊙ Sights

Brodick Castle   CASTLE
(NTS; www.nts.org.uk; castle & park adult/child £12.50/9, park only £6.50/5.50; ⊙ castle 11am-4pm May-Sep, 11am-3pm Apr & Oct, park 9.30am-sunset year-round) This elegant castle 2 miles north of Brodick evolved from 13th-century origins into a stately home and hunting lodge for the Dukes of Hamilton and was used until the 1950s. You enter via the hunting gallery, wallpapered with deer heads. The rest of the interior is characterised by fabulous 19th-century wooden furniture and an array of horses and hounds paintings. Helpful guides and laminated sheets – the kids' ones are more entertaining – add info.

The extensive grounds, now a country park with various trails among the rhododendrons, justify the steep entry fee.

Arran Aromatics   SOAP FACTORY
([📞] 01770-302595;   www.arranaromatics.com; ⊙ 9.30am-5.30pm or 6pm) Near the castle is this popular shop and visitor centre where you can purchase any number of scented items and watch the production line at work. There's also **Soapworks** (soapmaking from £6.50; ⊙ 10am-12.30pm & 1.30-4pm Apr-Oct, 10am-noon & 2-4pm Nov-Mar), a fun little place where kids (and adults...) can experiment by making their own soaps, combining colours and moulds to make weird and wonderful

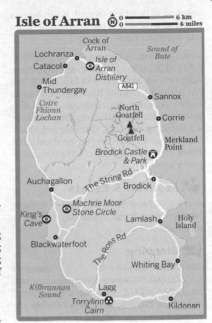

creations. There's a similar candle-dipping workshop (£3 for two candles).

Isle of Arran Brewery   BREWERY
([📞] 01770-302353; www.arranbrewery.com; tours £4; ⊙ 10am-5pm Mon-Sat, 12.30-5pm Sun Apr-Sep, variable hours Oct-Mar) A mile from town off the Lochranza road, this brewery produces the excellent-quality Arran beers, which include the addictive Arran Dark. Tours run daily: call for times as they vary by season. There's a good outdoors shop, **Arran Active** (www.arranactive.co.uk; ⊙ 9.30am-5pm Mon-Sat, 10.30am-5pm Sun), here too, if you're heading up Goatfell.

🏃 Activities

The 55-mile coastal circuit is popular with cyclists and has few serious hills – more in the south than the north. There are plenty of walking booklets and maps available and trails are clearly signposted around the island. Several leave from Lochranza, including the spectacular walk to the island's northeast tip, the **Cock of Arran**, finishing in the village of Sannox (8 miles one way).

Tackling **Goatfell** (the island's tallest peak) is 8 miles return (up to eight hours), starting in Brodick. If the weather's fine, there are superb views to Ben Lomond and the coast of Northern Ireland. It can be very cold and windy; take the appropriate maps and waterproof gear.

Arran Adventure Company OUTDOORS
(☑ 01770-303479; www.arranadventure.com; Auchrannie Rd; adult/teen/child £50/40/30) Run out of the Auchrannie Resort (which has an indoor pool and spa), this company offers loads of activities, including gorge walking, sea kayaking, climbing, abseiling and mountain biking. All activities run for about three hours. Drop in to see what's available while you're around.

🎉 Festivals & Events

Arran Folk Festival FOLK MUSIC
(www.arranevents.com) A four-day festival in mid-June.

🛏 Sleeping

Glen Rosa Campsite CAMPSITE £
(☑ 01770-302380; www.arrancamping.co.uk; sites per adult/child £4/2; P 🐾) In a lush glen 2 miles from Brodick, this campsite offers picturesque but basic camping in a large grassy riverside meadow, with cold water and toilets only. Take String Rd, then turn right almost immediately. After 400m, you'll see a white house on the left, where you register; the campground is 400m further.

Glenartney B&B ££
(☑ 01770-302220; www.glenartney-arran.co.uk; Mayish Rd; s/d £52/85; ⊘ Easter-Sep; P 🛜 🐾)
🐾 Uplifting bay views and genuine, helpful hosts make this a cracking option. Airy, stylish rooms make the most of the natural light available at the top of the town. Cyclists will appreciate bike wash, repair and storage facilities, while hikers can benefit from drying rooms and expert trail advice. They make big efforts to be sustainable.

Rothwell Lodge B&B ££
(☑ 01770-302208; www.rothwell-lodge.com; s £35-40, d £60-70; P 🛜) Sparklingly clean and luminous, this well-kept place offers an attractive modern environment with state-of-the-art bathrooms and numerous thoughtful touches at breakfast time. The upstairs en suite has heaps of space, and there's a large lounge. There are good discounts for multi-night stays and a self-catering apartment available downstairs. The owner was considering her future at last visit.

Belvedere Guest House B&B ££
(☑ 01770-302397; www.vision-unlimited.co.uk; Alma Rd; s £35, d £70-90; P 🛜) Overlooking town, bay and surrounding mountains, this has pleasant hosts and rooms are well-presented. Rooms are commodious but feel a smidgen overpriced; the two at the front are dearer but are en suite with great views. There's also a self-catering cottage as well as reiki and healing packages available.

★ Kilmichael Country House Hotel HOTEL £££
(☑ 01770-302219; www.kilmichael.com; s £95, d £163-204; ⊘ Apr-Oct; P 🛜 🐾) The island's best hotel is also the oldest building – one bit dates from 1650. Luxurious and tastefully decorated, it's a mile outside Brodick but seems a world away in deep countryside. With just eight spacious, very individual rooms and excellent four-course dinners (£45, open to nonguests), it's an ideal, utterly relaxing hideaway, which feels very classy without being overly formal.

In the grounds, patrolled by a sizeable muster of peacocks, there are also five self-catering cottages.

Douglas HOTEL £££
(☑ 01770-302968; www.thedouglashotel.co.uk; d/ superior d £149/179; P 🛜 🐾) Opposite the ferry, this hotel is a smart, stylish haven of island hospitality. Views are magnificent and luxurious rooms make the most of them. There are numerous thoughtful touches like binoculars to admire the vistas, and bathrooms are great. The downstairs bar (food served noon to 9pm) and bistro (6pm to 9.30pm) are also recommended. Prices drop midweek and in winter.

🍴 Eating & Drinking

Wineport CAFE £
(☑ 01770-302101; www.wineport.co.uk; Cladach Centre; mains £8-11; ⊘ 10am-5pm Apr-Oct) A mile-and-a-half from Brodick, next to the brewery, whose ales are offered on tap, this summer-only cafe-bar has great outdoor tables for sunny days and does a nice line in salads and pub grub. Opening hours are very changeable.

Ormidale Hotel PUB £
(☑ 01770-302293; www.ormidale-hotel.co.uk; Glen Cloy; mains £8-11; ⊘ food 5-9pm daily & 12.30-2.30pm Sat & Sun; 🖉 🐾) This hotel has decent bar food. Dishes change regularly, but there are always some good vegetarian options,

and daily specials. Quantities and value for money are high, and Arran beers are on tap.

★ **Brodick Bar** BRASSERIE ££
(☎ 01770-302169; www.brodickbar.co.uk; Alma Rd; mains £9-19; ☺ noon-2.30pm & 5.30-8.45pm or later Mon-Sat; ☜) Don't leave Brodick without dropping in here. The regularly changing blackboard menu brings modern French flair to this Arran pub, with great presentation, efficient service and delicious flavour combinations. You'll have a hard time choosing, as it's all brilliant. It's very buzzy on weekend evenings.

Fiddlers' Music Bar CAFE ££
(www.facebook.com/fiddlersmusicbar; Shore Rd; mains £9-12; ☺ meals 9am-9.30pm; ☜) Newly opened when we last passed by, this place was doing a good job serving decently priced food on gingham tablecloths and putting on live folk several times a week. Check out the appropriate toilet seats.

🛍 **Shopping**

Arran Cheese Shop FOOD
(www.arrancheese.com; Duchess Ct, Home Farm; ☺ 9am-5pm Mon-Sat, 10am-4.30pm Sun) Stop by this place to stock up on the famed local varieties. There are free samples and you can watch them make the stuff.

Corrie to Lochranza

The coast road continues north to small, pretty Corrie, where there's a **Goatfell** trailhead. After **Sannox**, with sandy beach and great mountain views, the road cuts inland. Heading to the very north, on the Island's main road, visitors weave through lush glens flanked by Arran's towering mountain splendour.

Pubs in Sannox and Corrie offer accommodation, food and drinks with sea views.

Lochranza

The village of Lochranza has a stunning location in a small bay at the island's north. On a promontory stands ruined 13th-century **Lochranza Castle** (HS; www.historic-scotland.gov.uk; ☺ 24hr) **FREE**, basically a draughty shell inside.

Isle of Arran Distillery (☎ 01770-830264; www.arranwhisky.com; tours adult/child £6/free) produces a light, aromatic single malt. The tour is a good one; it's a small set-up, and the whisky-making process is thoroughly explained. More expensive tours (£15) include extra tastings.

The Lochranza area bristles with red deer, who wander insouciantly into the village to crop the grass.

🛏 **Sleeping & Eating**

★ **Lochranza SYHA** HOSTEL £
(☎ 01770-830631; www.syha.org.uk; dm/d £19/50; ☺ mid-Mar–Oct plus Sat & Sun year-round; ℗@☜☜) 🦮 An excellent hostel in a charming place, with lovely views. Rooms sport chunky wooden furniture, keycards and lockers. Rainwater toilets, energy-saving heating solutions and an excellent wheelchair-accessible room show thoughtful design, while plush lounging areas, a kitchen you could run a restaurant out of, a laundry, a drying room, red deer in the garden, and welcoming management combine to make this a top option.

Castlekirk B&B ££
(☎ 01770-830202; www.castlekirkarran.co.uk; s £35-40, d £60-75; ☺ Mar–Oct; ℗☜☜) This unusual and warmly welcoming place to stay is a converted church chock-full of excellent artworks; there's a gallery downstairs, and paintings decorate the passageways and rooms. The breakfast area is dignified by a rose window, and there are great views of the castle opposite. Rooms are cosy under the sloping ceiling.

Apple Lodge B&B ££
(☎ 01770-830229; www.applelodgearran.co.uk; s/d/apt £50/78/90; ℗☜) Once the village manse, this rewarding choice is dignified and hospitable. Rooms are individually furnished and very commodious. One has a four-poster bed, while another is a self-contained apartment in the garden. The guest lounge is perfect for curling up with a good book, and courteous hosts mean you should book this one well ahead in summer.

Lochranza Hotel HOTEL ££
(☎ 01770-830223; www.lochranzahotel.co.uk; s/d £60/99; ℗☜) The only place in town for an evening meal (open noon to 9pm), this has somewhat overpriced but comfortable rooms: it's well worth paying the extra fiver for a larger front room, with super views. Showers are pleasingly powerful. The bar does toasties, jacket potatoes and the like, as well as fuller evening plates (dishes £10 to £13).

Catacol Bay Hotel
PUB £

(📞 01770-830231; www.catacol.co.uk; mains £8-11; 🕐 food noon-8.45pm, to 10pm summer; P 🛜 🐾 🐕) Genially run, and with a memorable position overlooking the water, this no-frills, somewhat rundown pub 2 miles south of Lochranza offers unpretentious bar food that comes out in generous portions. There's a Sunday lunch buffet (£13.95), and the beer garden is worth a contemplative pint with spirit-soothing views. Comfortable-enough rooms with shared bathroom are available (single/double £35/60).

West Coast

On the western side of the island is **Machrie Moor Stone Circle**, a pleasant 2-mile stroll (20 to 30 minute) from the parking area on the coastal road. There are actually several separate groups of stones of varying sizes, erected around 4000 years ago. You pass a Bronze Age burial cairn along the path.

Blackwaterfoot is the west coast's largest village, with shop and hotel. You can walk to **King's Cave** from here (6 miles) – Arran is one of several islands that claim the cave where Robert the Bruce had his famous arachnid encounter. This walk can easily be extended to the Machrie stones.

South Coast

The landscape in the south is gentler; the road drops into little wooded valleys, and it's particularly lovely around **Lagg**, where a 10-minute walk goes to **Torrylinn Cairn**, a chambered tomb over 4000 years old. **Kildonan** has pleasant sandy beaches, a gorgeous water outlook, a hotel, a campground and an ivy-clad ruined castle.

In genteel **Whiting Bay**, you'll find small sandy beaches and easy one-hour walks through the forest to the **Giant's Graves** and **Glenashdale Falls**, and back – keep an eye out for golden eagles and other birds of prey.

🛏 Sleeping & Eating

Sealshore Campsite
CAMPSITE £

(📞 01770-820320; www.campingarran.com; Kildonan; sites per adult/child £6/3, per tent £2-4; 🕐 Apr-Oct; P 🛜 🐕) Living up to its name, this excellent small campsite is right by sea (and the Kildonan Hotel) with one of Arran's finest views from its grassy camping area. There's a good washroom area with heaps of showers, kitchen facilities, and the breeze keeps the midges away. Cosy camping pods cost £30 for two people.

Kildonan Hotel
HOTEL ££

(📞 01770-820207; www.kildonanhotel.com; Kildonan; s/d/ste £75/99/135; P 🛜 🐕) Appealing rooms and a grounded attitude – dogs and kids are made very welcome – combine to make this one of Arran's better options. Oh, and it's right by the water, with seals basking on the rocks. The standard rooms could do with a pep-up but are decent; the suites – with private terrace or small balcony – are great.

Nearly all rooms have sea views; other attractions include great staff, a bar and restaurant serving tasty meals (mains £9 to £17; noon to 3pm and 6pm to 9pm), and live folk music.

Lagg Hotel
INN ££

(📞 01770-870255; www.lagghotel.com; Lagg, Kilmory; s/d £50/90; 🕐 Apr-Oct; P 🛜 🐕) This 18th-century coaching inn has a beautiful location and is the perfect place for a romantic weekend away from the cares of modern life. Rooms are smart; grab a superior one (£100) with garden views. There's also a cracking beer garden, a fine bar with log fire and an elegant restaurant (mains £9 to £13; noon to 3pm and 5.30pm to 9pm) with good veggie options.

Viewbank House
B&B ££

(📞 01770-700326; www.viewbank-arran.co.uk; Whiting Bay; s £30-35, d £62-79; P 🛜 🐕) Appropriately named, this friendly place does indeed have tremendous views from its vantage point high above Whiting Bay. Rooms, of which there are a variety with and without bathroom, are tastefully furnished and well kept. It's well signposted from the main road.

Coast
BISTRO ££

(📞 01770-700308; www.coastarran.co.uk; Shore Rd, Whiting Bay; mains £10-14; 🕐 10am-4pm daily, plus 6-9pm Thu-Sat; 🛜) Offering a sun-drenched conservatory on the water's edge, this serves grills, seafood and salads in the evening, with lighter offerings during the day. Opens Wednesday and Sunday evenings in summer too.

Lamlash

Lamlash is in a dazzling setting, strung along the beachfront. The bay was used as a safe anchorage by the navy during WW1 and WWII.

Just off the coast is **Holy Island**, owned by the Samye Ling Tibetan Centre and used as a retreat, but day visits are allowed. Depending on tides, the **ferry** ([☑] 01770-600998; tomin10@btinternet.com; adult/child return £12/6; ⊙ May-Sep, by arrangement Tue & Fri winter) makes around seven daily trips from Lamlash (15 minutes) between May and September. The same folk also run mackerel-fishing expeditions (£25).

No dogs, bikes, alcohol or fires are allowed on Holy Island. A good walk to the top of the hill (314m) takes two or three hours return. You can stay at the **Holy Island Centre for World Peace & Health** ([☑] 01770-601100; www.holyisle.org; dm/s/d £28/47/72; ⊙ Apr-Oct). Prices include full (vegetarian) board.

🛏 Sleeping & Eating

★ Glenisle Hotel
HOTEL **££**
([☑] 01770-600559; www.glenislehotel.com; Shore Rd; s/d/superior d £83/128/167; 🐾) This stylish hotel offers great service and high comfort levels. Rooms are decorated with contemporary fabrics; the 'cosy' ones under the sloping ceiling upstairs are a little cheaper. All feel fresh and include binoculars for scouring the seashore; upgrade to a superior for the best views over the water. Downstairs is excellent pub food (mains £10 to £13; 8am to 0pm, reduced hours in winter), with Scottish classics and a good wine list.

Lilybank Guest House
B&B **££**
([☑] 01770-600230; www.lilybank-arran.co.uk; Shore Rd; s/d £50/80; [P] 🐾) Built in the 17th century, Lilybank retains its heritage but has been refurbished for 21st-century needs. Rooms are clean and comfortable, with one adapted for disabled use. The front ones have great views over Holy Island. Breakfast includes organic porridge, oak-smoked kippers and other Arran goodies.

★ Drift Inn
PUB **££**
([☑] 01770-600608; www.driftinnarran.com; Shore Rd; mains £10-18; ⊙ food noon-9pm; 🐾🐾) Recently refurbished, this is now the island's best pub, with a plush interior with leather chairs and a fireplace, as well as a fabulous beer garden – enjoy magnificent views from both across to Holy Island. Great bar food is on offer – upmarket fare with thoughtful vegetarian options – as well as Arran ales on tap and soul and blues on the stereo.

Isle of Islay

POP 3200

The home of some of the world's greatest and peatiest whiskies, the names of which reverberate on the tongue like a pantheon of Celtic deities, Islay (*eye*-lah) is a wonderfully friendly place whose welcoming inhabitants offset its lack of scenic splendour. The distilleries are well-geared up for visits; even if you're not a fan of single malt, the birdlife, fine seafood, turquoise bays and basking seals are ample reason to visit. Locals are among Britain's most genial: a wave or cheerio to passers-by is mandatory, and you'll soon find yourself unwinding to relaxing island pace. The only drawback is that the waves of well-heeled whisky tourists have induced many sleeping and eating options to raise prices to eye-watering levels.

🧭 Tours

Islay Sea Safaris
BOAT TOURS
([☑] 01496-840510; www.islayseasafari.co.uk) Customised tours (£25 to £30 per person per hour) by sea from Port Ellen to spot some or all of Islay and Jura's distilleries in a single day, as well as birdwatching trips, coastal exploration, and trips to Jura's remote west coast and the Corryvreckan whirlpool.

🎉 Festivals & Events

Fèis Ìle
MUSIC, WHISKY
(Islay Festival; www.islayfestival.com) A week-long celebration of traditional Scottish music and whisky at the end of May. Events include *ceilidhs,* pipe-band performances, distillery tours, barbecues and whisky tastings.

Islay Jazz Festival
MUSIC
(www.islayjazzfestival.co.uk) This three-day festival takes place over the second weekend in September. A varied line-up of international talent plays at various venues across the island.

ℹ Information

Islay Tourist Office ([☑] 01496-810254; The Square, Bowmore; ⊙ 10am-5pm Mon-Sat, noon-3pm Sun Easter-Oct, 10am-3pm Mon-Fri Nov-Mar)

ℹ Getting There & Away

There are two ferry terminals: Port Askaig on the east coast, and Port Ellen in the south. Islay airport lies midway between Port Ellen and Bowmore.

AIR

Loganair/FlyBe (www.loganair.co.uk) flies daily from Glasgow to Islay, while **Hebridean Air Services** (☑ 0845 805 7465; www.hebridean air.co.uk) operates twice daily Tuesday and Thursday from Oban to Colonsay and Islay.

BOAT

CalMac (www.calmac.co.uk) runs ferries from Kennacraig to Port Ellen or Port Askaig (person/car £6.45/32, 2 to 2¼ hours, three to five daily). On Wednesday and Saturdays in summer you can continue to Colonsay (£3.95/16.55, 1¼ hours) and Oban (£11.10/54, four hours).

ⓘ Getting Around

BICYCLE

There are various places to hire bikes, including **Islay Cycles** (☑ 07760-196592; www.islaycycles.co.uk; bikes per day/week from £15/60) in Port Ellen.

BUS

A bus links Ardbeg, Port Ellen, Bowmore, Port Charlotte, Portnahaven and Port Askaig (limited service on Sunday). Pick up a copy of the *Islay & Jura Public Transport Guide* from the tourist office.

CAR

D&N MacKenzie (☑ 01496-302300; www.carhireonislay.co.uk; Islay Airport) offers car hire from £32 a day and can meet ferries.

TAXI

There are various drivers; **Carol** (☑ 01496-302155; www.carols-cabs.co.uk) can take bikes.

Port Ellen & Around

Port Ellen is Islay's principal entry point. The coast stretching northeast is one of the loveliest parts of the island, where within three miles you'll find three of whisky's biggest names: Laphroaig, Lagavulin and Ardbeg (see boxed text, p276).

A pleasant drive or ride leads past the distilleries to ruined **Kildalton Chapel**, 8 miles from Port Ellen. In the kirkyard is the exceptional late-8th-century Kildalton Cross. There are carvings of biblical scenes on one side and animals on the other.

The kelp-fringed *skerries* (small rocky islands or reefs) of the **Ardmore Islands**, near Kildalton, are a wildlife haven and home to Europe's second-largest colony of common seals.

🛏 Sleeping & Eating

Kintra Farm   CAMPSITE, B&B **£**
(☑ 01496-302051; www.kintrafarm.co.uk; tent sites £6-8, plus adult/child £4/2, s/d £50/80; ☺ Apr-Sep; Ⓟ) At the southern end of Laggan Bay, 3.5 miles northwest of Port Ellen, Kintra is a basic but beautiful campsite on buttercup-sprinkled turf amid the dunes, with a sunset view across the beach. There's also B&B available.

★**Oystercatcher B&B**   B&B **££**
(☑ 01496-300409; www.islay-bedandbreakfast.com; 63 Frederick Cres; s/d £60/80; 🔊) Two beautifully decorated upstairs rooms with a maritime theme and water views make inviting Islay bases in this excellent B&B. Thoughtful breakfast options and a super-welcoming host add appeal. If you want to dine here, you can organise to order in a seafood platter.

Old Kiln Café   CAFE **£**
(☑ 01496-302244; www.ardbeg.com; Ardbeg; mains £5-11; ☺ 10am-4.30pm daily May-Sep, Mon-Sat Apr & Oct, Mon-Fri Nov-Mar) Housed in the former malting kiln at Ardbeg distillery, this cafe serves homemade soups, tasty light meals, heartier daily specials and a range of desserts, including traditional clootie dumpling (a rich steamed pudding filled with currants and raisins).

Bowmore

This attractive Georgian village was built in 1768 to replace the village of Kilarrow, which just had to go – it was spoiling the view from the laird's house. Its centrepieces are the Bowmore distillery (p276) and distinctive **Round Church** at the top of Main St, built in circular form to ensure that the devil had no corners to hide in. He was last seen in one of Islay's distilleries.

🛏 Sleeping & Eating

Bowmore distillery offers a tempting range of self-catering cottages around the centre.

Lambeth House   B&B **££**
(☑ 01496-810597; lambethguesthouse@tiscali.co.uk; Jamieson St; s/d £60/94; 🔊) Cheerily welcoming, and with smart refurbished rooms with top-notch en suite bathrooms, this is a sound option in the centre of town. Breakfasts are reliably good. Rooms vary substantially in size.

Islay, Jura & Colonsay

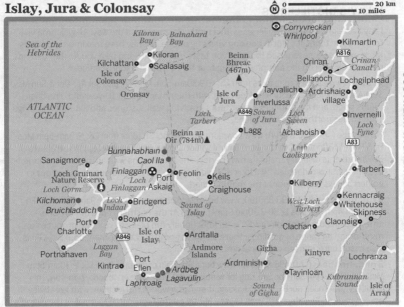

Bowmore House
B&B £££

(☑01496-810324; www.thebowmorehouse.co.uk; Shore St; s/d £75/150; 🅿🛜) This stately former bank offers plenty of character and super water views. It's top-level B&B here, with coffee machines in the rooms, an honesty minibar with bottles of wine and local ales, and plush king-sized beds. Rooms are spacious, high-ceilinged and light.

Harbour Inn
INN £££

(☑01496-810330; www.harbour-inn.com; The Square; s/d from £110/145; 🛜) The plush seven-room Harbour Inn, now owned by Bowmore whisky, is the poshest place in town. The restaurant (mains £19 to £26; open noon to 2pm and 6pm to 9pm) has harbour views and serves fresh local oysters, lobster and scallops, Islay lamb and Jura venison. It's tasty but feels a little overpriced.

Lochside Hotel
HOTEL £££

(☑01496-810244; www.lochsidehotel.co.uk; 19 Shore St; s/d £70/140; 🛜) Bedrooms at the Lochside are kitted out with chunky pine furniture, including one room adapted for wheelchair users. The conservatory dining room (mains £10 to £18; open 11am to 9pm) provides simple fare in generous portions with sweeping views over Loch Indaal, and the likeably boisterous bar boasts hundreds of single malts, including many rare bottlings.

Taste of Islay
DISTRO ££

(www.bowmore.com; School St; dishes £7-13; ⊙9am-5pm Mon-Sat, 11am-4pm Sun; 🛜) Alongside and owned by Bowmore distillery, this new spot offers appealing lunchtime fare, including good sandwiches and tasty seafood – local langoustine tails and other tempting morsels.

Port Charlotte and Around

Eleven miles from Bowmore, on the opposite shore of Loch Indaal, is attractive Port Charlotte.

👁 Sights & Activities

Museum of Islay Life
MUSEUM

(☑01496-850358; www.islaymuseum.org; Port Charlotte; adult/child £3/1; ⊙10.30am-4.30pm Mon-Fri Apr-Sep), Islay's long history is lovingly recorded in this museum, housed in an old church. Prize exhibits include an illicit still, 19th-century crofters' furniture, and a set of leather boots once worn by the horse that pulled the lawnmower at Islay House (so it wouldn't leave hoof prints on the lawn!).

ISLAY'S DISTILLERIES

Islay has eight working distilleries, with a ninth, Gartbreck, on the way. All welcome visitors and run tours. It's worth booking visits by phone, as they have maximum numbers. More expensive, specialised tours let you taste more malts and take you further behind the scenes. Pick up the pamphlet listing tour times from the tourist office.

Ardbeg (www.ardbeg.com; tours from £5; ⊗9.30am-5pm Mon-Fri, plus Sat Apr-Oct & Sun May-Sep) Ardbeg's iconic peaty whiskies start with their magnificent 10-year-old. The basic tour is good, and it also offers longer tours involving walks, stories and extended tastings. Three miles northeast of Port Ellen.

Bowmore (☑01496-810441; www.bowmore.com; School St; tours from £6; ⊗9am-5pm Mon-Fri & 9am-12.30pm Sat Oct-Mar, 9am-5pm Mon-Sat & noon-4pm Sun Apr-Sep) In the centre of Bowmore, this distillery malts its own barley. The tour begins with an overblown marketing video, but is redeemed by a look at (and taste of) the germinating grain laid out in golden billows on the floor of the malting shed.

Bruichladdich (☑01496-850190; www.bruichladdich.com; tours £5; ⊗9am-6pm Mon-Fri & 9.30am-4pm Sat, plus 12.30-3.30pm Sun Apr-Aug) At the northern edge of Port Charlotte, Bruichladdich (brook-laddy) is an infectiously fun place to visit and produces a mind-boggling range of bottlings; there's always some new experiment cooking. Gin is also made here, infused with local herbs.

Bunnahabhain (☑01496-840646; www.bunnahabhain.com; tours from £5; ⊗10am-5pm Mon-Sat, 11am-4pm Sun Apr-Sep, ring for winter hours) Pronounced 'boona-hah-ven', this distillery is 4 miles north of Port Askaig. It enjoys a wonderful location with great views across to Jura. The standard malt is very lightly peated compared to most of the island's whiskies.

Caol Ila (☑01496-302769; www.discovering-distilleries.com; tours from £6; ⊗9am-5pm daily mid-Apr–Aug, 9am-5pm Mon-Sat Sep-Oct, 10am-4pm Tue-Sat Nov–mid-Apr) Pronounced 'cull ee-lah', this distillery is a mile north of Port Askaig. It's a big, industrial set-up but enjoys a wonderful location with great views across to Jura. Tours are free if you sign up to Diageo's mailing list.

Kilchoman (☑01496-850011; www.kilchomandistillery.com; Rockfield Farm; tours from £6; ⊗10am-5pm Mon-Fri, plus Sat Apr-Oct) Likeable Kilchoman, set on a farm, is Scotland's second-smallest distillery, going into production in 2005. It grows and malts some of its own barley here and does its own bottling by hand. The tour is informative and the tasting generous. There's also a good cafe.

Lagavulin (www.discovering-distilleries.com; tours from £6; ⊗9am-7pm Mon-Fri, to 5pm Sat & Sun Jun-Sep, 9am-5pm daily Apr-May & Oct, 10am-4pm Mon-Sat Nov-Feb, 10am-4pm daily Mar) Peaty and powerful, this is one of the triumvirate of southern distilleries near Port Ellen. Tours are free if you sign up to Diageo's mailing list.

Laphroaig (www.laphroaig.com; tours from £6; ⊗9.45am-5pm daily Mar-Oct, 9.45am-4.30pm daily Nov & Dec, 9.45am-4.30pm Mon-Fri Jan-Feb) Famously peaty whiskies just outside Port Ellen. The 'Water to Whisky' tour (£82) is recommended – you see the water source, dig peat, have a picnic and try plenty of drams.

Islay Natural History Centre NATURE DISPLAY (www.islaynaturalhistory.org; Port Charlotte; adult/child £3/1.50; ⊗10am-4.30pm Mon-Fri May-Sep), next to the youth hostel, has displays explaining the island's natural history – with wildlife-watching advice – and hands-on exhibits for kids.

Six miles southwest of Port Charlotte the road ends at Portnahaven, a picturesque fishing village. For seal-spotting, you can't do better; there are frequently dozens of the portly beasts basking in the small harbour.

Seven miles north of Port Charlotte is Loch Gruinart Nature Reserve, where you can hear corncrakes in summer and see huge flocks of migrating ducks, geese and waders in spring and autumn; there's a hide with wheelchair access

🛏 Sleeping & Eating

Islay SYHA
HOSTEL £

(☎ 01496-850385; www.syha.org.uk; dm/q £19/80; ☺ Apr-Oct; @☎) This modern and comfortable hostel is housed in a former distillery building with views over the loch.

Port Mòr Campsite
CAMPSITE £

(☎ 01496-850441; www.islandofislay.co.uk; tent sites per adult/child £8/4; @☎) The sports field doubles as a campsite with toilets, showers, laundry and a children's play area in the main building. Open all year.

Distillery House
B&B ££

(☎ 01496-850495; mamak@btinternet.com; Port Charlotte; s £37.50, d £75-80; P ☎) For a taste of genuine islander hospitality at a fair price, head directly to this homely B&B on the right as you enter Port Charlotte. Set in part of the former Lochindaal distillery rooms are well-kept and most comfortable, with low beds. The cute single has sea views.

Port Charlotte Hotel
HOTEL £££

(☎ 01496-850360; www.portcharlottehotel.co.uk; s/d £115/190; P ☎☎) This lovely old Victorian hotel has stylish bedrooms with sea views, and a candlelit restaurant (mains £21 to £33; open 6.30pm to 9pm) serving local seafood, Islay beef, venison and duck. The bar (mains £10 to £16; meals noon to 2pm and 5.30pm to 8.30pm) also does great food, is well stocked with Islay malts and real ales, and has a nook at the back with a view over the loch towards the Paps of Jura.

Finlaggan

Loch Finlaggan, 3 miles southwest of Port Askaig, was once the most important settlement in the Hebrides, the central seat of power of the Lords of the Isles from the 12th to the 16th centuries. From the little island at the northern end of the loch they administered their island territories and entertained visiting chieftains in their great hall. Little remains now except the tumbled ruins of houses and a chapel, but the setting is beautiful and the history fascinating. A wooden walkway leads over the reeds and water lilies to the island, where information boards describe the remains.

Finlaggan Visitor Centre (www.finlaggan. com; adult/child £3/1; ☺10.30am-4.30pm Mon-Sat & 1.30-4.30pm Sun Apr-Sep) explains the site's history and archaeology. The island itself is open at all times.

Buses between Bowmore and Port Askaig stop at the road junction, from where it's a 15-minute walk to the loch.

Port Askaig & Around

Port Askaig is little more than a hotel, shop (with ATM), petrol pump and ferry pier, set in a picturesque nook halfway along the Sound of Islay. There are two distilleries within reach and ferry connections to the mainland and Jura, just across the strait.

Isle of Jura
POP 200

Jura lies long, dark and low off the coast like a vast Viking longship, its billowing sail the distinctive triple peaks of the Paps of Jura. A magnificently wild and lonely island, it's the perfect place to get away from it all – as George Orwell did in 1948. Orwell wrote his masterpiece *1984* while living at the remote farmhouse of Barnhill in the north of the island, describing it in a letter as 'a very un-get-at-able place'.

Jura takes its name from the Old Norse *dyr-a* (deer island) – an apt appellation, as the island supports a population of around 6000 red deer, outnumbering their human cohabitants by about 30 to one.

There's a shop but no ATM; you can get cashback with debit cards at the Jura Hotel.

◉ Sights

Apart from superb wilderness walking and wildlife-watching, there's not a whole lot to do except visit **Isle of Jura Distillery** (☎ 01496-820385; www.jurawhisky.com; Craighouse; tours from £6; ☺9.30am-4.30pm Mon-Sat Apr-Oct, 10am-2pm Mon-Fri Nov-Mar), near Craighouse, which includes a passenger return ferry ticket with each tour.

Jura Music Festival (www.juramusicfestival.com) in late September offers a convivial weekend of traditional Scottish folk music. The other big event is the **Isle of Jura Fell Race** (www.jurafellrace.org.uk) in late May, when around 250 hill runners converge on the island to race over the Paps.

🏃 Activities

There are few proper footpaths, and off-path exploration often involves rough going through giant bracken, knee-deep bogs and thigh-high tussocks. Most of the island is occupied by deer-stalking estates, and hill access may be restricted during the stalking season (July to February); the Jura Hotel can provide details.

Corryvreckan Viewpoint
WALKING

A good walk is to a viewpoint for the Corryvreckan Whirlpool. From the northern end of the public road (allow five to six hours for the 16-mile return trip from here) hike past Barnhill to Kinuachdrachd Farm (6 miles). Just before the farm a footpath forks left and climbs before traversing rough and boggy ground, a natural grandstand for viewing the turbulent waters of the Gulf of Corryvreckan.

If you have timed it right (check tide times at the Jura Hotel), you will see the whirlpool as a writhing mass of white water.

Evans Walk
WALKING

This is a stalkers' path leading 6 miles from the main road through a pass in the hills to a hunting lodge above the remote sandy beach at Glenbatrick Bay. The path leaves the road 4 miles north of Craighouse (just under a mile north of the bridge over the River Corran). Allow six hours for the 12-mile round trip.

The first 0.75 mile is hard going along an interwoven braid of faint, squelchy trails through lumpy bog; aim just left of the cairn on the near horizon. The path firms up and is easier to follow after you cross a stream. On the descent on the far side of the pass, look out for wild orchids and sundew, and keep an eye out for adders.

Paps of Jura
WALKING

Climbing the Paps is a truly tough hill walk over ankle-breaking scree that requires good fitness and navigational skills (allow eight hours for the 11 hard miles). One starting place is by the bridge over the River Corran, 3 miles north of Craighouse. The first peak you reach is Beinn a'Chaolais (734m), the second is Beinn an Oir (784m) and the third is Beinn Shiantaidh (755m). Most also climb Corra Bheinn (569m), before joining Evans Walk to return.

If you succeed in bagging all four, you can reflect on the fact that the record for the annual Paps of Jura fell race is just three hours!

🛏 Sleeping & Eating

Places to stay are very limited, so book ahead – don't rely on just turning up. As well as the hotel, there's a handful of B&B options and several self-catering cottages

that are let by the week (see www.juradevelopment.co.uk). One of these is **Barnhill** (☑ 01786-850274; www.escapetojura.com; per week from £600), where Orwell stayed at the far north of the island. It sleeps eight and is very remote: seven miles from the main road on a rough 4WD track, and 25 miles from the pub.

You can camp (£5 per person) in the field below the Jura Hotel; there's a new toilet and shower (small charge) block that walkers, yachties and cyclists can also use. From July to February, check on the deer-stalking situation before wild camping.

Jura Hotel
HOTEL ££

(☑ 01496-820243; www.jurahotel.co.uk; Craighouse; s £50-60, d £94-120; 🅿 �f0) The heart of Jura's community is this hotel, which is warmly welcoming and efficiently run. Rooms vary in size and shape, but all are renovated and feel inviting. The premier rooms – all of which have sea view – are just lovely, with understated elegance and polished modern bathrooms. You can eat (mains £9 to £14; noon to 2.30pm and 6.30pm to 8.30pm) in the elegant restaurant or the convivial pub.

Antlers
CAFE ££

(☑ 01496-820496; www.juradevelopment.co.uk; Craighouse; light meals £4-7; ⏱10am-5pm Mar-Oct, plus 6.30-8.30pm Fri) 🍽 This community-owned cafe has a craft shop and displays on Jura heritage. It does tasty home baking, sandwiches and the like, and is also open for more elaborate dinners on Fridays. Not licensed – £3 corkage.

ⓘ Getting There & Around

A car ferry shuttles between Port Askaig on Islay and Feolin on Jura (passenger/car/bicycle £1.60/8.55/free, five minutes, hourly Monday to Saturday, every two hours Sunday). There is no direct car-ferry connection to the mainland.

From April to September, **Jura Passenger Ferry** (☑ 07768-450000; www.jurapassengerferry.com; one-way £20; ⏱ mid-Apr–Sep) runs from Tayvallich on the mainland to Craighouse on Jura (one hour, one or two daily except Wednesday). Booking recommended.

The island's only **bus service** (☑ 01436-810200; www.garelochheadcoaches.co.uk) runs between the ferry slip at Feolin and Craighouse (20 minutes, three or four a day), timed to coincide with ferry arrivals and departures. One or two of the runs continue north as far as Inverlussa.

THE SCOTTISH MAELSTROM
....

The Gulf of Corryvreckan – the 1km-wide channel between the northern end of Jura and the island of Scarba – is home to one of the most notorious tidal whirlpools in the world.

On Scotland's west coast, the rising tide – the flood tide – flows northwards. As it moves up the Sound of Jura, to the east of the island, it is forced into a narrowing bottleneck jammed with islands and builds up to a greater height than the open sea to the west of Jura. As a result, millions of tonnes of seawater pour westwards through the Gulf of Corryvreckan at speeds of up to 8 knots – an average sailing yacht is going fast at 6 knots.

The **Corryvreckan Whirlpool** forms where this mass of moving water hits an underwater pinnacle, which rises from the 200m-deep seabed to within just 28m of the surface, and swirls over and around it. The turbulent waters create a magnificent spectacle, with white-capped breakers, standing waves, bulging boils and overfalls, and countless miniature maelstroms whirling around the main vortex.

Corryvreckan is at its most violent when a flooding spring tide, flowing west through the gulf, meets a westerly gale blowing in from the Atlantic. In these conditions, standing waves up to 5m high can form and dangerously rough seas extend more than 3 miles west of Corryvreckan, a phenomenon known as the Great Race.

You can see the whirlpool by making the long hike to the Corryvreckan Viewpoint at the northern end of Jura or by taking a boat trip from Islay or the Isle of Seil.

For tide times, see www.whirlpool-scotland.co.uk.

Hire bikes from **Jura Bike Hire** (☑ 07768-450000; www.jurabikehire.com; per day £12.50) in Craighouse.

Isle of Colonsay

POP 100

Legend has it that when St Columba set out from Ireland in 563, his first landfall was Colonsay. But on climbing a hill he found he could still see the distant coast of his homeland, and pushed on north to Iona, leaving behind only his name (Colonsay means 'Columba's Isle').

Colonsay is a little jewel-box of varied delights, none exceptional but each exquisite – an ancient priory, a woodland garden, a golden beach – set amid a Highland landscape in miniature: rugged, rocky hills, cliffs and sandy strands, machair and birch woods, even a trout loch.

◉ Sights & Activities

If tides are right, don't miss walking across the half-mile of cockleshell-strewn sand that links Colonsay to the smaller island of Oronsay. Here you can explore the 14th-century ruins of **Oronsay Priory**, one of Scotland's best-preserved medieval priories. There are two beautiful 15th-century stone crosses in the kirkyard, but the highlight is the collection of superb carved grave slabs in the Prior's House. The island is accessible

on foot for about 1½ hours either side of low tide; there are tide tables at the ferry terminal and hotel.

The **woodland garden** (☑ 01951-200211; www.colonsayestate.co.uk; Kiloran; ⊘ gardens dawn-dusk, walled garden 2-5pm Wed & noon-5pm Sat Easter-Sep) FREE at Colonsay House, 1.5 miles north of Scalasaig, is tucked in an unexpected fold of the landscape and is famous for its outstanding collection of hybrid rhododendrons and unusual trees. There's a cafe in the formal walled garden beside the house.

There are several good sandy beaches, but **Kiloran Bay** in the northwest, a scimitar-shaped strand of dark golden sand, is outstanding.

Back at Scalasaig, the **Colonsay Brewery** (☑ 01951-200190; www.colonsaybrewery.co.uk; Scalasaig; ⊘ ring for hours) offers you the chance to have a look at how it produces its handcrafted ales – the Colonsay IPA is a grand pint.

You can hire bikes from **Archie McConnell** (☑ 01951-200355; www.colonsaycottage.co.uk; Colnatarun Cottage, Kilchattan; per day/week £7.50/35) – book in advance and he'll deliver to the aerodrome or ferry.

🛏 Sleeping & Eating

Accommodation is limited and should be booked before coming to the island. Wild camping is allowed. See www.colonsay.org.uk for self-catering listings.

Backpackers Lodge
HOSTEL £

(☑ 01951-200312; www.colonsayestate.co.uk; Kiloran; dm/tw £19.50/50) Set in a former gamekeeper's house, this lodge is a 30-minute walk from the ferry (you can arrange to be picked up). Rates include use of the tennis court at nearby Colonsay House.

★ Colonsay Hotel
HOTEL ££

(☑ 01951-200316; www.colonsayestate.co.uk; s/d from £70/100; P 🛜) 🍴 This wonderfully laid-back hotel is set in an atmospheric old inn dating from 1750, a short walk uphill from the ferry pier. The stylish restaurant (mains £11 to £20) offers down-to-earth cooking using local produce as much as possible, from Colonsay oysters and lobsters to herbs and salad leaves from the Colonsay House gardens. The bar is a convivial melting pot of locals, guests, hikers, cyclists and yachties.

❶ Information

The ferry pier is at Scalasaig, the main village, with shop but no ATM. General information is available at the ferry waiting room, and at www.colonsay.org.uk.

Tiny **Colonsay Bookshop** (☑ 01951-200320; Scalasaig; ⊙ 3-5.30pm Mon-Sat, from noon Wed & Sat), in the same building as the microbrewery, has an excellent range of books on Hebridean history and culture.

❶ Getting There & Around

AIR

Hebridean Air Services (☑ 0845 805-7465; www.hebrideanair.co.uk) operates flights from Oban Airport (at North Connel) to Colonsay and Islay twice daily Tuesday and Thursday.

BOAT

CalMac (www.calmac.co.uk) runs from Oban to Colonsay (passenger/car £7/35.50, 2¼ hours, six weekly summer, three in winter). From April to October, on Wednesday and Saturdays, the ferry from Kennacraig to Islay continues to Colonsay and on to Oban. A day trip from Islay allows you six to seven hours on the island; the return fare from Islay to Colonsay per passenger/car is £7.90/33.10. A local minibus offers hop-on/hop-off service for day trippers.

OBAN & MULL

Oban
POP 8600

Oban, main gateway to many of the Hebridean islands, is a peaceful waterfront town on a delightful bay, with sweeping views to Kerrera and Mull. OK, that first bit about peaceful is true only in winter; in summer the town centre is jammed with traffic and crowded with holidaymakers and travellers headed for the islands. But the setting is still lovely, and Oban's brilliant seafood restaurants are marvellous places to be as the sun sets over the bay.

⊙ Sights

McCaig's Tower
HISTORIC BUILDING

(cnr Laurel & Duncraggan Rds; ⊙ 24hr) Crowning the hill above town is this Colosseum-like Victorian folly, commissioned in 1890 by local worthy John Stuart McCaig, with the philanthropic intention of providing work for unemployed stonemasons. To reach it on foot, make the steep climb up Jacob's Ladder (a flight of stairs) from Argyll St; the bay views are worth the effort.

Oban Distillery
DISTILLERY

(☑ 01631-572004; www.discovering-distilleries.com; Stafford St; tours £7.50; ⊙ noon-4.30pm Dec-Feb, 9.30am-5pm Mar-Jun & Oct-Nov, 9.30am-7.30pm Mon-Fri & 9.30am-5pm Sat & Sun Jul-Sep) This handsome distillery has been producing since 1794. The standard guided tour leaves regularly (worth booking) and includes a dram and a taste straight from the cask. Specialist tours (£35) run once daily in summer. Even without a tour, it's still worth a look at the small exhibition in the foyer.

Dunollie
CASTLE, MUSEUM

(☑ 01631-570550; www.dunollie.org; Dunollie Rd; adult/child £4/2; ⊙ 10am-4pm Mon-Sat & 1-4pm Sun Easter-Oct) A pleasant 1-mile stroll along the coast road leads to Dunollie Castle, built by the MacDougalls of Lorn in the 13th century and unsuccessfully besieged for a year during the 1715 Jacobite rebellion. It's very much a ruin, but the nearby 1745 House – seat of Clan MacDougall – is an intriguing museum of local and clan history. Ongoing improvement works are in progress.

Pulpit Hill VIEWPOINT

An excellent viewpoint to the south of Oban Bay; the footpath to the summit starts by Maridon B&B on Dunuaran Rd.

Activities

A tourist-office leaflet lists various local bike rides, including a 16-mile route to the Isle of Seil. Hire bikes from **Oban Cycles** (01631-566033; www.obancycleshop.com; 87 George St; per day/week £15/70; 10am-5pm Tue-Sat, plus Sun in summer), which also offers same-day repairs. Various operators offer boat trips to spot seals and other marine wildlife, departing from North Pier (adult/child £10/5).

Puffin Adventures DIVING

(01631-566088; www.puffin.org.uk; Port Gallanach) If you fancy exploring the underwater world, Puffin Adventures offers a 1½-hour package (£69) for complete beginners.

Sea Kayak Oban KAYAKING

(01631-565310; www.seakayakoban.com; Argyll St; 10am-5pm Mon-Fri, 9am-5pm Sat, 10am-4pm Sun) Has a well-stocked shop, great route advice and sea-kayaking courses, including an all-inclusive two-day intro for beginners (£170 per person). Also full equipment rental for experienced paddlers – trolley your kayak from the shop to the ferry (kayaks carried free) to visit the islands.

Tours

Basking Shark Scotland BOAT TRIP

(07975-723140; www.baskingsharkscotland. co.uk; May-Sep) Runs entertaining boat trips with optional snorkelling, focussed on finding and observing basking sharks – the world's second-largest fish – and other notable marine species.

Coastal Connection BOAT TOURS

(01631-565833; www.coastal-connection.co.uk) Runs wildlife-spotting trips, fast day trips to Tobermory, and custom excursions to many west coast islands.

West Coast Tours COACH TOURS

(01631-566809; www.westcoasttours.co.uk; 1 Queens Park Pl; Apr-Oct) Offers a Three Isles day trip (adult/child £60/30, 10 hours, daily) from Oban that visits Mull, Iona and Staffa. The crossing to Staffa is weather dependent. Without Staffa, the trip is £40/20 and takes eight hours. Also runs various trips on Mull.

Festivals & Events

Highlands and Islands Music & Dance Festival TRADITIONAL MUSIC

(www.obanfestival.org) At the beginning of May, this is an exuberant celebration of traditional Scottish music and dance. The town packs out.

West Highland Yachting Week SAILING

(www.whyw.co.uk) In late July/early August, Oban becomes the focus of one of Scotland's biggest yachting events. Hundreds of yachts cram into the harbour and the town's bars are jammed with thirsty sailors.

Argyllshire Gathering HIGHLAND GAMES

(www.obangames.com; adult/child £10/5) Held in late August, this is a key event in the Highland Games calendar and includes a prestigious pipe-band competition.

Sleeping

Despite having lots of B&B accommodation, Oban's beds can still fill up quickly in July and August, so try to book ahead. If you can't find a bed in Oban, consider Connel, 4 miles north.

Oban SYHA HOSTEL £

(01631-562025; www.syha.org.uk; Corran Esplanade; dm/tw £21/48; P@🖀) Set in a grand Victorian villa on the Esplanade, 0.75 miles north of the train station, this hostel is modernised to a high standard with comfy wooden bunks, lockers, good showers and a lounge with great views across Oban Bay. All dorms are en suite; the neighbouring lodge has three- and four-bedded rooms. Breakfast available

Oban Backpackers HOSTEL £

(01631-562107; www.obanbackpackers.com; Breadalbane St; dm £15-18; @🖀) Simple, colourful, relaxed and casual, this place has plenty of atmosphere. Dorms are cheap and cheerful – price varies according to the number of bunks – and there's a sociable downstairs lounge. Breakfast available for £2. Don't confuse with similarly named (also decent) Backpackers Plus situated across the road.

Jeremy Inglis Hostel HOSTEL £

(01631-565065; www.jeremyinglishostel.co.uk; 21 Airds Cres; dm/s £17/25; 🖀🍽) More eccentric B&B than a hostel – most 'dorms' have only two or three beds, and might come decorated with colourful duvets, original artwork, books, fresh flowers and more. It's

Oban

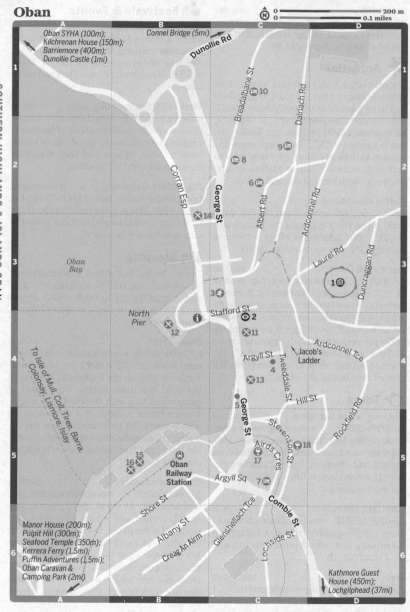

N
0 _____ 200 m
0 _____ 0.1 miles

Oban SYHA (100m);
Kilchrenan House (150m);
Barriemore (400m);
Dunollie Castle (1mi)

Connel Bridge (5mi)

Dunollie Rd

Breadalbane St

Dalriach Rd

Corran Esp

George St

Albert Rd

Ardconnel Rd

Laurel Rd

Duncraggan Rd

Oban
Bay

North
Pier

Stafford St

Argyll St

Jacob's
Ladder

Ardconnel Tce

Tweeddale St

Hill St

George St

Stevenson St

Rockfield Rd

To Isle of Mull,
Coll, Tiree, Barra,
Colonsay, Lismore, Islay

Oban
Railway
Station

Airds
Cres

Argyll Sq

Shore St

Albany St

Creag An Airm

Glenshellach Tce

Comble St

Lochside St

Manor House (200m);
Pulpit Hill (300m);
Seafood Temple (350m);
Kerrera Ferry (1.5mi);
Puffin Adventures (1.5mi);
Oban Caravan &
Camping Park (2mi)

Kathmore Guest
House (450m);
Lochgilphead (37mi)

grungy, friendly, decent value and there's a good kitchen/eating area. It won't be for everyone but the spirit of hospitality thrives here. Breakfast is included and features homemade jams. Wi-fi doesn't reach the rooms.

Oban Caravan & Camping Park CAMPSITE £

(☎ 01631-562425; www.obancaravanpark.com; Gallanachmore Farm; tent/campervan sites £15/20; ☺ Apr-Oct; ☻) This spacious campsite has a superb location overlooking the Sound of

Oban

Sights
1 McCaig's Tower........D3
2 Oban Distillery........C4

Activities, Courses & Tours
3 Oban Cycles........C3
4 Sea Kayak Oban........C4
5 West Coast Tours........C4

Sleeping
6 Heatherfield House........C2
7 Jeremy Inglis Hostel........C5
8 Oban Backpackers........C2
9 Old Manse Guest House........C2
10 Sandvilla Guesthouse........C1

Eating
11 Cuan Mór........C4
12 Ee-usk........B4
13 Kitchen Garden........C4
14 Oban Chocolate Company........B3
15 Oban Seafood Hut........B5
16 Waterfront Fishhouse Restaurant........B5

Drinking & Nightlife
17 Aulay's Bar........C5
18 Lorne Bar........C5

Kerrera, 2.5 miles south of Oban (two buses on schooldays). A one-person tent with no car is £8. No prebooking – it's first come, first served. There are also bungalows and camping pods that sleep up to four (for two/four £40/50).

★ **Old Manse Guest House** B&B ££
(☎01631-564886; www.obanguesthouse.co.uk; Dalriach Rd; s/d £65/90; P 📶) Set on the hillside above town, this B&B commands magnificent views over to Kerrera and Mull. It's run with genuine enthusiasm, and the owners are constantly adding thoughtful new features to the bright, cheerful rooms – think binoculars, DVDs, poetry, corkscrews and tartan hot-water bottles – and breakfast menus, with special diets catered for.

Barriemore GUESTHOUSE ££
(☎01631-566356; www.barriemore-hotel.co.uk; Corran Esplanade; s from £70, d £99-119; ⊙Mar-Nov; P 📶) With a grand location overlooking the entrance to Oban Bay, this place offers top-notch hospitality with tartan carpets on the stairs and plump Loch Fyne kippers on the breakfast menu. Rooms are all spacious, recently refurbished and full of features. The front ones – pricier but enormous – have fabulous vistas; there's also a great family suite up the back and solicitous service.

Sandvilla Guesthouse B&B ££
(☎01631-564483; www.holidayoban.co.uk; Breadalbane St; s/d £50/70; P 📶) Upbeat and modern, the rooms in this welcoming spot – all en suite by the time you read this – are lovely, bright and very well-kept. Enthusiastic owners guarantee a personal welcome and service with a smile. It's our favourite of several options on this street.

Kilchrenan House B&B ££
(☎01631-562663; www.kilchrenanhouse.co.uk; Corran Esplanade; s £50, d £70-110; P 📶) You'll get a warm welcome at the Kilchrenan, an elegant Victorian villa built for a textile magnate in 1883. Most of the rooms have views across Oban Bay, but rooms 5 and 9 are the best: room 5 has a huge free-standing bath tub, perfect for soaking weary bones.

Heatherfield House B&B ££
(☎01631-562806; www.heatherfieldhouse.co.uk; Albert Rd; s £50, d £80-115; P 📶) Welcoming Heatherfield House occupies a converted 1870s rectory set in extensive grounds and has six spacious rooms. One comes complete with fireplace, sofa and a view over the garden to the harbour.

Kathmore Guest House B&B ££
(☎01631-562104; www.kathmore.co.uk; Soroba Rd; s £35-50, d £60-75; P 📶) Warmly welcoming, this B&B combines traditional Highland hospitality and hearty breakfasts with a wee touch of boutique flair in its stylish bedspreads and colourful artwork. It's actually two adjacent houses combined, each has a comfortable lounge and shares an outdoor garden deck where you can enjoy a glass of wine on those long summer evenings. It's a 10-minute stroll from the centre.

Manor House HOTEL £££
(☎01631-562087; www.manorhouseoban.com; Gallanach Rd; r £170-235; P 📶 🐾) Built in 1780 for the Duke of Argyll, the old-fashioned Manor House is now one of Oban's finest hotels. It has small but elegant Georgian-style rooms – some with sea views – a posh bar frequented by local and visiting yachties, and a fine restaurant serving Scottish and

French cuisine. Children under 12 years are not welcome.

Eating

Oban Seafood Hut
SEAFOOD £

(www.obanseafoodhut.co.uk; Railway Pier; mains £3-13; ⊙10am-6pm Mar-Oct) If you want to savour superb Scottish seafood without the expense of an upmarket restaurant, head for Oban's famous seafood stall – it's the green shack on the quayside near the ferry terminal. Here you can buy fresh and cooked seafood to take away – excellent prawn sandwiches (£2.95), dressed crab (£4.95), and fresh oysters (95p each).

Kitchen Garden
DELI, CAFE £

(☑01631-566332; www.kitchengardenoban.co.uk; 14 George St; light meals £4-8; ⊙9am-5.30pm Mon-Sat, 10am-4.30pm Sun) A deli packed with delicious picnic food. Also has a great little cafe – good coffee, scones, cakes, homemade soups and sandwiches.

Oban Chocolate Company
SWEETS, CAFE £

(☑01631-566099; www.obanchocolate.co.uk; 34 Corran Esplanade; hot chocolate £3; ⊙10am-5pm Mon-Sat, 11am-5pm Sun Easter-Sep, shorter hours in winter, closed Jan; 📶) Specialises in hand-crafted chocolates (you can watch them being made) and also has a cafe serving excellent coffee and hot chocolate (try the chilli chocolate for a kick in the tastebuds), with big leather sofas in a window with a view of the bay. Open to 9pm Thursday to Saturday in July and August.

Waterfront Fishouse Restaurant
SEAFOOD ££

(☑01631-563110; www.waterfrontoban.co.uk; Railway Pier; mains £12-20; ⊙noon-2.15pm & 5.30-9.30pm Sun-Fri, noon-9.30pm Sat; 📶📶) Housed on the top floor of a converted seamen's mission, the Waterfront's stylish, unfussy decor in burgundy and brown, with dark wooden furniture, does little to distract from the superb seafood freshly landed at the quay just a few metres away. The menu ranges from classic haddock and chips to fresh oysters, scallops and langoustines. Best to book for dinner.

Cuan Mór
BISTRO ££

(☑01631-565078; www.cuanmor.co.uk; 60 George St; mains £9-14; ⊙10am-10pm; 📶📶) This always-busy bar and bistro brews its own beer, and sports a no-nonsense menu of old favourites – from haddock and chips or homemade lasagne to sausage and mash

with onion gravy – spiced with a few more sophisticated plates such as squat lobster carbonara, and a decent range of vegetarian dishes. And the sticky toffee pudding is not to be missed!

★ Seafood Temple
SEAFOOD £££

(☑01631-566000; www.obanseafood.com; Gallanach Rd; mains £16-25; ⊙6.15-8.30pm Apr-Sep, 6.15-8.30pm Wed-Sat Oct-Dec & Feb-Mar) 🌿 Locally sourced seafood is the god that's worshipped at this tiny temple, a former park pavilion with glorious views over the bay. Oban's smallest restaurant serves up whole lobster cooked to order, baked crab, plump langoustines and a seafood platter (£75 for two) which offers a taste of everything. Dinner is in two sittings, at 6.15pm and 8.30pm; bookings essential.

Ee-usk
SEAFOOD £££

(☑01631-565666; www.eeusk.com; North Pier; mains £12-24; ⊙noon-3pm & 5.45-9.30pm; 📶) 🌿 Bright and modern Ee'usk (it's how you pronounce *iasg*, Gaelic for 'fish') occupies a prime pier location. Floor-to-ceiling windows allow diners on two levels to enjoy sweeping views while sampling locally caught seafood ranging from fragrant fish cakes to langoustines and succulent fresh fish. A bevy of serving staff make it swift and efficient, and they make an effort to give you the best view available.

It's a little pricey, perhaps, but both food and location are first class. Closes 9pm in winter.

Drinking

Lorne Bar
PUB

(www.thelornebar.co.uk; Stevenson St; ⊙noon-11pm Mon-Wed, noon-2am Thu-Sun; 📶) A traditional pub with a lovely old island bar, polished brass fittings, stained glass and a beer garden, the Lorne serves local real ales, as well as above-average pub grub. You'll like it better before the disco lights come up on Friday and Saturday nights.

Aulay's Bar
PUB

(☑01631-562596; www.aulaysbar.com; 8 Airds Cres; ⊙11.30am-11pm) An authentic Scottish pub, Aulay's is cosy and low-ceilinged, its walls covered with old photographs of Oban ferries and other ships. It pulls in a mixed crowd of locals and visitors with its warm atmosphere and wide range of malt whiskies.

ℹ️ Information

Lorn & Islands District General Hospital
(☑01631-567500; Glengallan Rd) Southern end of town.

Oban Library (www.argyll-bute.co.uk; 77 Albany St; ☺10am-1pm & 2-7pm Mon & Wed, to 6pm Thu, to 5pm Fri, 10am-1pm Sat; 📶) Free internet.

Oban Tourist Office (☑01631-563122; www.oban.org.uk; 3 North Pier; ☺10am-5pm daily, extended weekday hours Apr-Oct) Helpful; on the waterfront.

ℹ️ Getting There & Away

Bus, train and ferry terminals are grouped conveniently together on the southern edge of the bay.

AIR

Hebridean Air (☑0845 805 7465; www.hebrideanair.co.uk) flies from Connel airfield to the islands of Coll, Tiree, Colonsay and Islay.

BOAT

CalMac (☑0800 066 5000; www.calmac.co.uk) ferries link Oban with the islands of Mull, Coll, Tiree, Lismore, Colonsay, Barra and South Uist. See each island section for details. Ferries to the Isle of Kerrera depart from a separate jetty, 2 miles southwest of Oban town centre.

BUS

Scottish Citylink (www.citylink.co.uk) operates most intercity coaches, while **West Coast Motors** (www.westcoastmotors.co.uk) runs local and regional services.

Fort William (via Appin and Ballachulish) £9.40, 1½ hours, two Monday to Saturday

Glasgow (via Inveraray and Arrochar) £23.10, 3¼ hours, three daily

TRAIN

Oban is at the terminus of a scenic route that branches off the West Highland line at Crianlarich. The train isn't much use for travelling north – to reach Fort William requires a long detour (3¾ hours). Take the bus instead.

Glasgow £22, three hours, three daily

Tyndrum/Crianlarich £10.70, one hour, three daily

ℹ️ Getting Around

Hazelbank Motors (☑01631-566476; www.obancarhire.co.uk; Lynn Rd; per day/week from £40/225; ☺8.30am-5pm Mon-Sat) hires cars.

Around Oban

Isle of Kerrera

POP 50

Some of the area's best walking is on Kerrera, which faces Oban across the bay. There's a 6-mile circuit (allow three hours), which follows tracks or paths and offers the chance to spot wildlife such as Soay sheep, wild goats, otters, golden eagles, peregrine falcons, seals and porpoises. At the island's southern end, there's a ruined castle.

Kerrera Bunkhouse (☑01631-566367; www.kerrerabunkhouse.co.uk; Lower Gylen; dm £15; ☺Easter-Sep) is a charming seven-bed bothy in a converted 18th-century stable a 2-mile walk south from the ferry. Booking ahead is recommended. You can get snacks and light meals at the neighbouring **Tea Garden** (☑01631-570223; www.kerrerabunkhouse.co.uk; Lower Gylen; light meals £3-9; ☺10.30am-4.30pm Easter-Sep).

There's a daily **passenger ferry** (☑01631-563665; www.kerrera-ferry.co.uk; ☺half-hourly 10.30am-12.30pm & 2-6pm Easter-Oct, plus 8.45am Mon-Sat, 6-7 daily Nov-Easter) from Gallanach, 2 miles southwest of Oban town centre (adult/child return £4.50/2, bicycle free, 10 minutes). You need to slide a signboard to summon the ferry.

Isle of Seil

POP 600

The small island of Seil, 10 miles southwest of Oban, is best known for its connection to the mainland – the graceful **Bridge over the Atlantic**, designed by Thomas Telford and opened in 1793.

◉ Sights

On the west coast is the pretty conservation village of **Ellenabeich**, with whitewashed cottages and rainwater barrels backed by a wee harbour and rocky cliffs. It was built to house local slate workers, but the industry collapsed in 1881 when the sea broke into the main quarry – the flooded pit can still be seen. The **Scottish Slate Islands Heritage Trust** (☑01852-300449; www.slateislands.org.uk; Ellenabeich; ☺10.30am-4.30pm Apr-Oct) **FREE** displays fascinating old photographs illustrating life in the village.

Coach tours flock to **Highland Arts** (☑ 01852-300273; www.highlandarts.co.uk; Ellenabeich; admission free; ⊘ 9am-7pm Apr-Sep, 9am-5pm Oct-Mar), a gift shop and a shrine to the eccentric output of the late 'poet, artist and composer' C John Taylor. Please, try to keep a straight face.

Just offshore is small **Easdale Island**, which has more old slate-workers' cottages and an interesting **folk museum** (☑ 01852-300370; www.easdalemuseum.org; adult/child £2.50/50p; ⊘ 11am-4.30pm Apr–mid-Oct, to 5pm Jul & Aug) with displays about the slate industry and social history. Climb to the top of the island (a 38m peak) for great views of the surrounding area. Confusingly, Ellenabeich is also referred to as Easdale, so 'Easdale Harbour', for example, is on the Seil side.

Anyone who fancies their hand at ducks and drakes should attend the **World Stone-Skimming Championships** (www.stoneskimming.com), held each year in an old quarry on the last Sunday in September.

A ferry hop from Seil's southern end takes you to neighbouring **Isle of Luing**, a quiet backwater with no real sights but appealing for wildlife walks and easygoing bike rides.

🏃 Activities

Sea Kayak Scotland   KAYAKING
(☑ 01852-300770; www.seakayakscotland.com; courses per person £80) Hire, instruction and guided sea kayaking trips run by an experienced operator.

👉 Tours

Sea.fari Adventures   BOAT TOURS
(☑ 01852-300003; www.seafari.co.uk; Ellenabeich; ⊘ Apr-Oct) Runs a series of exciting boat trips in high-speed rigid inflatables to Corryvreckan whirlpool (adult/child £38/29; call for dates of 'Whirlpool Specials', when the tide is at its strongest), as well as three-hour summer whale-watching (£48/36). There are also cruises to Iona and Staffa (£75/55), a weekly day trip to Colonsay (£48/36), plus trips to the remote Garvellach Islands (£48/36). Minimum of six out of season.

Sealife Adventures   BOAT TOURS
(☑ 01631-571010; www.sealife-adventures.com; 3-/4-/5-hour trip £49/58/65) Exciting boat trips, based on the eastern side of the island near the bridge. It has a large, comfortable boat offering wildlife cruises with knowledgeable guides and trips to the Corryvreckan whirlpool.

🍴 Eating

Oyster Bar   PUB
(www.seilislandpub.co.uk; Ellenabeich; half-dozen oysters £8; ⊘ food noon-2.15pm & 6-8pm, closed Mon evening; 🐾) This cute pub has a snug interior and a great back deck overlooking the water. With Fyne ales on tap and local oysters and other seafood, it's a great venue for a meal or drink.

ℹ Getting There & Around

West Coast Motors (www.westcoastmotors.co.uk) Bus 418 runs four times a day, except Sunday, from Oban to Ellenabeich (£3, 45 minutes) and on to North Cuan (£3, 53 minutes) for the ferry to Luing.

Easdale Ferry (☑ 0631-562125; http://seil.oban.ws/) Daily passenger-only ferry service from Ellenabeich to Easdale Island (£1.80 return, bicycles free, five minutes, every 30 minutes).

Luing Ferry (http://seil.oban.ws/; ⊘ return per person/car £1.80/7.20) Departs every 30 minutes for the three-minute trip.

Isle of Mull
POP 2800

From the rugged ridges of Ben More and the black basalt crags of Burg to the blinding white sand, rose-pink granite and emerald waters that fringe the Ross, Mull can lay claim to some of the finest and most varied scenery in the Inner Hebrides. Noble birds of prey soar over mountain and coast, while the western waters provide good whale-watching. Add a lovely waterfront 'capital', an impressive castle, the sacred island of Iona and easy access from Oban, and you can see why it's sometimes impossible to find a spare bed on the island.

👉 Tours

Mull's varied landscapes and habitats offer the chance to spot some of Scotland's rarest and most dramatic wildlife, including sea eagles, golden eagles, otters, dolphins and whales. Numerous operators offer walking or road trips to see them.

Staffa Tours   BOAT TOURS
(☑ 07831-885985; www.staffatours.com) Runs boat trips from Fionnphort to Staffa (adult/child £30/15, 2½ hours, daily April to October), or Staffa plus the Treshnish Isles (£55/27.50, five hours, Sunday to Friday May to July). It has options ex-Oban.

Mull, Coll & Tiree

Turus Mara BOAT TOURS
([☎]08000 858786; www.turusmara.com) Offers trips from Ulva Ferry in central Mull to Staffa and the Treshnish Isles (adult/child £57.50/29, 6½ hours), with an hour ashore on Staffa and two hours on Lunga, where you can see seals, puffins, kittiwakes, razorbills and many other species of seabird. It will do pick-ups from the Craignure ferry terminal.

Sea Life Surveys WILDLIFE WATCHING
([☎]01688-302916; www.sealifesurveys.com; Ledaig) Whale-watching trips head from Tobermory harbour to the waters north and west of Mull. An all-day whale-watch gives up to seven hours at sea (£80), and has a 95% success rate for sightings. The four-hour Wildlife Adventure cruise (adult/child £50/40) is better for young kids. Shorter seal-spotting excursions are also available.

Mull Wildlife Expeditions WILDLIFE WATCHING
([☎]01688-500121; www.scotlandwildlife.com; Ulva Ferry) Full-day Land Rover tours of the island with the chance of spotting red deer, golden eagles, peregrine falcons, white-tailed sea eagles, hen harriers, otters and perhaps dolphins and porpoises. Cost includes pick-up from accommodation or ferry, picnic lunch

and binoculars. Possible as a day trip from Oban.

Mull Magic WALKING TOURS
([☎]01688-301213; www.mullmagic.com) Offers guided walking tours in the Mull countryside to spot eagles, otters, butterflies and other wildlife, as well as customised tours. Check the website for the different itineraries available.

West Coast Tours BUS TOURS
([☎]01631-566809; www.westcoasttours.co.uk; tours £40-60) Various bus-and-boat day trips from Oban to Mull, with options that include Iona and Staffa.

★ Festivals & Events

Mull Music Festival MUSIC
(www.mishnish.co.uk) Last weekend of April; four days of foot-stomping traditional Scottish and Irish folk music at Tobermory's pubs.

Mendelssohn on Mull MUSIC
(www.mendelssohnonmull.com) A week-long festival of classical music in early July.

Mull Rally MOTORSPORT
(www.mullrally.org) Part of the Scottish Rally Championship, with around 150 cars

involved. Public roads are closed for parts of the early-October weekend.

ℹ Information

There's a bank with ATM in Tobermory, otherwise you can get cashback with a purchase from Co-op food stores.

Craignure Tourist Office (☎ 01680-812377; ⏰ 8.30am-5pm Mon-Sat, 10am-5pm Sun, to 7pm Jul & Aug) Opposite the ferry slip.

Explore Mull (☎ 01688-302875; www.explore-mull.com; Ledaig, Tobermory; ⏰ 9am-5pm Easter-Oct, to 7pm Jul-Aug; 🖥) In Tobermory car park. Local information, books all manner of island tours, hires bikes and has internet access.

ℹ Getting There & Away

Three **CalMac** (www.calmac.co.uk) car ferries link Mull with the mainland.

Lochaline to Fishnish (£3.30/14.45, 15 minutes, at least hourly) On the east coast of Mull.

Oban to Craignure (passenger/car £5.55/49.50, 40 minutes, every two hours) The busiest route – booking advised for cars.

Tobermory to Kilchoan (£5.30/27.50, 35 minutes, seven daily Monday to Saturday, plus five Sunday May to August) Links to the Ardnamurchan peninsula.

ℹ Getting Around

BICYCLE

You can hire bikes for around £15 per day from various places around the island, including Explore Mull in Tobermory.

BUS

West Coast Motors (☎ 01631-566809; www.westcoastmotors.co.uk) connects ferry ports and main villages. Its Discovery Day Pass (adult/child £15/7.50) is available from April to October and grants a day's unlimited bus travel.

Craignure to Fionnphort (£9/14 single/return, 1¼ hours, three to four Monday to Saturday, one Sunday)

Craignure to Tobermory (single/return £7/10, one hour, four to seven daily)

Tobermory to Dervaig and Calgary (£3/5.10 single/return, two to four Monday to Saturday)

CAR

Almost all of Mull's road network consists of single-track roads. There are petrol stations at Craignure, Fionnphort, Salen and Tobermory. **Mull Self Drive** (☎ 01680-300402; www.mullselfdrive.co.uk) rents small cars for £45/237 per day/week.

Craignure & Around

There's not much to see at Craignure, but three miles south is **Duart Castle** (☎ 01680-812309; www.duartcastle.com; adult/child £5.75/2.85; ⏰ 10.30am-5pm daily May–mid-Oct, 11am-4pm Sun-Thu Apr), the ancestral seat of the Maclean clan, enjoying a spectacular position on a rocky outcrop overlooking the Sound of Mull. Originally built in the 13th century, it was abandoned for 160 years before a 1912 restoration. As well as the dungeons, courtyard and battlements with memorable views, there's a lot of clan history – pantomime boos go to Lachlan Cattanach, who took his wife on an outing to an island in the strait, then left her there to drown when the tide came in. A bus to the castle meets the Oban ferry but it's a pretty walk too.

🛌 Sleeping

There's a handful of places to stay within 10 minutes' walk of the ferry.

Shieling Holidays CAMPSITE £ (☎ 01680-812496; www.shielingholidays.co.uk; Craignure; tent sites & 2 people £18, dm/d/d with en suite £13.50/33/49.50, cottages from £66; ⏰ mid-Mar–Oct; 🅿🖥📶) Walking distance from the Oban ferry is this well-equipped campsite with great views. Most of the permanent accommodation, including the hostel dorms and toilet block (dribbly showers), consists of 'cottage tents' made from heavy-duty tarpaulin, which gives the place a bit of a PVC-fetish feel.

Tobermory

POP 1000

Mull's main town is a picturesque little fishing and yachting port with brightly painted houses arranged around a sheltered harbour. The children's TV program *Balamory* was set here, and while the series stopped filming in 2004, regular repeats mean that the town still swarms in summer with toddlers (and nostalgic teenagers) towing parents around (you can get a *Balamory* info sheet from tourist offices).

⊙ Sights & Activities

Whale-watching boat trips run out of Tobermory harbour.

WALKING ON MULL

More information on the following walks can be obtained from the tourist offices in Oban, Craignure and Tobermory.

Ben More

Mull's highest peak, and the only island Munro outside Skye, Ben More (966m) offers spectacular views of surrounding islands. A trail leads up the mountain from Loch na Keal, by the bridge on the B8035 eight miles southwest of Salen – see Ordnance Survey (OS) 1:50,000 map sheet 49. Return the same way or continue down the narrow ridge to the eastern top, A'Chioch, then descend to the road via Gleann na Beinn Fhada. The glen can be wet and there's not much of a path. The return trip is 6.5 miles; allow five hours.

Carsaig Arches

One of the most adventurous walks is along the coast west of Carsaig Bay to the natural rock formation of Carsaig Arches at Malcolm's Point. There's a good path below the cliffs most of the way, but near the arches the route climbs and then traverses a very steep slope above a vertical drop into the sea (not for the unfit or faint-hearted). You'll see spectacular rock formations on the way, culminating in the arches themselves: the 'keyhole', a freestanding rock stack, and the 'tunnel', a huge natural arch. The western entrance is hung with curtains of columnar basalt – an impressive place. The return trip is 8 miles – allow three to four hours' walking time plus at least an hour at the arches.

Hebridean Whale & Dolphin Trust WILDLIFE EXHIBITION
(01688-302620; www.whaledolphintrust.co.uk; 28 Main St; 10am-5pm Mon-Fri, 11am-4pm Sun Apr-Oct, 11am-5pm Mon-Fri Nov-Mar) FREE This place has displays, videos and interactive exhibits on whale and dolphin biology and ecology, and is a great place for kids to learn about sea mammals. It also provides information about volunteering and reporting sightings of whales and dolphins. Opening is rather variable.

Mull Museum MUSEUM
(01688-302603; www.mullmuseum.org.uk; Main St; admission by donation; 10am-4pm Mon-Fri plus most Sat Easter-Oct) Places to go on a rainy day include Mull Museum, which records the history of the island. There are interesting exhibits on crofting, and on the *Tobermory Galleon*, a ship from the Spanish Armada that sank in Tobermory Bay in 1588 and has been the object of treasure seekers ever since.

Marine Visitor Centre MUSEUM
(www.tobermorymarinevisitorcentre.com; Ledaig; admission by donation; 9am-5pm Easter-Oct) By the harbour car park, this museum has good information on the local marine environment, and little touch pools with crabs and the like for the kids.

An Tobar Arts Centre GALLERY
(01688-302211; www.antobar.co.uk; Argyll Tce; 10am-5pm Mon-Sat May-Sep, 10am-4pm Tue-Sat Mar-Apr & Oct-Dec) FREE An art gallery and exhibition space in a former primary school with a good vegetarian-friendly cafe and top water views.

Tobermory Distillery DISTILLERY
(01688-302647; www.tobermorymalt.com; Ledaig; tours £6; 10am-5pm) This bijou distillery was established in 1798. It doesn't always open winter weekends; phone to check or book. There are two lines here, the standard Tobermory and the lightly peated Ledaig.

Sleeping

Tobermory has dozens of B&Bs, but the place can still be booked solid any time from May through to August, especially at weekends.

Tobermory SYHA HOSTEL £
(01688-302481; www.syha.org.uk; Main St; dm/q £19/84; Mar-Oct;) Great location in a Victorian house right on the waterfront, with dorms and good triples and quads for families. Was up for sale at time of writing so its future is uncertain but hopefully will remain a hostel.

Tobermory Campsite
CAMPSITE £

(☑ 01688-302624; www.tobermory-campsite. co.uk; Newdale, Dervaig Rd; tent sites per adult/child £7.50/3; ☺ Mar-Oct; 🅿🕸) 🏳 A quiet, family-friendly campsite 1 mile west of town on the road to Dervaig. It also has a self-catering house and static caravans available. Credit/debit cards not accepted.

Cuidhe Leathain
B&B ££

(☑ 01688-302504; www.cuidhe-leathain.co.uk; Breadalbane St; r £85; 🕾) A handsome 19th-century house in the upper town, Cuidhe Leathain (coo-lane), which means Maclean's Corner, exudes a cosily cluttered Victorian atmosphere. The rooms are beautifully plush, with plunger coffee and decent teas, breakfasts will set you up for the rest of the day, and the owners are a fount of knowledge about Mull and its wildlife. Minimum two-night stay.

Harbour View
B&B ££

(☑ 01688-301111; www.tobermorybandb.com; 1 Argyll Tce; s £65, d £80-90; 🕾) This beautifully renovated fishering cottage is perched on the edge of Tobermory's 'upper town'. Exposed patches of original stone walls add a touch of character, while a new extension provides the family suite (two adjoining rooms with shared bathroom, sleeps four) with an outdoor terrace that enjoys breathtaking views across the harbour.

Sonas House
B&B ££

(☑ 01688-302304; www.sonashouse.co.uk; The Fairways, Erray Rd; s/d £110/125, apt from £90; 🅿🛜🕸) Here's a first – a B&B with a heated, indoor 10m swimming pool! Sonas is a large, modern house – follow signs to the golf course – offering luxury B&B in a beautiful setting with superb views over Tobermory Bay; ask for the 'Blue Poppy' bedroom, which has its own balcony. There's also a self-contained studio apartment with double bed.

Harbour Guesthouse
B&B ££

(☑ 01688-302209; www.harbourguesthouse-tobermory.com; 59 Main St; s/d £37.50/78; ☺ Mar-Nov; 🕾) On the harbourfront, this B&B is friendly and offers rooms that vary in size and shape. The ones with water view are small, those without the vistas larger. It's got more rooms than most so can be a good option when things are booked; also, there aren't too many single beds around Tobermory, but there are a couple of compact ones here.

★ Highland Cottage
HOTEL £££

(☑ 01688-302030; www.highlandcottage.co.uk; Breadalbane St; d £150-165; ☺ Apr-mid-Oct; 🅿🛜🕸) Antique furniture, four-poster beds, embroidered bedspreads, fresh flowers and candlelight lend this small hotel (only six rooms) an appealingly old-fashioned cottage atmosphere, but with all mod cons including cable TV, full-size baths and room service. There's also an excellent restaurant here (dinner £39.50), and the personable owners are experts in guest comfort.

✗ Eating & Drinking

Fish & Chip Van
FISH & CHIPS £

(☑ 01688-301109; www.tobermoryfishandchipvan. co.uk; Main St; mains £6-9; ☺ 12.30-9pm Mon-Sat Apr-Dec, plus Sun Jun-Sep, 12.30-7pm Mon-Sat Jan-Mar) If it's a takeaway you're after, you can tuck into some of Scotland's best gourmet fish and chips down on the waterfront. And where else will you find a chip van selling freshly cooked scallops?

Pier Café
CAFE £

(The Pier; light meals £6-9; ☺ 10am-5pm, to 9pm Fri & Sat) A cosy wee corner with local art on the walls, tucked beneath Café Fish at the north end of the village, the Pier serves great coffee and breakfast rolls, plus tasty lunches such as haddock and chips, pasta and sandwiches.

★ Café Fish
SEAFOOD ££

(☑ 01688-301253; www.thecafefish.com; The Pier; mains £13-24; ☺ 11am-3pm & 5.30-9.30pm mid-Mar-Oct) Seafood doesn't come much fresher than the stuff served at this warm and welcoming little restaurant overlooking Tobermory harbour – as its motto says, 'The only thing frozen here is the fisherman'! Langoustines and squat lobsters go straight from boat to kitchen to join rich Tuscan-style seafood stew, fat scallops, fish pie and catch-of-the-day on the daily-changing menu, where confident use of Asian ingredients adds an extra dimension.

Mishnish Hotel
PUB ££

(☑ 01688-302009; www.mishnish.co.uk; Main St; mains £13-18; ☺ food noon-2pm & 6-9pm; 🕾) 'The Mish' is a favourite hang-out for visiting yachties and a good place for a pint, or a meal at the restaurant. Wood-panelled and flag-draped, this is a good old traditional pub where you can listen to live folk music, toast your toes by the open fire or challenge the locals to a game of pool.

North Mull

The road from Tobermory west to Calgary cuts inland, leaving most of Mull's north coast wild and inaccessible. It continues through the settlement of Dervaig to the beach at Calgary. From here onwards you are treated to spectacular coastal views; it's worth doing the route in reverse from Grunart for the best vistas.

◉ Sights

Glengorm Castle GALLERY, PARK
(☑01688-302321; www.glengormcastle.co.uk; Glengorm; ⊙10am-5pm May-Aug) FREE A long, single-track road leads north for 4 miles from Tobermory to majestic Glengorm Castle, with views across the sea to Ardnamurchan, Rum and the Outer Hebrides. The castle outbuildings house an **art gallery** featuring local artists, a **farm shop**, and an excellent cafe (p292). The castle, which offers upmarket B&B, is not open to the public, but you're free to explore the beautiful grounds, where several good walks are signposted.

Old Byre Heritage Centre MUSEUM
(☑01688-400229; www.old-byre.co.uk; Dervaig; adult/child £4/2; ⊙10.30am-6.30pm Wed-Sun Easter-late Oct) The curious and cheerful Old Byre brings Mull's heritage and natural history to life through a series of tableaux and half-hour film shows. The prize for most bizarre exhibit goes to the 40cm-long model of a midge. The centre's tearoom serves good, inexpensive snacks, and there's a kids' outdoor play area.

Calgary Art in Nature GALLERY
(☑01688-400256; www.calgaryartinnature.co.uk; ⊙10.30am-5pm) ✦ Run with enthusiasm and vision, this place just back from Calgary beach, as well as offering great self-catering accommodation, is an excellent art space. On-site silversmiths and wood sculptors ply their trade in their workshops, while a luminous gallery exhibits high-quality work from local artists. Other pieces dot the woodland ramble on the hill behind. There's also a good **tearoom** (www.calgary.co.uk; light meals £5-9; ⊙10.30am-5pm; ☎).

Calgary Beach BEACH
Mull's best (and busiest) silver-sand beach, flanked by cliffs and with views out to Coll and Tiree, is about 12 miles west of Tobermory. And yes – this is the place from which Canada's more famous Calgary takes its name.

🛏 Sleeping & Eating

Calgary Bay Campsite CAMPSITE
FREE You can camp for free in a lovely setting at the southern end of the beach at Calgary Bay. There are no facilities other than the public toilets across the road; water comes from the stream.

Dervaig Hostel HOSTEL £
(☑01688-400491; www.mull-hostel-dervaig.co.uk; Dervaig; dm/q £18/60, ᴾ☎) Basic but very comfortable bunkhouse accommodation in Dervaig's village hall, with self-catering kitchen and sitting room.

★ Calgary Farmhouse SELF-CATERING £ £
(☑01688-400256; www.calgary.co.uk; Calgary; per wk summer £400-1275; ᴾ☎) ✦ This brilliant complex near Calgary beach offers a number of fantastic apartments, cottages and a farmhouse, sleeping from two to nine, beautifully designed and fitted out with timber furniture and wood-burning stoves. The Hayloft is spectacular, with noble oak and

---

THAR SHE BLOWS!

The North Atlantic Drift – a swirling tendril of the Gulf Stream – carries warm water into the cold, nutrient-rich seas off the Scottish coast, resulting in huge plankton blooms. Small fish feed on the plankton, and bigger fish feed on the smaller fish; this huge seafood smorgasbord attracts large numbers of marine mammals, from harbour porpoises and dolphins to minke whales and even – though sightings are rare – humpback and sperm whales.

There are dozens of operators around the coast offering **whale-watching** boat trips lasting from a couple of hours to all day; some have sighting success rates of 95% in summer.

While seals, porpoises and dolphins can be seen year-round, minke whales are migratory. The best time to see them is from June to August, with August being the peak month for sightings. The website of the **Hebridean Whale & Dolphin Trust** (www.whaledolphintrust.co.uk) has lots of information on the species you are likely to see, and how to identify them.

local art. We loved romantic Kittiwake (one/three days £100/225), a beautiful wooden camping cabin among the trees, with bay views, boat for a ceiling and chemical toilet below decks.

The larger ones go by the week in summer, but smaller ones are available for shorter stays.

Achnadrish
APARTMENT ££

(☑01688-400388; www.achnadrish.co.uk; Dervaig Rd; 1-bedroom apt per week £300, 3-bedroom apt per week £700; P🗲) Achnadrish is a sympathetically restored shooting lodge that offers self-catering accommodation in two units: the cute little one-bedroomed White Cabin sleeps two; the three-bedroom West Wing, a range of former servants' quarters, sleeps six. Both have fully fitted kitchens, while the latter also has a large lounge with woodburning stove. The house is halfway between Tobermory and Calgary beach.

Bellachroy
HOTEL ££

(☑01688-400225; www.thebellachroy.co.uk; Dervaig; s/d £70/100; P🗲🐾) The Bellachroy is an atmospheric 17th-century droving inn with six plain but comfortable bedrooms. The bar is a focus for local social life and serves decent, if somewhat overpriced, food.

Glengorm Castle
B&B, SELF-CATERING £££

(☑01688-302321; www.glengormcastle.co.uk; r £165-215; ☺mid-Feb–mid-Dec; P🗲) Bristling with turrets as a real castle should, this special spot enjoys an unforgettable location; huge windows frame green fields sloping down to the water. The interior is very attractive: 20th-century art instead of stags' heads. The five bedrooms are all different, with lots of space and character. The place is run by lively, genuinely friendly owners, and kids will have a ball running around the grounds.There are also various self-catering cottages available (£495 to £920 per week).

Glengorm Coffee Shop
CAFE £

(www.glengormcastle.co.uk; Glengorm; light meals £3-8; ☺10am-5pm May-Aug; 🗲) 🍴 Set in a cottage courtyard in the grounds of Glengorm Castle, this licensed cafe serves superb lunches (from noon to 4.30pm) – the menu changes daily, but includes sandwiches and salads (much of the salad veg is grown on the Glengorm estate), soups and tasty specials.

Am Birlinn
SCOTTISH ££

(☑01688-400619; www.ambirlinn.com; Penmore, Dervaig; mains £13-23; ☺6-9pm Wed-Sun, plus noon-2pm Wed-Sun May-Oct) 🍴 Occupying a spacious modern wooden building between Dervaig and Calgary, this is an interesting dining option. Locally caught crustaceans and molluscs are the way to go here, though there are burgers, venison and other meat dishes available. Free pick-up and drop-off from Tobermory or other nearby spots is offered.

Central Mull

The central part of the island, between the Craignure–Fionnphort road and the narrow isthmus between Salen and Gruline, contains the island's highest peak, Ben More (966m) and some of its wildest scenery.

In tiny Gruline is the mausoleum of Lachlan Macquarie, enlightened fifth governor of New South Wales (Australia) and a Mull native. It's a 500m walk off the main road in attractive farmland.

The narrow B8035 along the southern shore of Loch na Keal squeezes past impressive cliffs before cutting south towards Loch Scridain. About 1 mile along the shore from Balmeanach, where the road climbs away from the coast, is Mackinnon's Cave, a deep spooky fissure in basalt cliffs that was once used as a refuge by Celtic monks. A big, flat rock inside, known as Fingal's Table, may have been their altar.

There's a very basic campsite (☑01680-300403; per person £4) at Killiechronan, 0.5 miles north of Gruline (toilets and water a five-minute walk away), and wild camping options on the south shore of Loch na Keal below Ben More.

South Mull

The road from Craignure to Fionnphort climbs through wild and desolate scenery before reaching the southwestern part of the island, which consists of a long peninsula called the Ross of Mull. The Ross has a spectacular south coast lined with black basalt cliffs that give way further west to white-sand beaches and pink granite crags. The cliffs are highest at Malcolm's Point, near the superb Carsaig Arches.

The village of Bunessan is home to the Ross of Mull Historical Centre (☑01681-700659; www.romhc.org.uk; admission £2; ☺10am-4pm Mon-Fri Easter-Oct, 10am-1pm

Mon-Thu Nov-Easter), a cottage museum by a ruined mill that houses displays on local history, geology, archaeology, genealogy and wildlife.

A minor road leads south from here to the beautiful white-sand bay of **Uisken**, with views of the Paps of Jura.

At the western end of the Ross, 35 miles from Craignure, is **Fionnphort** (*finn*-a-fort) and the Iona ferry. The coast here is a beautiful blend of pink granite rocks, white sandy beaches and vivid turquoise sea.

🛏 Sleeping & Eating

Fidden Farm   CAMPSITE £
(☑ 01681-700427; Fidden, Fionnphort; adult/child £7/4; ☺ Easter-Aug; ℗ 🐾) A basic but popular and beautifully situated campground, with views over pink granite reefs to Iona and Erraid. It's 1.25 miles south of Fionnphort. Opening months vary a little year to year.

★ Seaview   B&B ££
(☑ 01681-700235; www.iona-bed-breakfast-mull.com; Fionnphort; d £75-90; ☺ Mar-Oct; ℗ 🛜 🐾) 🍴 Just up from the ferry, this place has beautifully decorated bedrooms and a breakfast conservatory with grand views across to Iona. The owners are incredibly helpful and also offer tasty three-course dinners (£25 per person, not in summer), often based around local seafood. Breakfasts include locally sourced produce and the rooms are compact and charming, with gleaming modern bathrooms. Bikes available for guests to hire.

Staffa House   B&B ££
(☑ 01681-700677; www.staffahouse.co.uk; Fionnphort; s/d £53/76; ☺ Mar-Oct; ℗ 🛜) 🍴 This charming and hospitable B&B is packed with antiques and period features, and offers breakfast in a conservatory with a view of Iona. Solar panels top up the hot-water supply, and the hearty breakfasts and packed lunches (£6 to £8.50) make use of local and organic produce where possible. Rooms are designed for relaxation, with no TVs.

★ Ninth Wave   SCOTTISH £££
(☑ 01681-700757; www.ninthwaverestaurant.co.uk; Fionnphort; 3-/4-course dinner £44/52; ☺ 6-9pm Tue-Sun May-Oct) 🍴 Based in a former croft, this restaurant is owned and operated by a lobster fisherman and his Canadian wife. The daily menu makes use of locally landed shellfish and crustaceans, and vegetables and salad grown in the croft garden, served

in a stylishly converted bothy. It's excellent. Advance booking essential. No under-12s.

Isle of Iona
POP 200

Like an emerald teardrop off Mull's western shore, enchanting, idyllic Iona, holy island and burial ground of kings, is a magical place that lives up to its lofty reputation. From the moment you embark on the ferry towards its sandy shores and green fields, you'll notice something different about it. To appreciate its charms, spend the night: there are some excellent places to do it. Iona has declared itself a fair-trade island and actively promotes ecotourism.

History

St Columba sailed from Ireland and landed on Iona in 563, establishing a monastic community with the aim of Christianising Scotland. It was here that the *Book of Kells* – the prize attraction of Dublin's Trinity College – is believed to have been transcribed. It was taken to Ireland for safekeeping from 9th-century Viking raids.

The community was refounded as a Benedictine monastery in the early 13th century and prospered until its destruction during the Reformation. The ruins were given to the Church of Scotland in 1899, and by 1910 a group of enthusiasts called the Iona Community Council had reconstructed the abbey. It's still a flourishing spiritual community offering regular courses and retreats.

◉ Sights & Activities

Past the abbey, look for a footpath on the left signposted **Dun I** (dun-ee). An easy 15-minute walk leads to Iona's highest point, with fantastic 360 degree views.

Iona Abbey   HISTORIC BUILDING
(HS; ☑ 01681-700512; adult/child £7.10/4.30; ☺ 9.30am-5.30pm Apr-Sep, to 4.30pm Oct-Mar) Iona's ancient but heavily reconstructed abbey is the spiritual heart of the island. The spectacular nave, dominated by Romanesque and early Gothic vaults and columns is a powerful space; a door on the left leads to the beautiful cloister, where medieval grave slabs sit alongside modern religious sculptures. Out the back, the new museum displays fabulous carved high crosses and other inscribed stones, along with lots of background information. A replica of the

intricately carved St John's Cross stands outside the abbey.

Next to the abbey is an ancient graveyard where there's an evocative Romanesque chapel as well as a mound that marks the burial place of 48 of Scotland's early kings, including Macbeth; the ruined nunnery nearby was established at the same time as the Benedictine abbey.

Iona Heritage Centre MUSEUM
(☑ 01681-700576; adult/child £2.50/1.50; ⊙ 10.30am-5pm Mon-Sat Easter-Oct) Covers the history of Iona, crofting and lighthouses; there's a craft shop and cafe that serves delicious home baking.

☞ Tours

Alternative Boat Hire BOAT TOURS
(☑ 01681-700537; www.boattripsiona.com; ⊙ Mon-Thu Apr-Oct) Offers cruises in a traditional wooden sailing boat for fishing, birdwatching, picnicking, or just admiring the scenery. Three-hour afternoon trips cost £25/10 per adult/child; on Wednesday there's a full day cruise (10am to 5pm, £45/20). Booking essential.

MV Iolaire BOAT TOURS
(☑ 01681-700358; www.staffatrips.co.uk) Three-hour boat trips to Staffa (adult/child £30/15), departing Iona pier at 9.45am and 1.45pm, and from Fionnphort at 10am and 2pm, with one hour ashore on Staffa.

MV Volante WILDLIFE, FISHING
(☑ 01681-700362; www.volanteiona.com; ⊙ Jun-Oct) Four-hour sea-angling trips (£50 per person including tackle and bait), as well as 1½-hour round-the-island wildlife cruises (adult/child £15/8) and 3½-hour whale-watching trips (per person £40).

🛏 Sleeping & Eating

There are B&B options and a supermarket on the island.

★ Iona Hostel HOSTEL £
(☑ 01681-700781; www.ionahostel.co.uk; dm adult/child £21/17.50; 🅿 🛜) 🌱 This working ecological croft and environmentally sensitive hostel is one of Scotland's most rewarding and tranquil places to stay. Lovable black Hebridean sheep surround the building, which features pretty, practical and comfy dorms and an excellent kitchen-lounge. There's a fabulous beach nearby, and a hill to climb

for views. It's just over a mile from the ferry, past the abbey.

Iona Campsite CAMPSITE £
(☑ 01681-700112; www.ionacampsite.co.uk; tent sites per adult/child £6.50/3; ⊙ Apr-Oct; 🛜) Basic campsite about 1 mile west of the ferry.

★ Argyll Hotel HOTEL ££
(☑ 01681-700334; www.argyllhoteliona.co.uk; s £69, d £82-99; ⊙ Mar-Oct; @🛜🛜) 🌱 This cute, higgledy-piggledy warren of a hotel has great service and appealing snug rooms (a sea view costs more – £150 for a double), including good-value family options. Most of the rooms look out to the rear, where a huge organic garden supplies the country-house **restaurant** (lunch £6-8, dinner mains £12-16; ⊙ 12.15-2pm & 6.30-8pm; 🛜) 🌱 with wooden fireplace and antique tables and chairs. The menu includes home-grown salads, local seafood and Scottish beef and lamb.

❶ Getting There & Away

The passenger ferry from Fionnphort to Iona (£5.10 return, five minutes, hourly) runs daily. There are also various day trips available from Oban to Iona.

Isle of Tiree

POP 700

Low-lying Tiree (tye-ree) is a fertile sward of lush, green machair liberally sprinkled with grazing sheep and yellow buttercups, much of it so flat that, from a distance, the houses seem to rise out of the sea. It's one of the sunniest places in Scotland, but also one of the windiest. One major benefit – the constant breeze keeps away the midges.

The surf-lashed coastline here is scalloped with magnificent broad, sweeping beaches of white sand, hugely popular with windsurfers and kitesurfers. Others come for the birdwatching and lonely coastal walks.

◎ Sights

In the 19th century Tiree had a population of 4500, but poverty, food shortages and overcrowding led the Duke of Argyll to introduce a policy of assisted emigration. Between 1841 and 1881, more than 3600 left, many emigrating to Canada, the USA, Australia and New Zealand.

An Iodhlann
LIBRARY, EXHIBITION

(☑01879-220385; www.aniodhlann.org.uk; Scarinish; adult/child £3/free; ◷9am-1pm Mon & Wed-Thu, 10.30am-3.30pm Tue & Fri) A historical and genealogical library and archive, where some of the tens of thousands of descendants of Tiree emigrants come to trace their ancestry. The centre stages summer exhibitions on island life and history.

Skerryvore Lighthouse Museum
MUSEUM

(www.hebrideantrust.org; Hynish; ◷9am-5pm) FREE The picturesque harbour and hamlet of Hynish, near Tiree's southern tip, was built in the 19th century to house workers and supplies for the construction of lonely Skerryvore Lighthouse, 10 miles offshore. This museum occupies the old workshops by the sand-filled but flushable harbour; up the hill is the signal tower once used to communicate by semaphore with the lighthouse.

🏃 Activities

Reliable wind and big waves have made Tiree one of Scotland's top windsurfing venues. The annual Tiree Wave Classic (www.tireewaveclassic.co.uk) competition is held here in October.

Wild Diamond
WATERSPORTS

(☑01879-220399; www.wilddiamond.co.uk; Cornaig) Professional and friendly, this outfit runs courses in windsurfing (£30/100 per session/day), kitesurfing (£70/120 per half-day/full day), surfing, sand-yachting and stand-up paddleboarding, and rents out equipment, including surfboards.

Blackhouse Watersports
WATERSPORTS

(☑07711 807976; www.blackhouse-watersports. co.uk; Gott Bay; ◷Mar-Nov) Operates out of a beach hut at the far end of Gott Bay. Welcoming set-up that runs kitesurfing (£100) and surf (£35) lessons, hires kayaks (£25 for three hours including wetsuit), lends out fishing tackle and rents bikes (£10 per day).

🛏 Sleeping & Eating

Most of Tiree's accommodation is self-catering; make sure you have booked something before arriving.

Millhouse Hostel
HOSTEL £

(☑01879-220435; www.tireemillhouse.co.uk; Cornaig; dm/s/tw £21/33/46; ℗🛜) Housed in a converted barn next to an old ruined water mill, this small but comfortable hostel is 5 miles west from the ferry pier. The dorms have beds rather than bunks, there's a com-

ISLE OF STAFFA

Felix Mendelssohn, who visited the uninhabited island of Staffa in 1829, was inspired to compose his *Hebrides Overture* after hearing waves echoing in the impressive and cathedral-like Fingal's Cave. The cave walls and surrounding cliffs are composed of vertical, hexagonal basalt columns that look like pillars (Staffa is Norse for 'Pillar Island'). You can land and walk into the cave via a causeway. Nearby Boat Cave can be seen from the causeway, but you can't reach it on foot. Staffa also has a sizeable puffin colony, north of the landing place.

Northwest of Staffa lies a chain of uninhabited islands called the Treshnish Isles. The two main islands are curiously shaped Dutchman's Cap and Lunga. You can land on Lunga, walk to the top of the hill and visit the shag, puffin and guillemot colonies on the west coast at Harp Rock.

Unless you have your own boat, the only way to reach Staffa and the Treshnish Isles is on an organised boat trip from Ulva, Fionnphort or Iona.

mon area and it's cheaper if you stay more than one night.

Balinoe Croft Campsite
CAMPSITE £

(☑01879-220399; www.wilddiamond.co.uk; Balinoe; tent sites adult/child £12/6; ℗🛜🐕) A sheltered site with full facilities in the southwest of the island, near Balemartine, with great views of Mull. It's cheaper for multi-night stays or in the off-season.

Kirkapol House
B&B ££

(☑01879-220729; www.kirkapoltiree.co.uk; Kirkapol; s/d £38/70; ◷Apr-Sep; ℗🛜🐕) Set in a converted 19th-century church overlooking the island's biggest beach, the Kirkapol has six homely rooms with soothing sounds of waves, and a big lounge with a leather sofa. It's 2 miles north of the ferry terminal.

Scarinish Hotel
HOTEL ££

(☑01879-220308; www.tireescarinishhotel.com; Scarinish; s/d £70/90; ℗🛜🐕) The island's main hotel is looking a little tired these days, and the welcome is curtly professional rather than effusive, but it's an acceptable choice. Both the restaurant (two/

three-course dinner £22/26), with pleasant harbour views, and traditional lean-to bar (mains £6 to £9) do food, and you can get a packed lunch too. Food is served noon to 2.30pm and 5pm to 8.30pm.

Ceàbhar
SCOTTISH ££

(☏ 01879-220684; www.ceabhar.com; Sandaig; mains £8-15; ☺ 7-8.30pm Wed-Sat Easter-Oct, plus Tue Jul & Aug; P 🛜 🐕) 🍴 At Tiree's western end, this attractive restaurant looks out over the Atlantic towards the sunset. The cordial owners have the right attitude; they grow their own salads, eschew chips and have a nice line in good Fyne ales. The menu runs to handmade pizzas, soups, fish of the day and local lamb. A snug cottage sleeps up to eight people in five bedrooms.

ℹ Information

There's a bank (without ATM), post office and supermarket in Scarinish, the main village, half a mile south of the ferry pier. You can get cashback with debit-card purchases at the Co-op.

Some tourist information is available in the ferry terminal. A useful website is www.isleof tiree.com.

ℹ Getting There & Around

AIR

Loganair/FlyBe (www.loganair.co.uk) flies from Glasgow to Tiree daily. **Hebridean Air** (☏ 0845 805-7465; www.hebrideanair.co.uk) operates from Oban to Tiree via Coll (one-way from Oban/Coll £65/25, twice daily Monday and Wednesday plus once Friday and Sunday during school term).

BICYCLE & CAR

Rent bicycles (per day £10) and cars (per day £45) from **MacLennan Motors** (☏ 01879-220555; www.maclennanmotors.com; Gott) at the ferry pier. **Tiree Fitness** (☏ 01879-220421; www.tireefitness.co.uk; Sandaig; per day £15) has better bikes and will deliver them to the ferry (£5 extra).

BOAT

A **CalMac** (www.calmac.co.uk) ferry runs from Oban to Tiree (passenger/car £20.30/108 return, four hours, one daily) via Coll, except on Wednesday and Friday when the boat calls at Tiree first (three hours 20 minutes). The one-way fare from Coll to Tiree (one hour) is £3.30/14.90 per passenger/car. On Thursdays, the ferry continues to Barra in the Outer Hebrides (£8.60/44.50 one way, four hours), and stops again on the way back to Oban, allowing a long day trip to Tiree from the mainland.

Isle of Coll
POP 200

More ruged, Coll is Tiree's less populous neighbour. The northern part of the island is a mix of bare rock, bog and lochans (small lochs), while the south is swathed in golden shell-sand beaches and machair dunes up to 30m high. It's a gloriously relaxing place.

The island's main attraction is the peace and quiet – empty beaches, bird-haunted coastlines, and long walks along the shore. The biggest and most beautiful sandy beaches are at **Crossapol** in the south, and **Hogh Bay** and **Cliad** on the west coast.

In summer the corncrake's 'krek-krek' is heard at the **RSPB Reserve** at Totronald in the southwest of the island. From Totronald a sandy 4WD track runs north past the dunes backing Hogh Bay to the road at Totamore, allowing walkers and cyclists to make a circuit back to Arinagour rather than backtracking.

There are two castles about 6 miles southwest of Arinagour, both known as **Breachacha Castle**, built by the Macleans. The older, ruined towerhouse was replaced by a mid-18th century palace alongside, now gradually being restored.

🛏 Sleeping & Eating

You can wild camp for free on the hill above the Coll Hotel (no facilities); ask at the hotel first.

Coll Bunkhouse
HOSTEL £

(☏ 01879-230000; www.collbunkhouse.com; Arinagour; dm/tw £20/48; P 🛜) The gorgeous modern bunkhouse is in the main settlement, just a 10- to 15-minute walk from the ferry pier.

Tigh-na-Mara
B&B ££

(☏ 01879-230354; www.tighnamara.info; Arinagour; s £50-60, d £70-90; P 🛜) The first building you reach coming from the ferry is this lovely B&B, with a large front garden and magnificent views over the water. The owners are relaxed and welcoming, and the rooms have bird books and planispheres so you can do some spotting from your window. Wi-fi is fast for the Hebrides, and breakfast very tasty – try the stuffed tomato. There's also a self-catering option.

Coll Hotel

HOTEL **££**

(☎ 01879-230334; www.collhotel.com; Arinagour; s £65, d £100-125; P �) The island's only hotel is an atmospheric old place. Its quirkily shaped rooms have white-painted, wood-panelled walls, and some have lovely views over the manicured hotel gardens and the harbour. The hotel also has a lively public bar and good restaurant (mains £13 to £22; noon to 2pm and 6pm to 9pm) serving dishes prepared with regional smoked and fresh fish, shellfish and lamb. You can order smaller portions of the mains: not a bad idea, as they're sizeable.

Island Café

CAFE **££**

(Arinagour; mains £6-13; ⏱ 11am-2pm & 5-9pm Mon & Thu-Sat, noon-6pm Sun; ⏱) This cheerful spot serves hearty, homemade meals such as sausage and mash, haddock and chips, and vegetarian cottage pie, accompanied by organic beer, wine and cider. Sunday roasts are legendary on the island.

ℹ Information

Arinagour, 0.5 miles from the ferry pier, is Coll's only village, home to a shop, post office (with ATM), craft shops and aged petrol station. Coll has no reliable mobile-phone signal; there are payphones at the pier and in the hotel. For more information see www.visitcoll.co.uk.

ℹ Getting There & Around

AIR

Hebridean Air (☎ 0845 805-7465; www.hebrideanair.co.uk) operates flights from Connel Airfield (near Oban) to Coll (£65 one way, twice daily Monday and Wednesday plus once daily Friday and Sunday in school term).

BICYCLE

There is no public transport. Mountain bikes can be hired from the post office in Arinagour for £10 per day.

BOAT

CalMac (www.calmac.co.uk) runs from Oban to Coll (passenger/car £20.30/108 return, 2¾ hours, one daily) and continues to Tiree (one hour), except on Wednesday and Friday when the boat calls at Tiree first. The one-way fare from Coll to Tiree is £3.30/14.90 per passenger/car.

On Thursdays, you can take a ferry to Barra in the Outer Hebrides (£8.60/44.50 one way, four hours); it stops again on the way back to Oban, allowing a long day trip to Coll from the mainland.

NORTH ARGYLL

Loch Awe

Loch Awe is one of Scotland's most beautiful lochs, with rolling forested hills around its southern end and spectacular mountains in the north. It lies between Oban and Inveraray and is the longest loch in Scotland – about 24 miles – but is less than 1 mile wide for most of its length. At its northern end, it escapes to the sea through the narrow **Pass of Brander**, where Robert the Bruce defeated the MacDougalls in 1309. Here you can visit **Cruachan power station** (☎ 01866-822618; www.visitcruachan.co.uk; adult/child £7.50/2.50; ⏱ 9.30am-4.45pm Easter-Oct, 11am-3.45pm Mon-Fri Nov-Dec, Feb & Mar). Electric buses take you deep inside Ben Cruachan, allowing you to see the pump-storage hydro-electric scheme which occupies a vast cavern hollowed out of the mountain.

Also at the northern end of Loch Awe, a half-mile walk off the A85 are the scenic ruins of **Kilchurn Castle** (HS; ⏱ 9am-5pm Apr-Sep; FREE), built in 1440, which enjoys one of Scotland's finest settings; you can climb to the top of the four-storey castle tower.

Citylink (www.citylink.co.uk) buses from Glasgow to Oban go via Dalmally, Lochawe village and Cruachan power station. Trains from Glasgow to Oban stop at Dalmally and Lochawe village.

Connel & Taynuilt

Hemmed in by dramatic mountain scenery, **Loch Etive** stretches 17 miles from Connel to Kinlochetive (accessible by road from Glencoe). At Connel Bridge, 5 miles north of Oban, the loch joins the sea via a narrow channel partly blocked by an underwater rock ledge. When the tide flows in and out water pours through this bottleneck, creating spectacular white-water rapids known as the **Falls of Lora**. Park near the north end of the bridge and walk back into the middle to have a look.

Dunstaffnage Castle (HS; ☎ 01631-562465; www.historic-scotland.gov.uk; adult/child £4.50/2.70; ⏱ 9.30am-5.30pm Apr-Sep, to 4.30pm Oct), 2 miles west of Connel, looks like a schoolkid's drawing of what a castle should be – square and massive, with towers at the corners, perched on top of a rocky outcrop. It was built around 1260 and was captured by Robert the Bruce during the Wars of Independence. The haunted ruins of the nearby **chapel** contain lots of Campbell tombs. You reach the castle through a smart new European marine-research complex.

One of the region's most unusual historical sights is **Bonawe Iron Furnace** (HS; ✆ 01866-822432; www.historic-scotland.gov. uk; adult/child £4.50/2.70; ☉ 9.30am-5.30pm Apr-Sep), near Taynuilt. Dating from 1753, it felled the local birchwoods to make charcoal, needed for smelting. To produce Bonawe's annual output of 700 tons of pig iron took 10,000 acres of woodland. A fascinating self-guided tour leads you around the site.

From the nearby jetty, **Loch Etive Cruises** (✆ 01866-822430; 2-/3-hour cruises £10/15; ☉ 2-3 cruises Sun-Fri Easter-Oct) runs boat trips to the head of Loch Etive and back. You may spot eagles, otters, seals and deer, and at the head of the loch you can see the famous Etive slabs. Bookings essential.

Buses between Oban and Fort William or Glasgow, and trains between Oban and Glasgow, all stop in Connel and Taynuilt.

Appin & Around

The Appin region, once ruled over by the Stewarts from their stronghold at Castle Stalker, stretches north from the rocky shores of Loch Creran to the hills of Glencoe.

The **Scottish Sea Life Sanctuary** (✆ 01631-720386; www.sealsanctuary.co.uk; Barcaldine; adult/child £13.20/10.80; ☉ 10am-4pm Nov-Mar, 10am-5pm Apr-Oct) ✐, 10 miles north of Oban, provides a haven for orphaned seal pups. As well as seals there are tanks with herrings, rays and flatfish, touch pools for children, an otter sanctuary and displays on Scotland's marine environment. An outdoor nature trail is aimed at young 'uns.

North of Loch Creran, at Portnacroish, there's a wonderful view of **Castle Stalker** (www.castlestalker.com; adult/child £15/7; ☉ check website for summer guided tours) perched on a tiny offshore island. This spectacular tower house is only open for five weeks or so per year: book ahead. **Port Appin**, a couple of miles off the main road, is a pleasant spot with a passenger ferry to Lismore.

Scottish Citylink (www.citylink.co.uk) buses between Oban and Fort William stop at the Sea Life Sanctuary and Appin village.

🍴 Sleeping & Eating

Pierhouse Hotel   HOTEL **£££**
(✆ 01631-730302; www.pierhousehotel.co.uk; Port Appin; s/d from £75/140; P 🐾 📶) The quaint Pierhouse Hotel sits on the waterfront above the pier and has stylish modern rooms, a sauna and an excellent **restaurant** (mains £13-28; ☉ noon-2.30pm & 6.9pm; 📶) with views to Lismore, and specialises in local seafood and game. The bar offers cheaper fishy fare.

Lismore

POP 200

The island of Lismore (in Gaelic Lios Mor means 'Big Garden') is all lush grassland sprinkled with wildflowers. It's limestone that's the secret – it's rare in the Highlands, but it weathers to a very fertile soil.

In the middle of the island, **Lismore Gaelic Heritage Centre** (✆ 01631-760300; www.lismoregaelicheritagecentre.org; admission by donation; ☉ 11am-4pm Apr-Oct) ✐ has a museum with a fascinating exhibition on Lismore's history and culture; alongside stands a reconstruction of a crofter's cottage. The **cafe** (✆ 01631-760020; light meals £4-8; ☉ 11am-4pm Apr-Oct; ⊕) ✐ has an outdoor deck with a stunning view of the mainland mountains.

The romantic ruins of 13th-century **Castle Coeffin** have a lovely setting on the west coast. **Tirefour Broch**, a defensive tower with double walls reaching 4m in height, is directly opposite on the east coast. There is very little short-stay accommodation on Lismore. However, there are several self-catering options advertised on www. isleoflismore.com. Lismore is long and narrow – 10 miles long by 1 mile wide – with a road running almost its full length. There's a shop.

ℹ️ Getting There & Around

BICYCLE

You can hire **bikes** (✆ 01631-730391; per day adult/child £15/10) in Port Appin to bring across on the ferry.

BOAT

A **CalMac** (www.calmac.co.uk) car ferry runs from Oban to Achnacroish, with four to five sailings Monday to Saturday, two on Sunday (passenger/car return £6.60/55, 50 minutes).

Argyll & Bute Council (✆ 01631-569160; www.argyll-bute.gov.uk) operates the passenger ferry from Port Appin to Point (£1.60, 10 minutes, hourly). Bicycles are free.

Inverness & the Central Highlands

Best Places to Eat

➡ Lime Tree (p341)

➡ Café 1 (p305)

➡ Cross (p322)

➡ Lochleven Seafood Cafe (p339)

➡ Old Forge (p350)

Best Places to Stay

➡ Rocpool Reserve (p305)

➡ Lime Tree (p340)

➡ Lovat (p315)

➡ Eagleview Guest House (p322)

➡ Trafford Bank (p304)

Why Go?

From the subarctic plateau of the Cairngorms to the rolling hills of Highland Perthshire and the rugged, rocky peaks of Glen Coe, the central mountain ranges of the Scottish Highlands are testimony to the sculpting power of ice and weather. Here the landscape is at its grandest, with soaring hills of rock and heather bounded by wooded glens and rushing waterfalls.

Not surprisingly, this part of the country is an adventure playground for outdoor-sports enthusiasts. Aviemore, Glen Coe and Fort William draw hill walkers and climbers in summer, and skiers, snowboarders and ice climbers in winter. Inverness, the Highland capital, provides urban rest and relaxation, while nearby Loch Ness and its elusive monster add a hint of mystery.

From Fort William, base camp for climbing Ben Nevis, the Road to the Isles leads past the beaches of Arisaig and Morar to Mallaig, jumping-off point for the isles of Eigg, Rum, Muck and Canna.

When to Go
Inverness

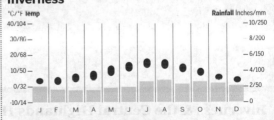

| **Apr–May** Mountain scenery is at its most spectacular, with snow lingering on the higher peaks. | **Jun** Fort William hosts the UCI Mountain Bike World Cup, pulling huge crowds. | **Sep** Ideal for hiking and hill walking: midges are dying off, but weather is still reasonably good. |

Inverness & the Central Highlands Highlights

1 Hiking among the hills, lochs and forests of beautiful **Glen Affric** (p308)

2 Wandering through the ancient Caledonian forest at **Rothiemurchus Estate** (p316)

3 Making it to the summit of **Ben Nevis** (p343) – and being able to see the view

4 Exploring the hills around gorgeous **Glen Lyon** (p335)

5 Keeping right on to the end of the road at bleak but beautiful **Rannoch Moor** (p332)

6 Rattling your teeth loose on the championship downhill mountain-bike course at **Nevis Range** (p343)

7 Taking in the stunning panorama from the summit of the **Sgurr of Eigg** (p352)

8 Soaking up the scenery (when you can see it!) in moody but magnificent **Glen Coe** (p336)

9 Venturing into the remote and rugged wilderness of the **Knoydart Peninsula** (p349)

ℹ Getting Around

For timetable information, call **Traveline Scotland** (☑ 0871 200 2233; www.travelinescotland.com).

BUS

Scottish Citylink (☑ 0871 266 3333; www.citylink.co.uk) Runs buses from Perth and Glasgow to Inverness and Fort William, and links Inverness to Fort William along the Great Glen.

Stagecoach (www.stagecoachbus.com) The main regional bus company, with offices in Aviemore, Inverness and Fort William. Dayrider tickets are valid for a day's unlimited travel on Stagecoach buses in various regions, including Inverness (£3.40), Aviemore and around (£6.50) and Fort William (£3.20).

TRAIN

Two railway lines serve the region: the Perth–Aviemore–Inverness line in the east, and the Glasgow–Fort William–Mallaig line in the west.

INVERNESS & THE GREAT GLEN

Inverness, one of the fastest growing towns in Britain, is the capital of the Highlands. It's a transport hub and jumping-off point for the central, western and northern Highlands, the Moray Firth coast and the Great Glen.

The Great Glen is a geological fault running in an arrow-straight line across Scotland from Fort William to Inverness. The glaciers of the last ice age eroded a deep trough along the fault line, which is now filled by a series of lochs – Linnhe, Lochy, Oich and Ness. The glen has always been an important communication route – General George Wade built a military road along the southern side of Loch Ness in the early 18th century, and in 1822 the various lochs were linked by the Caledonian Canal to create a cross-country waterway. The modern A82 road along the glen was completed in 1933 – a date that coincides with the first modern sightings of the Loch Ness Monster.

Inverness

POP 61,235

Inverness has a great location astride the River Ness at the northern end of the Great Glen. In summer it overflows with visitors intent on monster hunting at nearby Loch Ness, but it's worth a visit in its own right for a stroll along the picturesque River Ness, a cruise on Loch Ness, and a meal in one of the city's excellent restaurants.

Inverness was probably founded by King David in the 12th century, but thanks to its often violent history few buildings of real age or historical significance have survived – much of the older part of the city dates from the period following the completion of the Caledonian Canal in 1822. The broad and shallow River Ness, famed for its salmon fishing, runs through the heart of the city.

⊙ Sights & Activities

★ Ness Islands   PARK

The main attraction in Inverness is a leisurely stroll along the river to the Ness Islands. Planted with mature Scots pine, fir, beech and sycamore, and linked to the river banks and each other by elegant Victorian footbridges, the islands make an appealing picnic spot. They're a 20-minute walk south of the castle – head upstream on either side of the river (the start of the Great Glen Way), and return on the opposite bank.

On the way you'll pass the red-sandstone towers of **St Andrew's Cathedral** (11 Ardross St), dating from 1869, and the modern Eden Court Theatre (p306), which hosts regular art exhibits, both on the west bank.

Inverness Museum & Art Gallery   MUSEUM

(☑ 01463-237114; www.inverness.highland.museum; Castle Wynd; ⊙ 10am-5pm Tue-Sat Apr-Oct, Thu-Sat Nov-Mar) **FREE** Inverness Museum & Art Gallery has wildlife dioramas, geological displays, period rooms with historic weapons, Pictish stones and exhibitions of contemporary Highland arts and crafts.

Victorian Market   MARKET

(www.invernessvictorianmarket.co.uk; Academy St; ⊙ 9am-5pm Mon-Sat) If the rain comes down, you could opt for a spot of retail therapy in the Victorian Market, a shopping mall that dates from the 1890s and has rather more charm than its modern equivalents.

Inverness Castle   CASTLE

(Castle St) The hill above the city centre is topped by the picturesque Baronial turrets of Inverness Castle, a pink-sandstone confection dating from 1847 that replaced a medieval castle blown up by the Jacobites in 1746; it serves today as the Sheriff's Court. It's not open to the public, but there are good views from the surrounding gardens.

Inverness

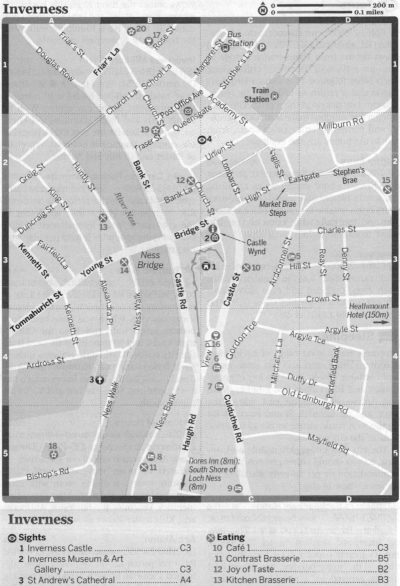

Inverness

⊙ Sights
1	Inverness Castle	C3
2	Inverness Museum & Art Gallery	C3
3	St Andrew's Cathedral	A4
4	Victorian Market	C2

🛏 Sleeping
5	Ardconnel House	C3
6	Bazpackers Backpackers Hotel	C4
	Glenmoriston Town House Hotel	(see 11)
7	Inverness Student Hotel	C4
8	MacRae Guest House	B5
9	Rocpool Reserve	C5

🍴 Eating
10	Café 1	C3
11	Contrast Brasserie	B5
12	Joy of Taste	B2
13	Kitchen Brasserie	B3
14	Rocpool	B3
15	Velocity Cafe	D2

🍸 Drinking & Nightlife
16	Castle Tavern	C4
17	Phoenix	B1

✪ Entertainment
18	Eden Court Theatre	A5
19	Hootananny	B2
20	Ironworks	B1

☞ Tours

Jacobite Cruises
BOAT TOURS

(☎ 01463-233999; www.jacobite.co.uk; Glenur-quhart Rd; adult/child £31.50/25; ⊙ daily Apr-Sep) Boats depart from Tomnahurich Bridge at 2pm for a 1½-hour 'Discovery' cruise along Loch Ness, followed by a visit to Urquhart Castle and a return to Inverness by coach. You can buy tickets at the tourist office and catch a free minibus to the boat. Other cruises and combined cruise/coach tours, from one to 6½ hours, are also available.

Happy Tours
WALKING TOURS

(☎ 07828 154683; www.happy-tours.biz; per person £6) Offers 1¼-hour guided walks exploring the town's history and legends. City history tours begin outside the tourist office at 11am, 1pm and 3pm daily, while 'crime and punishment' tours start at 7pm and 8.30pm.

Inverness Taxis
TOURS

(☎ 01463-222900; www.inverness-taxis.co.uk) Wide range of day tours to Urquhart Castle, Loch Ness, Culloden and even Skye. Fares per car (up to four people) range from £60 (two hours) to £240 (all day).

🛌 Sleeping

Inverness has a good range of backpacker accommodation, and also has some excellent boutique hotels. There are lots of guesthouses and B&Bs along Old Edinburgh Rd and Ardconnel St on the east side of the river, and on Kenneth St and Fairfield Rd on the west bank; all are within 10 minutes' walk of the city centre.

The city fills up quickly in July and August, so you should either prebook your accommodation or get an early start looking for somewhere to stay.

Bazpackers Backpackers Hotel
HOSTEL £

(☎ 01463-717663; www.bazpackershostel.co.uk; 4 Culduthel Rd; dm/tw £17/44; @ 🛜) This may be Inverness' smallest hostel (34 beds), but it's hugely popular. It's a friendly, quiet place – the main building has a convivial lounge centred on a wood-burning stove, and a small garden and great views (some rooms are in a separate building with no garden). The dorms and kitchen can be a bit cramped, but the showers are great.

Inverness Student Hotel
HOSTEL £

(☎ 01463-236556; www.scotlands-top-hostels.com; 8 Culduthel Rd; dm £18; P @ 🛜) Set in a rambling old house with comfy beds and

views across the River Ness, this hostel has a party atmosphere, and runs organised pub crawls in town. It's a 10-minute walk from the train station, just past the castle.

Inverness Millburn SYHA
HOSTEL £

(SYHA; ☎ 01463-231771; www.syha.org.uk; Victoria Dr; dm/tw £19/54; ⊙ Apr-Dec; P @ 🛜) Inverness' modern 166-bed hostel is 10 minutes' walk northeast of the city centre. With its comfy beds and flashy stainless-steel kitchen, some reckon it's the best SYHA hostel in the country. Booking is essential, especially at Easter and in July and August.

Bught Caravan Park & Campsite
CAMPSITE £

(☎ 01463-236920; www.invernesscaravanpark.com; Bught Lane; sites per person £10, campervan £16; ⊙ Easter-Sep; 🛜) A mile southwest of the city centre near Tomnahurich Bridge, this camping ground is hugely popular with backpackers.

★ Trafford Bank
B&B ££

(☎ 01463-241414; www.traffordbankguesthouse.co.uk; 96 Fairfield Rd; d £120-132; P 🛜) Lots of word-of-mouth rave reviews for this elegant Victorian villa, which was once home to a bishop, just a mitre-toss from the Caledonian Canal and 10 minutes' walk west from the city centre. The luxurious rooms include fresh flowers and fruit, bathrobes and fluffy towels – ask for the Tartan Room, which has a wrought-iron king-size bed and Victorian roll-top bath.

Ardconnel House
B&B ££

(☎ 01463-240455; www.ardconnel-inverness.co.uk; 21 Ardconnel St; r per person £35-40; 🛜) The six-room Ardconnel is one of our favourites – a terraced Victorian house with comfortable en suite rooms, a dining room with crisp white table linen, and a breakfast menu that includes Vegemite for homesick Antipodeans. Kids under 10 not allowed.

Ach Aluinn
B&B ££

(☎ 01463-230127; www.achaluinn.com; 27 Fairfield Rd; r per person £25-35; P) This large, detached Victorian house is bright and homely, and offers all you might want from a B&B:a a private bathroom, TV, reading lights, comfy beds with two pillows each and an excellent breakfast. Less than 10 minutes' walk west from the city centre.

Heathmount Hotel
BOUTIQUE HOTEL ££

(☎ 01463-235877; www.heathmounthotel.com; Kingsmills Rd; s/d from £75/115; P 🛜) Small and friendly, the Heathmount combines a popular local bar and restaurant with eight designer hotel rooms, each one different, ranging from a boldly coloured family room in purple and gold to a slinky black velvet four-poster double. Five minutes' walk east of the city centre.

MacRae Guest House B&B ££
(☑ 01463-243658; joycemacrae@hotmail.com; 24 Ness Bank; s/d from £45/64; P 🕏) This pretty, flower-bedecked Victorian house on the eastern bank of the river has smart, tastefully decorated bedrooms (one is wheelchair accessible), and vegetarian breakfasts are available. Minimum two-night bookings in July and August.

★**Rocpool Reserve** BOUTIQUE HOTEL £££
(☑ 01463-240089; www.rocpool.com; Culduthel Rd; s/d from £185/220; P 🕏) Boutique chic meets the Highlands in this slick and sophisticated little hotel, where an elegant Georgian exterior conceals an oasis of contemporary cool. A gleaming white entrance hall lined with red carpet and contemporary art leads to designer rooms in shades of chocolate, cream and gold; a restaurant by Albert Roux completes the luxury package.

Expect lots of high-tech gadgetry in the more expensive rooms, from iPod docks to balcony hot tubs with aquavision TV.

Glenmoriston Town House Hotel BOUTIQUE HOTEL £££
(☑ 01463-223777; www.glenmoristontownhouse. com; 20 Ness Bank; r from £180; P 🕏) Luxurious boutique hotel on the banks of the River Ness. Can organise golfing and fishing for guests.

✗ Eating

Velocity Cafe CAFE £
(☑ 01463-419956; http://velocitylove.co.uk; 1 Crown Ave; mains £4-7; ◷ 9am-5pm Fri-Mon & Wed, 10am-5pm Tue, 9am-9pm Thu; 🕏 🍴) 🍴 This cyclists' cafe serves soups, sandwiches and salads prepared with organic, locally sourced produce, as well as yummy cake and coffee. There's also a workshop where you can repair your bike or book a session with a mechanic.

★**Café 1** BISTRO ££
(☑ 01463-226200; www.cafe1.net; 75 Castle St; mains £10-24; ◷ noon-2.30pm & 5-9.30pm Mon-Fri, noon-2.30pm & 6-9.30pm Sat) 🍴 Café 1 is a friendly and appealing bistro with candlelit tables amid elegant blonde-wood and wrought-iron decor. There is an international menu based on quality Scottish produce,

from Aberdeen Angus steaks to crisp pan-fried sea bass and meltingly tender pork belly. The set lunch menu (two courses for £8) is served noon to 2.30pm Monday to Saturday.

Contrast Brasserie BRASSERIE ££
(☑ 01463-227889; www.glenmoristontownhouse. com; 22 Ness Bank; mains £17-26) Book early for what we think is one of the the best-value restaurants in Inverness: a dining room that drips designer style, with smiling professional staff and truly delicious food prepared using fresh Scottish produce. The two-course lunch menu (£11) and three-course early-bird menu (£16, 5pm to 6.30pm) are bargains.

Joy of Taste BRITISH ££
(☑ 01463-241459; www.thejoyoftaste.co.uk; 25 Church St; mains £15-19; ◷ noon-3pm & 5.30-10.30pm Mon-Sat, 5.30-9.30pm Sun) 🍴 Here's a novel concept – a restaurant run by a head chef and 25 volunteers who work a shift a week just for 'the love of creating a beautiful restaurant' (plus a share of the profits). And a very good job they have made of it, with a menu of classic British cuisine and a growing fan club of satisfied customers.

Rocpool MEDITERRANEAN ££
(☑ 01463-717274; www.rocpoolrestaurant.com; 1 Ness Walk; mains £18-25; ◷ noon-2.30pm & 5.45-10pm Mon-Sat) 🍴 Lots of polished wood, crisp white linen and leather booths and banquettes lend a nautical air to this relaxing bistro, which offers a Mediterranean-influenced menu that makes the most of quality Scottish produce, especially seafood. The two-course lunch is £15.

Kitchen Brasserie MODERN SCOTTISH ££
(☑ 01463-259119; www.kitchenrestaurant.co.uk; 15 Huntly St; mains £8-19; ◷ noon-10pm; 🕏 🍴) This spectacular glass-fronted restaurant offers a great menu and a view over the River Ness – try to get a table upstairs. Great value two-course lunch (£7, noon to 3pm) and early-bird menu (£12, 5pm to 7pm).

🍺 Drinking

Clachnaharry Inn PUB
(☑ 01463-239806; www.clachnaharryinn.co.uk; 17-19 High St; ◷ 11am-11pm, to midnight Fri & Sat) Just over a mile northwest of the city centre, on the bank of the Caledonian Canal just off the A862, this is a delightful old coaching inn (with beer garden out back) serving

an excellent range of real ales and good pub grub.

Castle Tavern PUB

(☑ 01463-718718; www.castletavern.net; 1-2 View Pl; ⏱ 11am-11pm) With a tasty selection of real ales, this pub has a wee suntrap of a terrace out the front. It's a great place for a pint on a summer afternoon.

Phoenix PUB

(☑ 01463-233685; 108 Academy St; ⏱ 11am-11pm) Recently refurbished, this is the most traditional of the pubs in the city centre, with a mahogany horseshoe bar and several real ales on tap, including beers from the Cairngorm, Cromarty and Isle of Skye breweries.

☆ Entertainment

Hootananny LIVE MUSIC

(☑ 01463-233651; www.hootananny.com; 67 Church St) Hootananny is the city's best live-music venue, with traditional folk- and/ or rock-music sessions nightly, including big-name bands from all over Scotland (and, indeed, the world). The bar is well stocked with a range of beers from the local Black Isle Brewery.

Eden Court Theatre THEATRE

(☑ 01463-234234; www.eden-court.co.uk; Bishop's Rd) The Highlands' main cultural venue (with theatre, art-house cinema and conference centre), Eden Court stages a busy program of drama, dance, comedy, music, film and children's events, and has a good bar and restaurant. Pick up a program from the foyer or check the website.

Ironworks LIVE MUSIC, COMEDY

(☑ 0871 789 4173; www.ironworksvenue.com; 122 Academy St) With live bands (rock, pop, tribute) and comedy shows two or three times a week, the Ironworks is the town's main venue for big-name acts.

❶ Information

Inverness Tourist Office (☑ 01463-252401; www.visithighlands.com; Castle Wynd; internet access per 20min £1; ⏱ 9am-6pm Mon-Sat, 9.30am-5pm Sun Jul & Aug, 9am-5pm Mon-Sat, 10am-4pm Sun Jun, Sep & Oct, 9am-5pm Mon-Sat Apr & May) Bureau de change and accommodation-booking service; also sells tickets for tours and cruises. Opening hours limited November to March.

❶ Getting There & Away

AIR

Inverness Airport (INV; ☑ 01667-464000; www.hial.co.uk/inverness-airport) At Dalcross, 10 miles east of the city, off the A96 towards Aberdeen. There are scheduled flights to Amsterdam, London, Manchester, Orkney, Shetland and the Outer Hebrides, as well as other places in the British Isles.

BUS

Services depart from **Inverness bus station** (Margaret St).

Aberdeen £12.50, 3¾ hours, hourly

Aviemore £9.80, 45 minutes, eight daily

Edinburgh £30, 3½ to 4½ hours, hourly

Fort William £11.20, two hours, five daily

Glasgow £30, 3½ to 4½ hours, hourly

London £45, 13 hours, one daily; more frequent services requiring a change at Glasgow. Operated by **National Express** (☑ 08717 81 81 78; www.gobycoach.com).

Portree £25, 3¼ hours, three daily

Thurso £19, three hours, three to five daily

Ullapool £12.80, 1½ hours, two daily except Sunday

If you book far enough in advance, **Megabus** (☑ 0871 266 3333; www.megabus.com) offers fares from as little as £1 for buses from Inverness to Glasgow and Edinburgh, and £10 to London.

TRAIN

Aberdeen £27, 2¼ hours, eight daily

Edinburgh £41, 3½ hours, eight daily

Glasgow £41, 3½ hours, eight daily

Kyle of Lochalsh £22, 2½ hours, four daily Monday to Saturday, two Sunday; one of Britain's great scenic train journeys

London £100, eight to nine hours, one daily direct; others require a change at Edinburgh

Wick £19, 4½ hours, four daily Monday to Saturday, one or two on Sunday; via Thurso

❶ Getting Around

TO/FROM THE AIRPORT

Stagecoach Jet (www.stagecoachbus.com) Buses run from the airport to Inverness bus station (£3.90, 20 minutes, every 30 minutes).

BICYCLE

Ticket to Ride (☑ 01463-419160; www.tickettoridehighlands.co.uk; Bellfield Park; per day from £22; ⏱ 9am-6pm Apr-Oct) Hire mountain bikes, hybrids and tandems; can be dropped off in Fort William. Will deliver bikes free to local hotels and B&Bs.

BUS

City services and buses to places around Inverness, including Nairn, Forres, the Culloden battlefield, Beauly, Dingwall and Lairg, are operated by Stagecoach (p479). An Inverness City Dayrider ticket costs £3.40 and gives unlimited travel for a day on buses throughout the city.

CAR

Focus Vehicle Rental (☑ 01463-709517; www.focusvehiclerental.co.uk; 6 Harbour Rd) The big boys charge from around £50 to £60 per day, but Focus has cheaper rates starting at £38 per day.

TAXI

Highland Taxis (☑ 01463-222222; www.highlandtaxisinverness.co.uk)

Around Inverness

Culloden Battlefield

The Battle of Culloden in 1746, the last pitched battle ever fought on British soil, saw the defeat of Bonnie Prince Charlie and the end of the Jacobite dream when 1200 Highlanders were slaughtered by government forces in a 68-minute rout. The Duke of Cumberland, son of the reigning King George II and leader of the Hanoverian army, earned the nickname 'Butcher' for his brutal treatment of the defeated Jacobite forces. The battle sounded the death knell for the old clan system, and the horrors of the Clearances soon followed. The sombre moor where the conflict took place has scarcely changed in the ensuing 260 years.

Culloden is 6 miles east of Inverness. Bus No 2 runs from Queensgate in Inverness to Culloden battlefield (£2.40, 30 minutes, hourly).

Culloden Visitor Centre   INTERPRETATION CENTRE
(NTS; www.nts.org.uk/culloden; adult/child £11/8.50; ☺ 9am-6pm Jun-Aug, to 5.30pm Apr, May, Sep & Oct, 10am-4pm Nov-Mar) This impressive visitor centre has everything you need to know about the Battle of Culloden in 1746, including the lead-up and the aftermath, with perspectives from both sides. An innovative film puts you on the battlefield in the middle of the mayhem, and a wealth of other audio presentations must have kept Inverness' entire acting community in business for weeks. The admission fee includes an audioguide for a self-guided tour of the battlefield itself.

Fort George

The headland guarding the narrows in the Moray Firth opposite Fortrose is occupied by the magnificent and virtually unaltered 18th-century artillery fortification of Fort George.

Fort George   FORTRESS
(HS; ☑ 01667-462777; adult/child £8.90/5.40; ☺ 9.30am-5.30pm Apr-Sep, to 4.30pm Oct-Mar) One of the finest artillery fortifications in Europe, Fort George was established in 1748 in the aftermath of the Battle of Culloden, as a base for George II's army of occupation in the Highlands. By the time of its completion in 1769 it had cost the equivalent of around £1 billion in today's money. It still functions as a military barracks; public areas have exhibitions on 18th-century soldiery, and the mile-plus walk around the ramparts offers fine views out to sea and back to the Great Glen.

Given its size, you'll need at least two hours to do the place justice. The fort is off the A96 about 11 miles northeast of Inverness; there is no public transport.

Nairn
POP 9775

Nairn is a popular golfing and seaside resort with a good sandy beach. The most interesting part of town is the old fishing village of **Fishertown**, down by the harbour, a maze of narrow streets lined with picturesque cottages. **Nairn Museum** (☑ 01667-456791; www.nairnmuseum.co.uk; Viewfield House; adult/child £3/50p; ☺ 10am-4.30pm Mon-Fri, to 1pm Sat Apr-Oct), a few minutes' walk from the tourist office, has displays on the history of Fishertown, as well as on local archaeology, geology and natural history.

You can spend many pleasant hours wandering along the **East Beach**, one of the finest in Scotland.

The big event in the town's calendar is the **Nairn Highland Games** (www.nairnhighlandgames.co.uk; ☺ mid-Aug), and there's also the **Nairn Book and Arts Festival** (www.nairnfestival.co.uk; ☺ Sep).

🛏 Sleeping & Eating

Glebe End   B&B ££
(☑ 01667-451659; www.glebe-end.co.uk; 1 Glebe Rd; r per person £35-45; ℗ 🛜) It's people as much as place that make a good B&B, and the owners here are all you could wish for –

helpful and welcoming. The house is lovely too, a spacious Victorian villa with home-away-from-home bedrooms and a sunny conservatory where breakfast is served.

Boath House Hotel
HOTEL £££

(☎01667-454896; www.boath-house.com; Auldearn; s/d from £190/260; P🐾) This beautifully restored Regency mansion, set in private woodland gardens 2 miles east of Nairn on the A96, is one of Scotland's most luxurious country-house hotels, and includes a spa offering holistic treatments and a Michelin-starred restaurant (three-/six-course dinner £45/70).

Classroom
GASTROPUB ££

(☎01667-455999; www.theclassroombistro.com; 1 Cawdor St; mains £14-25; ⊗noon-4.30pm & 5-10pm) 🍴 Done up in an appealing mixture of modern and traditional styles (lots of richly glowing wood with designer detailing) the Classroom doubles as cocktail bar and gastropub with a tempting menu that goes from Cullen skink (soup made with smoked haddock, potato, onion and milk) to Highland steak with peppercorn sauce.

❶ Information

Nairn has a **tourist information point** (☎01667-453476; Nairn Community Centre, King St; ⊗9am-5pm), banks with ATMs and a post office.

❶ Getting There & Away

Buses run hourly (less frequently on Sunday) from Inverness to Nairn (£5.50, 35 minutes) and on to Aberdeen. The bus station is just west of the town centre. The town also lies on the Inverness–Aberdeen railway line; there are five to seven trains a day from Inverness (£5.80, 15 minutes).

Cawdor Castle

Cawdor Castle
CASTLE

(☎01667-404615; www.cawdorcastle.com; adult/child £10/6.50; ⊗10am-5.30pm May-Sep) This was the 14th-century home of the thanes of Cawdor, one of the titles prophesied by the three witches for Shakespeare's Macbeth. But Macbeth couldn't have lived here, since the oldest part of the castle dates from the 14th century (the wings were 17th-century additions) and he died in 1057. The tour gives an insight into the 18th- and 19th-century lives of the Scottish

aristocracy; the castle is 5 miles southwest of Nairn.

Cawdor Tavern
PUB

(www.cawdortavern.co.uk; bar meals £9-21; ⊗11am-11pm Mon-Thu, 11am-midnight Fri & Sat, noon-11pm Sun, food served noon-9pm Mon-Sat, 12.30-9pm Sun) in the nearby village is worth a visit, though it can be difficult deciding what to drink as it stocks more than 100 varieties of whisky. There's also good pub food, with tempting daily specials.

West of Inverness

Beauly

POP 1365

Mary, Queen of Scots is said to have given this village its name in 1564 when she exclaimed, in French: *'Quel beau lieu!'* (What a beautiful place!). Founded in 1230, the red-sandstone **Beauly Priory** is now an impressive ruin, haunted by the cries of rooks nesting in a magnificent centuries-old sycamore tree.

The central **Priory Hotel** (☎01463-782309; www.priory-hotel.com; The Square; s/d £65/110; P🐾) has bright, modern rooms and serves good bar meals. However, the best place for lunch is across the street at the **Corner on the Square** (www.corneronthesquare.co.uk; 1 High St; mains £7-13; ⊗8.30am-5.30pm Mon-Fri, 8.30am-5pm Sat, 9.30am-5pm Sun), a superb little delicatessen and cafe that serves breakfast (till 11.30am), daily lunch specials (11.30am to 4.30pm) and excellent coffee.

Buses 28 and 28A from Inverness run to Beauly (£4.80, 30 to 45 minutes, hourly Monday to Saturday, five on Sunday), and it's on the Inverness–Thurso railway line.

Strathglass & Glen Affric

The broad valley of Strathglass extends about 18 miles inland from Beauly, followed by the A831 to **Cannich** (the only village in the area), where there's a grocery store and a post office.

Glen Affric (www.glenaffric.org), one of the most beautiful glens in Scotland, extends deep into the hills beyond Cannich. The upper reaches of the glen, now designated as **Glen Affric National Nature Reserve** (www.nnr-scotland.org.uk/glen-affric), is a scenic wonderland of shimmering lochs, rugged mountains and native Scots pine, home to pine martens, wildcats, otters, red squirrels and golden eagles.

About 4 miles southwest of Cannich is **Dog Falls**, a scenic spot where the River Affric squeezes through a narrow, rocky gorge. A circular walking trail (red waymarks) leads from Dog Falls car park to a footbridge below the falls and back on the far side of the river (2 miles, allow one hour).

The road continues beyond Dog Falls to a parking area and picnic site at the eastern end of **Loch Affric** where there are several short walks along the river and the loch shore. The circuit of Loch Affric (10 miles, allow five hours walking, two hours by mountain bike) follows good paths right around the loch and takes you deep into the heart of some very wild scenery.

It's possible to walk all the way from Cannich to **Glen Shiel** on the west coast (35 miles) in two days, spending the night at the remote Glen Affric SYHA Hostel. The route is now part of the newly waymarked **Affric-Kintail Way** (www.glenaffric.info), a 56-mile walking or mountain-biking trail leading from Drumnadrochit to Kintail via Cannich.

The minor road on the east side of the River Glass leads to the pretty little conservation village of **Tomich**, 3 miles southwest of Cannich, built in Victorian times as accommodation for estate workers. The road continues (unsurfaced for the last 2 miles) to a forestry car park, the starting point for a short (800m) walk to pretty **Plodda Falls**. A restored Victorian viewing platform extends over the top of the falls like a diving board, giving a dizzying view straight down the cascade into a remote and thickly forested river gorge. Keep your eyes peeled to see red squirrels and crossbills.

🛏 Sleeping & Eating

Glen Affric SYHA   HOSTEL £

(☑bookings 0845 293 7373; www.syha.org.uk; Allt Beithe; dm £22; ☺Apr–mid-Sep) This remote and rustic hostel is set amid magnificent scenery at the halfway point of the cross-country walk from Cannich to Glen Shiel, 8 miles from the nearest road. Facilities are basic and you'll need to take all supplies with you (and all litter away).

Book in advance. There is no phone, internet or mobile-phone signal at the hostel.

BCC Loch Ness Hostel   HOSTEL £

(☑01456-476296; www.bcclochnesshostel.co.uk; Glen Urquhart; s/d £25/45, tent sites per person £5, 2-person pods £30; 🅿🛜) Clean, modern, high-quality budget accommodation located halfway between Cannich and Loch Ness; advance booking recommended. There's also a good campsite with the option of luxury glamping pods.

Cannich Caravan & Camping Park   CAMPSITE £

(☑01456-415364; www.highlandcamping.co.uk; sites per person £7.50, pods s/d £22/30; 🛜) Good, sheltered site, with option of wooden camping 'pods' and on-site cafe. Mountain bikes for hire at £17 a day.

★ Kerrow House   B&B ££

(☑01456-415243; www.kerrow-house.co.uk; Cannich; per person £40-45; 🅿) 🍽 This wonderful Georgian hunting lodge has bags of old-fashioned character – it was once the home of Highland author Neil M Gunn – and has spacious grounds with 3.5 miles of private trout fishing. It's a mile south of Cannich on the minor road along the east side of the River Glass.

Tomich Hotel   HOTEL ££

(☑01456-415399; www.tomichhotel.co.uk; Tomich; s/d from £70/110; 🅿🛜🏊) About 3 miles southwest of Cannich on the southern side of the river, this Victorian hunting lodge has a blazing log fire, a Victorian restaurant, eight comfortable en suite rooms and – a bit of a surprise out here in the wilds – a small, heated indoor swimming pool.

❶ Getting There & Away

Stagecoach (www.stagecoachbus.com) buses 17 and 117 run from Inverness to Cannich (£5.40, one hour, three a day Monday to Saturday) via Drumnadrochit, and continue from Cannich to Tomich (10 minutes).

Ross's Minibuses (www.ross-minibuses.co.uk) From the first Monday in July to the 2nd Friday in September, runs a minibus from Inverness bus station to the Glen Affric car park via Drumnadrochit and Cannich (1½ hours, once daily Monday, Wednesday and Friday only). It shuttles between Cannich and Glen Affric (30 minutes) twice more on the same days. Check the website for the latest timetables.

Black Isle

The Black Isle – a peninsula rather than an island – is linked to Inverness by the Kessock Bridge.

Fortrose & Rosemarkie

At **Fortrose Cathedral** you'll find the vaulted crypt of a 13th-century chapter house and sacristy, and the ruinous 14th-century south aisle and chapel. **Chanonry Point**, 1.5 miles to the east, is a favourite dolphin-spotting vantage point; there are one-hour **dolphin-watching cruises** (☏ 01381-622383; www.dolphintripsavoch.co.uk; adult/child £14/9) departing from the harbour at Avoch (pronounced 'auch'), 3 miles southwest.

In Rosemarkie, the **Groam House Museum** (☏ 01381-620961; www.groamhouse.org.uk; High St; ⏱ 11am-4.30pm Mon-Fri, 2-4.30pm Sat & Sun Easter-Oct) **FREE** has a superb collection of Pictish stones engraved with designs similar to those on Celtic Irish stones.

From the northern end of Rosemarkie's High St, a short but pleasant signposted walk leads you through the gorges and waterfalls of the **Fairy Glen**.

Once you've worked up a thirst, retire to the bar at the **Anderson Hotel** (☏ 01381-620236; www.theanderson.co.uk; Union St) to sample its range of real ales (including Belgian beers and Somerset cider) and more than 200 single malt whiskies.

Cromarty

POP 725

The pretty village of Cromarty at the northeastern tip of the Black Isle has lots of 18th-century red-sandstone houses, and a lovely green park beside the sea for picnics and games. An excellent walk, known as the **100 Steps**, leads from the north end of the village to the headland viewpoint of South Sutor (4 miles round trip).

The 18th-century **Cromarty Courthouse** (☏ 01381-600418; www.cromarty-courthouse.org.uk; Church St; ⏱ noon-4pm daily Jul & Aug, Sun-Thu Easter-Jun & Sep) **FREE** details the town's history using contemporary references. Kids will enjoy the talking mannequins.

Near the courthouse is **Hugh Miller's Cottage & Museum** (www.hughmiller.org; Church St; adult/child £6.50/5; ⏱ noon-5pm daily Apr-Sep, Tue, Thu & Fri only Oct), the thatch-roofed birthplace of Hugh Miller (1802–56), a local stonemason and amateur geologist who later moved to Edinburgh and became a famous journalist and newspaper editor. The Georgian villa next door is home to a museum celebrating his life and achievements.

From Cromarty harbour, **Ecoventures** (☏ 01381-600323; www.ecoventures.co.uk; Cromarty Harbour; adult/child £26/20) runs 2½-hour boat trips into the Moray Firth to see bottlenose dolphins and other wildlife.

Also at the harbour, **Sutor Creek** (☏ 01381-600855; www.sutorcreek.co.uk; 21 Bank St; mains lunch £7-12, dinner £15-22; ⏱ 11am-9pm Wed-Sun) 🍴 is an excellent little cafe-restaurant serving wood-fired pizzas and fresh local seafood – if you can't get a table here, try its sister cafe, **Couper's Creek** (☏ 01381-600729; www.sutorcreek.co.uk; 20 Church St; mains £5-9; ⏱ 10am-5pm).

For something lighter, there are good tea and scones at the **Pantry** (1 Church St; ⏱ 10am-5pm Easter-Sep), or delicious filled rolls and savoury pies at the **Cromarty Bakery** (8 Bank St; ⏱ 9am-5pm Mon-Sat).

❶ Getting There & Away

Stagecoach buses 26 and 26A run from Inverness to Fortrose and Rosemarkie (£3.30, 30 to 40 minutes, twice hourly Monday to Saturday); half of them continue to Cromarty (£4.70, one hour).

Loch Ness

Deep, dark and narrow, Loch Ness stretches for 23 miles between Inverness and Fort Augustus. Its bitterly cold waters have been extensively explored in search of Nessie, the elusive Loch Ness monster, but most visitors see her only in cardboard-cutout form at Drumnadrochit's monster exhibitions. The busy A82 road runs along the northwestern shore, while the more tranquil and picturesque B862 follows the southeastern shore. A complete circuit of the loch is about 70 miles – travel anticlockwise for the best views.

🏃 Activities

The 79-mile **Great Glen Way** (www.greatglenway.com) long-distance footpath stretches from Inverness to Fort William, where walkers can connect with the **West Highland Way**. It is described in detail in *The Great Glen Way*, a guide by Jacquetta Megarry and Sandra Bardwell.

MONSTERS, MYTHS & LOCH NESS

Highland folklore is filled with tales of strange creatures living in lochs and rivers, notably the kelpie (water horse) that lures unwary travellers to their doom. The use of the term 'monster', however, is a relatively recent phenomenon, the origins of which lie in an article published in the *Inverness Courier* on 2 May 1933, entitled 'Strange Spectacle on Loch Ness'.

The article recounted the sighting of a disturbance in the loch by Mrs Aldie Mackay and her husband: 'There the creature disported itself, rolling and plunging for fully a minute, its body resembling that of a whale, and the water cascading and churning like a simmering cauldron.'

The story was taken up by the London press and sparked off a rash of sightings that year, including a notorious on-land encounter with London tourists Mr and Mrs Spicer on 22 July 1933, again reported in the *Inverness Courier*:

It was horrible, an abomination. About 50 yards ahead, we saw an undulating sort of neck, and quickly followed by a large, ponderous body. I estimated the length to be 25 to 30 feet, its colour was dark elephant grey. It crossed the road in a series of jerks, but because of the slope we could not see its limbs. Although I accelerated quickly towards it, it had disappeared into the loch by the time I reached the spot. There was no sign of it in the water. I am a temperate man, but I am willing to take any oath that we saw this Loch Ness beast. I am certain that this creature was of a prehistoric species.

The London newspapers couldn't resist. In December 1933 the *Daily Mail* sent Marmaduke Wetherall, a film director and big-game hunter, to Loch Ness to track down the beast. Within days he found 'reptilian' footprints in the shoreline mud (soon revealed to have been made with a stuffed hippopotamus foot). Then in April 1934 came the famous 'long-necked monster' photograph taken by the seemingly reputable Harley St surgeon Colonel Kenneth Wilson. The press went mad and the rest, as they say, is history.

In 1994, however, Christian Spurling – Wetherall's stepson, by then 90 years old – revealed that the most famous photo of Nessie ever taken was in fact a hoax, perpetrated by his stepfather with Wilson's help. Today, of course, there are those who claim that Spurling's confession is itself a hoax. And, ironically, the researcher who exposed the surgeon's photo as a fake still believes wholeheartedly in the monster's existence.

There have been regular sightings of the monster through the years (see www.lochnesssightings.com), with a peak in 1996–97 (the Hollywood movie *Loch Ness* was released in 1996), but reports have tailed off in recent years – there were no sightings at all in 2013.

Hoax or not, the bizarre mini-industry that has grown up around Loch Ness and its mysterious monster since that eventful summer three-quarters of a century ago is a spectacle in itself.

The Great Glen Way can also be ridden (strenuous!) by mountain bike, while the **Great Glen Mountain Bike Trails** at Nevis Range and Abriachan Forest offer challenging cross-country and downhill trails. (You can hire a mountain bike in Fort William and drop it off in Inverness, and vice versa.)

The **South Loch Ness Trail** (www.visitloch-ness.com/south-loch-ness-trail), opened in 2011, links a series of footpaths and minor roads along the less-frequented southern side of the loch. The 28 miles from Loch Tarff near Fort Augustus to Torbreck on the fringes of Inverness can be done on foot, by bike or on horseback.

There's also the option of the **Great Glen Canoe Trail** (www.greatglencanoetrail.info), a series of access points, waymarks and informal campsites that allow you to travel the length of the glen by canoe or kayak.

The climb to the summit of **Meallfuarvonie** (699m), on the northwestern shore of Loch Ness, makes an excellent short hill walk: the views along the Great Glen from the top are superb. It's a 6-mile round trip, so allow about three hours. Start from the car park at the end of the minor road leading south from Drumnadrochit to Bunloit.

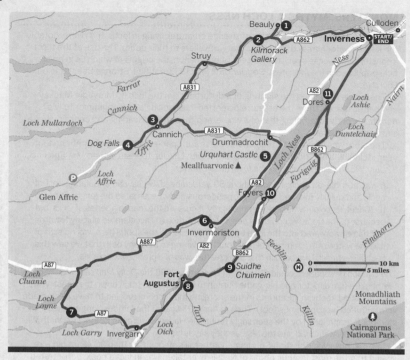

Driving Tour
A Loch Ness Circuit

START INVERNESS
FINISH INVERNESS
DISTANCE 130 MILES
DURATION FOUR HOURS

Head out of Inverness on the A862 to Beauly, arriving in time for breakfast at **1 Corner on the Square** (p308) in Beauly. Backtrack a mile and turn right on the A831 to Cannich, passing **2 Kilmorack Gallery**, which exhibits contemporary art in a converted church. The scenery gets wilder as you approach **3 Cannich**; turn right and follow the single-track road to the car park at **4 Dog Falls**. Take a stroll along the rushing river, or hike to the viewpoint (about a one-hour round trip; 2 miles) for a glimpse of remote Glen Affric.

Return to Cannich and turn right on the A831 to Drumnadrochit, then right on the A82 past picturesque **5 Urquhart Castle** (p314) and along the shores of Loch Ness. At **6 Invermoriston**, pause to look at the old bridge, built by engineer Thomas Telford

in 1813, then head west on the A887 towards Kyle of Lochalsh; after 16 miles go left on the A87 towards Invergarry. You are now among some of the finest mountain scenery in the Highlands; as the road turns east above Loch Garry, stop at the famous **7 viewpoint** (layby on right, signposted Glengarry Viewpoint). By a quirk of perspective, the lochs to the west appear to form the map outline of Scotland.

At Invergarry, turn left on the A82 to reach **8 Fort Augustus** and a late lunch at the Lovat or Lock Inn. Take the B862 out of town, following the line of General Wade's 18th-century military road, to another viewpoint at **9 Suidhe Chuimein**. A short (800m) walk up the well-worn path to the summit affords an even better panorama.

Ahead, you can choose the low road via the impressive **10 Falls of Foyers**, or stay on the the high road (B862) for more views; both converge on Loch Ness at the **11 Dores Inn** (p313), where you can sip a pint with a view along Loch Ness, and even stay for dinner before returning to Inverness.

✳️ Festivals & Events

RockNess Music Festival　　MUSIC
(www.rockness.co.uk; ☺Jun) A vast lochside
field at the village of Dores hosts this annual festival, a three-day smorgasbord of the
best in Scottish and international DJs and
bands. Recent headliners include Fat Boy
Slim, Basement Jaxx and Ellie Goulding.

Drumnadrochit

POP 1100

Seized by monster madness, its gift shops
bulging with Nessie cuddly toys, Drumnadrochit is a hotbed of beastie fever, with
two monster exhibitions battling it out for
the tourist dollar.

◉ Sights & Activities

Urquhart Castle　　CASTLE
(HS; ☎01456-450551; adult/child £7.90/4.80;
☺9.30am-6pm Apr-Sep, to 5pm Oct, to 4.30pm
Nov-Mar; Ⓟ) Commanding a brilliant location 1.5 miles east of Drumnadrochit, with
outstanding views (on a clear day), Urquhart Castle is a popular Nessie-watching
hot spot. A huge visitor centre (most of
which is beneath ground level) includes a
video theatre (with a dramatic 'unveiling'
of the castle at the end of the film) and displays of medieval items discovered in the
castle.

The castle was repeatedly sacked and rebuilt (and sacked and rebuilt) over the centuries; in 1692 it was blown up to prevent
the Jacobites from using it. The five-storey
tower house at the northern point is the
most impressive remaining fragment and

offers wonderful views across the water.
The site includes a huge gift shop and a
restaurant, and is often very crowded in
summer.

**Loch Ness Centre &
Exhibition**　　INTERPRETATION CENTRE
(☎01456-450573; www.lochness.com; adult/
child £7.45/4.95; ☺9.30am-6pm Jul & Aug, to 5pm
Easter-Jun, Sep & Oct, 10am-3.30pm Nov-Easter;
Ⓟ) This Nessie-themed attraction adopts
a scientific approach that allows you to
weigh the evidence for yourself. Exhibits
include the original equipment – sonar
survey vessels, miniature submarines, cameras and sediment coring tools – used in
various monster hunts, as well as original
photographs and film footage of sightings.
You'll find out about hoaxes and optical illusions, as well as learning a lot about the
ecology of Loch Ness – is there enough food
in the loch to support even one 'monster',
let alone a breeding population?

Nessieland　　EXHIBITION
(www.nessieland.co.uk; adult/child £6/3; ☺9am-
7pm Apr-Oct, to 5pm Nov-Mar; Ⓟ) This attraction is a miniature theme park aimed
squarely at the kids, though we suspect its
main function is to sell you Loch Ness monster souvenirs.

Nessie Hunter　　BOAT TOURS
(☎01456-450395; www.lochness-cruises.com;
adult/child £15/10; ☺Easter-Oct) One-hour
monster-hunting cruises, complete with
sonar and underwater cameras. Cruises
depart from Drumnadrochit hourly (except
1pm) from 9am to 6pm daily.

INVERNESS & THE CENTRAL HIGHLANDS LOCH NESS

WORTH A TRIP

DORES INN

While crowded tour coaches pour down the west side of Loch Ness to the hot spots of
Drumnadrochit and Urquhart Castle, the narrow B862 road along the eastern shore is
relatively peaceful. It leads to the village of Foyers, where you can enjoy a pleasant hike to
the **Falls of Foyers**.

But it's worth making the trip just for the **Dores Inn** (☎ 01463 751203; www.thedoresinn.
co.uk; Dores; mains £10-14; ☺ pub 10am-11pm, food served noon-2pm & 6-9pm; Ⓟ 🛜), a beautifully restored country pub furnished with recycled furniture, local landscape paintings
and fresh flowers. The menu specialises in quality Scottish produce, from haggis, turnips
and *tatties* (potatoes), and haddock and chips, to steaks, scallops and seafood platters.

The pub garden enjoys a stunning view along Loch Ness, and even has a dedicated
monster-spotting vantage point. The nearby campervan, emblazoned with Nessie-Serry
Independent Research, has been home to dedicated Nessie hunter Steve Feltham (www.
nessiehunter.co.uk) since 1991; he sells clay models of the monster, and is a font of fascinating stories about the loch.

LOCAL KNOWLEDGE

LOCH NESS & AROUND

The leader of the Loch Ness Project, and designer of the Loch Ness Centre & Exhibition, Adrian Shine, offers his recommendations for the Loch Ness area.

Urquhart Castle

If, having learned some of the inner secrets of the loch at the Loch Ness Centre & Exhibition (p313), you want to see it through new eyes, you cannot do better than visit Urquhart Castle (p313). Perched on a rocky promontory jutting into Loch Ness, its exhibits recount the castle's history from a vitrified Pictish fort to its role in the Scottish Wars of Independence. The view from the Grant Tower is truly breathtaking.

Fort Augustus Locks

At the southern end of the loch there is a flight of locks on the Caledonian Canal (p315) built by the great engineer Thomas Telford. It is always interesting to watch vessels being worked up this 'staircase' of water. British Waterways have a fascinating exhibition beside the locks.

Waterfall Walks

Starting from the car park at Invermoriston, cross the road to find a magnificent waterfall, then go back to take the path down the river through a mature beech wood to the shores of the loch. There is another famous waterfall at Foyers on the southeastern shore of Loch Ness, and Divach Falls up Balmacaan Rd at Drumnadrochit.

🛏 Sleeping & Eating

Loch Ness Backpackers Lodge HOSTEL **£**
(☑ 01456-450807; www.lochness-backpackers. com; Coiltie Farmhouse, East Lewiston; per person from £16; ℗ 🖥) This snug, friendly hostel housed in a cottage and barn has six-bed dorms, one double and a large barbecue area. It's about 0.75 miles from Drumnadrochit, along the A82 towards Fort William; turn left where you see the sign for Loch Ness Inn, just before the bridge.

Loch Ness SYHA HOSTEL **£**
(☑ 01320-351274; www.syha.org.uk; Glenmoriston; dm £20; ⊙ Apr-Sep, closed 10am-5pm daily; @) This hostel is housed in a big lodge overlooking Loch Ness, and many dorms have loch views. It's located on the A82 road, 13 miles southwest of Drumnadrochit, and 4 miles northeast of Invermoriston. Buses from Inverness to Fort William stop nearby.

Borlum Farm CAMPSITE **£**
(☑ 01456-450220; www.borlum.co.uk; sites per adult/child £6/4; ⊙ Mar-Oct) Basic campsite beside the main road 800m southeast of Drumnadrochit.

Loch Ness Inn INN **££**
(☑ 01456-450991; www.staylochness.co.uk; Lewiston; d/f £90/120; ℗ 🖥) The Loch Ness Inn ticks all the weary traveller's boxes, with comfortable bedrooms (the family suite sleeps two adults and two children), a cosy bar pouring real ales from the Cairngorm and Isle of Skye breweries, and a rustic restaurant (mains £9 to £19) serving hearty, wholesome fare such as whisky-flambéed haggis, and roast rump of Scottish lamb.

It's conveniently located in the quiet hamlet of Lewiston, between Drumnadrochit and Urquhart Castle.

Drumbuie Farm B&B **££**
(☑ 01456-450634; www.loch-ness-farm.co.uk; Drumnadrochit; s/d from £44/68; ℗) Drumbuie is a B&B in a modern house on a working farm – the surrounding fields are full of sheep and highland cattle – with views over Urquhart Castle and Loch Ness. Walkers and cyclists are welcome.

Fiddler's Coffee Shop & Restaurant CAFE, RESTAURANT **££**
(www.fiddledrum.co.uk; mains £11-18; ⊙ 11am-11pm; 🖥) The coffee shop does cappuccino and croissants, while the restaurant serves traditional Highland fare, such as venison and haggis, and a wide range of bottled Scottish beers. There's also a whisky bar with huge range of single malts.

ℹ Getting There & Away

Scottish Citylink (p302) and Stagecoach buses from Inverness to Fort William run along the shores of Loch Ness (six to eight daily, five on

Sunday); those headed for Skye turn off at Invermoriston. There are bus stops at Drumnadrochit (£3.20, 30 minutes), Urquhart Castle car park (£3.50, 35 minutes) and Loch Ness Youth Hostel (£9, 45 minutes).

Fort Augustus

POP 620

Fort Augustus, at the junction of four old military roads, was originally a government garrison and the headquarters of General George Wade's road-building operations in the early 18th century. Today it's a neat and picturesque little place, often overrun by coach-tour crowds in summer.

◎ Sights & Activities

Caledonian Canal   CANAL
(www.scottishcanals.co.uk) At Fort Augustus, boats using the Caledonian Canal are raised and lowered 13m by a 'ladder' of five consecutive locks. It's fun to watch, and the neatly landscaped canal banks are a great place to soak up the sun or compare accents with fellow tourists. The **Caledonian Canal Visitor Centre** (☑ 01320-366493; Ardchattan House, Canalside; ⊙ 10am-1.30pm & 2-5.30pm Apr-Oct) **FREE**, beside the lowest lock, showcases the history of the canal (p345).

Clansman Centre   MUSEUM
(www.scottish-swords.com; ⊙ 10am-6pm Apr-Oct) This exhibition of 17th-century Highland life has live demonstrations of how to put on a plaid (the forerunner of the kilt) and how the claymore (Highland sword) was made and used. There is also a workshop where you can purchase handcrafted reproduction swords, dirks and shields.

Cruise Loch Ness   BOAT TOURS
(☑ 01320-366277;   www.cruiselochness.com; adult/child £13.50/8; ⊙ hourly 10am-4pm Apr-Oct, 1 & 2pm only Nov-Mar) One-hour cruises on Loch Ness accompanied by the latest high-tech sonar equipment so you can keep an underwater eye open for Nessie. There are also one-hour evening cruises, departing 8pm daily (except Friday) April to August, and 90-minute speedboat tours.

🛏 Sleeping & Eating

Morag's Lodge   HOSTEL £
(☑ 01320-366289; www.moragslodge.com; Bunoich Brae; dm/tw/f from £21/50/69; P @ 🛜) This large and well-run hostel is based in a big Victorian house with great views of Fort Au-

gustus' hilly surrounds, and has a convivial bar with open fire. It's hidden away in the trees up the steep side road just north of the tourist-office car park.

Cumberland's Campsite   CAMPSITE £
(☑ 01320-366257;   www.cumberlands-campsite. com; Glendoe Rd; sites per adult/child £8/3; ⊙ Apr-Sep) Southeast of the village on the B862 towards Whitebridge; entrance beside Stravaigers Lodge.

Lorien House   B&B ££
(☑ 01320-366736; www.lorien-house.co.uk; Station Rd; s/d £60/74) Lorien is a cut above your usual B&B: the bathrooms come with bidets and the breakfasts with smoked salmon, and there's a library of walking, cycling and climbing guides in the lounge. No children under 12.

★ Lovat   HOTEL £££
(☑ 01456-459250;   www.thelovat.com;   Main Rd; d from £121; P 🛜) 🌱 A boutique-style makeover has transformed this former huntin'-and-shootin' hotel into a luxurious but ecoconscious retreat set apart from the tourist crush around the canal. The bedrooms are spacious and stylishly furnished, while the lounge is equipped with a log fire, comfy armchairs and grand piano. It has an informal brasserie and a highly acclaimed restaurant (five-course dinner £50), which serves top-quality cuisine.

Lock Inn   PUB ££
(Canal Side; mains £9-14; ⊙ meals noon-8pm) A superb little pub right on the canal bank, the Lock Inn has a vast range of malt whiskies and a tempting menu of bar meals, which includes Orkney salmon, Highland venison and daily seafood specials; the house speciality is beer-battered haddock and chips.

ℹ Information

There's an ATM and bureau de change in the post office beside the canal.

Fort Augustus Tourist Office (☑ 01320-366367; ⊙ 9am-6pm Mon-Sat & to 5pm Sun Easter-Oct) In the central car park.

ℹ Getting There & Away

Scottish Citylink (www.citylink.co.uk) and **Stagecoach** (www.stagecoachbus.com) buses from Inverness to Fort William stop at Fort Augustus (£6 to £10.20, one hour, five to eight daily Monday to Saturday, five on Sunday).

THE CAIRNGORMS

The Cairngorms National Park (www.cairngorms.co.uk) encompasses the highest landmass in Britain: a broad mountain plateau, riven only by the deep valleys of the Lairig Ghru and Loch Avon, with an average altitude of over 1000m and including five of the six highest summits in the UK. This wild mountain landscape of granite and heather has a sub-Arctic climate and supports rare alpine tundra vegetation and high-altitude bird species, such as snow bunting, ptarmigan and dotterel.

The harsh mountain environment gives way lower down to scenic glens softened by beautiful open forests of native Scots pine, home to rare animals and birds such as pine martens, wildcats, red squirrels, ospreys, capercaillies and crossbills.

This is prime hill-walking territory, but even couch potatoes can enjoy a taste of the high life by taking the Cairngorm Mountain Railway up to the edge of the Cairngorm plateau.

Aviemore

POP 3150

The gateway to the Cairngorms, Aviemore is the region's main centre for transport, accommodation, restaurants and shops. It's not the prettiest town in Scotland by a long stretch – the main attractions are in the surrounding area – but when bad weather puts the hills off limits, Aviemore fills up with hikers, cyclists and climbers (plus skiers and snowboarders in winter) cruising the outdoor-equipment shops or recounting their latest adventures in the cafes and bars. Add in tourists and locals and the eclectic mix makes for a lively little town.

Aviemore is on a loop off the A9 Perth–Inverness road; almost everything of note is to be found along the main drag, Grampian Rd; the train station and bus stop are towards its southern end.

The Cairngorm skiing area and funicular railway lie 9 miles southeast of Aviemore along the B970 (Ski Rd) and its continuation, past Coylumbridge and Glenmore.

⊙ Sights

Strathspey Steam Railway   HERITAGE RAILWAY
(☑ 01479-810725; www.strathspeyrailway.co.uk; Station Sq; return ticket per adult/child £13.95/6.98) Strathspey Steam Railway runs steam trains on a section of restored line between Aviemore and Broomhill, 10 miles to the northeast, via Boat of Garten. There are four or five trains daily from June to August, and a more limited service in April, May, September, October and December, with the option of enjoying afternoon tea, Sunday lunch or a five-course dinner on board.

An extension to Grantown-on-Spey is under construction (see www.railstograntown.org); in the meantime, you can continue from Broomhill to Grantown-on-Spey by bus.

★ Rothiemurchus Estate   FOREST
(www.rothiemurchus.net) The Rothiemurchus Estate, which extends from the River Spey at Aviemore to the Cairngorm summit plateau, is famous for having Scotland's largest remnant of **Caledonian forest**, the ancient forest of Scots pine that once covered most of the country. The forest is home to a large population of red squirrels, and is one of the last bastions of the Scottish wildcat.

The **Rothiemurchus Estate visitor centre** (☑ 01479-812345; ⊙ 9.30am-5.50pm) **FREE**, a mile southeast of Aviemore along the B970, sells an *Explorer Map* detailing more than 50 miles of footpaths and cycling trails, including the wheelchair-accessible 4-mile trail around **Loch an Eilein**, with its ruined castle and peaceful pine woods.

Craigellachie Nature Reserve   NATURE RESERVE
(www.nnr-scotland.org.uk/craigellachie; Grampian Rd; 🔊) A trail leads west from Aviemore Youth Hostel and passes under the A9 into the Craigellachie Nature Reserve, a great place for short hikes across steep hillsides covered in natural birch forest. Look out for wildlife, including the peregrine falcons that nest on the crags from April to July.

🏃 Activities

Bothy Bikes   MOUNTAIN BIKING
(☑ 01479-810111; www.bothybikes.co.uk; 5 Granish Way, Dalfaber; per half-/full day £16/20; ⊙ 9am-5.30pm) Located in northern Aviemore on the way to the golf course, this place rents out mountain bikes and can also advise on routes and trails; a good choice for beginners is the **Old Logging Way**, which runs from Aviemore to Glenmore, where you can make a circuit of Loch Morlich before returning. For experienced bikers, the whole of the Cairngorms is your playground. Booking recommended.

The Cairngorms

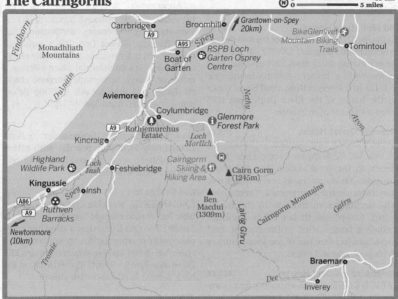

Rothiemurchus Fishery · FISHING

(☑ 01479-810703; www.rothiemurchus.net; Rothiemurchus Estate; ⏱ 9.30am-5pm Sep-May, to dusk Jun-Aug) Cast for rainbow trout at this loch at the southern end of the village; buy permits (from £10 for two hours to £30 per day, plus £5 for tackle hire) at the Fish Farm Shop. If you're a fly-fishing virgin, there's a beginner's package, including tackle hire, one hour's instruction and one hour's fishing, for £45 per person.

For experienced anglers, there's also salmon and sea-trout fishing on the River Spey – a day permit costs around £20; numbers are limited, so it's best to book in advance.

Cairngorm Sled-Dog Centre · DOG SLEDDING

(☑ 07767-270526; www.sled-dogs.co.uk; Ski Rd) This outfit will take you on a 30-minute sled tour of local forest trails in the wake of a team of huskies (adult/child £60/40), or a three-hour sled-dog safari (£175 per person). The sleds have wheels, so snow's not necessary. There are also one-hour guided tours of the kennels (adult/child £8/4). The centre is 3 miles east of Aviemore, signposted off the road to Loch Morlich.

Alvie & Dalraddy Estate · QUAD BIKING

(☑ 01479-810330; www.alvie-estate.co.uk; Dalraddy Holiday Park; per person £45) Join an hour-long cross-country quad-bike trek at this estate, 3 miles south of Aviemore on the B9152 (call first).

🛏 Sleeping

Aviemore Bunkhouse · HOSTEL £

(☑ 01479-811181, www.aviemore-bunkhouse.com; Dalfaber Rd; dm/d/f from £19/50/65; ℗@🛜) This independent hostel provides accommodation in bright, modern six- or eight-bed dorms, each with private bathroom, and one twin/family room. It has a drying room, secure bike storage and wheelchair-accessible dorms. From the train station, cross the pedestrian bridge over the tracks, turn right and walk south on Dalfaber Rd.

Aviemore SYHA · HOSTEL £

(☑ 01479-810345; www.syha.org.uk; 25 Grampian Rd; dm £20; ℗@🛜) Upmarket hostelling in a spacious, well-equipped building, five minutes' walk south of the village centre. There are four- and six-bed rooms, and a comfortable lounge with views of the mountains.

Rothiemurchus Camp & Caravan Park · CAMPSITE £

(☑ 01479-812800; www.rothiemurchus.net; Coylumbridge; sites per adult/child £11/2) The nearest camping ground to Aviemore is this year-round park, beautifully sited among

Scots pines at Coylumbridge, 1.5 miles along the B970.

Old Minister's House
B&B **££**

(☎ 01479-812181; www.theoldministershouse.co.uk; Rothiemurchus; s/d £70/110; P ≋) This former manse dates from 1906 and has four rooms with a homely, country-farmhouse feel. It's in a lovely setting amid Scots pines on the banks of the River Druie, just 0.75 miles southeast of Aviemore.

Ardlogie Guest House
B&B **££**

(☎ 01479-810747; www.ardlogie.co.uk; Dalfaber Rd; s/d from £40/62, Bothy per 3 nights £165; P ≋) Handy to the train station, the five-room Ardlogie has great views over the River Spey towards the Cairngorms. There's also self-catering accommodation in the Bothy, a cosy, two-person timber cabin. Facilities include a boules pitch in the garden, and guests can get free use of the local country club's pool, spa and sauna.

Ravenscraig Guest House
B&B **££**

(☎ 01479-810278; www.aviemoreonline.com; Grampian Rd; s/d £48/82; P ≋) Ravenscraig is a large, flower-bedecked Victorian villa with six spacious en suite rooms, plus another six in a modern chalet at the back (one wheelchair accessible). It serves traditional and veggie breakfasts in an attractive conservatory dining room.

Cairngorm Hotel
HOTEL **££**

(☎ 01479-810233; www.cairngorm.com; Grampian Rd; s/d from £61/104; P ≋) Better known as 'the Cairn', this long-established hotel is set in the fine old granite building with the pointy turret opposite the train station. It's a welcoming place with comfortable rooms and a determinedly Scottish atmosphere, all tartan carpets and stags' antlers. There's live music on weekends, so it can get a bit noisy – not for early-to-bedders.

✖ Eating & Drinking

★ Mountain Cafe
CAFE **£**

(www.mountaincafe-aviemore.co.uk; 111 Grampian Rd; mains £4-10; ☺ 8.30am-5pm Tue-Thu, to 5.30pm Fri-Mon; P ⅌ ⋒) The Mountain Cafe offers freshly prepared local produce with a Kiwi twist (the owner is from New Zealand): healthy breakfasts of muesli, porridge and fresh fruit (till 11.30am), hearty lunches of seafood chowder, burgers and imaginative salads, and home-baked breads, cakes and biscuits. Vegan, coeliac and nut-allergic diets catered for.

Ski-ing Doo
STEAKHOUSE **££**

(☎ 01479-810392; 9 Grampian Rd; mains £8-13, steaks £18-21; ☺ noon-9.30pm; ≋ ⋒) A long-standing Aviemore institution, the child-friendly Ski-ing Doo (it's a pun…ask the waiter!) is a favourite with family skiers and hikers. It's an informal place offering a range of hearty, homemade burgers, chicken dishes and juicy steaks; the Doo Below cafe-bar is open from 3pm to 11pm.

Winking Owl
PUB

(www.thewinkingowl.net; Grampian Rd; ☺ 11am-11pm) Lively local pub, popular with hikers and climbers, serving a good range of real ales and malt whiskies.

Old Bridge Inn
PUB

(☎ 01479-811137; www.oldbridgeinn.co.uk; 23 Dalfaber Rd; ☺ noon-midnight Sun-Thu, to 1am Fri & Sat; ≋) The Old Bridge has a snug bar, complete with roaring log fire in winter, and a cheerful, chalet-style **restaurant** (mains £10-24; ☺ noon-2pm & 6-9pm, to 10pm Fri & Sat) at the back serving quality Scottish cuisine.

❶ Information

There are ATMs outside the Tesco supermarket, and currency exchange at the post office and the tourist office, all located on Grampian Rd.

Aviemore Tourist Office (☎ 01479-810930; www.visitaviemore.com; The Mall, Grampian Rd; ☺ 9am-6pm Mon-Sat, 9.30am-5pm Sun Jul & Aug, 9am-5pm Mon-Sat, 10am-4pm Sun Easter-Jun, Sep & Oct) Hours are limited from October to Easter.

❶ Getting There & Away

BUS

Buses stop on Grampian Rd opposite the train station; buy tickets at the tourist office. Services include the following:

Edinburgh £26, four hours, five daily

Glasgow £26, 2¾ hours, five daily

Grantown-on-Spey £3.50, 35 minutes, five daily weekdays, two Saturday; bus 33 via Carrbridge (15 minutes)

Inverness £9.80, 45 minutes, eight daily

Perth £19.20, 2¼ hours, five daily

TRAIN

The train station is on Grampian Rd.

Edinburgh £40, three hours, six daily

Glasgow £40, three hours, six daily

Inverness £11.70, 40 minutes, 12 daily

ⓘ Getting Around

BICYCLE

Several places in Aviemore, Rothiemurchus Estate and Glenmore have mountain bikes for hire. An off-road cycle track links Aviemore with Glenmore and Loch Morlich.

Bothy Bikes (☑ 01479-810111; www.bothy-bikes.co.uk; 5 Granish Way, Dalfaber; ☺ 9am-5.30pm) Charges £20 a day for a quality bike with front suspension and disc brakes.

BUS

Bus 31 links Aviemore to Cairngorm car park (£2.50, 30 minutes, hourly) via Coylumbridge and Glenmore. A Strathspey Dayrider/Megarider ticket (£6.50/17) gives one/seven days unlimited bus travel from Aviemore as far as Cairngorm, Carrbridge and Kingussie (buy from the bus driver).

Around Aviemore

Cairngorm Mountain

Cairngorm Mountain Railway FUNICULAR RAILWAY
(☑ 01479-861261; www.cairngormmountain.org; adult/child return £10.50/6.80; ☺ every 20min, 10am-4pm May-Nov, 9am-4.30pm Dec-Apr) The region's most popular attraction is a funicular railway that will whisk you to the edge of the Cairngorm plateau (1085m) in just eight minutes. The bottom station is at the Coire Cas car park at the end of Ski Rd; at the top is an exhibition, a shop (of course) and a restaurant. Unfortunately, for environmental and safety reasons, you're not allowed out of the top station in summer unless you book a guided walk or mountain-bike descent.

From May to October, a 90-minute guided walk to the summit of Cairn Gorm (per person £6) departs twice a day, while a five-hour guided hill-walk runs twice a week. There's also the option of a guided mountain-bike descent (per person £25 to £35 including bike hire), Thursday to Sunday only. Check the website for details.

Cairngorm Mountain Ski Area SNOW SPORTS
(www.cairngormmountain.org; 1-day ski pass per adult/child £33.50/20) Aspen or Val d'Isère it ain't, but with 19 runs and 23 miles of piste Cairngorm is Scotland's biggest ski area. When the snow is at its best and the sun is shining you can close your eyes and imagine you're in the Alps; sadly, low cloud, high winds and horizontal sleet are more common. Ski or snowboard hire is around £23/17 per adult/child per day; there are lots of hire outlets at Coire Cas, Glenmore and Aviemore.

The season usually runs from December until the snow melts, which may be as late as the end of April, but snowfall here is unpredictable – in some years the slopes can be open in November, but closed for lack of snow in February. During the season the tourist office in Aviemore displays snow conditions and avalanche warnings. You can check the latest snow conditions at http://ski.visitscotland.com and www.winterhighland.info.

Loch Morlich

Six miles east of Aviemore, Loch Morlich is surrounded by some 8 sq miles of pine and spruce forest that make up the **Glenmore Forest Park**. Its attractions include a sandy beach (at the east end).

◉ Sights & Activities

The park's visitor centre at Glenmore has a small exhibition on the Caledonian forest and sells the *Glenmore Forest Park Map,* detailing local walks. The **circuit of Loch Morlich** (one hour) makes a pleasant outing; the trail is pram- and wheelchair-friendly.

★ **Glenmore Lodge** ADVENTURE SPORTS
(☑ 01479-861256; www.glenmorelodge.org.uk) One of Britain's leading adventure-sports training centres, offering courses in hill walking, rock climbing, ice climbing, canoeing, mountain biking and mountaineering. The centre's comfortable **B&B accommodation** (tw £76) is available to all, even if you're not taking a course, as is the indoor-climbing wall, gym and sauna.

Cairngorm Reindeer Centre GUIDED TOURS
(www.cairngormreindeer.co.uk; adult/child £12/6) The warden here will take you on a guided walk to see and feed Britain's only herd of reindeer, who are very tame and will even eat out of your hand. Walks take place at 11am daily year-round (weather-dependent), plus another at 2.30pm from May to September, and 3.30pm Monday to Friday in July and August.

Loch Morlich Watersports Centre WATER SPORTS
(☑ 01479-861221; www.lochmorlich.com; ☺ 9am-5pm May-Oct) This popular outfit rents out

Canadian canoes (£21 an hour), kayaks (£8), sailboards (£17.50), sailing dinghies (£25) and rowing boats (£21), and also offers instruction.

🛏 Sleeping

There is also accommodation at Glenmore Lodge (p319).

Cairngorm Lodge SYHA HOSTEL £
(☑ 01479-861238; dm/tw £17/45; ⊘ closed Nov & Dec; @ 🛜) Set in a former shooting lodge that enjoys a great location at the east end of Loch Morlich; prebooking is essential.

Glenmore Campsite CAMPSITE £
(☑ 01479-861271; www.campingintheforest.co.uk; tent & campervan sites £27) Campers can set up base at this attractive lochside site with pitches amid the Scots pines; rates include up to four people per tent/campervan.

❶ Getting There & Away

Bus 31 links Aviemore with Glenmore (£1.95, 30 minutes, hourly) .

Kincraig & Glen Feshie

Highland Wildlife Park WILDLIFE PARK
(☑ 01540-651270; www.highlandwildlifepark.org; adult/child £14.50/10.50; ⊘ 10am to 6pm Jul & Aug, to 5pm Apr-Jun & Sep-Oct, to 4pm Nov-Mar) It features a drive-through safari park and animal enclosures offering the chance to view rarely seen native wildlife, such as Scottish wildcats, capercaillies, pine martens and red squirrels, as well as species that once roamed the Scottish hills but have long since disappeared, including wolves, lynx, wild boars, beavers and European bison. Visitors without cars get driven around by staff (at no extra cost). It's near Kincraig, 6 miles southwest of Aviemore, and last entry is two hours before closing. Stagecoach bus 32 runs from Aviemore to Kincraig (10 minutes, five daily Monday to Saturday).

At Kincraig the Spey widens into Loch Insh, home of the **Loch Insh Watersports Centre** (☑ 01540-651272; www.lochinsh. com; Kincraig; day ticket per adult/child £32/25; ⊘ 8.30am-5.30pm), which offers canoeing, windsurfing, sailing, bike hire and fishing, as well as B&B accommodation. The food here is good, especially after 6.30pm when the lochside cafe becomes a cosy restaurant.

Beautiful, tranquil Glen Feshie extends south from Kincraig, deep into the Cairngorms, with Scots pine woods in its upper reaches surrounded by big, heathery hills. The 4WD track to the head of the glen makes a great mountain-bike excursion (25-mile round trip).

Carrbridge

POP 700

Carrbridge, 7 miles northeast of Aviemore, is a good alternative base for exploring the region. It takes its name from the graceful **old bridge** (spotlit at night), built in 1717, over the thundering rapids of the Dulnain.

The **Landmark Forest Adventure Park** (☑ 01479-841613; www.landmarkpark.co.uk; adult/child £15.50/13.50; ⊘ 10am-7pm mid-Jul–Aug, to 5 or 6pm Apr–mid-Jul & Sep, to 5pm Oct-Mar), set in a forest of Scots pines, is a theme park with a difference – the theme is timber. The main attractions are the Ropeworx high-wire adventure course, the Treetops Trail (a raised

---

MOUNTAIN WALKS IN THE CAIRNGORMS

The climb from the car park at the Coire Cas ski area to the summit of **Cairn Gorm** (1245m) is 2 miles and takes about two hours (one way). From there, you can continue south across the high-level plateau to Ben Macdui (1309m), Britain's second-highest peak. From the car park to the peak and then back is 12 miles and takes eight to 10 hours. It's a serious undertaking, and is for experienced and well-equipped walkers only.

The **Lairig Ghru trail**, which can take eight to 10 hours, is a demanding 24-mile walk from Aviemore through the Lairig Ghru pass (840m) to Braemar. An alternative to doing the full route is to make the six-hour return hike up to the summit of the pass and back to Aviemore. The path starts from Ski Rd, a mile east of Coylumbridge, and involves some very rough going.

Warning: the Cairngorm plateau is a sub-Arctic environment where navigation is difficult and weather conditions can be severe, even in midsummer. Hikers must have proper hill-walking equipment, and know how to use a map and compass. In winter it is a place for experienced mountaineers only. Trip durations are estimates only.

walkway through the forest canopy that allows you to view red squirrels, crossbills and crested tits), and the steam-powered sawmill.

Bus 34 runs from Inverness to Carrbridge (£4.65, 45 minutes, six daily Monday to Friday, three on Saturday) and onwards to Grantown-on-Spey (£2.50, 20 minutes) and Aviemore.

Boat of Garten

Boat of Garten is known as the Osprey Village because these rare and beautiful birds of prey nest nearby at the **RSPB Loch Garten Osprey Centre** (☑ 01479-831694; www.rspb.org.uk/lochgarten; Tulloch; osprey hide adult/child £5/2; ☺ osprey hide 10am-6pm Apr-Aug). The ospreys migrate here each spring from Africa and nest in a tall pine tree – you can watch from a hide as the birds feed their young. The centre is signposted about 2 miles east of the village.

There is flexible, good-quality home-stay accommodation at **Fraoch Lodge** (☑ 01479-831331; www.scotmountainholidays.com; Deshar Rd; per person £21-25; P 🛜), along with a wide range of outdoor activities, while the **Boat Hotel** (☑ 01479-831258; www.boathotel.co.uk; r from £100; P 🛜 🐾) offers luxurious accommodation and a superb restaurant.

Boat of Garten is 6 miles northeast of Aviemore. The most interesting way to get here is on the Strathspey Steam Railway (p316) from Aviemore.

Grantown-on-Spey

POP 2430

Grantown (*gran*-ton) is an elegant Georgian town on the banks of the Spey, a favoured haunt of anglers and the tweed-cap-and-green-wellies brigade. Thronged with tourists in summer, it reverts to a quiet backwater in winter. Most hotels can kit you out for a day of fly-fishing or put you in touch with someone who can.

🛏 Sleeping & Eating

⭐ **Brooklynn**   B&B ££
(☑ 01479-873113; www.woodier.com; Grant Rd; r per person £38-44; P 🛜) 🍃 This beautiful Victorian villa features original stained glass and wood panelling, and seven spacious, luxurious rooms (all doubles have en suites). The food – dinner is available as well as breakfast – is superb too.

Chaplin's Coffee House & Ice Cream Parlour   CAFE £
(High St; ☺ 10am-5pm May-Sep, closed Sun Oct-Apr) Traditional family cafe selling delicious homemade ice cream.

ℹ Getting There & Away

Bus 34 runs from Inverness to Aviemore via Grantown-on-Spey (£5.90, 1¼ hours, six daily Monday to Friday, three on Saturday).

Kingussie & Newtonmore

The gracious old Speyside towns of Kingussie (kin-*yew*-see) and Newtonmore sit at the foot of the great heather-clad humps known as the Monadhliath Mountains. Newtonmore is best known as the home of the excellent Highland Folk Museum; the road west from Newtonmore to Spean Bridge passes Ardverikie Estate and Loch Laggan, famous as the setting for the BBC TV series *Monarch of the Glen*.

⊙ Sights & Activities

Highland Folk Museum   MUSEUM
(☑ 01540-673551; www.highlandfolk.museum; Kingussie Rd, Newtonmore; ☺ 10.30am-5.30pm Apr-Aug, 11am-4.30pm Sep & Oct) 🅵🆁🅴🅴 The open air Highland Folk Museum comprises a collection of historical buildings and artefacts revealing many aspects of Highland culture and lifestyle. Laid out like a farming township, it has a community of traditional thatch-roofed cottages, a sawmill, a schoolhouse, a shepherd's bothy (hut) and a rural post office. Actors in period costume give demonstrations of woodcarving, wool-spinning and peat-fire baking. You'll need at least two to three hours to make the most of a visit here.

Ruthven Barracks   RUIN
(HS; ☺ 24hr) 🅵🆁🅴🅴 Ruthven Barracks was one of four garrisons built by the British government after the first Jacobite rebellion of 1715, as part of a Hanoverian scheme to take control of the Highlands. Ironically, the barracks were last occupied by Jacobite troops awaiting the return of Bonnie Prince Charlie after the Battle of Culloden. Perched dramatically on a river terrace and clearly visible from the main A9 road near Kingussie, the ruins are spectacularly floodlit at night.

Laggan Wolftrax
MOUNTAIN BIKING

(http://scotland.forestry.gov.uk/visit/laggan-wolftrax; Strathmashie Forest; trails free, parking £3; ⊙10am-6pm Mon, 9.30am-5pm Tue, Thu & Fri, 9.30am-6pm Sat & Sun) Ten miles southwest of Newtonmore, on the A86 road towards Spean Bridge, this is one of Scotland's top mountain-biking centres, with purpose-built trails ranging from open-country riding to black-diamond downhills with rock slabs and drop-offs. By the time you read this, there will be a new centre with a cafe and bike shop or similar.

Highland All Terrain
ADVENTURE TOUR

(☑0845 094 5513; http://quadbiketours.co.uk; Kinloch Laggan; from per person £45) Join an off-road quad-bike tour of Ardverikie Estate, which appears as Glen Bogle in the TV series *Monarch of the Glen*. Tours range from one hour to 3½ hours, and take in many of the TV locations.

🍴 Sleeping & Eating

★Eagleview Guest House
B&B ££

(☑01540-673675; www.eagleviewguesthouse.co.uk; Perth Rd, Newtonmore; r per person £39-40; P🗦) Welcoming Eagleview is one of the best places to stay in the area, with beautifully decorated bedrooms, super-king-size beds, spacious bathrooms with power showers (except room 4, which has a Victorian slipper bath!), and nice little touches such as cafetières (coffee plungers) with real coffee – and fresh milk – on your hospitality tray, and Scottish kippers on the breakfast menu.

Hermitage
B&B ££

(☑01540-662137; www.thehermitage-scotland.com; Spey St, Kingussie; s/d from £40/70; P🗦) The five-bedroom Hermitage is a lovely old house with plenty of character, filled with Victorian period features – ask for room 5 (superior king), with double bed, Chesterfield sofa, and a view of the hills. The lounge has deep sofas arranged by a log fire, and there are good views of the Cairngorms from the breakfast room and garden.

★Cross
SCOTTISH £££

(☑01540-661166; www.thecross.co.uk; Tweed Mill Brae, off Ardbroilach Rd, Kingussie; 2-course lunch £23, 3-course dinner £60; ⊙noon-2pm & 7-8.30pm; P🗦) 🌿 Housed in a converted water mill, the Cross is one of the finest restaurants in the Highlands. The intimate, low-raftered dining room has an open fire and a patio overlooking the stream, and serves a daily-changing menu of fresh Scottish produce accompanied by a superb wine list. If you want to stay the night, there are eight stylish rooms (double or twin £100 to £180) to choose from.

ℹ️ Getting There & Away

BUS

Kingussie and Newtonmore are served by **Scottish Citylink** (☑0871 266 3333; www.citylink.co.uk) buses:

Aviemore £7.70, 25 minutes, five to seven daily

Inverness £13.40, one hour, six to eight Monday to Saturday, three Sunday

Perth £16.30, 1¾ hours, five daily

TRAIN

Kingussie's train station is at the southern end of town. Kingussie and Newtonmore are served by the following:

Edinburgh £35, 2½ hours, seven a day Monday to Saturday, two Sunday

Inverness £11.70, 50 minutes, eight a day Monday to Saturday, four Sunday

Eastern Cairngorms

Tomintoul & Around

This high-altitude (345m) village was built by the Duke of Gordon in 1775 on the old military road that leads over the Lecht pass from Corgarff, a route now followed by the A939 (usually the first road in Scotland to be blocked by snow when winter closes in). The duke hoped that settling the dispersed population of his estates in a proper village would help to stamp out cattle stealing and illegal distilling.

Tomintoul (tom-in-*towel*) is a pretty, stone-built village with a grassy, tree-lined main square (the museum here was closed at the time of writing, but it is hoped that it will reopen soon).

The surrounding **Glenlivet Estate** (now the property of the Crown) has lots of walking and cycling trails – the estate's **tourist office** (☑01479-870070; www.glenlivetestate.co.uk; Main St; ⊙9am-5pm Mon-Fri) distributes free maps of the area – and a spur of the **Speyside Way** long-distance footpath runs between Tomintoul and Ballindalloch, 15 miles to the north.

There's excellent mountain biking at the new **BikeGlenlivet** (www.glenlivetestate.co.uk; trails free, parking £3) trail centre, 4.5 miles north of Tomintoul, off the B9136 road. Custom-built trails range from the 9km blue run for beginners to the 22km red route for more experienced riders. Cafe, showers and bike hire on site.

🛏 Sleeping & Eating

Accommodation for walkers includes the **Smugglers Hostel** (☎01807-580364; www.thesmugglershostel.co.uk; Main St; dm £15-18; 🛜), housed in the old village school; the highly recommended **Argyle Guest House** (☎01807-580766; www.argyletomintoul.co.uk; 7 Main St; d/f £64/110) is a more comfortable alternative (best porridge in the Cairngorms!).

For something to eat, try the **Clockhouse Restaurant** (The Square; mains £10-13; ⊗noon-2pm & 6-8pm), which serves light lunches and bistro dinners, or the **Coffee Still** (☎07599 973845; BikeGlenlivet Trail Centre; mains £6-8; ⊗11am-5pm Tue-Fri, 10am-5.30pm Sat & Sun; P), which specialises in home baking and mouth-watering homemade burgers.

❶ Getting There & Away

There is a very limited bus service to Tomintoul, once a week from Elgin via Aberlour (£6, 1½ hours, one a day, Thursday only), and from Keith via Dufftown (£4.50, one hour, one a day, Tuesday only); check with the tourist office in Elgin for the latest timetables. Outside these times, there is a **Dial-a-Bus** service (call ☎01343-562533 Monday to Friday to book a seat).

Cockbridge-Tomintoul Road

The A939, known as the Cockbridge–Tomintoul road – a magnificent rollercoaster of a route much loved by motorcyclists – crosses the Lecht pass (637m), where there's a small skiing area with lots of short easy and intermediate runs.

Corgarff Castle   CASTLE
(HS; ☎01975-651460; adult/child £5.50/3.30; ⊗9.30am-5.30pm Apr-Sep) In the wild hills of the eastern Cairngorms, near the A939 from Cockbridge to Tomintoul, is the impressive fortress of Corgarff Castle. The tower house dates from the 16th century, but the star-shaped defensive curtain wall was added in 1748 when the castle was converted to a military barracks in the wake of the Jacobite rebellion.

Lecht 2090   WINTER SPORTS
(www.lecht.co.uk) In winter, you can hire skis, boots and poles for £20 a day; a one-day lift pass is £29. In summer (weekends only), the chairlift serves mountain-biking trails (day ticket £29); there are no bike-hire facilities, though, so you'll need to bring your own.

Southern Cairngorms

Royal Deeside

The upper valley of the River Dee stretches west from Aboyne to Braemar, closely paralleled by the A93 road. Made famous by its long association with the monarchy (today's royal family still holiday at Balmoral Castle, built for Queen Victoria in 1855) the region is often called Royal Deeside.

The River Dee, renowned around the world for its **salmon fishing**, has its source in the Cairngorm Mountains west of Braemar, the starting point for long walks into the hills. The **FishDee website** (www.fishdee.co.uk) has all you need to know about fishing on the river.

BALLATER
POP 1530
The attractive little village of Ballater owes its 18th-century origins to the curative waters of nearby Pannanich Springs (now bottled commercially as Deeside Natural Mineral Water), and its prosperity to nearby Balmoral Castle.

The **tourist office** (☎01339-755306; Station Sq; ⊗9am-6pm Jul & Aug, 10am-5pm Sep-Jun) is in the Old Royal Station.

◉ Sights & Activities

When Queen Victoria travelled to Balmoral Castle she would alight from the royal train at Ballater's **Old Royal Station** (☎01339-755306; Station Sq; admission £2; ⊗10am-6pm Jul & Aug, to 5pm Sep-Jun). The station has been beautifully restored and now houses the tourist office, a cafe and a museum with a replica of Victoria's royal coach (the original is in the National Railway Museum in York).

Also on Station Sq is **Dee Valley Confectioners** (☎01339-755499; www.dee-valley.co.uk; Station Sq; admission free; ⊗9am-noon & 2-4.30pm Mon-Thu Apr-Oct), where you can drool over the manufacture of traditional Scottish sweeties. Note the crests on the shop fronts along the main street proclaiming 'By Royal Appointment' – the village is a major supplier of provisions to Balmoral.

As you approach Ballater from the east the hills start to close in, and there are many pleasant walks in the surrounding area. The steep woodland walk up **Craigendarroch** (400m) takes just over one hour. **Morven** (871m) is a more serious prospect, taking about six hours, but offers good views from the top; ask at the tourist office for more info.

You can hire bikes from **CycleHighlands** ([🏷] 01339-755864; www.cyclehighlands.com; The Pavilion, Victoria Rd; bicycle hire per day £18; ⊗ 9am-6pm) and **Bike Station** ([🏷] 01339-754004; www.bikestationballater.co.uk; Station Sq; bicycle hire per 3hr/day £12/18; ⊗ 9am-6pm), which also offers guided bike rides and advice on local trails.

🛏 Sleeping & Eating

Habitat   HOSTEL £
([🏷] 01339-753752; www.habitat-at-ballater.com; Bridge Sq; dm/tw from £20/45; 🛜) 🍴 Tucked up a lane near the bridge over the River Dee, Habitat is an attractive and ecofriendly hostel with three eight-bed bunk rooms (with personal lockers and reading lamps), and a comfortable lounge with big, soft sofas and a wood-burning stove.

★ Auld Kirk   HOTEL ££
([🏷] 01339-755762; www.theauldkirk.com; Braemar Rd; s/d from £65/100; P 🛜 🐾) Here's something a little out of the ordinary – a seven-bedroom hotel housed in a converted 19th-century church. The interior blends original features with sleek modern decor – the pulpit now serves as the reception desk, while the breakfast room is bathed in light from leaded gothic windows.

Rock Salt & Snails   CAFE £
([🏷] 07834 452583; 2 Bridge St; mains £4-8; ⊗ 10am-5pm Mon-Sat, 11am-5pm Sun; 🛜 📶) A great litte cafe serving excellent coffee, and tempting lunch platters composed of locally sourced deli products (cheese, ham, salads etc), including a kids' platter.

❶ Getting There & Away

Bus 201 runs from Aberdeen to Ballater (£11, 1¾ hours, hourly Monday to Saturday, six on Sunday) via Crathes Castle, and continues to Braemar (£5.60, 30 minutes) every two hours.

BALMORAL CASTLE

Eight miles west of Ballater lies **Balmoral Castle** ([🏷] 01339-742334; www.balmoralcastle.com; adult/child £11/5; ⊗ 10am-5pm Apr-Jul, last admission 4.30pm), the Queen's Highland holiday home, screened from the road by a thick curtain of trees. Built for Queen Victoria in 1855 as a private residence for the royal family, it kicked off the revival of the Scottish Baronial style of architecture that characterises so many of Scotland's 19th-century country houses.

The admission fee includes an interesting and well thought-out audioguide, but the tour is very much an outdoor one through garden and grounds; as for the castle itself, only the ballroom, which displays a collection of Landseer paintings and royal silver, is open to the public. Don't expect to see the Queen's private quarters! The main attraction is learning about Highland estate management, rather than royal revelations.

You can buy a booklet that details several waymarked walks within Balmoral Estate; the best is the climb to **Prince Albert's Cairn**, a huge granite pyramid that bears the inscription 'To the beloved memory of Albert the great and good, Prince Consort. Erected by his broken hearted widow Victoria R. 21st August 1862'.

The massive pointy-topped mountain that looms to the south of Balmoral is **Lochnagar** (1155m), immortalised in verse by Lord Byron, who spent his childhood years in Aberdeenshire:

England, thy beauties are tame and domestic
To one who has roamed o'er the mountains
afar.
Oh! for the crags that are wild and majestic:
The steep frowning glories of dark Lochnagar.

Lord Byron, Lochnagar

Balmoral is beside the A93 at Crathie and can be reached on the Aberdeen–Braemar bus.

BRAEMAR
POP 450

Braemar is a pretty little village with a grand location on a broad plain ringed by mountains where the Dee valley and Glen Clunie meet. In winter this is one of the coldest places in the country – temperatures as low as -29°C have been recorded – and during spells of severe cold, hungry deer wander the streets looking for a bite to eat. Braemar is an excellent base for hill walking, and there's also skiing at nearby Glenshee.

The **tourist office** (☎01399-741600; The Mews, Mar Rd; ⏰9am-6pm Aug, 9am-5pm Jun, Jul, Sep & Oct, 10am-5pm Mon-Sat, 2-5pm Sun Nov-May), opposite the Fife Arms Hotel, has lots of useful info on walks in the area. There's a bank with an ATM in the village centre, an outdoor equipment shop and a **grocery store** (⏰7.30am-9pm Mon-Sat, 9am-6pm Sun).

⦿ Sights & Activities

Just north of the village, turreted **Braemar Castle** (www.braemarcastle.co.uk; adult/child £8/4; ⏰10am-4pm Sat & Sun Jun-Sep, also Wed Jul-mid-Sep, daily Aug, 11am-3pm Sat-Sun May & Oct) dates from 1628 and served as a government garrison after the 1745 Jacobite rebellion. It was taken over by the local community in 2007, and now offers guided tours of the historic castle apartments.

An easy walk from Braemar is up **Creag Choinnich** (538m), a hill to the east of the village above the A93. The 1-mile route is waymarked and takes about 1½ hours. For a longer walk (4 miles; about three hours) and superb views of the Cairngorms, head for the summit of **Morrone** (859m), southwest of Braemar. Ask at the tourist office for details of these and other walks.

You can hire mountain bikes from **Braemar Mountain Sports** (☎01339-741242; www.braemarmountainsports.com; 5 Invercauld Rd; bike hire per day £18; ⏰9am-6pm) for £18 per 24 hours. It also rents skiing and mountaineering equipment.

🛏 Sleeping

★Rucksacks Bunkhouse   HOSTEL £
(☎01339-741517; 15 Mar Rd; bothies £7; dm £12-15, tw £36; 🅿) An appealing cottage with a comfy dorm, and cheaper beds in an alpine-style bothy (shared sleeping platform for 10 people; bring your own sleeping bag). Extras include a drying room (for wet-weather gear), a laundry and even a sauna (£10 an hour). The friendly owner is a font of knowledge about the local area.

Braemar SYHA   HOSTEL £
(☎01339-741659; www.syha.org.uk; 21 Glenshee Rd; dm/tw £18.50/44; ⏰Feb-Oct; @) This hostel is housed in a grand former shooting lodge just south of Braemar village centre on the A93 to Perth. It has a comfy lounge with a pool table, and a barbecue in the garden.

Braemar Caravan & Camping Park   CAMPSITE £
(☎01339-741373; www.braemarcaravansite.co.uk; tent sites incl 2 people £12.50; ⏰closed mid-Oct-mid-Dec; 🛜) There is good camping here, or you can camp wild (no facilities) along the minor road on the east bank of the Clunie Water, 3 miles south of Braemar.

Craiglea   B&B ££
(☎01339-741641; www.craigleabraemar.com; Hillside Dr; d/f from £74/105; 🅿🛜) Craiglea is a homely B&B set in a pretty stone cottage with three en suite bedrooms. Vegetarian breakfasts are available and the owners can give advice on local walks.

St Margarets   B&B ££
(☎01339-741697; soky37@hotmail.com; 13 School Rd; s/tw £34/56; 🛜) Grab this place if you can, but there's only one room, a twin with a serious sunflower theme. The genuine warmth of the welcome is delightful. It's tucked behind the church on the south side of the A93 road.

Braemar Lodge Hotel   HOTEL, BUNKHOUSE ££
(☎01339-741627; www.braemarlodge.co.uk; Glenshee Rd; dm from £12, s/d £75/120; 🅿) This Victorian shooting lodge on the southern outskirts of Braemar has bags of character, not least in the wood-panelled Malt Room bar, which is as well stocked with mounted deer heads as it is with single malt whiskies. There's a good restaurant with views of the hills, plus a 12-berth hikers' bunkhouse in the hotel grounds.

✗ Eating

Taste   CAFE £
(☎01339-741425; www.taste-braemar.co.uk; Airlie House, Mar Rd; mains £4-7; ⏰10am-5pm Tue-Sat; ♿) 𝒫 Taste is a relaxed little cafe with armchairs in the window, serving homemade soups, sandwiches, coffee and cakes.

★Gathering Place   BISTRO ££
(☎01339-741234; www.the-gathering-place.co.uk; 9 Invercauld Rd; mains £12-19; ⏰6-9pm Tue-Sat; 🛜) This bright and breezy bistro is an unexpected corner of culinary excellence, with a welcoming dining room and sunny conservatory, tucked below the main road junction at the entrance to Braemar village.

ⓘ Getting There & Away

Bus 201 runs from Aberdeen to Braemar (£11, 2¼ hours, every two hours Monday to Saturday, five on Sunday). The 50-mile drive from Perth to Braemar is beautiful, but there's no public transport on this route.

MAR LODGE ESTATE

West of Braemar spreads the National Trust for Scotland's Mar Lodge Estate (NTS; www.nts.org.uk/property/mar-lodge-estate; ⊘24hr year round) FREE, one of the country's most important nature conservation areas, covering 7% of the Cairngorms National Park. The £4-million legacy that allowed the trust to purchase the property in 1995 stipulated that, as well as promoting conservation and public access, the trust should continue to run Mar Lodge as a sporting estate. So, alongside walking trails and forest regeneration there is salmon fishing and deer stalking.

Several easy, waymarked walks start from the Linn of Dee car park, 6.5 miles west of Braemar, including the Linn of Dee, a narrow gorge that extends downstream from the road bridge, and Glen Lui. Numerous long mountain walks (for experienced hill walkers only) also start from here, including the adventurous 24-mile walk through the Lairig Ghru pass to Aviemore.

Another short walk (3 miles, 1½ hours) begins 4 miles beyond the Linn of Dee at the Linn of Quoich – a waterfall that thunders through a narrow slot in the rocks. Head uphill on a footpath on the east bank of the stream, past the Punch Bowl (a giant pothole) to a modern bridge that spans the narrow gorge, and return via a 4WD road on the far bank. A longer walk (10 miles) is to follow the 4WD road up Glen Quoich to a beautiful remnant of Caledonian pine forest (return the same way).

GLENSHEE

The route along the A93 from Braemar to Blairgrowrie through Glenshee is one of the most scenic drives in the country. It's fantastic walking country in summer, and there's skiing in winter. Blairgowrie and Braemar are the main accommodation centres for the Glenshee resort, although there is a small settlement 5 miles south of the ski runs at Spittal of Glenshee with a couple of good sleeping options.

Glenshee Ski Resort   SNOW SPORTS
(☑ 01339-741320; www.ski-glenshee.co.uk; 1-day lift pass £29) With 22 lifts and 36 runs Glenshee is one of Scotland's largest skiing areas. When the sun burns through the clouds after a good fall of snow, you'll be in a unique position to drink in the beauty of the country; the skiing isn't half bad either. The chairlift, which also opens in July and August for walkers and mountain bikers, can whisk you up to 910m, near the top of the Cairnwell (933m).

The Angus Glens

Five scenic glens – Isla, Prosen, Clova, Lethnot and Esk – cut into the hills along the southern fringes of the Cairngorms National Park, accessible from Kirriemuir in Angus. All have attractive scenery, though each glen has its own distinct personality: Glen Clova and Glenesk are the most beautiful, while Glen Lethnot is the least frequented. You can get detailed information on walks in the Angus Glens from the tourist office in Kirriemuir and from the Glen Clova Hotel in Glen Clova.

There is no public transport to the Angus Glens other than a limited school-bus service along Glen Clova; ask at the tourist office in Kirriemuir (p223) for details.

GLEN ISLA

At Bridge of Craigisla at the foot of the glen is a spectacular, 24m waterfall called Reekie Linn; the name Reekie (Scottish for 'smoky') comes from the billowing spray that rises from the falls.

A 5-mile walk beyond the road end at Auchavan leads into the wild and mountainous upper reaches of the glen, where the Caenlochan National Nature Reserve protects rare alpine flora on the high plateau.

GLEN PROSEN

Near the foot of Glen Prosen, 6 miles north of Kirriemuir, there's a good forest walk up to the Airlie monument on Tulloch Hill (380m); start from the eastern road, about a mile beyond Dykehead.

From Glenprosen Lodge, at the head of the glen, a 9-mile walk along the Kilbo Path leads over a pass between Mayar (928m) and Driesh (947m), and descends to Glendoll Lodge at the head of Glen Clova (allow five hours).

Prosen Hostel (☑ 01575-540238; www.prosenhostel.co.uk; dm £20; ⊘year round; P @) is an 18-bed bunkhouse with excellent facilities (including a red squirrel viewing area in the lounge). It's 7 miles up the glen, just beyond Prosen village (no public transport).

GLEN CLOVA

The longest and loveliest of the Angus Glens stretches north from Kirriemuir for 20 miles, broad and pastoral in its lower reaches but growing narrower and craggier as the steep, heather-clad Highland hills close in around its head.

The minor road beyond the Glen Clova Hotel ends at a Forestry Commission car park at Glen Doll with a **visitor centre** (☑01575-550233; Glen Doll; ☺9am-6pm Apr-Sep, to 4.30 Oct-Mar) and **picnic area**, which is the trailhead for a number of strenuous walks through the hills to the north.

Jock's Road is an ancient footpath that was much used by cattle drovers, soldiers, smugglers and shepherds in the 18th and 19th centuries; 700 Jacobite soldiers passed this way during their retreat in 1746, en route to defeat at Culloden. From the car park the path strikes west along Glen Doll, then north across a high plateau (900m) before descending steeply into Glen Callater and on to Braemar (15 miles; allow five to seven hours). The route is hard going and should not be attempted in winter; you'll need OS 1:50,000 map numbers 43 and 44.

An easier walk leads from Glen Doll car park to **Corrie Fee**, a spectacular glacial hollow in the edge of the mountain plateau (4.5 miles round trip, waymarked).

Glen Clova Hotel (☑01575-550350; www. clova.com; s/d from £65/90, bunkhouse per person £17; ☑) is a lovely old drover's inn near the head of the glen and a great place to get away from it all. As well as 10 comfortable, country-style, en suite rooms (one with a four-poster bed), it has a bunkhouse out the back, a rustic, stone floored climbers' bar with a roaring log fire, and a bay-windowed **restaurant** (mains £9-16; ☺noon-8.15pm Sun-Thu, to 8.45pm Fri & Sat, shorter hr Nov-Mar; ☑) with views across the glen. The menu includes haggis, venison casserole and vegetarian lasagne, and there's a separate children's menu.

GLEN LETHNOT

This glen is noted for the **Brown & White Caterthuns** – two extraordinary Iron Age hill forts, defended by ramparts and ditches, perched on twin hilltops at its southern end. A minor road crosses the pass between the two summits, and it's an easy walk to either fort from the parking area in the pass; both are superb viewpoints.

GLENESK

The most easterly of the Angus Glens, Glenesk runs for 15 miles from Edzell to lovely **Loch Lee**, surrounded by beetling cliffs and waterfalls. Ten miles up the glen from Edzell is **Glenesk Folk Museum** (www.gleneskretreat.co.uk; ☺10am-5pm Mon-Fri, to 6pm Sat & Sun Apr-Oct) **FREE**, an old shooting lodge that houses a fascinating collection of antiques and artefacts documenting the local culture of the 17th, 18th and 19th centuries. It also has a tearoom, restaurant and gift shop, and has public internet access.

Five miles further on, the public road ends at **Invermark Castle**, an impressive ruined tower guarding the southern approach to the Mounth, a hill track to Deeside.

HIGHLAND PERTHSHIRE

ⓘ Getting Around

Away from the main A9 Perth to Inverness road public transport is thin on the ground, and often geared to the needs of local schools. On Tuesdays, Wednesdays and Sundays from June to mid-October, the **Ring of Breadalbane Explorer** (☑01828-626262; www.facebook. com/breadalbaneexplorer) bus service operates on a circular route taking in Crieff, Comrie, Lochearnhead, Killin, Kenmore and Aberfeldy, with four circuits a day in each direction. It also runs on Saturdays in July and August. The £10 fare allows unlimited hop-on/hop-off travel for one day.

Dunkeld to Blair Atholl

There are a number of major sights strung along the busy but scenic A9, the main route north from Perth to the Cairngorms and Inverness.

Dunkeld & Birnam

POP 1005

The Tay runs like a story-book river between the twin towns of Dunkeld and Birnam, nestled in the heart of Perthshire's Big Tree Country. As well as Dunkeld's lovely cathedral, there's much walking to be done in this area of magnificent forested hills. These same walks were one of the inspirations for Beatrix Potter to create her children's tales.

⊙ Sights & Activities

Dunkeld Cathedral
CHURCH

(HS; www.dunkeldcathedral.org.uk; High St; ⊙9.30am-6.30pm Apr-Sep, to 4pm Oct-Mar) **FREE** Situated on the grassy banks of the River Tay, Dunkeld Cathedral is one of the most beautifully sited churches in Scotland; don't miss it on a sunny day, when there are few lovelier places to be. Half the cathedral is still in use as a church; the rest is in ruins. It partly dates from the 14th century, having suffered damaged during the Reformation and the battle of Dunkeld (Jacobites vs government) in 1689.

The Wolf of Badenoch, a fierce 14th-century noble who burned towns and abbeys to the ground in protest at his excommunication, is buried here – undeservedly – in a fine medieval tomb behind the wooden screen in the church.

Dunkeld House Grounds
GARDENS

(⊙24hr) **FREE** Waymarked walks lead upstream from Dunkeld Cathedral through the gorgeous grounds of Dunkeld House Hotel, formerly a seat of the dukes of Atholl. In the 18th and early 19th centuries the 'planting dukes', as they became known, planted more than 27-million conifers on their estates 'for beauty and profit', introducing species such as larch, Douglas fir and sequoia, and sowing the seeds of Scottish forestry.

The abundance of vast, ancient trees here has given rise to the nickname Big Tree Country (www.perthshirebigtreecountry.co.uk). Just west of the cathedral is the 250-year-old 'parent larch', the lone survivor of several planted in 1738, and said to have provided the seed stock for all Scottish larch trees. On the far side of the river is Niel Gow's Oak, another ancient tree said to have provided inspiration for legendary local fiddler Niel Gow (1727–1807).

Birnam
VILLAGE

Across the bridge from Dunkeld is Birnam, a name made famous by *Macbeth*. There's not much left of Birnam Wood, but there is a small, leafy Beatrix Potter Park (the children's author, who wrote the evergreen story of *Peter Rabbit*, spent childhood holidays in the area). Next to the park, in the Birnam Arts Centre (www.birnaminstitute.com; Station Rd; admission £1.50; ⊙10am-5pm mid-Mar–Nov, 10am-4.30pm Mon-Sat, 11am-4.30pm Sun Dec–mid-Mar), is a small exhibition on Potter and her characters.

Loch of the Lowes Wildlife Centre
WILDLIFE RESERVE

(☑01350-727337; www.swt.org.uk; adult/child £4/50p; ⊙10am-5pm Mar-Oct, 10.30am-4pm Fri-Sun Nov-Feb) Loch of the Lowes, 2 miles east of Dunkeld off the A923, has a visitor centre devoted to red squirrels and the majestic osprey. There's a birdwatching hide (with binoculars provided), where you can see the birds nesting during breeding season (late April to August).

🛏 Sleeping & Eating

★ Jessie Mac's
HOSTEL, B&B £

(☑01350-727324; www.jessiemacs.co.uk; Murthly Tce, Birnam; dm/d £18/70; 🛜) 🅿 Set in a Victorian manse complete with baronial turret, Jessie Mac's is a glorious cross between B&B and luxury hostel, with three gorgeous doubles and five shared rooms with bunks. Guests make good use of the country-style lounge, sunny dining room and well-equipped kitchen, and breakfasts are composed of local produce, from organic eggs to Dunkeld smoked salmon.

Erigmore Estate
LODGE £££

(☑01350-727236; www.erigmore.co.uk; Birnam; d for 2 nights from £380; 🅿🐕🏊) Scattered around the wooded, riverside grounds of Erigmore House, the former country retreat of a wealthy clipper ship's captain, these luxury timber lodges provide cossetted comfort complete with outdoor deck and – at the more expensive end of the range – a private hot tub. The house itself contains shared facilities, including a bar, restaurant and swimming pool.

★ Taybank
PUB £

(☑01350-727340; www.thetaybank.co.uk; Tay Tce; mains £6-9; ⊙11am-11pm Mon-Thu, to midnight Fri & Sat, 12.30-11pm Sun) Top choice for a sunkissed pub lunch by the river is the Taybank, a regular meeting place and performance space for musicians of all creeds and a wonderfully welcoming bar serving ales from the local Strathbraan Brewery. There's live music several nights per week, and the menu runs to burgers and stovies (stewed potato and onion with meat or other ingredients).

❶ Information

Dunkeld Tourist Office (☑01350-727688; www.dunkeldandbirnam.org.uk; The Cross; ⊙9am-5pm Apr-Oct, Fri-Sun Nov-Mar) Has information on local hiking and biking trails.

ℹ Getting There & Away

Dunkeld is 15 miles north of Perth. Citylink buses running between Glasgow/Edinburgh (£16.60, two hours, five daily) and Inverness stop at the Birnam Hotel. **Stagecoach** (www.stage-coachbus.com) runs hourly buses (only five on Sunday) between Perth and Dunkeld (£2.50, 40 minutes), continuing to Aberfeldy.

There are also buses from Dunkeld to Blair-gowrie (£2.50, 35 minutes), twice daily on Tuesday, Thursday and Saturday only.

Pitlochry

POP 2780

Pitlochry, with the scent of the Highlands already in the air, is a popular stop on the way north. In summer the main street can be a conga line of tour groups, but linger a while and it can still charm – on a quiet spring evening it's a pretty place with salmon leaping in the Tummel and good things brewing at the Moulin Hotel.

◉ Sights

One of Pitlochry's attractions is its beautiful riverside; the River Tummel is dammed here, and if you're lucky you might see salmon swimming up the fish ladder to Loch Faskally above (May to November, best month is October).

★ Edradour Distillery   DISTILLERY

(☑ 01796 472095; www.edradour.co.uk; tours adult/child £7.50/2.50; ⊙ 10am-5pm Mon-Sat Apr-Oct; ☑ ♿) This is proudly Scotland's smallest and most picturesque distillery and one of the best to visit: you can see the whole process, easily explained, in one building. It's 2.5 miles east of Pitlochry by car, along the Moulin road, or a pleasant 1-mile walk.

Bell's Blair Athol Distillery   DISTILLERY

(☑ 01796-482003; www.discovering-distilleries.com; Perth Rd; standard tour £6.50; ⊙ 10am-5pm Apr-Oct, to 4pm Nov-Mar, closed Sun Jan-Mar) Tours here focus on whisky making and the blending of this well-known dram. More detailed private tours give you greater insights and superior tastings.

Explorers Garden   GARDENS

(☑ 01796-484600; www.explorersgarden.com; Foss Rd; adult/child £4/1; ⊙ 10am-5pm Apr-Oct) This gem of a garden is based around plants brought to Scotland by 18th- and 19th-century Scottish botanists and explorers such as David Douglas (after whom the Douglas fir is named), and celebrates 300 years of collecting and the 'plant hunters' who tracked down these exotic species.

Wild Space   GALLERY

(www.jmt.org/wildspace.asp; Tower House, Station Rd; ⊙ 10am-4.30pm Mon-Fri, 10.30am-4.30pm Sat, 11am-4pm Sun May-Sep, shorter hr winter) **FREE** This combined art gallery, interpretation centre and bookshop is run by environmental charity the John Muir Trust. It stages exhibitions of contemporary landscape art, and sells maps, walking guides and wildlife-and evironment-related books.

🎉 Festivals & Events

Winter Words   LITERATURE

(www.pitlochry.org/whats_on; ⊙ Feb) A 10-day literary festival, with a packed program of talks by authors, poets and broadcasters. Past guests have included novelist Louis de Bernieres and mountaineer/author Sir Chris Bonington.

Étape Caledonia   CYCLING

(www.etapecaledonia.co.uk; ⊙ mid-May) This 81-mile charity cycling event brings competitors of all standards onto the beautiful Highland roads between Pitlochry and Tummel Bridge. It's grown into a huge event, with more than 5000 participants; you'll have to prebook accommodation when its on.

Enchanted Forest   LIGHT SHOW

(www.enchantedforest.org.uk; adult £14-18, child £7-9, ⊙ Oct) This spectacular three-week sound-and-light show staged in a forest near Pitlochry is a major family hit.

🛏 Sleeping

Ashleigh   B&B £

(☑ 01796-470316; www.realbandbpitlochry.co.uk; 120 Atholl Rd; s/d £30/57; ⊛) Genuine welcomes don't come much better than Nancy's, and her place on the main street makes a top Pitlochry pit stop. Two comfortable doubles share an excellent bathroom, and there's an open kitchen stocked with goodies where you make your own breakfast in the morning. A home away from home and a standout budget choice. Cash only; no kids.

She also has a good self-catering apartment with great views, available by the night.

Pitlochry Backpackers Hotel   HOSTEL £

(☑ 01796-470044; www.scotlands-top-hostels.com; 134 Atholl Rd; dm/tw/d £18/47/52; ⊙ Apr–mid-Nov; ☑ @ ⊛) Friendly, laid-back and very comfortable, this is a cracking hostel smack bang in the middle of town, with three- to eight-bed dorms that are in mint condition. There are also good-value en suite twins and doubles, with beds, not bunks. Cheap breakfast and a pool table add to the convivial party atmosphere. No extra charge for linen.

Pitlochry SYHA   HOSTEL £
(☎ 01796-472308; www.syha.org.uk; Knockard Rd; dm/tw £17/45; ☺ Mar-Oct; P @ ☎) Great location overlooking the town centre. Popular with families and walkers.

★ Craigatin House   B&B ££
(☎ 01796-472478; www.craigatinhouse.co.uk; 165 Atholl Rd; s £80, d standard/deluxe £90/100; P @ ☎) Several times more tasteful than the average Pitlochry lodging, this elegant house and garden is set back from the main road. Chic contemporary fabrics covering expansive beds offer a standard of comfort above and beyond the reasonable price; the rooms in the converted stable block are particularly inviting. A fabulous breakfast and lounge area gives views over the lush garden.

Breakfast choices include whisky-laced porridge, smoked-fish omelettes and apple pancakes. Kids not allowed.

Tir Aluinn   B&B ££
(☎ 01796-473811; www.tiraluinn.co.uk; 10 Higher Oakfield Rd; per person £35-37; P ☎) Tucked away above the main street, this is a little gem of a place with bright rooms and easy-on-the-eye furniture, and a warm personal welcome. Breakfasts are a pleasure too.

Knockendarroch House   HOTEL £££
(☎ 01796-473473; www.knockendarroch.co.uk; Higher Oakfield; d incl dinner from £208; P ☎ ☀) Top of the town and boasting the best views, this genteel, well-run hotel has a range of luxurious rooms with huge windows that take advantage of the Highland light. The standard rooms have better views than the larger, slightly pricier superior ones. A couple of rooms have great little balconies, perfect for a sundowner. Meals are highly recommended.

✗ Eating & Drinking

★ Moulin Hotel   PUB ££
(☎ 01796-472196; www.moulinhotel.co.uk; Kirkmichael Rd; mains £8-12; P ☎ ☀) A mile away from town but a world apart, this atmospheric inn was trading centuries before the tartan tack came to Pitlochry. With its low ceilings, ageing wood and booth seats, the Moulin is a wonderfully romantic spot for

a house-brewed ale and a portion of Highland comfort food: try the mince and tatties, or venison stew. It's a pleasant uphill stroll from Pitlochry, and an easy roll down afterwards.

Port-na-Craig Inn   BAR, BISTRO ££
(☎ 01796-472777; www.portnacraig.com; Port Na Craig; mains £13-22, 2-/3-course lunch £13/15; ☺ 11am-8.30pm; P ☀) Across the river from the town centre, this cute little cottage sits in what was once a separate hamlet. Top-quality main meals are prepared with confidence and panache; there are also simpler sandwiches, kids' meals and light lunches. Or you could just sit outdoors by the river with a pint and watch the anglers.

McKay's   PUB
(www.mckayshotel.co.uk; 138 Atholl Rd; ☺ 11am-11pm Sun-Thu, to 12.30am Fri-Sat) This is the place to go to meet locals and have a big night out. Live music at weekends, weekly karaoke and DJs make this Pitlochry's most popular place. The action moves from the spacious front bar (which serves food) to the boisterous dance floor out the back.

☆ Entertainment

★ Pitlochry Festival Theatre   THEATRE
(☎ 01796-484626; www.pitlochryfestivaltheatre.com; Port-na-Craig; tickets £26-35) Founded in 1951 (in a tent!), this famous and much-loved theatre is the focus of Highland Perthshire's cultural life. The summer season, from May to mid-October, stages a different play each night of the week except Sunday.

ⓘ Information

Pitlochry Tourist Office (☎ 01796-472215; www.perthshire.co.uk; 22 Atholl Rd; ☺ 9am-5pm Mar-Oct, Mon-Sat Nov-Feb) Good information on local walks.

ⓘ Getting There & Away

Citylink (www.citylink.co.uk) Buses run every two hours to Inverness (£16.60, 2¼ hours), Perth (£10.70, 40 minutes), Edinburgh (£16.60, two to 2½ hours) and Glasgow (£16.60, 2¼ hours).

Megabus (☎ 0871 266 3333; www.megabus.com) Offers discounted fares to Inverness, Perth, Edinburgh and Glasgow.

Stagecoach (www.stagecoachbus.com) Buses run to Aberfeldy (£2, 30 minutes, three Sunday), Dunkeld (£2, 30 minutes, hourly Monday to Saturday) and Perth (£3.40, 1¼ hours, hourly Monday to Saturday).

Pitlochry is on the main railway line from Perth (£13.20, 30 minutes, nine daily Monday to Saturday, five on Sunday) to Inverness.

❶ Getting Around

Escape Route (☏ 01796-473859; www.escape-route.co.uk; 3 Atholl Rd; bike hire per half/full day from £16/24; ☉9am-5.30pm Mon-Sat, 10am-5pm Sun) Rents out bikes and provides advice on local trails; it's worth booking ahead at weekends.

Killiecrankie

The beautiful, rugged pass of Killiecrankie, 3.5 miles north of Pitlochry, where the River Garry tumbles through a narrow gorge, was the site of the 1689 battle that ignited the Jacobite rebellion. The **Killiecrankie visitor centre** (NTS; ☏01796-473233; www.nts.org.uk; admission free, parking £2; ☉10am-5.30pm Apr-Oct) has great interactive displays on Jacobite history and local flora and fauna. There's plenty to touch, pull and open – great for kids. There are some stunning walks into the wooded gorge too; keep an eye out for red squirrels. Also here, **Highland Fling** (☏0845 366 5844; www.bungeejumpscotland.co.uk; per person £75, repeat jumps £30) offers breathtaking 40m bungee jumps off the bridge over the gorge at weekends, plus Wednesday and Friday from May to September.

A standout choice, the **Killiecrankie House Hotel** (☏01796-473220; www.killiecrankiehotel.co.uk; d standard/superior dinner, bed & breakfast £240/290; ☉Mar-Dec; P❒❒❒) offers faultless hospitality in a peaceful setting. There's interesting art on the walls, and rooms are relaxing retreats with views over the lovely gardens. The best things about the Scottish country-house experience are here without the musty feel that sometimes goes with it; the food is also excellent. Two-night minimum stay at busy times; B&B-only rates are sometimes available.

Local buses between Pitlochry and Blair Atholl stop at Killiecrankie (£1.50, 10 minutes, three to seven daily).

Blair Castle & Blair Atholl

One of the most popular tourist attractions in Scotland, magnificent **Blair Castle** (☏01796-481207; www.blair-castle.co.uk; adult/child/family £9.90/5.95/26.75; ☉9.30am-5.30pm Apr-Oct, 10am-4pm Sat & Sun Nov-Mar; P❒), and the 108 sq miles it sits on, is the seat of the duke of Atholl, head of the Murray clan. It's an impressive white building set beneath forested slopes above the River Garry. Thirty rooms are open to the public and they present a wonderful picture of upper-class Highland life from the 16th century on.

The original tower was built in 1269, but the castle has undergone significant remodelling since. The dining room is sumptuous – check out the nine-pint wine glasses – and the ballroom is a vaulted chamber that's a virtual stag cemetery. The current duke visits the castle every May to review the **Atholl Highlanders**, Britain's only private army.

For a great walk, drive or cycle (strenuous!), take the steep, winding road to **Glenfender** and Loch Moraig from Blair Atholl. It's about 3 miles on a long, narrow uphill road to a farmhouse; the view of the peaks Beinn a'Ghlo at the top is spectacular.

The **Atholl Arms Hotel** (☏01796-481205; www.athollarms.co.uk; s/d from £70/86; P❒❒), near the castle, is a traditional place with darkish rooms and comfortably old-fashioned decor. The Bothy Bar here is the sibling pub of the Moulin Hotel in Pitlochry, snug with booth seating, low-slung roof, bucketloads of character and an enormous fireplace.

Blair Atholl is 6 miles northwest of Pitlochry, and the castle a further mile beyond it. Local buses run between Pitlochry and Blair Atholl (£2, 25 minutes, three to seven daily). Four buses a day (Monday to Saturday) go directly to the castle. There are trains from Perth (£13.20, 40 minutes, nine daily Monday to Saturday, five on Sunday).

Lochs Tummel & Rannoch

The scenic route along Lochs Tummel and Rannoch (www.rannochandtummel.co.uk) is worth doing any way you can – by foot, bicycle or car. Hillsides shrouded with ancient birchwoods and forests of spruce, pine and larch make up the fabulous **Tay Forest Park**. These wooded hills roll into the glittering waters of the lochs; a visit in autumn is recommended, when the birch leaves are at their finest.

The **Queen's View Visitor Centre** (www.forestry.gov.uk; admission free, parking £2; ☉visitor centre 10am-6pm late Mar–mid-Nov) at the eastern end of Loch Tummel provides access to a magnificent viewpoint along the loch to

RANNOCH MOOR

Beyond Rannoch Station, civilisation fades away and Rannoch Moor begins. This is the largest area of moorland in Britain, stretching west for eight barren, bleak and uninhabited miles to the A82 Glasgow–Fort William road. A triangular plateau of blanket bog occupying more than 50 sq miles, the moor is ringed by high mountains and puddled with countless lochs, ponds and peat hags. Water covers 10% of the surface, and it has been canoed across, swum across and even skated across in winter.

Despite the appearance of desolation, the moor is rich in wildlife, with curlews, golden plovers and snipe darting among the tussocks, black-throated divers, goosanders and mergansers on the lochs, and – if you're lucky – ospreys and golden eagles overhead. Herds of red deer forage alongside the railway, and otters patrol the loch shores. And keep an eye out for the sundew, a tiny, insect-eating plant with sticky-fingered leaves.

A couple of excellent (and challenging) walks start from Rannoch Station: north to Corrour Station (11 miles, four to five hours), from where you can return by train; and west along the northern edge of the moor to the King's House Hotel at the eastern end of Glen Coe (11 miles, four hours).

the conical peak of **Schiehallion** (1083m). A new cafe and shop was under construction here at the time of writing.

Waterfalls, mountains and a shimmering loch greet visitors in **Kinloch Rannoch**. It's a great base for walks and cycle trips around **Loch Rannoch**, including the hike up Schiehallion (6.5 miles return), a relatively straightforward climb from Braes of Foss rewarded by spectacular views. See www.jmt. org/east-schiehallion-estate.asp for more information. Loch Rannoch can be fished for brown trout, Arctic char and pike; you can get permits (£8 per day) at the Country Store in Kinloch Rannoch.

Eighteen miles west, the road ends at romantic, isolated **Rannoch Station**, which is on the Glasgow–Fort William railway line. Beyond is desolate, intriguing **Rannoch Moor**. There's a tearoom on the platform, and a welcoming small hotel alongside.

Rannoch Station is a dead end, and there's no petrol in this area; the closest pumps are at Aberfeldy, Pitlochry, and Blair Atholl.

🛏 Sleeping & Eating

Kilvrecht Campsite　　　　　CAMPSITE £

(☏ 01350-727284; tent sites with/without car £8/5; ⊗ Apr–mid-Oct) This basic but beautiful campsite (toilet block, but no hot water) is 2 miles west of Kinloch Rannoch on the south shore of the loch. Hiking and mountain-biking trails begin from the site.

Moor of Rannoch Hotel　　　　HOTEL ££

(☏ 01882-633238; www.moorofrannoch.co.uk; Rannoch Station; s/d £80/114; ⊗ mid-Feb–Oct; P 🐾) At the end of the road beside Rannoch train station, this is one of Scotland's most isolated places (no internet, no TV, only fleeting mobile-phone reception), but luckily this hotel is here to keep your spirits up with cosy rooms and great walks right from the doorstep – a magical getaway. It does good dinners (three courses £29), and can prepare a packed lunch.

Gardens B&B　　　　　　　　B&B ££

(☏ 01882-632434; www.thegardensdunalastair. co.uk; Dunalastair; per person £40-45; P) Off the beaten track between Kinloch Rannoch and Tummel Bridge, this place has just two rooms – a double and a twin. But what rooms they are: effectively suites, each with their own bathroom and sitting room. The conservatory space is great for soaking up the sun and contemplating the stunning view of Schiehallion.

Loch Tummel Inn　　　　　　　PUB ££

(☏ 01882-634272; www.lochtummelinn.co.uk; dinner mains £10-17; ⊗ 12.15-2.30pm & 5.30-8.30pm Tue-Sat, 12.15-8pm Sun Apr-Oct; P 🐾) This old coaching inn is a snug spot for a decent feed, the menu ranging from pub classics to more ambitious meat and game dishes. The friendly bar serves locally brewed beer and is a top spot for a quiet pint at the outdoor tables with a view over Loch Tummel. The inn is about 3 miles east of the village of Tummel Bridge.

❶ Getting There & Away

Broons Buses (☏ 01882-632331) Runs between Kinloch Rannoch and Rannoch Station

(£2.50, 35 minutes, two to four a day Monday to Friday).

Elizabeth Yule Coaches (☎ 01796-47229) From April to October operates a bus service from Pitlochry to Kinloch Rannoch (£3.50, 50 minutes, three to five a day Monday to Saturday) via Queen's View and Loch Tummel Inn.

There are two to four trains daily from Rannoch station north to Fort William (£10.10, one hour) and Mallaig, and south to Glasgow (£23.10, 2¾ hours).

Strathtay

From Ballinluig, south of Pitlochry, the valley of the River Tay arcs westward through Aberfeldy towards the scenic delights of Kenmore and Loch Tay. This is the heart of Highland Perthshire.

Aberfeldy

POP 1895

Aberfeldy is a peaceful, pretty place on the banks of the Tay; adventure sports, art and castles all feature on the menu here, but if it's moody lochs and glens that steal your heart, you may want to push a little further west.

◉ Sights & Activities

The **Birks of Aberfeldy**, made famous by a Robert Burns poem, offer a great short walk from the centre of town, following a vigorous burn upstream past several picturesque cascades. The B846 road towards Fortingall crosses the Tay via the elegant **Wade's Bridge**, built in 1733 as part of the network of military roads designed to tame the Highlands.

Dewar's World of Whisky DISTILLERY (www.dewarsworldofwhisky.com; tours adult/child £7/4; ⊙10am-6pm Mon-Sat & noon-4pm Sun Apr-Oct, 10am-4pm Mon-Sat Nov-Mar) At the eastern end of Aberfeldy, this home of the famous blend offers a good tour, fully 90 minutes long. After the usual overblown film, there's a museum section with audioguide, and an entertaining interactive blending session, as well as the tour of the whisky-making process. More expensive tours allow you to try venerable Aberfeldy single malts and others.

Watermill GALLERY, BOOKSHOP (www.aberfeldywatermill.com; Mill St; ⊙10am-5pm Mon-Sat, 11am-5pm Sun, to 5.30pm daily May-Sep) **FREE** You could while away several hours at this converted watermill, which houses a cafe, bookshop and art gallery exhibiting contemporary works of art. The shop has the biggest range of titles in the Highlands, with a great selection of books on Scottish history, landscape and wildlife.

Castle Menzies CASTLE (www.castlemenzies.org; adult/child £6/2.50; ⊙10.30am-5pm Mon-Sat, 2-5pm Sun Easter-Oct; Ⓟ) Castle Menzies is the 16th-century seat of the chief of Clan Menzies (*ming*-iss), magnificently set against a forest backdrop. Inside it reeks of authenticity, despite extensive restoration work. Check out the fireplace in the dungeon-like kitchens, and the gaudy great hall with windows revealing a ribbon of lush, green countryside extending into wooded hills beyond the estate. You get

---

SALMON FISHING ON THE TAY

The Tay is Scotland's longest river (117 miles) and the most powerful in Britain, discharging more water into the sea each year than the Thames and Severn combined. It is also Europe's most famous salmon river, attracting anglers from all over the world (the season runs from 15 January to 15 October). The British record rod-caught salmon, weighing in at 64lb (29kg), was hooked in the Tay near Dunkeld in 1922, by local girl Georgina Ballantine.

Salmon fishing has an air of exclusivity, and can be expensive, but anyone, even complete beginners, can have a go. There is lots of information on the FishTay website (www. fishtay.co.uk), but novices will do best to hire a guide.

Fishinguide Scotland (☎ 07714 598848; www.fishinguide.co.uk;) A lifetime's experience of exploring his native rivers, lochs and coastline means there isn't much that professional guide Duncan Pepper doesn't know about Scottish fishing. Though based near the Tay, he leads fishing trips all over Scotland for salmon, trout, pike, pollack and more. Packages cost from £200 per person per day, including travel, instruction, permits, tackle and a lavish picnic lunch.

in for free if you share a surname with the castle. It's about 1.5 miles west of Aberfeldy, off the B846.

Highland Safaris
TOURS

(📞 01887-820071; www.highlandsafaris.net; ⊙ 9am-5pm, closed Sun Nov-Jan; 🚗) This outfit offers an ideal way to spot some wildlife or simply enjoy Perthshire's magnificent countryside. Standard trips include the 2½-hour Mountain Safari (adult/child £40/20), which includes whisky and shortbread in a mountain bothy; and the four-hour Safari Trek (adult/child £65/45), culminating with a walk in the mountains and a picnic. You may spot wildlife such as golden eagles, osprey and red deer. There's also gold panning for kids (£5) and mountain-bike hire (per day £20).

Splash
RAFTING

(📞 01887-829706; www.rafting.co.uk; Dunkeld Rd; ⊙ 9am-9pm; 🚗) Splash offers family-friendly white-water rafting on the River Tay (adult/child £40/30, Wednesday to Sunday year-round) and more advanced adult trips on the Tummel (grade 3/4, June to September) and the Orchy (grade 3/5, October to March). It also offers pulse-racing descents on river bugs (£60), canyoning (£55) and mountain-bike hire (per half-/full day £15/20).

🛏 Sleeping & Eating

Tigh'n Eilean Guest House
B&B ££

(📞 01887-820109; www.tighneilean.com; Taybridge Dr; s/d £48/75; 🅿 🛜 🌐) Everything about this property screams comfort. It's a gorgeous place overlooking the Tay, with individually designed rooms: one has a jacuzzi, while another is set on its own in a cheery yellow summer house in the garden, giving you a bit of privacy. The garden itself is fabulous, with hammocks for lazing in, and the riverbank setting is delightful.

Balnearn Guest House
B&B ££

(📞 01887-820431; www.balnearnhouse.com; Crieff Rd; s/d/f from £48/69/80; 🅿 🛜 🌐) Balnearn is a sedate, refined and luxurious mansion near the centre of town, with space to spare. Most rooms have great natural light, and there's a particularly good family room downstairs. Breakfast has been lavishly praised by readers, and the attentive, cordial hosts are helpful while respecting your privacy.

ⓘ Information

Aberfeldy Tourist Office (📞 01887-829010; The Square; ⊙ 9.30am-5pm Apr-Oct, closed Thu & Sun Nov-Mar) In an old church on the central square.

ⓘ Getting There & Away

Stagecoach (www.stagecoachbus.com) bus 23 runs from Perth to Aberfeldy (1½ hours, hourly Monday to Saturday, fewer on Sunday) via Dunkeld; from Pitlochry (£3.40, 40 minutes), you'll need to change buses at Ballinluig. There's no regular bus link west to Killin, but see also the Ring of Breadalbane Explorer (p327).

Local buses run a circular route from Aberfeldy through Kenmore, Fortingall and back to Aberfeldy once each way on school days only.

Kenmore

The picturesque village of Kenmore lies at Loch Tay's eastern end, 6 miles west of Aberfeldy. Dominated by a striking archway leading to **Taymouth Castle** (not open to the public), it was built by the third Earl of Breadalbane in 1760 to house his estate workers.

Kenmore is a good activity base, and **Loch Tay Boat House** (📞 07923 540826; www.loch-tay.co.uk; Pier Rd; ⊙ mid-Mar–mid-Oct) can have you speeding off on a mountain bike (per half-/full day £15/20) or out on the loch itself, in anything from a canoe to a cabin cruiser that'll sleep a whole family.

The heart of the village, **Kenmore Hotel** (📞 01887-830205; www.kenmorehotel.com; The Square; r from £89; 🅿 @ 🛜 🌐) has a bar with a roaring fire and some verses scribbled on the chimneypiece by Robert Burns in 1787, when the inn was already a couple of centuries old. There's also a riverbank beer garden, great views from the restaurant and a wide range of accommodation.

Loch Tay

Loch Tay is the heart of the ancient region known as Breadalbane (from the Gaelic *Bràghad Albainn*, 'the heights of Scotland') – mighty **Ben Lawers** (1214m), looming over the loch, is the highest peak outside the Ben Nevis and Cairngorms regions. Much of the land to the north of Loch Tay falls within the **Ben Lawers National Nature Reserve** (www.nnr-scotland.org.uk/ben-lawers), known for its rare alpine flora. The minor road along the south shore is narrow and twisting (unsuitable for large vehicles), but offers great views of the hills to the north.

The main access point for the **ascent of Ben Lawers** is the car park 1½ miles off the A827, on the minor road from Loch Tay to Bridge of Balgie. The climb is 6.5 miles and can take up to five hours (return): pack wet-weather gear, water and food, and a map and compass. There's also an easier nature trail here.

Less than a mile south of Kenmore is the fascinating **Scottish Crannog Centre** (☑ 01887-830583; www.crannog.co.uk; tours adult/child £8/6; ☺ 10am-5.30pm Apr-Oct), perched on stilts above the loch. Crannogs – effectively artificial islands – were a favoured form of defensive dwelling from the 3rd millennium BC onwards. This superb re-creation (based on studies of Oakbank crannog, one of 18 discovered in Loch Tay) offers a guided tour that includes an impressive demonstration of fire making and Iron Age crafts.

Culdees Bunkhouse (☑ 01887-830519; www.culdeesbunkhouse.co.uk; dm/tw/f £18/50/69; P@☎☜☝) is a wonderfully offbeat hostel with majestic vistas: the whole of the loch stretches out below you. It's fine base for hill walking or for mucking in with the volunteers who help run the sustainable farm here. It's half a mile above the village of Fearnan, 4 miles west of Kenmore.

Fortingall

Fortingall is one of the prettiest villages in Scotland, with 19th-century thatched cottages in a tranquil setting. The church has impressive wooden beams and a 7th-century monk's bell; in the churchyard, there's a 2000-year-old yew tree that was around when the Romans camped in the meadows by the River Lyon. Popular if unlikely tradition says that Pontius Pilate was born here. Today the tree is a shell of its former self – at its zenith it had a girth of over 17m, but souvenir hunters have reduced it to two much smaller trunks.

Fortingall Hotel (☑ 01887-830367; www.fortingall.com; s/d £120/165; P☎☜☝) ✆ is a peaceful, old-fashioned country hotel furnished with quiet good taste. The spotless bedrooms have huge beds, modern bathrooms and thoughtful little extras, and look out over green meadows; in all, a perfect spot for doing very little except enjoying the clean air and excellent food.

WORTH A TRIP

UPPER STRATHEARN

The Highland villages of **Comrie** and **St Fillans** in upper Strathearn are surrounded by forests and bare, craggy hilltops where deer and mountain hares live in abundance. St Fillans enjoys an excellent location at the eastern end of **Loch Earn**, which reflects the silhouettes of distant peaks.

The **Four Seasons** (☑ 01765-685333; www.thefourseasonshotel.co.uk; St Fillans; d from £122; ☺ Mar-Dec; P☎☜☝) is a historic hotel – the Beatles stayed here while on tour in 1964 – that has been given a classy modern makeover. Two beautifully appointed lounges and an atmospheric wee bar enjoy great views over the loch. The superior rooms – worth the upgrade – have the best vistas, and there are many activities to choose from, including waterskiing, quad biking and pony trekking. There are also six chalets nestled in the slopes behind the hotel, plus a noted fine-dining restaurant.

Comrie is 24 miles west of Perth, and St Fillans is about 5 miles further west. Buses run from Perth via Crieff to Comrie (£3.60, one hour, roughly hourly Monday to Saturday, every two hours Sunday) and St Fillans (£6.20, 1½ hours, five daily Monday to Saturday).

Glen Lyon

This remote and romantic glen stretches for 34 unforgettable miles of rickety stone bridges, Caledonian pine forest and heather-clad peaks. It becomes wilder and more uninhabited as it snakes its way west, and is proof that hidden treasures still exist. The ancients believed it to be a gateway to Faerieland, and even the most sceptical of visitors will be entranced by the valley's magic.

From Fortingall, a narrow road winds up the glen, while another from Loch Tay crosses the hills to **Bridge of Balgie**, halfway along. The road continues as far as the dam on Loch Lyon, passing a memorial to Robert Campbell (1808–94; a Canadian explorer and fur trader, who was born in the glen). Cycling through Glen Lyon is a wonderful way to experience this special place.

There are no villages in the valley – the majestic and lonely scenery is the main reason to be here – just a cluster of houses at Bridge of Balgie, where the **Bridge of Balgie Tearoom** (☎ 01887-866221; Bridge of Balgie; snacks £3-5; ⊙ 10am-5pm Apr-Oct) serves homemade cakes, sandwiches and soups to hungry walkers and cyclists.

★**Milton Eonan** (☎ 01887-866337; www.miltoneonan.com; Bridge of Balgie; per person £43; P ⊜ ⊛) is a must for those seeking tranquillity in a glorious natural setting. On a bubbling stream where a watermill once stood, it's a working rare-breed croft with a romantic one-bedroom self-catering cottage (breakfast available) at the bottom of the garden. The lively owners offer packed lunches and evening meals (£20) using local and home-grown produce. It's signposted to the right a short distance beyond Bridge of Balgie, on the road towards Loch Tay.

There is no public transport in the glen.

WEST HIGHLANDS

This region extends from the bleak blanket bog of the Moor of Rannoch to the west coast beyond Glen Coe and Fort William, and includes the southern reaches of the Great Glen. The scenery is grand throughout, with high and wild mountains dominating the glens. Great expanses of moor alternate with lochs and patches of commercial forest. Fort William, at the inner end of Loch Linnhe, is the only sizeable town in the area.

Since 2007 the region has been promoted as **Lochaber Geopark** (www.lochabergeopark. org.uk), an area of outstanding geology and scenery.

Glen Coe

Scotland's most famous glen is also one of the grandest and – in bad weather – the grimmest. The approach to the glen from the east, watched over by the rocky pyramid of **Buachaille Etive Mor** – the Great Shepherd of Etive – leads over the Pass of Glencoe and into the narrow upper valley. The southern side is dominated by three massive, brooding spurs, known as the **Three Sisters**, while the northern side is enclosed by the continuous steep wall of the knife-edged **Aonach Eagach** ridge, a classic mountaineering challenge. The main road threads its lonely way through the middle of all this mountain grandeur, past deep gorges and crashing waterfalls, to the more pasto-ral lower reaches of the glen around Loch Achtriochtan and Glencoe village.

Glencoe was written into the history books in 1692 when the resident MacDonalds were murdered by Campbell soldiers in what became known as the Glencoe Massacre.

🏃 Activities

There are several short, pleasant walks around **Glencoe Lochan**, near the village. To get there, turn left off the minor road to the youth hostel, just beyond the bridge over the River Coe. There are three walks (40 minutes to an hour), all detailed on a signboard at the car park. The artificial lochan was created by Lord Strathcona in 1895 for his homesick Canadian wife Isabella and is surrounded by a North American–style forest.

A more strenuous hike, but well worth the effort on a fine day, is the climb to the **Lost Valley**, a magical mountain sanctuary still haunted by the ghosts of the murdered MacDonalds (only 2.5 miles round trip, but allow three hours). A rough path from the car park at Allt na Reigh (on the A82, 6 miles east of Glencoe village) bears left down to a footbridge over the river, then climbs up the wooded valley between Beinn Fhada and Gearr Aonach (the first and second of the Three Sisters). The route leads steeply up through a maze of giant, jumbled, moss-coated boulders before emerging – quite unexpectedly – into a broad, open valley with an 800m-long meadow as flat as a football pitch. Back in the days of clan warfare, the valley – invisible from below – was used for hiding stolen cattle; its Gaelic name, Coire Gabhail, means 'corrie of capture'.

The summits of Glen Coe's mountains are for experienced mountaineers only. The Cicerone guidebook *Ben Nevis & Glen Coe* by Ronald Turnbull, available in most bookshops and outdoor-equipment shops, details everything from short easy walks to challenging mountain climbs.

East of the Glen

Glencoe Mountain Resort OUTDOORS
(☎ 01855-851226; www.glencoemountain.com; Kingshouse; ⊙ 9am-8.30pm) A few miles east of Glen Coe proper is the Glencoe Mountain Resort, where commercial skiing in Scotland first began back in 1956. The **chairlift** (adult/child £10/5; ⊙ 9am-4.30pm Mon-Fri, 8.30am-4.30pm Sat & Sun) continues to operate in summer – there's a grand view over the

Moor of Rannoch from the top – providing access to mountain-biking trails. The **Lodge Café-Bar** has comfy sofas where you can soak up the view through the floor-to-ceiling windows. In winter a lift pass costs £30 a day; equipment hire is £25.

Two miles west of the ski centre, a minor road leads along peaceful and beautiful **Glen Etive**, which runs southwest for 12 miles to the head of Loch Etive. On a hot summer's day the River Etive contains many tempting pools for swimming in, and there are lots of good picnic sites.

Kings House Hotel   HOTEL, PUB **££**
(☎01855-851259; www.kingy.com; Kingshouse; s/d £45/100; P) This remote hotel claims to be one of Scotland's oldest licensed inns, dating from the 17th century. It has long been a favourite meeting place for climbers, skiers and walkers (it's on the West Highland Way); accommodation is basic, but there is good pub grub and real ale. The rustic **Climbers Bar** (bar meals £8-12; ⊙11am-11pm) round the back is more relaxed than the lounge.

The hotel lies on the old military road from Stirling to Fort William, and after the Battle of Culloden it was used as a Hanoverian garrison – hence the name.

Glencoe Village

POP 360

The little village of Glencoe stands on the south shore of Loch Leven at the western end of the glen, 16 miles south of Fort William.

◉ Sights & Activities

Glencoe Folk Museum   MUSEUM
(☎01855-811664; www.glencoemuseum.com; adult/child £3/free; ⊙10am-4.30pm Mon-Sat Easter-Oct) This small, thatched museum houses a varied collection of military memorabilia, farm equipment, and tools of the woodworking, blacksmithing and slate-quarrying trades.

Glencoe Visitor Centre   INTERPRETATION CENTRE
(NTS; ☎01855-811307; www.glencoe-nts.org.uk; adult/child £6.25/5; ⊙9.30am-5.30pm Easter-Oct, 10am-4pm Thu-Sun Nov-Easter; P) ⊘ The centre provides comprehensive information on the geological, environmental and cultural history of Glencoe via high-tech interactive and audiovisual displays, charts the history of mountaineering in the glen, and

tells the story of the Glencoe Massacre in all its gory detail. It's 1.5 miles east of Glencoe village.

Steven Fallon Mountain Guides   OUTDOORS
(☎07795 146400; www.stevenfallon.co.uk; per person from £50) If you lack the experience or confidence to tackle Glen Coe's challenging mountains alone, then you can join a guided hill walk or hire a private guide from this outfit.

🛏 Sleeping

Glencoe Independent Hostel   HOSTEL **£**
(☎01855-811906; www.glencoehostel.co.uk; dm £13-16.50, bunkhouse £12.50-14.50; P@🛜) This handily located hostel, just 1.5 miles southeast of Glencoe village, is set in an old farmhouse with six- and eight-bed dorms, and a bunkhouse with another 16 bed spaces in communal, alpine-style bunks. There's also a cute little wooden cabin that sleeps up to three (£19 to £25 per person per night).

Glencoe SYHA   HOSTEL **£**
(☎08155-811219; www.syha.org.uk; dm/tw £21/56; P@🛜🐕) Very popular with hikers, though the atmosphere can be a little institutional. It's a 1.5-mile walk from the village along the minor road on the northern side of the river.

Invercoe Caravan & Camping Park   CAMPSITE **£**
(☎01855-811210; www.invercoe.co.uk; tent sites without car per person £9, campervan sites £22) Our favourite official camping ground in Glencoe, this place has great views of the surrounding mountains and is equipped with antimidge machines and a covered area for campers to cook in.

Clachaig Inn   HOTEL **££**
(☎01855-811252; www.clachaig.com; per person from £51; P🛜) The Clachaig has long been a favourite haunt of hill walkers and climbers. As well as comfortable en suite accommodation, there's a smart, wood-panelled lounge bar with lots of sofas and armchairs, mountaineering photos, and climbing magazines to leaf through.

Climbers usually head for the lively **Boots Bar** (mains £9-18) on the other side of the hotel – it has log fires, serves real ale and good pub grub, and has live Scottish music on Saturday nights. It's 2 miles southeast of Glencoe village.

THE GLENCOE MASSACRE

Glen Coe – Gleann Comhann in Gaelic – is sometimes (wrongly) said to mean 'the glen of weeping', a romantic mistranslation that gained popularity in the wake of the brutal murders that took place here in 1692 (the true origin of the name is pre-Gaelic, its meaning lost in the mists of time).

Following the Glorious Revolution of 1688, in which the Catholic King James VII/II (VII of Scotland, II of England) was replaced on the British throne by the Protestant King William II/III, supporters of the exiled James – known as Jacobites, most of them Highlanders – rose up against William in a series of battles. In an attempt to quash Jacobite loyalties, King William offered the Highland clans an amnesty on the condition that all clan chiefs took an oath of loyalty to him before 1 January 1692.

Maclain, the elderly chief of the MacDonalds of Glencoe, had long been a thorn in the side of the authorities. Not only was he late in setting out to fulfil the king's demand, but he mistakenly went first to Fort William before travelling slowly through winter mud and rain to Inveraray, where he was three days late in taking the oath before the Sheriff of Argyll.

The secretary of state for Scotland, Sir John Dalrymple, decided to use the fact that Maclain had missed the deadline to punish the troublesome MacDonalds, and at the same time set an example to other Highland clans, some of whom had not bothered to take the oath.

A company of 120 soldiers, mainly from the Campbell territory of Argyll, were sent to the glen under cover of collecting taxes. It was a long-standing tradition for clans to provide hospitality to travellers and, since their commanding officer was related to Maclain by marriage, the troops were billeted in MacDonald homes.

After they'd been guests for 12 days, the government order came for the soldiers to 'fall upon the rebels the MacDonalds of Glencoe and put all to the sword under 70. You are to have a special care that the Old Fox and his sons do upon no account escape'. The soldiers turned on their hosts at 5am on 13 February, killing Maclain and 37 other men, women and children. Some of the soldiers alerted the MacDonalds to their intended fate, allowing them to escape; many fled into the snow-covered hills, where another 40 people perished in the cold.

The ruthless brutality of the incident caused a public uproar, and after an inquiry several years later Dalrymple lost his job. There's a monument to Maclain in Glencoe village, and members of the MacDonald clan still gather here on 13 February each year to lay a wreath.

✕ Eating

★ Glencoe Café
CAFE £

(☑ 01855-811168; www.glencoecafe.com; mains £4-8; ☺ 10am-4pm, to 5pm May-Sep, closed Nov) This friendly cafe is the hub of Glencoe village, serving breakfast fry-ups till 11.30am (including vegetarian versions), light lunches based around local produce (think Cullen skink, smoked salmon quiche, venison burgers) and the best cappuccino in the glen.

Crafts & Things
CAFE £

(☑ 01855-811325; www.craftsandthings.co.uk; Annat; mains £3-7; ☺ 10am-5pm Mon-Fri, 9.30am-5pm Sat & Sun; ℗ ⓐ) Just off the main road between Glencoe village and Ballachulish, the coffee shop in this craft shop is a good spot for a lunch of homemade lentil soup with crusty rolls, ciabatta sandwiches, or just coffee and carrot cake. There are tables outdoors and a box of toys to keep the little ones occupied.

ⓘ Getting There & Away

Scottish Citylink (☑ 0871 266 3333; www.citylink.co.uk) Buses run between Fort William and Glencoe (£7.80, 30 minutes, eight daily) and from Glencoe to Glasgow (£21, 2½ hours, eight daily). Buses stop at Glencoe village, Glencoe Visitor Centre and Glencoe Mountain Resort.

Stagecoach (www.stagecoachbus.com) Bus 44 links Glencoe village with Fort William (£3.70, 35 minutes, hourly Monday to Saturday, three on Sunday) and Kinlochleven (£2, 25 minutes).

Kinlochleven

POP 900

Kinlochleven is hemmed in by high mountains at the head of beautiful Loch Leven, about 7 miles east of Glencoe village. The aluminium smelter that led to the town's development in the early 20th century has long since closed, and the opening of the Ballachulish Bridge in the 1970s allowed the main road to bypass the town completely. Decline was halted by the opening of the West Highland Way, which now brings a steady stream of hikers through the village.

The final section of the **West Highland Way** stretches for 14 miles from Kinlochleven to Fort William. The village is also the starting point for easier walks up the glen of the River Leven, through pleasant woods to the **Grey Mare's Tail waterfall**, and harder mountain hikes into the **Mamores**.

🏃 Activities

Ice Factor   ADVENTURE SPORTS
(☑ 01855-831100; www.ice-factor.co.uk; Leven Rd; ⊙ 9am-10pm Tue & Thu, to 7pm Mon, Wed & Fri-Sun; ⛶) If you fancy trying your hand at ice climbing, even in the middle of summer, the world's biggest indoor ice-climbing wall offers a one-hour beginner's 'taster' session for £30. You'll also find a rock-climbing wall, an aerial adventure course, a sauna and steam room, and a cafe and bar-bistro.

Via Ferrata   ADVENTURE SPORTS
(☑ 01397-747111; www.verticaldescents.com; per person £65) Scotland's first via ferrata – a 500m climbing route equipped with steel ladders, cables and bridges – snakes through the crags around the Grey Mare's Tail waterfall, allowing nonclimbers to experience the thrill of climbing (you'll need a head for heights, though!).

🛏 Sleeping & Eating

Blackwater Hostel   HOSTEL, CAMPSITE £
(☑ 01855-831253; www.blackwaterhostel.co.uk; Lab Rd; dm/tw £16.50/40, tent sites per person £7, pods from £35; ☎) This 40-bed hostel has spotless dorms with en suite bathrooms and TV, and a level, well-sheltered camping ground with the option of wooden 'glamping' pods.

★**Lochleven Seafood Cafe**   SEAFOOD ££
(☑ 01855-821048; www.lochlevenseafoodcafe. co.uk; mains £11-22, whole lobster £40; ⊙ noon-3pm & 6-9pm Apr-Oct; ℗) This outstanding place serves superb shellfish freshly plucked from live tanks – oysters on the half shell, razor clams, scallops, lobster and crab – plus a daily fish special and some nonseafood dishes. For warm days, there's an outdoor terrace with a view across the loch to the Pap of Glencoe, a distinctive conical mountain.

❶ Getting There & Away

Stagecoach (www.stagecoachbus.com) bus 44 runs from Fort William to Kinlochleven (£4.70, 50 minutes, hourly Monday to Saturday, three on Sunday) via Ballachulish and Glencoe village.

Fort William

POP 9910

Basking on the shores of Loch Linnhe amid magnificent mountain scenery, Fort William has one of the most enviable settings in the whole of Scotland. If it wasn't for the busy dual carriageway crammed between the town centre and the loch, and one of the highest rainfall records in the country, it would be almost idyllic. Even so, the Fort has carved out a reputation as 'Outdoor Capital of the UK' (www.outdoorcapital.co.uk), and easy access by rail and bus makes it a good place to base yourself for exploring the surrounding mountains and glens.

Magical **Glen Nevis** begins near the northern end of the town and wraps itself around the southern flanks of **Ben Nevis** (1344m), Britain's highest mountain and a magnet for hikers and climbers. The glen is also popular with movie makers – parts of *Braveheart*, *Rob Roy* and the *Harry Potter* movies were filmed there.

History

There is little left of the fort from which the town derives its name. The first castle here was constructed by General Monck in 1654 and called Inverlochy, but the meagre ruins by the loch are those of the fort built in the 1690s by General Mackay and named after King William II/III. In the 18th century it became part of a chain of garrisons (along with Fort Augustus and Fort George) that controlled the Great Glen in the wake of the Jacobite rebellions; it was pulled down in the 19th century to make way for the railway.

Originally a tiny fishing village called Gordonsburgh, the town adopted the name of the fort after the opening of the railway in 1901 (in Gaelic it is known as An Gearasdan, 'the garrison'). The juxtapostion of the railway and the Caledonian Canal saw the town grow into a major tourist centre. Its position has been consolidated in the last three decades by the huge increase in popularity of climbing, skiing, mountain biking and other outdoor sports.

◎ Sights

Jacobite Steam Train HERITAGE RAILWAY
(☑ 0844 850 4685; www.westcoastrailways.co.uk; day return adult/child £34/19; ☺ daily Jul & Aug, Mon-Fri mid-May–Jun & Sep-Oct) The Jacobite Steam Train, hauled by a former LNER K1 or LMS Class 5MT locomotive, travels the scenic two-hour run between Fort William and Mallaig. Classed as one of the great railway journeys of the world, the route crosses the historic Glenfinnan Viaduct, made famous in the *Harry Potter* films – the Jacobite's owners supplied the steam locomotive and rolling stock used in the film.

Trains depart from Fort William train station in the morning and return from Mallaig in the afternoon. There's a brief stop at Glenfinnan station, and you get 1½ hours in Mallaig.

West Highland Museum MUSEUM
(☑ 01397-702169; www.westhighlandmuseum.org.uk; Cameron Sq; ☺ 10am-5pm Mon-Sat Apr-Oct, to 4pm Mar & Nov-Dec, closed Jan & Feb) **FREE** This small but fascinating museum is packed with all manner of Highland memorabilia. Look out for the secret portrait of Bonnie Prince Charlie – after the Jacobite rebellions all things Highland were banned, including pictures of the exiled leader, and this tiny painting looks like nothing more than a smear of paint until viewed in a cylindrical mirror, which reflects a credible likeness of the prince.

☞ Tours

Crannog Cruises CRUISE
(☑ 01397-700714; www.crannog.net/cruises; adult/child £14/7) Operates four daily 1½-hour wildlife cruises on Loch Linnhe, visiting a seal colony and a salmon farm.

☆☆ Festivals & Events

UCI Mountain Bike
World Cup MOUNTAIN BIKING
(www.fortwilliamworldcup.co.uk) In June, Fort William pulls in crowds of more than 18,000 spectators for this World Cup downhill mountain-biking event. The gruelling downhill course is at nearby Nevis Range ski area.

▭ Sleeping

It's best to book well ahead in summer, especially for hostels.

Calluna APARTMENT £
(☑ 01397-700451; www.fortwilliamholiday.co.uk; Heathercroft, Connochie Rd; dm/tw £16/36, 6- to 8-person apt per week £550; ℗ ☎) Run by well-known mountain guide Alan Kimber and wife Sue, the Calluna offers self-catering apartments geared to groups of hikers and climbers, but also takes individual travellers prepared to share; there's a fully equipped kitchen and an excellent drying room for your soggy hiking gear.

Bank Street Lodge HOSTEL £
(☑ 01397-700070; www.bankstreetlodge.co.uk; Bank St; dm/tw from £17/55; ℗) Part of a modern hotel and restaurant complex, the Bank Street Lodge offers the most central budget beds in town, only 250m from the train station. It has kitchen facilities and a drying room.

Fort William Backpackers HOSTEL £
(☑ 01397-700711; www.scotlands-top-hostels.com; Alma Rd; dm/tw £18/47; ℗ @ ☎) A 10-minute walk from the bus and train stations, this lively and welcoming hostel is set in a grand Victorian villa, perched on a hillside with great views over Loch Linnhe.

★ Grange B&B ££
(☑ 01397-705516; www.grangefortwilliam.com; Grange Rd; r per person £65-70; ℗ ☎) An exceptional 19th-century villa set in its own landscaped grounds, the Grange is crammed with antiques and fitted with log fires, chaise longues and Victorian roll-top baths. The Turret Room, with its window seat in the turret overlooking Loch Linnhe, is our favourite. It's 500m southwest of the town centre. No children.

★ Lime Tree HOTEL ££
(☑ 01397-701806; www.limetreefortwilliam.co.uk; Achintore Rd; s/d from £100/110; ℗) Much more interesting than your average guesthouse, this former Victorian manse overlooking Loch Linnhe is an 'art gallery with rooms', decorated throughout with the artist-owner's atmospheric Highland landscapes. Foodies rave about the restaurant, and the gallery space – a triumph of sensitive design – stages everything from serious exhibitions (works by David Hockney and Andy Goldsworthy have appeared) to folk concerts.

St Andrew's Guest House
B&B ££

(✆ 01397-703038; www.standrewsguesthouse.co.uk; Fassifern Rd; s/d £55/68; P 🛜) Set in a lovely 19th-century building that was once a rectory and choir school, St Andrew's retains period features, such as carved masonry, wood panelling and stained-glass windows. It has six spacious bedrooms those at the front have stunning views.

No 6 Caberfeidh
B&B ££

(✆ 01397-703756; www.6caberfeidh.com; Fassifern Rd, 6 Caberfeidh; d/f £70/110; 🛜) Friendly owners and comfortable accommodation make a great combination; add a good central location and you're all set. Choose from one of two family rooms (one double and one single bed) or a romantic double with four-poster. Freshly prepared breakfasts include scrambled egg with smoked salmon.

Crolinnhe
B&B £££

(✆ 01397-703795; www.crolinnhe.co.uk; Grange Rd; r £130-140; ⊗ Easter-Oct; P) This grand 19th-century villa enjoys a lochside location, beautiful gardens and sumptuous accommodation – a welcome dose of luxury at the end of the West Highland Way. Breakfast porridge comes with cream and a wee jug of whisky!

✗ Eating & Drinking

Sugar and Spice
CAFE £

(✆ 01397-705005; 147 High St; mains £8-11; ⊗ 11am-4pm Mon-Wed, to 9pm Thu-Sat; 🛜🚻) Enjoy what is probably the best coffee in town at this colourful cafe, just a few paces from the official finishing line of the West Highland Way. In the evening (Thursday to Saturday only) it serves authentic Thai dishes (BYOB).

Crannog Seafood Restaurant
SEAFOOD ££

(✆ 01397-705589; www.crannog.net; Town Pier; mains £15-20; ⊗ noon-2.30pm & 6-9pm) ⌀ The Crannog wins the prize for best location in town – perched on the Town Pier, giving window-table diners an uninterrupted view down Loch Linnhe. Informal and unfussy, it specialises in fresh local fish – there are three or four daily fish specials plus the main menu – though there are lamb, venison and vegetarian dishes too. Two-course lunch £15.

Grog & Gruel
MEXICAN ££

(✆ 01397-705078; www.grogandgruel.co.uk; 66 High St; mains £9-18; ⊗ bar meals noon-9pm, restaurant 5-9pm; 🛜🚻) Upstairs from the Grog & Gruel real-ale pub is a lively Tex-Mex restaurant, with a crowd-pleasing menu of tasty enchiladas, burritos, fajitas, burgers, steaks and pizza.

★ Lime Tree
SCOTTISH £££

(✆ 01397-701806; www.limetreefortwilliam.co.uk; Achintore Rd; mains £14-23; ⊗ 6.30-9.30pm; P) ⌀ Fort William is not overendowed with great places to eat, but the restaurant at this small hotel and art gallery has put the UK's Outdoor Capital on the gastronomic map. The chef turns out delicious dishes built around fresh Scottish produce, ranging from partan bree (crab soup) to roast cod to venison sausage.

Ben Nevis Bar
PUB

(✆ 01397-702295; 105 High St; ⊗ 11am-11pm) The lounge here enjoys a good view over the loch, and the bar exudes a relaxed, jovial atmosphere where climbers and tourists can work off leftover energy jigging to live music (Thursday and Friday nights).

ℹ Information

Belford Hospital (✆ 01397-702481; Belford Rd) Opposite the train station.

Fort William Tourist Office (✆ 01397-703781; www.visithighlands.com; 15 High St; internet per 20min £1; ⊗ 9am-6pm Mon-Sat, 10am-5pm Sun Apr-Sep, limited hours Oct-Mar) Internet access.

Post Office (✆ 0845 722 3344; 5 High St)

ℹ Getting There & Away

Both bus and train station are next to the huge Morrisons supermarket, reached from the town centre via an underpass next to the Nevisport shop.

BUS

Scottish Citylink (✆ 0871 266 3333; www.citylink.co.uk) buses link Fort William with other major towns and cities:

Edinburgh £34, 4½ hours, one daily direct, seven with a change at Glasgow; via Glencoe and Crianlarich

Glasgow £23, three hours, eight daily

Inverness £11.20, two hours, six daily

Oban £9.40, 1½ hours, three daily

Portree £30, three hours, three daily

Shiel Buses (✆ 01397-700700; www.shielbuses.co.uk) service no 500 runs to Mallaig (£6.10, 1½ hours, three daily Monday to Friday) via Glenfinnan (30 minutes) and Arisaig (one hour).

CAR

Easydrive Car Hire (☑ 01397-701616; www.easydrivescotland.co.uk; Unit 36a, Ben Nevis Industrial Estate, Ben Nevis Dr) Hires out small cars from £32/175 a day/week, including tax and unlimited mileage, but not Collision Damage Waiver (CDW).

TRAIN

The spectacular West Highland line runs from Glasgow to Mallaig via Fort William. The overnight **Caledonian Sleeper** (www.scotrail.co.uk/sleeper) service connects Fort William and London Euston (from £113 sharing a twin-berth cabin, 13 hours).

There's no direct rail connection between Oban and Fort William – you have to change at Crianlarich, so it's faster to use the bus.

Edinburgh £42, five hours; three daily, two on Sunday; change at Glasgow's Queen St station

Glasgow £28, 3¾ hours, three daily, two on Sunday

Mallaig £11.80, 1½ hours, four daily, three on Sunday

❶ Getting Around

BICYCLE

Alpine Bikes (☑ 01397-704008; www.lochaberbikehire.com; 117 High St; ☉ 9am-5.30pm Mon-Sat, 10am-5.30pm Sun) Mountain-bike rental from £20 a day; bikes can be hired here and dropped off in Inverness. Also hires out full-suspension downhill bikes and body armour for use on Nevis Range trails.

BUS

The Fort Dayrider ticket (£3.20) gives unlimited travel for one day on Stagecoach bus services in the Fort William area. Buy from the bus driver.

TAXI

There's a taxi rank on the corner of High St and the Parade.

Around Fort William

Glen Nevis

You can walk the 3 miles from Fort William to scenic Glen Nevis in about an hour or so. The **Glen Nevis Visitor Centre** (☑ 01397-705922; www.bennevisweather.co.uk; ☉ 8.30am-6pm Jul-Aug, 9am-5pm Apr-Jun & Sep-Oct, 9am-3pm Nov-Mar) FREE is situated 1.5 miles up the glen, and provides information on walking, weather forecasts and specific advice on climbing Ben Nevis.

From the car park at the far end of the road along Glen Nevis, there is an excellent 1.5-mile walk through the spectacular Nevis Gorge to **Steall Meadows**, a verdant valley dominated by a 100m-high bridal-veil waterfall. You can reach the foot of the falls by crossing the river on a wobbly, three-cable wire bridge: one cable for your feet and one for each hand – a real test of balance!

🛏 Sleeping & Eating

★ Ben Nevis Inn   HOSTEL £

(☑ 01397-701227; www.ben-nevis-inn.co.uk; Achintee; dm £15.50; ☉ pub noon-11pm daily Apr-Oct, Thu-Sun only Nov-Mar; ℗) This great barn of a pub serves real ale and tasty bar meals (mains £9 to £15, food served noon to 9pm), and has a comfy 24-bed bunkhouse downstairs. It's at the start of the path from Achintee up Ben Nevis, and only a mile from the end of the West Highland Way.

Achintee Farm   B&B, HOSTEL £

(☑ 01397-702240; www.achinteefarm.com; Achintee; per person hostel £21, B&B £39-45; ℗ 🐾) This attractive farmhouse offers excellent B&B accommodation and also has a small hostel attached. It's at the start of the path up Ben Nevis.

Glen Nevis SYHA   HOSTEL £

(SYHA; ☑ 01397-702336; www.syha.org.uk; dm/tw £22/55; @🐾) Large, impersonal and reminiscent of a school camp, this hostel is 3 miles from Fort William, right beside one of the starting points for the tourist track up Ben Nevis.

Glen Nevis Caravan
& Camping Park   CAMPSITE £

(☑ 01397-702191; www.glen-nevis.co.uk; tent sites £7.20, incl car £11, campervan £12.10, plus per person £3.50; ☉ mid-Mar–Oct; 🐾) This big, well-equipped site is a popular base camp for Ben Nevis and the surrounding mountains. The site is 2.5 miles from Fort William, along the Glen Nevis road.

❶ Getting There & Away

Bus 41 runs from Fort William bus station to the Glen Nevis SYHA (£2, 15 minutes, two daily year round, five daily Monday to Saturday June to September). Check at the tourist office for the latest timetable, which is liable to alteration.

Nevis Range

Nevis Range OUTDOORS
([☎]01397-705825; www.nevisrange.co.uk; gondola return trip per adult/child £11.50/6.75; ⊙10am-5pm summer, 9.30am-dusk winter, closed mid-Nov-mid-Dec) The Nevis Range ski area, 6 miles north of Fort William, spreads across the northern slopes of Aonach Mor (1221m). The gondola that gives access to the bottom of the ski area at 655m operates year round (15 minutes each way). At the top there's a restaurant and a couple of hiking trails through nearby Leanachan Forest, as well as excellent mountain-biking trails.

During the ski season a one-day lift pass costs £30/18.50 per adult/child; a one-day package, including equipment hire, lift pass and two hours' instruction, costs £64.

Bus 41 runs from Glen Nevis youth hostel and Fort William bus station to Nevis Range (£1.95, 20 minutes, five daily Monday to Saturday, three on Sunday, limited service October to April). Check at the tourist office for the latest timetable, which is liable to alteration.

Nevis Range Downhill & Witch's Trails MOUNTAIN BIKING
([☎]01397-705825; bike.nevisrange.co.uk; single/multitrip ticket £13/31; ⊙10.15am-3.45pm mid-May–mid-Sep) A world championship downhill mountain-bike trail – for experienced riders only – runs from the Snowgoose restaurant at the Nevis Range ski area to the base station; bikes are carried up on a rack on the gondola cabin. A multitrip ticket gives unlimited uplift for a day; full-suspension bike hire costs from £40/70 per single run/full day.

There's also a 4-mile XC red trail that begins at the Snowgoose, and the Witch's Trails, 25 miles of waymarked forest road and singletrack in the nearby forest, including a 5-mile world-championship loop.

CLIMBING BEN NEVIS

As the highest peak in the British Isles, Ben Nevis (1344m) attracts many would-be ascensionists who would not normally think of climbing a Scottish mountain – a staggering (often literally) 100,000 people reach the summit each year.

Although anyone who is reasonably fit should have no problem climbing Ben Nevis on a fine summer's day, an ascent should not be undertaken lightly. Every year people have to be rescued from the mountain. You will need proper walking boots (the path is rough and stony, and there may be snow on the summit), warm clothing, waterproofs, a map and compass, and plenty of food and water. And don't forget to check the weather forecast (see www.bennevisweather.co.uk).

Here are a few facts to mull over before you go racing up the tourist track: the summit plateau is bounded by 700m-high cliffs and has a sub-Arctic climate; at the summit it can snow on any day of the year; the summit is wrapped in cloud nine days out of 10; in thick cloud, visibility at the summit can be 10m or less; and in such conditions the only safe way off the mountain requires careful use of a map and compass to avoid walking over those 700m cliffs.

The tourist track (the easiest route to the top) was originally called the Pony Track. It was built in the 19th century for the pack ponies that carried supplies to a meteorological observatory on the summit (now in ruins), which was manned continuously from 1883 to 1904.

There are three possible starting points for the tourist track ascent – Achintee Farm; the footbridge at Glen Nevis SYHA; and, if you have a car, the car park at Glen Nevis Visitor Centre. The path climbs gradually to the shoulder at Lochan Meall an t-Suidhe (known as the Halfway Lochan), then zigzags steeply up beside the Red Burn to the summit plateau. The highest point is marked by a trig point on top of a huge cairn beside the ruins of the old observatory; the plateau is scattered with countless smaller cairns, stones arranged in the shape of people's names and, sadly, a fair bit of litter.

The total distance to the summit and back is 8 miles; allow at least four or five hours to reach the top, and another 2½ to three hours for the descent. Afterwards, as you celebrate in the pub with a pint, consider the fact that the record time for the annual Ben Nevis Hill Race is just under 1½ hours – up *and* down. Then have another pint.

Corpach to Loch Lochy

Corpach lies at the southern entrance to the Caledonian Canal, 3 miles north of Fort William; there's a classic picture-postcard view of Ben Nevis from the mouth of the canal. Nearby is the award-winning **Treasures of the Earth** (☎01397-772283; www.treasuresoftheearth.co.uk; Corpach; adult/child £5/3; ⊙9.30am-6pm Jul-Sep, 10am-5pm Apr-Jun & Oct, shorter hours Nov-Feb) exhibition, a rainy-day diversion with a great collection of gemstones, minerals, fossils and other geological curiosities.

A mile east of Corpach, at Banavie, is **Neptune's Staircase**, an impressive flight of eight locks that allows boats to climb 20m to the main reach of the **Caledonian Canal**. The B8004 road runs along the west side of the canal to Gairlochy at the south end of Loch Lochy, offering superb views of Ben Nevis; the canal towpath on the east side makes a great walk or bike ride (6.5 miles).

From Gairlochy the B8005 continues along the west side of Loch Lochy to Achnacarry and the **Clan Cameron Museum** (☎01397-712480; www.clan-cameron.org; Achnacarry; adult/child £3.50/free; ⊙11am-5pm Jul & Aug, 1.30-5pm Easter-Jun & Sep–mid-Oct), which records the history of the clan and its involvement with the Jacobite rebellions, including items of clothing that once belonged to Bonnie Prince Charlie.

From Achnacarry the **Great Glen Way** continues along the roadless western shore of Loch Lochy, and a dead-end minor road leads west along remote but lovely **Loch Arkaig**.

There are a couple of backpacker hostels in Corpach. At **Farr Cottage Lodge** (☎01397-772315; www.farrcottage.com; Corpach; dm/tw £16.50/50; [P@☎]) bike hire is also available, while the folk at **Blacksmiths Backpackers Hostel** (☎01397-772467; www.highland-mountain-guides.co.uk; Corpach; dm £17; [P☎]) can organise courses in climbing, kayaking and other sports.

Glen Spean & Glen Roy

Near Spean Bridge, at the junction of the B8004 and A82, 2.5 miles east of Gairlochy, stands the **Commando Memorial**, which commemorates the WWII special forces soldiers who trained in this area.

Four miles further east, at Roy Bridge, a minor road leads north up Glen Roy, which is noted for its intriguing, so-called parallel roads. These prominent horizontal terraces contouring around the hillside are actually ancient shorelines formed during the last ice age by the waters of an ice-dammed glacial lake. The best viewpoint is at a car park just over 3 miles up Glen Roy, where there's an interpretation board explaining the landscape features you can see.

Ardnamurchan

Ten miles south of Fort William, a **car ferry** (car £7.60, bicycle & foot passenger free; ⊙5 min, every 30min) makes the short crossing to Corran Ferry. The drive from here to **Ardnamurchan Point** (www.ardnamurchan.com), the most westerly point on the British mainland, is one of the most beautiful in the western Highlands, especially in late spring and early summer when much of the narrow, twisting road is lined with the bright pink and purple blooms of rhododendrons.

The road clings to the northern shore of Loch Sunart, going through the pretty villages of **Strontian** – which gave its name to the element strontium, first discovered in ore from nearby lead mines in 1790 – and **Salen**.

The mostly single-track road from Salen to Ardnamurchan Point is only 25 miles long, but it'll take you 1½ hours each way. It's a dipping, twisting, low-speed roller coaster of a ride through sun-dappled native woodlands draped with lichen and fern. Just when you're getting used to the views of Morvern and Mull to the south, it makes a quick detour to the north for a panorama over the islands of Rum and Eigg.

◉ Sights

Nádurra Visitor Centre   WILDLIFE CENTRE
(☎01972-500209; www.nadurracentre.co.uk; Glenmore; adult/child £4.50/2.25; ⊙10am-5.30pm Mon-Sat, 11am-5.30pm Sun Apr-Oct, 10am-4pm Tue-Fri, 11.30am-4pm Sun Nov-Mar; [⊞]) This fascinating centre – midway between Salen and Kilchoan – was originally devised by a wildlife photographer and tries to bring you face to face with the flora and fauna of the Ardnamurchan peninsula. The Living Building exhibit is designed to attract local wildlife, with a mammal den that is occasionally occupied by hedgehogs or pine martens, an owl nest-box, a mouse nest and a pond.

If the beasties are not in residence, you can watch recorded video footage of the animals. There's also seasonal live CCTV coverage of local wildlife, ranging from nesting herons to a golden eagle feeding site.

Ardnamurchan Distillery DISTILLERY
(www.adelphidistillery.com; Glenbeg) A brand-new whisky distillery went into production on the shores of Loch Sunart in summer 2014, complete with visitor centre and tasting room. Although you will be able to see the whisky-making process, the finished product will be matured in casks until at least 2020 before being bottled as a single malt.

Ardnamurchan Lighthouse HISTORIC BUILDING
(☑01972-510210; www.ardnamurchanlighthouse. com; Ardnamurchan Point; visitor centre adult/child £3/2, guided tours £6/4; ☉10am-5pm Apr-Oct; ⊞) The final 6 miles of road from Kilchoan to Ardnamurchan Point end at the 36m-high, grey granite tower of Ardnamurchan Lighthouse, built in 1849 by the 'Lighthouse Stevensons' – family of Robert Louis – to guard the westernmost point of the British mainland. There's a tearoom, and the visitor centre will tell you more than you'll ever need to know about lighthouses, with lots of hands-on stuff for kids.

The guided tour (every half-hour 11am to 4.30pm) includes a trip to the top of the lighthouse. But the main attraction here is the expansive view over the ocean – this is a superb sunset viewpoint, provided you don't mind driving back in the dark.

Kilchoan VILLAGE
The scattered crofting village of Kilchoan, the only village of any size west of Salen, is best known for the scenic ruins of 13th-century Mingary Castle. The village has a tourist office (☑01972-510222; Pier Rd, Kilchoan; ☉9am-5pm Mon-Sat Easter-Oct), a shop, a hotel and a campsite, and there's a ferry to Tobermory on the Isle of Mull.

🛏 Sleeping & Eating

Ardnamurchan Campsite CAMPSITE £
(☑01972-510766; www.ardnamurchanstudycentre. co.uk; Kilchoan; sites per adult/child £8/3; ☉May-Sep; ☎) Basic but beautifully situated campsite, with the chance of seeing otters from your tent. It's along the Ormsaig road, 2 miles west of Kilchoan village.

Salen Hotel INN ££
(☑01967-431661; www.salenhotel.co.uk; Salen; r £70-100; ℗☎) A traditional Highland inn with views over Loch Sunart, the Salen Hotel has three rooms in the pub (two with sea views) and another three rooms (all en suite) in a modern chalet out the back. The cosy lounge has a roaring fire and comfy

---

THE CALEDONIAN CANAL

Running for 59 miles from Corpach, near Fort William, to Inverness via Lochs Lochy, Oich and Ness, the Caledonian Canal links the east and west coasts of Scotland, avoiding the long and dangerous sea passage around Cape Wrath and through the turbulent Pentland Firth. Designed by Thomas Telford and completed in 1822 at a cost of £900,000 – a staggering sum then – the canal took 20 years to build, including 29 locks, four aqueducts and 10 bridges.

Conceived as a project to ease unemployment and bring prosperity to the Highlands in the aftermath of the Jacobite rebellions and the Clearances, the canal proved to be a commercial failure – the locks were too small for the new breed of steamships which came into use soon after its completion. But it proved to be a success in terms of tourism, especially after it was popularised by Queen Victoria's cruise along the canal in 1873. Today the canal is used mainly by yachts and pleasure cruisers, though since 2010 it has also been used to transport timber from west-coast forestry plantations to Inverness.

Much of the Great Glen Way (p310) follows the line of the canal; it can be followed on foot, by mountain bike or on horseback, and 80% of the route has even been done on mobility scooters. An easy half-day hike or bike ride is to follow the canal towpath from Corpach to Gairlochy (10 miles), which takes you past the impressive flight of eight locks known as Neptune's Staircase, and through beautiful countryside with grand views to the north face of Ben Nevis.

If you're cycling the length of the Great Glen Way, you can hire mountain bikes from Alpine Bikes (p342) in Fort William and drop them off at Ticket to Ride (p306) in Inverness, or vice versa.

INVERNESS & THE CENTRAL HIGHLANDS ARDNAMURCHAN

sofa, and the bar meals, including seafood, venison and other game dishes, are very good.

Inn at Ardgour INN ££

(☏ 01855-841225; www.ardgour.biz; Corran Ferry; d/tw/f £100/120/140; Ⓟ) This pretty, white-washed coaching inn, draped in colourful flower baskets, makes a great place for a lunch break or overnight stop. The restaurant (mains £9 to £17) is set in the row of cottages once occupied by the Corran ferrymen, and serves traditional, homemade Scottish dishes.

Antler Tearoom CAFE £

(Nàdurra Visitor Centre, Glenmore; mains £4-7; ⊙10am-5.30pm Mon-Sat, 11am-5.30pm Sun Apr-Oct, 10am-4pm Tue-Fri, 11.30am-4pm Sun Nov-Mar; Ⓟ🛜♿) The cafe at this wildlife centre serves coffee, home baking and lunch dishes, including fresh salads and sandwiches and homemade soup.

❶ Getting There & Away

Shiel Buses (☏ 01397-700700; www.shielbuses. co.uk) bus 506 runs from Fort William to Acharacle, Salen and Kilchoan (£7.50, 3½ hours, one daily Monday to Saturday) via Corran Ferry. There's a car ferry between Kilchoan and Tobermory on the Isle of Mull.

Salen to Lochailort

The A861 road from Salen to Lochailort passes through the low, wooded hills of Moidart. A minor road (signposted Dorlin) leads west from the A861 at Shiel Bridge to a parking area looking across to the picturesque roofless ruin of 13th-century Castle Tioram. The castle sits on a tiny island in Loch Moidart, connected to the mainland by a narrow strand that is submerged at high tide (the castle's name, pronounced *chee*-ram, means 'dry'). It was the ancient seat of the Clanranald Macdonalds, but the Clanranald chief ordered it to be burned (to prevent it falling into the hands of Hanoverian troops) when he set off to fight with the Jacobites in the 1715 rebellion. You can walk to the island at low tide, but signs warn that the castle is dangerous to enter.

As the A861 curls around the north shore of Loch Moidart you will see a line of three huge beech trees (one badly damaged) and two obvious stumps between the road and the shore. Known as the Seven Men of Moidart (four have been blown down by gales and replaced with saplings), they were planted in the late 18th century to commemorate the seven local men who accompanied Bonnie Prince Charlie from France and acted as his bodyguards at the start of the 1745 rebellion.

Road to the Isles

The 46-mile A830 road from Fort William to Mallaig is traditionally known as the Road to the Isles, as it leads to the jumping-off point for ferries to the Small Isles and Skye, itself a stepping stone to the Outer Hebrides. This is a region steeped in Jacobite history, having witnessed both the beginning and the end of Bonnie Prince Charlie's doomed attempt to regain the British throne in 1745–46.

The final section of this scenic route, between Arisaig and Mallaig, has been upgraded to a fast straight road. Unless you're in a hurry, opt instead for the more scenic old road (signposted Alternative Coastal Route).

Between the A830 and the A87 far to the north lie Knoydart and Glenelg – forming Scotland's 'Empty Quarter' – a rugged landscape of wild mountains and lonely sea lochs roughly 20 miles by 30 miles in size, mostly uninhabited and penetrated only by two minor roads (along Lochs Arkaig and Quoich). If you want to get away from it all, this is the place to go.

❶ Getting Around

BUS

Shiel Buses (☏ 01397-700700; www.shielbuses. co.uk) Bus 500 runs from Fort William to Mallaig (£6.10, 1½ hours, three daily Monday to Friday, one on Saturday) via Glenfinnan (30 minutes) and Arisaig (one hour).

TRAIN

The Fort William–Mallaig railway line has four trains a day (three on Sunday), with stops at many points along the way, including Corpach, Glenfinnan, Lochailort, Arisaig and Morar.

Glenfinnan

POP 100

Glenfinnan is hallowed ground for fans of Bonnie Prince Charlie; the monument here marks where he raised his Highland army. It is also a place of pilgrimage for steam-train enthusiasts and *Harry Potter* fans – the famous railway viaduct features in the films, and is regularly traversed by the Jacobite Steam Train (p340).

⊙ Sights & Activities

Glenfinnan Monument
MONUMENT

This tall column, topped by a statue of a kilted Highlander, was erected in 1815 on the spot where Bonnie Prince Charlie first raised his standard and rallied the Jacobite clans on 19 August 1745, marking the start of his ill-fated campaign, which would end in disaster at Culloden 14 months later. The setting, at the north end of Loch Shiel, is hauntingly beautiful.

Glenfinnan Visitor Centre
INTERPRETATION CENTRE

(NTS; adult/child £3.50/2.50; ⊙ 9.30am-5pm Jul & Aug, 10am-5pm Easter-Jun, Sep & Oct) This centre recounts the story of the '45, as the Jacobite rebellion of 1745 is known, when Bonnie Prince Charlie's loyal clansmen marched and fought their way from Glenfinnan south via Edinburgh to Derby, then back north to final defeat at Culloden.

Glenfinnan Station Museum
MUSEUM

(www.glenfinnanstationmuseum.co.uk; admission 80p; ⊙ 9am-5pm May-Oct; P) This fascinating little museum is dedicated to the great days of steam on the West Highland line. The famous 21-arch **Glenfinnan Viaduct**, just east of the station, was built in 1901, and featured in several *Harry Potter* movies. A pleasant walk of around 0.75 miles east from the station (signposted) leads to a viewpoint for the viaduct and for Loch Shiel.

Loch Shiel Cruises
CRUISE

(⊡ 07801 537617; www.highlandcruises.co.uk; ⊙ Apr-Sep) Offers boat trips along Loch Shiel, with the opportunity of spotting golden eagles and other wildlife. There are one- to 2½-hour cruises (£10 to £18 per person) daily except Saturday and Wednesday. On Wednesday the boat goes the full length of the loch to **Acharacle** (£17/25 one way/return), calling at Polloch and Dalilea, allowing for a range of walks and bike rides using the forestry track on the eastern shore. The boat departs from a jetty near Glenfinnan House Hotel.

🛏 Sleeping & Eating

Sleeping Car Bunkhouse
HOSTEL £

(⊡ 01397-722295; www.glenfinnanstationmuseum.co.uk; Glenfinnan Station; per person £14, entire coach £120; ⊙ May-Oct; P) Two converted railway carriages at Glenfinnan Station house this unusual 10-berth bunkhouse and the atmospheric **Dining Car Tearoom** (snacks £3-5; ⊙ 9am 4.30pm May-Oct), which serves scones with cream and jam and pots of tea. There are superb views of the mountains above Loch Shiel.

★ Prince's House Hotel
INN £££

(⊡ 01397-722246; www.glenfinnan.co.uk; s/d from £80/130; P) A delightful old coaching inn from 1658, the Prince's House is a great place to pamper yourself – ask for the spacious, tartan-clad Stuart Room (£190), complete with four-poster bed, if you want to stay in the oldest part of the hotel. The relaxed but well-regarded restaurant specialises in Scottish produce (four-course dinner £43.50).

There's no documentary evidence that Bonnie Prince Charlie actually stayed here in 1745, but it was the only sizeable house in Glenfinnan at that time, so...

Arisaig & Morar

The five miles of coast between Arisaig and Morar is a fretwork of rocky islets, inlets and gorgeous silver-sand beaches backed by dunes and machair, with stunning sunset views across the sea to the silhouetted peaks of Eigg and Rum. The **Silver Sands of Morar**, as they are known, draw crowds of bucket-and-spade holidaymakers in July and August, when the many camping grounds scattered along the coast are filled to overflowing.

⊙ Sights & Activities

Camusdarach Beach
BEACH

Fans of the movie *Local Hero* still make pilgrimages to Camusdarach Beach, just south of Morar, which starred in the film as Ben's beach. To find it, look for the car park 800m north of Camusdarach campsite; from here, a wooden footbridge and a 400m walk through the dunes lead to the beach. (The village that featured in the film is on the other side of the country, at Pennan.)

Land, Sea & Islands Visitor Centre
MUSEUM

(www.arisaigcentre.co.uk; Arisaig; ⊙ 10am-6pm Mon-Fri, 10-4pm Sat, 2-5pm Sun Apr-Oct, shorter hours Sat-Mon only Nov-Mar; P) **FREE** This centre in Arisaig village houses exhibits on the cultural and natural history of the region, plus a small but fascinating exhibition on the part played by the local area as a base for training spies for the Special Operations Executive (SOE, forerunner of MI6) during WWII.

WORTH A TRIP

INN PEACE

....

Glenuig Inn (☑ 01687-470219; www.glenuig.com; Glenuig; bunkhouse per person £28, B&B s/d/q from £65/105/145; P 🕏) Set on a peaceful bay on the Arisaig coast, halfway between Lochailort and Acharacle on the A830, the Glenuig Inn is a great place to get away from it all. As well as offering comfortable accommodation, good food (served noon to 9pm), and real ale on tap, it's a great base for exploring Arisaig, Morar and the Loch Shiel area.

Arisaig Marine   CRUISE
(☑ 01687-450224; www.arisaig.co.uk; Arisaig Harbour; ☉ Apr-Sep) Runs cruises from Arisaig harbour to Eigg (£18 return, one hour, six a week), Rum (£25 return, 2½ hours, two or three a week) and Muck (£20 return, two hours, three a week), with four hours ashore on Eigg, or two to three hours on Rum or Muck. The trips include whale-watching, with up to an hour for close viewing.

🛏 Sleeping & Eating

There are at least a half-dozen camping grounds between Arisaig and Morar; all are open in summer only, and are often full in July and August, so book ahead. Several are listed on www.road-to-the-isles.org.uk.

Garramore House   B&B ££
(☑ 01687-450268; r per person £25-35; P 🐾) Built as a hunting lodge in 1840, this house served as an HQ for the SOE during WWII. Today it's a wonderfully atmospheric, old-fashioned guest-house set in lovely woodland gardens with resident peacocks and great views to the Small Isles and Skye. Garramore is signposted off the coastal road, 4 miles north of Arisaig village.

Camusdarach Campsite   CAMPSITE £
(☑ 01687-450221; Arisaig; tent/campervan sites £8/15, plus per person £3; ☉ Mar-Oct; 🕏) 🐾 A small and nicely landscaped site with good facilities, only three minutes' walk from the *Local Hero* beach (via gate in northwest corner).

Old Library Lodge & Restaurant SCOTTISH ££
(☑ 01687-450651; www.oldlibrary.co.uk; Arisaig; mains £10-19; P 🕏) 🐾 The Old Library is a charming restaurant with rooms (B&B

single/double £75/120) set in converted 200-year-old stables overlooking the waterfront in Arisaig village. The lunch menu concentrates on soups, burgers and smoked fish or meat platters, while dinner is a more sophisticated affair offering local seafood, beef and lamb.

Mallaig

POP 800

If you're travelling between Fort William and Skye, you may find yourself overnighting in the bustling fishing and ferry port of Mallaig (*mahl*-ig). Indeed, it makes a good base for a series of day trips by ferry to the Small Isles and Knoydart.

⊙ Sights & Activities

Loch Morar   LAKE
(www.lochmorar.org.uk) A minor road from Morar village, 2.5 miles south of Mallaig, leads to scenic 11-mile-long Loch Morar, which at 310m is the deepest body of water in the United Kingdom. Reputed to be inhabited by its own version of Nessie – Morag, the Loch Morar monster – the loch and its surrounding hills are the haunt of otters, wildcats, red deer and golden eagles.

A 5-mile signposted footpath leads along the north shore of the loch from the road-end at Bracorina, 3 miles east of Morar village, to Tarbet on Loch Nevis, from where you can catch a passenger ferry (p350) back to Mallaig (departs 3.40pm June to September).

Mallaig Heritage Centre INTERPRETATION CENTRE
(☑ 01687-462085; www.mallaigheritage.org.uk; Station Rd; ☉ 11am-4pm Tue-Fri, noon-4pm Sat) **FREE** The village's rainy-day attractions are limited to this heritage centre, which covers the archaeology and history of the region, including the heart-rending tale of the Highland Clearances in Knoydart.

MV Grimsay Isle   FISHING, BOAT TOURS
(☑ 07780 815158; Apr-Sep; adult/child £20/10) The MV *Grimsay Isle* provides entertaining, two-hour customised sea-fishing trips and wildlife-watching tours (book at the tourist office).

🛏 Sleeping & Eating

Seaview Guest House   B&B ££
(☑ 01687-462059; www.seaviewguesthousemallaig.com; Main St; r per person £30-38; ☉ Mar–mid-Nov; P) This comfortable five-bedroom B&B

has grand views over the harbour, not only from the upstairs bedrooms but also from the breakfast room. There's also a cute little cottage next door that offers self-catering accommodation (www.selfcateringmallaig. com; one double and one twin room) for £400 to £495 a week.

Springbank Guest House   B&B ££
(☑ 01687-462459; www.springbank-mallaig.co.uk; East Bay; s/d £35/65; [P] [?]) The Springbank is a traditional West Highland house with six homely guest bedrooms, with superb views across the harbour to the Cuillin of Skye.

Fish Market Restaurant   SEAFOOD ££
(☑ 01687-462299; Station Rd; mains £10-21) 🍴 At least half-a-dozen signs in Mallaig advertise 'seafood restaurant', but this bright, modern bistro-style place next to the harbour is our favourite, serving simply prepared scallops, smoked salmon, mussels, and fresh Mallaig haddock fried in breadcrumbs, as well as the tastiest Cullen skink on the west coast.

Upstairs is a **coffee shop** (mains £6-7; ☺ 11am-5pm) that serves delicious hot roast-beef rolls with horseradish sauce, and scones with clotted cream and jam.

Tea Garden   CAFE £
(☑ 01687-462764; www.mallaigteagarden.co.uk; Harbour View; mains £6-12; ☺ 9am-6pm, to 9pm May-Sep) On a sunny day the Tea Garden's terrace cafe, with its flowers, greenery and cosmopolitan backpacker staff, can feel more like the Med than Mallaig. The coffee is good, and the speciality of the house is a pint glass full of Mallaig prawns with dipping sauce (£12.50). From late May to September the cafe opens in the evening with a bistro menu.

Jaffy's   FISH & CHIPS £
(www.jaffys.co.uk; Station Rd; mains £4-8; ☺ noon-2.30pm & 5-8pm daily May Oct, 5-8pm Thu-Sat only Nov-Apr) Owned by a third-generation fish-merchant's family, Mallaig's chippy serves superbly fresh fish and chips, as well as kippers, prawns and other seafood.

❶ Information

Mallaig has a **tourist office** (☑ 01687-462170; East Bay; ☺ 10am-5.30pm Mon-Fri, 10.15am-3.45pm Sat, noon-3.30pm Sun), a post office, a bank with ATM and a **co-op supermarket** (☺ 8am-10pm Mon-Sat, 9am-9pm Sun).

❶ Getting There & Away

BOAT
Ferries run from Mallaig to the Small Isles, the Isle of Skye, Knoydart and South Uist. See the relevant sections for details.

BUS
Shiel Buses (☑ 01397-700700; www.shielbuses.co.uk) bus 500 runs from Fort William to Mallaig (£6.10, 1½ hours, three daily Monday to Friday, one on Saturday) via Glenfinnan (30 minutes) and Arisaig (one hour).

TRAIN
The West Highland line runs between Fort William and Mallaig (£11.80, 1½ hours) four times a day (three on Sunday).

Knoydart Peninsula
POP 150

The Knoydart peninsula is the only sizeable area in Britain that remains inaccessible to the motor car, cut off by miles of rough country and the embracing arms of Lochs Nevis and Hourn – Gaelic for the lochs of Heaven and Hell. No road penetrates this wilderness of rugged hills – **Inverie**, its sole village, can only be reached by ferry from Mallaig, or on foot from the remote road's end at Kinloch Hourn (a tough 16-mile hike).

The main reasons for visiting are to climb the remote 1020m peak of **Ladhar Bheinn** (*laar*-ven), which affords some of the west coast's finest views, or just to enjoy the feeling of being cut off from the rest of the world. There are no shops, no TV and no mobile-phone reception (although there *is* internet access); electricity is provided by a private hydroelectric scheme – truly 'off the grid' living! For more information and full accommodation listings, see www.knoydart-foundation.com.

🛏 Sleeping & Eating

Knoydart Foundation Bunkhouse   HOSTEL £
(☑ 01687-462163; www.knoydart-foundation. com; Inverie; dm adult/child £17/10; @ [?]) 🍴 A 15-minute walk east of Inverie ferry pier, this is a cosy hostel with wood-burning stove, kitchen and drying room.

Long Beach   CAMPSITE £
(Long Beach; per tent & 1 person £4, per extra person £3) Basic but beautiful campsite, a 10-minute walk east of the ferry; water supply and composting toilet, but no showers. Ranger comes around to collect fees.

Knoydart Lodge B&B ££

(☑ 01687-460129; www.knoydartlodge.co.uk; Inverie; s/d £68/95; ☎⊛) This must be some of
the most spacious and luxurious B&B accommodation on the whole west coast, let alone
in Knoydart. On offer are five large, stylish
bedrooms in a fantastic, modern timber-
built lodge reminiscent of an Alpine chalet,
just a short stroll from the beach.

★ **Old Forge** PUB, RESTAURANT ££

(☑ 01687-462267; www.theoldforge.co.uk; Inverie;
mains £10-20; ⊙food served 12.30-3pm & 6.30-
9.30pm; ☎⊛) ∥ The Old Forge is listed in
the *Guinness Book of Records* as Britain's
most remote pub. It's surprisingly sophisticated – as well as having real ale on tap,
there's an Italian coffee machine for those
wilderness lattes and cappuccinos. The
house special is a seafood platter (£30), all
ingredients sourced within 7 miles of the
pub.

In the evening you can sit by the fire, pint
of beer in hand and join the impromptu
ceilidh (an evening of traditional Scottish
entertainment including music, song and
dance) that seems to take place just about
nightly.

❶ Getting There & Away

Sea Bridge Knoydart (☑ 01687-462916;
www.knoydartferry.com; one way/return
£11/20) From April to October this fast
passenger ferry service runs from Mallaig to
Inverie eight times daily Monday to Friday,
four times Saturday and Sunday (25 minutes),
and will carry bikes, canoes and kayaks at
no extra charge. From November to March,
there are four crossings on weekdays, two on
weekends.

Western Isles Cruises (☑ 01687-462233;
westernislescruises.co.uk; 1 way/day return
£10/15) Passenger ferry linking Mallaig to
Inverie (45 minutes) twice daily Monday to
Saturday from April to October. Taking the
morning boat gives you up to 5½ hours ashore
in Knoydart before the return trip. There's
also an afternoon sailing between Inverie and
Tarbet on the south side of Loch Nevis, allowing
walkers to hike along the northern shore of
Loch Morar to Tarbet and return by boat (£15
Tarbet–Inverie–Mallaig).

It's also possible to join the boat just for the
cruise, without going ashore (£20 for Mallaig–
Inverie–Tarbet–Mallaig).

SMALL ISLES

The scattered jewels of the Small Isles – Rum,
Eigg, Muck and Canna – lie strewn across
the silvery-blue cloth of the Cuillin Sound to
the south of the Isle of Skye. Their distinctive outlines enliven the glorious views from
the beaches of Arisaig and Morar.

Rum is the biggest and boldest of the
four, a miniature Skye of pointed peaks
and dramatic sunset silhouettes. Eigg is the
most pastoral and populous, dominated by
the miniature sugarloaf mountain of the
Sgurr. Muck is a botanist's delight with its
wildflowers and unusual alpine plants, and
Canna is a craggy bird sanctuary made of
magnetic rocks.

If your time is limited and you can only
visit one island, choose Eigg; it has the most
to offer on a day trip.

❶ Getting There & Away

The main ferry operator is **CalMac** (www.cal-
mac.co.uk), which operates the passenger-only
ferry from Mallaig:

Canna £23.75 return, two hours, six a week

Eigg £12.80 return, 1¼ hours, four a week

Muck £19.50 return, 1½ hours, five a week

Rum £18.90 return, 1¼ hours, five a week

You can also hop between the islands without
returning to Mallaig, but the timetable is complicated and it requires a bit of planning – you
would need at least five days to visit all four.
Bicycles are carried for free.

In summer Arisaig Marine (☑ 01687-450224;
www.arisaig.co.uk; Arisaig Harbour; ⊙Apr-Sep)
operates day cruises from Arisaig harbour to
Eigg (£18 return, one hour, six a week), Rum
(£25 return, 2½ hours, two or three a week) and
Muck (£20 return, two hours, three a week). The
trips include whale-watching, with up to an hour
for close viewing. Sailing times allow four or
five hours ashore on Eigg, two or three hours on
Muck or Rum.

Isle of Rum

POP 22

The Isle of Rum – the biggest and most
spectacular of the Small Isles – was once
known as the Forbidden Island. Cleared of
its crofters in the early 19th century to make
way for sheep, from 1888 to 1957 it was the
private sporting estate of the Bulloughs,
a nouveau riche Lancashire family who
made their fortune in the textile industry.
Curious outsiders who ventured too close
to the island were liable to find themselves

staring down the wrong end of a gamekeeper's shotgun.

The island was sold to the Nature Conservancy in 1957 and has since been a reserve noted for its deer, wild goats, ponies, golden and white-tailed eagles, and a 120,000-strong nesting colony of Manx shearwaters. Its dramatic, rocky mountains, known as the Rum Cuillin for their similarity to the peaks on neighbouring Skye, draw hill walkers and climbers.

◎ Sights & Activities

★ Kinloch Castle   CASTLE

(☑ 01687-462037; www.isleofrum.com; adult/child £9/4.50; ⊘ guided tours daily Apr-Oct, to coincide with ferry times) When George Bullough – a dashing, Harrow-educated cavalry officer – inherited Rum along with half his father's fortune in 1891, he became one of the wealthiest bachelors in Britain. Bullough blew half his inheritance on building his dream bachelor pad – the ostentatious Kinloch Castle. Since the Bulloughs left, the castle has survived as a perfect time capsule of upper-class Edwardian eccentricity – the guided tour should not be missed.

Bullough shipped in pink sandstone from Dumfriesshire and 250,000 tonnes of Ayrshire topsoil for the gardens, and paid his workers a shilling extra a day to wear tweed kilts – just so they'd look more picturesque. Hummingbirds were kept in the greenhouses and alligators in the garden, and guests were entertained with an orchestrion, the Edwardian equivalent of a Bose hi-fi system (one of only six that were ever made).

Nature Trails   WALKING

There's some great coastal and mountain walking on the island, including a couple of easy, waymarked nature trails in the woods around Kinloch. The first path on the left after leaving the pier leads to an **otter hide** (signposted).

Glen Harris is a 10-mile round trip from Kinloch, on a rough 4WD track; allow four to five hours' walking. The climb to the island's highest point, **Askival** (812m), is a strenuous hike and involves a bit of rock scrambling (allow six hours for the round trip from Kinloch).

You can hire bikes from the **Craft Shop** (☑ 01687-462744; www.rumbikehire.co.uk; per day £15) near Kinloch Castle.

🛏 Sleeping

Accommodation on Rum is strictly limited – at the time of writing there was only the Castle Hostel, one B&B and the campsite; a new bunkhouse should be open by the time you read this. Booking is essential for the hostel, though not for campers. There are also two bothies (unlocked cottages with no facilities, for the use of hikers) on the island, and wild camping is permitted.

Kinloch Castle Hostel   HOSTEL £

(☑ 01687-462037; www.isleofrum.com; dm/d £10.50/74; ◉ Mar-Oct, 🐾) The castle hostel has 32 beds in four-bed dorms. There are two self-catering kitchens and a comfortable lounge.

Kinloch Village Campsite   CAMPSITE £

(☑ 01687-460328; www.isleofrum.com; sites per adult/child £6/3) Situated between the pier and Kinloch Castle, this basic camping ground has toilets, a water supply and hot showers (from April to October). There are also two wooden camping cabins (£22 for two persons), which must be booked in advance.

ℹ Information

Kinloch, where the ferry lands, is the island's only settlement; it has a small **grocery shop** (⊘ 5-7pm), post office and public telephone, and a **tourist office** (⊘ 8.30am-5pm Apr-Oct) near the pier where you can get information and leaflets on walking and wildlife. There's a **tearoom** (⊘ noon-6pm Mon-Sat Apr-Sep; 🐾) in the village hall, with wi-fi and internet access. The hall itself is open at all times for people to shelter from the rain (or the midges!). For more information see www.isleofrum.com.

Isle of Eigg

POP 83

The Isle of Eigg made history in 1997 when it became the first Highland estate to be bought out by its inhabitants. The island is now owned and managed by the **Isle of Eigg Heritage Trust** (www.isleofeigg.org), a partnership among the islanders, Highland Council and the Scottish Wildlife Trust.

◎ Sights & Activities

The island takes its name from the Old Norse *egg* (edge), a reference to the Sgurr of Eigg (393m), an impressive minimountain that towers over Galmisdale. Ringed by vertical cliffs on three sides, it's composed of pitchstone lava with columnar jointing similar to that seen on the Isle of Staffa and at the Giant's Causeway in Northern Ireland.

The climb to the summit of the **Sgurr of Eigg** (4.5 miles round trip; allow three to four hours) begins on the road that leads steeply uphill from the pier, which continues through the woods to a red-roofed cottage. Go through the gate to the right of the cottage and turn left; just 20m along the road a cairn on the right marks the start of a boggy footpath that leads over the eastern shoulder of the Sgurr, then traverses beneath the northern cliffs until it makes its way up onto the summit ridge.

On a fine day the views from the top are magnificent – Rum and Skye to the north, Muck and Coll to the south, Ardnamurchan Lighthouse to the southeast and Ben Nevis shouldering above the eastern horizon. Take binoculars – on a calm summer's day there's a good chance of seeing minke whales feeding down below in the Sound of Muck.

A shorter walk (2 miles; allow 1½ hours round trip, and bring a torch) leads west from the pier to the spooky and claustrophobic **Uamh Fraing** (Massacre Cave). Start as for the Sgurr of Eigg, but 800m from the pier turn left through a gate and into a field. Follow the 4WD track and fork left before a white cottage to pass below it. A footpath continues across the fields to reach a small gate in a fence; go through it and descend a ridge towards the shore.

The cave entrance is tucked inconspicuously down to the left of the ridge. The entrance is tiny – almost a hands-and-knees job – but the cave opens out inside and runs a long way back. Go right to the back, turn off your torch, and imagine the cave packed shoulder to shoulder with terrified men, women and children. Then imagine the panic as your enemies start piling firewood into the entrance. Almost the entire population of Eigg – around 400 people – sought refuge in this cave when the MacLeods of Skye raided the island in 1577. In an act of inhuman cruelty, the raiders lit a fire in the narrow entrance and everyone inside died of asphyxiation. There are more than a few ghosts floating around in here.

🛏 Sleeping & Eating

All accommodation should be booked in advance. For a full listing of self-catering accommodation, see www.iseofeigg.org.

Glebe Barn HOSTEL £
(☏01687-482417; www.glebebarn.co.uk; dm/tw £17/40; @🛜) Excellent bunkhouse accommodation in the middle of the island, with a smart, maple-floored lounge with central fireplace, modern kitchen, laundry, drying room, and bright, clean dorms and bedrooms.

Sue Holland's Croft CAMPSITE £
(☏01687-482480; www.eiggorganics.co.uk; Cleadale; per tent £5, yurt £35-40; 🛜) This organic croft in the north of the island has a campsite with basic facilities, and also offers accommodation for two in a Mongolian yurt.

Lageorna B&B ££
(☏01687-460081; www.lageorna.co.uk; Cleadale; per person incl dinner £65; 🛜) 🍴 This converted croft house and lodge in the island's northwest is Eigg's most luxurious accommodation. Rooms are fitted with beautiful, locally made, 'driftwood-style' timber beds, and even have iPod docks (but no mobile-phone reception). Evening meals are part of the package, with the menu heavy on locally grown vegetables, seafood and venison.

Galmisdale Bay CAFE £
(www.galmisdale-bay.com; Galmisdale; mains £4-9; ⏰10am-5pm Mon-Sat, 11am-4.30pm Sun May-Sep, longer hours Jul-Aug, shorter hous Oct-Apr) 🍴 There's a good cafe-bar above the ferry pier. Winter opening hours coincide with ferry arrivals and departures.

ℹ Information

The ferry landing is at Galmisdale in the south.
An Laimhrig (www.isleofeiggshop.co.uk; ⏰10am-5pm Mon-Wed & Fri, 10am-3pm Thu, 11am-5pm Sat, noon-1pm & 3.30-5pm Sun May–mid-Oct, shorter hours winter) An Laimhrig, the building above the pier, houses a grocery store, post office, craft shop and cafe. You can hire **bikes** (☏07833 701493; www.eiggadventures.co.uk; per day £15) here too.

Isle of Muck

POP 27

The tiny island of Muck (www.isleofmuck.com), measuring just 2 miles by 1 mile, has exceptionally fertile soil, and the island is carpeted with wildflowers in spring and early summer. It takes its name from the Gaelic *muc* (pig), and pigs are still raised here.

Ferries call at the southern settlement of Port Mor. There's a **tearoom and craft** shop (⊙11am-4pm Jun-Aug, shorter hours May & Sep) above the pier, which also acts as a tourist office.

It's an easy 15-minute walk along the island's only road from the pier to the sandy beach at Gallanach on the northern side of the island. A longer and rougher hike (3.5 miles; 1½ hours round trip) goes to the top of Beinn Airein (137m) for the best views. Puffins nest on the cliffs at the western end of Camas Mor, the bay to the south of the hill.

The cosy six-bed Isle of Muck Bunkhouse (☑01687-462042; dm £15), with self-catering kitchen, is just above the pier, while the gorgeous, new Gallanach Lodge (☑01687-462365; lodge@isleofmuck.com; per person incl dinner £85; ☎) ✏ enjoys stunning views over Gallanach Bay on the west side of the island.

You can camp on the island for free – but ask at the craft shop first. For a full accommodation listings see www.isleofmuck.com.

Isle of Canna

POP 12

The island of Canna (www.theisleofcanna.com) is a moorland plateau of black basalt rock, just 5 miles long and 1.25 miles wide; it was gifted to the National Trust for Scotland in 1981 by its owner, the Gaelic scholar and author John Lorne Campbell. Compass Hill (143m), at the northeastern corner, contains enough magnetite (an iron oxide mineral) to deflect the navigation compasses in passing yachts.

The ferry arrives at the hamlet of A'Chill at the eastern end of the island, where visiting yachts people have left extensive graffiti on the rock face south of the harbour. There's a tearoom and craft shop by the harbour, and a tiny post office in a hut. There is no mobile-phone reception.

You can walk to An Coroghon, just east of the ferry pier, a medieval stone tower perched atop a sea cliff, and continue to Compass Hill, or take a longer hike along the southern shore past Canna House (guided tour £5; ⊙1-2.30pm Wed, 4-5.30pm Sat Apr-Sep), the former home of John Lorne Campbell, and an ornately decorated early Christian stone cross. In 2012 a *bullaun* (cursing stone), with an inscribed cross was discovered nearby; these are common in Ireland, but this was the first to be found in Scotland.

Accommodation is very limited. Tighard (☑01687-462474; www.tighard.co.uk; s/d £80/120; ☎) is the only B&B, and cafe-restaurant Gille Brighde (☑1687 482488; www.cafecanna. co.uk; mains £9-18; ⊙12.30-8.30pm Wed-Mon Apr-Oct, longer hours Jun-Aug) the only eating place (booking recommended for dinner). Check www.theisleofcanna.co.uk for self-catering accommodation. Wild camping is allowed.

354

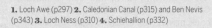

1. Loch Awe (p297) 2. Caledonian Canal (p315) and Ben Nevis
(p343) 3. Loch Ness (p310) 4. Schiehallion (p332)

JOE CORNISH / GETTY IMAGES ©

SIMON BUTTERWORTH / GETTY IMAGES ©

2

Lochs & Mountains

Since the 19th century, when the first tourists started to arrive, the Scottish Highlands have been famed for their wild nature and majestic scenery, and today the country's biggest draw remains its magnificent landscape. At almost every turn is a vista that will stop you in your tracks – keep your camera close at hand.

Ben Nevis

Scotland's highest peak is a perennial magnet for hillwalkers and ice climbers, but it's also one of the country's most photographed mountains. The classic viewpoints for the Ben include Corpach Basin at the entrance to the Caledonian Canal, and the B8004 road between Banavie and Gairlochy, from where you can see the precipitous north face.

Loch Ness

Scotland's largest loch by volume (it contains more water than all the lakes in England and Wales added together) may be most famous for its legendary monster, but it is also one of Scotland's most scenic. The minor road along the southeastern shore reveals a series of classic views.

Schiehallion

From the Gaelic *Sìdh Chailleann* (Fairy Hill of the Caledonians), this is one of Scotland's most distinctive mountains, its conical peak a prominent feature of views along Loch Tummel and Loch Rannoch. It's also one of the easier Munros, and a hike to the summit is rewarded with a superb panorama of hills and lochs.

Loch Awe

Loch Awe is a little off the beaten track, but is well worth seeking out for its gorgeous scenery. Dotted with islands and draped with native woodlands of oak, birch and alder, its northern end is dominated by the evocative ruins of Kilchurn Castle, with the pointed peaks of mighty Ben Cruachan reflected in its shifting waters.

4

Northern Highlands & Islands

Best Places to Eat

➡ Albannach (p374)

➡ Three Chimneys (p395)

➡ Côte du Nord (p370)

➡ Plockton Shores (p382)

Best Places to Stay

➡ The Torridon (p380)

➡ Gearrannan Holiday Cottages (p400)

➡ Toravaig House Hotel (p390)

➡ Pennyland House (p368)

➡ Mackays Rooms (p372)

➡ Mey House (p367)

Why Go?

Scotland's vast and melancholy soul is here: an epic land with a stark beauty that imprints the hearts of those who journey through it. Mist and mountains, rock and heather; long summer evenings are the pay-off for so many days of horizontal rain. It's simply magical.

The chambered cairns of Caithness and structures of the Western Isles are testament to the skills of prehistoric builders; cragtop castles and broken walls of abandoned crofts tell of the Highlands' turbulent history.

Outdoors is the place to be, whatever the weather; there's nothing like comparing windburn or mud-ruined boots over a well-deserved dram by the fire of a Highland pub. The landscape lends itself to activity, be it woodland strolls, thrilling mountain-bike descents, sea-kayaking, Munro-bagging, beachcombing or birdwatching. Best are the locals, big-hearted and straight-talking; make it your business to get to know them.

When to Go?
Portree

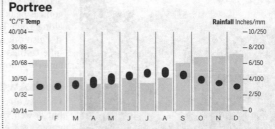

Jun Long evenings bathe achingly sublime landscapes in dreamy light.

Jul The Hebridean Celtic Festival is a top time to experience the culture of the Outer Hebrides.

Sep Less busy than summer, the midges have gone and temperatures are (maybe!) still OK.

EAST COAST

The east coast landscapes of the old counties of Ross and Sutherland unfold real wilderness and Highland character. While the interior is dominated by mournful moor-and-mountain landscapes, along the coast great heather-covered hills heave themselves out of the wild North Sea. Rolling farmland drops suddenly into icy waters, and small, historic towns are moored precariously alongside.

Strathpeffer

POP 1100

Strathpeffer is a charming old Highland spa town, creaking pavilions and grandiose hotels dripping with faded grandeur. It rose to prominence during Victorian times, when the fashionable flocked here in huge numbers to bathe in, wash with and drink the sulphurous waters. The tourist influx led to the construction of grand buildings and architectural follies.

☉ Sights & Activities

Locals have put together excellent interactive tours of Strathpeffer: download them to your phone at www.strathpeffer.org, or pick up a tablet from participating places around town.

The **Eagle Stone** (follow signs from the main drag) is well worth a look. It's a pre-7th-century Pictish stone connected to a figure from local history – the Brahan Seer, who predicted many future events.

There are many good signposted walking trails around Strathpeffer.

The **Strathpeffer & District Pipe Band** plays in the town square every Saturday from 8.30pm, mid-May to mid-September. There's Highland dancing and a festive air.

Highland Museum of Childhood   MUSEUM
(☏01997-421031; www.highlandmuseumof-childhood.org.uk; Old Train Station; adult/child £2.50/1.50; ☉10am-5pm Mon-Sat, 2-5pm Sun Apr-Oct) Strathpeffer's former train station houses a wide range of social-history displays about childhood, and also has activities for children, including a dressing-up box and toy train. There's a good gift shop for presents for a little somebody, and a peaceful cafe.

Spa Pavilion & Upper Pump Room   HISTORIC BUILDINGS

(www.strathpefferpavilion.org; Golf Course Rd; ☉Pump Room 10am-5pm Jun-Aug, 1-5pm Tue-Thu & Sat-Sun Sep-May) FREE In Strathpeffer's heyday, the Pavilion was the social centre, venue for dances, lectures and concerts. These days it's been renovated as a performing arts venue. Alongside, the Upper Pump Room has some splendid displays showing the bizarre lengths Victorians went to for a healthy glow, and exhibitions of local art, as well as artisanal sweets and tourist information in the friendly shop.

Square Wheels Cycles   BICYCLE RENTAL
(☏01997-421000; www.squarewheels.biz; The Square; half-/full day £12/20; ☉10am-6pm Tue-Sat, noon-4pm Sun) Hires out mountain bikes and gives route information; prices decrease with multiday hire.

⛏ Sleeping & Eating

There are a couple of large hotels geared to coach tours of retirees.

★**Craigvar**   B&B ££
(☏01997-421622; www.craigvar.com; The Square; s/d £60/90; P🐾) Luxury living with a refined touch is what you'll find in this delightful Georgian house in the village's heart. Classy little extras are all here, such as a welcome drink, Highland-Belgian chocolates, bathrobes and fresh fruit. The owner offers a wonderfully genuine welcome. Light, elegant rooms are great, with fabulous new bathrooms. One double has a particularly pleasing outlook and a sensational bed – you'll need to collapse back into it after the gourmet breakfast.

Coul House Hotel   HOTEL £££
(☏01997-421487; www.coulhouse.com; s/d £95/170; P@🐾🐶) At Contin, south of Strathpeffer on the A835, Coul House dates from 1821 but has a light, airy feel in contrast to many country houses of this vintage. It's family run, and very cordial. Beautiful dining and lounge areas are complemented by elegant rooms with views over the lovely gardens; superiors look out to the mountains beyond. There are forest trails for walking or mountain biking right on the doorstep and a good restaurant. You can often find lower prices on the website.

Northern Highlands & Islands Highlights

1 Gorging on fresh, succulent seafood in the delightful town of **Ullapool** (p376), with its picture-perfect harbour

2 Dipping your toes in the water at some of the world's most beautiful beaches on **Harris** (p401)

3 Shouldering the challenge of the **Cuillin Hills** (p391), with their rugged silhouettes brooding over the skyscape of Skye

4 Picking your jaw up off the floor as you marvel at the epic Highland scenery of the **far northwest** (p372)

5 Taking the trip out to **Cape Wrath** (p374), Britain's gloriously remote northwestern shoulder

6 Relaxing in postcard-pretty **Plockton** (p381), where the Highlands meet the Caribbean

7 Launching yourself in a sea kayak to explore the otter-rich waters around the **Isle of Skye** (p384)

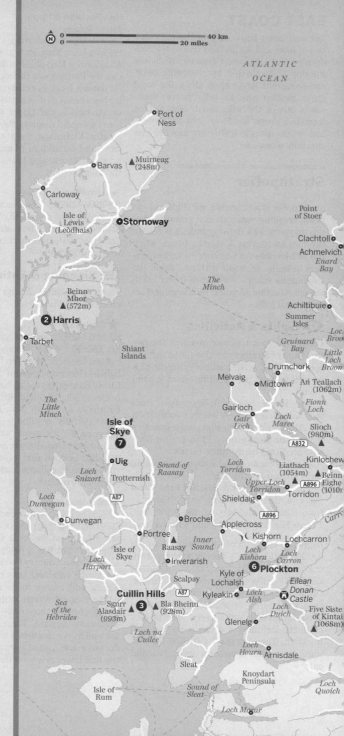

Red Poppy

BISTRO ££

(☑ 01997-423332; www.redpoppyrestaurant.co.uk; Main Rd; mains £14-20; ☺ 11.30am-9pm Tue-Sat, noon-3.30pm Sun; ☞) On the main road opposite the spa buildings, this is comfortably Strathpeffer's best eatery. The casual modern interior with its bright red chairs is the venue for confident, well-presented dishes covering game and other classic British ingredients. It's a little cheaper at lunchtime, when set-priced menus are available.

🛈 Getting There & Around

BUS

Stagecoach (www.stagecoachbus.com) operates from Inverness to Strathpeffer (£5.20, 45 minutes, hourly Monday to Saturday, four on Sunday). Inverness to Gairloch and Durness services, plus some Inverness to Ullapool buses, also drop in.

Tain

POP 3700

Scotland's oldest royal burgh, Tain is a proud sandstone town that rose to prominence as pilgrims descended to venerate the relics of St Duthac, who is commemorated by the 12th-century ruins of St Duthac's Chapel, and St Duthus Church.

◉ Sights

Tain Through Time

MUSEUM

(☑ 01862-894089; www.tainmuseum.org.uk; Tower St; adult/child £3.50/2.50; ☺ 10am-5pm Mon-Fri Apr-Oct, also Sat Jun-Aug) Set in the grounds of St Duthus Church is Tain Through Time, an entertaining heritage centre with a colourful and educational display on St Duthac, King James IV and key moments in Scottish history. Another building focuses on the town's fine silversmithing tradition. Admission includes an audioguided walk around town.

Glenmorangie

DISTILLERY

(www.glenmorangie.com; tours £5; ☺ 10am-5pm Mon-Fri, plus 10am-4pm Sat & noon-4pm Sun Jun-Aug) Located on Tain's northern outskirts, Glenmorangie (emphasis on the second syllable) produces a fine lightish malt, subjected to a number of different cask finishes for variation. The tour is less in-depth than some but finishes with a free dram. A special tour is £30.

🛌 Sleeping & Eating

Golf View House

B&B ££

(☑ 01862-892856; www.bedandbreakfasttain. co.uk; 13 Knockbreck Rd; s/d £60/85; ℗☞) Set in an old manse in a secluded location just off the main drag, this spot offers magnificent views over fields and water. Impeccable rooms are very cheerful and bright, and there's an upbeat feel, with delicious breakfasts and welcoming hospitality. It's worth the extra for a room with a view.

Royal Hotel

HOTEL ££

(☑ 01862-892013; www.royalhoteltain.co.uk; High St; s/d £55/90; ☞✱) So much the heart of town that the main street has to detour around it, the refurbished Royal has good-sized spruce rooms. For only a tenner more, you get a four-poster room in the older wing; these have a choice of colour schemes, and are well worth the upgrade. The restaurant is the best in town and bar meals are also decent.

🛈 Getting There & Away

Stagecoach (www.stagecoachbus.com) buses run from Inverness (£9.70, 50 minutes, roughly hourly); some continue north as far as Thurso.

Trains run daily to Inverness (£13.50, 1¼ hours) and Thurso (£16.50, 2¾ hours).

Portmahomack

POP 600

Portmahomack is a former fishing village in a flawless spot – off the beaten track, gazing across the water at sometimes snowcapped peaks.

Tarbat Discovery Centre

MUSEUM

(☑ 01862-871351; www.tarbat-discovery.co.uk; Tarbatness Rd; adult/child £3.50/1; ☺ 10am-5pm Mon-Sat May-Sep, 2-5pm Mon-Sat Apr & Oct, plus 2-5pm Sun Jun-Oct) This intruiging museum has great carved Pictish stones. The foundations of an Iron Age settlement were discovered around the village church; ongoing investigation revealed a Pictish monastery with evidence of manuscript production. The exhibition is excellent and includes the church's spooky crypt.

Oystercatcher Restaurant

SEAFOOD ££

(☑ 01862-871560; www.the-oystercatcher.co.uk; Main St; lunch mains £8-14, dinner mains £15-20; ☺ 12.15-2.45pm Thu-Sun, plus 6.30-8.30pm Wed-Sat Mar-Oct; ℗☞⊞). Seafood aficionados shouldn't miss this bright and cheerful place where a lunchtime bistro menu lets you choose your serving size, and a classy brasserie evening menu includes lots of lobster among other temptations. Fourteen-course tasting menus (£60) are a delight, with invention and quality given levity by the whimsical dish names. It also offers three cosy rooms (single/double £52/108). Rates include what has to be Scotland's most amazing breakfast, with numerous gourmet options.

Stagecoach (www.stagecoachbus.com) runs from Tain to Portmahomack (£1.95, 25 minutes, four to five Monday to Friday).

Bonar Bridge & Around

The A9 crosses Dornoch Firth by bridge and causeway, near Tain. An alternative route goes around the firth via Ardgay and Bonar Bridge, where the A836 to Lairg branches west.

⊙ Sights & Activities

Croick VILLAGE
From Ardgay, a single-track road leads 10 miles up Strathcarron to Croick, the scene of notorious evictions during the 1845 Clearances. You can still see the evocative messages scratched by refugee crofters from Glencalvie on the eastern windows of **Croick Church**.

Kyle of Sutherland Trails MOUNTAIN BIKING
(☑01408-634063; scotland.forestry.gov.uk/visit/carbisdale) Mountain bikers will find two networks of forest trails around Bonar Bridge. From the car park below Carbisdale Castle, there's a red and a blue trail with great views. At Balblair, a mile from Bonar Bridge off the Lairg road, 7 miles of black track will test expert bikers.

🛏 Sleeping

Carbisdale Castle SYHA HOSTEL £
(☑01549-421232; www.syha.org.uk; ⊙mid-Mar–Oct; ℗@🛜) This castle, 10 minutes' walk north of Culrain train station, was Scotland's most opulent hostel, but its future was in doubt at time of writing, as spiralling maintenance costs had closed it. It may or may not reopen: check the website.

❶ Getting There & Away

Trains from Inverness to Thurso stop at Culrain (£15.20, 1½ hours), half a mile from Carbisdale Castle.

THE RIGHT SIDE OF THE TRACKS

Sleeperzzz.com (☑01408-641343; www.sleeperzzz.com; dm £16-20; ⊙Mar–Sep; ℗) Scotland has some unusual hostels and this is one of them. Set in three caringly converted railway carriages, an old bus and a beautiful wooden caravan parked up in a siding by Rogart station, it has cute two-person bedrooms, kitchenettes and tiny lounges. The owners make an effort to run the hostel on sustainable lines.

There's a local pub that does food, as well as beautifully lonely Highland scenery in the vicinity. It's on the A839, 10 miles east of Lairg, but is also easily reached by train on the Inverness–Wick line (10% discount if you arrive this way or by bike).

Lairg & Around

POP 900
Lairg is an attractive village, although the tranquillity can be rudely interrupted by the sound of military jets roaring overhead (Loch Shin valley is frequently used by the RAF for low-flying exercises). Located at the southern end of Loch Shin, it's a remote but important Highlands crossroad, gateway to central Sutherland's remote mountains and loch-speckled bogs.

⊙ Sights & Activities

Ferrycroft Visitor Centre MUSEUM
(☑01549-402160; www.highland.gov.uk/ferrycroft; ⊙10am-4pm Apr-Oct; 🛅) On the opposite side of the river from the town centre, this visitor centre has displays on local history, wildlife and a tourist information desk. A short walk leads from the centre to the **Ord Hut Circles and Chambered Cairns**, a collection of prehistoric roundhouses and tombs.

Falls of Shin WATERFALL
(www.fallsofshin.co.uk; 🛅) FREE Four miles south of Lairg, the picturesque Falls of Shin is one of the best places in the Highlands to see salmon leaping on their way upstream to spawn (June to September). A short and easy footpath leads to a viewing terrace overlooking the waterfall. There are waymarked forest trails here; other attractions

were closed at last research after the visitor centre burned down.

🛏 Sleeping

Lochview
B&B ££

(☏ 01549-402578; www.lochviewlairg.co.uk; Lochside; s/d £40/84; P 🛜) Years of experience have made the kindly owners here absolute experts in ensuring guest comfort. Huge rooms with seating areas and great facilities overlook the loch; the lounge gives onto the grassy garden that stretches down to it. Bathrooms are modern and sparklingly clean: in all, it's a very impressive set-up.

ℹ Getting There & Away

Trains from Inverness to Thurso stop at Lairg (£16.30, 1¾ hours). Four buses run Monday to Saturday to Tain via Bonar Bridge and Ardgay (one via the Falls of Shin). Three buses run Monday to Friday to Helmsdale via Rogart and Golspie.

Dornoch

POP 1200

On the north shore of Dornoch Firth, two miles off the A9, this attractive old market town is one of the east coast's most pleasant settlements. Dornoch is best known for its championship golf course, but there's a fine cathedral among other noble buildings. Other historical oddities: the last witch to be executed in Scotland was boiled alive in hot tar here in 1722 and Madonna married Guy Ritchie here in 2000.

◉ Sights & Activities

Have a walk along Dornoch's golden-sand beach, which stretches for miles. South of Dornoch, seals are often visible on the sandbars of Dornoch Firth.

Dornoch Cathedral
CHURCH

(www.dornoch-cathedral.com; St Gilbert St; ⊙9am-7pm or later) FREE Consecrated in the 13th century, Dornoch Cathedral is an elegant Gothic edifice with an interior softly illuminated through modern stained-glass windows. The controversional first Duke of Sutherland, whose wife restored the church in the 1830s, lies in a sealed burial vault beneath the chancel.

By the western door is the sarcophagus of Sir Richard de Moravia, who died fighting the Danes at the battle of Embo in the 1260s. Until he met his maker, the battle had been going rather well for him; he'd managed to slay the Danish commander with the unattached leg of a horse that was to hand.

Historylinks
MUSEUM

(www.historylinks.org.uk; The Meadows; adult/child £2.50/free; ⊙10am-4pm daily Jun-Sep, Mon-Fri Apr, May & Oct, Wed & Thu only Nov-Mar; ⚑) Historylinks is a child-friendly museum focusing on local history. Displays cover geology, the Picts, the building of the cathedral and the development of the golf course – and you can add to your background knowledge of the area through a selection of audiovisuals.

Royal Dornoch
GOLF

(☏ 01862-810219; www.royaldornoch.com; Golf Rd, Dornoch; summer green fee £120) One of Scotland's most famous links, described by Tom Watson as 'the most fun I have ever had on a golf course'. It's public, and you can book a slot online. Twilight rates are the most economical. A golf pass (www.dornochfirthgolf.co.uk) lets you play several courses in the area at a good discount.

🛏 Sleeping

★ Dornoch Castle Hotel
HOTEL ££

(☏01862-810216; www.dornochcastlehotel.com; Castle St; s/d £73/125, superior/deluxe d £169/250; P🛜) This 16th-century former bishop's palace makes a wonderful place to stay, particularly if you upgrade to one of the superior rooms, which have views, space, whisky and chocolates on the welcome tray and (some) a four-poster bed; the deluxe rooms are unforgettable. Cheaper rooms (single/double £50/65), simpler, without the historic atmosphere, are also available in adjoining buildings.

2 Quail
B&B ££

(☏ 01862-811811; www.2quail.com; Castle St; s £80, d £90-100; 🛜) Intimate and upmarket, 2 Quail offers a warm main-street welcome. Tasteful, spacious chambers are full of old-world comfort, with sturdy metal bedframes, plenty of books and plump duvets. The downstairs guest lounge is an absolute delight. It's best to book ahead, especially in winter. It also offers a self-catering cottage sleeping six.

Trevose Guest House
B&B ££

(☏ 01862-810269; jamackenzie@tiscali.co.uk; Cathedral Sq; s/d £40/64; ⊙May-Sep; 🛜⚑) First impressions deceive at Trevose Guest House, a lovely stone cottage right by the cathedral. It looks compact but actually boasts very spacious rooms with significant comfort and well-loved old wooden furnishings. Character oozes from every pore of the place and a benevolent welcome is a given.

✖ Eating

Luigi   ITALIAN £
(www.luigidornoch.com; Castle St; light meals £5-9; ⊙ 10am-5pm daily, plus 6.45-9pm Fri & Sat, dinner daily in summer) The clean lines of this contemporary Italian-American cafe make a break from the omnipresent heritage and history of this coastline. Ciabattas and salads stuffed with tasty deli ingredients make it a good lunch stop; more elaborate dinners (£14 to £19) usually include fine seafood choices.

Eagle Hotel   PUB £
(✆ 01862-810008; www.eagledornoch.co.uk; Castle St; bar meals £8-11; ⊙ food noon-9pm) Nobody on the streets of Dornoch after 7pm? You'll find most of them in this cosy, welcoming pub, which looks after its customers with good service and a menu of very solid fare – reliably tasty burgers, haggis sausages, fish and chips or daily roasts – at fair prices. It packs out at weekends so book.

Dornoch Castle Hotel   SCOTTISH £££
(✆ 01862-810216; www.dornochcastlehotel.com; Castle St; mains £18 22; ⊙ noon-2.30pm & 6-9pm) In the evening, toast your toes in the cosy bar, which has decent real ales and a substantial malt selection, before dining in style at this hotel restaurant, tucking into dishes featuring plenty of game and seasonal produce. Bar meals are also available during the day.

ⓘ Information

Tourist Office (✆ 01862-810594; Castle St; ⊙ 9am-12.30pm & 1.30-4pm Mon Fri, plus 10am 4pm Sat May-Aug & 10am-4pm Sun Jul & Aug) In the council building alongside Dornoch Castle Hotel.

ⓘ Getting There & Away

There are buses roughly hourly from Inverness (£10.20, 1¼ hours), with some services continuing north to Wick or Thurso.

Golspie

POP 1400

Golspie is a pretty little village most visited for nearby Dunrobin Castle. There are good facilities and a pleasant beach: it's a congenial place to spend a day or two.

⊙ Sights & Activities

There are several good local walks, including the classic 3.75 mile (return) hike climbing steeply to the summit of **Ben Bhraggie** (394m), crowned by a massive monument to the Duke of Sutherland, notorious for his leading role in the Highland Clearances.

★ Dunrobin Castle   CASTLE
(✆ 01408-633177; www.dunrobincastle.co.uk; adult/child £10.50/5.75; ⊙ 10.30am-4.30pm Mon-Sat & noon-4.30pm Sun Apr, May & Sep–mid-Oct, 10am-5pm daliy Jun & Aug) Magnificent Dunrobin Castle, a mile past Golspie, is the Highlands' largest house. Although it dates to 1275, most of what you see was built in French style between 1845 and 1850. A home of the dukes of Sutherland, it's richly furnished and offers an intriguing insight into the aristocratic lifestyle. The beautiful castle inspires mixed feelings locally; it was once the seat of the first Duke of Sutherland, notorious for some of the cruellest episodes of the Highland Clearances.

The duke's estate was, at over 6000 square kilometres, the largest privately owned area of land in Europe. He evicted around 15,000 people from their homes to make way for sheep.

This classic fairy-tale castle is adorned with towers and turrets, but only 22 of its 187 rooms are on display, with hunting trophies much to the fore. Beautiful formal gardens, where impressive falconry displays take place two or three times a day, extend down to the sea. In the gardens is a museum with an eclectic mix of archaeological finds, natural-history exhibits, more non-PC animal remains and an excellent collection of Pictish stones.

Highland Wildcat   MOUNTAIN BIKING
(www.highlandwildcat.com; ⊙ dawn-dusk) FREE
The expert-only black trail at Highland Wildcat is famous for having the highest single-track descent in the country (a 390m drop over 7km). There's plenty for beginners and families too, with a scenic blue trail and easy forest routes. No facilities; grab the map off the website.

⊨ Sleeping

Blar Mhor   B&B ££
(✆ 01408-633609; www.blarmhor.co.uk; Drummuie Rd; s/d/f £35/60/80; P 🛈 🞿 🞿) On the

approach into Golspie from Dornoch, this excellent guesthouse has large, beautifully kept rooms with swish modern bathrooms in a towering Victorian mansion. There are beautifully landscaped gardens and cheerful hosts will brighten your stay with little extras like chocolates on the bed.

ℹ Getting There & Away

Both trains (£18.20, 2¼ hours, two or three daily) and buses (£11.60, 1½ hours) between Inverness and Wick/Thurso stop in Golspie and at Dunrobin Castle.

Helmsdale

POP 700

Surrounded by breathtaking coastline and gorse-covered hills that explode mad-yellow in spring, this sheltered fishing town, like many on this coast, was a major emigration point during the Clearances and a booming herring port.

Timespan Heritage Centre (www.timespan.org.uk; Dunrobin St; adult/child £4/2; ⊙ 10am-5pm Easter-Oct, 10am-3pm Sat & Sun & 2-4pm Tue Nov-Easter) has an impressive display covering local history (including the 1869 gold rush) and Barbara Cartland, queen of romance novels, who was a Helmsdale regular. There are also local art exhibitions, a geology garden and a cafe.

The River Helmsdale offers some of the best Highland **salmon fishing**. Permits, tackle and advice can be obtained from **Helmsdale Tackle Company** (☑ 01431-821372; www.helmsdalecompany.com; 15-17 Dunrobin St; ⊙ 9am-5pm Mon-Sat), which also hires rods and boats.

🛏 Sleeping & Eating

Helmsdale Hostel   HOSTEL £
(☑ 07971-516287, 01431-821636; www.helmsdale-hostel.co.uk; Stafford St; dm/tw/f £19/45/60; ⊙ Apr-Sep; ☜🐾) This caringly run hostel is in very good nick, well-equipped and spotlessly clean; it makes a cheerful, comfortable budget base for exploring Caithness. Dorms have mostly cosy single beds rather than bunks, and en suite rooms are great for families. The lofty central space has a lounge with wood stove and good kitchen.

Customs House   B&B £
(☑ 01431-821648; Shore St; r per person £22; P) Old-fashioned, cordial and top value, this has a great location opposite the little har-

bour, and fluffy, comfortable rooms with heaps of cushions and big cosy beds. Breakfast is great, with fresh fruit, cheese, abundant coffee and juice, plus cooked options.

La Mirage   BISTRO £
(☑ 01431-821615; www.lamirage.org; 7 Dunrobin St; mains £7-12; ⊙ 11am-8.45pm Mon-Sat, noon-8.45pm Sun; ☜) Created in homage to Barbara Cartland, this is a '70s throwback with pink walls, kitschy installations and a retro menu. Meals aren't gourmet – think chicken Kiev – but portions are huge. Fish and chips are also available takeaway; eat 'em by the pretty harbour.

ℹ Getting There & Away

Buses from Inverness (£11.60, 1¾ hours) and Thurso stop in Helmsdale, as do trains (from Inverness £18.20, 2½ hours, two to three daily).

CAITHNESS

Once you pass Helmsdale, you are entering Caithness, a place of jagged gorse-and-grass-topped cliffs hiding tiny fishing harbours. Scotland's top corner was once Viking territory, historically more connected to Orkney and Shetland than the rest of the mainland. It's a mystical, ancient land peopled with wise folk with long memories who are fiercely proud of their Norse heritage.

Helmsdale to Lybster

Seven miles north of Helmsdale is **Badbea**, an abandoned crofting village established during the Highland Clearances in the early 19th century. The village of **Dunbeath** is spectacularly set in a deep glen; the **Heritage Centre** (☑ 01593-731233; www.dunbeath-heritage.org.uk; The Old School, Dunbeath; adult/child £2.50/free; ⊙ 10am-5pm Sun-Fri Apr-Sep, 11am-3pm Mon-Fri Oct-Mar) has a stone carved with runic graffiti, and a display on Neil Gunn, whose wonderful novels evoke the Caithness of his boyhood.

Two miles north is **Laidhay Croft Museum** (☑ 0756-370 2321; www.laidhay.co.uk; adult/child £2.50/50p; ⊙ 10am-5pm Mon-Sat Jun-Sep), which recreates crofting life from the mid-1800s to WWII. At **Clan Gunn Heritage Centre** (☑ 01593-741700; www.clangunnsociety.org; Latheron; adult/child £2.50/50p; ⊙ 11am-1pm & 2-4pm Mon-Sat Jun-Sep) in **Latheron**, a mile beyond, there's information on the Gunn clan, from its Viking origins to the present day. It's worth pulling into the car park on a fine day to admire the stunning views.

Lybster & Around

Lybster is a purpose-built fishing village dating from 1810, with a stunning harbour area surrounded by grassy cliffs. In its heyday, it was Scotland's third-busiest port. Things have changed – now there are only a couple of boats – but there are several interesting prehistoric sites in the area.

Sights & Activities

Waterlines   MUSEUM
($\boxed{J}$ 01593-721520; The Harbour; adult/child £2.50/50p; ☺ 11am-5pm May-Oct) At the picturesque harbour in Lybster, this museum has an exhibition on the town's fishing heritage, a smokehouse and a cafe.

Whaligoe Steps   CLIFFS
At Ulbster, 5 miles north of Lybster, this staircase cut into the cliff provides access to a tiny natural harbour, with an ideal grassy picnic spot, ringed by vertical cliffs and echoing with the cackle of nesting fulmars. The path begins at the end of the minor road opposite the road signposted 'Cairn of Get'. There's a cafe at the top.

Cairn o'Get   PREHISTORIC SITE
The Cairn o'Get, a prehistoric burial cairn, is signposted off the road in Ulbster. It's a mile's boggy walk from the car park.

Achavanich Stone Setting   PREHISTORIC SITE
Six miles to the northwest of Lybster and a mile off the A9, these 30 standing stones date from around 2000 BC. These crumbling monuments of the distant past still capture the imagination with their desolate location. Nearby are the remains of a burial cairn, another millennium older.

Grey Cairns of Camster   PREHISTORIC SITE
Dating from between 4000 BC and 2500 BC, these burial chambers are hidden in long, low mounds rising from an evocatively lonely moor. The **Long Cairn** measures 60m by 21m. You can enter the main chamber, but must first crawl into the well-preserved **Round Cairn**, which has a corbelled ceiling.

From a turn-off a mile east of Lybster on the A99, the cairns are 4 miles north. You can continue 7 further miles to approach Wick on the A882.

Hill o'Many Stanes   PREHISTORIC SITE
Two miles beyond the Camster turn-off on the A99 is a curious, fan-shaped arrangement of 22 rows of small stones, probably from around 2000 BC. Staggeringly, there were 600 in the original pattern. On a sunny day, the views from this hill are stunning.

ℹ️ Getting There & Away

Stagecoach buses between Thurso and Inverness run via Lybster and Dunbeath. The Wick–Helmsdale service also stops at these places.

Wick

POP 7200

More gritty than pretty, Wick has been down on its luck since the collapse of the herring industry. It was once the world's largest fishing port for the 'silver darlings', but when the market dropped off after WWII, job losses were huge and the town hasn't totally recovered. It's worth a visit though, particularly for its excellent museum and attractive, spruced-up harbour area.

Sights & Activities

A path leads a mile south to the ruined 12th-century **Old Wick Castle** (☺ 24hr) **FREE**, with spectacular cliffs a little further south. In good weather, it's a fine coastal walk, but take care on the final approach. Three miles northeast of Wick is the magnificently located clifftop ruin of **Castle Sinclair** (☺ 24hr).

⭐ **Wick Heritage Centre**   MUSEUM
($\boxed{J}$ 01955-605393; www.wickheritage.org; 20 Bank Row; adult/child £4/50p; ☺ 10am-5pm Apr-Oct, last entry 3.45pm) Tracking the rise and fall of the herring industry, this great town museum displays everything from fishing equipment to complete herring boats. It's absolutely huge inside, and is crammed with memorabilia and extensive displays describing Wick's heyday in the mid-19th century.

The Johnston collection is the star exhibit. From 1863 to 1977, three generations photographed everything that happened around Wick; the 70,000 photographs are an amazing record.

Old Pulteney   DISTILLERY
($\boxed{J}$ 01955-602371; www.oldpulteney.com; Huddart St; tours £6; ☺ 10am-4pm Mon-Fri Oct-Apr, 10am-5pm Mon-Fri & 10am-4pm Sat May-Sep) The most northerly distillery on mainland Scotland

runs excellent tours twice daily, with more expensive visits available for aficionados.

Tours

Caithness Seacoast　　BOAT TOURS
(☑01955-609200; www.caithness-seacoast.co.uk; ⊙Apr-Oct) This outfit will take you out to sea to inspect the rugged coastline of the northeast. Various options include a half-hour jaunt (adult/child £17/11) to a three-hour return trip down to Lybster (adult/child £45/35).

Sleeping & Eating

Seaview　　B&B £
(☑01955-602735; www.wickbb.co.uk; 14 Scalesburn; s/d £40/60; P�🖥🐾) On the water, though not in its prettiest part, this offers genuine, bend-over-backwards hospitality from cheerful June. It's reliably comfortable, with compact rooms, two of which share a bathroom. The little conservatory lounge is a top spot for lazy moments with river views.

Mackays Hotel　　HOTEL ££
(☑01955-602323; www.mackayshotel.co.uk; Union St; s/d £89/119; 🖥) Hospitable Mackays is Wick's best hotel by a long stretch. Attractive, mostly refurbished rooms vary in layout and size, so ask to see a few; prices are usually lower than these rack rates. On-site **No 1 Bistro** (Union St; mains £11-17; ⊙noon-2pm & 5-9pm; 🖥) is a fine option for lunch or dinner. The world's shortest street, 2.06m-long Ebenezer Place, is on one side of the hotel.

Bord de l'Eau　　FRENCH ££
(☑01955-604400; 2 Market St; mains £14-19; ⊙noon-2.30pm & 6-9pm Tue-Sat, 6-9pm Sun) This serene, relaxed French restaurant is Wick's best place to eat. It overlooks the river and serves a changing menu of mostly meat-and-game French classics, backed up by daily fish specials. Starters are great value, and mains include a huge assortment of vegetables, so you won't go hungry. The conservatory dining room with water views is lovely on a sunny evening.

❶ Information

Wick Tourist Office (☑01955-602547; www.visithighlands.com; 66 High St; ⊙9am-5.30pm Mon-Sat) Good selection of information; upstairs in McAllans Clothing Store.

❶ Getting There & Away

AIR
Wick is a Caithness transport gateway. **Flybe/Loganair** (☑0871 700 2000; www.flybe.com) flies from Edinburgh; **Eastern Airways** (☑0870 366 9100; www.easternairways.com) from Aberdeen.

BUS
Stagecoach (p361) and Citylink (www.citylink.co.uk) operate to/from Inverness (£19, three hours, six daily) and Stagecoach to Thurso (£3.30, 35 minutes, hourly). There's also connecting service to John O'Groats and Gills Bay (£3.30, 40 minutes, two to three daily) for the passenger and car ferries to Orkney.

TRAIN
Trains service Wick from Inverness (£19.30, 4¼ hours, four daily).

John O'Groats

POP 300

Though not the northernmost point of the British mainland (that's Dunnet Head), John O'Groats still serves as the end point of the 874-mile trek from Land's End in Cornwall, a popular if arduous route for cyclists and walkers, many of whom raise money for charitable causes. There's a passenger ferry from here to Orkney. Most of the settlement is taken up by a stylish modern self-catering complex, which has given a dose of new life to the once-tawdry locale.

◉ Sights & Activities

Ninety-minute wildlife cruises to the island of Stroma or Duncansby Head cost £18 (late June to August).

Duncansby Head　　LOOKOUT
Two miles east, Duncansby Head has a small lighthouse and 60m-high cliffs sheltering nesting fulmars. A 15-minute walk through a sheep paddock yields spectacular views of the sea-surrounded monoliths known as Duncansby Stacks.

Sleeping & Eating

There's a campsite and several B&Bs in and around John O'Groats.

Natural Retreats　　SELF-CATERING ££
(☑0844 384-3166; www.naturalretreats.com; apt £125-250; P🖥🐾) Nearly all of John O'Groats is now taken up by this company, which has erected a series of modern wooden holiday

chalets offering spectacular views, and transformed the old hotel – with the addition of some eye-catchingly colourful giant Scandi-modern 'fish warehouses' – into self-catering apartments. All are stylish and well-equipped. There's a minimum two-night stay.

Teuchters
B&B ££

(📞01955-611323; www.teuchtersbandb.co.uk; Gills; s/d £40/60; P🎧📶🐾) By the Gills Bay ferry, 3 miles west of John O'Groats, this purpose-built B&B offers excellent rooms, plenty of space, modern comfort and stunning water views across to Stroma and Orkney. It has a lock-up shed for bikes and motorbikes.

Storehouse
CAFE £

(www.naturalretreats.com; light meals £5-10; ⊙8am-5pm; 📶) The best of the eating options, this modern cafe does pizzas, panini, sandwiches on tasty thick-cut bread, and deli platters with Arran cheeses and local smoked salmon.

ℹ Information

John O'Groats Tourist Office (📞01955-611373; www.visithighlands.com; ⊙11am-3pm Nov-Mar, 10am-4pm Apr, 10am-5pm May & Sep-Oct, 9am-6pm Jun-Aug) Has a fine selection of local novels and nonfiction.

ℹ Getting There & Away

BOAT

From May to September, a passenger ferry (p409) shuttles across to Burwick in Orkney. Three miles west, a car ferry (p409) runs from Gills Bay to St Margaret's Hope in Orkney.

BUS

Stagecoach (p361) runs between John O'Groats and Wick (£3.30, 40 minutes, two to three daily) or Thurso (£4, 40 minutes, regular Monday to Saturday).

Mey

The **Castle of Mey** (www.castleofmey.org.uk; adult/child £11/6.50; ⊙10.20am-5pm May-Sep, last admission 4pm), a big crowd-puller for its Queen Mother connections, is 6 miles west of John O'Groats. The exterior is grand but inside it feels domestic and everything is imbued with the Queen Mum's character. The highlight is the genteel guided tour, with various anecdotes recounted by staff who once worked for her. In the grounds there's a farm zoo, an unusual walled garden that's worth a stroll and lovely views over the Pentland Firth. The castle normally closes for a couple of weeks at the end of July for royal visits.

On the main road nearby, excellent **Hawthorns** (📞01847-851710; www.thehawthornsbnb.co.uk; s/d £50/75; P🎧📶🐾) is a modern, easygoing B&B with contemporary artistic flair, a genuine welcome and very spruce, super-spacious ground floor rooms with mini-fridges. There are good options for families. Also just off the main road, **Mey House** (📞01847 851852; www.meyhouse.co.uk; East Mey; r £100-120; ⊙Easter-Oct; P🎧) is beautifully situated among green fields running down to the water with majestic views of Orkney and Dunnet Head. This modern top-drawer sleep is a welcoming, sumptuous place to stay. They've thought it all through: huge, luxurious rooms have arty designer decor, excellent custom-made beds, Nespresso machines, big flatscreens, sound bar and stunning modern bathrooms with shower and tub. There's fast satellite wi-fi and transfers: free for nearby ferries and inexpensive for Wick or Thurso. No toddlers are allowed, as there's an interior balcony.

Dunnet Head

Eight miles east of Thurso a minor road leads to dramatic Dunnet Head, the most northerly point on the British mainland. There are majestic cliffs dropping into the turbulent Pentland Firth, inspiring views of Orkney, basking seals and nesting seabirds below, and a lighthouse built by Robert Louis Stevenson's grandad. Also on the headland, near the main road, is **Mary-Ann's Cottage** (adult/child £3/0.50; ⊙2-4.30pm Jun-Sep). Mary-Ann lived in this 19th-century croft for nigh on a century; in-depth guided tours take you round her humble but cosy farm and house: a fascinating back-in-time experience.

Just west, **Dunnet Bay** offers one of Scotland's finest beaches, backed by high dunes, as well as **Seadrift** (📞01847-821531; ⊙2-5pm Sun-Tue, Thu & Fri May-Sep, from 10.30am Jul & Aug) FREE a small wildlife display, and a caravan-dominated **campsite** (📞01847-821319; www.caravanclub.co.uk; site £5.10, plus adult member/nonmember £6.20/16.20; ⊙Apr-Sep; P) backing the beach.

Thurso

POP 7900

Britain's most northerly mainland town, Thurso makes a handy overnight stop if you're heading west or across to Orkney. There's a pretty town beach, riverbank strolls and a good museum. Ferries for Orkney leave from Scrabster, 2.5 miles away.

⊙ Sights

Caithness Horizons MUSEUM
(www.caithnesshorizons.co.uk; High St; ⊙10am-6pm Mon-Sat, also 11am-4pm Sun Apr-Sep) FREE
This museum brings Caithness history and lore to life through excellent displays. Fine Pictish cross-slabs greet the visitor downstairs; the main exhibition is a wide-ranging look at local history using plenty of audiovisuals – check out the wistful account of the now-abandoned island of Stroma. There's also a gallery space, an exhibition on the Dounreay nuclear reactor, tourist information and a cafe.

🏃 Activities

Thurso is an unlikely surfing centre but the nearby coast has arguably the best and most regular surf on mainland Britain. There's an excellent right-hand reef break on the eastern side of town, directly in front of the castle (closed to the public), and another shallow reef break 5 miles west at **Brimms Ness**. Pack a drysuit: this is no Hawaii. **Thurso Surf** (☑0844 802 5750; www.thurso-surf.com; half-day lessons £35-50) gives lessons, normally at Dunnet Bay east of town.

🛏 Sleeping

Sandra's Hostel HOSTEL £
(☑01847-894575; www.sandras-backpack-ers.co.uk; 24 Princes St; dm/d/f £16/38/60; P@🛜) In the heart of town above a chip shop, this budget backpacker option offers en suite dorms, mostly four-berthers with elderly mattresses, a spacious kitchen and traveller-friendly facilities such as internet and help-yourself cereals and toast. It's not luxurious but it's a reliable cheap sleep.

★Pennyland House B&B ££
(☑01847-891194; www.pennylandhouse.co.uk; s/d/tr £60/80/90; P🛜🐾) A super conversion of an historic house, this is a standout B&B choice. It offers phenomenal value for this level of accommodation, with huge oak-furnished rooms named after golf cours-es: we especially loved St Andrews – super-spacious, with a great chessboard-tiled bathroom. Hospitality is enthusiastic and helpful, and there's an inviting breakfast space, garden and terraced area with views across to Hoy. Two-night minimum stay in summer.

Marine B&B ££
(☑01847-890676; www.themarinethurso.co.uk; 38 Shore St, s £75, d £90-99; P🛜) Tucked away in Thurso's most appealing corner you'll find a top spot right by the pretty town beach, offering spectacular vistas over it and across to Orkney. Surfers can study the breakers from the stunning conservatory-lounge, and rooms are just fabulous, with a designer's touch and a subtle maritime feel. Two rooms in the adjacent house make a great family option.

Murray House B&B ££
(☑01847-895759; www.murrayhousebb.com; 1 Campbell St; s/d/f £35/70/80; P🛜) A solid, handsome 19th-century town house on a central corner, Murray House gives a good first impression with a genuine welcome and ample dimensions. It continues with smart rooms with solid wooden furniture and modern bathrooms, two of which offer secluded sloping-ceiling spaces on the top floor. No credit cards.

Forss House Hotel HOTEL £££
(☑01847-861201; www.forsshousehotel.co.uk; s/d/superior d £99/135/175; P🛜🐾) Tucked into trees 5 miles west of Thurso is a Georgian mansion offering elegant accommodation with both character and style. Sumptuous upstairs rooms are preferable to basement rooms as they have lovely garden views. There are also beautifully appointed suites in the garden itself, providing both privacy and tranquillity. Thoughtful extras like CDs and books in every room add appeal. It's right alongside a beautiful salmon river – the hotel can sort out permits and equipment – and if you've had a chilly day in the waders, some 300 malt whiskies await in the hotel bar.

🍴 Eating

Cups CAFE £
(www.cups-scrabster.co.uk; Scrabster; light meals £4-8; ⊙10am-4pm Mon-Sat, 11am-4pm Sun) Set in a converted chapel, it's all about teas and delicious home-baked scones and cakes at

this place near the ferry. It also does a nice line in baked potatoes and sandwiches.

Y-Not
PUB £

(www.facebook.com/Ynotthurso; Meadow Lane; mains £7-12; ☺food 11.30am-9pm; ☎) Just off the pedestrian strip, this looks grim from outside but gets better once you're in, offering a cavernous split-level eating and lounging space with live music at weekends, and a cosier lounge bar. Food is pretty decent, with good-value pub standards and a few more ambitious daily specials. It also offers accommodation.

Holborn Hotel
BISTRO, PUB ££

(☏ 01847-892771; www.holbornhotel.co.uk; 16 Princes St; bar meals £8-11, restaurant mains £13-20; ☺noon-2pm & 6-8pm or 9pm; ☎) A trendy, comfortable place decked out in light wood, the Holborn contrasts starkly with more traditional Thurso watering holes. In the bar, uncomplicated but decent meals are available, while quality seafood – including delicious home-smoked salmon – is the mainstay of a short but solid menu fleshed out by specials at **Red Pepper restaurant**, where desserts are excellent too. Service can be slow when busy.

Le Bistro
BISTRO ££

(☏ 01847-893737; 2 Traill St; lunch £6-10, dinner mains £11-17; ☺10am-3pm Tue-Sat, 5-9pm Thu-Sat) This eatery buzzes with chatter on weekend evenings as locals of all ages chow down on its simple meat-and-carb creations. What it does, it does well: respectably sized steaks come on a sizzling platter and service has a smile.

★Captain's Galley
SEAFOOD £££

(☏ 01847-894999; www.captainsgalley.co.uk; Scrabster; 5-course dinner £49; ☺7-9pm Tue-Sat) ✐ By the Scrabster ferry, this is classy but friendly, offering a short, seafood-based menu featuring local and sustainably sourced produce prepared in relatively simple ways, letting natural flavours shine through. The chef picks the best fish off the local boats, and the menu describes exactly which fishing grounds your morsel came from. Cheaper, quality fish 'n' chips are also available to take away from 4.30pm until 6.30pm.

ℹ Information

Thurso Tourist Office (☏ 01847-893155; www. visithighlands.com; High St; ☺10am-6pm Mon-Sat, plus 11am-4pm Sun Apr-Sep) In the Caithness Horizons museum.

ℹ Getting There & Around

It's a 2-mile walk from Thurso train station to the ferry at Scrabster; there are buses from Olrig St.

BUS

From Inverness, Stagecoach/Citylink run to Thurso/Scrabster (£19, three hours, five daily). There are buses roughly hourly to Wick, as well as every couple of hours to John O'Groats (£4, 40 minutes, Monday to Saturday). There's one bus on Tuesdays and Fridays westwards to Tongue via Bettyhill; it also runs some Saturdays.

TRAIN

There are four daily trains from Inverness (£19.30, 3¾ hours), with a connecting bus to Scrabster.

NORTH & WEST COAST

Quintessential wilderness such as this, marked by single-track roads, breathtaking emptiness and a wild, fragile beauty, makes this perhaps Scotland's most evocative region. The scenic majesty is never forgotten.

Thurso to Durness

It's 80 winding – and utterly spectacular – coastal miles from Thurso to Durness.

Dounreay & Melvich

Ten miles west of Thurso, **Dounreay nuclear power station** was the first in the world to supply mains electricity; it's currently being decommissioned. The clean-up is planned to be finished by 2023; it's still a major employment source for the region.

Beyond, **Melvich** overlooks a fine beach and there are great views from **Strathy Point** (a 2-mile drive from the coast road, then a 15-minute walk).

Bettyhill

POP 500

Bettyhill is a crofting community of resettled tenant farmers kicked off their land during the Clearances; the spectacular panorama of a sweeping, sandy beach backed by velvety green hills with rocky outcrops makes a sharp contrast to that sad history.

Strathnaver Museum (☎ 01641-521418; www.strathnavermuseum.org.uk; adult/child £2/1; ⊙ 10am-5pm Mon-Sat Apr-Oct), housed in an old church, tells the story of the Strathnaver Clearances through posters written by local kids. The museum contains Clan Mackay memorabilia, crofting equipment and a boat-shaped container that was used by St Kildans to send messages to the mainland. Outside the back door is the **Farr Stone**, a fine carved Pictish cross-slab.

A good B&B option is **Farr Cottage** (☎ 01641-521755; www.bettyhillbedandbreakfast. co.uk; Farr; s/d £40/64; P ⌂), a welcoming white bungalow amid the bleating of sheep and beautiful scenery a mile off the main road (follow signs to Farr). Rooms are modern and compact, with sparkling bathrooms. Good dinners (£16 for two courses) as well as packed lunches are available.

An extraordinary place to eat, **Côte du Nord** (☎ 01641-521773; www.cotedunord.co.uk; The School House, Kirtomy; degustation £39; ⊙ 7-9pm Wed, Fri & Sat Apr-Oct) ✿, is in the nearby village of Kirtomy. Brilliantly innovative cuisine, local ingredients and wonderfully whimsical presentation are the highlights of the excellent degustation menu here. It's an unlikely spot to find such a gourmet experience and the chef is none other than the local GP who forages for wild herbs and flavours in between patients. Top value. It's tiny, so reserve well ahead.

Bettyhill **tourist office** (☎ 01641-521244; www.visithighlands.com; ⊙ 10.45am-4.30pm Mon-Thu, 10.45am-4pm Fri, 11am-4pm Sat) has good information on the area and the **cafe** (☎ 01641-521244; mains £5-9; ⊙ 10.30am-4pm Mon-Thu, 10.30am-4pm & 5-7.30pm Fri, 11am-4pm & 5-7.30pm Sat) here serves home baking and light meals.

Tongue & Around

POP 500

Coldbackie has outstanding views over sandy beaches, turquoise waters and offshore islands. Two miles further is Tongue, with the evocative 14th-century ruins of Castle Varrich, once a Mackay stronghold. To get to the castle, take the trail next to the Royal Bank of Scotland – it's an easy stroll.

🛏 Sleeping & Eating

Kyle of Tongue Hostel & Holiday Park   HOSTEL, CAMPSITE £
(☎ 01847-611789; www.tonguehostelandholiday-park.co.uk; dm £18, d £42-50; P ⌂) In a won-

derful spot right by the causeway across the Kyle of Tongue, a mile west of town, this is the top budget option in the area, with clean, spacious dorms, great family rooms, views, a decent kitchen and a cosy lounge. It's bright and helpful, and there's a bike shed as well as camping (£7 per person).

Cloisters   B&B ££
(☎ 01847-601286; www.cloistertal.demon.co.uk; Talmine; s/d £38/65; P ⌂ ☺) Superbly located, this has three en suite twin rooms and absolutely brilliant views over the Kyle of Tongue and offshore islands. Breakfast is in the artistically converted church alongside, and it can do evening meals at weekends. From Tongue, cross the causeway and take the right-hand turn to Melness; Cloisters is a couple of miles down this road.

Tongue Hotel   HOTEL ££
(☎ 01847-611206; www.tonguehotel.co.uk; s/d/superior d £75/110/130; P ⌂) A stalwart of the north coast, this former hunting lodge is looking very spruce again and offers attractive, roomy chambers, including plush superiors with top views, and classic standards, some with recently renovated bathrooms. It has a restaurant, plus bar meals in the snug Brass Tap basement bar, a good spot to chat with locals. Food is served noon to 2pm and 6pm to 9pm.

Tigh-nan-Ubhal   B&B ££
(☎ 01847-611281; www.tigh-nan-ubhal.com; Main St; d £60-70; P ⌂ ☺) In the middle of Tongue, and within stumbling distance of two pubs, is this charming B&B. There are snug, loft-style rooms with plenty of natural light, but the basement double with spa is the pick of the bunch – it's the biggest en suite we've seen in northern Scotland. There's also a caravan in the garden and a cheaper room (£50) that shares a bathroom.

Craggan Hotel   SCOTTISH ££
(☎ 01847-601278; www.thecraggan.co.uk; Talmine; mains £10-21; ⊙ 11am-9.15pm) On the side road to Melness, across the causeway from Tongue village, the Craggan Hotel doesn't look much from outside, but go in and you'll find smart, formal service and a menu ranging from exquisite burgers to classy game and local scallops, crab and langoustines, presented beautifully. It also does pizzas and curries to take away and the wine list's not bad either.

Getting There & Away

One bus runs to Tongue Tuesday and Friday to/from Thurso. A postbus runs Monday to Saturday to Lairg. For Durness a bus runs schooldays from Talmine, stopping just west of the causeway across the kyle. It also goes on to Lairg.

Tongue to Durness

From Tongue it's 30 miles to Durness – the main road follows a causeway across the **Kyle of Tongue**, while the old road goes around the head of the kyle, with beautiful views of **Ben Loyal**. Continuing west, you cross a desolate moor to the northern end of freshwater **Loch Hope**. Beyond Loch Hope, as the main road descends towards the sea, there are stunning views over **Loch Eriboll**, Britain's deepest sea inlet and a shelter for ships during WWII.

Durness

POP 400

Scattered Durness (www.durness.org) is wonderfully located, strung out along cliffs rising from a series of pristine beaches. When the sun shines, the effects of blinding white sand, the cry of seabirds and the spring-green-coloured seas combine in a magical way. There are shops, an ATM, petrol and plenty of accommodation options.

Sights & Activities

Walking around the sensational sandy coastline is a highlight, as is a visit to Cape Wrath. Durness' beautiful beaches include Rispond to the east, Sango Sands below town and Balnakeil to the west. At **Balnakeil**, under a mile beyond Durness, a craft village occupies a onetime early-warning radar station. A walk along the beach to the north leads to **Faraid Head**, where you can see puffin colonies in early summer. You can hire bikes from a shed on the square.

Smoo Cave CAVE

(www.smoocave.org) A mile east of the centre is a path down to Smoo Cave. From the vast main chamber, you can head through to a smaller flooded cavern where a waterfall sometimes cascades from the roof. There's evidence the cave was inhabited about 6000 years ago. You can take a **boat trip** (☎01971-511704; adult/child £4/2; ⊙11am-4pm Apr-May & Sep, 10am-5pm Jun-Aug) to explore a little further into the interior.

OFF THE BEATEN TRACK

DETOUR – FORSINARD & STRATHNAVER

Though it's tough to tear yourself away from the coast, we recommend plunging down the A897 just east of Melvich. After 14 miles you reach the railway at **Forsinard**. On the platform is **Forsinard Flows Visitor Centre** (☎01641-571225; www.rspb.org.uk; ⊙9am-5pm Apr-Oct) FREE, with a small nature exhibition. There's a live hen-harrier cam, plus guided walks and 4x4 excursions available – phone for dates. A 1-mile trail introduces you to the Flows peatland; 4 miles north is a 4-mile trail crossing golden plover and dunlin nesting grounds. The deep peat blanket bog is a rare and important habitat, at risk from climate change. A larger visitor centre is in the works.

Past here, the epic peaty moorscapes stir the heart with their desolate beauty. Take a right at Kinbrace onto the B871, which covers more jaw-dropping scenery before arriving at Syre. Turn right to follow the Strathnaver (valley) back to the coast near Bettyhill. Strathnaver saw some of the worst of the Clearances; the **Strathnaver Trail** is a series of numbered points of interest along the valley relating to both this and various prehistoric sites.

Accommodation options on this lonely detour include **Cornmill Bunkhouse** (☎01641-571219; www.achumore.co.uk; dm £15; P), a comfortable, modern hostel occupying a picturesque old mill on a working croft in the middle of nowhere; it's on the A897 4 miles south of the coast road. Turning left instead of right at Syre, you'll eventually reach the remote **Altnaharra Hotel** (☎01549-411222; www.altnaharra.com; s/d/superior d £65/130/150; ⊙Mar-Dec; P).

Sleeping

Lazy Crofter Bunkhouse HOSTEL £

(☎01971-511202; www.durnesshostel.com; dm £17.50;) Durness' best budget accommodation is here, opposite the supermarket. A bothy vibe gives it a very Highland feel. Inviting dorms have plenty of room and lockers, and there's also a sociable shared table for meals and board games, and a great wooden deck with sea views, perfect for midge-free evenings.

Sango Sands Oasis CAMPSITE £

(☑ 01971-511222; www.sangosands.com; sites per adult/child £7/5; P 🐕) You couldn't imagine a better location for a campsite: great grassy areas on the edge of cliffs, descending to two lovely sandy beaches. Facilities are good and very clean and there's a pub next door. Electric hookup is an extra £4. You can camp free from November to March but don't complain about the cold.

★ Mackays Rooms HOTEL ££

(☑ 01971-511202; www.visitdurness.com; d standard/deluxe £125/139; ☺ Easter-Oct; P 🛜🐕) You really feel you're at the furthest corner of Scotland here, where the road turns through 90 degrees. But whether heading south or east, you'll go far before you find a better place to stay than this haven of Highland hospitality. With big beds, contemporary colours and soft fabrics, it's a romantic spot with top service and numerous boutique details. The same owners run **Croft 103** (☑ 01971-511202; www.croft103.com; Port na Con, Laid; per week £1600; P 🛜), a stunning, modern self-catering option for couples 6 miles east, right on Loch Eriboll. There are two cottages, both immaculate.

Morven B&B ££

(☑ 01971-511252; s/d £40/60; P 🐕) Cheery owners, a handy next-to-pub location and a serious border collie theme to the decor are key features of this ultra-cosy place. Rooms, which are upstairs and share a downstairs bathroom, have been recently renovated and feel new and super-comfortable. One is especially spacious and has a top coastal vista.

Glengolly B&B B&B ££

(☑ 01971-511255; www.glengolly.com; d £72-76; ☺ Apr-Oct; P 🛜) This working croft provides comfortable rooms with good space in a traditional B&B atmosphere. Apart from the handy central location, there are other advantages: a superior breakfast menu, with smoked fish and fortified porridge options, and a chance to see a demonstration of sheepdogs at work.

✕ Eating

★ Cocoa Mountain CAFE £

(☑ 01971-511233; www.cocoamountain.co.uk; Balnakeil; hot chocolate £3.75, 10 truffles £9.50; ☺ 9am-6pm high season, 10am-5pm low season) ✿ At the Balnakeil craft village, this up-beat cafe and chocolate maker offers handmade treats including a chilli, lemongrass and coconut white-chocolate truffle, plus many more unique flavours. Tasty espresso and hot chocolate warm the cockles on those blowy horizontal-drizzle days. It offers light lunches and home-baking too, plus chocolate-making workshops.

Sango Sands Oasis PUB FOOD £

(www.sangosands.com; mains £7-12; ☺ food noon-2.30pm & 6.30-8pm Mon-Sat, 12.30-3pm & 6.30-8pm Sun) On the clifftops in the centre of town, this pub by the campsite offers great views from its window tables. A cosy restaurant area does decent bar food in generous quantities.

Smoo Cave Hotel PUB ££

(www.smoocavehotel.co.uk; mains £9-15; ☺ food 11.30am-9.30pm; 🛜) Signposted off the main road at the eastern end of town, this amiable local offers quality bar food in hefty portions. Haddock or daily seafood specials are an obvious and worthwhile choice; there's also a restaurant area with clifftop views.

ℹ Information

Durness Tourist Office (☑ 01971-511368; www.visithighlands.com; ☺ 10am-4.30pm Mon-Sat & 10am-3pm Sun Easter-Jun & Sep, 9.30am-5.30pm Mon-Sat & 10am-4pm Sun Jul-Aug, 10am-4.30pm Mon-Sat Oct) Very helpful. Phone for possible winter opening.

ℹ Getting There & Away

From mid-May to mid-September, one **bus** (☑ 01463-222444; www.decoaches.co.uk) runs daily Monday to Saturday from Durness to Inverness (£16.70) via Ullapool (£12.50). You can take bikes (£6) but they must be booked ahead (during office hours). Another, year-round **bus** (☑ 07782-110007; www.thedurnessbus.com) heads daily Monday to Saturday to Lairg (£7.85), which has a train station. On Saturday a bus heads to either Inverness or Thurso.

Durness to Ullapool

Perhaps Scotland's most spectacular road, the 69 miles connecting Durness to Ullapool is a smorgasbord of dramatic scenery, almost too much to take in. From Durness you pass through a broad heathered valley with the looming grey bulk of Foinaven and Arkle to the southeast. Heather gives way to a rockier landscape of Lewisian gneiss pockmarked with hundreds of small lochans, and gorse-covered hills prefacing the magnificent Torridonian sandstone mountains of Assynt and Coigach, including Suilven's distinctive sugarloaf, ziggurat-like Quinag and pinnacled Stac Pollaidh. The area has been named **Northwest Highlands Geopark** (www.nwhgeopark.com).

Scourie & Handa Island

Scourie (www.scourie.co.uk) is a pretty crofting community halfway between Durness and Ullapool. A few miles north lies **Handa Island** (www.scottishwildlifetrust.org.uk), a nature reserve run by the Scottish Wildlife Trust. The island's western cliffs support important seabird breeding populations. The **boat** (☑ 07775-625890; adult/child £13.50/7; ⊘ outbound 9am-2pm Mon-Sat Apr-Aug, last ferry back 5pm) to Handa leaves from Tarbet Pier, 5.5 miles north of Scourie.

Scourie Lodge (☑ 01971-502248; www.scourielodge.co.uk; s/d £55/90; ⊘ Apr-Oct; P✆), in a gorgeous building overlooking the bay, has old-style comfort and hospitality in a lovely setting. The welcoming owners have been doing this for decades so they know all about guests' comfort. Rooms are traditionally styled and good-sized. The separate 'coach-house' twin is a lovely space. Best is the spectacular walled garden, a gloriously peaceful haven; palm trees are proof of the Gulf Stream's good works. Cards aren't taken.

Kylesku & Loch Glencoul

Hidden away on the shores of Loch Glencoul, tiny Kylesku served as a ferry crossing on the route north until it was made redundant by beautiful Kylesku Bridge in 1984. It's a good base for walks; you can hire bikes too.

◉ Sights & Activities

Eas a'Chuil Aluinn   WATERFALL
Five miles southeast of Kylesku, in wild, remote country lies 213m-high Eas a'Chuil Aluinn, Britain's highest waterfall. You can hike to the top of the falls from a parking area at a sharp bend in the main road 3 miles south of Kylesku (6 miles return; allow five hours).

Kylesku Boat Tours   BOAT TOURS
(☑ 01971-502239; www.rachaelclare.com; adult/child £25/18; ⊘ mid-May–Sep) By the Kylesku Hotel, this little boat runs trips out to see

WORTH A TRIP

SANDWOOD BAY
....

The road from Durness meets the sea again at Rhiconich, from where a minor road leads past Kinlochbervie, one of Scotland's premier fish-landing ports, to Blairmore. This is the starting point for the walk (four miles each way) to **Sandwood Bay**, one of Scotland's best and most isolated beaches, guarded at one end by the spectacular rock pinnacle **Am Buachaille**.

the Eas a'Chuil Aluinn waterfall and local seal colonies.

🍴 Sleeping & Eating

★ **Kylesku Hotel**   INN ££
(☑ 01971-502231; www.kyleskuhotel.co.uk; s £68-89, d £97-120; ⊘ Mar-Oct; 🛜🐾) ✆ Run with pride and enthusiasm, this is a great place to stay, or to gorge yourself on delicious sustainable seafood in the convivial bar (mains £10 to £19; food served noon to 9pm). Local langoustines and mussels are a speciality. There's a variety of rooms; the small extra charge for loch views is well worthwhile.

Achmelvich & Around

Not far south of Kylesku, a 30-mile detour on the narrow B869 rewards with spectacular views and fine beaches. From the lighthouse at Point of Stoer, a one-hour cliff walk leads to the **Old Man of Stoer**, a spectacular sea stack. On this stretch is **Clachtoll Beach Campsite** (☑ 01571-855377; www.clachtollbeachcampsite.co.uk; tent site £6-14, plus per adult/child £4/1; ⊘ Apr-Sep; P🛜🐾), a great coastal spot, and **Achmelvich Beach SYHA** (☑ 01571-844480; www.syha.org.uk; dm/tw £18/46; ⊘ Apr-Sep), a whitewashed cottage beside a great beach. Dorms are simple with privacy curtains separating bunks, and there's a sociable common kitchen/eating area. It does breakfasts and sells heat-up dinners; there's a basic summer shop and chip van at the adjacent campsite. It's a 4-mile walk from Lochinver; some buses from Ullapool and Lochinver stop here.

Lochinver & Assynt

With its otherworldly scenery of isolated peaks rising above a sea of crumpled, lochan-spattered gneiss, Assynt epitomises

WORTH A TRIP

CAPE WRATH

Though its name actually comes from the Norse word for 'turning point', there is something daunting and primal about Cape Wrath, the remote north-western point of the British mainland, crowned by a lighthouse built by the famous Stevenson family of engineers and close to the seabird colonies of **Clo Mor**, Britain's highest coastal cliffs. Getting to Cape Wrath involves a **boat ride** (☎01971-511284; www. capewrathferry.co.uk; single/return £4/6; ☺Easter-Oct) – passengers and bikes only – across the Kyle of Durness (10 minutes), connecting with a **minibus** (☎01971-511284; www.visitcapewrath.com; single/return £7/12; ☺Easter-Oct) running 11 miles to the cape (40 minutes). This combination is a friendly but eccentric, sometimes shambolic service with limited capacity, so plan on waiting in high season, and ring beforehand to make sure the ferry is running. The ferry leaves from two miles southwest of Durness, and runs twice or more daily from April to September. If you eschew the minibus, it's a spectacular 11-mile ride or hike from boat to cape over bleak scenery occasionally used by the Ministry of Defence as a firing range. A cafe at the lighthouse serves soup and sandwiches.

An increasingly popular walking route, the **Cape Wrath Trail** (www. capewrathtrail.co.uk), runs from Fort William up to Cape Wrath (200 miles). It's unmarked, so you may want to do it guided – **C-n-Do** (www.cndoscotland. com) is one operator – or buy the *Cape Wrath Trail* guidebook (www.cicerone. co.uk).

the northwest's wild magnificence. Glaciers have sculpted the hills of Suilven (731m), Canisp (846m), Quinag (808m) and Ben More Assynt (998m) into strange, wonderful silhouettes.

Lochinver is the main settlement, a busy little fishing port that's a popular port of call with its laid-back atmosphere, good facilities and striking scenery.

🏃 Activities

NorWest Sea Kayaking KAYAKING
(☎01571-844281; www.norwestseakayaking.com) This outfit offers three-day introductory sea-kayaking courses and guided kayaking tours around the Summer Isles and in the Lochinver/Ullapool area. It also hires kayaks in Lochinver.

🛏 Sleeping & Eating

Veyatie B&B ££
(☎01571-844424; www.veyatie-scotland.co.uk; Lochinver; s/d £70/90; [P][🖥][🐾]) This choice, at the end of the road across the bay, has perhaps the finest views of all, best enjoyed from the grassy garden or conservatory lounge on a sunny day. There are two enormous rooms with lovely plush beds, great en suites, flatscreens and iPod docks. Breakfast is highly recommended.

⭐ **Albannach** HOTEL £££
(☎01571-844407 www.thealbannach.co.uk; Lochinver; s/d/ste incl dinner £220/300/380; ☺Tue-Sun Mar-Dec; [P][🐾]) 🍴 One of the Highlands' top places to stay and eat, this hotel combines old-fashioned country-house elements – steep creaky stairs, stuffed animals, fireplaces, and noble antique furniture – with strikingly handsome showroom-class rooms that range from a sumptuous four-poster to more modern spaces with things like underfloor heating and, in one case, a private deck with outdoor spa.

The restaurant serves a table d'hôte (tailored to your needs) that's famed throughout Scotland (£68 for nonresidents); the welcoming owners grow lots of their own produce and focus on organic and local ingredients. Glorious views, spacious grounds and great walks in easy striking distance make this a perfect base.

Lochinver Larder & Riverside Bistro CAFE, BISTRO ££
(☎01571-844356; www.lochinverlarder.co.uk; 3 Main St, Lochinver; pies £5, mains £11-20; ☺10am-7.45pm, to 8.30pm Jun-Sep; 📞) This offers an outstanding menu of inventive food made with local produce. The bistro turns out delicious seafood dishes in the evening, while the takeaway counter (open till 7pm) sells delicious pies with a wide range of gourmet fillings: try the wild boar and apricot. It also does quality meals to take away and heat up: great for hostellers and campers.

Caberfeidh
PUB ££

(☎01571-844321; www.caberfeldhlochinver.co.uk; Main St, Lochinver; tapas £6-8; ☺food noon-2.30pm & 6-8.45pm; ☎) ✦ This convivial pub (with riverside beer garden) serves a range of real ales and some excellent food. The menu is based around tapas-sized portions like venison meatballs or local langoustines. A sustainable, low food-mile philosophy is at work and the quality shines through.

🔒 Shopping

Highland Stoneware
CERAMICS

(www.highlandstoneware.com; Lochinver; ☺9am-5.30pm Mon-Fri Jan-Easter, 9am-6pm Mon-Fri & 9am-5pm Sat Easter-Oct, plus 11am-3pm Sun Jun-Sep) Using local landscapes as inspiration, Highland Stoneware ensures you can relive the northwest's majesty every time you have a cuppa. Even better are the mosaics outside, especially the car. You can watch the potters at work here on weekdays.

ⓘ Information

Assynt Visitor Centre (☎01571-844194; www.discoverassynt.co.uk; Main St; ☺10am-4.30pm Mon-Sat & 11am-3pm Sun Easter-Jun, Sep &Oct, 9.30am-5pm Mon-Sat & 10am-4pm Sun Jul & Aug) Has leaflets on hill walks in the area and a display on the story of Assynt.

ⓘ Getting There & Away

There are usually one to three bus services of some sort between Ullapool and Lochinver (50 minutes to 1½ hours) Mondays to Saturdays, including a summer bus that goes on to Durness.

Coigach

The region south of Assynt, west of the main A835 road from Ullapool to Ledmore Junction, is known as Coigach (www.coigach.com). A lone, single-track road penetrates this wilderness, leading through gloriously wild scenery to remote settlements. At the western end of Loch Lurgainn, a branch leads north to Lochinver, a scenic backroad so narrow and twisting that it's nicknamed the **Wee Mad Road**.

Coigach is a wonderland for walkers and wildlife enthusiasts, with a patchwork of sinuous silver lochs dominated by the isolated peaks of Cul Mor (849m), Cul Beag (769m), Ben More Coigach (743m) and Stac Pollaidh (613m). The main settlement is the straggling township of **Achiltibuie**,

15 miles from the main road, with the gorgeous Summer Isles moored just off the coast, and silhouettes of mountains skirting the bay.

◎ Sights & Activities

Stac Pollaidh
WALKING

Despite its diminutive size, Stac Pollaidh provides one of the most exciting hill walks in the Highlands, with some good scrambling on its narrow sandstone crest. Begin at the car park overlooking Loch Lurgainn, 5 miles west of the A835, and follow a clearly marked and well-made footpath around the eastern end of the hill to ascend from the far side; return by the same route (3 miles return, two to four hours).

🧭 Tours

Summer Isles Seatours
BOAT TOURS

(☎07927-920592; www.summerisles-seatours.co.uk; adult/child £25/15; ☺Mon-Sat May-Sep) Three cruises daily to the Summer Isles from Achiltibuie, with time ashore on Tanera Mor, where the post office issues its own Summer Isles stamps.

🛏 Sleeping & Eating

Achininver SYHA
HOSTEL £

(☎01854-622482; www.syha.org.uk; dm £18; ☺May-Aug) The rudimentary 20-bed Achininver hostel, a half-mile walk off the main road, is designed for walkers and outdoor enthusiasts. Its remote, serene location has to be one of the country's best.

★ Summer Isles Hotel
HOTEL £££

(☎01854-622282; www.summerisleshotel.co.uk, Achiltibuie; s £125-190, d £165-240; ☺Easter-Oct; P☎☎☎) This is a special place, with wonderfully romantic, commodious rooms — one themed on Charlie Chaplin, who stayed here, others suites in separate cottages – plus cracking views and a snug bar with outdoor seating. 'Courtyard view' rooms are darkish: it's worth upgrading to one with vistas. It's the perfect spot for a romantic getaway or some quality time off life's treadmill.

The restaurant (noon to 3pm and 6pm to 9pm; dinner £59) is of high quality, with local lobster usually featuring, plus the renowned cheese and dessert trolleys – and there's a great wine list considering you're in the middle of nowhere.

❶ Getting There & Around

There are one to two daily buses Monday to Saturday from Ullapool to Badenscallie (half a mile from Achininver SYHA) and Achiltibuie (1¼ hours).

Ullapool

POP 1500

This pretty port on the shores of Loch Broom is the largest settlement in Wester Ross and one of the most alluring spots in the Highlands, a wonderful destination in itself as well as a gateway to the Western Isles. Offering a row of whitewashed cottages arrayed along the harbour and special views of the loch and its flanking hills, the town has a very distinctive appeal. The harbour served as an emigration point during the Clearances, with thousands of Scots watching Ullapool recede behind them as the diaspora cast them across the world.

◎ Sights & Activities

Ullapool is a great centre for walking. Good walking books and leaflets are available at the tourist office.

Ullapool Museum MUSEUM
(www.ullapoolmuseum.co.uk; 7 West Argyle St; adult/child £3.50/free; ◎10am-5pm Mon-Sat Apr-Oct) Housed in a converted Telford church, this museum relates the prehistoric, natural and social history of the town and Lochbroom area, with a particular focus on the emigration to Nova Scotia and other places. There's also a genealogy section if you want to trace your Scottish roots.

An Talla Solais GALLERY
(☑01854-612310; www.antallasolais.org; Market St; ◎10am-4pm Wed-Sun mid-Apr–mid-Oct) FREE This community-run gallery stages changing exhibitions of works by Highland artists, from paintings and photography to ceramics and textiles. Opening hours vary, so check the website for exhibition dates and times. There's a decent cafe here.

☞ Tours

Seascape BOAT TOURS
(☑01854-633708; www.sea-scape.co.uk; adult/child £30/20; ◎Jun-Aug) Runs enjoyable two-hour tours out to the Summer Isles in an orange rigid inflatable boat (RIB).

Summer Queen BOAT TOURS
(☑01854-612472; www.summerqueen.co.uk; ◎Mon-Sat May-Sep) The stately *Summer Queen* takes you out (weather permitting) around Isle Martin (£20/10 per adult/child, two hours) or to the Summer Isles (£30/15, four hours), with a stop on Tanera Mor.

✬ Festivals & Events

Ullapool Guitar Festival MUSIC
(www.ullapoolguitarfestival.com) Held in early October, this features a series of concerts and workshops over a weekend, with late-night club sessions and some high-quality musicians on show.

⌷ Sleeping

Note that during summer Ullapool is very busy and finding accommodation can be tricky – book ahead.

Ullapool SYHA HOSTEL £
(☑01854-612254; www.syha.org.uk; Shore St; dm/tw/q £20/45/88; ◎Apr-Oct; �***) You've got to hand it to the SYHA; it's chosen some very sweet locations for its hostels. This is as close to the water as it is to the town's best pub: about four seconds' walk. The front rooms have harbour views but the busy dining area and little lounge are also good spots for contemplating the water.

Ceilidh Clubhouse HOSTEL £
(☑01854-612103; www.theceilidhplace.com; West Lane; s/tw/f £23-30/58/68; P�***) Opposite the Ceilidh Place, which runs it, this annexe offers no-frills accommodation for walkers, journeyers and staff. A big building, it has hostel-style rooms with sturdy bunks and basins. Though shared showers and toilets are a little institutional, rooms are private: if you're woken by snores, at least they'll be familiar ones. Prices drop substantially outside high summer.

Broomfield Holiday Park CAMPSITE £
(☑01854-612020; www.broomfieldhp.com; West Lane; tent sites £15-19, sites solo campers £8-12; ◎Apr-Sep; P***) Great grassy headland location, very close to centre. Midge-busting machines in action.

★West House B&B ££
(☑01854-613126; www.ullapoolaccommodation.net; West Argyle St; s £60, d £75-85; P***) ⊘ Slap bang in the centre, this solid white house, once a manse, offers excellent rooms with contemporary style and great bathrooms.

Breakfast is continental: rooms come with a fridge stocked with fresh fruit, cheeses, yoghurts, homemade bread, proper coffee and juice so you can eat at your leisure in your own chamber. Most rooms have great views, as well as iPod docks and other conveniences. The owners also have tempting self-catering options in the Ullapool area.

★Tamarin Lodge   B&B ££
(☑ 01854-612667; www.tamarinullapool.com; The Braes; s/d £42/84; P 🕸 🍴) Effortlessly elegant modern architecture in this hilltop house is noteworthy in its own right, but the glorious vistas over the hills opposite and water far below are unforgettable. All rooms face the view; some have a balcony, and all are very spacious, quiet and utterly relaxing, with unexpected features and gadgets. The great lounge and benevolent hosts are a delight. Follow signs for Braes from the Inverness road.

Point Cottage   B&B ££
(☑ 01854-335062; www.pointcottagebandb.co.uk; 22 West Shore St; d £70; P 🕸) If you've just arrived by ferry, you've probably already admired Ullapool's line of shorefront cottages; this is one of them. It's a romantic option for couples, with impeccable modernised rooms with plush bedding, preserving their cottage feel. An upmarket continental breakfast is served in-room: it's a pleasure to eat at your little window table with loch views.

★Ceilidh Place   HOTEL £££
(☑ 01854-612103; www.theceilidhplace.com; 14 West Argyle St; s £58-92, d £140-164; ⊘ Feb-Dec; P 🕸 🍴) This hotel, which includes a bookshop, is a celebration of Scottish culture: we're talking literature and traditional music, not tartan and Nessie dolls. It's one of the Highlands' more unusual and delightful places to stay. Rooms go for character over modernity: instead of TV they come with a selection of books chosen by Scottish literati, eclectic artwork and cosy touches. The sumptuous lounge has sofas, chaises longues and an honesty bar.

🍴 Eating & Drinking

Arch Inn   PUB ££
(☑ 01854-612454; www.thearchinn.co.uk; West Shore St; mains £10-18; ⊘ food noon-2.30pm & 5-9pm Mon-Sat, 12.30-2.30pm & 5-9pm Sun; 🕸) There's pleasing pub food to be had at this shorefront establishment, where the cosy bar and restaurant area dishes up generous well-presented mains that range from tender chicken and fish dishes to more advanced blackboard specials with local seafood a highlight. Service is helpful and efficient. The outdoor tables right beside the lapping water are a top spot for a pint.

Ceilidh Place   SCOTTISH ££
(☑ 01854-612103; 14 West Argyle St; mains £10-18; ⊘ 8am-9pm Feb-Dec; 🕸) Serves up inventive dishes that focus on fresh local seafood backed up by stews, plus lighter meals like pies and burgers during the day. Presentation and quality are high, and it's an atmospheric place, cosy with outdoor seating, good wines by the glass and regular live music and events.

Ferry Boat Inn   PUB ££
(☑ 01854-612431; www.ferry-boat-inn.com; Shore St; mains £9-15; ⊘ food 7.30am-9.30pm; 🕸) Known as the FBI, this character-laden waterfront inn is a little less traditional looking these days with its bleached wood and nonstained carpet, but it's still a place where locals and visitors mingle. Management and chefs seem to change frequently, but if things are going well it's an atmospheric venue for local seafood. Drop by for a drink either way.

ℹ Information

Ullapool Bookshop (☑ 01854-612918; www. ullapoolbookshop.co.uk; Quay St; ⊘ 9am-6pm Mon-Sat, 10am-5pm Sun) Lots of books on Scottish topics and local maps. Internet access £1 per 15 minutes.

Ullapool Tourist Office (☑ 01854-612486; ullapool@visitscotland.com; Argyle St, ⊘ 9.30am-5pm Mon-Sat Easter-Oct, plus 10am-3pm Sun Jun-Aug) Can book ferries and buses.

Ullapool Library (☑ 01854-612543; Mill St; ⊘ 9am-5pm Mon-Fri, plus 6-8pm Tue & Thu, closed Mon & Wed during holidays; 🕸) Free internet access.

ℹ Getting There & Around

Citylink (www.citylink.co.uk) has one to three daily buses from Inverness to Ullapool (£12.80, 1½ hours), connecting with the Lewis ferry (p397).

Ullapool to Kyle of Lochalsh

Although it's less than 50 miles as the crow flies from Ullapool to Kyle of Lochalsh, it's more like 150 miles along the circuitous coastal road – but don't let that put you off. It's a deliciously remote region and there are fine views of beaches and bays backed by mountains all the way along.

If you're hurrying to Skye, head inland on the A835 (towards Inverness) and catch up with the A832 further south, near Garve.

Braemore & Around

Twelve miles southeast of Ullapool at Braemore, the A832 doubles back towards the coast as it heads for Gairloch (the A835 continues southeast across the wild, sometimes snowbound, Dirrie More pass to Garve and Inverness).

Just west of the junction, a car park gives access to the Falls of Measach, which spill 45m into spectacularly deep and narrow Corrieshalloch Gorge. You can cross the gorge on a swaying suspension bridge, and walk west for 250m to a viewing platform that juts out dizzyingly above a sheer drop. The thundering falls and misty vapours rising from the gorge are very impressive.

Gairloch & Around

POP 1000

Gairloch is a group of villages (comprising Achtercairn, Strath and Charlestown) around the inner end of a loch of the same name. Gairloch is a good base for whale- and dolphin-watching excursions and the surrounding area has beautiful sandy beaches, good trout fishing and birdwatching.

⊙ Sights & Activities

The B8056 runs along Loch Gairloch's southern shore, past the cute little harbour of Badachro, to end at the gorgeous pink-sand beach of Red Point – a perfect picnic spot. Another coastal road leads north from Gairloch 11 miles to the settlement of Melvaig. From here a private road (open to walkers and cyclists) continues 3 miles to Rua Reidh Lighthouse (building and grounds off limits to non-guests).

Gairloch Heritage Museum   MUSEUM

(www.gairlochheritagemuseum.org; adult/child £4/1; ⊙10am-5pm Mon-Fri & 11am-3pm Sat Apr-Oct) This has interesting displays on life in the West Highlands from Pictish times to the present, including locally built fishing boats and a faithful re-creation of a crofter's cottage.

Inverewe Garden   GARDENS

(NTS; www.nts.org.uk; adult/concession £10.50/7.50; ⊙10am-3pm Nov-Mar, to 5pm Apr & Sep, to 5.30pm May, to 6pm Jun-Aug, to 4pm Oct) Six miles north of Gairloch, this splendid garden is a welcome splash of colour on this otherwise bleak coast. The climate here is warmed by the Gulf Stream, which allowed Osgood MacKenzie to create this exotic woodland garden in 1862. There are free guided tours on weekdays at 1.30pm (March to October). The cafe has great cakes.

Gairloch Marine Wildlife Centre   NATURE DISPLAY

(☑01445-712636; www.porpoise-gairloch.co.uk; Pier Rd; ⊙10am-4pm Easter-Oct) 🏷 FREE This has audiovisual and interactive displays, lots of charts, photos and knowledgeable staff. Cruises (☑01445-712636; www.porpoise-gairloch.co.uk; adult/child £20/15) run from the centre up to three times daily (weather permitting); during the two-hour trips you may see basking sharks, porpoises and minke whales. The crew collects data on water temperature and conditions, and monitors cetacean populations, so you are subsidising important research.

Gairloch Trekking Centre   HORSE RIDING

(☑01445-712652; www.gairlochtrekkingcentre.co.uk; Flowerdale Mains; ⊙Fri-Wed Mar-Oct) Offers riding lessons, pony trekking and guided treks in the ample grounds of Gairloch Estate.

👉 Tours

Hebridean Whale Cruises   BOAT TOURS

(☑01445-712458; www.hebridean-whale-cruises.com; Pier Rd; cruises 2½/4hr £45/75) Based at the harbour, this set-up runs close-in trips to see seals, otters and seabirds, or trips further out to feeding grounds where you might see dolphins, minke whales or orca. It operates two boats, one a cabin cruiser, the other a zippy rigid inflatable.

🛏 Sleeping

Wayside Guest House   B&B £

(☑01445-712008; issmith@msn.com; Strath; s/d £40/60; 🐾) Cosy and compact, this offers comfortable and welcoming accommodation in Strath, the spiritual heart of Gairloch. The spotless rooms come with either en suite bathroom or fabulous view; you decide what's more important. It offers excellent value and hosts full of kind thoughts.

Rua Reidh Lighthouse
LODGE ££

(✆01445-771263; www.stayatalighthouse.co.uk; d/f £60/110; ☺Easter-Oct; P🖘🐾) Three miles down a private road beyond Melvaig (11 miles north of Gairloch), this simple, excellent lodge gives a taste of a lighthouse keeper's life. It's a wild, lonely location great for walking and birdwatching. Breakfast is included and tasty evening meals are available. It's open Easter to October, but there's a self-catering apartment open almost year-round. Book well ahead.

Gairloch View Guest House
B&B ££

(✆01445-712666; www.gairlochview.com; s/d £55/80; P🖘) The unique selling point of this unassuming modern house is a patio with a stunning view over the sea to Skye – a view you can also enjoy from your breakfast table. The three bedrooms, with plenty of natural light, are comfortably furnished in classic country style, and the residents' lounge has satellite TV and a small library of books and games.

✖ Eating

Mountain Coffee Company
CAFE £

(Strath Sq, Strath; light meals £4-7; ☺9am-5.30pm, shorter hours low season; 🖘) ✔ More the sort of place you'd expect to find on the gringo trail in the Andes, this offbeat and cosy spot is a shrine to all things mountaineering and travelling. It sells tasty savoury bagels, home baking and a range of decadent coffees and hot chocolates. The conservatory is the place to lap up the sun, while the attached Hillbillies Bookshop is worth a browse.

Badachro Inn
PUB ££

(✆01445-741255; www.badachroinn.com; Badachro; light meals £5-8, mains £11-16; ☺food noon-3pm & 6-9pm, from 12.30pm Sun; P) ✔ Set in an enchanting location, overlooking a sheltered yacht harbour at Badachro, 5 miles southwest of Gairloch, this old Highland inn serves local real ales and platters of fresh local seafood: crab, scallops and langoustines, some landed right alongside. There are also tasty panini and sandwiches; eating out on the deck on a sunny day here is a real treat.

Na Mara
BISTRO ££

(www.namararestaurant.co.uk; Strath Sq, Strath; mains £10-18; ☺5-8pm Thu-Tue; ♿) On the square in Strath, this brings a light, cheery smile to west-coast eating with its inclusive menu that starts at burgers, pastas and curries and includes steaks and seafood dishes in classic bistro style with a range of influences. Good value, but check opening times ahead.

ℹ Information

Gairloch Tourist Office (✆01445-712071; ☺10am-4pm Mon-Sat Oct–Apr, 10am-5pm Mon-Sat & 10am-4pm Sun May-Sep) In the wooden Gale Centre, on the road through town, this has good walking pamphlets. Opening hours are slightly variable.

ℹ Getting There & Away

Public transport to Gairloch is very limited. **Westerbus** (✆01445-712255) runs Monday to Saturday to/from Inverness (£10, 2¼ hours), and Thursday to/from Ullapool.

Loch Maree & Around

Stretching 12 miles between Poolewe and Kinlochewe, **Loch Maree** is considered one of Scotland's prettiest lochs. At its southern end, tiny **Kinlochewe** makes a good base for outdoor activities. **Beinn Eighe Visitor Centre** (✆01445-760254; www.nnr-scotland.org.uk/beinn-eighe; ☺9am-5pm Easter-Oct; ♿) FREE, a mile north, has interactive kid-friendly displays on local geography, ecology, flora and fauna, and provides information on local walking routes, including the **Beinn Eighe Mountain Trail**. This is a waymarked 4-mile return walk to a plateau and cairn on the side of Beinn Eighe, offering magnificent views over Loch Maree.

Kinlochewe Hotel (✆01445-760253; www.kinlochewehotel.co.uk; Kinlochewe; dm £15.50, s £50, d £90-98; P🖘🐾) ✔ is a well-run, welcoming place that's very walker-friendly. As well as comfortable, spotless rooms – 'economy' ones share a bathroom – there are nice features like a handsome lounge well stocked with books, a great bar with real ales on tap and a thoughtful menu of locally sourced food. There's also a bunkhouse with one no-frills 12-bed dorm (BYO sleeping bag and towels), a decent kitchen and clean bathrooms.

The **Whistle Stop Cafe** (Kinlochewe; meals £6-13; ☺9am-9pm Mon-Sat Apr-Oct, to 6pm midweek Mar & Nov; 🖘), a colourful presence in the former village hall, is a tempting place to drop by for anything from a coffee to enticing bistro fare. It's very friendly, and used to pumping life back into chilled walkers and cyclists. Unlicensed, but you can take your own wine.

Torridon & Around

The road southwest from Kinlochewe passes through Glen Torridon, amid some of Britain's most beautiful scenery. Carved by ice from massive layers of ancient sandstone that takes its name from the region, the mountains here are steep, shapely and imposing, whether flirting with autumn mists, draped in dazzling winter snows, or reflected in the calm blue waters of Loch Torridon on a summer day.

The road reaches the sea at spectacularly sited Torridon village, then continues westwards to lovely Shieldaig, which boasts an attractive main street of whitewashed houses right on the water, before turning south to Applecross, Lochcarron and Kyle of Lochalsh.

◉ Sights & Activities

The Torridon Munros – Liathach (1054m; pronounced '*lee*-agakh', Gaelic for 'the Grey One'), Beinn Eighe (1010m; 'ben *ay*', 'the File') and Beinn Alligin (986m; 'the Jewelled Mountain') – are big, serious mountains for experienced hill walkers only. Though not technically difficult, their ascents are long and committing, often over rough and rocky terrain. Information is available at the NTS Countryside Centre (NTS; ☑ 01445-791221; www.nts.org.uk; ⊙ 10am-5pm Sun-Fri Easter-Sep) FREE in Torridon; rangers offer guided mountain walks (£25 per person, weekdays only, advance booking necessary) in July and August. You can buy food here for a nearby red-deer herd.

Torridon Sea Tours   BOAT TRIPS
(☑ 01520-755353; www.torridonseatours.com) Runs various trips from Shieldaig, including 90-minute morning or evening cruises on Loch Torridon (adult/child £25/15) and half- or full-day cruises around offshore islands.

🛏 Sleeping & Eating

There's a free campsite at the entrance to Torridon village and a decent shop and cafe in the village itself.

Torridon SYHA   HOSTEL £
(☑ 01445-791284; www.syha.org.uk; dm £20, tw £45-49; ⊙ Mar-Oct, plus weekends Nov-Feb; P@🐶📶) This spacious hostel has enthusiastic, can-do management and sits in a magnificent location, surrounded by spectacular mountains. Spacious dorms and privates (twins have single beds) are allied to a huge kitchen and convivial lounge area, with ales on sale. It's a very popular walking base, with great advice from the in-house mountain rescue team, so book ahead. As well as breakfasts, packed lunches and heat-up dinners are offered.

Ferroch   B&B ££
(☑ 01445-791451; www.ferroch.co.uk; s/d £75/98; P📶) Just outside town, on the road to Shieldaig, this offers most memorable vistas from its pleasant garden and top-floor double. All rooms are very spacious and comfortable, and it's a welcoming place, with a lounge with fire and music, afternoon tea served on the grass and excellent breakfasts and dinners featuring homemade yoghurt, cheese and bread, among other goodies. No cards.

Torridon Inn   INN ££
(☑ 01445-791242; www.thetorridon.com; s/d/q £100/110/175; ⊙ daily May-Oct, Thu-Sun Nov, Dec, Mar & Apr, closed Jan & Feb; P📶🐶) Adjacent to The Torridon hotel, this convivial but upmarket walkers' hang-out offers excellent modern rooms that vary substantially in size and layout, and a sociable bar offering all-day food. Rooms for groups (up to six) offer more value.

★ The Torridon   HOTEL £££
(☑ 01445-791242; www.thetorridon.com; r standard/superior/master £235/290/440; ⊙ closed Jan, plus Mon & Tue Nov, Dec, Feb & Mar; P@📶🐶) If you prefer the lap of luxury to the sound of rain beating on your tent, head for this lavish Victorian shooting lodge with a romantic lochside location. Sumptuous contemporary rooms with awe-inspiring views and top bathrooms and a cheery Highland cow atop the counterpane couldn't be more inviting. This is one of Scotland's top country hotels, always luxurious but never pretentious.

Master suites are lavish in size and comfort, with a more classic decor and bay windows making the most of the panoramas. Service is excellent, with muddy boots positively welcomed, and dinners are sumptuous affairs, open to non-residents (£55). Friendly staff can organise any number of activities on land or water.

Tigh an Eilean Hotel   HOTEL £££
(☑ 01520-755251; www.tighaneilean.co.uk; Shieldaig; s/d £80/160; ⊙ Feb-Dec; 📶) With a lovely waterfront position, this is an appealing destination for a relaxing stay, offering not luxury but comfortable old-style rooms.

You'll feel it offers better value if you manage to get a loch-view one – the vistas are gloriously soothing. Service is very helpful, and there's a cosy lounge with honesty bar. Dinner (£45) features regional produce, local seafood and delicious Scottish cheeses. Book ahead in winter.

Shieldaig Bar and Coastal Kitchen SEAFOOD ££
(www.shieldaigbarandcoastalkitchen.co.uk; Shieldaig; mains £9-17; ⊙noon-2.30pm & 6-9pm Sep-May, noon-9pm Jun-Aug) This attractive pub has real ales and waterside tables plus a great upstairs dining room and outdoor deck for more casual dining, with an emphasis on local seafood and bistro-style meat dishes like steak-frites or sausages and mash. Blackboard specials feature the daily catch.

Applecross

POP 200

The delightfully remote seaside village of Applecross feels like an island retreat due to its isolation and the magnificent views of Raasay and the hills of Skye that set the pulse racing, particularly at sunset. On a clear day it's an unforgettable place, though the campsite and pub fill to the brim in school holidays.

A road leads here 25 winding miles from Shieldaig, but more spectacular (accessed from further south on the A896) is the magnificent **Bealach na Ba** (626m; Pass of the Cattle), the third-highest motor road in the UK, and the longest continuous climb. Originally built in 1822, it climbs steeply and hair-raisingly via hairpin bends perched over sheer drops, with gradients up to 25%, then drops dramatically to the village with views of Skye. **Mountain & Sea Guides** (✐01250-744394; www.applecross.uk.com) runs short sea-kayaking, hill-walking and mountaineering excursions, as well as more serious expeditions.

🛏 Sleeping & Eating

Applecross Campsite CAMPSITE £
(✐01520-744268; www.applecross.uk.com; sites per adult/child £9/4.50, 2-person hut £45; ⊙Mar-Oct; 🅿🛜🐾) Offers green grassy plots, cute little wooden cabins and a good greenhouse-like cafe.

⭐**Applecross Inn** INN ££
(✐01520-744262; www.applecross.uk.com; Shore St; s/d £85/130, mains £9-18; ⊙food noon-9pm;

🅿🛜🐾) 🍴 The hub of the spread-out community and the perfect shoreside location for a sunset pint, this inn is famous for its food – mostly daily blackboard specials concentrate on local seafood and venison – and sports seven snug bedrooms. All have a view of the Skye hills and the sea.

Lochcarron

POP 900

Appealing, whitewashed Lochcarron is a veritable metropolis in these parts, with good services and a long lochside shoreline.

The **Old Manse** (✐01520-722208; www.theoldmanselochcarron.com; Church St; s/d £40/65, tw with loch view £75; 🅿🛜🐾) is a top-notch Scottish guesthouse, beautifully appointed and in a prime lochside position. Rooms are traditional in style and simply gorgeous with elegant furniture. Those overlooking the water are larger and well worth the extra tenner. Evening meals (£12 for two courses) are available. Take the road towards Strome.

On the main waterfront road through town, **Rockvilla** (✐01520-722379; www.therockvilla.com; Main St; s £61, d £72-86; ⊙Easter-Sep; 🅿🛜) has very welcoming hosts and lovely modernised rooms with heaps of space and dreamy views over the water. The restaurant here serves inventive bistro fare at fair prices.

Four miles west of town on the A896, **Kishorn Seafood Bar** (✐01529-733240; www.kishornseafoodbar.co.uk; A896, Kishorn; mains £10-16; ⊙10am-5pm Mar-Nov, to 9pm Fri & Mon-Sat Jul-Sep) 🍴 is a cute pale-blue bungalow which serves the freshest of local seafood simply and well, with very fair prices. Views are spectacular, and you've got the satisfaction of knowing that much of your meal was caught in Loch Kishorn just below.

Plockton

POP 400

Idyllic little **Plockton** (www.plockton.com), with its perfect cottages lining a perfect bay, looks like it was designed as a film set. And it has indeed served as just that – scenes from *The Wicker Man* (1973) were filmed here, and the village became famous as the location for the 1990s TV series *Hamish Macbeth*.

With all this picture-postcard perfection, it's hardly surprising that Plockton is a tourist hot spot, crammed with day trippers and holidaymakers in summer. But there's no denying its appeal, with 'palm trees' (actually hardy New Zealand cabbage palms) lining the waterfront, a thriving small-boat sailing scene and several good places to stay, eat and drink. The big event of the year is the **Plockton Regatta** (www.plockton-sailing.com), a fortnight of boat races culminating in a concert and *ceilidh*.

🏃 Activities

Hire canoes and rowboats on the waterfront to explore the bay.

Sea Kayak Plockton   KAYAKING
(☑ 01599-544422; www.seakayakplockton.co.uk) Offers everything from beginners' lessons to multi-day trips around Skye to highly challenging odysseys right out to St Kilda.

👉 Tours

Calum's Seal Trips   BOAT TOURS
(☑ 01599-544306; www.calums-sealtrips.com; adult/child £10/6; ⊙ Apr-Oct) Runs seal-watching cruises – there are swarms of the slippery fellas just outside the harbour, and the trip comes with an excellent commentary. Trips leave several times daily. You may even spot otters, and there's a longer dolphin-watching trip available.

🛏 Sleeping

The village has some excellent places to stay, but it's popular. Best to book ahead.

Tigh Arran   B&B £
(☑ 01599-544307; www.plocktonbedandbreakfast. com; Duirinish; s/d £50/60; P 🖘 😹) It's hard to decide which is better at this sweet spot in Duirinish, two miles from the Plockton shorefront. The warm personal welcome is a highlight, but it's matched by absolutely stunning views across to Skye. All three of the en suite rooms – with appealing family options – enjoy them, as does the comfy lounge. A top spot, far from stress and noise; and great value.

Plockton Station Bunkhouse   HOSTEL £
(☑ 01599-544235; mickcoe@btInternet.com; dm £15; P 🖘) Airily set in the former train station (the new one is opposite), this has cosy four-bed dorms, a garden and kitchen-lounge with plenty of light and good perspectives over the frenetic comings-and-goings (OK, that last bit's a lie) of the platforms below. It can get a bit cramped when there are lots of folk in. The owners also do good-value B&B

(single/double £30/50) next door in inaccurately named 'Nessun Dorma'.

Plockton Hotel   INN ££
(☑ 01599-544274; www.plocktonhotel.co.uk; 41 Harbour St; s/d £90/130, cottage s/d £55/80; 🖘) 🕊 Black-painted Plockton Hotel is one of those classic Highland spots that manages to make everyone happy, whether it's thirst, hunger or fatigue that brings you knocking. Assiduously tended rooms are a delight, with excellent facilities and thoughtful touches. Those without a water view are consoled with more space and a balcony with rock-garden perspectives. The cottage nearby offers simpler comfort. The cosy bar, or wonderful beer garden on a sunny day, are memorable places for a pint, and food ranges from sound-value bar meals to seafood platters and local langoustines brought in on the afternoon boat (mains £6 to £12).

Shieling   B&B ££
(☑ 01599-544282; jane@shieling282.freeserve. co.uk; s/d £40/65; ⊙ late May-late Sep; P 🖘) A short stroll across the little causeway from the waterfront strip, characterful Shieling is surrounded by an expertly trimmed garden and has pleasing rooms with views and big beds as well as a lovely lounge with water outlook. Next door is an historic thatched blackhouse. A kindly welcome is guaranteed.

Duncraig Castle   B&B ££
(☑ 01599-544295; www.duncraigcastle.co.uk; P) Duncraig Castle offers luxurious, offbeat hospitality, as long as stuffed animals don't offend you. At time of research it was closed for substantial renovation, but should open for the 2016 season. It's very close to Plockton but has its own train station.

🍴 Eating

⭐ **Plockton Shores**   SEAFOOD ££
(☑ 01599-544263; www.plocktonshoresrestaurant.com; 30 Harbour St; mains £11-18; ⊙ noon-2.30pm & 6-8.30pm Mon-Sat, from 11am Sun; 🖉) 🕊 This welcoming restaurant attached to a shop sports a tempting menu of local seafood, including good-value platters with langoustines, mussels, crab, squat lobster and more, or succulent hand-dived tempura scallops. There's also a very tasty line in venison, steaks and a small selection of tasty vegetarian dishes that are more than an afterthought. Breakfast, teas and snacks from morning until night are served.

Plockton Inn
SEAFOOD ££

(☑ 01599-544222; www.plocktoninn.co.uk; mains £10-18; ⊘ noon-2.15pm & 6-9pm; 🔊) Offering a wide range from haggis to local langoustines (Plockton prawns) and daily seafood specials, this offers welcoming service. A range of rooms – some substantially more spacious than others, and some in an annexe – are available at a decent price.

Kyle of Lochalsh
POP 700

Before the bridge was opened in 1995, this was Skye's main ferry port. Visitors now tend to buzz through town, but Kyle has some good boat trips if you're interested in marine life.

◎ Sights & Activities

Seaprobe Atlantis
BOAT TOURS

(☑ 0800 980 4846; www.seaprobeatlantis.com; adult/child from £13/7; ⊘ Easter-Oct) A glass-hulled boat takes you on a spin around the kyle to spot seabirds, seals and maybe an otter. The basic trip includes entertaining commentary and plenty of beautiful jellyfish; longer trips also take in a WWII shipwreck. Book at the tourist office.

🛏 Sleeping & Eating

There's a string of B&Bs just outside of town on the road to Plockton.

Buth Bheag
SEAFOOD £

(salads £3-6; ⊘ 10am-5pm Tue-Fri, 10am-3pm Sat) This tiny place by the water, near the tourist office, has great takeaway fresh seafood salads and rolls for a pittance. Munch them sitting by the harbour.

Waverley
SCOTTISH ££

(☑ 01599-534337; www.waverleykyle.co.uk; Main St; mains £12-21; ⊘ 5.30-9.30pm Fri-Tue) This is an intimate place with excellent service; try the Taste of Land and Sea, combining Aberdeen Angus fillet steak with fresh local prawns, or one of several other reliably good fish options. Blackboard specials offer a dinner deal if you eat before 7pm.

❶ Information

Kyle of Lochalsh Tourist Office (☑ 01599-534276; ⊘ 9.30am-4.30pm Easter-Oct) Beside the main seafront car park; stocks information on Skye. Next to it is one of Scotland's most lavishly decorated public toilets.

❶ Getting There & Away

Citylink runs two to three daily buses from Inverness (£19.90, two hours) and three from Glasgow (£36.20, five to six hours).

The train route between Inverness and Kyle of Lochalsh (£22, 2½ hours, up to four daily) is marvellously scenic.

Kyle to the Great Glen

It's 55 miles southeast via the A87 from Kyle to Invergarry, which lies between Fort William and Fort Augustus, on Loch Oich.

Eilean Donan Castle

Photogenically sited at the entrance to Loch Duich, near Dornie, Eilean Donan (☑ 01599-555202; www.eileandonancastle.com; adult/child/family £6.50/5.50/16; ⊘ 10am-6pm Feb-Dec, from 9am Jul & Aug) is one of Scotland's most evocative castles, and must be represented in millions of photo albums. It's on an islet linked to the mainland by a stone-arched bridge. It's very much a re-creation inside, with an excellent introductory exhibition. Keep an eye out for the photos of castle scenes from *Highlander;* there's also a sword that was used at Culloden in 1746. The castle, though built in the early 13th century by the Mackenzies, was bombarded into ruins by government ships in 1719 when Jacobite forces were defeated at the Battle of Glenshiel. It was rebuilt between 1912 and 1932 by the Macraes, who own it.

Citylink buses to or from Skye will stop opposite the castle.

Glen Shiel & Glenelg

From Eilean Donan Castle, the A87 follows Loch Duich into spectacular Glen Shiel, with 1000m-high peaks soaring on either side of the road. Here in 1719, a Jacobite army was defeated by Hanoverian government forces. Among those fighting on the rebel side were clansmen led by famous outlaw Rob Roy MacGregor, and 300 soldiers loaned by the king of Spain; the mountain above the battlefield is still called Sgurr nan Spainteach (Peak of the Spaniard).

At Shiel Bridge, home to a famous wild-goat colony, a narrow side road goes over the Bealach Ratagain (pass), with great views of the Five Sisters of Kintail peaks, to Glenelg, where there's a community-run ferry to Skye. From palindromic Glenelg round

MADDENING MIDGES

Forget Nessie; the Highlands have a real monster. A voracious bloodsucking female fully 3mm long named *culicoides impunctatus*, or the Highland midge. The bane of campers and as much a symbol of Scotland as the kilt or dram, they drive sane folk to distraction, descending in biting clouds.

Though normally vegetarian, the female midge needs a dose of blood in order to lay her eggs. And, like it or not, if you're in the Highlands between June and August, you just volunteered as a donor. Midges especially congregate near water, and are most active in the early morning, though squadrons also patrol in the late evening.

Repellents and creams are reasonably effective, though some walkers favour midge veils. Light-coloured clothing also helps. Many pubs and campsites have midge-zappers. Check www.midgeforecast.co.uk for activity levels by area, but don't blame us: we've been eaten alive when the forecast said moderate too.

to the road-end at Arnisdale, the scenery becomes even more spectacular, with great views across Loch Hourn to the remote Knoydart peninsula. Along this road are two fine ruined Iron Age brochs.

🏃 Activities

There are several good walks in the area, including the two-day, cross-country hike from Morvich to Cannich via scenic **Gleann Lichd** and Glen Affric SYHA (35 miles). A traverse of the **Five Sisters of Kintail** is a classic but seriously challenging hill-walking expedition, taking in three Munro summits; start at the parking area just east of the Glen Shiel battlefield and finish at Morvich (eight to 10 hours).

🛏️ Sleeping & Eating

Ratagan SYHA HOSTEL £

(☎01599-511243; www.syha.org.uk; Ratagan; dm £18.50; ⊙mid-Mar–Oct; P@🛜) This hostel has excellent facilities and a to-die-for spot on the south shore of Loch Duich. Cheap meals are on offer, and there's a licensed bar. A bus runs Monday to Friday from Kyle of

Lochalsh, otherwise it's a 2-mile walk from Shiel Bridge on the main road.

Kintail Lodge Hotel INN, BOTHY ££

(☎01599-511275; www.kintaillodgehotel.co.uk; Shiel Bridge; dm/s/d £16/95/130; P🛜) With most of the fine rooms here facing the loch, you'd be unlucky not to get a decent outlook. Tasty bar meals (£9 to £16), including local venison and seafood, are available for lunch (noon to 2.30pm) and dinner (6pm to 9pm). There are also two bunkhouses with self-catering facilities, each sleeping six; linen is £6 extra.

Glenelg Inn INN ££

(☎01599-522273; www.glenelg-inn.com; Glenelg; mains £11-19; ⊙food 12.30-2.30pm & 6.30-9pm; P🛜🐾) One of the Highlands' most picturesque places for a pint or a romantic away-from-it-all stay (doubles £120), the Glenelg Inn has tables in a lovely garden with cracking views of Skye. The elegant dining room and cosy bar area serves up posh fare, with the local catch always featuring. Service variable.

ℹ️ Getting There & Away

BOAT

At Glenelg, a picturesque community-owned vehicle **ferry** (www.skyeferry.com; foot passenger/bike/car with passengers £3/4/15; ⊙10am-6pm Easter–mid-Oct) runs across to Kylerhea on Skye. This is a highly recommended way of reaching the island; it runs every 20 minutes and doesn't need booking.

BUS

Citylink buses between Fort William/Inverness and Skye travel along the A87. A bus runs Monday to Friday from Kyle of Lochalsh to Arnisdale, via Shiel Bridge, Ratagan and Glenelg. Check www.skyeways.co.uk for new Glenelg services.

ISLE OF SKYE

POP 10,000

The Isle of Skye (an t-Eilean Sgiathanach in Gaelic) takes its name from the old Norse *sky-a*, meaning 'cloud island', a Viking reference to the often-mist-enshrouded Cuillin Hills. It's the second-largest of Scotland's islands, a 50-mile-long patchwork of velvet moors, jagged mountains, sparkling lochs and towering sea cliffs. The stunning scenery is the main attraction, but when the mist closes in there are plenty of castles, crofting museums and cosy pubs and restaurants;

there are also dozens of art galleries and craft studios (ask at Portree tourist office for the free *Gallery & Studio Trails* booklet).

Along with Edinburgh and Loch Ness, Skye is one of Scotland's top-three tourist destinations. However, the hordes tend to stick to Portree, Dunvegan and Trotternish – it's almost always possible to find peace and quiet in the island's further-flung corners. Come prepared for changeable weather: when it's fine it's very fine indeed, but all too often it isn't.

🏃 Activities

Walking

Skye offers some of the finest – and in places, the roughest and most difficult – walking in Scotland. There are many detailed guidebooks available, including a series of four walking guides by Charles Rhodes, available from the Aros Experience (p392) and the tourist office in Portree. You'll need Ordnance Survey (OS) 1:50,000 maps 23 and 32. Don't attempt the longer walks in bad weather or in winter.

Easy, low-level routes include: through **Strath Mor** from Luib (on the Broadford–Sligachan road) and on to Torrin (on the Broadford–Elgol road; allow 1½ hours, 4 miles); from **Sligachan to Kilmarie** via Camasunary (four hours, 11 miles); and from **Elgol to Kilmarie** via Camasunary (2½ hours, 6.5 miles). The walk from **Kilmarie to Coruisk** and back via Camasunary and the 'Bad Step' is superb but slightly harder (11 miles round trip, allow five hours). The **Bad Step** is a rocky slab poised above the sea that you have to scramble across; it's easy in fine, dry weather, but some walkers find it intimidating.

Skye Wilderness Safaris   WALKING
(☑ 01470-552292; www.skye-wilderness-safaris. com; per person £295; ☺ May-Sep) Runs two-day guided hiking trips through the Cuillin Hills or along the Trotternish ridge; meals and luxury camping accommodation included.

Climbing

The Cuillin Hills is a playground for rock climbers, and the two-day traverse of the Cuillin Ridge is the finest mountaineering expedition in the British Isles. There are several mountain guides in the area who can provide instruction and safely introduce inexperienced climbers to the more difficult routes.

Skye Guides   ROCK CLIMBING
(☑ 01471-822116; www.skyeguides.co.uk) A two-day introduction-to-rock-climbing course costs around £380, and a private mountain guide can be hired for £200 a day (both rates are for two clients).

Sea Kayaking

The sheltered coves and sea lochs around the coast of Skye provide water lovers with magnificent sea-kayaking opportunities. The centres listed here can provide kayaking instruction, guiding and equipment hire for both beginners and experts. It costs around £40 to £50 for a half-day kayak hire with instruction.

Whitewave Outdoor Centre   KAYAKING
(☑ 01470-542414; www.white-wave.co.uk; 19 Linicro, Kilmuir; ☺ Mar-Oct) Provides kayaking instruction, guiding and equipment hire for both beginners and experts.

Skyak Adventures   KAYAKING
(☑ 01471-820002; www.skyakadventures.com; 29 Lower Breakish, Breakish) Expeditions and courses to take both beginners and experienced paddlers to otherwise inaccessible places.

☞ Tours

There are several operators who offer guided tours of Skye, covering history, culture and wildlife. Rates are from £150 to £200 for a six-hour tour for up to six people.

Skye Tours   BUS TOURS
(☑ 01471-822716; www.skye tours.co.uk; adult/ child £35/30; ☺ Mon-Sat) Five-hour sightseeing tours of Skye in a minibus, departing from the tourist office car park in Kyle of Lochalsh (close to Kyle of Lochalsh train station).

Skye Light Images   4WD TOURS
(☑ 07909-706802; www.skyejeepsafaris.co.uk; ☺ Oct-Easter) Offers 4WD winter safaris in the wilder areas of Skye with tuition on landscape and wildlife photography.

ℹ️ Information

INTERNET ACCESS

The Portree Tourist Office (p387) has internet access for £1 per 20 minutes.

Columba 1400 Community Centre (Staffin; per hr £1; ☺ 10am-8pm Mon-Sat Apr-Oct; ☏)

Seamus's Bar (Sligachan Hotel; per 15min £1; ☺ 11am-11pm; ☏)

Skye & Outer Hebrides

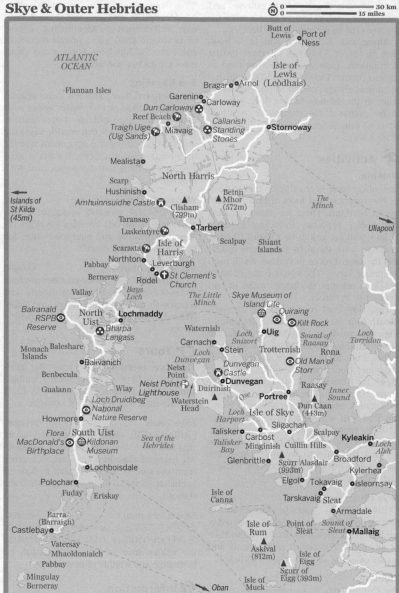

MEDICAL SERVICES

Portree Community Hospital (☏ 01478-613200; Fancyhill) There's a casualty department and dental surgery here.

MONEY

Only Portree and Broadford have banks with ATMs, and Portree's tourist office has a currency exchange desk.

TOURIST INFORMATION

Portree Tourist Office (☎ 01478-612137; Bayfield Rd, Portree; internet per 20min £1; ⊙9am-6pm Mon-Sat & 10am-4pm Sun Jun-Aug, 9am-5pm Mon-Fri & 10am-4pm Sat Apr, May & Sep, shorter hours Oct-Mar) The only tourist office on the island; provides internet access (£1 per 20 minutes) and currency exchange.

ⓘ Getting There & Away

BOAT

Despite the bridge, there are still a couple of ferry links between Skye and the mainland. Ferries also operate from Uig on Skye to the Outer Hebrides.

Mallaig to Armadale (www.calmac.co.uk; per person/car £4.65/23.90) The Mallaig to Armadale ferry (30 minutes, eight daily Monday to Saturday, five to seven on Sunday) is very popular on weekends and in July and August, so book ahead if you're travelling by car.

Glenelg to Kylerhea (www.skyeferry.co.uk; car with up to four passengers £15; ⊙Easter-mid-Oct) Runs a tiny vessel (six cars only) on the short Kylerhea to Glenelg crossing (five minutes, every 20 minutes). The ferry operates from 10am to 6pm daily (till 7pm June to August).

BUS

Glasgow to Portree £41, seven hours, three daily

Glasgow to Uig £41, 7½ hours, two daily; via Crianlarich, Fort William and Kyle of Lochalsh

Inverness to Portree £24, 3¼ hours, three daily

CAR & MOTORCYCLE

The Isle of Skye became permanently tethered to the Scottish mainland when the Skye Bridge opened in 1995. The controversial bridge tolls were abolished in 2004 and the crossing is now free.

There are petrol stations at Broadford (open 24 hours), Armadale, Portree, Dunvegan and Uig.

ⓘ Getting Around

Getting around the island by public transport can be a pain, especially if you want to explore away from the main Kyleakin–Portree–Uig road. Here, as in much of the Highlands, there are fewer buses on Saturday and only a handful of Sunday services.

BUS

Stagecoach (p360) operates the main bus routes on the island, linking all the main villages and towns. Its **Skye Dayrider/Megarider** ticket gives unlimited bus travel for one day/seven days for £8/32. For timetable info, call **Traveline** (☎ 0871 200 22 33).

TAXI

Kyle Taxi Company (☎ 01599-534323; www.skyecarhire.co.uk) You can order a taxi or hire a car from Kyle Taxi Company. Car hire costs from around £40 a day, and you can arrange for the car to be waiting at Kyle of Lochalsh train station.

Kyleakin (Caol Acain)

POP 100

Poor wee Kyleakin had the carpet pulled from under it when the Skye Bridge opened – it went from being the gateway to the island to a backwater bypassed by the main road. It's now a pleasant, peaceful little place, with a harbour used by yachts and fishing boats.

The community-run **Bright Water Visitor Centre** (☎ 01599-530040; www.eileanban.org; The Pier; adult/child £1/free; ⊙10am-4pm Mon-Fri Easter-Sep) serves as a base for tours of **Eilean Ban** – the island used as a stepping stone by the Skye Bridge – where Gavin Maxwell (author of *Ring of Bright Water*) spent the last 18 months of his life in 1968–69, living in the lighthouse keeper's cottage. The island is now a nature reserve and tours (£7 per person) are available in summer (must be booked in advance). The visitor centre also houses a child-friendly exhibition on Maxwell, the lighthouse and the island's wildlife. Tours run twice daily on weekdays, at 11am and 2pm.

There are two hostels and a couple of B&Bs in the village. The friendly **Skye Backpackers** (☎ 01599-534510; www.skyebackpackers.com; dm/tw £18/47; @ ⊚) is our favourite, with even cheaper beds (£13) in caravans out back. For something to eat, **Harry's Coffee Shop** (The Pier; mains £3-6; ⊙10am-8pm May-Sep, shorter hours winter) serves great coffee and cake, breakfast rolls and hot lunches.

About 3 miles southwest of Kyleakin, a minor road leads southwards to **Kylerhea**, where there's a 1½-hour nature trail to a shorefront **otter hide**, where you stand a good chance of seeing these elusive creatures. A little further on is the jetty for the **car ferry to Glenelg** on the mainland.

A shuttle bus runs half-hourly between Kyle of Lochalsh and Kyleakin (£1.20, five minutes), and there are eight to 10 buses daily (except Sunday) to Broadford (£2.40,

15 minutes), and three or four to Portree (£6.20, one hour).

Broadford (An T-Ath Leathann)

POP 750

Broadford is a service centre for the scattered communities of southern Skye. The long, straggling village has a 24-hour petrol station, a large **Co-op supermarket** (⊘ 8am-10pm Mon-Sat, 9am-6pm Sun) with an ATM, a laundrette and a bank.

There are lots of B&Bs in and around Broadford and the village is well placed for exploring southern Skye by car.

🛏 Sleeping & Eating

★ Tigh an Dochais   B&B ££

(📞 01471-820022; www.skyebedbreakfast.co.uk; 13 Harrapool; d £90; 🅿) 🍴 A cleverly designed modern building, Tigh an Dochais is one of Skye's best B&Bs – a little footbridge leads to the front door, which is on the 1st floor. Here you'll find the dining room (gorgeous breakfasts) and lounge offering a stunning view of sea and hills; the bedrooms (downstairs) open onto an outdoor deck with that same wonderful view.

Berabhaigh   B&B ££

(📞 01471-822372; www.isleofskye.net/berabhaigh; 3 Lime Park; r per person £38; ⊘ Mar-Oct; 🅿🛜) This is a lovely old croft house with bay views located just off the main road at the east end of the village, not far from Creelers.

Luib House   B&B ££

(📞 01471-820334; www.luibhouse.co.uk; Luib; r per person £33-35; 🅿🛜) This is a large, comfortable and well-appointed B&B 6 miles north of Broadford.

Broadford Hotel   HOTEL £££

(📞 01471-822204; www.broadfordhotel.co.uk; Torrin Rd; s/d from £120/140; 🅿🛜) The Broadford Hotel is a stylish retreat with luxury fabrics and designer colour schemes. There's a formal restaurant and the more democratic **Gabbro Bar** (mains £7-12; ⊘ food served noon-9pm), where you can enjoy a bar meal of smoked haddock chowder or steak pie washed down with Isle of Skye Brewery ale.

Creelers   SEAFOOD ££

(📞 01471-822281; www.skye-seafood-restaurant.co.uk; Lower Harrapool; mains lunch £10, dinner £14-19; ⊘ noon-9.30pm Mon-Sat Mar-Nov; ♿) 🍴

Broadford has several places to eat but one really stands out: Creelers is a small, bustling, no-frills restaurant that serves some of the best seafood on Skye. The house speciality is a rich, spicy seafood gumbo. Best to book ahead.

Cafe Sia   CAFE, PIZZERIA ££

(📞 01471-822616; www.cafesia.co.uk; mains £6-12; ⊘ 9.30am-9pm Sun-Thu, to 10pm Fri-Sat; 🛜♿) 🍴 Serving everything from eggs Benedict and cappuccino to cocktails and seafood specials, this appealing new cafe specialises in wood-fired pizzas (also available to take away) and artisan coffee (yes, that's a coffee roaster sitting in the corner). There's also an outdoor deck with great views of the Red Cuillin.

Sleat

If you cross over the sea to Skye on the ferry from Mallaig you arrive in Armadale, at the southern end of the long, low-lying peninsula known as Sleat (pronounced 'slate'). The landscape of Sleat itself is not exceptional, but it provides a grandstand for ogling the magnificent scenery on either side – take the steep and twisting minor road that loops through Tarskavaig and Tokavaig for stunning views of the Isle of Rum, the Cuillin Hills and Bla Bheinn.

Armadale

Armadale, where the ferry from Mallaig arrives, is little more than a store, a post office and a couple of houses. There are six or seven buses a day Monday to Saturday (three on Sunday) from Armadale to Broadford (£3.50, 30 minutes) and Portree (£6.80, 1¼ hours).

⦿ Sights & Activities

Museum of the Isles   MUSEUM

(📞 01471-844305; www.clandonald.com; adult/child £8/6.50; ⊘ 9.30am-5.30pm Apr-Oct, occasionally shorter hours Oct; 🅿) Just along the road from Armadale pier is the part-ruined **Armadale Castle**, former seat of Lord MacDonald of Sleat. The neighbouring museum will tell you all you ever wanted to know about Clan Donald, as well as providing an easily digestible history of the Lordship of the Isles. Prize exhibits include rare portraits of clan chiefs, and a wine glass that was once used by Bonnie Prince Charlie. The

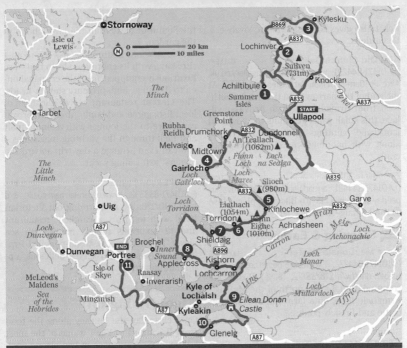

Driving Tour
Wee Roads & Mighty Mountains

START ULLAPOOL
FINISH PORTREE
DISTANCE 320 MILES
DURATION 3–4 DAYS

Starting in Ullapool, this drive takes in some of the lesser-known roads and the most majestic Highland scenery, leaving you on the Isle of Skye in summer, or in Glenelg in winter.

Leave your bags in the hotel, because the first day is a long round trip from Ullapool. Head north on the A835, and left turn to ❶ **Achiltibuie**, where after gaping at impressive lochside Stac Pollaidh en route, you can admire the outlook over the Summer Isles. From here, backtrack 6 miles then turn left up the Wee Mad Road, a narrow, tortuous but scenic drive north to pretty ❷ **Lochinver**. From here, the B869 winds north past spectacular beaches at Achmelvich and Clachtoll to ❸ **Kylesku**, where the hotel makes a great lunch stop. Return south to Ullapool on the main road (A894-A837-A835), with classic northwestern scenery and things to see such as Inchnadamph Caves, Ardvreck Castle and Knockan Crag along the way.

The next day head inland along the A835 before taking the A832 ❹ **Gairloch** turn-off, following the long, circuitous coast road with plenty of options from whale-watching trips to a botanic garden to hill walking around scenic Loch Maree. At ❺ **Kinlochewe** turn back coastwards on the A896, descending a spectacular pass to ❻ **Torridon**, where the rugged beauty is simply breathtaking. There are good overnight stops all along this route.

From ❼ **Shieldaig**, take the coastal road to sublime little ❽ **Applecross**, then brave the Bealach na Ba pass to get you back to the main road. A loop around Loch Carron will eventually bring you to the A87. Turn left, passing ❾ **Eilean Donan Castle** (p383) and, reaching Glen Shiel, take the right turn to ❿ **Glenelg**, a scenic, out-of-the-way place with a wonderfully rustic summer ferry crossing to Skye. Disembark at Kylerhea and enjoy the vistas on one of the island's least-trafficked roads before hitting the A87 again. From here, ⓫ **Portree** is an easy drive, but numerous picturesque detours – to Sleat or Elgol for example – mean you might take a while to reach it yet.

ticket also gives admission to the lovely castle gardens.

Aird Old Church Gallery
GALLERY

(☎ 01471-844291; www.airdoldchurchgallery.co.uk; Aird; ⏰ 10am-5pm Mon-Sat Easter-Sep) FREE At the end of the narrow road that leads southwest from Armadale through Ardvasar village, this small gallery exhibits the powerful landscape paintings of Peter McDermott, along with handmade jewellery and other crafts.

Armadale Bikes
CYCLING

(☎ 01471-844421; armadalebikes.co.uk; Ardvasar; per day adult/child £15/10) Bike hire place close to the Mallaig–Armadale ferry.

🛏 Sleeping & Eating

Flora MacDonald Hostel
HOSTEL £

(☎ 01471-844272; www.skye-hostel.co.uk; The Glebe; dm/tw/q £18/38/72; P🐕) Rustic accommodation 3 miles north of the Mallaig–Armadale ferry, on a farm full of Highland cattle and Eriskay ponies.

Shed
CAFE ££

(☎ 01471-844222; The Pier; mains £7-15; ⏰ 9am-6pm) A cute little wooden shed with some outdoor tables, that serves good seafood salads, pizzas, fish and chips, and coffees – you can sit in or take away.

Isleornsay

This pretty harbour, 8 miles north of Armadale, is opposite Sandaig Bay on the mainland, where Gavin Maxwell lived and wrote his much-loved memoir *Ring of Bright Water*.

◉ Sights

Gallery An Talla Dearg
GALLERY

(www.eileaniarmain.co.uk; ⏰ 10am-6pm Mon-Fri, to 4pm Sat & Sun Apr-Oct) FREE This gallery exhibits the works of artists who were inspired by Scottish landscapes and culture.

🛏 Sleeping & Eating

⭐ Toravaig House Hotel
HOTEL ££

(☎ 01471-820200; www.skyehotel.co.uk; d £99-130; P🐕) This hotel, 3 miles south of Isleornsay, is one of those places where the owners know a thing or two about hospitality – as soon as you arrive you'll feel right at home, whether relaxing on the sofas by the log fire in the lounge or admiring the view across

the Sound of Sleat from the lawn chairs in the garden.

The spacious bedrooms – ask for room 1 (Eriskay), with its enormous sleigh bed – are luxuriously equipped, from the crisp bed linen to the huge, high-pressure shower heads. The elegant restaurant serves the best of local fish, game and lamb. After dinner you can retire to the lounge with a single malt and flick through the yachting magazines – you can even arrange a day trip aboard the owners' 42ft sailing yacht.

Hotel Eilean Iarmain
HOTEL £££

(☎ 01471-833332; www.eilean-iarmain.co.uk; s/d from £110/170; P) A charming old Victorian hotel with log fires, a candlelit restaurant and 12 luxurious rooms, many with sea views. The hotel's cosy, wood-panelled **Praban Bar** (mains £9-16) serves delicious, upmarket pub grub.

Elgol (Ealaghol)

On a clear day, the journey along the road from Broadford to Elgol is one of the most scenic on Skye. It takes in two classic postcard panoramas – the view of Bla Bheinn across **Loch Slapin** (near Torrin), and the superb view of the entire Cuillin range from **Elgol pier**.

Just west of Elgol is the **Spar Cave**, famously visited by Sir Walter Scott in 1814 and mentioned in his poem *Lord of the Isles*. The 80m-deep cave is wild, remote and filled with beautiful flowstone formations. It is a short walk from the village of Glasnakille, but the approach is over seaweed-covered boulders and is only accessible for one hour either side of low water. Check tide times and route information at the tearoom in Elgol.

Bus 55 runs from Broadford to Elgol (£3.20, 45 minutes, three daily Monday to Friday, two Saturday).

👉 Tours

Bella Jane
BOAT TOURS

(☎ 0800 731 3089; www.bellajane.co.uk; ⏰ Apr-Oct) Bella Jane offers a three-hour cruise (adult/child £24/13, three daily) from Elgol harbour to the remote **Loch na Cuilce**, an impressive inlet surrounded by soaring peaks. On a calm day, you can clamber ashore here to make the short walk to Loch Coruisk in the heart of the Cuillin Hills. You get 1½ hours ashore and visit a seal colony en route.

Aquaxplore　　　　　　　　BOAT TOURS
(☎ 0800 731 3089; www.aquaxplore.co.uk; ☺ Apr-Oct) Runs 1½-hour high-speed boat trips from Elgol to an abandoned shark-hunting station on the island of Soay (adult/child £28/20), once owned by *Ring of Bright Water* author Gavin Maxwell. There are longer trips (adult/child £54/44, four hours) to Rum, Canna and Sanday to visit breeding colonies of puffins, with the chance of seeing minke whales on the way.

Misty Isle　　　　　　　　　BOAT TOURS
(☎ 01471-866288; www.mistyisleboattrips.co.uk; adult/child £20/10; ☺ Apr-Oct) The pretty, traditional wooden launch *Misty Isle* offers cruises to Loch Coruisk with 1½ hours ashore (no Sunday service).

Cuillin Hills

The Cuillin Hills are Britain's most spectacular mountain range (the name comes from the Old Norse *kjöllen*, meaning 'keel-shaped'). Though small in stature (Sgurr Alasdair, the highest summit, is only 993m), the peaks are near-alpine in character, with knife-edge ridges, jagged pinnacles, scree-filled gullies and hectares of naked rock. While they are a paradise for experienced mountaineers, the higher reaches of the Cuillin are off limits to the majority of walkers.

The good news is that there are also plenty of good low-level hikes within the ability of most walkers. One of the best (on a fine day) is the steep climb from Glenbrittle campsite to Coire Lagan (6 miles round trip; allow at least three hours). The impressive upper corrie contains a lochan for bathing (for the hardy!), and the surrounding cliffs are a playground for rock climbers – bring your binoculars.

Even more spectacular, but much harder to reach on foot, is Loch Coruisk (from the Gaelic Coir'Uisg, the Water Corrie), a remote loch ringed by the highest peaks of the Cuillin. Accessible by boat trip (p390) from Elgol, or via an arduous 5.5-mile hike from Kilmarie, Coruisk was popularised by Sir Walter Scott in his 1815 poem *Lord of the Isles*. Crowds of Victorian tourists and landscape artists followed in Scott's footsteps, including JMW Turner, whose watercolours were used to illustrate Scott's works.

There are two main bases for exploring the Cuillin – Sligachan to the north (on the Kyle of Lochalsh–Portree bus route), and Glenbrittle to the south (no public transport).

🛏 Sleeping & Eating

Sligachan Bunkhouse　　　　　　HOSTEL £
(☎ 01478-650458; www.sligachanselfcatering.co.uk; Sligachan; dm £18; 🅿) Comfortable and modern bunkhouse opposite the Sligachan Hotel. Bed linen £4 extra.

Sligachan Campsite　　　　　　CAMPSITE £
(Sligachan; sites per person £6; ☺ Apr-Oct) Across the road from the Sligachan Hotel is this basic campsite; be warned – this spot is a midge magnet. No bookings.

Glenbrittle SYHA　　　　　　　HOSTEL £
(☎ 01478-640278; Glenbrittle; dm £18.50; ☺ Apr-Sep) Scandinavian-style timber hostel that quickly fills up with climbers on holiday weekends.

Glenbrittle Campsite　　　　　CAMPSITE £
(☎ 01478-640404; Glenbrittle; sites per adult/child incl car £8/5; ☺ Apr-Sep) Excellent site, close to mountains and sea, with a shop selling food and outdoor kit; the midges can be diabolical, though.

Sligachan Hotel　　　　　　　HOTEL £££
(☎ 01478-650204; www.sligachan.co.uk; Sligachan; per person £68-78; 🅿 @ 🛜) The Slig, as it has been known to generations of climbers, is a near village in itself, encompassing a comfortable hotel, a microbrewery, self-catering cottages, a small mountaineering museum, a big barn of a pub – Seamus's Bar – and an adventure playground.

Seamus's Bar　　　　　　　　PUB £
(Sligachan Hotel; mains £8-13; ☺ food served 11am-9.30pm; 🛜 ♿) This place dishes up decent bar meals, including haggis, neeps and tatties, and fish and chips, and serves real ales from its own microbrewery. It also has a range of 200 malt whiskies in serried ranks above the bar.

Minginish

Loch Harport, to the north of the Cuillin, divides the Minginish Peninsula from the rest of Skye. On its southern shore lies the village of Carbost, home to Talisker malt whisky, produced at Talisker Distillery. Magnificent Talisker Bay, 5 miles west of

Carbost, is framed by a sea stack and a waterfall.

◉ Sights

Talisker Distillery   DISTILLERY
(☎01478-614308; www.discovering-distilleries.com; guided tour £7; ⊙9.30am-5pm Mon-Sat Apr-Oct, 11am-5pm Sun Jul & Aug, 10am-4.30pm Mon-Fri Nov-Mar) Skye's only distillery produces smooth, sweet and smoky Talisker single-malt whisky; the guided tour includes a free dram.

🛏 Sleeping & Eating

Skyewalker Independent Hostel   HOSTEL £
(☎01478-640250; www.skyewalkerhostel.com; Fiskavaig Rd, Portnalong; dm £17; P) Three miles northwest of Carbost, this excellent hostel is housed in the old village school, with cosy lounge, well-equipped kitchen, and superb gardens with glass-domed outdoor seating area. No wi-fi or mobile phone signal.

Old Inn   B&B, HOSTEL ££
(☎01478-640205; www.theoldinnskye.co.uk; Carbost; s/d £48/76; P) The Old Inn is an atmospheric wee pub, offering accommodation in bright B&B bedrooms and an appealing chalet-style bunkhouse (from £17 per person). The bar is a favourite with walkers and climbers from Glenbrittle, and serves excellent pub grub (£10 to £16, noon to 10pm), from fresh oysters to haddock and chips. There's an outdoor patio at the back with great views over Loch Harport.

Oyster Shed   SEAFOOD £
(www.skyeoysterman.co.uk; Carbost; mains £4-8; ⊙11am-6pm Mon-Fri, noon-6pm Sat Apr-Oct, shorter hours winter) 🍴 A farm shop selling fresh local seafood to take away, including oysters, cooked mussels and scallops, and seafood platters.

ℹ Getting There & Away

There's one bus a day (school days only) from Portree to Carbost (£3.70, 40 minutes) via Sligachan.

Portree (Port Righ)

POP 2320

Portree is Skye's largest and liveliest town. It has a pretty harbour lined with brightly painted houses, and there are great views of the surrounding hills. Its name (from the Gaelic for King's Harbour) commemorates James V, who came here in 1540 to pacify the local clans.

◉ Sights & Activities

Aros Centre   INTERPRETATION CENTRE
(☎01478-613649; www.aros.co.uk; Viewfield Rd, Portree; sea-eagle exhibition £4.75; ⊙9am-5.30pm; P♿) On the southern edge of Portree, the Aros Centre is a combined visitor centre, book and gift shop, restaurant, theatre and cinema. The visitor centre (Easter to October) offers a look at fascinating, live CCTV images from local sea-eagle nests, and a wide-screen video of Skye's impressive scenery (it's worth waiting for the aerial shots of the Cuillin).

The centre is a useful rainy-day retreat, with an indoor, soft play area for children.

MV Stardust   BOAT TOURS
(☎07798 743858; www.skyeboat-trips.co.uk; Portree Harbour; adult/child £18/9) MV *Stardust* offers one- to two-hour boat trips to the Sound of Raasay, with the chance to see seals, porpoises and – if you're lucky – white-tailed sea eagles. On Saturday there are longer cruises to the Isle of Rona (£30 per person). You can also arrange to be dropped off for a hike on the Isle of Raasay and picked up again later.

✯ Festivals & Events

Isle of Skye Highland Games   HIGHLAND GAMES
(www.skye-highland-games.co.uk) These annual games are held in Portree in early August.

🛏 Sleeping

Portree is well supplied with B&Bs, but accommodation fills up fast in July and August, so be sure to book ahead.

Bayfield Backpackers   HOSTEL £
(☎01478-612231; www.skyehostel.co.uk; Bayfield; dm £18; P@🛜) Clean, central and modern, this hostel provides the best backpacker accommodation in town. The owner really makes you feel welcome, and is a fount of advice on what to do and where to go in Skye.

Torvaig Campsite   CAMPSITE £
(☎01478-612209; www.portreecampsite.co.uk; Torvaig; per adult/child £7/3; ⊙Apr-Oct; 🛜) An attractive, family-run campsite located 1.5 miles north of Portree, on the road to Staffin.

Ben Tianavaig B&B   B&B ££
(☎01478-612152; www.ben-tianavaig.co.uk; 5 Bosville Tce; r £75-88; P🛜) 🍴 A warm welcome

awaits from the Irish-Welsh couple who run this appealing B&B bang in the centre of town. All four bedrooms have a view across the harbour to the hill that gives the house its name and breakfasts include free-range eggs and vegetables grown in the garden. Two-night minimum stay April to October; no credit cards.

Woodlands
B&B **££**
(☎ 01478-612980; www.woodlands-portree.co.uk; Viewfield Rd; r £70; ☺ Mar-Oct; 🅿 🤖) A great location, with views across the bay, and unstinting hospitality make this modern B&B, a half-mile south of the town centre, a good choice.

Rosedale Hotel
HOTEL **££**
(☎ 01478-613131; www.rosedalehotelskye.co.uk; Beaumont Cres; s/d from £60/90; ☺ Easter-Oct; 🤖) The Rosedale is a cosy, old-fashioned hotel – you'll be welcomed with a glass of whisky or sherry when you check in – delightfully situated down by the waterfront. Its three converted fishermen's cottages are linked by a maze of narrow stairs and corridors, and the restaurant has a view of the harbour.

Peinmore House
B&B **£££**
(☎ 01478-612574; www.peinmorehouse.co.uk; r £135-145; 🅿 🤖) Signposted off the main road about 2 miles south of Portree, this former manse has been cleverly converted into a guest house that is more stylish and luxurious than most hotels. The bedrooms and bathrooms are huge (one bathroom has an armchair in it!), as is the choice of breakfast (kippers and smoked haddock on the menu), and there are panoramic views to the Old Man of Storr.

Cuillin Hills Hotel
HOTEL **£££**
(☎ 01478-612003; www.cuillinhills-hotel-skye.co.uk; Scorrybreac Rd; r £210-310; 🅿 🤖) Located on the eastern fringes of Portree, this luxury hotel enjoys a superb outlook across the harbour towards the Cuillin mountains. The more expensive rooms cosset guests with four-poster beds and panoramic views, but everyone can enjoy the scenery from the glass-fronted restaurant and well-stocked whisky bar.

✖ Eating & Drinking

Café Arriba
CAFE **£**
(☎ 01478-611830; www.cafearriba.co.uk; Quay Brae; mains £5-10; ☺ 7am-6pm daily May-Sep, 8am-5pm Thu-Sat Oct-Apr; 🖋) 🍴 Arriba is a funky little cafe, brightly decked out in primary colours and offering delicious flatbread melts (bacon, leek and cheese is our favourite) as well as the best choice of vegetarian grub on the island, ranging from a veggie breakfast fry-up to falafel wraps with hummus and chilli sauce. Also serves excellent coffee.

★ Harbour View Seafood Restaurant
SEAFOOD **££**
(☎ 01478-612069; www.harbourviewskye.co.uk; 7 Bosville Tce; mains £14-19; ☺ noon-3pm & 5.30-11pm Tue-Sun) 🍴 The Harbour View is Portree's most congenial place to eat. It has a homely dining room with a log fire in winter, books on the mantelpiece and bric-a-brac on the shelves. And on the table, superb Scottish seafood such as fresh Skye oysters, seafood chowder, king scallops, langoustines and lobster.

Sea Breezes
SEAFOOD **££**
(☎ 01478-612016; www.seabreezes-skye.co.uk; 2 Marine Buildings, Quay St; mains £12-20; ☺ noon-2pm & 5-9.30pm Apr-Oct) 🍴 Sea Breezes is an informal, no-frills restaurant specialising in local fish and shellfish fresh from the boat – try the impressive seafood platter, a small mountain of langoustines, crab, oysters and lobster (£48 for two). Book early, as it's often hard to get a table.

L'Incontro
CAFE
(The Green; ☺ 4-11pm Tue-Sun May-Sep) This adjunct to a popular pizza restaurant (upstairs beside the Royal Hotel) serves excellent Italian espresso, and also has an extensive range of Italian wines.

Isles Inn
PUB
(☎ 01478-612129; Somerled Sq; ☺ 11am-11pm Mon-Thu, 11am-midnight Fri-Sat, 12.30-11pm Sun; 🦿) Portree's pubs are nothing special, but the Isles Inn is more atmospheric than most. The Jacobean bar, with its flagstone floor and open fires, pulls in a lively mix of young locals, backpackers and tourists.

ℹ Getting There & Around

BICYCLE
Island Cycles (☎ 01478-613121; www.island-cycles-skye.co.uk; The Green; ☺ 9am-5pm Mon-Sat) You can hire bikes here for £8.50/15 per half-/full day.

BUS
The main bus stop is in Somerled Sq. There are six Scottish Citylink buses every day from Kyle

of Lochalsh to Portree (£6.50, one hour) continuing to Uig.

Local buses (mostly six to eight Monday to Saturday, three on Sunday) run from Portree to:

Armadale (£6.80, 1¼ hours) Connecting with the ferry to Mallaig

Broadford (£5.20, 40 minutes)

Dunvegan Castle (£4.65, 40 minutes, one daily)

There are also three buses a day on a circular route around Trotternish (in both directions), taking in Flodigarry (£4.65, 45 minutes), Kilmuir (£4.65, 45 minutes) and Uig (£3.50, 30 minutes).

Dunvegan (Dun Bheagain)

Skye's most famous historic building, and one of its most popular tourist attractions, is **Dunvegan Castle** (☑ 01470-521206; www.dunvegancastle.com; adult/child £10/7; ⊙ 10am-5.30pm Apr–mid-Oct; ℗), seat of the chief of Clan MacLeod. It has played host to Samuel Johnson, Sir Walter Scott and, most famously, Flora MacDonald. The oldest parts are the 14th-century keep and dungeon but most of it dates from the 17th to 19th centuries.

In addition to the usual castle stuff – swords, silver and family portraits – there are some interesting artefacts, most famous being the Fairy Flag, a diaphanous silk banner that dates from some time between the 4th and 7th centuries. Bonnie Prince Charlie's waistcoat and a lock of his hair, donated by Flora MacDonald's granddaughter, share a room with Rory Mor's Drinking Horn, a beautiful 16th-century vessel of Celtic design that could hold 2.2L of claret. Upholding the family tradition, in 1956, John MacLeod – the 29th chief, who died in 2007 – downed the contents in one minute and 57 seconds 'without setting down or falling down'.

From the end of the minor road beyond Dunvegan Castle entrance, an easy 1-mile walk leads to the **Coral Beaches** – a pair of blindingly white beaches composed of the bleached exoskeletons of coralline algae known as *maerl*.

On the way to Dunvegan from Portree you'll pass **Edinbane Pottery** (☑ 01470-582234; www.edinbane-pottery.co.uk; ⊙ 9am-6pm daily Easter-Oct, Mon-Fri Nov-Easter), one of the island's original craft workshops, established in 1971, where you can watch potters at work creating beautiful and colourful stoneware.

Duirinish & Waternish

The Duirinish peninsula to the west of Dunvegan, and Waternish to the north, boast some of Skye's most atmospheric hotels and restaurants, plus an eclectic range of artists' studios and crafts workshops.

◉ Sights & Activities

The sparsely populated Duirinish peninsula is dominated by the distinctive flat-topped peaks of Helabhal Mhor (469m) and Helabhal Bheag (488m), known locally as **MacLeod's Tables**. There are some fine walks from Orbost, including the summit of Helabhal Bheag (allow 3½ hours return) and the 5-mile trail from Orbost to **MacLeod's Maidens**, a series of pointed sea stacks at the southern tip of the peninsula.

It's worth making the long drive beyond Dunvegan to the west side of the Duirinish Peninsula to see the spectacular sea cliffs of **Waterstein Head**, and to walk down to **Neist Point lighthouse** with its views to the Outer Hebrides.

🛏 Sleeping & Eating

★ **Red Roof Café** CAFE £
(☑ 01470-511766; www.redroofskye.co.uk; Glendale; mains £6-9; ⊙ 11am-5pm Sun-Fri Apr-Oct; ℗ 🍴) 🍂 Tucked away up a glen, a mile off the main road, this restored 250-year-old byre is a wee haven of home-grown grub. As well as great coffee and cake, there are lunch platters (noon to 3pm) of Skye seafood, game or cheese served with salad leaves and edible flowers grown just along the road.

Stein Inn PUB ££
(☑ 01470-592362; www.steininn.co.uk; Stein; mains £8-18; ⊙ food noon-4pm & 6-9.30pm Mon-Sat, 12.30-4pm & 6.30-9pm Sun Easter-Oct; ℗) This old country inn dates from 1790 and has a handful of bedrooms (per person £37 to £55), all with sea views, a lively little bar and a delightful beer garden beside the loch – a real suntrap on warm summer afternoons. The bar serves real ales from the Isle of Skye Brewery and excellent bar meals. Food is served in winter too, but call ahead to check.

Lochbay Seafood Restaurant SEAFOOD ££
(☑ 01470-592235; www.lochbay-seafood-restaurant.co.uk; Stein; 3-course dinner £33, lobster £11 extra; ⊙ 6.30-9pm Wed-Sat Easter–mid-Oct; ℗) This is one of Skye's most romantic restau-

rants, a cosy farmhouse kitchen of a place with terracotta tiles and a wood-burning stove, and a menu that includes most things that either swim in the sea or live in a shell. Best to book ahead.

★ **Three Chimneys** MODERN SCOTTISH £££
(☑ 01470-511258; www.threechimneys.co.uk; Colbost; 3-course lunch/dinner £37/60; ⊙ 12.15-1.45pm Mon-Sat mid-Mar–Oct, plus Sun Easter-Sep, 6.15-9pm daily year-round; P) ◢ Halfway between Dunvegan and Waterstein, the Three Chimneys is a superb romantic retreat combining a gourmet restaurant in a candlelit crofter's cottage with sumptuous five-star rooms (double £345) in the modern house next door. Book well in advance, and note that children are not welcome in the restaurant in the evenings.

🔒 Shopping

Dandelion Designs ARTS & CRAFTS
(www.dandelion-designs.co.uk; Captain's House, Stein; ⊙ 11am-5pm Easter-Oct, shorter hours Nov-Mar; 🐾) At Stein on the Waternish Peninsula, Dandelion Designs is an interesting little gallery with a good range of colour and monochrome landscape photography, lino prints by Liz Myhill and a range of handmade arts and crafts.

Shilasdair Yarns KNITWEAR
(www.theskyeshilasdairshop.co.uk; Carnach; ⊙ 10am-6pm Apr-Oct) The couple who run this place, a few miles north of Stein, moved to Skye in 1971 and now raise sheep, hand-spin woollen yarn, and hand-dye a range of wools and silks using natural dyes. You can see the dyeing process and try hand-spinning in the exhibition area behind the studio, which sells finished knitwear as well as yarns.

Trotternish

The Trotternish Peninsula to the north of Portree has some of Skye's most beautiful – and bizarre – scenery. A loop road allows a circular driving tour of the peninsula from Portree, passing through the village of Uig, where the ferry to the Outer Hebrides departs. The following sights are described travelling anticlockwise from Portree.

◉ Sights & Activties

Old Man of Storr ROCK FORMATION
The 50m-high, pot-bellied pinnacle of crumbling basalt known as the Old Man of Storr

is prominent above the road 6 miles north of Portree. Walk up to its foot from the car park in the woods at the northern end of Loch Leathan (round trip 2 miles). This seemingly unclimbable pinnacle was first scaled in 1955 by English mountaineer Don Whillans, a feat that has been repeated only a handful of times since.

Quiraing ROCK FORMATION
Staffin Bay is dominated by the dramatic basalt escarpment of the Quiraing: its impressive land-slipped cliffs and pinnacles constitute one of Skye's most remarkable landscapes. From a parking area at the highest point of the minor road between Staffin and Uig you can walk north to the Quiraing in half an hour.

Duntulm Castle CASTLE
Near the tip of the Trotternish Peninsula is the ruined MacDonald fortress of Duntulm Castle, which was abandoned in 1739, reputedly because it was haunted. From the red telephone box 800m east of the castle, a faint path leads north for 1.5 miles to **Rubha Hunish coastguard lookout**, now restored as a tiny but cosy bothy overlooking the northernmost point of Skye.

Skye Museum of Island Life MUSEUM
(☑ 01470-552206; www.skyemuseum.co.uk; adult/child £2.50/50p; ⊙ 9.30am-5pm Mon-Sat Easter-Oct; P) The peat-reek of crofting life in the 18th and 19th centuries is preserved in the thatched cottages, croft houses, barns and farm implements of the Skye Museum of Island Life. Behind the museum is Kilmuir Cemetery, where a tall Celtic cross marks the grave of Flora MacDonald; the cross was erected in 1955 to replace the original monument, of which 'every fragment was removed by tourists'.

Fairy Glen NATURAL FORMATION
Just south of Uig, a minor road (signposted 'Sheader and Balnaknock') leads in a mile or so to the Fairy Glen, a strange and enchanting natural landscape of miniature conical hills, rocky towers, ruined cottages and a tiny roadside lochan.

🍴 Sleeping & Eating

Dun Flodigarry Hostel HOSTEL £
(☑ 01470-552212; www.hostelflodigarry.co.uk; Flodigarry; dm/tw £18/40, tent sites per person £9; P @ 🛜) A bright and welcoming hostel that enjoys a stunning location above the sea, with views across Raasay to the mainland

mountains. A nearby hiking trail leads to the Quiraing (2.5 miles away), and there's a hotel bar barely 100m from the door. You can also camp nearby and use all the hostel facilities.

Uig SYHA HOSTEL £

(☎01470-542746; Uig; dm £18.50; ⊙Mar-Sep; P@) Sociable hostel with fantastic sunset views over Uig Bay. You have to vacate the place between 10.30am and 5pm, even when it's raining!

Flodigarry Hotel HOTEL £££

(☎01470-552203; www.hotelintheskye.co.uk; Flodigarry; r £130-250; P) From 1751 to 1759 Flora MacDonald lived in a cottage which is now part of this atmospheric hotel. You can stay in the cottage itself (there are four bedrooms here), or in the more spacious rooms in the main hotel; nonresidents are welcome at the stylish bar and restaurant, with great views over the sea.

Isle of Raasay

POP 160

Raasay (www.raasay.com) is the rugged, 10-mile-long island that lies off Skye's east coast. The island's fascinating history is recounted in the book *Calum's Road* by Roger Hutchinson.

There are several good walks here, including one to the flat-topped conical hill of **Dun Caan** (443m), and another to the extraordinary ruin of **Brochel Castle**, perched on a pinnacle at the northern end of Raasay. The Forestry Commission publishes a free leaflet (available in the ferry waiting room) with suggested walking trails.

Set in a rustic cottage high on the hill overlooking Skye, **Raasay SYHA** (☎01478-660240; Creachan Cottage; dm £17.50; ⊙May-Aug) is a 1.5-mile walk from the ferry pier and makes a good base for exploring the island. Beautifully renovated **Raasay House** (☎01478-660266; www.raasay-house.co.uk; dm £25, s/d £105/125; P) provides outdoor-activity courses, and accommodation ranging from hostel bunks to luxury B&B. It also has the island's only bar and restaurant (mains £12 to £20), serving quality pub grub and locally brewed beers.

A **CalMac ferry** (www.calmac.co.uk; return passenger/car £6.45/24.80) runs from Sconser, on the road from Portree to Broadford, to Raasay (25 minutes, nine daily Monday to Saturday, twice daily Sunday). There are no petrol stations on the island.

OUTER HEBRIDES

POP 27,670

The Western Isles, or Na h-Eileanan an Iar in Gaelic – also known as the Outer Hebrides – are a 130-mile-long string of islands lying off the northwest coast of Scotland. There are 119 islands in total, of which the five main inhabited islands are Lewis and Harris (two parts of a single island, although often described as if they are separate islands), North Uist, Benbecula, South Uist and Barra. The middle three (often referred to simply as 'the Uists') are connected by road-bearing causeways.

The ferry crossing from Ullapool or Uig to the Western Isles marks an important cultural divide – more than a third of Scotland's registered crofts are in the Outer Hebrides, and no less than 60% of the population are Gaelic speakers. The rigours of life in the old island blackhouses are still within living memory.

Religion still plays a prominent part in public and private life, especially in the Protestant north, where shops and pubs close their doors on Sundays and some accommodation providers prefer guests not to arrive or depart on the Sabbath. The Roman Catholic south is a little more relaxed about these things.

If your time is limited, head straight for the west coast of Lewis with its prehistoric sites, preserved blackhouses and beautiful beaches. As with Skye, the islands are dotted with arts and crafts studios – the tourist offices can provide a list.

ℹ Information

INTERNET RESOURCES

CalMac (www.calmac.co.uk) Ferry timetables.

Visit Hebrides (www.visithebrides.com)

MEDICAL SERVICES

Uist & Barra Hospital (☎01870-603603; Balivanich, Benbecula)

Western Isles Hospital (☎01851-704704; MacAulay Rd, Stornoway, Lewis)

MONEY

There are banks with ATMs in Stornoway (Lewis), Tarbert (Harris), Lochmaddy (North Uist), Balivanich (Benbecula), Lochboisdale (South Uist) and Castlebay (Barra). Elsewhere, some hotels and shops offer cash-back facilities.

TOURIST INFORMATION

Castlebay Tourist Office (☎01871-810336; Main St, Castlebay; ⏱9am-1pm & 2-5pm Mon-Sat & noon-4pm Sun Apr-Oct)

Lochboisdale Tourist Office (☎01878-700286; Pier Rd, Lochboisdale, South Uist; ⏱9am-5pm Mon-Sat Apr-Oct)

Stornoway Tourist Office (☎01851-703088; www.visithebrides.com; 26 Cromwell St, Stornoway; ⏱9am-6pm Mon-Sat year-round)

Tarbert Tourist Office (☎01859-502011; Pier Rd, Tarbert; ⏱9am-5pm Mon-Sat Apr-Oct)

❶ Getting There & Away

AIR

There are airports at Stornoway (Lewis), Benbecula and Barra. Flights operate to Stornoway from Edinburgh, Inverness, Glasgow and Aberdeen. There are also two flights a day (Tuesday to Thursday only) between Stornoway and Benbecula.

There are daily flights from Glasgow to Barra, from Tuesday to Thursday only to Benbecula. At Barra, the planes land on the hard-sand beach at low tide, so the timetable depends on the tides.

Eastern Airways (☎0870 366 9100; www. easternairways.com)

FlyBe/Loganair (☎01857-873457; www. loganair.co.uk)

BOAT

There are two or three ferries a day to Stornoway, one or two a day to Tarbert and Lochmaddy, and one a day to Castlebay and Lochboisdale. You can also take the ferry from Lochboisdale to Castlebay (car/passenger £22.90/7.95, 1½ hours, one daily Monday, Tuesday and Thursday) and from Castlebay to Lochboisdale (one daily Wednesday, Friday and Sunday).

Standard one-way fares on CalMac (p403) ferries:

CROSSING	DURATION (HOURS)	CAR	DRIVER/ PASSENGER
Ullapool–Stornoway	2¾	£48	£9.15
Uig–Lochmaddy	1¾	£29	£6
Uig–Tarbert	1½	£29	£6
Oban–Castlebay	4¾	£65	£14.25
Oban–Lochboisdale	6¾	£65	£14.25

Advance booking for cars is recommended (essential in July and August); foot and bicycle passengers should have no problems. Bicycles are carried free.

❶ Getting Around

Despite their separate names, Lewis and Harris are actually one island. Berneray, North Uist, Benbecula, South Uist and Eriskay are all linked by road bridges and causeways. There are car ferries between Leverburgh (Harris) and Berneray; Tarbert (Harris) and Lochmaddy (North Uist); Eriskay and Castlebay (Barra); and Lochboisdale (South Uist) and Castlebay (Barra).

The local council publishes timetables of all bus and ferry services within the Outer Hebrides, available at tourist offices. Or look online at www.cne-siar.gov.uk/travel.

BICYCLE

Bikes can be hired for around £10 to £15 a day or £60 to £80 a week in Stornoway (Lewis), Uig (Lewis), Leverburgh (Harris), Howmore (South Uist) and Castlebay (Barra).

Harris Outdoor Adventure (☎07788 425157; www.harrisoutdoor.co.uk; Pier Rd, Leverburgh) Can deliver bikes to your accommodation.

Rothan Cycles (☎07740 364093; www. rothan.com; Howmore, South Uist) Offers a delivery and pick-up service at various points between Eriskay and Stornoway.

BUS

The bus network covers almost every village in the islands, with around four to six buses a day on all the main routes; however, there are no buses at all on Sunday. You can pick up timetables from tourist offices, or call **Stornoway bus station** (☎01851-704327) for information.

CAR & MOTORCYCLE

Apart from the fast, two-lane road between Tarbert and Stornoway, most roads are single track. The main hazard is posed by sheep wandering about or sleeping on the road. Petrol stations are far apart (almost all of those on Lewis and Harris are closed on Sunday), and fuel is about 10% more expensive than on the mainland.

There are petrol stations at Stornoway, Barvas, Borve, Uig, Breacleit (Great Bernera), Ness, Tarbert and Leverburgh on Lewis and Harris; Lochmaddy and Cladach on North Uist; Balivanich on Benbecula; Howmore, Lochboisdale and Daliburgh on South Uist; and Castlebay on Barra.

Cars can be hired from around £35 per day.

Arnol Motors (☎018510-710548; www. arnolmotors.com; Arnol, Lewis; ⏱8am-5pm Mon-Sat)

Lewis Car Rentals (☎01851-703760; www. lewis-car-rental.co.uk; 52 Bayhead St, Stornoway; ⏱8am-5pm Mon-Sat)

Lewis (Leodhais)

POP 21,000 (INCLUDING HARRIS)

The northern part of Lewis is dominated by the expanse of the Black Moor, a vast, undulating peat bog dimpled with glittering lochans, seen clearly from the Stornoway–Barvas road. But Lewis' finest scenery is on the west coast, from Barvas southwest to Mealista, where the rugged landscape of hill, loch and sandy strand is reminiscent of the northwestern Highlands. The Outer Hebrides' most evocative historic sites – Callanish Standing Stones, Dun Carloway and Arnol Blackhouse Museum – are also here.

Stornoway (Stornabhagh)

POP 5715

Stornoway is the bustling 'capital' of the Outer Hebrides. The only real town in the whole archipelago, it's a surprisingly busy little place. Though set on a beautiful natural harbour, the town isn't going to win any prizes for beauty or atmosphere, but it's a pleasant introduction to this remote corner.

◎ Sights

Lews Castle   CASTLE
The Baronial mansion across the harbour from Stornoway town centre was built in the 1840s for the Matheson family, then owners of Lewis; it was gifted to the community by Lord Leverhulme in 1923. A major redevelopment sees the new **Museum nan Eilean** (Museum of the Isles) opening here from summer 2015, covering the history of the Outer Hebrides and exploring traditional island life. The beautiful wooded grounds are open to the public and host the Hebridean Celtic Festival in July.

An Lanntair Arts Centre   ARTS CENTRE
(☑ 01851-703307; www.lanntair.com; Kenneth St; ⊙10am-9pm Mon-Wed, to 10pm Thu, to midnight Fri & Sat) FREE The modern, purpose-built An Lanntair (Gaelic for 'lighthouse'), complete with art gallery, theatre, cinema and restaurant, is the centre of the town's cultural life; it hosts changing exhibitions of contemporary art and is a good source of information on cultural events.

Lewis Loom Centre   MUSEUM
(☑ 01851-704500; 3 Bayhead; adult/child £1/50p; ⊙9.30am-5.30pm Mon-Sat) This appealingly ramshackle exhibition records the history of Harris Tweed; the 40-minute guided tour

(£2.50 extra) includes wool-spinning and weaving demonstrations.

✹ Festivals & Events

Hebridean Celtic Festival   MUSIC
(www.hebceltfest.com) A four-day extravaganza of folk/rock/Celtic music held in the second half of July.

⌂ Sleeping

Heb Hostel   HOSTEL £
(☑ 01851-709889; www.hebhostel.co.uk; 25 Kenneth St; dm £18; @ 🕿) The Heb is a friendly, easygoing hostel close to the ferry, with comfy wooden bunks, a convivial living room with peat fire and a welcoming owner who can provide all kinds of advice on what to do and where to go.

Laxdale Holiday Park   CAMPSITE £
(☑ 01851-703234; www.laxdaleholidaypark.com; 6 Laxdale Lane; tent sites £8-10, plus per person £3.50; ⊙Mar-Oct; 🕿) This campsite, 1.5 miles north of town off the A857, has a sheltered woodland setting, though the tent area is mostly on a slope – get there early for a level pitch. There are also wooden camping pods (per night £32 to £40), and a bunkhouse (£17 per person) that stays open year-round.

Hal o' the Wynd   B&B ££
(☑ 01851-706073; www.halothewynd.com; 2 Newton St; s/d from £60/80; 🕿) Touches of tartan and Harris Tweed lend a tradtional air to this welcoming B&B, conveniently located directly opposite the ferry pier. Most rooms have views over the harbour to Lews Castle. There's also a cafe on the premises.

Park Guest House   B&B ££
(☑ 01851-702485; www.theparkguesthouse.co.uk; 30 James St; s/d from £58/110; @ 🕿) A charming Victorian villa with a conservatory and eight luxurious rooms (mostly en suite), the Park Guest House is comfortable and central and has the advantage of an excellent **restaurant** specialising in Scottish seafood, beef and game plus one or two vegetarian dishes (3-course dinner £30). Rooms overlooking the main road can be noisy on weekday mornings.

Royal Hotel   HOTEL ££
(☑ 01851-702109; www.royalstornoway.co.uk; Cromwell St; s/d from £79/99; P 🕿) The 19th-century Royal is the most appealing of Stornoway's hotels – the rooms at the front retain period features such as wood panelling, and enjoy a view across the harbour

to Lews Castle. Ask to see your room first, though, as some are a bit cramped.

Braighe House B&B £££
(☎ 01851-705287; www.braighehouse.co.uk; 20 Braighe Rd; s/d from £115/130; ℗) This spacious and luxurious guesthouse, 3 miles east of the town centre on the A866, has stylish, modern bedrooms and a great seafront location. Good bathrooms with powerful showers, hearty brakfasts and genuinely hospitable owners round off the perfect package.

✕ Eating

Thai Café THAI £
(☎ 01851-701811; www.thai-cafe-stornoway.co.uk; 27 Church St; mains £5-10; ⊙ noon-2.30pm & 5.30-11pm Mon-Sat; ☎) Here's a surprise – authentic, inexpensive Thai food in the heart of Stornoway. This spick-and-span, no-frills restaurant has a genuine Thai chef and serves some of the most delicious, best-value Asian food in the Hebrides. If you can't get a table, it does takeaway.

An Lanntair Arts Centre BISTRO ££
(Kenneth St; mains lunch £6-12, dinner £13-19; ⊙ cafe 10am-late, restaurant noon-2.30pm Mon-Sat, 5-8.30pm Thu-Sat; ☎ ✎ 🕮) The stylish and family-friendly cafe and restaurant at the arts centre serves a broad range of freshly prepared dishes, from tasty bacon rolls at breakfast to burgers, salads or fish and chips for lunch, and char-grilled steaks or local scallops for dinner.

★ Digby Chick BISTRO £££
(☎ 01851-700026; www.digbychick.co.uk; 5 Bank St; mains £17-25, 2-course lunch £13.50; ⊙ noon-2pm & 5.30-9pm Mon-Sat; 🕮) 🖋 A modern restaurant that dishes up bistro cuisine such as haddock and chips, slow-roast pork belly or roast vegetable panini at lunchtime. The Digby Chick metamorphoses into a candlelit gourmet restaurant in the evening, serving dishes such as grilled langoustines, seared scallops, venison and steak. Three-course early-bird menu (5.30pm to 6.30pm) for £19.

🛍 Shopping

Baltic Bookshop BOOKS
(☎ 01851-702802; 8-10 Cromwell St; ⊙ 9am-5.30pm Mon-Sat) Good for local history books and maps.

Sandwick Road Petrol Station FOOD & DRINK
(Engebret Ltd; ☎ 01851-702304; Sandwick Rd; ⊙ 6am-11pm Mon-Sat, 10am-4pm Sun) The only shop in town that's open on a Sunday, selling groceries, alcohol, hardware, fishing tackle and outdoor kit; the Sunday papers arrive around 2pm.

ⓘ Getting There & Away

The bus station is on the waterfront, next to the ferry terminal (left luggage desk £1.50 per piece). Bus W10 runs from Stornoway to Tarbert (£4.40, one hour, four or five daily Monday to Saturday) and Leverburgh (£6.20, two hours).

The Westside Circular bus W2 runs a circular route from Stornoway through Callanish (£2.50, 30 minutes), Carloway, Garenin and Arnol; the timetable means you can visit one or two of the sites in a day.

Butt of Lewis (Rubha Robhanais)

The Butt of Lewis – the extreme northern tip of the Hebrides – is windswept and rugged, with a very imposing lighthouse, pounding surf and large colonies of nesting fulmars on the high cliffs. There's a bleak sense of isolation here, with nothing but the grey Atlantic between you and Canada.

Just before the turn-off to the Butt at Eoropie (Eoropaidh), you'll find **St Moluag's Church** (Teampull Mholuidh), an austere, barnlike structure believed to date from the 12th century but still used by the Episcopal Church. The main settlement here is **Port of Ness** (Port Nis) with an attractive harbour. To the west of the village is the sandy beach of **Traigh**, which is popular with surfers and has a kids' adventure playground nearby.

Arnol

One of Scotland's most evocative historic buildings, the **Arnol Blackhouse** (HS; ☎ 01851-710395; adult/child £4.50/2.70; ⊙ 9.30am-5.30pm Mon-Sat Apr-Sep, to 4.30pm Oct-Mar; ℗) is not so much a museum as a perfectly preserved fragment of a lost world. Built in 1885, this traditional blackhouse – a combined byre, barn and home – was inhabited until 1964 and has not been changed since the last inhabitant moved out. The staff faithfully rekindle the central peat fire every morning so you can experience the distinctive peat-reek; there's no chimney, and the smoke finds its own way out through the turf roof, windows and door – spend too long inside and you might feel like you've been kippered! The museum is just off the A858, about 3 miles west of Barvas.

At nearby Bragar, a pair of whalebones forms an arch by the road, with the rusting harpoon that killed the whale dangling from the centre.

Garenin (Na Gearrannan)

The picturesque and fascinating Gearrannan Blackhouse Village is a cluster of nine restored thatch-roofed blackhouses perched above the exposed Atlantic coast. One of the cottages is home to the Blackhouse Museum (☎ 01851-643416; www.gearrannan. com; adult/child £3/1; ◎ 9.30am-5.30pm Mon-Sat Apr-Sep), a traditional 1955 blackhouse with displays on the village's history, while another houses the Taigh an Chocair Cafe (mains £3-6; ◎ 9.30am-5.30pm Mon-Sat).

The other blackhouses in the village are let out as self-catering holiday cottages (☎ 01851-643416; www.gearrannan.com; 2-person cottage for 3 nights £226), offering the chance to stay in a unique and luxurious modernised blackhouse with attached kitchen and lounge. There's a minimum five-night stay from June to August.

Carloway (Carlabagh)

Dun Carloway (Dun Charlabhaigh) is a 2000-year-old, dry-stone broch, perched defiantly above a beautiful loch with views to the mountains of North Harris. The site is clearly signposted along a minor road off the A858, a mile southwest of Carloway village. One of the best-preserved brochs in Scotland, its double walls (with internal staircase) still stand to a height of 9m and testify to the engineering skills of its Iron Age architects.

The tiny, turf-roofed Doune Broch Centre (☎ 01851-643338; ◎ 10am-5pm Mon-Sat Apr-Sep) FREE nearby has interpretative displays and exhibitions about the history of the broch and the life of the people who lived there.

Callanish (Calanais)

The Callanish Standing Stones, 15 miles west of Stornoway on the A858 road, form one of the most complete stone circles in Britain. It is one of the most atmospheric prehistoric sites anywhere; its ageless mystery, impressive scale and undeniable beauty leave a lasting impression. Sited on a wild and secluded promontory overlooking Loch Roag, 13 large stones of beautifully banded gneiss are arranged, as if in worship, around a 4.5m-tall central monolith. Some 40 smaller stones radiate from the circle in the shape of a cross, with the remains of a chambered tomb at the centre. Dating from 3800 to 5000 years ago, the stones are roughly contemporary with the pyramids of Egypt.

The nearby Calanais Visitor Centre (☎ 01851-621422; www.callanishvisitorcentre.co.uk; admission free, exhibition £2.50; ◎ 9.30am-8pm Mon-Sat Jun-Aug, 10am-6pm Mon-Sat Apr, May, Sep & Oct, 10am-4pm Tue-Sat Nov-Mar; ℗) is a tour de force of discreet design. Inside is a small exhibition that speculates on the origins and purpose of the stones, and an excellent cafe (mains £4-7).

If you plan to stay the night, you have a choice of Eshcol Guest House (☎ 01851-621357; www.eshcol.com; 21 Breascleit; r per person £43; ℗) and neighbouring Loch Roag Guest House (☎ 01851-621357; www.lochroag. com; 22a Breascleit; r per person £39-55; ℗ 🛜), half a mile north of Callanish. Both are modern bungalows with the same friendly owner, who is very knowledgeable about the local area (evening meals available).

Great Bernera

This rocky island is connected to Lewis by a bridge built by the local council in 1953 – the islanders had originally planned to blow up a small hill with explosives and use the material to build their own causeway. On a sunny day, it's worth making the long detour to the island's northern tip for a picnic at the perfect little sandy beach of Bosta (Bostadh).

In 1996 archaeologists excavated an entire Iron Age village at the head of Bosta beach. Afterwards, the village was reburied for protection, but a reconstruction of an Iron Age house (☎ 01851-612331; Bosta; adult/child £3/1; ◎ noon-4pm Mon-Fri May-Sep; ℗) now sits nearby. Stand around the peat fire, with strips of mutton being smoked above, while the custodian explains the domestic arrangements – truly fascinating, and well worth the trip.

There are five buses a day between Stornoway and the hamlet of Breacleit (£3.10, one hour) on Great Bernera; two or three a day will continue to Bosta on request. Alternatively, there's a signposted 5-mile coastal walk from Breacleit to Bosta.

Miavaig (Miaghaig) & Mealista (Mealasta)

The B8011 road (signposted Uig, on the A858 Stornoway–Callanish road) from Garrynahine to Timsgarry (Timsgearraidh) meanders through scenic wilderness to some of Scotland's most stunning beaches. At Miavaig, a loop road detours north through the Bhaltos Estate to the pretty, mile-long white strand of Reef Beach; there's a basic but spectacular campsite (Traigh na Beirigh; tent sites £10; ☉ Apr-Oct) in the machair behind the beach.

From April to September, SeaTrek (www.seatrek.co.uk) runs two-hour boat trips (adult/child £35/25, Monday to Saturday) in a high-speed RIB to spot seals and nesting seabirds. In June and July it also runs more adventurous, all-day trips (£95 per person, two per month) in a large motor boat to the Flannan Isles, a remote group of tiny, uninhabited islands 25 miles northwest of Lewis. Puffins, seals and a ruined 7th-century chapel are the main attractions, but the isles are most famous for the mystery of the three lighthouse keepers who disappeared without trace in December 1900. There's also a 12-hour round trip to remote St Kilda (£180, once or twice weekly, May to September, weather permitting).

From Miavaig, the road continues west through a rocky defile to Timsgarry and the vast, sandy expanse of Traigh Uige (Uig Sands). The famous 12th-century Lewis chess pieces, made of walrus ivory, were discovered in the sand dunes here in 1831. Of the 78 pieces, 67 are in the British Museum in London, with 11 in Edinburgh's National Museum of Scotland (p57); you can buy replicas at various outlets on the isle of Lewis.

There's a basic campsite (sites per person £2) on the south side of the bay (signposted 'Ardroil Beach') and a superb guesthouse, Baile-na-Cille (☎ 01851-672242; www.bailenacille.co.uk; Timsgarry, Uig; per person £55; P ☎), on the north side.

At the southwestern end of Traigh Uig is Auberge Carnish (☎ 01851-672459; www.aubergecarnish.co.uk; Carnais; s/d from £85/120; P), a beautifully designed timber building that houses a luxury B&B and restaurant (3-course dinner £35; booking essential) with a stunning outlook over the sands.

The minor road that continues south from Timsgarry to Mealista passes a few smaller, but still spectacular, white-sand and boulder beaches on the way to a remote dead end; on a clear day you can see St Kilda on the horizon.

There are two or three buses a day from Stornoway to Uig (£4.40, 50 minutes).

Harris (Na Hearadh)

Harris, to the south of Lewis, is the scenic jewel in the necklace of islands that comprise the Outer Hebrides. It has a spectacular blend of rugged mountains, pristine beaches, flower-speckled machair and barren rocky landscapes. The isthmus at Tarbert splits Harris neatly in two: North Harris is dominated by mountains that rise forbiddingly above the peat moors to the south of Stornoway – Clisham (799m) is the highest point. South Harris is lower-lying, fringed by beautiful white-sand beaches in the west and a convoluted rocky coastline to the east.

Harris is famous for Harris Tweed, a high-quality woollen cloth still hand-woven in islanders' homes. The industry employs around 400 weavers; staff at Tarbert tourist office can tell you about weavers and workshops you can visit.

Tarbert (An Tairbeart)

POP 480

Tarbert is a harbour village with a spectacular location, tucked into the narrow neck of land that links North and South Harris. It has ferry connections to Uig on Skye. Under construction beside the ferry pier at the time of research, the Isle of Harris Distillery will be open to visitors daily (except Sunday) from spring 2015. Village facilities include two petrol stations, a bank, ATM and two general stores.

🛏 Sleeping & Eating

Tigh na Mara　　　　　　　　　D&B £

(☎ 01859-502270; East Tarbert; per person £25-30; P) Excellent-value B&B (though the single room is a bit cramped) just five minutes from the ferry – go up the hill above the tourist office and turn right. The owner bakes fresh cakes every day, to enjoy in the conservatory with a view over the bay.

Harris Hotel　　　　　　　　　HOTEL ££

(☎ 01859-502154; www.harrishotel.com; s/d from £70/98; P @ ☎) Run since 1903 by four generations of the Cameron family, Harris Hotel is a 19th-century sporting hotel, built in 1865

NORTHERN HIGHLANDS & ISLANDS HARRIS (NA HEARADH)

for visiting anglers and deer stalkers, and retains a distinctly old-fashioned atmsophere. It has spacious, comfy rooms and a decent restaurant; look out for JM Barrie's initials scratched on the dining-room window (the author of *Peter Pan* visited in the 1920s).

Hotel Hebrides   HOTEL £££
(☑ 01859-502364; www.hotel-hebrides.com; Pier Rd; s/d/f £75/150/180; 🛜) The location and setting don't look promising – a nondescript building squeezed between ferry pier and car park – but this modern establishment brings a dash of urban glamour to Harris, with flashy fabrics and wall coverings, luxurious towels and toiletries, and a stylish restaurant and lounge bar.

Hebscape   CAFE £
(www.hebscapegallery.co.uk; Ardhasaig; mains £3-7; ⊙ 10am-4.30pm Mon-Sat Apr-Oct; 🅿🛜) 🍃 This stylish new cafe-cum-art gallery, a couple of miles outside Tarbert on the road north towards Stornoway, occupies a hilltop site with breathatking views over Loch A Siar. Enjoy home-baked cakes or scones with Suki tea or freshly brewed espresso, or a hearty bowl of homemade soup, while admiring the gorgeous landscape photography of co-owner Darren Cole.

First Fruits   CAFE £
(☑ 01880-502439; www.firstfruits-tearoom.co.uk; Pier Rd; mains £3-10; ⊙ 10.30am-4pm Mon, Wed & Fri, 10am-4pm Tue & Thu & 10am-3pm Sat Apr-Sep) A cosy little cottage tearoom near the tourist office – handy while you wait for a ferry.

North Harris

Magnificent North Harris is the most mountainous region of the Outer Hebrides. There are few roads here, but many opportunities for climbing, walking and birdwatching.

The B887 leads west, from a point 3 miles north of Tarbert, to **Hushinish**, where there's a lovely silver-sand beach. Along the way the road passes an old whaling station, one of Lord Leverhulme's failed development schemes, and the impressive shooting lodge of **Amhuinnsuidhe Castle**, now an exclusive hotel. Between the two, at Miavaig, a parking area and gated track gives hikers access to a golden eagle observatory, a 1.3-mile walk north from the road. On Wednesdays from April to September, local rangers lead a 3½-hour **guided walk** (£5 per person) in search of eagles; details from Tarbert tourist office or www.north-harris.org.

South Harris

The west coast of South Harris has some of the most beautiful beaches in Scotland. The blinding white sands and turquoise waters of **Luskentyre** and **Scarasta** would be major holiday resorts if they were transported to somewhere with a warm climate; as it is, they're usually deserted.

The east coast is a complete contrast to the west – a strange, rocky moonscape of naked gneiss pocked with tiny lochans, the bleakness lightened by the occasional splash of green around the few crofting communities. Film buffs will know that the psychedelic sequences depicting an alien landscape in *2001: A Space Odyssey* were shot from an aircraft flying low over the east coast of Harris.

The narrow, twisting road that winds its way along this coast is known locally as the **Golden Road**, because of the vast amount of money it cost per mile. It was built in the 1930s to link all the tiny communities known as 'The Bays'.

🎯 Sights & Activities

Clò Mòr   MUSEUM
(☑ 01859-511189; Old School, Drinishader; ⊙ 9am-5.30pm Mon-Sat; 🅿) **FREE** The Campbell family has been making Harris Tweed for 90 years, and this exhibition (behind the family shop) celebrates the history of the fabric known in Gaelic as *clò mòr* (the 'big cloth'); ask about live demonstrations of tweed weaving on the 70-year-old Hattersley loom. Drinishader is 5 miles south of Tarbert on the east coast road.

Seallam! Visitor Centre   MUSEUM
(www.seallam.com; Northton; adult/child £2.50/2; ⊙ 10am-5pm Mon-Sat; 🅿) The culture and landscape of the Hebrides are celebrated in the fascinating exhibition (*Seallam* is Gaelic for 'Let me show you'). The centre, which is in Northton, 3 miles north of Leverburgh, also has a genealogical research centre for people who want to trace their Hebridean ancestry.

St Clement's Church   HISTORIC BUILDING
(Rodel; ⊙ 9am-5pm Mon-Sat) **FREE** At the southernmost tip of the east coast of Harris stands the impressive 16th-century St Clement's Church, built by Alexander MacLeod of Dunvegan between the 1520s and 1550s, only to be abandoned after the Reformation. There are several fine tombs inside, includ-

ing the cenotaph of Alexander MacLeod, finely carved with hunting scenes, a castle, a birlinn (the traditional longboat of the islands) and various saints, including St Clement clutching a skull.

Sleeping & Eating

Am Bothan
HOSTEL £
(☎01859-520251; www.ambothan.com; Ferry Rd, Leverburgh; dm £20; P🐾) An attractive, chalet-style hostel, Am Bothan has small, neat dorms and a great porch where you can enjoy morning coffee with views over the creek. The hostel offers bike hire and can arrange wildlife-watching boat trips.

Lickisto Blackhouse Camping
CAMPSITE £
(☎01859-530485; www.freewebs.com/vanvon; Liceasto; tent sites per adult/child £12/6, yurt £70) Remote and rustic campsite on an old croft, with pitches set among heather and outcrops with chickens running wild. Campers can use a communal kitchen/lounge in a converted blackhouse, and there are two yurts with woodburning stove and gas cooker (no electricity). Bus W13 from Tarbert to Leverburgh stops at the entrance.

Carminish House
B&B ££
(☎01859-520400; www.carminish.com; 1a Strond, Leverburgh; s/d £60/80; P🐾) One of the few B&Bs in Harris that is open all year, the welcoming Carminish is a modern house with three comfy bedrooms. There's a view of the ferry from the dining room, and lots of nice little touches such as handmade soaps, a carafe of drinking water in the bedroom and fresh fruit salad at breakfast.

Sorrel Cottage
B&B ££
(☎01859-520319; www.sorrelcottage.co.uk; 2 Glen, Leverburgh; s/d from £48/72; 🐾) Sorrel Cottage is a pretty crofter's house, about 1.5 miles west of the ferry at Leverburgh. Vegetarians and vegans are happily catered for. Bike hire available.

Rodel Hotel
INN £££
(☎01859-520210; www.rodelhotel.co.uk; Rodel; s/d from £85/130; ☉Apr-Oct; P🐾) Don't be put off by the rather grey and grim-looking exterior of this remote hotel – the interior has been refurbished to a high standard and offers four large, luxurious bedrooms; the one called Iona (a twin room) has the best view, across the little harbour towards Skye. The hotel restaurant (mains lunch £9-11, dinner £15-20; ☉noon-3pm & 5.30-9.30pm) serves delicious local seafood, steak and venison.

Skoon Art Café
CAFE £
(☎01859-530268; www.skoon.com; Geocrab; mains £4-7; ☉10am-4.30pm Tue-Sat Apr-Sep, shorter hours Oct-Mar; P) Set halfway along the Golden Road, this neat little art gallery doubles as an excellent cafe serving delicious homemade soups, sandwiches, cakes and desserts (try the marmalade and ginger cake).

Getting There & Around

A CalMac (☎0800 066 5000; www.calmac.co.uk) car ferry zigzags through the reefs of the Sound of Harris from Leverburgh to Berneray (pedestrian/car £7.35/33.50, one hour, three or four daily Monday to Saturday, two or three Sunday).

There are two to four buses a day (except Sunday) from Tarbert to Leverburgh; W10 takes the main road along the west coast (£2.90, 40 minutes), while W13 winds along the Golden Road on the east (one hour).

Berneray (Bearnaraigh)
POP 138
Berneray was linked to North Uist by a causeway in October 1998, but that hasn't altered the peace and beauty of the island. The beaches on its west coast are some of the most beautiful and unspoilt in Britain, and seals and otters can be seen in Bays Loch on the east coast.

The basic but atmospheric Gatliff Hostel (www.gatliff.org.uk; dm adult/child £12/7, camping per person £8), housed in a pair of restored blackhouses right by the sea, is the place to stay. You can camp outside, or on the grass above the gorgeous white-sand beach just to the north.

The Nurse's Cottage (www.isleofberneray.com; ☉11am-3pm Mon-Fri Jun-Aug) provides tourist information and internet access.

Bus W19 runs from Berneray (Gatliff Hostel and Harris ferry) to Lochmaddy (£2.10, 20 to 30 minutes, eight daily Monday to Saturday). There are daily ferries to Leverburgh (Harris).

North Uist (Uibhist A Tuath)
POP 1255
North Uist, an island half-drowned by lochs, is famed for its trout fishing but also has some magnificent beaches on its north and west coasts. For birdwatchers this is

paradise, with regular sightings of waders and wildfowl ranging from redshank to red-throated diver to red-necked phalarope. The landscape is less wild and mountainous than Harris but it has a sleepy, subtle appeal. Little Lochmaddy is the first village you hit after arriving on the ferry from Skye. There's a tourist office, a couple of stores, a bank with an ATM, a petrol station, a post office and a pub.

◉ Sights

Balranald RSPB Reserve WILDLIFE RESERVE
FREE Birdwatchers flock to this RSPB nature reserve, 18 miles west of Lochmaddy, in the hope of spotting the rare red-necked phalarope or hearing the distinctive call of the corncrake. There's a **visitor centre** (admission free; ☺9am-6pm Apr-Aug) with a resident warden who offers 1½-hour guided walks (£5, depart visitor centre 10am Tuesday, May to September).

Taigh Chearsabhagh ARTS CENTRE, MUSEUM
(☎01876-500293; www.taigh-chearsabhagh.org; Lochmaddy; arts centre free, museum £3; ☺10am-5pm Mon-Sat; ℗) Taigh Chearsabhagh is a museum and arts centre that preserves and displays the history and culture of the Uists, and is also a thriving community centre, post office and meeting place. The centre's **cafe** (mains £3 to £7) dishes up homemade soups, sandwiches and cakes.

Bharpa Langass & Pobull Fhinn HISTORIC SITES
A waymarked circular path beside the Langass Lodge Hotel (just off the A867, 6 miles southwest of Lochmaddy) leads to the chambered Neolithic burial tomb of **Bharpa Langass** and the stone circle of **Pobull Fhinn** (Finn's People); both are reckoned to be around 5000 years old. There are lovely views over the loch, where you may be able to spot seals and otters.

⛏ Sleeping & Eating

Rushlee House B&B **££**
(☎01876-500274; www.rushleehouse.co.uk; Lochmaddy; s/d £50/75; ℗) A lovely modern bungalow with three luxuriously appointed bedrooms and great views of the hills to the south. No evening meals, but it's just a short walk to the restaurant at Hamersay House. The B&B is 0.75 miles from the ferry pier; take the first road on the right, then first left.

Langass Lodge Hotel HOTEL **££**
(☎01876-580285; www.langasslodge.co.uk; Locheport; s/d from £80/109; ℗🛜) The delightful Langass Lodge Hotel is a former shooting lodge set in splendid isolation overlooking Loch Langais. Refurbished and extended, it now offers a dozen appealing rooms, many with sea views, and one of the Hebrides' best **restaurants** (mains £13-23; ☺noon-2pm & 6-9pm), noted for its fine seafood and game.

Hamersay House HOTEL **£££**
(☎01876-500700; www.hamersayhouse.co.uk; Lochmaddy; s/d £95/135; ℗🛜) Hamersay is Lochmaddy's most luxurious accommodation, with eight designer bedrooms, a lounge with sofas around an open fire, and a good restaurant with sea views from the terrace.

ℹ Getting There & Around

Buses from Lochmaddy to Lochboisdale (£4.80, 1¾ hours), Eriskay Pier (£5.60, 2½ hours), Berneray, Langass, Clachan na Luib, Benbecula and Daliburgh run five to eight times a day Monday to Saturday.

Benbecula (Beinn Na Faoghla)

POP 1305

Benbecula is a low-lying island with a flat, lochan-studded landscape that's best appreciated from the summit of **Rueval** (124m), the island's highest point. There's a path around the south side of the hill (signposted from the main road; park beside the landfill site) that is said to be the route taken to the coast by Bonnie Prince Charlie and Flora MacDonald during the prince's escape in 1746. The main village, Balivanich, has a bank with an ATM, a post office, a large **Co-op supermarket** (☺8am-8pm Mon-Sat, 11am-6pm Sun) and a petrol station (open on Sunday). It is also the location of **Benbecula airport**.

South Uist (Uibhist A Deas)

POP 1755

South Uist is the second-largest island in the Outer Hebrides and saves its choicest corners for those who explore away from the main north–south road. The low-lying west coast is an almost unbroken stretch of white-sand beach and flower-flecked machair – a waymarked hiking trail, the **Machair Way**, follows the coast – while the multitude of inland lochs provide excellent trout fishing. The east coast, riven by four large sea lochs, is hilly and remote, with spectacular **Beinn Mhor** (620m) the highest point.

Driving south from Benbecula you cross from the predominantly Protestant northern half of the Outer Hebrides into the mostly Roman Catholic south, a religious transition marked by the granite statue of **Our Lady of the Isles** on the slopes of Rueval (the hill with the military radomes on its summit) and the presence of many roadside shrines.

The ferry port of **Lochboisdale** is the island's largest settlement, with a tourist office, a bank with an ATM, a grocery store and a petrol station.

⊙ Sights & Activties

Loch Druidibeg National Nature Reserve
WILDLIFE RESERVE

FREE Loch Druidibeg National Nature Reserve is an important breeding ground for birds such as dunlin, redshank, ringed plover, greylag goose and corncrake; you can take a 5-mile self-guided walk through the reserve. Ask for details at the Scottish Natural Heritage office on the main road beside the loch.

Kildonan Museum
MUSEUM

(☑ 01878-710343; www.kildonanmuseum.co.uk; Kildonan; adult/child £2/free; ☉ 10am-5pm Apr-Oct; ℗) Six miles north of Lochboisdale, Kildonan Museum explores the lives of local crofters through its collection of artefacts, an absorbing exhibition of black-and-white photography and first-hand accounts of harsh Hebridean conditions. There's also an excellent **tearoom** (mains £3-8; ☉ 11am-4pm) and craft shop.

Amid Milton's ruined blackhouses, half a mile south of the museum, a cairn marks the site of **Flora MacDonald's birthplace**.

🛏 Sleeping & Eating

Tobha Mor Crofters' Hostel
HOSTEL £

(www.gatliff.org.uk; Howmore; dm adult/child £12/7) Atmospheric hostel housed in a restored thatched blackhouse, about 12 miles north of Lochboisdale.

Wireless Cottage
B&B £

(☑ 01878-700660; www.wirelesscottage.co.uk; Lochboisdale; per person from £25; ☎) This pretty little cottage, which once housed the local telephone exchange, is now a welcoming and good-value B&B a short (300m) walk

from the ferry, with just two bedrooms (one double, one family).

★ Polochar Inn
INN ££

(☑ 01878-700215; www.polocharinn.com; Polochar; s/d from £70/90; ℗ ☎) This 18th-century inn has been transformed into a stylish, welcoming hotel with a stunning location looking out across the sea to Barra. The excellent restaurant and bar menu (mains £14 to £18) includes fish chowder, haddock and chips, local salmon and Uist lamb. Polochar is 7 miles southwest of Lochboisdale, on the way to Eriskay.

Lochside Cottage
B&B ££

(☑ 01878-700472; www.lochside-cottage.co.uk; Lochboisdale; r per person £30; ℗ ☎) Lochside Cottage is a friendly B&B, 1.5 miles west of the ferry, and has rooms with views and a sun lounge barely a fishing-rod's length from its own trout loch.

❶ Getting There & Around

CalMac (p403) ferries run between Lochmaddy and Uig (Skye), and Lochboisdale and Oban.

Bus W17 runs about four times a day (not Sunday) between Berneray and Eriskay via Lochmaddy, Balivanich and Lochboisdale. The trip from Lochboisdale to Lochmaddy (£4.80) takes 1¾ hours.

Eriskay (Eiriosgaigh)

POP 143

In 1745 Bonnie Prince Charlie first set foot in Scotland on the west coast of Eriskay, on the sandy beach (immediately north of the ferry terminal) still known as **Prince's Strand** (Coilleag a'Phrionnsa).

More recently the SS *Politician* sank just off the island in 1941. The islanders salvaged much of its cargo of around 250,000 bottles of whisky and, after a binge of dramatic proportions, the police intervened and a number of the islanders landed in jail. The story was immortalised by Sir Compton Mackenzie in his comic novel *Whisky Galore,* later made into a famous film.

A car ferry links Eriskay with Ardmhor at the northern end of Barra.

Barra (Barraigh)

POP 1175

With its beautiful beaches, wildflower-clad dunes, rugged little hills and strong sense of community, diminutive Barra – just 14 miles

CROFTING & THE CLEARANCES

The wild empty spaces up here are among Europe's least populated zones, but this wasn't always so. Ruins of cottages in desolate areas are mute witnesses to one of the most heartless episodes of Scottish history: the Highland Clearances.

Until the 19th century the most common form of farming settlement here was the baile, a group of a dozen or so families who farmed the land granted to them by the local chieftain in return for military service and a portion of the harvest. The arable land was divided into strips called rigs, which were allocated to different families by annual ballot so that each took turns at getting the poorer soils; this system was known as runrig. The families worked the land communally and their cattle shared grazing land.

After Culloden, however, the king banned private armies and new laws made the clan chiefs actual owners of their traditional lands, often vast tracts of territory. With the prospect of unimagined riches allied to a depressing failure of imagination, the lairds decided that sheep were more profitable than agriculture and proceeded to evict tens of thousands of farmers. These desperate folk were forced to head for the cities in the hope of finding work or to emigrate to the Americas or southern hemisphere. Those who stayed were forced to eke a living from narrow plots of marginal agricultural land, often close to the coast. This form of smallholding became known as crofting. The small patch of land barely provided a living and had to be supplemented by other work such as fishing and kelp-gathering. It was always precarious, as rights were granted on a year-by-year basis, so at any moment a crofter could lose not only the farm but also the house they'd built on it.

The late 19th-century economic depression meant many couldn't pay their rent. This time, however, they resisted expulsion, instead forming the Highland Land Reform Association and their own political party. Their resistance led the government to accede to several demands, including security of tenure, fair rents and eventually the supply of land for new crofts. Crofters now have the right to purchase their farmland and 2004 laws finally abolished the feudal system, which created so much misery.

in circumference – is the Outer Hebrides in miniature. For a great view of the island, walk up to the top of **Heaval** (383m), a mile northeast of Castlebay. **Castlebay** (Bagh a'Chaisteil), in the south, is the largest village. There's a tourist office (p397), a bank with an ATM, a post office and two grocery stores.

◎ Sights

Kisimul Castle   CASTLE
(HS; ☑ 01871-810313; Castlebay; adult/child incl ferry £5.50/3.30; ⊙ 9.30am-5.30pm Apr-Sep) Castlebay takes its name from the island fortress of Kisimul Castle, first built by the MacNeil clan in the 11th century. A short boat trip takes you out to the island, where you can explore the fortifications. The castle was restored in the 20th century by American architect Robert MacNeil, who became the 45th clan chief; he gifted the castle to Historic Scotland in 2000 for an annual rent of £1 and a bottle of whisky (Talisker single malt, if you're interested).

Traigh Mor   BEACH
This vast expanse of firm golden sand (the name means 'Big Strand') serves as Barra's airport (a mile across at low tide, and big enough for three 'runways'), the only beach airport in the world that handles scheduled flights. Watching the little Twin Otter aircraft come and go is a popular spectator sport. In between flights, locals gather cockles, a local seafood speciality, from the sands.

Barra Heritage Centre   MUSEUM
(☑ 01871-810413; www.barraheritage.com; Castlebay; adult/child £3/1; ⊙ 10.30am-4.30pm Mon-Sat Apr-Oct) This heritage centre has Gaelic-themed displays about the island, local art exhibitions and a tearoom.

🛏 Sleeping & Eating

Accommodation on Barra is limited, so make a reservation before committing to a night on the island. Wild camping (on foot or by bike) is allowed almost anywhere; campervans and car campers are restricted to official sites – check www.isleofbarra.com.

Dunard Hostel
HOSTEL **£**

(☑ 01871-810443; www.dunardhostel.co.uk; Castlebay; dm/tw from £18/40; **P**) Dunard is a friendly, family-run hostel just five minutes' walk from the ferry terminal. The owners can organise sea-kayaking tours for £35/65 a half-/full day.

Borve Camping & Caravan Site
CAMPSITE **£**

(www.barracamping.co.uk; Borve; sites 2-person tent £14, campervan £18; ☉ Mar-Oct) An attractive campsite on the west coast of the island, close to Barra's best sandy beaches.

Castlebay Hotel
HOTEL **££**

(☑ 01871-810223; www.castlebayhotel.com; Castlebay; s/d from £65/110; **P** ☎) The Castlebay Hotel offers spacious bedrooms decorated with a subtle tartan motif – it's worth paying a bit extra for a sea view – and there's a comfy lounge and conservatory with grand views across the harbour to the islands south of Barra. The hotel bar is the hub of island social life, with regular sessions of traditional music, and the restaurant specialises in local seafood and game.

Tigh na Mara
B&B **££**

(☑ 01871-810304; www.tighnamara-barra.co.uk; Castlebay; per person from £35; ☉ Apr-Oct; **P** ☎) A lovely cottage B&B with a brilliant location just above the ferry pier, looking out over the bay and Kisimul Castle. Ask for the en suite double bedroom with bay view.

Deck
CAFE **£**

(Castlebay; mains £4-6; ☉ 10am-6pm Mon-Sat & noon-5pm Sun May-Sep) There are only outdoor seats at this cafe (attached to a toffee factory), on a wooden deck overlooking the bay, but it's worth waiting for a fine day to sample the freshly baked scones and homemade cakes.

❶ Getting There & Around

AIR

There are two daily flights from Glasgow to Barra airport

BOAT

A CalMac (p403) car ferry (pedestrian/car £8/22.90, 40 minutes, three to five daily) links Eriskay with Ardmhor at the northern end of Barra. Ferries also run from Castlebay to Oban and Lochboisdale.

BICYCLE

You can hire bikes from **Barra Cycle Hire** (☑ 01871-810284; Castlebay; per day £12), at the east end of Castlebay.

BUS

A bus service links ferry arrivals and departures at Ardmhor with Castlebay (£1.60, 20 minutes). Bus W32 makes a circuit of the island up to five times daily (not Sunday), and also connects with flights at the airport.

Orkney & Shetland

Includes ➡

Best Places to Eat

➡ Creel (p417)
➡ Foveran (p415)
➡ Hay's Dock (p430)

Best Places to Stay

➡ Scalloway Hotel (p432)
➡ Brinkies Guest House (p421)
➡ Albert Hotel (p414)
➡ West Manse (p426)
➡ Almara (p435)
➡ Busta House Hotel (p434)

Why Go?

Up here at Britain's top end it can feel more Scandinavian than Scottish, and no wonder. For the Vikings, the jaunt across the North Sea from Norway was as easy as a stroll down to the local mead hall and they soon controlled these windswept, treeless archipelagos, laying down longhouses alongside stony remains of ancient prehistoric settlements.

An ancient magic hovers in the air above Orkney and Shetland, endowing them with an allure that lodges firmly in the soul. It's in the misty seas, where seals, whales and porpoises patrol lonely coastlines; it's in the air, where squadrons of seabirds wheel above huge nesting colonies; and it's on land, where standing stones catch late summer sunsets and strains of folk music disperse in the air before the wind gusts shut the pub door. These islands reward the journey.

When to Go
Lerwick

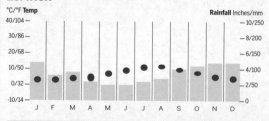

Jan Shetland's Up Helly Aa (p431): horned helmets and burning Viking ships on the beach.

Jun Orkney rocks to the St Magnus Festival (p413): book accommodation ahead.

Jul Summer sunlight and Scotland's longest daylight hours.

ORKNEY

There's a magic to Orkney that you begin to feel as soon as the Scottish mainland slips astern. Only a few short miles of ocean separate Stromness from Scrabster, but the Pentland Firth is one of Europe's most dangerous waterways, a graveyard of ships that adds an extra mystique to these islands shimmering in the sea mists.

An archipelago of mostly flat, green-topped islands stripped bare of trees and ringed with red sandstone cliffs, its heritage dates back to the Vikings whose influence is still strong today. Famed for ancient standing stones and prehistoric villages, for sublime sandy beaches and spectacular coastal scenery, it's a region whose ports tell of lives shared with the blessings and rough moods of the sea, and a destination where seekers can find melancholy wrecks of warships and the salty clamour of remote seabird colonies.

⚐ Tours

Orkney Archaeology Tours   GUIDED TOURS
(✆01856-721450; www.orkneyarchaeologytours.co.uk) Specialises in all-inclusive multi-day tours focusing on Orkney's ancient sites with an archaeologist guide. Also runs private full-day (£420 for up to four) tours.

Wildabout Orkney   GUIDED TOURS
(✆01856-877737; www.wildaboutorkney.com) Operates tours covering Orkney's history, ecology, folklore and wildlife. Day trips operate year-round and cost £59, with pick-ups in Stromness and Kirkwall.

John O'Groats Ferries   BUS TOURS
(✆01955-611353; www.jogferry.co.uk; ⊙May-Sep) For the hurried; runs a one-day tour of the main sites for £58, including the ferry from John O'Groats. You can do the whole thing as a long day trip from Inverness.

❶ Getting There & Away

AIR
Flybe (✆0871 700 2000; www.flybe.com) flies daily from Kirkwall to Aberdeen, Edinburgh, Glasgow, Inverness and Sumburgh (Shetland). Most summers it also serves Bergen (Norway).

BOAT
During summer, book car spaces ahead. Peak season fares are quoted here.

John O'Groats Ferries (✆01955-611353; www.jogferry.co.uk; single £15, incl bus to Kirkwall £17; ⊙May-Sep) Passenger-only service from

John O'Groats to Burwick, on the southern tip of South Ronaldsay, with connecting bus to Kirkwall. Two to three departures daily.

Northlink Ferries (✆0845 6000 449; www.northlinkferries.co.uk) Operates ferries from Scrabster to Stromness (passenger/car £19.15/58, 1½ hours, two to three daily), from Aberdeen to Kirkwall (passenger/car £31/110, six hours, three or four weekly) and from Kirkwall to Lerwick (passenger/car £24.30/101, six to eight hours, three or four weekly) on Shetland. Fares are up to 30% lower off-season.

Pentland Ferries (✆01856-831226, 0800 688-8998; www.pentlandferries.co.uk; adult/child/car/bike £15/7/35/free) Leave from Gills Bay, 3 miles west of John O'Groats, and head to St Margaret's Hope on South Ronaldsay three to four times daily.

BUS
Citylink (www.citylink.co.uk) runs daily from Inverness to Scrabster, connecting with the Stromness ferries. John O'Groats Ferries has summer-only 'Orkney bus' service from Inverness to Kirkwall. Tickets (one-way/return £40/55, five hours) include bus-ferry-bus travel from Inverness to Kirkwall. There are two daily from June to August.

❶ Getting Around

The *Orkney Transport Guide* details all island transport and is free from tourist offices.

The largest island, Mainland, is linked by causeways to four southern islands; others are reached by air and ferry.

AIR
Loganair (✆01856-873457; www.loganair.co.uk) operates interisland flights from Kirkwall.

BICYCLE
Various locations on Mainland hire bikes, including **Cycle Orkney** (✆01856-875777; www.cycleorkney.com; Tankerness Lane, Kirkwall; per day/3 days/week £15/30/60; ⊙9am-5.30pm Mon-Sat) and **Orkney Cycle Hire** (✆01856-850255; www.orkneycyclehire.co.uk; 54 Dundas St, Stromness; per day £10-12.50). Both offer out-of-hours pick-ups.

BOAT
Orkney Ferries (✆01856-872044; www.orkneyferries.co.uk) Operates car ferries from Mainland to the islands. See individual islands for details. An Island Explorer pass costs £42 for a week's passenger travel. Bikes are carried free.

BUS
Stagecoach (✆01856-878014; www.stagecoachbus.com) Runs buses on Mainland and connecting islands. Most don't operate on Sunday. Dayrider (£8.30) and 7-Day Megarider (£18.55) tickets allow unlimited travel.

Orkney & Shetland Highlights

1 Shaking your head in astonishment at extraordinary **Skara Brae** (p419) and **Maes Howe** (p418), prehistoric perfection that predates the pyramids

2 Soaking up the glorious scenery of **Hoy** and make the hike to the spectacular **Old Man of Hoy** (p422)

3 Island-hopping the magical **Northern Islands** of Orkney (p422), where crystal azure waters lap against glittering white-sand beaches

4 Diving the sunken warships of **Scapa Flow** (p418)

5 Discovering your inner Viking at Lerwick's **Up Helly Aa** (p431) festival

6 Capering with puffins and dodging dive-bombing skuas at Shetland's nature reserves of **Hermaness** (p436), **Fetlar** (p438) or **Noss** (p431)

7 Staying in one of Shetland's romantic **lighthouse cottages** (p432); one of the best is at spectacular **Sumburgh**

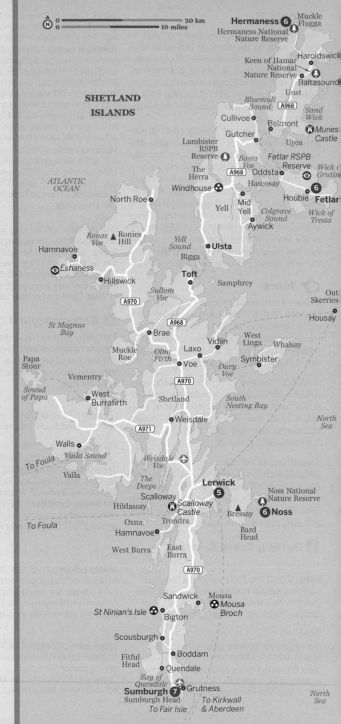

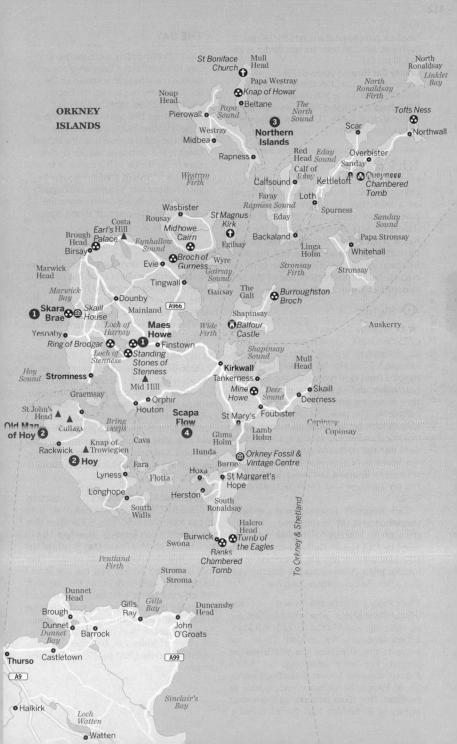

ORKNEY ISLANDS

North Ronaldsay
Linklet Bay

St Boniface Church
Mull Head
Papa Westray
Knap of Howar
Beltane
Noup Head
Papa Sound
The North Sound
North Ronaldsay Firth
Tofts Ness
Pierowall
Scar
Northwall
Westray
Midbea
Rapness
3 **Northern Islands**
Red Head
Eday Sound
Overbister
Sanday
Westray Firth
Calfsound
Calf of Eday
Kettletoft
Quoyness Chambered Tomb
Faray
Loth
Rapness
Rapness Sound
Eday
Spurness
Sanday Sound
Wasbister
St Magnus Kirk
Linga Holm
Papa Stronsay
Costa Hill
Rousay
Midhowe Cairn
Egilsay
Backaland
Whitehall
Earl's Palace
Eynhallow Sound
Brough Head
Birsay
Broch of Gurness
Wyre
Stronsay Firth
Stronsay
Marwick Head
Evie
Gairsay Sound
Tingwall
Gairsay
The Galt
Burroughston Broch
Marwick Bay
Dounby
Maes Howe
Wide Firth
Shapinsay
Auskerry
1 Skara Brae
Skaill House
Mainland
A966
Balfour Castle
Yesnaby
Loch of Harray
Shapinsay Sound
Ring of Brodgar
1 Finstown
Mull Head
Hoy Sound
Loch of Stenness
Standing Stones of Stenness
Kirkwall
Stromness
Mid Hill
Tankerness
Deer Sound
Skaill
Deerness
Graemsay
Orphir
Mine Howe
Foubister
St John's Head
Houton
Scapa Flow
St Mary's
Copinsay
Old Man of Hoy **2**
Bring Deeps
Cullags
Cava
St Margaret's Hope
Copinsay
Rackwick
Knap of Trowieglen
Hunda
Orkney Fossil & Vintage Centre
2 Hoy
Fara
Hoxa
Burray
Lyness
Flotta
Herston
Longhope
South Walls
South Ronaldsay
Halcro Head
Burwick
Tomb of the Eagles
Swona
Banks Chambered Tomb
Pentland Firth
Stroma
Stroma
To Orkney & Shetland
Dunnet Head
Gills Bay
Gills Bay
Duncansby Head
Brough
Dunnet
Dunnet Bay
Barrock
John O'Groats
Thurso
Castletown
A99
A9
Sinclair's Bay
Halkirk
Loch Watten
Watten

CAR

Small-car rates begin at around £35/190 per day/week, although there are specials for as low as £30 per day.

Orkney Car Hire (☑ 01856-872866; www. orkneycarhire.co.uk; Junction Rd, Kirkwall) Recommended. Close to Kirkwall bus station.

WR Tullock (☑ 01856-875500; www.orkney-carrental.co.uk; Castle St, Kirkwall) Opposite Kirkwall bus station.

Kirkwall

POP 7000

Orkney's capital is a bustling market town on a wide bay. Kirkwall's long, winding, paved main street and twisting wynds (lanes) are very atmospheric, and the town has a magnificent cathedral. Founded in the early 11th century, when Earl Rognvald Brusason established his kingdom here, the original part of Kirkwall is one of the best examples of an ancient Norse town.

◉ Sights

★**St Magnus Cathedral**   CATHEDRAL
(☑ 01856-874894; www.stmagnus.org; Broad St; ⊙9am-6pm Mon-Sat, 1-6pm Sun Apr-Sep, 9am-1pm & 2-5pm Mon-Sat Oct-Mar) FREE Constructed from local red sandstone, Kirkwall's centrepiece, dating from the early 12th century, is among Scotland's most interesting cathedrals. The powerful atmosphere of an ancient faith pervades the impressive interior. Lyrical and melodramatic epitaphs of the dead line the walls and emphasise the serious business of 17th- and 18th-century bereavement. Tours of the upper level (£7.25) run on Tuesdays and Thursdays; phone to book.

Earl Rognvald Brusason commissioned the cathedral in 1137 in the name of his martyred uncle, Magnus Erlendsson, who was killed by Earl Hakon Paulsson on Egilsay in 1117. Magnus remains are entombed in an interior pillar. Another notable interment is that of the Arctic explorer John Rae.

Earl's Palace & Bishop's Palace   RUIN
(HS; ☑ 01856-871918; www.historic-scotland.gov.uk; Watergate; adult/child £4.50/2.70; ⊙9.30am-5.30pm Apr-Sep, to 4.30pm Oct) These two adjacent ruined palaces are worth poking around. The more intriguing, the **Earl's Palace**, was once known as the finest example of French Renaissance architecture in Scotland. One room features an interesting history of its builder, Earl Patrick Stewart,

THE BA'

Every Christmas Day and New Year's Day, Kirkwall holds a staggering spectacle: a crazy ball game known as The Ba'. Two enormous teams, the Uppies and the Doonies, fight their way, no holds barred, through the streets, trying to get a leather ball to the other end of town. The ball is thrown from the Market Cross to the waiting crowd; the Uppies have to get the ba' to the corner of Main St and Junction Rd, the Doonies must get it to the water. Violence, skulduggery and other stunts are common and the event, fuelled by plenty of strong drink, can last hours.

executed in Edinburgh for treason. He started construction in about 1600, but ran out of money and never completed it.

The **Bishop's Palace** was built in the mid-12th century for Bishop William the Old. There's a good cathedral view from the tower.

Orkney Museum   MUSEUM
(☑ 01856-873191; www.orkney.gov.uk; Broad St; ⊙10.30am-12.30pm & 1.30-5pm Mon-Sat) FREE In a former merchant's house is this labyrinthine display. It has an overview of Orcadian history and prehistory, including Pictish carvings and a display on the Ba'. Most engaging are the last rooms, covering 19th- and 20th-century social history. Note, the museum is open 10.30am to 5.30pm in summer.

★**Highland Park Distillery**   DISTILLERY
(☑ 01856-874619; www.highlandpark.co.uk; Holm Rd; tour adult/child £7.50/free; ⊙10am-5pm Mon-Sat, noon-5pm Sun May-Aug, 10am-5pm Mon-Fri Apr & Sep, 1-5pm Mon-Fri Oct-Mar) South of the centre, this distillery is great to visit. They malt their own barley; you can see it and the peat kiln used to dry it on the excellent, well-informed hour-long tour. The standard 12-year-old is a soft, balanced malt, great for novices and aficionados alike; the 18-year-old is among the world's finest drams. This and older whiskies can be tasted on more specialised tours (£20 to £75), which you can prearrange.

Kirkwall

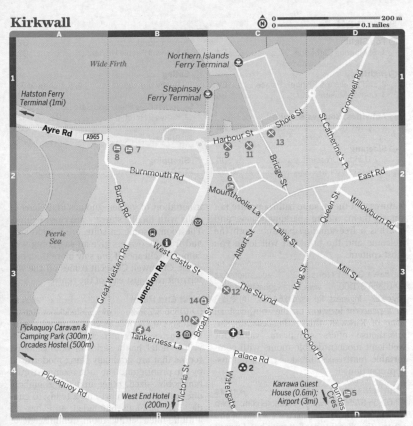

✖ Festivals & Events

St Magnus Festival ARTS, MUSIC
(☏ 01856 871445; www.stmagnusfestival.com) A colourful celebration of music and the arts in late June.

🛏 Sleeping

Orcades Hostel HOSTEL £
(☏ 01856-873745; www.orcadeshostel.com; Muddisdale Rd; dm/s/d £20/40/52; P@🛜) Book ahead to get a bed in this cracking hostel on the western edge of town. It's a guesthouse conversion so there's a very smart kitchen and lounge, and great-value doubles. Comfortable dorms with just four bunks make for sound sleeping; young, enthusiastic owners give the place spark.

Kirkwall Peedie Hostel HOSTEL £
(☏ 01856-875477; www.kirkwallpeediehostel.com; Ayre Rd; dm/s/d £15/20/30; P🛜) Nestling into a corner at the end of the Kirkwall water-

front, this cute hostel set in former fisherfolk's cottages squeezes in all the necessary features for a comfortable stay. Despite the compact appearance, the dorms actually have plenty of room – and there are three tiny kitchens so you should find some elbow room. A separate 'bothy' sleeps four.

Pickaquoy Caravan & Camping Park CAMPSITE £
(☏ 01856-879900; www.pickaquoy.co.uk; Muddisdale Rd; sites per adult/child/tent £9.95/4.95/4.85; ⏱ Apr-Oct; P🛜🐾🏊) No view, but plenty of grass and excellent modern facilities. If unattended, check in at the adjacent leisure centre.

2 Dundas Crescent B&B ££
(☏ 01856-874805; www.twodundas.co.uk; 2 Dundas Cres; s/d £40/75; P🛜) This former manse is a magnificent building with four enormous rooms blessed with large windows and sizeable beds. There are plenty of period

Kirkwall

features, but the en suite bathrooms are not among them: they're sparklingly new, and one has a free-standing bathtub. Both the welcome and the breakfast will leave you most content.

Karrawa Guest House   GUESTHOUSE ££
(📞01856-871100; www.karrawaguesthouseorkney.co.uk; Inganess Rd; s/d £64/68; 🅿🛜🐕) In a peaceful location on the southeastern edge of Kirkwall, this enthusiastically-run guesthouse offers significant value for well-kept modern double rooms with comfortable mattresses. Breakfast is generously proportioned.

Lynnfield Hotel   HOTEL ££
(📞01856-872505; www.lynnfieldhotel.com; Holm Rd; s £90-100, d £115-155; 🅿🛜🐕) South of the centre, this sizeable yet intimate hotel is run with a professional touch. Rooms are individually decorated, and feature handsome furniture and plenty of character. Deluxe rooms have enormous bathrooms and opulent four-posters; others might showcase a Jacuzzi or antique desk. Public areas include a cosy dark-wood drawing room and large, well-regarded **restaurant** (dinner mains £16 to £19; noon to 1.45pm and 6pm to 8.45pm).

Ayre Hotel   HOTEL ££
(📞01856-873001; www.ayrehotel.co.uk; Ayre Rd; s/d £90/120; 🅿🛜) Right on the waterfront, this 200-year-old hotel has been recently renovated, leaving its low-ceilinged, large-bedded rooms looking very spruce. It's definitely worth paying the extra few pounds to grab one with a sea view.

Lerona   B&B ££
(📞01856-874538; Cromwell Cres; s/d £33/66; 🅿) Guests come first here, but the wee folk –

a battalion of garden gnomes and clans of dolls with lifelike stares – are close behind. The rooms, some en suite, are a good size, and friendly owners give an easygoing welcome. It's cheaper if you stay more than one night. Cromwell Crescent comes off the waterfront road just east of the centre.

West End Hotel   HOTEL ££
(📞01856-872368; www.westendkirkwall.co.uk; Main St; s/d £72/105; 🅿🛜🐕) Run with gentle courtesy, this attractive pale-blue-and-yellow hotel has a series of old-fashioned rooms that are gradually being modernised by the proprietors. The attic rooms are cute but hobbit-sized; other updated chambers offer plenty of comfort and a teddy to cuddle. The fabulous but faded suite has an antique-filled sitting room, reminiscent of stays at some great-uncle's place.

⭐ **Albert Hotel**   HOTEL £££
(📞01856-876000; www.alberthotel.co.uk; Mounthoolie Lane; s/d £96/135; 🛜) Stylishly refurbished in plum and grey, this central but peaceful hotel is Kirkwall's finest address. Comfortable contemporary rooms in a variety of categories sport superinviting beds and smart bathrooms. A great Orkney base, with the more-than-decent Bothy Bar downstairs. Walk-in prices often cheaper.

✖ Eating & Drinking

Reel   CAFE £
(www.facebook.com/thereelkirkwall; Albert St; sandwiches £3-6; ⊙9am-6pm Mon-Sat; 🛜) Part music shop and part cafe, Kirkwall's best coffee-stop sits alongside the cathedral, and bravely puts tables outside at the slightest threat of sunshine. It's a relaxed spot, good for morning-after debriefing, a quiet Orkney ale, or lunchtime panini and musically

named sandwiches (plus the cheese-and-mushroom Skara Brie). It's a local folk musicians' centre, with regular evening sessions.

Judith Glue Real Food Cafe   CAFE £
(www.judithglue.com; 25 Broad St; light meals £5-10; ⏰9am-6pm Mon-Sat, 10am-6pm Sun year-round, to 10pm Fri & Sat May plus Mon-Sat Jun-Sep; 🔊) 🍴 At the back of a lively craft shop opposite the cathedral, this cafe serves toothsome sandwiches and salads, as well as daily specials and succulent seafood platters. There's an open kitchen and a strong emphasis on sustainable and organic ingredients, but put the feel-good factor aside for a moment and fight for a table. Check Facebook for regular events.

Bothy Bar   PUB £
(☎01856-876000; www.alberthotel.co.uk; Mounthoolie Lane; mains £7-12; ⏰noon-2pm & 5-9pm; 🔊) In the Albert Hotel, the Bothy looks very smart these days with its modish floor and B&W photos of old-time Orcadian farming, but its low tables provide old-time cheer and sustaining food. Think sausages, haddock and stews: good pub grub.

★Foveran   ORCADIAN ££
(☎01856-872389; www.thefoveran.com; St Ola; mains £15-23; ⏰6.30-8.30pm mid-Apr–mid-Oct, Fri & Sat only plus other days by arrangement off-season; 🔊) 🍴 Three miles down the Orphir road, one of Orkney's best dining options is surprisingly affordable for the quality. Tranquilly located, with a cosy eating area overlooking the sea, it shines presenting classic Orcadian ingredients – the steak with haggis and whisky sauce is feted throughout, while North Ronaldsay lamb comes in four different, deliciously tender cuts.

A medley of toothsome vegetables accompanies the mains, and interesting wines complement the dishes. If you like the spot – and why wouldn't you? – there are compact, comfortable, Laura Ashley-decorated rooms available (single/double £78/116).

Shore   GASTROPUB ££
(www.theshore.co.uk; 6 Shore St; bar meals £8-10, restaurant mains £12-18; ⏰food 11am-9.30pm; 🔊) This popular harbourside eatery offers bar meals combined with more adventurous evening fare in the restaurant section. It's run with a customer-comes-first attitude, and the seafood is especially good.

Kirkwall Hotel   PUB, SCOTTISH ££
(☎01856-872232; www.kirkwallhotel.com; Harbour St; mains £8-16; ⏰noon-2pm & 6-9pm; 🔊) This grand old waterfront hotel is one of Kirkwall's better dining places. The elegant bar and eating area packs out; it's a favourite spot for an evening out with the clan. A fairly standard pub-food list is complemented by a seasonal menu featuring local seafood and meat – the lamb is delicious. The more modern bar down the side, Skippers, also does food.

Helgi's   PUB ££
(www.helgis.co.uk; 14 Harbour St; mains £10-12; ⏰food noon-9pm, from 12.30pm Sun; 🔊) There's a traditional cosiness about this place, but the decor has moved beyond the time-honoured beer-soaked carpet to a comfortable contemporary slate floor and quotes from the *Orkneyinga Saga* plastering the walls. It's more find-a-table than jostle-at-the-bar and serves cheerful, well-priced comfort food – light bites only between 2pm and 5pm. Take your pint upstairs for quiet harbour contemplation.

🛍 Shopping

Kirkwall has some gorgeous jewellery and crafts along Albert St. The Longship (☎01856-888790; www.olagoriejewellery.com; 7 Broad St; ⏰10am-5pm Mon-Sat Sep-May, 9am-5.30pm daily Oct-Apr), established in 1859, has Orkney-made crafts, food, gifts and exquisite designer jewellery across adjacent shops.

ℹ Information

Balfour Hospital (☎01856-888000; www.ohb. scot.nhs.uk; New Scapa Rd) Follow Junction Road south out of town and you'll see it on your right.

Kirkwall Tourist Office (☎01856-872856; kirkwall@visitscotland.com; West Castle St; ⏰9am-6pm daily Jun-Sep, 9am-5pm Mon-Fri & 10am-2pm Sat Oct-Apr, 9am-6pm Mon-Sat & 10am-2pm Sun May) Has a good range of Orkney info. Shares building with the bus station.

ℹ Getting There & Away

AIR
Flybe (p409) and Loganair (p409) services use **Kirkwall Airport** (www.hial.co.uk), located a few miles east of town and served by bus 4.

BOAT
Ferries to the Northern Islands depart from the town harbour; however, ferries to Aberdeen and

Shetland use the Hatston terminal, 1 mile north-west. Bus X10 shuttles out there regularly.

BUS

All services leave from the **bus station** (West Castle St);

Bus X1 Stromness (£3, 30 minutes, hourly, seven Sunday); St Margaret's Hope (£2.80)

Bus 2 Orphir and Houton (£2.70, 20 minutes, four or five daily Monday to Saturday)

Bus 5 Evie (£2.70, 30 minutes, three to five daily Monday to Saturday), Tingwall (Rousay ferry) and Birsay.

East Mainland to South Ronaldsay

After a German U-boat sank battleship HMS *Royal Oak* in 1939, Winston Churchill had causeways of concrete blocks erected across the channels on the eastern side of Scapa Flow, linking Mainland to the islands of Lamb Holm, Glims Holm, Burray and South Ronaldsay. The Churchill Barriers, flanked by rusting wrecks of blockships, now support the main road from Kirkwall to Burwick.

ℹ Getting There & Away

Bus 3 from Kirkwall runs to Deerness in East Mainland (£2.70, 30 minutes, three to five Monday to Saturday), some via Tankerness. Bus X1 goes to South Ronaldsay's St Margaret's Hope (£2.80, 30 minutes, almost hourly Monday to Saturday).

East Mainland

At Tankerness is the mysterious Iron Age site of **Mine Howe** (☑ 01865-861234; www.minehowe.com; adult/child £4/2; ⊙ 10am-4pm daily Jun-Aug, 11am-3pm Tue & Fri Sep & May), an eerie underground construction of unknown function. In the centre of an earthen mound ringed by a ditch, a claustrophobic, precarious flight of narrow steps descends steeply to a stone-lined chamber about 1.5m in diameter and 4m high. At the time of research it was closed due to storm damage but will hopefully reopen.

Lamb Holm

This tiny island's **Italian Chapel** (☑ 01865-781268; ⊙ 9am-dusk) FREE was once in a POW camp housing Italian soldiers working on the Churchill Barriers. They built the chapel in their spare time, using Nissen huts, scrap metal and considerable artistic skills. It's an extraordinary monument to human ingenuity.

Alongside is the enthusiastic shop of **Orkney Wine Company** (☑ 01856-781736; www.orkneywine.co.uk; ⊙ 10am-5pm Mon-Sat May-Sep, plus noon-4pm Sun Jul & Aug, reduced hours Mar-Apr & Oct-Dec, closed Jan & Feb), which produces handmade wines made from berries, flowers and vegetables, all naturally fermented. Get stuck into some strawberry-rhubarb wine or blackcurrant port – unusual flavours but surprisingly delicious.

Burray

POP 400

This small island has a fine beach at Northtown on the east coast, where you may see seals.

⊙ Sights

Orkney Fossil & Vintage Centre　　MUSEUM
(☑ 01865-731255;　www.orkneyfossilcentre.co.uk; adult/child £4/2.50; ⊙ 10am-5pm mid-Apr–Sep) A quirky collection of household and farming relics, 360-million-year-old Devonian fish fossils found locally and galleries devoted to the world wars, including a display on the Churchill Barriers. There's an excellent coffee shop here. It's on the left half a mile after crossing to Burray, coming from Kirkwall.

🛏 Sleeping & Eating

Sands Hotel　　HOTEL **££**
(☑ 01856-731298; www.thesandshotel.co.uk; s/d/ste £90/115/165; P 🐕 🔊) This commodious refurbished 19th-century herring station is right on the pier in Burray village. Rooms have stylish furnishings, and all have great water views. Families and groups should consider a suite: brilliant two-level self-contained flats that sleep four and have a kitchen. There's a good restaurant (noon to

---

BLACKENINGS

Some attractive Orcadian caught your eye? Think twice, because weddings up here are traditionally preceded by a 'blackening'. The groom (and these days, often the bride) is stripped naked by friends, painted with treacle, floured, feathered and paraded around town before being bound to the Mercat Cross with clingfilm. You have been warned.

2pm and 6pm to 9pm) with a genteel nautical feel.

South Ronaldsay

POP 900

South Ronaldsay's main village, pristine St Margaret's Hope, was named after the Maid of Norway, who died here in 1290 on her way to marry Edward II of England (strictly a political affair: Margaret was only seven years old). The ferry from Gills Bay on mainland Scotland docks here, while the passenger ferry from John O'Groats lands at Burwick, at the island's southern tip.

⊙ Sights & Activities

★ **Tomb of the Eagles**   ARCHAEOLOGICAL SITE
(☑ 01865-831339;   www.tomboftheeagles.co.uk; Liddel; adult/child £7.50/3.50; ⊙ 9.30am-5.30pm Apr-Sep, 10am-noon Mar, 9.30am-12.30pm Oct) Two significant archaeological sites were found here by a farmer on his land. The first is a Bronze Age stone building with a firepit, indoor well and plenty of seating: a communal cooking site or the original Orkney pub? Beyond, in a spectacular clifftop position, the neolithic tomb (wheel yourself in prone on a trolley) is an elaborate stone construction which held the remains of up to 340 people who died some five millennia ago.

An excellent personal explanation is given to you at the visitor centre; you meet a few spooky skulls and can handle some of the artefacts found, plus absorb information on the mesolithic period. It's about a mile's airy walk to the tomb from the centre, which is near Burwick.

Banks Chambered Tomb   ARCHAEOLOGICAL SITE
(Tomb of the Otters; www.bankschamberedtomb. co.uk; Cleat; adult/child £6/free; ⊙ 10am-5pm Apr-Oct) Discovered while digging a car park, this 5000-year-old chambered tomb is still being investigated but has yielded a vast quantity of human bones, well preserved thanks to the saturation of the earth. The

tomb is dug into bedrock and makes for an atmospheric if claustrophobic visit. The guided tour from the guy who found it mixes homespun archaeological theories with astute observations.

In the visitor centre, which is a good bistro too, you can handle finds of stones and bones, including the remains of otters, who presumably used this as a den. Follow signs for Tomb of the Eagles.

🛏 Sleeping & Eating

St Margaret's Hope Backpackers   HOSTEL £
(☑ 01856-831225,   www.orkneybackpackers.com, dm £15; ℗) Just a stroll from the Gills Bay ferry, this hostel is a lovely stone cottage offering small, simple rooms with up to four berths – great for families. There's a lounge, kitchen, laundry and good, hot showers. Book in at the Trading Post shop next door.

★ **Bankburn House**   B&B ££
(☑ 01856-831310;   www.bankburnhouse.co.uk; A961; s/d £52/68, without bathroom £41/62; ℗ @ 🐾 🖵) 🐾 This large rustic house does everything right, with smashing good-sized rooms and engaging owners who put on quality breakfasts and take pride in constantly innovating to improve guests' comfort levels. The huge lawn overlooks St Margaret's Hope and the bay – perfect for sunbathing on shimmering Orkney summer days. Prices drop substantially for multinight stays.

Skerries Bistro   SEAFOOD ££
(☑ 01856-831605; www.skerriesbistro.co.uk; Cleat; lunches £5-9, dinner mains £10-18; ⊙ 11am-5pm & 6-9pm Apr-Oct) Helpful and friendly, this cafe-bistro occupies a smart, modern glass-walled building with great clifftop views near the island's southern tip. Meals range from soups and sandwiches to daily fish and shellfish specials. It's all delicious. Dinner should be booked ahead. A romantic little separate pod is available for seafood feasts.

★ **Creel**   SEAFOOD £££
(☑ 01856-831311; www.thecreel.co.uk; Front Rd, St Margaret's Hope; 2-/3-course dinner £33/40; ⊙ 7-9pm Tue-Sat Apr–mid-Oct; 🖵) 🐾 On the waterfront in an unassuming house, on unpretentious wooden tables, some of Scotland's best seafood has been served up for well over 20 years. Upstairs, three most comfortable rooms (singles/doubles £75/110) face the spectacular sunset over the water. Wooden ceilings and plenty of space give

---

ⓘ ORKNEY EXPLORER PASS

The Orkney Explorer Pass covers all Historic Scotland sites in Orkney, including Maes Howe, Skara Brae, the Broch of Gurness, the Brough of Birsay and the Bishop's Palace and Earl's Palace in Kirkwall; it costs £18/10.80/36 per adult/child/family.

them an airy feel. It was up for sale at the time of research, so fingers crossed.

West & North Mainland

This part of the island is sprinkled with outstanding prehistoric monuments: the journey to Orkney is worth it for these alone. It would take the best part of a day to see all of them – if pushed for time, visit Skara Brae then Maes Howe, but book your visit to the latter in advance.

◉ Sights

★ Maes Howe ARCHAEOLOGICAL SITE
(HS; ☎ 01856-761606; www.historic-scotland.gov. uk; adult/child £5.50/3.30; ⊗ tours hourly 10am-4pm) Egypt has pyramids, Scotland has Maes Howe. Constructed about 5000 years ago, it's an extraordinary place, a Stone Age tomb built from enormous sandstone blocks, some of which weighed many tonnes and were brought from several miles away. Creeping down the long stone passageway to the central chamber, you feel the indescribable gulf of years that separate us from the architects of this mysterious place. Though nothing is known about who and what was interred here, the scope of the project suggests it was a structure of great significance.

In the 12th century, the tomb was broken into by Vikings searching for treasure. A couple of years later, another group sought shelter in the chamber from a three-day blizzard. Waiting out the storm, they carved runic graffiti on the walls. As well as the some-things-never-change 'Olaf was 'ere' and 'Thorni bedded Helga', there are also more intricate carvings, including a particularly fine dragon and a knotted serpent.

Buy tickets in Tormiston Mill across the road. Entry is by 45-minute guided tours on the hour: reserve your tour slot ahead by phone. Oversized groups mean guides tend to only show a couple of the Viking inscriptions, but they'll happily show more if asked.

Standing Stones of Stenness ARCHAEOLOGICAL SITE
(HS; www.historic-scotland.gov.uk; ⊗ 24hr) FREE Within sight of Maes Howe, four mighty stones remain of what was once a circle of 12. Recent research suggests they were perhaps erected as long ago as 3300 BC, and they impose by their sheer size; the tallest measures 5.7m in height. The narrow strip of land they're on, the Ness of Brodgar, separates the Harray and Stenness lochs and was the site of a large settlement, inhabited throughout the neolithic period (3500–1800 BC).

Barnhouse Neolithic Village RUIN
(HS; www.historic-scotland.gov.uk; ⊗ 24hr) FREE Alongside the Standing Stones of

---

DIVING SCAPA FLOW

One of the world's largest natural harbours, Scapa Flow has been in near-constant use by fleets from the Vikings onwards. After WWI, 74 German ships were interned here; when the armistice dictated a severely reduced German navy, Admiral von Reuter, in charge of the fleet, took matters into his own hands. A secret signal was passed around and the British watched incredulously as every German ship began to sink. Fifty-two of them went to the bottom, with the rest left aground in shallow water.

Most were salvaged, but seven vessels remain to attract divers. There are three battleships – the *König*, the *Kronprinz Wilhelm* and the *Markgraf*. The first two were partially blasted for scrap, but the *Markgraf* is undamaged and considered one of Scotland's best dives.

Numerous other ships rest on the sea bed. HMS *Royal Oak*, sunk by a German U-boat in October 1939 with the loss of 833 crew, is a war grave and diving is prohibited.

It's worth prebooking diving excursions far in advance. **Scapa Scuba** (☎ 01856-851218; www.scapascuba.co.uk; Lifeboat House, Stromness; beginner's try dive £80, 2 guided dives £125-145; ⊗ noon-7pm Mon-Fri & 3-6pm Sat & Sun May-Sep) is an excellent operator that caters for both beginners – with 'try dives' around the Churchill barriers – and tried-and-tested divers. You'll need plenty of experience to dive the wrecks, some of which are 47m deep, plus have recent drysuit experience: this can be organised for you. **Diving Cellar** (☎ 01856-850055; www.divescapaflow.co.uk; Pierhead, Stromness; week diving incl B&B £485) offers intensive week-long packages, including accommodation, for experienced divers.

NESS OF BRODGAR

Ongoing excavations on the **Ness of Brodgar**, between the Stenness standing stones and the Ring of Brodgar, are rapidly revealing that this was a neolithic site of huge importance. Probably a major power and religious centre and used for over a millennium, the settlement had a mighty wall, a large building (a temple or palace?) and as many as 100 other structures, some painted. Each dig season reveals new, intriguing finds. During the season, mid-July to late August, free guided tours of the excavation run at 11am, 1pm and 3pm.

Stenness are the excavated remains of a village thought to have been inhabited by the builders of Maes Howe. Don't skip this: it brings the area to life. The houses are well preserved and similar to Skara Brae with their stone furnishings. One of the buildings was entered by crossing a fireplace: possibly of ritual significance.

Ring of Brodgar ARCHAEOLOGICAL SITE
(HS; www.historic-scotland.gov.uk; ☺24hr) **FREE**
A mile north of Stenness is this wide circle of standing stones, some over 5m tall. The last of the three Stenness monuments to be built (2500–2000 BC), it remains a most atmospheric location. Twenty-one of the original 60 stones still stand among the heather. On a grey day with dark clouds thudding low across the sky, the stones are a spine-tingling sight.

Orkney Folklore & Storytelling Visitor Centre FOLKLORE
(☏01856-841207; www.orkneyattractions.com) Located between Brodgar and Skara Brae, this offbeat centre focuses on the islands' folkloric tradition. The best way to experience it is on one of its atmospheric storytelling evenings, Peatfire Tales of Orkney (Sunday, Tuesday and Friday at 8.30pm March to October, adult/child £10/6) where local legends are told with musical accompaniment around a peat fire. It also runs interesting guided walks of the coastline and of Stromness (£7) and offers B&B.

⭐**Skara Brae** ARCHAEOLOGICAL SITE
(HS; www.historic-scotland.gov.uk; joint ticket with Skaill House adult/child £7.10/4.30; ☺9.30am-5.30pm Apr-Sep, to 4.30pm Oct-Mar)

Idyllically situated by a sandy bay 8 miles north of Stromness, and predating Stonehenge and the pyramids of Giza, extraordinary Skara Brae is northern Europe's best-preserved prehistoric village. Even the stone furniture – beds, boxes and dressers – has survived the 5000 years since a community lived and breathed here. It was hidden under dunes until an 1850 storm exposed the houses underneath.

There's an excellent interactive exhibit and short video, arming visitors with facts and theory, which will enhance the impact of the site. You then enter a reconstructed house, giving the excavation, which you head on to next, more meaning.

The joint ticket also gets you into **Skaill House** (HS; ☺Apr-Sep), a mansion built for the bishop in 1620. It's a bit anticlimactic catapulting straight from the neolithic to the 1950s decor, but you can see a smart hidden compartment in the library as well as the bishop's original 17th-century four-poster bed.

Buses run to Skara Brae from Kirkwall and Stromness a few times weekly in summer, but not all are useful to visit the site. It's possible to walk along the coast from Stromness to Skara Brae (9 miles), or it's an easy taxi (£15), hitch or cycle from Stromness. If you ring before 3pm the day before, you can book **Octobus** (☏01856-871536; www.octocic.co.uk) from Kirkwall (£3.20 each way).

Orkney Brewery BREWERY
(☏01856-841777; www.orkneybrewery.co.uk; Quoyloo; tour adult/child £6/3.50; ☺10am-4.30pm Mon-Sat & 11am-4.30pm Sun Apr-Oct plus most of Dec, winter opening by arrangement) These folk have been producing their brilliant Orcadian beers – Dark Island is a standout, while Skullsplitter lives up to its name – for years now, but this new visitor centre is a great place to come and try them. Tours run regularly and explain the brewing process, while, fashionably decked out in local stone, the cafe-bar is atmospheric.

Birsay

The small village of Birsay is 6 miles north of Skara Brae.

⊙ Sights & Activities

Earl's Palace RUIN
(☺24hr) **FREE** The ruins of this palace, built in the 16th century by the despotic Robert Stewart, earl of Orkney, dominate the village

of Birsay. Today it's a mass of half walls and crumbling columns; the size of the palace is impressive, matching the reputed ego and tyranny of its former inhabitant.

Brough of Birsay ARCHAEOLOGICAL SITE
(HS; www.historic-scotland.gov.uk; adult/child £4.50/2.70; ☺9.30am-5.30pm mid-Jun–Sep) At low tide – check tide times at any Historic Scotland site – you can walk out to this windswept island, site of extensive Norse ruins, including a number of longhouses and 12th-century St Peter's Church. There's also a replica of a Pictish stone found here. St Magnus was buried here after his murder on Egilsay in 1117, and the island became a pilgrimage place. The attractive lighthouse has fantastic views. Take a picnic, but don't get stranded...

🛏 Sleeping & Eating

Birsay Hostel HOSTEL, CAMPSITE £
(📖after hours 01856-721470, office hours 01856-873535; www.orkney.gov.uk; tent sites 1/2 people £6.45/10.25, dm/tw £16.60/46; 🅿🐾) A former activity centre and school now has dorms that vary substantially in spaciousness – go for two- or four-bedded ones. There's a big kitchen and a grassy camping area; kids and families sleep substantially cheaper. It's on the A967 south of Birsay village.

Birsay Bay Tearoom CAFE £
(www.birsaybaytearoom.co.uk; Birsay; light meals £3-6; ☺11am-3.30pm Fri-Sun Oct-Mar, 11am-4.30pm Wed-Sun Apr, 11am-6pm Wed-Mon May-Sep; 📶) A pleasant spot with sweeping views over green grass, black cows and blue-grey sea, this serves teas, coffees, home-baking and light meals. It's a good spot to wait for the tide to go out before crossing to the Brough, in plain sight.

Evie

On an exposed headland at Aikerness, 1.5 miles northeast from the village of Evie, the Broch of Gurness (HS; www.historic-scotland.gov.uk; adult/child £5.50/3.30; ☺9.30am-12.30pm & 1.30-5.30pm Apr-Sep) is a fine example of the drystone fortified towers that were both a status symbol for powerful farmers and useful protection from raiders some 2200 years ago. The imposing entranceway and sturdy stone walls – originally 10m high – are impressive; inside you can see the hearth and where a mezzanine floor would have fitted. Around the broch are a number of well-preserved outbuildings, including a curious shamrock-shaped house. The visitor centre has some interesting displays on the culture that built these remarkable fortifications.

Stromness

POP 1800

This appealing grey-stone port has a narrow, elongated, flagstone-paved main street and tiny alleys leading down to the waterfront between tall houses. It lacks Kirkwall's size but makes up for that with bucketloads of character, having changed little since its heyday in the 18th century, when it was a busy staging post for ships avoiding the troublesome English Channel during European wars. Stromness is ideally located for trips to Orkney's major prehistoric sites.

◉ Sights

The main recreation in Stromness is simply strolling up and down the narrow, atmospheric main street, where cars and pedestrians move at the same pace.

★Stromness Museum MUSEUM
(📖01856-850025; www.stromnessmuseum.co.uk; 52 Alfred St; adult/child £4.50/1; ☺10am-5pm daily Apr-Sep, 11am-3.30pm Mon-Sat Oct-Mar) A superb museum full of knick-knacks from maritime and natural-history exhibitions covering whaling, the Hudsons Bay Company and the sunk German fleet. You can happily nose around for a couple of hours. Across the street is the house where local poet and novelist George Mackay Brown lived.

Pier Arts Centre GALLERY
(📖01856-850209; www.pierartscentre.com; 30 Victoria St; ☺10.30am-5pm Tue-Sat, plus Mon Jun-Aug) FREE This gallery has really rejuvenated the Orkney modern-art scene with its sleek lines and upbeat attitude. It's worth a look as much for the architecture as its high-quality collection of 20th-century British art and the changing exhibitions.

🎭 Festivals & Events

Orkney Folk Festival MUSIC
(www.orkneyfolkfestival.com) A four-day event in late May, with folk concerts, *ceilidhs* and casual pub sessions. Stromness packs out, and late-night buses from Kirkwall are laid on. Book tickets and accommodation ahead.

🛏 Sleeping

Hamnavoe Hostel
HOSTEL £

(☎01856-851202; www.hamnavoehostel.co.uk; 10a North End Rd; dm/s/tw £20/22/44; 🛜) This well-equipped hostel is efficiently run and boasts excellent facilities, including a fine kitchen and a lounge room with great perspectives over the water. The dorms are very commodious, with duvets, decent mattresses and reading lamps (bring a pound coin for the heating), and the showers are good. Ring ahead as the owner lives off-site.

Brown's Hostel
HOSTEL £

(☎01856-850661; www.brownsorkney.co.uk; 45 Victoria St; s £20, d £36-45; @🛜) On the main street, this handy, sociable place has cosy private rooms – no dorms, no bunks – at a good price. There's an inviting common area, where you can browse the free internet or swap pasta recipes in the open kitchen. There are en suite rooms in a house up the street, with self-catering options available.

Point of Ness Caravan & Camping Park
CAMPSITE £

(☎office hrs 01856-873535, site 01856-850532; www.orkney.gov.uk; Ness Rd; tent sites 1/2 people £7.20/11.20; ☺Apr-Sep; P🛜⛺) This breezy, fenced-in campground has a super location overlooking the bay at the southern end of town and is as neat as a pin. There's free wi-fi.

★ Brinkies Guest House
B&B ££

(☎01856 851881; www.brinkiesguesthouse.co.uk; s £50, d £75-80; P🛜) Just a short walk from the centre, but with a lonely, king-of-the-castle position overlooking the town and bay, this exceptional place offers five-star islander hospitality. Compact, modern rooms are handsome, stylish and comfortable, public areas are done out most attractively in wood, but above all it's the charming owner's flexibility and can-do attitude that makes this so special.

Breakfast is 'continental Orcadian' – a stupendous array of quality local cheese, smoked fish and homemade bere bannocks. Want a lie-in? No problem, saunter down at 10am. Don't want breakfast? How about packed lunch instead? Take Outertown Rd off Back Rd, turn right on to Brownstown Rd, and keep going.

Burnside Farm
B&B ££

(☎01856-850723; www.burnside-farm.com; North End Rd; s £50, d £80-95; P🛜) A most pleasing option on a working dairy farm on the edge of Stromness, this offers lovely views over green fields, the town and harbour. Rooms are elegant, and maintain the style from when the house was built in the late 1940's, with elegant period furnishings. The top-notch bathrooms, however, are sparklingly contemporary. Breakfast is served with vistas, and the kindly owner couldn't be more welcoming.

Ferry Inn
INN ££

(☎01856-850280; www.ferryinn.com; 10 John St; s £52, d £70-90; 🛜) With a wide variety of rooms divided between the pub itself and a guesthouse opposite, the Ferry is a useful accommodation option in Stromness, which can fill up fast. New owners have renovated the chambers, and they are mostly a good size, with attractive modern decor and OK bathrooms.

🍴 Eating & Drinking

Ferry Inn
PUB £

(☎01856-850280; www.ferryinn.com; 10 John St; mains £7-14; ☺food noon-2pm & 5-9pm Mon-Fri, noon-9pm Sat & Sun; 🛜) Every port has its pub, and in Stromness it's the Ferry. Convivial and central, it warms the cockles with folk music, local beers and characters, and pub food that offers plenty of value in a dining area done out like the deck of a ship. The fish 'n' chips are excellent, and a few blackboard specials fill things out. It's also open for breakfasts.

Hamnavoe Restaurant
SEAFOOD ££

(☎01856-850606; 35 Graham Pl; mains £15-22; ☺6-9pm Tue-Sun Jun-Aug) Tucked away off the main street, this Stromness favourite specialises in excellent local seafood in an intimate, cordial atmosphere. There's always something good off the boats, and the chef prides himself on his lobster. Booking is a must. It usually opens weekends off-season.

Stromness Hotel
SEAFOOD, PUB ££

(☎01856-850298; www.stromnesshotel.com; 15 Victoria St; mains £10-19; ☺6-9pm daily, plus noon-2pm Sat & Sun; 🛜) This central hotel does decent local seafood dishes plus a few Indian curries and skewers, with some vegetarian options. There's a lounge bar with harbour views, or the earthier, convivial Flattie Bar downstairs.

ℹ Information

Stromness Tourist Office (☎01856-850716; www.visitorkney.com; Ferry Rd; ⏱10am-4pm Mon-Fri & 8.30am-2.30pm Sat Apr-May, 9am-5pm daily Jun-Oct) In the ferry terminal.

ℹ Getting There & Around

BOAT

Northlink Ferries (p409) runs services from Stromness to Scrabster on the mainland (high season passenger £19.15, car £58, 1½ hours, two to three daily).

BUS

Bus X1 runs regularly to Kirkwall (£3, 30 minutes) and on to St Margaret's Hope.

Hoy

POP 400

Orkney's second-largest island, Hoy (meaning 'High Island'), got the lion's share of the archipelago's scenic beauty. Shallow turquoise bays lace the east coast and massive sea cliffs guard the west, while peat and moorland cover Orkney's highest hills. Much of the north is a reserve for breeding seabirds. Book ahead for the car ferry to Hoy.

◎ Sights & Activities

Scapa Flow Visitor Centre MUSEUM
(☎01856-791300; www.orkney.gov.uk; Lyness; admission by donation; ⏱9am-4.30pm Mon-Fri Mar-Oct, plus 9am-4.30pm Sat May-Oct, 1st ferry arrival to 4pm Sun May-Sep) Lyness was an important naval base during both world wars, when the British Grand Fleet was based in Scapa Flow. This fascinating museum and photographic display, located in an old pumphouse that once fed fuel to the ships, is a must-see for anyone interested in Orkney's military history. Take your time to browse the exhibits and have a look at the folders of supplementary information: letters home from a seaman lost when the *Royal Oak* was torpedoed are particularly moving.

Old Man of Hoy ROCK FORMATION
Hoy's best-known sight is this spectacular 137m-high rock stack jutting from the ocean off the tip of an eroded headland. It's a tough ascent for experienced climbers only but a great walk from Rackwick (6 miles return). You can see it from the Scrabster–Stromness ferry.

🛏 Sleeping & Eating

Hoy Centre HOSTEL £
(☎office hours 01856-873535, warden 01856-791315; www.orkney.gov.uk; dm/tw £18/49; ℗) This clean, bright modern hostel has an enviable location, around 15 minutes' walk from Moaness Pier, at the base of the rugged Cuilags. Rooms are all en suite and include good-value family options; there's also a spacious kitchen and DVD lounge. The same people run a simpler hostel at Rackwick, five miles away.

Wild Heather B&B ££
(☎01856-791098; www.wildheatherbandb.co.uk; Lyness; s/d £43/69; ℗) Turn right from the Lyness ferry to reach this great place right on the bay. The lovely room is frilly and spotless, with soul-soothing water views from your own wee conservatory, where you also tuck into breakfast. Packed lunches and three-course dinners (£16.50) are available, as well as cycle storage and a genuine welcome. The owners' daughter runs a cute craft shop alongside.

Stromabank Hotel PUB ££
(☎01856-701494; www.stromabank.co.uk; Longhope; ⏱6-9pm Sat, 12.30-2pm & 6-9pm Sun Sep-May, plus 6-9pm Mon-Wed & Fri Jun-Aug; ℗🐾) Perched on the hill above Longhope, the small atmospheric Stromabank has very acceptable, refurbished en suite rooms (s/d £45/70), as well as tasty home-cooked meals, including seafood and steaks (£7 to £14) using lots of local produce. The owners were looking to sell, so details may change.

ℹ Getting There & Away

Orkney Ferries (p409) runs a passenger/bike ferry (adult £4.25, 30 minutes, two to six daily) between Stromness and Moaness at Hoy's northern end, and a car ferry to Lyness from Houton on Mainland (passenger/car £4.25/13.60, 40 minutes, up to seven daily Monday to Friday, two or three Saturday and Sunday); book cars in advance. Sunday service is May to September only.

A bus meets the ferries and runs to Hoy's main settlements.

Northern Islands

The group of windswept islands north of Mainland is a haven for birds, rich in archaeological sites, and blessed with wonderful white-sand beaches and azure seas. Some give a real sense of what Orkney was like before the modern world infringed upon island life.

Note that the 'ay' at the end of island names (from the Old Norse for 'island') is pronounced 'ee'.

❶ Getting There & Away

Orkney Ferries (☑ 01856-872044; www. orkneyferries.co.uk) and **Loganair** (☑ 01857-873457; www.loganair.co.uk) enable you to make day trips to many of the islands from Kirkwall. That said, it's really best to stay and soak up the slow, easy pace of life.

Shapinsay

POP 300

Just a short ferry hop from Kirkwall, Shapinsay is an intensively cultivated island whose southern end is dominated by 19th-century **Balfour Castle** and good beaches along its western edge. About 4 miles from the pier, at the island's northeastern corner, Iron Age **Burroughston Broch** is one of the best preserved of these defensive towers in Orkney.

❶ Getting There & Away

Orkney Ferries (p409) operates a ferry from Kirkwall (passenger/car £4.25/13.60, 25 minutes). Services are limited in winter.

Rousay

POP 200

Off the north coast of Mainland, Rousay makes a great day trip, but you'll feel like staying longer. This hilly island is famous for its numerous excellent archaeological sites.

◉ Sights & Activities

You can hire a bike (£7 per day) at Trumland Farm and make the hilly 14-mile circuit of the island. You can walk from the ferry pier to Midhowe Broch, taking in all the main historic sites (12 miles return, allow six hours).

The major archaeological sites are clearly labelled from the road ringing the island. Heading west from the ferry, you soon come to **Taversoe Tuick**, an intriguing burial cairn constructed on two levels, with separate entrances – perhaps a joint tomb for different families; a semidetached solution in posthumous housing. Not far beyond are two other significant cairns: **Blackhammer**,

then **Knowe of Yarso**, the latter a fair walk up the hill but with majestic views.

★ Midhowe Cairn
& Broch ARCHAEOLOGICAL SITES
(HS; www.historic-scotland.gov.uk; ⊘24hr) FREE
Six miles from the ferry, mighty **Midhowe Cairn** has been dubbed the 'Great Ship of Death'. Built around 3500 BC and enormous, it's divided into compartments, in which the remains of 25 people were found. Covered by a protective stone building, it's nevertheless memorable. Adjacent **Midhowe Broch**, whose sturdy stone lines echo the rocky shoreline's striations, is a muscular Iron Age fortified compound with a mezzanine floor. The sites are on the water, a 10-minute walk downhill from the main road.

🛏 Sleeping & Eating

Trumland Farm HOSTEL £
(☑01856-821252; trumland@btopenworld.com; sites £5, dm £12-14; ℗ 🐾) 🐾 An easy stroll from the ferry (turn left at the main road), this organic farm has a wee hostel with two dorms and a pretty little kitchen and common area. You can pitch tents and use the facilities; there's also well-equipped self-catering in a cottage and various farm buildings.

Taversoe Hotel HOTEL ££
(☑01856-821325; www.taversoehotel.co.uk; s/d £50/80; ℗) Two miles west from the ferry pier, the island's only hotel is a low-key place, with neat, simple doubles with water vistas that share a bathroom and a twin with en suite but no view. The best views are from the dining room, which serves good-value meals (noon to 5pm Monday, noon to 9pm Tuesday to Saturday and noon to 7.30pm Sunday in summer). The friendly owners will collect you from the ferry.

❶ Getting There & Around

BOAT
A small **ferry** (☑01856-751360; www.orkneyferries.co.uk) connects Tingwall on Mainland with Rousay (return passenger/bicycle/car £8.50/free/27.20, 30 minutes, up to six daily) and the nearby islands of Egilsay and Wyre. Vehicle bookings are compulsory.

TAXI
Rousay Tours (☑01856-821234; www.rousaytours.co.uk; adult/child £30/10) offers taxi service and recommended guided tours of the island, including wildlife-spotting (seals and

otters), visits to the prehistoric sites and optional tasty packed lunch.

Stronsay

POP 350

Stronsay attracts walkers and cyclists for its lack of serious inclines and the beautiful landscapes of its four curving bays. You can spot wildlife here: chubby seals basking on the rocks, puffins and other seabirds.

🛏 Sleeping & Eating

Stronsay Hotel   HOTEL ££
(☎ 01857-616213; www.stronsayhotelorkney.co.uk; s/d £50/79; 🛜🏠) The island's watering hole is near the ferry and has immaculate refurbished rooms. There's also recommended pub grub in the bar.

ℹ Getting There & Away

AIR

Loganair (p423) flies from Kirkwall to Stronsay (£37 one way, 20 minutes, one or two daily).

BOAT

A **ferry** (☎ 01856-872044; www.orkneyferries. co.uk) links Kirkwall with Stronsay (passenger/car £8.35/19.70, 1½ hours, two to three daily) and Eday.

Eday

POP 150

This slender island was extensively cut for peat to supply the surrounding islands. The interior is hilly and covered in peat bog, while the coast and the north of the island are low-lying and green.

◉ Sights

Eday Heritage & Visitor Centre   MUSEUM
(☎ 01857-622283; www.visiteday.com; ◷ 9am-5.30pm daily May-Sep, 10am-5pm Sun Oct-Apr) FREE Has a range of local history exhibits, as well as an audiovisual about tidal energy initiatives: there's a big test project just offshore.

👉 Tours

Eday Minibus Tour   GUIDED TOURS
(☎ 01857-622206; adult/child £14/12) Offers taxi service and 2¼-hour guided tours from the ferry pier on Monday, Wednesday and Friday from May to mid-September.

OUT TO THE ISLANDS

It's well worth getting out to explore Orkney's further-flung islands, accessible by reasonably priced ferry or plane. Though you can see 'the sights' in a matter of hours, the key is to stay a day or two and relax into the pace of island life.

Though some are hillier than others, all offer a broadly similar landscape of flattish green farmland running down to scenic coastline.

Nearly all have places where you can camp, hire bikes and sleep cheaply. Most islands offer a bus service that meets ferries: you may have to call to book this. The *Islands of Orkney* magazine, available from tourist offices, has detailed listings and maps for every island.

🛏 Sleeping & Eating

Eday Hostel   HOSTEL £
(☎ 07977-281084; dm £12-15; 🅿@🛜) Four miles north of the ferry pier, this recently renovated, community-run hostel is a simple but comfortable place to stay. You can camp alongside too at no cost and there are bikes available to hire.

ℹ Getting There & Away

AIR

There's a Monday and Wednesday flight from Kirkwall (one-way £37, 30 minutes) to London airport – that's London, Eday.

BOAT

Ferries sail from Kirkwall, sometimes via Stronsay or Sanday (passenger/car £8.35/19.70, two hours, two to three daily).

Sanday

POP 500

Aptly named, blissfully quiet flat Sanday is ringed by Orkney's best beaches – with dazzling-white sand of the sort you'd expect in the Caribbean. It's a peaceful, green, pastoral landscape with the sea revealed at every turn.

ORKNEYINGA SAGA

Written around 1200, this saga is a rich tale of sorcery, political intrigue, and cunning and unscrupulous acts among the Viking earls of Orkney. Part myth and part historical fact, it begins with the capture of the islands by the king of Norway and recounts the tumultuous centuries until they become part of Scotland. It's a wonderful piece of medieval literature and well worth a read. I lead to the Orkneyinga Saga Centre (⊙9am-6pm late May-late Oct) FREE in the south coast village of Orphir for more background.

⊙ Sights

Quoyness Chambered Tomb
ARCHAEOLOGICAL SITE

(⊙24hr) FREE There are several archaeological sites on Sanday, the most impressive being the Quoyness chambered tomb, similar to Maes Howe and dating from the 3rd millennium BC. It has triple walls, a main chamber and six smaller cells.

Sanday Heritage Centre
MUSEUM

(Lady; entry by donation; ⊙9am-5pm Mar-Oct) This new museum in the former temperance hall has intriguing displays on various aspects of island history, including fishing, the wars, archaeology and shipwrecks. In an adjacent field, a typical croft house is preserved.

🛏 Sleeping & Eating

Two adjacent pubs in the main settlement, Kettletoft, offer accommodation and basic bar meals.

Ayre's Rock Hostel & Campsite
HOSTEL, CAMPSITE £

(☎01857-600410; www.ayres-rock-hostel-orkney. com; tent sites 1-/2-person £7/9, pods per person £10, dm/s/tw £15/18/30; P🛜🐕) This super-friendly spot six miles north of the ferry by a beach offers a cosy hostel with three rooms sleeping two or four in beds, and a sweet grassy campsite by the water. As well as tent pitches, there are heated two-person pods and a static caravan. There's a craft shop and Saturday chip shop on-site, and the hosts are extremely helpful.

Backaskaill
B&B ££

(☎01857-600305; www.bedandbreakfastsanday-orkney.com; s/d £45/75; P🛜) Set on a working cattle farm by the sea, this offers comfortable accommodation in a noble stone farmhouse. The polished interior features an eclectic collection of art and curios and cordial, professional hospitality. Rooms feel light and modern, and there's a fabulous guest lounge. The island's best meals (mains £9 to £16) are here and can be booked by non-guests.

ℹ Getting There & Away

AIR

There are flights from Kirkwall to Sanday (one way £37, 20 minutes, once or twice daily).

BOAT

Ferries run from Kirkwall (passenger/car £8.35/19.70, 1½ hours), with a link to Eday. A bus meets the boat.

Westray
POP 600

If you've time to visit only one of Orkney's Northern Islands, make Westray (www.westraypapawestray.co.uk) the one. The largest of the group, it has rolling farmland, handsome sandy beaches, great coastal walks and several appealing places to stay.

⊙ Sights & Activities

Noup Head
NATURE RESERVE

FREE This bird reserve at Westray's north-western tip is a dramatic area of sea cliffs with vast numbers of breeding seabirds from April to July. You can walk here along the clifftops from a car park, passing the impressive chasm of Ramni Geo, and return via the lighthouse access road (4 miles).

Westray Heritage Centre
MUSEUM

(☎01857-677414; www.westrayheritage.co.uk; Pierowall; adult/child £3/50p; ⊙10am-noon Tue-Sat & 2-5pm Sun May-Sep) This has displays on local history, nature dioramas and archaeological finds, with some famous neolithic carvings (including the 5000-year-old 'Westray Wife'). These small sandstone figurines are the oldest known depictions of the human form so far found in the British Isles.

★ Noltland Castle
CASTLE

(⊙8am-8pm) FREE A half-mile west of Pierowall stands this sturdy ruined towerhouse, built in the 16th century by Gilbert Balfour, aide to Mary, Queen of Scots. The castle is super-atmospheric and bristles with shot holes, part of the defences of the deceitful Balfour, who plotted to murder Cardinal Beaton and, after being exiled, the king of Sweden. Like a pantomime villain, he met a sticky end.

Tours

Westraak
GUIDED TOURS

(☎ 01857-677777; www.westraak.co.uk; Quarry Rd, Pierowall) Runs informative and engaging trips around the island, covering everything from Viking history to puffin mating habits.

Sleeping & Eating

★ West Manse
B&B £

(☎ 01857-677482; www.westmanse.co.uk; Westside; r per person £20; P🖥🐾) ✎ No timetables reign at this imposing house with arcing coastal vistas; make your own breakfast when you feel like it. Your welcoming hosts have introduced a raft of green solutions for heating, fuel and more. Kids will love this unconventional place, its play nooks and hobbit house, while art exhibitions, cooking and blacksmithing classes, venerably comfortable furniture and clean air are drawcards for parents.

Chalmersquoy & The Barn
B&B, HOSTEL £

(☎ 01857-677214; http://chalmersquoywestray. co.uk; Pierowall; dm £20, apt per night £60-100, tent sites £5-8 plus per adult/child £2/1; P🖥) This excellent, intimate, modern hostel is an Orcadian gem. It's heated throughout and has pristine kitchen facilities and an inviting lounge; rooms sleep two or three in comfort. Out the front, the lovely owners have top self-catering apartments with great views, and three spacious en suite B&B rooms. There's also a campground on-site. A recommended all-round choice.

Bis Geos
SELF-CATERING £

(☎ 01857-677420; www.bisgeos.co.uk; per week from £350; P) Stunning views at this spectacular, quirky and cosy self-catering option between Pierowall and Noup Head.

Braehead Manse
B&B, SELF-CATERING ££

(☎ 01857-677861; www.braeheadmanse.co.uk; Braehead; s/d £65/90; P🖥) ✎ A top-notch conversion of a former village hall behind the church in the middle of the island, this has two luminous, high-ceilinged rooms with modern en suite bathrooms and a swish open-plan kitchen/living/dining area.

You can either take it as self-catering – perfect for a family of four – or B&B.

Pierowall Hotel
PUB £

(☎ 01857-677472; www.pierowallhotel.co.uk; Pierowall; mains £8-11; ⊙ food noon-1.30pm & 5-8.30pm; 🖥) The heart of this island community, the refurbished local pub is famous throughout Orkney for its popular fish and chips – whatever has turned up in the day's catch by the hotel's boats is displayed on the blackboard. There are also some curries available, but the sea is the way to go here. It also has rooms, hires bikes and offers internet access.

ⓘ Getting There & Around

AIR

There are daily flights from Kirkwall to Westray (one way £37, 20 minutes).

BOAT

A ferry (p409) links Kirkwall with Rapness (passenger/car £8.35/19.70, 1½ hours, daily). A bus to the main town, Pierowall, meets the ferry.

Papa Westray

POP 90

Known locally as Papay, this exquisitely peaceful, tiny island (4 miles by 1 mile) is home to possibly Europe's oldest domestic building, the **Knap of Howar** (⊙24hr) **FREE** (5500 years old), and largest arctic tern colony. Plus the two-minute hop from Westray is the world's shortest scheduled air service. The island was the cradle of Christianity in Orkney – **St Boniface Kirk** (⊙24hr) **FREE** was founded in the 8th century, though most of it dates to the 12th.

Sleeping & Eating

Beltane House
GUESTHOUSE, HOSTEL £

(☎ 01857-644224; www.papawestray.co.uk; dm/ s/d £17/25/35; P🖥🐾) Owned by the local community co-op, this comprises a 20-bed hostel and a guesthouse with four simple and immaculate rooms with en suite and self-catering kitchen access. It's just over a mile north of the ferry. You can camp here (£5/3 per adult/child).

ⓘ Getting There & Away

AIR

There are daily flights to Papa Westray (£18, 15 minutes) from Kirkwall, and a special £21 return fare if you stay overnight. Some of the Kirkwall flights go via Westray (£17, 2 minutes) or North Ronaldsay (£17, 10 minutes).

BOAT

A passenger-only ferry runs from Pierowall on Westray to Papa Westray (£4.15, 25 minutes, three to six daily in summer); the crossing is free if you travel direct from the Rapness ferry from Westray. From October to April the boat sails by arrangement (☑ 01857-677216).

North Ronaldsay

POP 70

North Ronaldsay is a real outpost surrounded by rolling seas and big skies. Delicious peace-and-quiet and excellent birdwatching lure visitors. There are enough semiferal sheep to seize power, but a 13-mile drystone wall running around the island keeps them off the grass; they make do with seaweed, which gives their meat a unique flavour.

☞ Tours

North Ronaldsay Tour　　　　GUIDED TOURS
(☑ 07703-112224; lighthouse or mill adult/child £6/4, combined £9/7) Offers excellent tours of one of North Ronaldsay's two lighthouses and a wool mill.

🛏 Sleeping

Observatory Guest House HOSTEL, CAMPSITE **££**
(☑ 01857-633200; www.nrbo.co.uk; sites £4.50, dm/s/d £17.50/40.50/81; P @ 🛜) ✐ Powered by wind and solar energy, this offers first-rate accommodation and ornithological activities next to the ferry pier. There's a cafe-bar with lovely coastal views and convivial communal dinners (£14.50) in a sun-kissed (sometimes) conservatory; if you're lucky, local lamb might be on the menu. You can also camp here.

ⓘ Getting There & Away

AIR

There are two or three daily flights to North Ronaldsay (£18, 20 minutes) from Kirkwall. The £21 return offer (you must stay overnight) is great value.

BOAT

A ferry runs from Kirkwall on Tuesday and Friday (passenger/car £8.35/19.70, 2½ hours).

SHETLAND

Close enough to Norway geographically and historically to make nationality an ambiguous concept, the Shetland Islands are Britain's most northerly outpost. There's a Scandinavian lilt to the local accent, and streets named King Haakon or St Olaf remind that Shetland was under Norse rule until 1469, when it was gifted to Scotland in lieu of the dowry of a Danish princess.

Though the stirringly bleak setting still feels uniquely Scottish, Shetland is far from a backwater: offshore oil makes it quite a busy, well-heeled place, with hotels frequently block-booked for workers. Nevertheless, nature still rules the seas and islands, and the birdlife is spectacular: pack binoculars.

ⓘ Getting There & Away

AIR

The main **airport** (LSI; ☑ 01950-461000; www.hial.co.uk) is at Sumburgh, 25 miles south of Lerwick. **Flybe** (☑ 0871 700 2000; www.flybe.com) runs daily services to Aberdeen, Kirkwall, Inverness, Edinburgh and Glasgow, and summer services to Bergen (Norway).

BOAT

Northlink Ferries (☑ 0845 600 0449; www.northlinkferries.co.uk; 🛜) runs daily overnight car ferries between Aberdeen and Lerwick (high-season one-way passenger/car £41/144, 12 to 15 hours), some stopping at Kirkwall, Orkney. With a basic ticket you can sleep in recliner chairs or the bar area. It's £36 for a berth in a shared cabin and up to £137 for a comparatively luxurious double cabin. Sleeping pods (£18) are comfortable, reclinable seats. There's a cafe, bar, paid lounge and cinema on-board plus slow wi-fi.

ⓘ Getting Around

AIR

Interisland flights are operated by **DirectFlight** (☑ 01595-840246; www.directflight.co.uk) from Tingwall airport, 6.5 miles northwest of Lerwick. There are big discounts for under-25s.

BOAT

Ferry services run by **Shetland Islands Council** (www.shetland.gov.uk/ferries) link Mainland to other islands.

BICYCLE

You can hire bikes from several places, including Grantfield Garage (p428; per day/week £12.50/50) in Lerwick.

BUS

An extensive bus network, coordinated by **ZetTrans** (www.zettrans.org.uk), radiates from Lerwick to all corners of Mainland, and on (via ferry) to the islands of Yell and Unst. Schedules aren't great for day tripping from Lerwick.

CAR & MOTORCYCLE

Shetland has broad, well-made roads (think 'oil money'). Car hire is fuss-free, and vehicles can be delivered to transport terminals. Prices are usually around £35/180 for a day/week.

Bolts Car Hire (☑ 01595-693636; www.boltscarhire.co.uk; 26 North Rd, Lerwick) Also has an office at Sumburgh airport.

Grantfield Garage (☑ 01595-692709; www.grantfieldgarage.co.uk; North Rd, Lerwick; ⊙ 9am-5.30pm Mon-Sat) The cheapest. A short walk towards town from the Northlink ferry terminal.

Star Rent-a-Car (☑ 01595-692075; www.starrentacar.co.uk; 22 Commercial Rd, Lerwick) Opposite the bus station. Has an office at Sumburgh airport.

Lerwick

POP 7000

Built on the herring trade, Lerwick is Shetland's only real town, home to a third of the islands' population. It has a solidly maritime feel, with aquiline oilboats competing for space in the superb natural harbour with the dwindling fishing fleet. Wandering along atmospheric Commercial St is a delight, and the excellent museum provides cultural background.

⊙ Sights

★ **Shetland Museum**   MUSEUM
(☑ 01595-695057; www.shetland-museum.org.uk; Hay's Dock; ⊙ 10am-5pm Mon-Sat, noon-5pm Sun) **FREE** This is an impressive recollection of 5000 years' worth of culture, people and their interaction with this ancient landscape. Comprehensive but never dull, the display covers everything from the archipelago's geology to its fishing industry, via local mythology – find out about scary *nyuggles* (ghostly horses) or detect *trows* (fairies). Pictish carvings and replica jewellery are among the finest pieces; the museum also includes a working lighthouse mechanism, small gallery, boat-building workshop, and archive for tracing Shetland ancestry.

Böd of Gremista   MUSEUM
(Shetland Textile Museum; www.shetlandtextilemuseum.com; Gremista Rd; admission £2; ⊙ noon-5pm Tue-Sat, to 7pm Thu May–mid-Oct) A mile north of the centre, this house, birthplace of P&O founder Arthur Anderson, was also once a fish-curing station. It now holds a display on the knitted and woven textiles

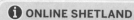

ⓘ ONLINE SHETLAND

The excellent website www.visit.shetland.org has good info on accommodation, activities and more.

and patterns that take their name from the islands.

Clickimin Broch   ARCHAEOLOGICAL SITE
FREE This fortified site, just under a mile southwest of the town centre, was occupied from the 7th century BC to the 6th century AD. It's impressively large, and its setting on a small loch gives it a feeling of being removed from the present day.

Fort Charlotte   FORTRESS
(Charlotte St; ⊙ 9.30am-sunset) **FREE** Built in 1781, this occupies the site of an earlier fortification built in 1665 to protect the harbour from the Dutch navy. The five-sided fortress never saw action, but today houses local volunteer units and provides excellent views over the harbour.

☞ Tours

Shetland Geotours   GUIDED TOURS
(☑ 01595-859218;   www.shetlandgeotours.com; per person from £45) Runs daily excursions and guided walks, focusing on geology, history and archaeology, but including some nature-watching. Check the website for the schedule.

⁂ Festivals & Events

Shetland Folk Festival   MUSIC
(www.shetlandfolkfestival.com) Held in late April or early May.

⊫ Sleeping

Lerwick has very average hotels but excellent B&Bs. It fills year-round; book ahead. There's no campsite within 15 miles.

Islesburgh House Hostel   HOSTEL £
(☑ 01595-745100;   www.islesburgh.org.uk;   King Harald St; dm/tw/q £20/40/60; ⊙ Apr-Sep; P @ ⊚) This typically grand Lerwick mansion houses an excellent hostel, with comfortable dorms, a shop, a laundry, a cafe and an industrial kitchen. Electronic keys offer excellent security and no curfew. It's wise to book ahead, and ask about winter availability as it sometimes opens for groups.

Lerwick

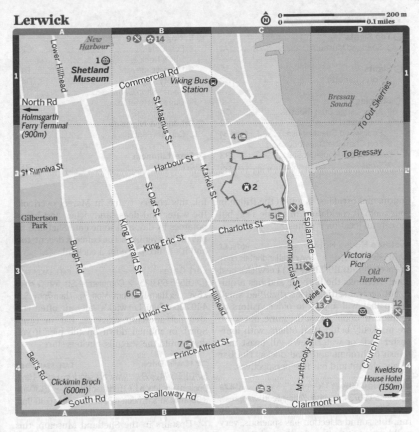

Woosung
B&B £

(☎01595-693687; conroywoosung@hotmail.com; 43 St Olaf St; s without bathroom £30-35, d without bathroom £50-55; 🛜🖵) A budget gem in the heart of Lerwick B&B-land, this has a wise and welcoming host, and comfortable, clean, good-value rooms that share a bathroom. The solid stone house dates from the 19th century, built by a clipper captain who traded tea out of the Chinese port it's named after.

★ Alder Lodge Guesthouse
B&B ££

(☎01595-695705; www.alderlodgeguesthouse. com; 6 Clairmont Pl; s/d £35/75; 🖵🛜) This stone former bank is a delightful place to stay. Imbued with a sense of space and light, the rooms are large and very well furnished, with good en suites, fridges and DVD player. Excellent hosts really make the effort to help you feel at home, and do a great breakfast, with a smoked fish option and special di-

ets catered for. There is also a self-catering house nearby.

★ Fort Charlotte Guesthouse
B&B ££

(☎01595-692140; www.fortcharlotte.co.uk; 1 Charlotte St; s/d £35/70; 🛜🖵) Sheltering under the fortress walls, this friendly place offers summery en suite rooms, including great singles. Views down the pedestrian street are on offer in some; sloping ceilings and oriental touches add charm to others. There's a bike shed and local salmon for breakfast. Very popular; book ahead.

Brentham House
B&B ££

(☎01950-460201; www.brenthamhouse.com; 7 Harbour St; s/d/apt £65/80/130; 🛜) This staffless place – pick up the keys from the restaurant on the corner – offers attractive rooms with comfy seats, decent bathrooms – big towels and powerful showers – and limited harbour views. There's a posh self-catering apartment (the Bressay Suite) also.

Lerwick

Continental breakfast is left in the fridge in your room. It could do with a little TLC, but the central location is a plus.

Kveldsro House Hotel HOTEL ££
(☎ 01595-692195; www.shetlandhotels.com; Greenfield Pl; s/d £110/135; P ☞) Lerwick's best hotel overlooks the harbour and has a quiet but central setting. It's a dignified small set-up that will appeal to older visitors or couples. All doubles cost the same, but some are markedly better than others, with four-poster beds or water views. All boast new stylish bathrooms and iPod docks. The bar area is elegant and has fine perspectives.

Eddlewood Guest House B&B ££
(☎ 01595-696734; http://eddlewood.wordpress.com; 8 Clairmont Pl; s/d £50/70; ☞) Cheerfully run, this sound selection has spacious, very well-kept en suite rooms with good showers. The top-floor rooms have plenty of character, with a cosy attic feel and good sea views. The friendly owner runs a welcoming, relaxed ship.

✖ Eating

Peerie Shop Cafe CAFE £
(☎ 01595-692816; www.peerieshopcafe.com; Esplanade; light meals £3-8; ☉ 9am-6pm Mon-Sat; ☞) If you've been craving proper espresso since leaving the mainland, head to this gem, with art exhibitions, wire-mounted halogens and industrial-gantry chic. Newspapers, scrumptious cakes and sandwiches, hot chocolate that you deserve after that blasting wind outside, and – more rarely – outdoor seating give everyone a reason to be here.

Mareel Cafe CAFE £
(Mareel; light meals £3-5; ☉ 10am-11pm Sun-Thu, 10am-1am Fri & Sat; ☞) Buzzy, arty and colour-

ful, this cheery venue in Mareel overlooks the water and does sandwiches and baked potatoes by day, and some cute Shetland tapas in the evenings. The coffee is decent, too, and it's a nice place for a cocktail.

Fort Café CAFE, TAKEAWAY £
(☎ 01595-693125; 2 Commercial St; fish & chips £6-8; ☉ 11am-10.30pm Mon-Fri, 11am-7pm Sat, 4-10.30pm Sun) Lerwick's salty air often creates fish-and-chip cravings. Eat in (until 8pm), or munch down on the pier if you don't mind the seagulls' envious stares.

★ **Hay's Dock** CAFE, SEAFOOD ££
(☎ 01595-741569; www.haysdock.co.uk; Hay's Dock; mains lunch £7-11, dinner £15-22; ☉ 10.30am-3.30pm Mon-Sat, noon-4.30pm Sun, plus 6.30-9pm Fri & Sat year-round & Tue-Thu Jun-Aug; ☞ 👶) ☕ Upstairs in the Shetland Museum, this sports a wall of picture windows and a fair-weather balcony that overlooks the harbour. Clean lines and pale wood recall Scandinavia, but the menu relies on carefully selected local and Scottish produce. Lunch ranges from delicious fish and chips to chowder, while evening menus concentrate on seafood and steak.

Queen's Hotel SCOTTISH ££
(☎ 01595-692826; www.kgqhotels.co.uk; Commercial St; mains £15-22; ☉ noon-2pm & 5.30-9.30pm; ☞) The dining room in this slightly run-down hotel wins marks for its harbour views – book one of the window tables. It's best visited for beautifully presented, classy local seafood dishes.

Monty's Bistro BRITISH ££
(☎ 01595-696555; www.montys-shetland.co.uk; 5 Mounthooly St; mains lunch £8-10, dinner £13-17; ☉ 5-9pm Mon, noon-2pm & 5-9pm Tue-Sat, noon-9.30pm Sun; ☞) ☕ Though well hidden away

behind the tourist office, Monty's is far from a secret and Shetlanders descend on it with alacrity. The upstairs dining room, with proper floorboards and an upbeat atmosphere, is a cheerful venue for good-quality British bistro fare.

Drinking & Entertainment

Check what's on at **Mareel** (☑ 01595-745555; www.mareel.org), a swish new arts venue near the museum.

Captain Flint's PUB
(2 Commercial St; ⊙11am-1am; 🔊) This portside bar – Lerwick's liveliest – throbs with happy conversation, loud music and has a distinctly nautical, creaky-wooden feel. There's a cross-section of young 'uns, tourists, boat folk and older locals. There's live music some nights and a pool table upstairs.

Shopping

Best buys are the woollen cardigans and sweaters for which Shetland is world famous. Check www.shetlandsartsandcrafts. co.uk for outlets around the islands, or grab the *Shetland Craft Trail* brochure from the tourist office.

❶ Information

There are several free wi-fi networks around the centre.
Gilbert Bain Hospital (☑ 01595-743000; www. shb.scot.nhs.uk/; South Rd)
Lerwick Tourist Office (☑ 01595-693434; lerwick@visitscotland.com; cnr Commercial St & Mounthooly St; ⊙9am-5pm Mon-Sat & 10am-4pm Sun Apr-Sep, 10am-4pm Mon-Sat

---

UP HELLY AA!!

Shetland's long Viking history has rubbed off in more ways than just street names and square-shouldered locals. Most villages have a fire festival, a continuation of Viking midwinter celebrations of the rebirth of the sun. The most spectacular happens in Lerwick.

Up Helly Aa (www.uphellyaa.org) takes place on the last Tuesday in January. Squads of *guizers* dress in Viking costume and march through the streets with blazing torches, dragging a replica longship, which they then surround and burn, bellowing out Viking songs from behind bushy beards.

Oct-Mar) Helpful, with a good range of books and maps.

❶ Getting There & Away

BOAT
Northlink Ferries (p427) dock at Holmsgarth terminal, a 15-minute walk northwest from the town centre.

BUS
From **Viking bus station** (☑ 01595-694100; Commercial Rd), buses service various corners of the archipelago, including regular services to/ from Sumburgh Airport.

Bressay & Noss
POP 400

These islands lie across Bressay Sound just east of Lerwick. Bressay (*bress*-ah) has interesting walks, especially along the cliffs and up Ward Hill (226m), which has good views of the islands. Much smaller Noss is a nature reserve.

⊙ Sights & Activities

★**Isle of Noss** NATURE RESERVE
(☑ 0800-107-7818; www.nnr-scotland.org.uk/noss; boat adult/child £3/1.50; ⊙10am-5pm Tue, Wed & Fri-Sun mid-Apr–Aug) Little Noss, 1.5 miles wide, lies just east of Bressay. High sea cliffs harbour over 100,000 pairs of breeding seabirds, while inland heath supports hundreds of pairs of great skua.

Access is by dinghy from Bressay; phone in advance to check that it's running. Walking anticlockwise around Noss is easier, with better cliff viewing. There's a small visitor centre by the dock.

Seabirds & Seals CRUISE
(☑ 07595-540224; www.seabirds-and-seals.com; adult/child £45/25; ⊙10am & 2pm mid-Apr–mid-Sep) Runs three-hour wildlife cruises around Bressay and Noss, departing from Lerwick. Includes underwater viewing. Trips run year-round, weather permitting; book by phone or at Lerwick tourist office.

🛏 Sleeping & Eating

Northern Lights Holistic Spa B&B ££
(☑ 01595-820257; www.shetlandspa.com; Uphouse; s/d £75/125; 🅿🔊) Offering huge, colourful rooms and marvellous views back over the sound towards Lerwick, this unusual place is appealingly decorated with Asian art. Room rates include sauna, steam

room and jacuzzi; massages and elaborate dinners (£37.50; BYOB) are available. Head for Uphouse; it's the big yellow building near the crest of the hill.

❶ Getting There & Away

Ferries (passenger/car return £5.20/12.80, seven minutes, frequent) link Lerwick and Bressay. The Noss crossing is 2.5 miles across the island.

Central & West Mainland

Scalloway

POP 1200

Surrounded by bare, rolling hills, Scalloway (*scall*-o-wah) – Shetland's former capital – is a busy fishing and yachting harbour with a thriving seafood-processing industry. It's 6 miles from Lerwick.

There are pretty beaches and pleasant walks on the nearby islands, linked by bridges, of Trondra and East and West Burra.

◉ Sights & Activities

Scalloway Museum   MUSEUM
(www.scallowaymuseum.org; Castle St; adult/child £3/1; ⊙11am-4pm Mon-Sat, 2-4pm Sun May-Sep; ⊞) This enthusiastic modern museum has an excellent display on Scalloway life and history, with prehistoric finds, witch-burnings and local lore all featuring. There's a detailed section on the Shetland Bus, and a fun area for kids.

Scalloway Castle   CASTLE
(HS; www.historic-scotland.co.uk; ⊙24hr) FREE The town's most promient landmark is Scalloway Castle, built around 1600 by Earl Patrick Stewart. The turreted and corbelled tower house is fairly well preserved. If locked, get keys from Scalloway Museum or Scalloway Hotel.

Shetland Bus Memorial   MONUMENT
(Main St) During WWII a fleet of small boats – the Shetland Bus – shuttled from Scalloway to occupied Norway, carrying agents and supplies for the Norwegian resistance, and returning with refugees, recruits for Free Norwegian forces and Christmas trees. The memorial, built of stones from both countries, is a moving tribute.

Shetland offers intriguing options for getting off the beaten accommodation track. There's a great network of *bōds* – simple rustic cottages or huts with peat fires. They cost £10 per person, or £8 for the ones without electricity, and are available March to October. Contact and book via **Shetland Amenity Trust** (✆01595-694688; www.camping-bods. com; ⊙9am-5pm Mon-Thu, 9am-4pm Fri).

The same organisation runs three **Lighthouse Cottages** (✆01595-694688; www.shetlandlighthouse.com; per three days £277-320, per week £600-700), commanding dramatic views of rugged coastline: one, recently renovated and classy, at Sumburgh, one on the island of Bressay near Lerwick, and one at Eshaness. They sleep six to seven, and prices drop substantially off-season.

🛏 Sleeping & Eating

★**Scalloway Hotel**   HOTEL ££
(✆01595-880444; www.scallowayhotel.com; Main St; s/d £80/115; 🅿🛜) One of Shetland's best, this energetically run waterfront place has very stylish rooms featuring sheepskins, local tweeds and other fabrics, and views over the harbour. Some are larger than others; the best is the fabulous superior, with handmade furniture, artworks and a top-of-the-line mattress on its four-poster bed. The **restaurant** (mains £11 to £15) is good for quality seafood and Scottish cheeses.

❶ Getting There & Away

Buses run from Lerwick (£1.90, 20 minutes, roughly hourly Monday to Saturday, two Sunday) to Scalloway, stopping on Main St.

South Mainland

From Lerwick, it's 25 miles down this narrow, hilly tail of land to Sumburgh Head. The lapping waters are an inviting turquoise – if it weren't for the raging Arctic gales, you'd be tempted to have a dip.

Sandwick & Around

Opposite scattered Sandwick is the small isle of **Mousa**, an RSPB reserve protecting some 7000 breeding pairs of storm petrels.

DON'T MISS

SEA KAYAKING

Paddling is great for exploring Shetland's tortuous coastline, and allows you to get up close to seals and bird life. **Sea Kayak Shetland** (☏ 01595-840272; www.seakayakshetland.co.uk; beginner session/half-day/day £25/40/75) is a reliable operator catering for beginners and experts alike, and offering various guided trips.

It's also home to rock-basking seals and impressive **Mousa Broch**. Rising to 13m, it's an imposing double-walled structure with a spiral staircase to access a 2nd floor. It features in Viking sagas as a hideout for eloping couples.

👉 Tours

Mousa Boat   BOAT TOURS
(☏ 07901-872339; www.mousa.co.uk; ⊙ Apr–mid-Sep) This operator runs daily boat trips to Mousa (adult/child return £16/7, 15 minutes) from Sandwick, allowing three hours ashore on the island. It also offers night petrel-viewing trips (dates on website).

Bigton & Around

Three buses from Lerwick (not Sunday) stop in Bigton, whence it's another couple of miles to the largest shell-and-sand tombolo (sand or gravel isthmus) in Britain. Walk across to beautiful, emerald-capped **St Ninian's Isle**, where you'll find the ruins of a 12th-century church where a famous hoard of silver Pictish treasure was found. The treasure is now kept in Edinburgh's Museum of Scotland (p57), with replicas in Lerwick's Shetland Museum (p428)

Boddam & Scousburgh

From small Boddam a side road leads to the **Shetland Crofthouse Museum** (☏ 01950-460557; www.shetlandheritageassociation.com; ⊙ 10am-1pm & 2-5pm May-Sep) **FREE**, a restored, rethatched 19th-century dwelling furnished with period fittings and utensils. The Lerwick–Sumburgh bus stops right outside.

West of Boddam, Shetland's best beach is gloriously white **Scousburgh Sands**. The nearby **Spiggie Hotel** (☏ 01950-460409; www.thespiggiehotel.co.uk; s/d £70/130, self-catering s/d from £80/100; ℗ ☏) has compact rooms, self-catering annexes and tasty seafood and bar meals (lunch Wednesday to Sunday, dinner daily; mains £9 to £19). The rooms and dining room boast great views down over the local loch.

Sumburgh

With sea cliffs, and grassy headlands jutting out into sparkling blue waters, Sumburgh is one of the most scenic places on the island, with a far greener landscape than the peaty north.

◎ Sights

⭐**Old Scatness**   ARCHAEOLOGICAL SITE
(☏ 01595-694688; www.shetland-heritage.co.uk; adult/child £5/4; ⊙ 10am-5pm Mon mid-May–Aug; 🐾) This dig brings Shetland's prehistory vividly to life; it's a must-see for archaeology buffs, but fun for kids, too. Clued-up guides in Iron Age clothes show you the site, which has provided important clues on the Viking takeover and dating of Shetland material. There's an impressive broch from around 300 BC, roundhouses and later wheelhouses. Best of all is the reconstruction with peat fire and working loom. At time of research, lack of funding had restricted opening to Mondays.

Jarlshof   ARCHAEOLOGICAL SITE
(HS; ☏ 01950-460112; www.historic-scotland.gov. uk; adult/child £5.30/3.30; ⊙ 9.30am-5.30pm Apr-Sep, 9.30am-4.30pm Oct-Mar) Old and new collide here, with Sumburgh airport right by this picturesque, instructive archaeological site. Various periods of occupation from 2500 BC to AD 1500 can be seen; the complete change upon the Vikings' arrival is obvious: their rectangular longhouses present a marked contrast to the preceding brochs, roundhouses and wheelhouses. Atop the site is 16th-century Old House, named 'Jarlshof' in a novel by Sir Walter Scott. There's an informative audio tour included with admission.

⭐**Sumburgh Head**
Visitor Centre   LIGHTHOUSE, MUSEUM
(☏ 01595-694688; www.sumburghhead.com; adult/child £6/2; ⊙ 10am-4pm May-Aug) High on the cliffs at Sumburgh Head, this excellent new attraction is set across several buildings. Displays explain about the lighthouse, foghorn and radar station that operated here, while there's a good exhibition on the

local marine life and bird life. You can visit the lighthouse itself on a guided tour.

Sumburgh Head BIRDWATCHING

(www.rspb.org.uk) At Mainland's southern tip, these spectacular cliffs offer a good chance to get up close to puffins, and huge nesting colonies of fulmars, guillemots and razorbills. If you're lucky, you might spot dolphins, minke whales or orcas. Also here is an excellent visitor centre, in the lighthouse buildings.

🛏 Sleeping & Eating

Betty Mouat's BÖD £

(☏ 01595-694688; www.camping-bods.com; Dunrossness; dm £10; ☺ Mar-Oct; 🅿) This is a simple and comfortable hostel run by the Shetland Amenity Trust, with fridge, peat fire (£5 a bag), power and decent hot-water bathrooms.

Sumburgh Hotel HOTEL ££

(☏ 01950-460201; www.sumburghhotel.com; s/d £85/110; 🅿@🛜📺) A reliable country-style hotel. Rooms have been recently renovated and feature soft duvets, attractive colour schemes and big towels. Larger sea-view rooms looking out to Fair Isle cost a tenner more. This is handy for the airport or Sumburgh Head birdwatching, though food is mediocre.

Another option is Sumburgh Lighthouse Cottage (p432).

ℹ Getting There & Away

To get to Sumburgh from Lerwick, take the airport bus (£2.60 to Sumburgh, £3 to the airport; 45 minutes, four to six daily).

North Mainland

Northern Mainland is very photogenic – jumbles of cracked, peaty brown hills, blending with grassy pastureland, extend like bony fingers into the icy grey waters of the North Sea.

Brae & Around

The crossroads settlement of Brae has several accommodation options. Book in advance, as they fill with oil workers.

🛏 Sleeping & Eating

★ Busta House Hotel HOTEL ££

(☏ 01806-522506; www.bustahouse.com; s/d £99/115; 🅿@🛜📺) 🍴 This genteel, characterful hotel has a long, sad history and inevitable rumours of a (friendly) ghost. Built in the late 18th century (though the oldest part dates from 1588), its refurbished rooms – all individually decorated – are compact and retain a classy but homey charm. Sea views and/or four-poster bed cost a bit more. There are excellent dinners with local produce for £35. Food is served noon to 2.30pm and 6pm to 9pm.

Frankie's Fish & Chips CAFE, TAKEAWAY £

(☏ 01806-522700; www.frankiesfishandchips.com; mains £6-9; ☺9.30am-8pm Mon-Sat, noon-8pm Sun; 🛜) 🍴 This famous Shetland chippie

---

WESTERN ISLANDS

Off West Mainland is **Papa Stour** (population 15), home to huge colonies of auks, terns and skuas. Buckled volcanic strata have been wonderfully eroded to dramatic caves, arches and stacks. There's limited self-catering accommodation, and a small campsite. The island is served by Tuesday-only flights (p427) from Tingwall (return £65, day return possible) and **ferries** (☏ 01595-745804; www.shetland.gov.uk/ferries/) from West Burrafirth (passenger/car single £5.20/1.50, one hour).

Fifteen miles out in the Atlantic stands windswept **Foula**, perhaps Britain's most isolated community. Thirty-eight people are joined by 500,000 seabirds, including the rare Leach's petrel and Manx shearwater, and the world's largest colony of great skuas. There's no shop, but **Leraback** (☏ 01595-753226; www.originart.eu/leraback/leraback.html; Foula; B&B incl dinner per person £40; 🅿) offers B&B and evening meals.

DirectFlight (p427) flies to Foula from Tingwall (£74.50 return), with day trips possible from March to mid-October. There are **ferries** (☏ 01595-840208; www.bkmarine.co.uk) from Walls (person/car single £5.20/19.60); bookings are essential. You can day trip to Foula from Scalloway with **Cycharters** (☏ 01595-696598; www.cycharters.co.uk).

uses only locally sourced and sustainable seafood. As well as chip-shop standards, the menu runs to plump Shetland mussels in garlicky sauces and, when available, scallops. It also does breakfast rolls and fry-ups. Eat in or take away.

ℹ️ Getting There & Away

Buses from Lerwick to North Roe and Mossbank stop in Brae (£2.70, 45 minutes, four to seven daily Monday to Saturday).

Eshaness & Hillswick

Eleven miles northwest of Brae the road ends at the red basalt cliffs of Eshaness, some of Shetland's most impressive coastal scenery. When the wind subsides there is superb walking and panoramic views from the headland lighthouse.

A mile east, a side road leads to **Tangwick Haa Museum** (☑️ 01806-503389; ⊙ 11am-5pm mid-Apr–Sep; **FREE**), in a restored 17th-century house. The wonderful collection of ancient black-and-white photos captures the sense of community here.

🛏️ Sleeping & Eating

Braewick Cafe & Caravan Park CAMPSITE £
(☑️ 01806-503345; www.eshaness.shetland.co.uk; sites for 1/2/wigwams £6/8/42; ⊙ mid-Mar–mid-Sep; 🅿️ 🛜 🌡️) ⊘ Decent tent pitches and tasty light meals served in a cafe (dishes £4 to £10; 10am to 5pm Thursday to Monday mid-March to mid-September, daily in July and August) with stunning views over St Magnus Bay's weird and wonderful rock formations, are on offer here. Much food is sourced from the owners' croft next door. It also has 'wigwams' – wooden huts with fridge and kettle that sleep four (six at a pinch). It's on the road between Hillswick and Eshaness.

Johnnie Notions' BÖD £
(☑️ office 01595-694688, warden 01806-503362; www.camping-bods.co.uk; dm £8; ⊙ Mar-Oct) There are four spacious berths in this cute wee stone *böd*, 3.5 miles east of Eshaness, with its challengingly low door. It's very basic, with no showers or electricity. This was the birthplace of Johnnie 'Notions' Williamson, an 18th-century blacksmith who inoculated several thousand people against smallpox using a self-devised serum.

★**Almara** B&B ££
(☑️ 01806-503261; www.almara.shetland.co.uk; s/d £35/70; 🅿️ 🛜) ⊘ Follow the puffin signpost a mile short of Hillswick to find Shetland's finest welcome. With sweeping views over the bay, this house has a great lounge, unusual features in the excellent rooms and bathrooms (including thoughtful extras such as USB chargers) and a good eye on the environment. You'll feel completely at home and appreciated; this is B&B at its best.

St Magnus Bay Hotel HOTEL ££
(☑️ 01806-503372; www.stmagnusbayhotel.co.uk; Hillswick; s/d £80/90; 🅿️ 🛜 🌡️) This hotel in Hillswick occupies a wonderful wooden mansion built in 1896. The owners are involved in an ongoing renovation process – a major job – to return it to former glories, so availability of rooms is variable, but if you can grab a renovated one, they are great. There's a sauna plus bar and restaurant meals.

ℹ️ Getting There & Away

An evening bus from Lerwick (Monday to Saturday) runs to Hillswick (£2.90, 1¼ hours), Eshaness (1½ hours) and North Roe (1½ hours). Two morning buses run the return route.

The North Isles

Yell, Unst and Fetlar make up the North Isles, connected by ferry, as is Yell to Mainland. All are great for nature-watching; Unst has the most to offer overall. If you're going to spend a night on both Yell and Fetlar/Unst, do Yell on the way back, as the second ferry is free if you are coming from Mainland that same day.

Yell

POP 1000

Yell if you like but nobody will hear; the desolate peat moors here are typical Shetland scenery. The bleak landscape has an undeniable appeal.

⊙ Sights & Activities

Lumbister RSPB Reserve NATURE RESERVE
(www.rspb.org.uk) At this nature reserve red-throated divers, merlins, skuas and other bird species breed. The area is home to a large otter population, too, best viewed around Whale Firth, where you may also spot common and grey seals.

Old Haa Museum · MUSEUM

(☎ 01957-702431; ⊙ 10am-4pm Tue-Thu & Sat & 2-5pm Sun Apr-Sep) **FREE** This has a medley of curious objects (pipes, piano, dolls-in-cradles, tiny bibles, ships in bottles and a sperm-whale jaw) as well as an archive of local history, and a tearoom. It's in Burravoe, 4 miles east of the southern ferry terminal in Ulsta.

Shetland Gallery · GALLERY

(www.shetlandgallery.com; Sellafirth, Yell; ⊙ 11am-5pm Tue-Sat & 2-5pm Sun Easter-Sep) Not far from the ferry to Unst and Fetlar, this has rotating exhibitions of Shetland artists.

Windhouse · RUIN

Northwest of the small settlement of Mid Yell, on the hillside above the main road, stand the reputedly haunted ruins of Windhouse, dating from 1707. It's been uninhabited since the 1920s, although there are plans to refurbish it. Look out for the Lady in Silk, the most famous of the ruins' several ghostly presences.

🛏 Sleeping & Eating

Lots of excellent self-catering cottages are dotted around the island; check www.visitscotland.com for options.

Windhouse Lodge · BÖD £

(☎ office 01595-694688, warden 01957-702350; www.camping-bods.co.uk; dm £10) Below the haunted ruins of Windhouse, and on the A968, you'll find this well-kept, clean, snug camping *böd* with power and a pot-belly stove to warm your toes. It's one of the cosiest, with a modern interior. Mattresses are thin. Book via phone or the website.

Pinewood House · B&B ££

(☎ 01957-702092; www.pinewoodhouseshetland.co.uk; Aywick; s/d £35/70; [P][🐾][🌐][❄]) Next to Aywick shop, this three-roomer boasts glorious water views from the lounge and bedrooms, and offers a warm welcome and optional, very tasty evening meals (£16).

❶ Getting There & Away

BOAT

Yell is connected with Mainland by **ferries** (☎ 01595-745804; www.shetland.gov.uk/ferries) between Toft and Ulsta (passenger/car return £5.20/7.60, 20 minutes, frequent). It's wise to book car space in summer.

OFF THE BEATEN TRACK

FAIR ISLE

Halfway to Orkney, remote Fair Isle is best known for birdwatching and its patterned knitwear, still produced in the island's cooperative. Smart **Fair Isle Lodge & Bird Observatory** (☎ 01595-760258; www.fairislebirdobs.co.uk; s/d incl full board £70/130; ⊙ May-Oct; [P][@][🌐]) offers good en suite rooms. Rates are full board, and there are free guided walks and other bird-related displays and activities. From Tingwall, Direct-Flight (p427) operates flights to Fair Isle (£79 return, 25 minutes). Ferries sail from Grutness (near Sumburgh) and some from Lerwick (one-way person/car £5.20/19.60, three hours) two to three times weekly.

BUS

Buses run Monday to Saturday from Lerwick to Yell (£4.60), connecting with ferries to Fetlar and Unst; connecting services cover other parts of the island.

Unst

POP 600

You're fast running out of Scotland once you cross to rugged Unst (www.unst.org). Scotland's most northerly inhabited island is prettier than Yell, with bare, velvety-smooth hills and settlements clinging to waterside locations, fiercely resisting the buffeting winds.

◎ Sights & Activities

Muness Castle · CASTLE

(Muness; ⊙ 24hr) **FREE** This picturesque, sturdy 16th-century tower-house in the island's southeastern corner was built by Laurence Bruce, *foud* (magistrate) of Shetland, who was, by all accounts, a nasty piece of work, overtaxing locals and replacing their elected officials with his cronies. It's an atmospheric visit; grab a torch from under the information panel to explore.

★**Hermaness Nature Reserve** · NATURE RESERVE

(www.nnr-scotland.org.uk) At marvellous Hermaness headland, a 4.5-mile round walk takes you to cliffs where gannets, fulmars and guillemots nest, and numerous puffins frolic. You can see Scotland's most northerly point, the rocks of **Out Stack**, and **Muckle Flugga**, with its lighthouse built by Robert Louis Stevenson's uncle. Duck into the **visitor centre** (📞01595-711278; ⏱9am-5pm May-early Sep) **FREE**, with its poignant story about long-time resident Albert Ross. To visit Muckle Flugga, you can charter **boats** (📞01806-522447; www.muckleflugga.co.uk; 2-hr charter £150; ⏱Jun-Aug) in summer.

The path to the cliffs is guarded by a squadron of great skuas who nest in the nearby heather, and dive-bomb at will if they feel threatened. They're damn solid birds too, but don't usually make contact.

⭐**Unst Bus Shelter**   LANDMARK
(www.unstbusshelter.shetland.co.uk; Baltasound) At the turn-off to Littlehamar, just past Baltasound, is Britain's most impressive bus stop. Enterprising locals, tired of waiting in discomfort, decided to do a job on it, and it now boasts posh seating, novels, numerous decorative features and a visitors' book to sign. The theme and colour scheme changes yearly.

Unst Heritage Centre   MUSEUM
(📞01957-755244, 01957-711528; www.unstheritage.com; Haroldswick; adult/child £3/free, combined ticket with Unst Boat Haven £5; ⏱11am-4pm May-Sep) This heritage centre houses a modern museum with a history of the Shetland pony and a re-creation of a croft house.

Unst Boat Haven   MUSEUM
(📞01957-755282, 01957-711528; Haroldswick; adult/child £3/free, combined ticket with Unst Heritage Centre £5; ⏱11am-4pm May-Sep) This large shed is a boaty's delight, packed with a beautifully cared-for collection of Shetland rowing and sailing boats, all with a backstory. Old photos and maritime artefacts speak of the glory days of Unst fishing.

Skidbladner Longship   MUSEUM
(📞01595-694688; www.vikingshetland.com; Haroldswick; ⏱24hr) **FREE** Unst has the highest concentration of Viking longhouse sites in the country. The Viking Unst project manages three excavation sites, and has as its centrepiece this replica Viking longship. A recreated longhouse is alongside.

🛏 Sleeping & Eating

⭐**Gardiesfauld Hostel**   HOSTEL **£**
(📞01957-755279; www.gardiesfauld.shetland.co.uk; 2 East Rd, Uyeasound; tent sites per adult/child £6/2, dm £15; ⏱Apr-Sep; 🅿🛜) This spotless hostel has very spacious dorms with lockers, family rooms, a garden, an elegant lounge and a wee conservatory dining area with great bay views. You can camp here too, with separate areas for tents and vans. The bus stops right outside. Bring 20p for a shower.

Saxa Vord   HOSTEL **£**
(📞01957-711711; www.saxavord.com; Haroldswick; s/d £21/42; ⏱late May-early Sep; 🅿🛜) This former RAF base is not the most atmospheric lodging, but the barracks-style rooms offer great value. The restaurant dishes out reasonable local food, and there's a bar – Britain's northernmost, by our reckoning – and a friendly, helpful atmosphere. Self-catering houses (£450 to £595 per week) are good for families and available year-round.

Prestegaard   B&B **££**
(📞01957-755234; prestegaard@postmaster.co.uk; Uyeasound; s/d £34/60; ⏱May-Sep; 🅿🛜) This solid old manse near the water makes a great base. Rooms are spacious and comfy, with sea views and separate (but private) bathroom – we particularly like the upstairs one. The breakfast room with Up Helly Aa memorabilia will bring out the Viking in you, and the kindly owner is helpful. Continental breakfast (and porridge!) only.

WILDLIFE-WATCHING IN SHETLAND

For birdwatchers, Shetland is paradise – a stopover for migrating Arctic species and host to vast seabird breeding colonies; June is the height of the season.

Every bird has its own name here: rain geese are red-throated divers, bonxies are great skuas, and alamootics are storm petrels. Clownish puffin antics are a highlight. The RSPB (p471) maintains several reserves plus there are National Nature Reserves at **Hermaness**, **Keen of Hamar** and **Noss**. **Foula** and **Fair Isle** also support large seabird populations.

Keep an eye on the sea: sea otters, orcas and other cetaceans are regularly sighted. Latest sightings are logged at useful www.nature-shetland.co.uk.

Shetland Nature Festival (www.shetlandamenity.org) in early July has guided walks, talks, boat trips, open days and workshops.

Baltasound Hotel
HOTEL, PUB ££

(☑ 01957-711334; www.baltasoundhotel.co.uk; Baltasound; s £45-60, d £90-100; ⊙ May–mid-Oct; P 🛜) Brightly decorated, commodious rooms – some bigger than others – are complemented by wooden chalets arrayed around the lawn. It's worth the tenner upgrade to the 'large doubles', which sport good modern bathrooms. There's a lovely country outlook, and evening bar meals (mains £7 to £12; food served 6pm to 8pm) in a dining room dappled by the setting sun.

❶ Getting There & Around

BICYCLE

Hire **bikes** (☑ 01957-711393; www.unstcyclehire.co.uk; Haroldswick; per day/week £7.50/30; ⊙ 11.30am-5pm Mon-Sat, 1-4pm Sun, can hire out of hours) in the chocolate shop at the Saxa Vord complex in Haroldswick.

BOAT

Unst is connected with Yell and Fetlar by a small ferry (p436) between Gutcher and Belmont (free if coming from Mainland that day, otherwise passenger/car £5.20/7.60 return, 10 minutes, frequent).

BUS

Buses run Monday to Saturday from Lerwick to the Unst ferry (£4.60, 2½ hours). There are connecting services around Unst itself (£1.70 to £1.80).

Fetlar

POP 60

Fetlar is the smallest but most fertile of the North Isles. Its name is derived from the Viking term for 'fat land'.

◉ Sights & Activities

There's great birdwatching – Fetlar is home to three-quarters of Britain's breeding population of red-necked phalaropes, which nest around the **Loch of Funzie** (pronounced 'finnie') in the southeast of the island. From April to October, you can view them from an RSPB hide.

Excellent **Fetlar Interpretive Centre** (☑ 01957-733206; www.fetlar.com; adult/child £3/free; ⊙ 11am-4pm Mon-Fri & noon-4pm Sat & Sun May-Sep) has photos, audio recordings and videos on the island and its history. You'll find it right in the middle of the island, 4½ miles from the ferry.

🛏 Sleeping

Friendly **Gord B&B** (☑ 01957-733227; nicboxall@btinternet.com; r per person incl dinner £50; P) has terrific sea views and two twin rooms and one double, all with en suite. There's also Aithbank **camping böd** (☑ 01595-694688; www.camping-bods.com; dm £10) by the water, handily close to the Loch of Funzie.

❶ Information

There's no petrol on Fetlar, but there's a part-time shop in Houbie.

❶ Getting There & Away

Four to nine daily ferries (p436; free if coming from Mainland that day, otherwise passenger/car £5.20/7.60 return, 25 minutes) connect Fetlar with Gutcher on Yell and Belmont on Unst.

Understand
Scotland

Scotland Today

Although an integral part of Great Britain since 1707, Scotland has maintained a separate and distinct identity throughout the last 300 years, which strengthened with the return of a devolved Scottish parliament to Edinburgh in 1999. Since then, Scottish politics has diverged significantly from Westminster, culminating in September 2014 when a referendum on whether Scotland should become an independent country resulted in a narrow majority voting to remain part of the UK.

Best in Print

Raw Spirit (Iain Banks; 2003) An enjoyable jaunt around Scotland in search of the perfect whisky.

Mountaineering in Scotland (WH Murray; 1947) Classic account of climbing in Scotland in the 1930s, when just getting to Glen Coe was an adventure in itself.

Adrift in Caledonia (Nick Thorpe; 2006) An insightful tale of hitchhiking around Scotland on a variety of vessels.

The Poor Had No Lawyers (Andy Wightman; 2010) A penetrating (and fascinating) analysis of who owns land in Scotland, and how they got it.

Best on Film

Whisky Galore! (1949) Classic Ealing comedy about wily Scottish islanders outfoxing the government when a cargo of whisky gets shipwrecked.

Local Hero (1983) Gentle Bill Forsyth comedy-drama sees American oil executive beguiled by the Highland landscape and eccentric locals.

Trainspotting (1996) 'Who needs reasons when you've got heroin?' Danny Boyle's second film dives into the gritty underbelly of life among Edinburgh drug addicts.

Scottish Independence

From the Red Clydeside movement of the 1920s to the 1997 UK elections when the country returned no Conservative MPs at all, Scotland's politics have always been more left-wing and communitarian than England's (or, at least, the south of England's).

Since the return of the devolved Scottish parliament to Edinburgh in 1999, policies that have been applied in Scotland but not in the rest of the UK include free long-term care for the elderly, the abolition of tuition fees for university students, and higher pay for teachers. A perceived disconnect between Scotland's social-democratic aspirations and what voters felt was an increasingly authoritarian and right-wing Westminster government led to the Scottish National Party's (SNP) 2011 victory at Holyrood and its commitment to put the question of Scottish independence to the vote.

The implications of Scotland breaking away from the UK were hotly debated in the year leading up to the 2014 referendum. Would the Scots need a new currency, or be able to keep using the pound? Would there be border controls with England? Would Scotland be able to remain in the EU? How would North Sea oil revenues be divided? Would the Queen still be head of state?

The referendum took place on 18 September 2014, posing the question: 'Should Scotland be an independent country?' The result was that 55% voted to maintain the status quo (from a turnout of 85%). What this means for the future of Scotland remains unclear. Will there be increased powers for the Scottish parliament in Edinburgh? Will there be a collapse in support for the SNP? The closeness of the result promises that there will be wrangling for years to come.

Renewable Energy

One of the central planks of the SNP's vision for an independent Scotland was its energy policy. The party leader, Alex Salmond, said that he wanted the country to be the 'Saudi Arabia of renewable energy' – becoming self-sufficient in energy by 2020, and a net exporter of 'clean' electricity.

In the first half of the 20th century the Scottish Highlands were one of the first regions in the world to develop hydroelectric power on a large scale, and since 2000 wind turbines have sprung up all over the place. By 2009, renewables provided 27% of Scotland's energy consumption, a figure that rose to 40% in 2013; the government's target is to reach 100% by 2020.

However, the future of Scotland's energy industry lies not on land, but in the sea: Scotland has access to 25% of Europe's available tidal energy, and 10% of its wave power. The country is at the leading edge of developing wave, tidal and offshore wind power, and in 2012 the waters around Orkney and the Pentland Firth were designated as a Marine Energy Park.

Development vs Conservation

In 2010 the Scottish government gave the go-ahead to a 135-mile, high voltage overhead power line from Beauly (near Inverness) to Denny in Stirlingshire, to connect wind- and marine-generated electricity from the north to the heart of the national grid. Construction is under way on 600 giant pylons marching through some of the Highlands' most scenic areas, including Strathglass, Fort Augustus and Bridge of Tummel.

Supporters point out that the scheme also involves the removal of almost 60 miles of low-voltage pylons from the Cairngorms National Park; opponents claim that a seabed cable, while more expensive, would have been a better alternative. The debate reflects a larger tension that exists across the Highlands and Islands – between those keen to develop the region's resources and conservationists who want to keep the area unspoiled.

POPULATION: **5.3 MILLION**

AREA: **78,722 SQ KM**

UNEMPLOYMENT: **7.2%** **(2013)**

ANNUAL WHISKY EXPORTS: **1.26 BILLION BOTTLES** **(2013)**

....

if Scotland were 100 people

98 would be white
1 would be South Asian
1 would be other

....

belief systems
(% of population)

43
Church of Scotland

28
Non-Religious

16
Roman Catholic

6.8
Other Christian

6.2
Other

....

population per sq mile

SCOTLAND   USA   ENGLAND

= 80 people

History

Despite its geographical isolation, Scotland has taken a full part in the flow of European history, being forged from the melting-pot of several cultures and in turn growing to wield great cultural, scientific and manufacturing influence right around the globe. From the decline of the Vikings onwards, Scottish history has been predictably and often violently bound to that of its southern neighbour, England. Battles and border raids were commonplace until shared kingship, then political union, drew the two together. Even then, Jacobite risings reflected divisions in Scottish and British society. More recently, an increasing trend towards self-determination led to the devolved Scottish parliament of 1999, and the 2014 independence referendum.

Early Days

Top Prehistoric Sites

Jarlshof, Shetland

Skara Brae, Orkney

Maes Howe, Orkney

Kilmartin Glen, Argyll

Callanish, Lewis

Tomb of the Eagles, Orkney

Scottish Crannog Centre, Kenmore

Hunters and gatherers have left fragments of evidence of Scotland's earliest human habitation. These people came in waves from northern Europe and Ireland as glaciers retreated in the wake of the last Ice Age around 10,000 BC.

The Neolithic was similarly launched by arrivals from mainland Europe. Scotland's Stone Age has left behind an astonishing diary of human development, unforgettable memories in stone of a distant past. Caithness, Orkney and Shetland have some of the world's best-preserved prehistoric villages, burial cairns and standing stones. Further south, crannogs (round structures built on stilts over a loch) were a favoured form of defensible dwelling through the Bronze Age.

The Iron Age saw the construction of a remarkable series of defence-minded structures of a different sort. Brochs (again a northeastern island development) were complex, muscular stone fortresses, some of which still stand well over 10m high.

Romans & Picts

The Roman occupation of Britain began in AD 43, almost a century after Julius Caesar first invaded. However, the Roman onslaught ground to a halt in the north, not far beyond the present-day Scottish border. Between AD 78 and 84, governor Agricola marched northwards and

TIMELINE	4000 BC	2200 BC	AD 43
	Neolithic farmers move to Scotland from mainland Europe; sites from these ancient days dot Scotland, with the best concentrated in Orkney.	Beaker culture arrives in Scotland. The Bronze Age produces swords and shields. Construction of hill forts, crannogs and mystifying stone circles.	Claudius begins the Roman conquest of Britain, almost a century after Julius Caesar first invaded. By AD 80 a string of forts is built from the Clyde to the Forth.

spent several years trying to subdue tribes the Romans called the Picts (from the Latin *pictus,* meaning 'painted'). By the 2nd century Emperor Hadrian, tired of fighting in the north, decided to cut his losses and built the wall (AD 122–28) that bears his name across northern England. Two decades later Hadrian's successor, Antoninus Pius, invaded Scotland again and built a turf rampart, the Antonine Wall, between the Firth of Forth and the River Clyde. In northern Britain, the Romans had met their match.

Little is known about the Picts, who inhabited northern and eastern Scotland. The Roman presence probably helped forge disparate Celtic tribes into a unified group; we can assume they were fierce fighters given the trouble the hardy Roman army had with them. The main material evidence of their culture is their fabulous carved symbol stones, found across eastern Scotland.

Eventually the Romans left Britain and at this time there were at least two indigenous peoples in the northern region of the British Isles: the Picts in the north and east, and the Britons in the southwest. A new group, the Celtic Scots probably arrived around AD 500, crossing from Ireland and establishing a kingdom called Dál Riata in Argyll. St Ninian was the earliest recorded bringer of Christianity to the region, establishing a mission in Whithorn in Scotland's southwest. In the 6th century, St Columba, Scotland's most famous missionary, resumed St Ninian's work. Columba was a scholar and monk exiled, tradition has it, after involvement in a bloody battle. After fleeing Ireland in 563, he established a monastery on Iona – an island that retains an ancient, mystical aura – and also travelled northeast to take his message to the Picts. By the late 8th century most of Scotland had converted.

The First Kings of Scotland

The Picts and Scots were drawn together by the threat of a Norse invasion and by political and spiritual power from their common Christianity. Kenneth MacAlpin, first king of a united Scotland, achieved power using a mixture of blood ties and diplomacy. He set his capital in Pictland at Scone and brought to it the sacred Stone of Destiny, used in the coronation of Scottish kings.

Nearly two centuries later, MacAlpin's descendant Malcolm II (r 1005–18) defeated the Northumbrian Angles, a Germanic tribe who had settled in eastern England, at the Battle of Carham (1018) bringing Edinburgh and Lothian under Scottish control and extending Scottish territory as far south as the Tweed.

But the Highland clans, inaccessible in their glens, remained a law unto themselves for another 700 years. A cultural and linguistic divide

Top Pictish Stones

St Vigeans Museum, Arbroath

Aberlemno Stones, Angus

Dupplin Cross, Dunning

Groam House Museum, Rosemarkie

Meigle Museum, Meigle

Inverness Museum, Inverness

Tarbat Discovery Centre, Portmahomack

Elgin Museum, Elgin

AD 142	AD 397	5th century	Early 500s
Building of Antonine Wall marks the northern limit of the Roman Empire. It is patrolled for about 40 years, but after this the Romans decide northern Britain is too difficult to conquer.	The first Christian mission beyond Hadrian's Wall, in Whithorn, is initiated by St Ninian. The earliest recorded church in Scotland is built to house his remains.	Roman soldiers are recalled to Rome as the Empire faces attack from barbarian tribes. The last Romans depart and Emperor Honorius tells Britons to fend for themselves.	A Celtic tribe, the Scots, cross the sea from northern Ireland and establish a kingdom in Argyll called Dál Riata.

grew up between the Gaelic-speaking Highlanders and the Lowlanders who spoke the Scots tongue.

Robert the Bruce & William Wallace

When Alexander III fell to his death in Fife in 1286, the succession was disputed by no less than 13 claimants, but in the end it came down to two: Robert de Brus, lord of Annandale, and John Balliol, lord of Galloway. King Edward I of England was asked to arbitrate. He chose Balliol, whom he thought he could manipulate more easily.

Seeking to tighten his feudal grip on Scotland, Edward – known as the 'Hammer of the Scots' – treated the Scots king as vassal rather than equal. The humiliated Balliol finally turned against him and allied Scotland with France in 1295, thus beginning the enduring 'Auld Alliance' and ushering in the Wars of Independence.

Edward's response was bloody. In 1296 he invaded Scotland and Balliol was incarcerated in the Tower of London; in another blow to Scots pride, Edward removed the Stone of Destiny from Scone and took it back to London.

Enter William Wallace. Bands of rebels were attacking the English occupiers and Wallace led one such band to defeat the English at Stirling Bridge in 1297. After Wallace's execution, Robert the Bruce, grandson of Robert de Brus, saw his chance, defied Edward (whom he had previously aligned himself with), murdered his rival John Comyn and had himself crowned king of Scotland at Scone in 1306. Bruce mounted a campaign to drive the English out of Scotland but suffered repeated defeats. Persistence paid off and he went on to secure an illustrious victory over the English at Bannockburn, enshrined in Scottish legend as one of the finest moments in the country's history.

Scottish independence was eventually won in 1328, though 'the Bruce' died the next year. Wars with England and civil strife continued, however. In 1371 Robert the Bruce's grandson, Robert II, acceded to the

THE DECLARATION OF ARBROATH

During the Wars of Independence, a group of Scottish nobles sent a letter to Pope John XXII requesting support for the cause of Scottish independence. Having railed against Edward I's tyranny and sung the praises of Robert the Bruce, the declaration famously states: 'For so long as a hundred of us remain alive, we will yield in no least way to English dominion. For we fight, not for glory nor for riches nor for honours, but only and alone for freedom, which no good man surrenders but with his life.' The Pope initially supported the Scottish cause but English lobbying changed his mind.

685	780	848	1040
The Pictish king Bridei defeats the Northumbrians at Nechtansmere in Angus, an against-the-odds victory that sets the foundations for Scotland as a separate entity.	From the 780s onwards, Norsemen in longboats from Scandinavia begin to pillage the Scottish coast and islands, eventually taking control of Orkney, Shetland and the Western Isles.	Kenneth MacAlpin unites the Scottish and Pictish thrones, thus uniting Scotland north of the Firth of Forth into a single kingdom.	Macbeth takes the Scottish throne after defeating Duncan. This, and the fact that he was later killed by Duncan's son Malcolm, are the only parallels to the Shakespeare version.

throne, founding the Stewart (Stuart) dynasty, which was to rule Scotland and, in time, the rest of Britain, until 1714.

The Renaissance

James IV (r 1488–1513) married the daughter of Henry VII of England, the first of the Tudor monarchs, thereby linking the two royal families through 'the Marriage of the Thistle and the Rose'. This didn't prevent the French from persuading James to go to war with his in-laws, and he was killed at the Battle of Flodden in 1513, along with some 10,000 of his subjects. Renaissance ideas, in particular Scottish poetry and architecture, flourished during this time; some of the finest Scottish Renaissance buildings can be seen within the fortress of Stirling Castle.

Mary, Queen of Scots & the Reformation

In 1542 King James V, childless, lay on his deathbed broken-hearted, it is said, after his defeat by the English at Solway Moss. Then news came that his wife had given birth to a baby girl. Fearing the end of the Stewart dynasty, and recalling its origin through Robert the Bruce's daughter, James sighed, 'It cam' wi' a lass, and it will gang wi' a lass'. He died shortly thereafter, leaving his week-old daughter, Mary, to inherit the throne as Queen of Scots.

She was sent to France at an early age and Scotland was ruled by regents, who rejected overtures from Henry VIII of England urging them to wed the infant queen to his son. Furious Henry sent his armies to take vengeance on the Scots. The 'Rough Wooing', as it was called, failed to win hearts and minds and in 1558 Mary was married to the French dauphin and became queen of France as well as Scotland.

While Mary was in France, being raised Catholic, the Reformation tore through Scotland, to where, following the death of her sickly husband, the 18-year-old returned in 1561. She was formally welcomed to her capital city and held a famous audience with John Knox. The great reformer harangued the young queen and she later agreed to protect the budding Protestant Church in Scotland while continuing to practise Catholicism in private.

She married Lord Darnley in the Chapel Royal at Holyrood and gave birth to a son (later James VI) in 1565. Any domestic bliss was short-lived and, in a scarcely believable train of events, Darnley was involved in the murder of Mary's Italian secretary Rizzio (rumoured to be her lover), before he himself was murdered, probably by Mary's new lover and third-husband-to-be, the earl of Bothwell.

The Scots had had enough; Mary's enemies – an alliance of powerful nobles – finally confronted her at Carberry Hill, east of Edinburgh, and Mary was forced to abdicate in 1567 and thrown into prison at Castle

MARY, QUEEN OF SCOTS

Mary Queen of Scots by Antonia Fraser is the classic biography of Scotland's ill-starred queen, digging deep behind the myths to discover the real woman caught up in the labyrinthine politics of the period.

1263	1296	1298–1305	1314
Norse power is finally broken at the Battle of Largs, which marks the retreat of Viking influence and eventually the handing back of the western isles to Scotland.	King Edward I marches on Scotland with an army of 30,000 men, razing ports, butchering citizens and capturing the castles of Berwick, Edinburgh, Roxburgh and Stirling.	William Wallace is made Guardian of Scotland in March 1298. After Edward's defeat of the Scots at the Battle of Falkirk, Wallace resigns as guardian and goes into hiding, but is fatally betrayed after his return in 1305.	Robert the Bruce wins a famous victory over the English at the Battle of Bannockburn – a victory which would turn the tide in favour of the Scots for the next 400 years.

Leven. She escaped, met her enemies in battle at Langside but was defeated and fled to England, where she was imprisoned for 19 years by Elizabeth I then finally executed in 1587.

Her son James VI (r 1567–1625) had meanwhile been crowned at Stirling, and a series of regents ruled in his place. In England, Elizabeth died childless, and the English, desperate for a male monarch, soon turned their attention north. James VI of Scotland became James I of England and moved his court to London. His plan to politically unite the two countries, however, failed. For the most part, the Stewarts (Stuarts) ignored Scotland from then on.

The Royal Stuarts: A History of the Family that Shaped Britain (2010) is a gripping portrait of the dynasty by Scottish journalist Allan Massie.

Union with England

Civil war and 17th-century religious conflict left the country and its economy ruined. Scotland couldn't compete in this new era of European colonialism and, to add to its woes, during the 1690s, famine killed up to a third of the population in some areas. Anti-English feeling ran high: the Protestant king William, who had replaced the exiled Catholic James VII/II to the chagrin of many in Scotland, was at war with France and employing Scottish soldiers and taxes – many Scots, sympathetic to

THE LORDS OF THE ISLES

In medieval times, when overland Highland travel was slow, difficult and dangerous, the sea lochs, firths (estuaries), kyles (narrow sea channels) and sounds of the west coast were the motorways of their time. Cut off from the rest of Scotland, but united by these sea roads, the west coast and islands were a world unto themselves.

Descended from the legendary Somerled (a half-Gaelic, half-Norse warrior of the 12th century), the chiefs of Clan Donald claimed sovereignty over this watery kingdom. It was John MacDonald of Islay who first styled himself Dominus Insularum (Lord of the Isles) in 1353. He and his descendants ruled their vast territory from their headquarters at Finlaggan in Islay, backed up by fleets of swift *birlinns* and *nyvaigs* (Hebridean galleys), an intimate knowledge of the sea routes of the west and a network of coastal castles.

Clan Donald held sway over the isles, often in defiance of the Scottish kings, from 1350 to 1493. At its greatest extent, in the second half of the 15th century, the Lordship of the Isles included all the islands on the west coast of Scotland, the west-coast mainland from Kintyre to Ross-shire, and the Antrim coast of northern Ireland. But in a greedy grab for territory, Clan Donald finally pushed its luck too far. John MacDonald made a secret pact with the English king Edward IV to divide Scotland between them. When this treason was discovered 30 years later, the Lordship was forfeited to King James IV of Scotland, and the title has remained in possession of the Scottish, and later British, royal family ever since. Lord of the Isles is one of the many titles held today by Prince Charles, heir to the British throne.

1328	1410	1468–69	1488–1513
Continuing raids on northern England force Edward III to sue for peace and the Treaty of Northampton gives Scotland its independence, with Robert I, the Bruce, as king.	One of Europe's most venerable educational institutions, The University of St Andrews, is founded.	Orkney and then Shetland are mortgaged to Scotland as part of a dowry from Danish King Christian I, whose daughter is to marry the future King James III of Scotland.	The Scottish Renaissance produces an intellectual climate that encourages Protestantism, a reaction against the perceived wealth and corruption of the medieval Roman Catholic Church.

the French, disapproved. This feeling was exacerbated by the failure of the Darien Scheme, an investment plan designed to establish a Scottish colony in Panama, which resulted in widespread bankruptcy in Scotland.

The failure made it clear to wealthy Scottish merchants and stockholders that the only way they could gain access to the lucrative markets of developing colonies was through union with England. The English parliament favoured union through fear of Jacobite sympathies in Scotland being exploited by its enemies, the French.

On receiving the Act of Union in Edinburgh, the chancellor of Scotland, Lord Seafield – leader of the parliament that the Act of Union abolished – is said to have murmured under his breath, 'Now there's an end to an auld sang'. Robert Burns later castigated the wealthy politicians who engineered the union in characteristically stronger language: 'We're bought and sold for English gold – such a parcel of rogues in a nation!'

The Jacobites

The Jacobite rebellions of the 18th century sought to displace the Hanoverian monarchy (chosen by the English parliament in 1701 to ensure a Protestant succession to the childless Stuart queens Mary II and Anne) and restore a Catholic Stuart king to the British throne.

James Edward Stuart, known as the Old Pretender, was the son of James VII/II. With French support he arrived in the Firth of Forth with a fleet of ships in 1708, but was seen off by English men-of-war.

The earl of Mar led another Jacobite rebellion in 1715 but proved an ineffectual leader; his campaign fizzled out soon after the inconclusive Battle of Sheriffmuir.

The Old Pretender's son, Charles Edward Stuart, better known as Bonnie Prince Charlie or the Young Pretender, landed in Scotland for the final uprising. He had little military experience, didn't speak Gaelic and had a shaky grasp of English. Nevertheless, supported by an army of Highlanders, he marched southwards and captured Edinburgh, except for the castle, in September 1745. He got as far south as Derby in England, but success was short-lived; an Hanoverian army led by the duke of Cumberland harried him all the way back to the Highlands, where Jacobite dreams were finally extinguished at the Battle of Culloden in 1746.

Although a heavily romanticised figure, Bonnie Prince Charlie was partly responsible for the annihilation of Highland culture, given the crackdown following his doomed attempt to recapture the crown. After returning to France he gained a reputation for drunkenness and mistreatment of mistresses. France had serious plans to invade Britain during the mid-18th century, but eventually ceased to regard the prince as a serious character.

Jacobite, a term derived from the Latin for 'James', is used to describe the political movement committed to the return of the Catholic Stuart kings to the thrones of England and Scotland.

Bonnie Prince Charlie's flight after the Battle of Culloden is legendary. He lived in hiding in the remote Highlands and islands for months before being rescued by a French frigate.

His narrow escape from Uist to Skye, dressed as Flora MacDonald's maid, is the subject of the 'Skye Boat Song'.

1513	1567	1603	1692
James IV invades northern England and is soundly defeated in Northumberland at the Battle of Flodden. It marks a watershed in war history, with artillery on the upswing and archery on the way out.	Mary, Queen of Scots is deposed and thrown in prison. Though her last stand is still to come, the days of wilful royal action in Scotland seem to be over.	James VI of Scotland inherits the English throne in the so-called Union of the Crowns, becoming James I of Great Britain.	The Massacre of Glencoe causes further rifts between those clans loyal to the crown and those loyal to the old ways.

The Highland Clearances

In the aftermath of the Jacobite rebellions, Highland dress, the bearing of arms and the bagpipes were outlawed. The Highlands were put under military control and private armies were banned.

John Prebble's wonderfully written book *The Highland Clearances* tells the terrible story of how the Highlanders were driven out of their homes and forced into emigration.

The clansmen, no longer of any use as soldiers and uneconomical as tenants, were evicted from their homes and farms by the Highland chieftains to make way for flocks of sheep. A few stayed to work the sheep farms; many more were forced to seek work in the cities, or to eke a living from crofts (smallholdings) on poor coastal land. Men who had never seen the sea were forced to take to boats to try their luck at herring fishing, and many thousands emigrated – some willingly, some under duress – to the developing colonies of North America, Australia and New Zealand.

If you do much walking in the Highlands and islands, you are almost certain to come across a pile of stones among the bracken, all that remains of a house or cottage. Look around and you'll find another, and another, and soon you'll realise that this was once a crofting settlement. It's one of the saddest sights you'll see in Scotland – this emptiness, where once there was a thriving community.

The Scottish Enlightenment

During the period known as the Scottish Enlightenment (roughly 1740–1830) Edinburgh became known as 'a hotbed of genius'. Philosophers David Hume and Adam Smith and sociologist Adam Ferguson emerged as influential thinkers, nourished on generations of theological debate. Medic William Cullen produced the first modern pharmacopoeia, chemist Joseph Black advanced the science of thermodynamics and geologist James Hutton challenged long-held beliefs about the age of the Earth.

TARTAN

There was a revival in Scottish history and literature. The writings of Sir Walter Scott and the poetry of Robert Burns achieved lasting popularity. The clichéd images that spring to mind when you say 'Scotland' – bagpipes, haggis, tartans, misty glens – owe much to their romantic depictions of the country.

Most clan tartans are in fact a 19th-century invention (long after the demise of the clan system), partly inspired by the writings of Sir Walter Scott.

The Industrial Revolution

The development of the steam engine ushered in the Industrial Revolution. Glasgow, deprived of its lucrative tobacco trade following the American War of Independence (1776–83), developed into an industrial powerhouse, the 'second city' of the British Empire. Cotton mills, iron and steelworks, chemical plants, shipbuilding yards and heavy-engineering works proliferated along the River Clyde in the 19th century, powered by southern Scotland's abundant coal mines.

1707	1745–46	1740s–1830s	1914–1932
Despite popular opposition, the Act of Union, which brings England and Scotland under one parliament, one sovereign and one flag, takes effect on 1 May.	The culmination of the Jacobite rebellions: Bonnie Prince Charlie lands in Scotland, gathers an army and marches south. Though he gains English territory, he is eventually defeated at the Battle of Culloden.	Cultural and intellectual life flourishes during the Scottish Enlightenment. Meanwhile, the Industrial Revolution brings preeminence in production of textiles, iron, steel and coal – and above all in shipbuilding.	Scottish industry slumps during WWI and collapses in its aftermath in the face of overseas competition and the Great Depression. About 400,000 Scots emigrate between 1921 and 1931.

The Clearances and the Industrial Revolution had shattered the traditional rural way of life, and though manufacturing cities and ports thrived in these decades of Empire, wealth was generated for a select few by an impoverished many. Deep poverty forced many into emigration and others to their graves. The depopulation was exacerbated by WWI, which took a heavy toll on Scottish youth. The ensuing years were bleak and marked by labour disputes.

War & Peace

Scotland largely escaped the trauma and devastation wrought by WWII on the industrial cities of England (although Clydebank was bombed). Indeed, the war brought a measure of renewed prosperity to Scotland as the shipyards and engineering works geared up to supply material. But the postwar period saw the collapse of shipbuilding and heavy industry, on which Scotland had become over-reliant.

After the discovery of North Sea oil off the Scottish coast, excitement turned to bitterness for many Scots, who felt that revenues were being siphoned off to England. This issue, along with takeovers of Scots companies by English ones (which then closed the Scots operation, asset-stripped and transferred jobs to England), fuelled increasing nationalist sentiment. The Scottish National Party (SNP) developed into a third force (later, a second as they eclipsed the Conservatives, and then first as they won power from the Labour Party) in Scottish politics.

Devolution

In 1979 a referendum was held on whether to set up a directly elected Scottish Assembly. Fifty-two per cent of those who voted said 'yes' to devolution, but Labour Prime Minister James Callaghan decided that everyone who didn't vote should be counted as a 'no', so the Scottish Assembly was rejected.

From 1979 to 1997 Scotland was ruled by a Conservative government in London for which the majority of Scots hadn't voted. Separatist feelings, always present, grew stronger. Following the landslide victory of the Labour Party in 1997, another referendum was held on the creation of a Scottish parliament. This time the result was overwhelmingly and unambiguously in favour.

Elections were held and the Scottish parliament convened for the first time in 1999 in Edinburgh, with Labour's Donald Dewar, who died in office the very next year, becoming First Minister. Labour held power until 2007, when the pro-independence Scottish National Party formed government. They were overwhelmingly re-elected in 2011 and pushed for a referendum on independence. In September 2014, the Scots voted against becoming an independent nation.

Between 1904 and 1931 around one million people emigrated from Scotland to begin a new life in North America and Australasia.

A well-presented and easily absorbed introduction to Scottish history can be found at www.bbc.co.uk/history/scottishhistory. The accompanying images of historical sites help bring it to life.

1941–45	1970s	1999–2004	2014
Clydebank is blitzed by German bombers in 1941 with 1200 deaths; by 1945 one out of four males in the workforce is employed in heavy industries to support the war effort.	The discovery of oil and gas in the North Sea brings new prosperity to Aberdeen and the surrounding area, and also to the Shetland Islands.	Scottish parliament is convened after a three-century hiatus in May 1999. The new parliament building is opened in Edinburgh by Queen Elizabeth II in 2004.	Scotland votes on and rejects becoming a fully independent nation and so remains part of the United Kingdom.

The Scottish Larder

Traditional Scottish cookery is all about basic comfort food: solid, nourishing fare, often high in fat, that will keep you warm on a winter's day spent in the fields or out fishing, and sweet treats to come home to in the evening. But a new culinary style known as Modern Scottish has emerged over the last two decades. It's a style that should be familiar to fans of Californian Cuisine and Mod Oz. Chefs take top-quality Scottish produce – from Highland venison, Aberdeen Angus beef and freshly landed seafood, to root vegetables, raspberries and Ayrshire cheeses – and prepare it simply, in a way that enhances the natural flavours, often adding a French, Italian or Asian twist. Scotland's traditional drinks – whisky and beer – have also found a new lease of life in recent years, with single malts being marketed like fine wines, and a new breed of microbreweries springing up all over the country.

Breakfast, Lunch & Dinner

Haggis may be the national dish for which Scotland is most famous, but when it comes to what Scottish people actually cook and eat most often, the hands-down winner has to be mince and tatties (potatoes). Minced beef, browned in the pan and then stewed slowly with onion, carrot and gravy, is served with mashed potatoes (with a splash of milk and a knob of butter added during the mashing) – it's tasty, warming and you don't even have to chew.

A Caledonian Feast by Annette Hope is a fascinating and readable history of Scottish cuisine, providing a wealth of historical and sociological background.

The Full Scottish

Surprisingly few Scots eat porridge for breakfast – these days a cappuccino and a croissant is just as likely – and even fewer eat it in the traditional way; that is, with salt to taste, but no sugar. The breakfast offered in a B&B or hotel usually consists of fruit juice and cereal or muesli, followed by a choice of bacon, sausage, black pudding (a type of sausage made from dried blood), grilled tomato, mushrooms and a fried egg or two.

Fish for breakfast may sound strange, but was not unusual in crofting (smallholding) and fishing communities where seafood was a staple; many hotels still offer grilled kippers (smoked herrings) or smoked haddock (poached in milk and served with a poached egg) for breakfast – delicious with lots of buttered toast.

PRICE BANDS

Eating choices are flagged with price indicators, based on the cost of an average main course from the dinner menu.

➡ £ Budget place where a main dish is less than £9

➡ ££ Midrange; mains are £9 to £18

➡ £££ Top end; mains are more than £18

Lunch mains are often cheaper than dinner mains, and many places offer an 'early bird' special with lower prices (usually available between 5pm and 7pm).

SSSSSSMOKIN'!

Scotland is famous for its smoked salmon, but there are many other varieties of smoked fish – plus smoked meats and cheeses – to enjoy. Smoking food to preserve it is an ancient art that has recently undergone a revival, but this time it's more about flavour than preservation.

There are two parts to the process – first the cure, which involves covering the fish in a mixture of salt and molasses, or soaking it in brine; and then the smoke, which can be either cold smoking (at less than 34°C), which results in a raw product, or hot smoking (at more than 60°C), which cooks it. Cold-smoked products include traditional smoked salmon, kippers and Finnan haddies. Hot-smoked products include *bradan rost* ('flaky' smoked salmon) and Arbroath smokies.

Arbroath smokies are haddock that have been gutted, beheaded and cleaned, then salted and dried overnight, tied together at the tail in pairs, and hot-smoked over oak or beech chippings for 45 to 90 minutes. Finnan haddies (named after the fishing village of Findon in Aberdeenshire) are also haddock, but these are split down the middle like kippers, and cold smoked.

Kippers (smoked herring) were invented in Northumberland, in northern England, in the mid-19th century, but Scotland soon picked up the technique, and both Loch Fyne and Mallaig were famous for their kippers.

There are dozens of modern smokehouses scattered all over Scotland, many of which offer a mail-order service as well as an on-site shop; here are a few recommended ones:

Hebridean Smokehouse (☏01876-580209; www.hebrideansmokehouse.com; Clachan, North Uist; ☉8am-5.30pm Mon-Fri year-round, 9am-5pm Sat Easter-Oct) Peat-smoked salmon and sea trout.

Inverawe Smokehouse & Fishery (☏0844 8475 49; www.smokedsalmon.co.uk; Inverawe, nr Oban; ☉8.30am-5.30pm Mar-Oct) Delicate smoked salmon, plump juicy kippers.

Marrbury Smokehouse (☏01671-840241; www.visitmarrbury.co.uk; Carsluith Castle, Dumfries & Galloway; ☉10.30am-5pm Tue-Sat) Supplier to Gleneagles Hotel and other top restaurants.

Loch Duart Artisan Smokehouse (☏01870-610324; www.lochduartsmokedsalmon. com; Lochcarnan, South Uist; ☉8.30am-4.30pm Mon-Fri) Famous for its flaky, hot-smoked salmon.

Broth, Skink & Bree

Scotch broth, made with mutton stock, barley, lentils and peas, is nutritious and tasty, while cock-a-leekie is a hearty soup made with chicken and leeks. Warming vegetable soups include leek and potato soup, and lentil soup (traditionally made using ham stock – vegetarians beware!).

Seafood soups include the delicious Cullen skink, made with smoked haddock, potato, onion and milk, and *partan bree* (crab soup).

Surf & Turf

Steak eaters will enjoy a thick fillet of world-famous Aberdeen Angus beef, and beef from Highland cattle is much sought after. Venison, from the red deer, is leaner and appears on many menus. Both may be served with a wine-based or creamy whisky sauce. Then there's haggis, Scotland's much-maligned national dish...

Scottish salmon is famous worldwide, but there's a big difference between the now-ubiquitous farmed salmon and the leaner, more expensive, wild fish. Also, there are concerns over the environmental impact of salmon farms on the marine environment.

Smoked salmon is traditionally dressed with a squeeze of lemon juice and eaten with fresh brown bread and butter. Trout, salmon's smaller

Scottish food writer Sue Lawrence's book *A Cook's Tour of Scotland* contains 120 recipes based on the use of fresh, seasonal Scottish produce.

HAGGIS – SCOTLAND'S NATIONAL DISH

Scotland's national dish is often ridiculed by foreigners because of its ingredients, which admittedly don't sound promising – the finely chopped lungs, heart and liver of a sheep, mixed with oatmeal and onion and stuffed into a sheep's stomach bag. However, it actually tastes surprisingly good.

Haggis should be served with *champit tatties* and *bashed neeps* (mashed potatoes and turnips), with a generous dollop of butter and a good sprinkling of black pepper.

Although it's eaten year-round, haggis is central to the Burns Night celebrations of 25 January, in honour of Scotland's national poet, Robert Burns, when Scots worldwide unite to revel in their Scottishness. A piper announces the arrival of the haggis and Burns' poem *Address to a Haggis* is recited to this 'Great chieftan o' the puddin-race'. The bulging haggis is then lanced with a dirk (dagger) to reveal the steaming offal within, 'warm, reekin, rich'.

Vegetarians (and quite a few carnivores, no doubt) will be relieved to know that veggie haggis is available in some restaurants.

cousin – whether wild, rod-caught brown trout or farmed rainbow trout – is delicious fried in oatmeal.

As an alternative to kippers, you may be offered Arbroath smokies (lightly smoked fresh haddock), traditionally eaten cold. Herring fillets fried in oatmeal are good, if you don't mind picking out a few bones. Mackerel pâté and smoked or peppered mackerel (both served cold) are also popular.

Juicy langoustines (also known as Dublin Bay prawns), crabs, lobsters, oysters, mussels and scallops are also widely available.

Clootie & Cranachan

Traditional Scottish puddings are irresistibly creamy, high-calorie concoctions. Cranachan is whipped cream flavoured with whisky, and mixed with toasted oatmeal and raspberries. Atholl brose is a mixture of cream, whisky and honey, flavoured with oatmeal. Clootie dumpling is a rich steamed pudding filled with currants and raisins (so called for being wrapped in a 'cloot', or linen cloth, for steaming).

HAGGIS

It has been illegal to import haggis into the USA since 1971, when the US Department of Agriculture declared that sheep's lungs are unfit for human consumption.

Vegetarians & Vegans

Scotland has the same proportion of vegetarians as the rest of the UK – around 8% to 10% of the population – and vegetarianism is now firmly in the mainstream. Even the most remote Highland pub usually has at least one vegetarian dish on the menu, and there are many dedicated vegetarian restaurants in the cities. If you get stuck, there's almost always an Italian or Indian restaurant where you can get meat-free pizza, pasta or curry. Vegans, though, may find the options a bit limited outside of Edinburgh and Glasgow.

One thing to keep in mind is that lentil soup, a seemingly vegetarian staple of Scottish pub and restaurant menus, is traditionally made with ham stock.

Eating with Kids

Following the introduction of the ban on smoking in public places in 2006, many Scottish pubs and restaurants have had to broaden their appeal by becoming more family friendly. As a result, especially in the cities and more popular tourist towns, many restaurants and pubs now have family rooms and/or play areas.

In this guide we have indicated restaurants that offer children's menus, high chairs and other child-friendly facilities with a family-friendly icon.

You should be aware that children under the age of 14 are not allowed into the majority of Scottish pubs, even those that serve bar meals; and in family-friendly pubs (those in possession of a Children's Certificate), under-14s are only allowed in between 11am and 8pm, and must be accompanied by an adult aged 18 or older.

Cookery Courses

There are more than a dozen places that offer courses in Scottish cookery. These are two of the most famous:

Kinloch Lodge Hotel (☎01471-833333; www.kinloch-lodge.co.uk; Kinloch, Isle of Skye) Courses in Scottish cookery and demonstrations using fresh, seasonal Scottish produce by Lady Claire Macdonald, author of *Scottish Highland Hospitality* and *Celebrations*. Fees include three nights accommodation at the hotel.

Nick Nairn Cook School (☎01877-389900; www.nairnscookschool.com; 15 Back Wynd, Aberdeen) Two-day courses in modern Scottish cooking at the school owned by Scotland's top TV chef, Nick Nairn, author of *Wild Harvest* and *Island Harvest*.

What Are Ye Drinkin'?

A Pint...

Scottish breweries produce a wide range of beers. The market is dominated by multinational brewers, but smaller local breweries generally create tastier brews, some of them very strong. The aptly named Skull Splitter from Orkney is a good example, at 8.5% alcohol by volume.

Many Scottish beers use old-fashioned 'shilling' categories to indicate strength (the number of shillings was originally the price per barrel; the stronger the beer, the higher the price). The usual range is from 60 to 80 shillings (written 80/-). You'll also see IPA, which stands for India Pale Ale, a strong, hoppy beer first brewed in the early 19th century for export to India (the extra alcohol meant that it kept better on the long sea voyage).

Draught beer is served in pints (usually costing from £2.40 to £3.50) or half pints; alcoholic content generally ranges from 3% to 6%. What the English call bitter, Scots call heavy, or export. Caledonian 80/- and Belhaven 80/- are worth trying, but Deuchar's IPA from Edinburgh's Caledonian Brewery is our favourite.

The website www.scottishbrewing.com has a comprehensive list of Scottish breweries, both large and small.

Scottish Ales

The increasing popularity of real ales and a backlash against the bland conformity of globalised multinational brewing conglomerates has seen a huge rise in the number of artisan brewers and microbreweries springing up all over Scotland. They take pride in using only natural ingredients, and many try to revive ancient recipes, such as heather- and seaweed-flavoured ales.

These beers are sold in pubs, off-licences and delicatessens. Here are a few of our favourites:

Black Isle Brewery (www.blackislebrewery.com; Old Allangrance, Black Isle) Range of organic beers.

Cairngorm Brewery (☎01479 812222; www.cairngormbrewery.com; Dalfaber Industrial Estate) Creator of multi-award-winning Trade Winds ale.

Colonsay Brewery (☎01951 200190; www.colonsaybrewery.co.uk; Isle of Colonsay) Produces lager, 80/- and IPA.

IRN BRU

Scotland's most famous soft drink is Barr's Irn Bru: a sweet fizzy drink, radioactive orange in colour, that smells like bubble gum and almost strips the enamel from your teeth. Many Scots swear by its restorative effects as a cure for a hangover.

Islay Ales (www.islayales.com; Isle of Islay; ⏰10.30am-5pm Mon-Sat Apr-Sep, to 4pm Oct-Mar) Refreshing and citrusy Saligo Ale.

Orkney Brewery (📞01856-841777; www.orkneybrewery.co.uk; Quoyloo; tour adult/child £6/3.50; ⏰10am-4.30pm Mon-Sat & 11am-4.30pm Sun Apr-Oct plus most of Dec, winter opening by arrangement) Famous for its rich, chocolatey Dark Island ale, and the dangerously strong Skull Splitter.

Traquair House Brewery (📞01896 830323; www.traquair.co.uk; Traquair House, Innerleithen) Traquair House Ale, at 7.2% alcohol, is rich, dark and strong.

Williams Bros (📞01259-725511; www.williamsbrosbrew.com; New Alloa Brewery, Kelliebank, Alloa) Produces historic beers flavoured with heather flowers, seaweed, Scots pine and elderberries.

...Or a Wee Dram?

Scotch whisky (always spelt without an 'e' – whiskey with an 'e' is Irish or American) is Scotland's best-known product and biggest export. The spirit has been distilled in Scotland at least since the 15th century.

As well as whiskies, there are whisky-based liqueurs such as Drambuie. If you must mix your whisky with anything other than water, try a whisky-mac (whisky with ginger wine). After a long walk in the rain there's nothing better to put a warm glow in your belly.

HOW TO BE A MALT WHISKY BUFF

'Love makes the world go round? Not at all! Whisky makes it go round twice as fast'. *Whisky Galore, Compton Mackenzie (1883–1972)*

Whisky tasting today is almost as popular as wine tasting was in the yuppie heyday of the late 1980s. Being able to tell your Ardbeg from your Edradour is de rigueur among the whisky-nosing set, so here are some pointers to help you impress your friends.

What's the difference between malt and grain whiskies?

Malts are distilled from malted barley – that is, barley that has been soaked in water, then allowed to germinate for around 10 days until the starch has turned into sugar – while grain whiskies are distilled from other cereals, usually wheat, corn or unmalted barley.

So what is a single malt?

A single malt is a whisky that has been distilled from malted barley and is the product of a single distillery. A pure (or vatted) malt is a mixture of single malts from several distilleries, and a blended whisky is a mixture of various grain whiskies (about 60%) and malt whiskies (about 40%) from many different distilleries.

Why are single malts more desirable than blends?

A single malt, like a fine wine, somehow captures the essence of the place where it was made and matured – a combination of the water, the barley, the peat smoke, the oak barrels in which it was aged and (in the case of certain coastal distilleries) the sea air and salt spray. Each distillation varies from the one before, like different vintages from the same vineyard.

How should a single malt be drunk?

Either neat, or preferably with a little water added. To appreciate the aroma and flavour to the utmost, a measure of malt whisky should be cut (diluted) with one-third to two-thirds as much spring water (still, bottled spring water will do). Ice, tap water and (God forbid) mixers are for philistines. Would you add lemonade or ice to a glass of Chablis?

Where can I learn more?

If you're serious about spirits, the **Scotch Malt Whisky Society** (📞0131-554 3451; www. smws.com) has branches all around the world. Membership of the society costs from £122 for the first year (£59 a year thereafter) and includes use of members' rooms in Edinburgh and London.

At a bar, older Scots may order a 'half' or 'nip' of whisky as a chaser to a pint or half pint of beer (a 'hauf and a hauf'). Only tourists ask for 'Scotch' – what else would you be served in Scotland? The standard measure in pubs is either 25mL or 35mL.

Top 10 Single Malt Whiskies – Our Choice

After a great deal of diligent research (and not a few sore heads), Lonely Planet's *Scotland* authors have selected their 10 favourite single malts from across the country.

Ardbeg (www.ardbeg.com; Islay; tours from £5; ☺9.30am-5pm Mon-Fri, plus Sat Apr-Oct & Sun May-Sep) The 10-year-old from this noble distillery is a byword for excellence. Peaty but well balanced. Hits the spot after a hill walk.

Bowmore (☐01496-810441; www.bowmore.com; School St, Islay; tours from £6; ☺9am-5pm Mon-Fri & 9am-12.30pm Sat Oct-Mar, 9am-5pm Mon-Sat & noon-4pm Sun Apr-Sep) Smoke, peat and salty sea air – a classic Islay malt. One of the few distilleries that still malts its own barley.

Bruichladdich (☐01496-850190; www.bruichladdich.com; Islay; tours £5; ☺9am-6pm Mon-Fri & 9.30am-4pm Sat, plus 12.30-3.30pm Sun Apr-Aug) A visitor-friendly distillery with a quirky, innovative approach – famous for very peaty special releases.

Glendronach (Speyside) Only sherry casks are used here, so the creamy, spicy result tastes like grandma's Christmas trifle.

Highland Park (☐01856-874619; www.highlandpark.co.uk; Holm Rd, Orkney; tour adult/child £7.50/free; ☺10am-5pm Mon-Sat & noon-5pm Sun May-Aug, 10am-5pm Mon-Fri Apr & Sep, 1-5pm Mon-Fri Oct-Mar) Full and rounded, with heather, honey, malt and peat. Award-winning distillery tour.

Isle of Arran (☐01770-830264; www.arranwhisky.com; Arran; tours adult/child £6/free; ☺10am-5.30pm Apr-Oct, 11am-4pm Mon-Sat Nov-Mar) One of Scotland's newer distilleries, offering a lightish, flavoursome malt with flowery, fruity notes.

Macallan (☐01340-872280; www.themacallan.com; Speyside; tours £15; ☺9.30am-6pm Mon-Sat Easter-Oct, 9.30am-5pm Mon-Fri Nov-Mar) The king of Speyside malts, with sherry and bourbon finishes. Distillery set amid waving fields of Golden Promise barley.

Springbank (☐01586-552009; www.springbankwhisky.com; 85 Longrow, Campbeltown; tours from £6.50; ☺tours 10am & 2pm Mon-Sat) Complex flavours – sherry, citrus, pear drops, peat – with a salty tang. The entire production process from malting to bottling takes place on site.

Talisker (☐01478-614308; www.discovering-distilleries.com; Skye; guided tour £7; ☺9.30am-5pm Mon-Sat Apr-Oct, 11am-5pm Sun Jul & Aug, 10am-4.30pm Mon-Fri Nov-Mar) Brooding, heavily peated nose balanced by a satisfying sweetness from this lord of the isles. Great postdinner dram.

The Balvenie (Speyside) Rich and honeyed, this Speysider is liquid gold for those with a sweet tooth.

Top Seafood Restaurants

Ondine, Edinburgh

Café Fish, Tobermory

Waterfront Fishhouse Restaurant, Oban

Silver Darling, Aberdeen

Tolbooth Restaurant, Stonehaven

Lochleven Seafood Cafe, Kinlochleven

Seafood Restaurant, St Andrews

Plockton Shores, Plockton

Starfish, Tarbert

Seafood Temple, Oban

Scottish Culture

Arts

The notion of 'the Scottish arts' often conjures up clichéd images of bagpipe music, incomprehensible poetry and romanticised paintings of Highland landscapes. But Scottish artists have given the world a wealth of unforgettable treasures, from the songs and poems of Robert Burns and the novels of Walter Scott, to the architecture of Charles Rennie Mackintosh.

For a guide to Scottish film locations, check out www.scotlandthemovie.com.

Literature

Scotland has a long and distinguished literary history, from the days of the medieval makars ('makers' of verses, ie poets) to the modern 'rat pack' of Iain Banks, Irvine Welsh and Ian Rankin.

SCOTS & GAELIC

From the 8th to the 19th centuries the common language of central and southern Scotland was **Lowland Scots** (sometimes called Lallans), which evolved from Old English and has Dutch, French, Gaelic, German and Scandinavian influences. As distinct from English as Norwegian is from Danish, it was the official language of state in Scotland until the Act of Union in 1707.

Following the Union, English rose to predominance as the language of government, church and polite society. The spread of education and literacy in the 19th century eventually led to Lowland Scots being perceived as backward and unsophisticated – children were often beaten for speaking Scots in school instead of English.

The Scots tongue persisted, however, and has undergone a revival – there are now Scots language dictionaries, university degree courses in Scots language and literature, and Scots is studied as part of the school curriculum.

Scottish Gaelic (*Gàidhlig* – pronounced 'gallic') is spoken by about 80,000 people in Scotland, mainly in the Highlands and islands. It is a member of the Celtic family of languages, which includes Irish Gaelic, Manx, Welsh, Cornish and Breton.

Gaelic culture flourished in the Highlands until the Jacobite rebellions of the 18th century. After the Battle of Culloden in 1746 many Gaelic speakers were forced from their ancestral lands, and Gaelic was regarded as little more than a 'peasant' language of no modern significance.

It was only in the 1970s that Gaelic began to make a comeback. After two centuries of decline, the language is now being encouraged through financial help from government agencies and the EU, and Gaelic education is flourishing at every level from playgroups to tertiary institutions.

Burns & Scott

Scotland's most famous literary figure is, of course, Robert Burns (1759–96). His works have been translated into dozens of languages and are known the world over. Burns wrote in Lowland Scots, or Lallans; in fact, his poetry was instrumental in keeping Lallans alive to the present day. He was also very much a man of the people, satirising the upper classes and the church for their hypocrisy. Although he is best known for the comical tale of *Tam O'Shanter* and for penning the words to *Auld Lang Syne*, his more political poems – including *Such A Parcel Of Rogues In A Nation* (about the 1707 Act of Union) and *A Man's A Man for a' That* (about class and solidarity) – reveal his socialist leanings.

The son of an Edinburgh lawyer, Sir Walter Scott (1771–1832) was Scotland's greatest and most prolific novelist. Scott was born in Edinburgh and lived at various New Town addresses before moving to his country house at Abbotsford. His early works were rhyming ballads, such as *The Lady of the Lake*, and his first historical novels – Scott effectively invented the genre – were published anonymously. Plagued by debt in later life, he wrote obsessively in order to make money, but will always be best remembered for classic tales such as *Waverley, The Heart of Midlothian, Ivanhoe, Redgauntlet* and *Castle Dangerous*.

RLS & Sherlock Holmes

Along with Scott, Robert Louis Stevenson (1850–94) ranks as Scotland's best-known novelist. Born at 8 Howard Pl in Edinburgh into a family of famous lighthouse engineers, Stevenson studied law at Edinburgh University but was always intent on pursuing the life of a writer. An inveterate traveller, but dogged by ill health, he finally settled in Samoa in 1889, where he was loved by the local people and known as 'Tusitala' – the teller of tales. Stevenson is known and loved around the world for those tales: *Kidnapped, Catriona, Treasure Island, The Master of Ballantrae* and *The Strange Case of Dr Jekyll and Mr Hyde*.

Sir Arthur Conan Doyle (1859–1930), the creator of Sherlock Holmes, was born in Edinburgh and studied medicine at Edinburgh University. He based the character of Holmes on one of his lecturers, the surgeon Dr Joseph Bell, who had employed his forensic skills and powers of deduction on several murder cases in Edinburgh.

MacDiarmid to Muriel Spark

Scotland's finest modern poet was Hugh MacDiarmid (born Christopher Murray Grieve; 1892–1978). Originally from Dumfriesshire, he moved to Edinburgh in 1908, where he trained as a teacher and a journalist, but spent most of his life in Montrose, Shetland, Glasgow and Biggar. His masterpiece is 'A Drunk Man Looks at the Thistle', a 2685-line Joycean monologue.

The poet and storyteller George Mackay Brown (1921–96) was born in Stromness in the Orkney Islands, and lived there almost all his life. Although his poems and novels are rooted in Orkney, his work, like that of Burns, transcends local and national boundaries. His best-known novel *Greenvoe* (1972) is a warm, witty and poetic evocation of everyday life in an Orkney community.

Dame Muriel Spark (1918–2006) was born in Edinburgh and educated at James Gillespie's High School for Girls, an experience that provided material for perhaps her best-known novel, *The Prime of Miss Jean Brodie*, a shrewd portrait of 1930s Edinburgh.

Six Essential Scottish Novels

Waverley (Sir Walter Scott, 1814)

The Silver Darlings (Neil M Gunn, 1941)

A Scots Quair (Lewis Grassic Gibbon, trilogy 1932–34)

The Prime of Miss Jean Brodie (Muriel Spark, 1961)

Greenvoe (George Mackay Brown, 1972)

Trainspotting (Irvine Welsh, 1993)

TRADITIONAL MUSIC

The Contemporary Scene

The most widely known Scots writers today include Iain Banks (1954–2013; *The Crow Road*), Irvine Welsh (1961–; *Trainspotting*), Janice Galloway (1955–; *The Trick Is To Keep Breathing*) and Liz Lochhead (1947–; *Mary Queen of Scots Got Her Head Chopped Off*). The grim realities of modern Glasgow are vividly conjured in the short story collection *Not Not While the Giro* by James Kelman (1946–), whose controversial novel *How Late It Was, How Late* won the 1994 Booker Prize.

The Scottish crime-writing charts are topped by Val McDermid (1955–) and Ian Rankin (1960–). McDermid's novels feature private investigator Kate Brannigan, and psychologist Tony Hill; *Wire in the Blood* became a successful TV series. Rankin's Edinburgh-based crime novels, featuring the hard-drinking, introspective Detective Inspector John Rebus, are sinister, engrossing mysteries that explore the darker side of Scotland's capital city. He has a growing international following (his books have been translated into 22 languages).

Music

Traditional Music

Scotland has always had a strong folk tradition. In the 1960s and 1970s Robin Hall and Jimmy MacGregor, the Corries and the hugely talented Ewan McColl worked the pubs and clubs up and down the country. The Boys of the Lough, headed by Shetland fiddler Aly Bain, was one of the first professional bands to promote the traditional Celtic music of Scotland and Ireland. It was followed by the Battlefield Band, Alba, Capercaillie and others.

The Scots folk songs that you will often hear sung in pubs and at *ceilidhs* (evenings of traditional Scottish entertainment, including music, song and dance) draw on Scotland's rich history. A huge number of them relate to the Jacobite rebellions in the 18th century and, in particular, to Bonnie Prince Charlie – 'Hey Johnnie Cope', the 'Skye Boat Song' and 'Will Ye No Come Back Again', for example – while others relate to the Covenanters and the Highland Clearances.

In recent years there has been a revival in traditional music, often adapted and updated for the modern age. Bands such as Runrig pioneered with their own brand of Gaelic rock, while Shooglenifty blend Scottish folk music with anything from indie rock to electronica, producing a hybrid that has been called 'acid croft'.

But perhaps the finest modern renderings of traditional Scottish songs come from singer-songwriter Eddi Reader, who rose to fame with the band Fairground Attraction and their 1988 hit 'Perfect'. Her album *Eddi Reader Sings the Songs of Robert Burns* (2003, re-released with extra tracks in 2009) is widely regarded as one of the best interpretations of Burns' works.

Bagpipes

The traditional Highland bagpipe consists of a leather bag held under the arm, kept inflated by blowing through the blowstick; the piper forces air through the pipes by squeezing the bag with the forearm. Three of the pipes, known as drones, play a constant note (one bass, two tenor) in the background; the fourth pipe, the chanter, plays the melody.

Highland soldiers were traditionally accompanied into battle by the skirl of the pipes, and the Scottish Highland bagpipe is unique in being the only musical instrument ever to be classed as a weapon. The playing of the pipes was banned – under pain of death – by the British government in 1747 as part of a scheme to suppress Highland culture in the

The Traditional Music & Song Association (www.tmsa.org.uk) website has listings of music, dance and cultural festivals around Scotland.

The Living Tradition (www.livingtradition.co.uk) is a bimonthly magazine covering the folk and traditional music of Scotland and the British Isles, as well as Celtic music, with features and reviews of albums and live gigs.

wake of the Jacobite uprising of 1745. The pipes were revived when the Highland regiments were drafted into the British Army towards the end of the 18th century.

Bagpipe music may not be to everyone's taste, but Scotland's most famous instrument has been reinvented by bands such as the Red Hot Chilli Pipers, who use pipes, drums, guitars and keyboards to create rock versions of trad tunes. They feature regularly at festivals throughout the country.

Ceilidhs

The Gaelic word *ceilidh* (*kay*-lay) means 'visit'. A *ceilidh* was originally a social gathering in the house after the day's work was over, enlivened with storytelling, music and song. These days, a *ceilidh* means an evening of traditional Scottish entertainment including music, song and dance. To find one, check the village noticeboard, or just ask at the local pub; visitors are always welcome to join in.

Rock & Pop

It would take an entire book to list all the Scottish artists and bands that have made it big in the world of rock and pop. From Glasgow-born King of Skiffle, Lonnie Donegan, in the 1950s, to the chart-topping Dumfries DJ Calvin Harris today, the roll call is long and impressive, and only a few can be mentioned here.

The '90s saw the emergence of three bands that took the top three places in a 2005 vote for the best Scottish band of all time – melodic indie-pop songsters Belle and Sebastian, Brit-rock band Travis, and indie rockers Idlewild, who opened for the Rolling Stones in 2003. Scottish artists who have made an international impression in more recent times include award-winning Glasgow band Glasvegas; Ayrshire rockers Biffy Clyro; and indie rock group Frightened Rabbit.

The airwaves are awash with female singer-songwriters, but few are as gutsy and versatile as Edinburgh-born, St Andrews–raised KT Tunstall. Although she's been writing and singing since the late 1990s, it was her 2005 debut album *Eye to the Telescope* that introduced her to a wider audience. And then there's Glasgow-born Amy Macdonald, who was only 20 years old when her first album *This is the Life* (2007) sold 3 million copies; her third, *Life in a Beautiful Light*, was released in 2012.

As far as male singer-songwriters are concerned, few are more popular than bespectacled twin brothers Craig and Charlie Reid, better known as The Proclaimers. Nine studio albums from 1987 to 2012 provided ample material for the hugely successful movie based on their music, *Sunshine On Leith* (2013).

Painting

Perhaps the most famous Scottish painting is the portrait Reverend Robert Walker Skating on Duddingston Loch by Sir Henry Raeburn (1756–1823), in the National Gallery of Scotland. This image of a Presbyterian minister at play beneath Arthur's Seat, with all the poise of a ballerina and the hint of a smile on his lips, is a symbol of Enlightenment Edinburgh, the triumph of reason over wild nature.

Scottish portraiture reached its peak during the Scottish Enlightenment in the second half of the 18th century with the paintings of Raeburn and his contemporary Allan Ramsay (1713–84), while Sir David Wilkie (1785–1841), whose genre paintings depicted scenes of rural Highland life, was one of the greatest artists of the 19th century.

In the early 20th century the Scottish painters most widely acclaimed outside of the country were the group known as the Scottish Colourists –

Top Five Scottish Pop Playlist

Franz Ferdinand, 'Take Me Out'

KT Tunstall, 'Suddenly I See'

The Proclaimers, 'Letter from America'

The View, 'Same Jeans'

Biffy Clyro, 'Bubbles'

Amy Macdonald, 'This is the Life'

Runrig, 'Loch Lomond'

The Rezillos, 'Top of the Pops'

Simple Minds, 'Don't You (Forget About Me)'

Texas, 'Say What You Want'

SJ Peploe (1871–1935), Francis Cadell (1883–1937), Leslie Hunter (1877–1931) and JD Fergusson (1874–1961) – whose striking paintings drew on French post-Impressionist and Fauvist influences. Peploe and Cadell, active in the 1920s and 1930s, often spent the summer painting together on the Isle of Iona, and reproductions of their beautiful landscapes and seascapes appear on many a print and postcard.

Cinema

Top Five Scottish Films

....

The 39 Steps (1935)

....

Whisky Galore! (1949)

....

Local Hero (1983)

....

Rob Roy (1995)

....

Trainspotting (1996)

Perthshire-born John Grierson (1898–1972) is acknowledged around the world as the father of the documentary film. His legacy includes the classic *Drifters* (about the Scottish herring fishery) and *Seaward the Great Ships* (about Clyde shipbuilding). Writer-director Bill Forsyth (1946–) is best known for *Local Hero* (1983), a gentle comedy about an oil magnate seduced by the beauty of the Highlands, and *Gregory's Girl* (1980), about an awkward teenage schoolboy's romantic exploits.

In the 1990s the rise of the director-producer-writer team of Danny Boyle (English), Andrew Macdonald and John Hodge (both Scottish) – who wrote the scripts for *Shallow Grave* (1994), *Trainspotting* (1996) and *A Life Less Ordinary* (1997) – marked the beginnings of what might be described as a home-grown Scottish film industry.

Other Scottish directorial talent includes Kevin Macdonald, who made *Touching the Void* (2003), *The Last King of Scotland* (2006) and *State of Play* (2009), and Andrea Arnold, who directed *Red Road* (2006) and the BAFTA-winning *Fish Tank* (2009).

Scottish Actors

Scotland's most famous actor is, of course, Sir Sean Connery (1930–), the original and arguably best James Bond, and star of dozens of other hit films including *Highlander* (1986), *The Name of the Rose* (1986), *Indiana Jones and the Last Crusade* (1989), *The Hunt for Red October* (1990) and *The League of Extraordinary Gentlemen* (2003). Connery started life as 'Big Tam' Connery, sometime milkman and brickie, born in a tenement in Fountainbridge, Edinburgh.

Other Scottish actors who have achieved international recognition include Robert Carlyle, who starred in *Trainspotting* (1996), *The Full Monty* (1997), *The World Is Not Enough* (1999) and *28 Weeks Later* (2007); Ewan McGregor, who appeared in *Trainspotting*, the more recent Star Wars films, *Salmon Fishing in the Yemen* (2012) and *August: Osage County* (2013); and Kelly Macdonald, yet another *Trainspotting* alumna who went on to appear in *Gosford Park* (2001), *No Country for Old Men* (2007) and TV series *Boardwalk Empire,* and voiced heroine Merida in *Brave* (2012).

Architecture

Despite dodgy Scottish accents from Liam Neeson and Jessica Lange, *Rob Roy* is a witty and moving cinematic version of Sir Walter Scott's tale of the outlaw MacGregor.

The leading Scottish architects of the 18th century were William Adam (1684–1748) and his son Robert Adam (1728–92), whose revival of classical Greek and Roman forms influenced architects throughout Europe. Among the many neoclassical buildings they designed are Hopetoun House, Culzean Castle and Edinburgh's Charlotte Sq, possibly the finest example of Georgian architecture anywhere.

Alexander 'Greek' Thomson (1817–75) changed the face of 19th-century Glasgow with his neoclassical designs, while in Edinburgh, William Henry Playfair (1790–1857) continued Adam's tradition in the Greek temples of the National Monument on Calton Hill, the Royal Scottish Academy and the National Gallery of Scotland.

The 19th-century resurgence of interest in Scottish history and identity, led by writers such as Sir Walter Scott, saw architects turn to the towers, pointed turrets and crow-stepped gables of ancient castles for inspiration. The Victorian revival of the Scottish Baronial style, which first made an appearance in 16th-century buildings such as Craigievar Castle, produced many fanciful abodes such as Balmoral Castle, Scone Palace and Abbotsford.

Scotland's best known 20th-century architect and designer was Charles Rennie Mackintosh (1868–1928), one of the most influential exponents of the art-nouveau style. His finest building is the Glasgow School of Art (1896), which still looks modern more than a century after it was built.

Sport

Football

Football (soccer) in Scotland is not so much a sport as a religion, with thousands turning out to worship their local teams on Wednesdays and weekends throughout the season (August to May). Sacred rites include standing in the freezing cold of a February day, drinking hot Bovril and eating a Scotch pie as you watch your team getting gubbed.

Scotland's top 10 clubs play in the Scottish Premier League (www.scot-prem.com), but two teams – Glasgow Rangers and Glasgow Celtic – have dominated the competition. On only 18 occasions since 1890 has a team other than Rangers or Celtic won the league; the last time was when Aberdeen won in 1985.

However, Rangers made headlines in 2012 when they were forced into liquidation over a tax dispute and kicked out of the SPL. Celtic are having an easy run while their traditional rivals claw their way back into the premier league.

Rugby Union

Traditionally, football was the sport of Scotland's urban working classes, while rugby union (www.scottishrugby.org) was the preserve of middle-class university graduates and farmers from the Borders. Although this distinction is breaking down – rugby's popularity soared after the 1999 World Cup was staged in the UK, and the middle classes have invaded the football terraces – it persists to some extent.

Each year, from January to March, Scotland takes part in the Six Nations Rugby Championship. The most important fixture is the clash against England for the Calcutta Cup – it's always an emotive event; Scotland has won twice and drawn once in the last 10 years.

At club level, the season runs from September to May, and among the better teams are those from the Borders such as Hawick, Kelso and Melrose. At the end of the season, teams play a rugby sevens (seven-a-side) variation of the 15-player competition.

Golf

Scotland is the home of golf. The game was probably invented here in the 12th century, and the world's oldest documentary evidence of a game being played (dating from 1456) was on Bruntsfield Links in Edinburgh.

Today, there are more than 550 golf courses in Scotland – that's more per capita than in any other country (see www.scottishgolfcourses.com). The sport is hugely popular and much more egalitarian than in other countries, with lots of affordable, council-owned courses. There are many world-famous championship courses too, from Muirfield in East Lothian and Turnberry and Troon in Ayrshire, to Carnoustie in Angus and St Andrews' Old Course in Fife.

CASTLES

SCOTTISH CULTURE SPORT

Scotland's Castles by Chris Tabraham is an excellent companion for anyone touring Scottish castles – a readable, illustrated history detailing how and why they were built.

Shinty (*camanachd* in Gaelic) is a fast and physical ball-and-stick sport similar to Ireland's hurling, with more than a little resemblance to clan warfare. It's an indigenous Scottish game played mainly in the Highlands, and the most prized trophy is the Camanachd Cup. For more information, see www.shinty.com.

TARTAN

This distinctive checked pattern, traditionally associated with the kilt, has become the definitive symbol of Scotland, inspiring skirts, scarves, blankets, ties, key-fobs and a thousand other saleable souvenirs. The pattern is thought to date back to at least the Roman period, though it has become romantically associated with the Gaels, who arrived from Ireland in the 6th century. What is certain is that a tartan plaid had become the standard uniform of Highlanders by the start of 18th century. Following the Battle of Culloden in 1746, the Disarming Act banned the wearing of Highland dress in an attempt to stamp out Gaelic culture.

In the 19th century, tartan got caught up in the cult of so-called 'Balmorality' – Queen Victoria's patronage of Scottish culture – and many of the setts (tartan patterns) now associated with particular clans were created out of thin air by a pair of brothers known as the Sobieski Stuarts, who claimed descent from Bonnie Prince Charlie. The brothers' setts were based on a 'lost' document dating back to the 15th century and they published a hugely successful book of invented tartans, *The Costume of the Clans*, which became established as the genuine tartans of many Highland clans before their elaborate fraud was exposed. Today every clan, and indeed every football team, has one or more distinctive tartans, though few date back more than 150 years.

You can search for your own clan tartan at www.tartansauthority.com.

Highland Games

Highland games are held in Scotland throughout the summer, and not just in the Highlands. You can find dates and details of Highland games held all over the country on the Scottish Highland Games Association website (www.shga.co.uk).

The traditional sporting events are accompanied by piping and dancing competitions and attract locals and tourists alike. Some events are peculiarly Scottish, particularly those that involve trials of strength: tossing the caber (heaving a tree trunk into the air), throwing the hammer and putting the stone. The biggest Highland games are staged at Dunoon, Oban and Braemar.

Natural Scotland

Visitors revel in rural Scotland's solitude and dramatic scenery. Soaring peaks, steely blue lochs, deep inlets, forgotten beaches and surging peninsulas evince astonishing geographic diversity. Scotland's wild places harbour Britain's most majestic wildlife, from the emblematic osprey to the red deer, its bellow reverberating among large stands of native forest. Seals, dolphins and whales patrol the seas, islands moored in the rough Atlantic are havens for species long hunted to extinction further south, while the northeastern archipelagos clamour with seabird colonies of extraordinary magnitude.

The Land

Scotland's mainland divides neatly into thirds. The Southern Uplands, ranges of grassy rounded hills bounded by fertile coastal plains, occupy the south, divided from the Lowlands by the Southern Uplands Fault.

The central Lowlands lie in a broad band stretching from Glasgow and Ayr in the west to Edinburgh and Dundee in the east. This area is underlain by sedimentary rocks, including beds of coal that fuelled Scotland's Industrial Revolution. It's only a fifth of the nation by land area, but has most of the country's industry, its two largest cities and 80% of the population.

Another geological divide – the Highland Boundary Fault – marks the southern edge of the Scottish Highlands. These hills – most of their summits around 900m to 1000m – were scoured by Ice Age glaciers, creating a series of deep, U-shaped valleys, some now flooded by the long, narrow sea lochs that today are such a feature of west Highland scenery. The Highlands form 60% of the Scottish mainland, and are cut in two by the Great Glen, a long, glacier-gouged valley running southwest to northeast.

Despite their pristine beauty, the wild, empty landscapes of the western and northern Highlands are artificial wildernesses. Before the Highland Clearances many of these empty corners of Scotland supported sizeable rural populations.

Offshore, some 800 islands are concentrated in four main groups: the Shetland Islands, the Orkney Islands, the Outer Hebrides and the Inner Hebrides.

Scottish Natural Heritage (www.snh.gov.uk) is the government agency responsible for the conservation of Scotland's wildlife, habitats and landscapes. A key initiative is to reverse biodiversity loss.

The Water

It rains a lot in Scotland – some parts of the western Highlands get over four metres of it a year, compared to 2.3 metres in the Amazon Basin – so it's not surprising there's plenty of water about. Around 3% of Scotland's land surface is fresh water; the numerous lochs, rivers and burns (streams) form the majority of this, but about a third is in the form of wetlands: the peat bogs and fens (mires) that form a characteristic Highland and island landscape.

But it's salt water that really shapes the country. Including the islands, there are more than 10,000 miles of tortuous, complex Scottish shoreline.

Some 90% of Britain's surface fresh water is found in Scotland, and Loch Lomond is Britain's biggest body of fresh water.

Wildlife

Scotland's wildlife is one of its big attractions, and the best way to see it is to get out there. Pull on the boots and sling on the binoculars, go quietly and see what you can spot. Many species that have disappeared from, or are rare in, the rest of Britain survive here.

Animals

While the Loch Ness monster still hogs headlines, Scotland's wild places harbour a wide variety of animals. Britain's largest land animal, the red deer, is present in numbers – recent figures estimate as many as 400,000 – as is the more common roe deer. You'll see them if you spend any time in the Highlands: some are quite content to wander down the village street in the evening and crop at the lawns.

Otters are found in most parts of Scotland, around the coast and along salmon and trout rivers. The best places to spot them are in the north-west, especially in Skye and the Outer Hebrides.

Scotland is home to 75% of Britain's red squirrels, pushed out elsewhere by the dominant greys, native to North America. The greys often carry a virus that's lethal to the reds, so measures are in place to try to prevent their further encroachment.

Other small mammals include the Orkney vole and various bats, as well as stoats and weasels. The blue mountain hare swaps a grey-brown summer coat for a pure-white winter one.

Rarer beasts slaughtered to the point of near-extinction in the 19th century include pine martens, polecats and Scottish wildcats. Populations of these are small and remote, but are slowly recovering.

Of course, most animals you'll see will be in fields or obstructing you on single-track roads. Several indigenous sheep varieties are still around, smaller and stragglier than the purpose-bred supermodels to which we're accustomed. Other emblematic domestic animals include the Shetland pony and gentle Highland cow with its horns and shaggy reddish-brown coat and fringe.

The waters are rich in marine mammals. Dolphins and porpoises are fairly common, and in summer minke whales are regular visitors. Orcas are regularly sighted around Shetland and Orkney. Seals are widespread. Both the Atlantic grey and common seal are easily seen on coasts and islands.

Birds

Scotland has an immense variety of birds. For birdwatchers, the Shetland Islands are paradise. Twenty-one of the British Isles' 24 seabird species are found here, breeding in huge colonies; being entertained by the puffins' clownish antics is a highlight for visitors.

A beautifully written book about Scotland's wildlife, penned by a man who lived and breathed alongside the country's critters in a remote part of the Highlands, is *A Last Wild Place* by Mike Tomkies.

One of the best-loved pieces of Scottish wildlife writing is *Ring of Bright Water* by Gavin Maxwell, in which the author describes life on the remote Glenelg peninsula with his two pet otters in the 1950s.

JOURNEY OF THE SALMON

One of Scotland's most thrilling sights is the salmon's leap up a fast-flowing cascade, resolutely returning to the river of its birth. The salmon's life begins in early spring, hatching in a stretch of fresh water in some Scottish glen. Called fry at this stage and only an inch long, it stays for a couple of years, growing through the 'parr' stage to become smolt, when it heads out to sea.

Its destination could be anywhere in the North Atlantic, but it eventually, sometimes after several years, returns home – using the earth's magnetic field to navigate – to reproduce. Arriving all through the year, but most commonly in late spring and autumn, salmon regain strength after the arduous journey and spawn from November to January. That job done, the salmon normally dies and the cycle begins anew.

Large numbers of red grouse – a popular game bird – graze the heather on the moors. The ptarmigan plays the Arctic trick of changing its plumage from mottled brown in summer to dazzling white in winter. In heavily forested areas you may see capercaillie, a black, turkey-like bird and the largest member of the grouse family. Millions of greylag geese winter on Lowland stubble fields.

The **Royal Society for the Protection of Birds** (RSPB; www.rspb.org. uk) is very active in Scotland. As well as the successful reintroduction of species, the population of several precariously placed bird species has stabilised.

The majestic osprey (absent for most of the 20th century) nests in Scotland from mid-March through to September, after migrating from West Africa. There are around 200 breeding pairs and you can see nesting sites throughout the country, including at Loch Garten and Loch of the Lowes. Other protected birds of prey, such as golden eagles, white-tailed eagles, peregrine falcons and hen harriers, are slowly recovering.

The habitat of the once-common corncrake was almost completely wiped out by modern farming methods but farmers now mow in corncrake-friendly fashion and numbers have recuperated. Listen for its distinctive call – like a thumbnail drawn along the teeth of a comb – in the Uists and on Islay.

> Seventeen per cent of Scotland is forested, compared with England's 7%, Finland's 74% and a worldwide average of 30%.

Plants & Trees

Although the thistle is Scotland's national flower, more characteristic are the Scottish bluebell (harebell), carpeting native woodlands in spring; and heather, the tiny pink and purple flowers of which emerge on the moors in August. Vivid pink rhododendrons are introduced but grow vigorously, and bright yellow gorse flowers in late spring.

Only 1% of Scotland's ancient woodlands, which once covered much of the country, survive, and these are divided into small parcels across the land. Managed regeneration forests are slowly covering more of the landscape, especially in the Highlands. The government's **Forestry Commission** (www.forestry.gov.uk), conducts managed logging and dedicates large woodland areas to sustainable recreational use. The vast majority of this tree cover is coniferous, and there's a plan to increase it to 25% of land area by 2050.

National Parks

Scotland has two national parks – **Loch Lomond & the Trossachs** (www.lochlomond-trossachs.org) and the **Cairngorms** (www.cairngorms. co.uk). There's a huge range of other protected areas: forty-seven **National Nature Reserves** (www.nnr-scotland.org.uk) span the country, and there are also marine areas under various levels of protection.

> Scotland accounts for one-third of the British mainland's surface area, but it has a massive 80% of Britain's coastline and only 10% of its population.

Environmental Issues

Scotland's abundance of wind and water means the government hasn't had to look far for sources of renewable energy. The ambitious grand plan is to generate 100% of the country's energy needs from renewable sources by 2020. Things are going well, with a level close to 50% at time of research, and a solid commitment against fracking and nuclear power.

Though a major goal is to halt a worrying decline in biodiversity, climate change is a huge threat to existing species. Temperature rises would leave plenty of mountain plants and creatures with no place to go; a steady decline in Scotland's seabird population is also surmised to have been partly caused by a temperature-induced decrease of plankton.

The main cause, however, of the worrying level of fish stocks is clear: we've eaten them all. In 2010 the Marine (Scotland) Act was passed. It's a compromise solution that tries to both protect vulnerable marine stocks and sustain the flagging fishing industry. It may well be too little, too late.

Scottish Environment LINK (www. scotlink.org), the umbrella body for Scotland's voluntary environmental organisations, includes 36 bodies committed to environmental sustainability.

Survival Guide

Directory A–Z

Accommodation

Scotland provides a comprehensive choice of accommodation to suit all visitors.

For budget travel, the options are campsites, hostels and cheap B&Bs.

Above this price level is a plethora of comfortable B&Bs, pubs and guesthouses (£25 to £45 per person per night). Midrange hotels are present in most places, while in the higher price bracket (£65-plus per person per night) there are some superb hotels, the most interesting being converted castles and mansions, or chic designer options in cities.

If you're travelling solo, expect to pay a supplement in hotels and B&Bs, meaning you'll often be forking out over 75% of the price of a double for your single room.

Almost all B&Bs, guesthouses and hotels (and even some hostels) include breakfast – either full Scottish or a continental style – in the room price. If you don't want it, you may be able to negotiate a lower price, but not often.

Prices increase over the peak tourist season (June to September) and are at their highest in July and August. Outside of these months, and particularly in winter, special deals are often available at guesthouses and hotels.

If you're going to be in Edinburgh in August (festival month) or at Hogmanay (New Year), book as far in advance as you can – a year if possible – as the city will be packed.

For a few extra pounds, tourist offices have an accommodation booking service, which can be handy over summer. However, note that they can only book the ever-decreasing number of places that are registered with **VisitScotland** (☑0845 859 1006; www.visitscotland.com/accommodation). There are many other fine accommodation options that, mostly due to the hefty registration fee, choose not to register with the tourist board. Registered places tend to be a little pricier

PRACTICALITIES

Newspapers Leaf through Edinburgh's **The Scotsman** (www.scotsman.com) newspaper or Glasgow's **The Herald** (www.heraldscotsman.com); the latter is well into its third century. Have a giggle at rival tabloids the *Daily Record* and the *Scottish Sun,* or try the old-fashioned *Sunday Post* for a nostalgia trip.

Television Watch BBC1 Scotland, BBC2 Scotland and ITV stations STV or Border. Channels Four and Five are UK-wide channels with unchanged content for Scotland. BBC Alba is a widely available digital channel broadcasting in Scottish Gaelic.

Radio Find out what's hitting the headlines on **BBC Radio Scotland** (www.bbc.co.uk/radioscotland) by listening to *Good Morning Scotland* from 6am weekdays.

Smoking In Scotland you can't smoke in any public place that has a roof and is at least half enclosed. That means pubs, bus shelters, restaurants and hotels – basically, anywhere you might want to.

Weights & Measurements Use the metric system for weights and measures, with the exception of road distances (in miles) and beer (in pints). The pint is 568mL, more than the US version.

than nonregistered ones. VisitScotland's star system is based on a rather arbitrary set of criteria, so don't set too much store by it.

Most hotels and a rapidly increasing percentage of B&Bs can be found on the big discount sites such as the following:

➜ www.hotels.com

➜ www.booking.com

➜ www.lastminute.com

➜ www.laterooms.com

B&Bs & Guesthouses

B&Bs – bed and breakfasts – are an institution in Scotland. At the bottom end you get a bedroom in a private house, a shared bathroom and the 'full Scottish' (juice, coffee or tea, cereal and cooked breakfast – bacon, eggs, sausage, baked beans and toast). Midrange B&Bs have en suite bathrooms, TVs in each room and more variety (and healthier options) for breakfast. Almost all B&Bs provide hospitality trays (tea- and coffee-making facilities) in bedrooms. Common B&B options range from urban houses to pubs and farms.

Guesthouses, often large converted private houses, are an extension of the B&B concept. They are normally larger and less personal than B&Bs.

Camping & Caravan Parks

Free 'wild' camping became a legal right under the Land Reform Bill. However, campers are obliged to camp on unenclosed land, in small numbers and away from buildings and roads.

Commercial camping grounds are often geared to caravans and vary widely in quality. There are numerous campsites across Scotland; **VisitScotland** (☑0845 859 1006; www.visitscotland.com/accommodation) lists a good selection of them on its website and on a free map, available at tourist offices.

Homestays & Hospitality Exchange

A convenient and increasingly popular holiday option is to join an international house-exchange organisation. You sign up for a year and place your home on a website giving details of what you're looking for, where and for how long. You organise the house swap yourself with people in other countries and arrange to swap homes, rent free, for an agreed period. Shop around, as registration costs vary between organisations. Check out **Home Link International** (www.homelink.org.uk) and **Home Base Holidays** (www.home-base-hols.com) for starters.

Organisations such as **Couchsurfing** (www.couchsurfing.org) or **Hospitality Club** (www.hospitalityclub.org) put people in contact for more informal free accommodation offers – a bit like blind-date couch-surfing. Even if you're not comfortable crashing in a stranger's house, these sites are a great way to meet locals just to go out for a pint or two.

Airbnb (www.airbnb.com) is a community that has a whole range of options, from couches to smart private rooms in people's flats to top-value holiday rentals and almost anything else you can think of.

Hostels

Numerous hostels offer cheap, sociable accommodation and in Scotland the standard of facilities is generally very good. The more upmarket hostels have en suite bathrooms in their dorms, and all manner of luxuries that give them the feel of hotels, if it weren't for the bunk beds.

Hostels nearly always have facilities for self-catering, and, apart from very remote ones, internet access of some kind. Many can arrange activities and tours.

In Highland areas you'll find bothies – simple walkers' hostels and shelters – and in the Shetlands there are *bōds* (characterful but basic shared accommodation).

INDEPENDENT & STUDENT HOSTELS

There are a large number of independent hostels, most with prices around £12 to £20 per person. Facilities vary considerably. **Scottish Independent Hostels** (www.hostel-scotland.co.uk) is an affiliation of over 100 hostels in Scotland, mostly in the north. You can browse them online or pick up their free *Scottish Independent Hostels* map-guide from tourist offices.

SCOTTISH YOUTH HOSTEL ASSOCIATION

The **SYHA** (☑0845 293 7373; www.syha.org.uk) has a network of decent, reasonably priced hostels and produces a free booklet available from SYHA hostels and tourist offices. There are dozens to choose from around the country, ranging from basic walkers' digs to mansions

SELF-CATERING IN SCOTLAND

Self-catering accommodation is very popular in Scotland and staying in a house in a city or cottage in the country gives you an opportunity to get a feel for a region and its community. The minimum stay is usually one week in the summer peak season, and three days or less at other times.

Accommodation of this type varies very widely, from rustic one-bedroom cottages with basic facilities and sheep cropping the grass outside to castles, historic houses and purpose-built designer retreats with every mod-con.

We've only listed limited self-catering options. The best place to start looking for this kind of accommodation is the website of **VisitScotland** (☎0845 859 1006; www. visitscotland.com/accommodation), which lists numerous options all over Scotland. These also appear in the regional accommodation guides available from tourist offices. A quick internet search will reveal many websites listing thousands of self-catering places all across the country.

Expect a week's rent for a two-bedroom cottage to cost from £200 in winter, and up to £400 or more July to September.

The following are other places to search:

Embrace Scotland (Association of Scotland's Self-Caterers; www.embracescotland.com) Association of self-catering properties with a searchable database of over 2500 across Scotland.

Homeaway (www.homeaway.co.uk) A good choice for self-catering, with a wide portfolio and guest reviews.

LHH Scotland (☎01381-610496; www.lhhscotland.com) Has an upmarket portfolio of mostly larger houses and mansions, including some castle options.

Cottages and Castles (☎01738-451610; www.cottages-and-castles.co.uk) Offers a wide range of self-catering accommodation, as the name suggests.

Cottage Guide (www.cottageguide.co.uk) Lots of Scottish cottages to browse online.

NTS Holidays (☎0844 493 2108; www.nts.org.uk/holidays) The National Trust for Scotland has an excellent portfolio of upmarket accommodation, including historic houses, lighthouse cottages and more.

Ecosse Unique (☎01835-822277; www.uniquescotland.com) Offers holiday homes all over Scotland.

Landmark Trust (☎01628-825925; www.landmarktrust.org.uk) A building-preservation charity that restores historic buildings and rents them out as accommodation.

and castles. You've got to be an HI member to stay, but nonmembers can pay a £3 supplement per night that goes towards the £10 membership fee. Prices vary according to the month, but average around £16 to £20 per adult in high season.

Most SYHA hostels close from around mid-October to early March but can be rented out by groups.

Hotels

There are some wonderfully luxurious places, including rustic country-house hotels in fabulous settings, and castles complete with crenellated battlements, grand staircases and the obligatory rows of stag heads. Expect all the perks at these places, often including a gym, a sauna, a pool and first-class service. Even if you're on a budget, it's worth splashing out for a night at one of the classic Highland hotels, which are the hubs of the local community, incorporating the local pub and restaurant.

In the cities, dullish chain options dominate the midrange category, though there are some quirkier options to be had in Glasgow and Edinburgh.

Increasingly, hotels use an airline-style pricing system, so it's worth booking well ahead to take advantage of the cheapest rates. The website www.moneysavingexpert.com has a good guide to finding cheap hotel rooms.

University Accommodation

Many Scottish universities offer their student accommodation to visitors during the holidays. Most rooms are comfy, functional single bedrooms, some with shared

bathroom, but there are also twin and family units, self-contained flats and shared houses. Full-board, half-board, B&B and self-
catering options are often available. Rooms are usually let out from late June to mid-September.

Activities

Scotland is a brilliant place for outdoor recreation and has something to offer everyone, from those who enjoy a short stroll to full-on adrenalin junkies. Although hiking, golf, fishing and cycling are the most popular activities, there is an astonishing variety of things to do.

Most activities are well organised and have clubs and associations that can give visitors invaluable information and, sometimes, substantial discounts. **VisitScotland** (www.visitscotland.com) has information on most activities. Its website has useful pages on fishing, golf, skiing, cycling and adventure sports. It also produces a good booklet, *Active in Scotland*, available at tourist offices.

Birdwatching

The **Royal Society for the Protection of Birds** (RSPB; www.rspb.org.uk) should be any birdwatcher's first port of call. The **Scottish Wildlife Trust** (www.swt.org.uk) manages several nature reserves, and the **Scottish Ornithologists' Club** (www.the-soc.org.uk) website has useful sections on where to watch birds.

Cycling

There are many excellent routes throughout the country. **Sustrans** (www.sustrans.

org.uk/scotland/national-cycle-network) is the first place to go for more information. For mountain biking, check out the **7Stanes** (www.7stanes-mountainbiking.com) website if you're going to be in the south of the country. There are top-class mountain-biking trails all over the country now – the Where to Ride link on www.dmbins.com covers them all.

Fishing

Seasons and permits vary according to locality. Permits can usually be obtained at the local tackle shop. **VisitScotland** (www.visitscotland.com) produces a useful magazine, *Fishing in Scotland*, available free in tourist offices. Its website also has some useful information on permits and seasons. Comprehensive fishing information can also be found at www.fishpal.com/scotland.

Children

Scotland offers a range of child-friendly accommodation and activities suitable for families.

It's worth asking in tourist offices for local family-focused publications. *The List* magazine (available at newsagents and bookshops) has a section on children's activities and events in and around Glasgow and Edinburgh.

The **National Trust for Scotland** (NTS; ✆0844-493 2100; www.nts.org.uk) and **Historic Scotland** (HS; ✆0131-668 8831; www.historic-scotland.gov.uk) organise family-friendly activities at their properties throughout the summer.

Children are generally well received around Scotland, and every area has some

child-friendly attractions and B&Bs. Even dryish local museums usually make an effort with an activity sheet or child-focused information.

A lot of pubs are family-friendly and some have great beer gardens where kids can run around and exhaust themselves while you have a quiet pint. However, be aware that many Scottish pubs, even those that serve bar meals, are forbidden by law to admit children under 14. In family-friendly pubs (ie those in possession of a Children's Certificate), accompanied under-14s are admitted between 11am and 8pm. There's no clear indication on which is which: just ask the bartender first.

Children under a certain age can often stay free with their parents in hotels, but be prepared for hotels and B&Bs (normally upmarket ones) that won't accept children; call ahead to get the low down. More hotels and guesthouses these days provide child-friendly facilities, including cots. Many restaurants (especially the larger ones) have highchairs and decent children's menus available.

Breastfeeding in public is accepted and is actively encouraged by government campaigns.

The larger car-hire companies can provide safety seats for children, but they're worth booking well ahead.

See also Lonely Planet's *Travel with Children*.

Customs Regulations

Travellers arriving in the UK from EU countries don't have to pay tax or duty on goods for personal use, and can bring in as much EU duty-paid alcohol and tobacco as they like. However, if you bring in more than the following, you'll probably be asked some questions:

➜ 800 cigarettes
➜ 1kg of tobacco

➡ 10L of spirits

➡ 90L of wine

➡ 110L of beer.

Travellers from outside the EU can bring in, duty-free:

➡ 200 cigarettes or 100 cigarillos or 50 cigars or 250g of tobacco

➡ 16L of beer

➡ 4L of nonsparkling wine

➡ 1L of spirits or 2L of fortified wine or sparkling wine

➡ £390 worth of all other goods, including perfume, gifts and souvenirs.

Anything over this limit must be declared to customs officers on arrival. Check www.hmrc.gov.uk/customs for further details, and for information on reclaiming VAT on items purchased in the UK by non-EU residents.

Electricity

230V/50Hz

Discount Cards

Historic Sites

Membership of Historic Scotland (HS) and the National Trust for Scotland (NTS) is worth considering, espe-

cially if you're going to be in Scotland for a while. Both are nonprofit organisations dedicated to the preservation of the environment, and both care for hundreds of spectacular sites. You can join up at any of their properties.

Historic Scotland (HS; ☎0131-668 8831; www.historic-scotland.gov.uk) A nonprofit organisation that cares for hundreds of sites of historical importance. A year's membership costs £48/89 per adult/family, and gives free entry to HS sites (half-price entry to sites in England and Wales). Also offers a short-term Explorer Pass – three days out of five for £29, seven days out of 14 for £38. Can be great value, particularly if you visit both Edinburgh and Stirling castles.

National Trust for Scotland (NTS; ☎0844 493 2100; www.nts.org.uk) NTS looks after hundreds of sites of historical, architectural or environmental importance. A year's membership, costing £50/87 for an adult/family, offers free access to all NTS and National Trust properties (in the rest of the UK). If you're 25 or under, it's a great deal at only £21.

Hostel Cards

If travelling on a budget, membership of the **Scottish Youth Hostel Association/ Hostelling International** (SYHA; ☎0845 293 7373; www.syha.org.uk) is a must (annual membership over/under 16 years is £10/free, life membership is £100).

Senior Cards

Discount cards for those over 60 years are available for train travel (p469).

Student & Youth Cards

The most useful card is the **International Student Identity Card** (ISIC; www.isic.org), which displays your photo. This gives you discounted entry to many attractions and on many forms of transport.

There's a global industry in fake student cards, and many places now stipulate a maximum age for student discounts or substitute a 'youth discount' for 'student discount'. If under 30 but not a student, you can apply for the **European Youth Card** (www.europeanyouthcard.org), which goes by various names in different countries, or an International Youth Travel Card (IYTC), also issued by ISIC. These cards are available through student unions, hostelling organisations or youth travel agencies.

Food

Eating choices are flagged with price indicators, based on the cost of an average main course from the dinner menu.

➡ **£** Budget place where a main dish is less than £9

➡ **££** Midrange; mains are £9 to £18

➡ **£££** Top end; mains are more than £18

Lunch mains are often cheaper than dinner mains, and many places offer an 'early bird' special with lower prices (usually available between 5pm and 7pm).

Gay & Lesbian Travellers

Although many Scots are fairly tolerant of homosexuality, couples overtly displaying affection away from acknowledged 'gay' venues or districts may encounter disapproval.

Edinburgh and Glasgow have small but flourishing gay scenes. The website and monthly magazine *Scotsgay* (www.scotsgay.co.uk) keeps gays, lesbians and bisexuals informed about gay-scene issues.

Health

➡ If you're an EU citizen, a European Health Insurance Card (EHIC) – available from health centres or, in the UK, post offices – covers you for most medical care. An EHIC will not cover you for non-urgent cases, or emergency repatriation.

➡ Citizens from non-EU countries should find out if there is a reciprocal arrangement for free medical care between their country and the UK.

➡ If you do need health insurance, make sure you get a policy that covers you for the worst possible scenarios, including emergency flights home.

➡ No jabs (vaccinations) are required to travel to Scotland.

➡ The most painful problems facing visitors to the Highlands and islands are midges.

Insurance

This not only covers you for medical expenses, theft or loss, but also for cancellation of, or delays in, any of your travel arrangements.

Lots of bank accounts give their holders automatic travel insurance – check if this is the case for you.

Always read the small print carefully. Some policies specifically exclude 'dangerous activities', such as scuba diving, motorcycling, skiing, mountaineering and even trekking.

There's a variety of policies and your travel agent can give recommendations. Make sure the policy includes health care and medication in the countries you may visit on your way to/from Scotland.

You may prefer a policy that pays doctors or hospitals directly rather than forcing you to pay on the spot and claim the money back later. If you have to claim later, make sure you keep all documentation. Some policies ask you to call back (reverse charges) to a centre in your home country where an immediate assessment of your problem is made.

Not all policies cover ambulances, helicopter rescue or emergency flights home. Most policies exclude cover for pre-existing illnesses.

Worldwide travel insurance is available at www.lonelyplanet.com/travel_ser-

vices. You can buy, extend and claim online any time – even if you're already on the road.

Internet Access

If you're travelling with a laptop, you'll find a wide range of places offering a wi-fi connection. These range from cafes to B&Bs and public spaces.

We've indicated accommodation and eating and drinking options that have wi-fi with the 🛜 symbol in the text. Wi-fi is often free, but some places (typically, upmarket hotels) charge.

There are increasingly good deals on pay-as-you-go mobile internet from mobile network providers.

If you see the @ symbol, then the place has an internet terminal.

If you don't have a laptop or smartphone, the best places to check email and surf the internet are public libraries – nearly all of which have at least a couple of computer terminals, and they are free to use, though there's often a time limit.

Internet cafes also exist in the cities and larger towns and are generally good value, charging approximately £2 to £3 per hour.

Many of the larger tourist offices across the country also have internet access.

Language Courses

Scotland is a popular place to learn English, and there are numerous places to do it. Dedicated language academies offer intensive tuition at a price and can also arrange accommodation in residences or with local families. Much cheaper are colleges, some of which even offer free English classes for foreigners.

A good resource to start you off is the **English UK Scotland website** (www.englishukscotland.com), which has

---

MIDGES

If you've never been to the Scottish Highlands and islands before, be prepared for an encounter with the dreaded midge. These tiny, 2mm long blood-sucking flies appear in huge swarms in summer, and can completely ruin a holiday if you're not prepared to deal with them.

They proliferate from late May to mid-September, but especially mid-June to mid-August – which unfortunately coincides with the main tourist season – and are most common in the western and northern Highlands. Midges are at their worst during the twilight hours, and on still, overcast days – strong winds and bright sunshine tend to discourage them.

The only way to combat them is to cover up, particularly in the evening. Wear long-sleeved, light-coloured clothing (midges are attracted to dark colours) and, most importantly, use a reliable insect repellent.

details of many colleges and language schools, mostly in Edinburgh and Glasgow.

Legal Matters

The 1707 Act of Union preserved the Scottish legal system as separate from the law in England and Wales.

Police have the power to detain, for up to six hours, anyone suspected of having committed an offence punishable by imprisonment (including drugs offences).

If you need legal assistance, contact the **Scottish Legal Aid Board** (☏0845 122 8686; www.slab.org.uk; 44 Drumsheugh Gardens, Edinburgh).

Possession of cannabis is illegal, with a spoken warning for first offenders with small amounts. Fines and prison sentences apply for repeat offences and larger quantities. Possession of harder drugs is much more serious. Police have the right to search anyone they suspect of possessing drugs.

Maps

If you're about to tackle Munros, you'll require maps with far greater detail than the maps in this guide, or the ones supplied by tourist offices. The Ordnance Survey (OS) caters to walkers, with a wide variety of maps at 1:50,000 and 1:25,000 scales. Alternatively, look out for the excellent walkers' maps published by Harveys; they're at scales of 1:40,000 and 1:25,000.

Money

The British currency is the pound sterling (£), with 100 pence to a pound. 'Quid' is the slang term for pound.

Three Scottish banks issue their own banknotes, meaning there's quite a variety of different notes in circulation. They are legal

currency in England too, but you'll sometimes run into problems changing them. They are also harder to exchange once you get outside the UK.

Euros are accepted in Scotland only at some major tourist attractions and a few upmarket hotels – it's always better to have sterling cash.

ATMs

ATMs (called cashpoints in Scotland) are widespread and you'll usually find at least one in small towns and villages. You can use Visa, MasterCard, Amex, Cirrus, Plus and Maestro to withdraw cash from ATMs belonging to most banks and building societies in Scotland.

Cash withdrawals from some ATMs may be subject to a small charge, but most are free. If you're not from the UK, your home bank will likely charge you for withdrawing money overseas; it pays to be aware of how much, as it may be much better to withdraw larger amounts less often.

Credit Cards

Visa and MasterCard cards are widely recognised, although many places will charge a small amount for accepting them. Charge cards such as Amex and Diners Club may not be accepted in smaller establishments. Many smaller B&Bs do not take cards.

Moneychangers

Be careful using bureaux de change; they may offer good exchange rates but frequently levy outrageous commissions and fees. The best-value place to change money in the UK is at post offices, but only the ones in larger towns and cities offer this service. Larger tourist offices also have exchange facilities.

Tipping

Tip 10% in sit-down restaurants, but not if there's

already a service charge on the bill.

In classy places, staff may expect closer to 15%.

Service is at your discretion: even if the charge is added to the bill, you don't have to pay it.

Don't tip in pubs: if the service has been exceptional over the course of an evening, you can say 'have one for yourself'.

In taxis, round up to the nearest pound.

Opening Hours

In the Highlands and islands Sunday opening is restricted, and it's common for there to be little or no public transport.

Opening hours are as follows:

Banks 9.30am to 4pm or 5pm Monday to Friday; some are open 9.30am to 1pm Saturday.

Nightclubs 9pm or 10pm to 1am, 2am or later. Often only open Thursday to Saturday.

Post offices 9am to 6pm Monday to Friday, 9am to 12.30pm Saturday (main branches to 5pm Saturday).

Pubs & Bars 11am to 11pm Monday to Thursday, 11am to 1am Friday and Saturday, 12.30pm to 11pm Sunday; lunch is served noon to 2.30pm, dinner 6pm to 9pm daily.

Shops 9am to 5.30pm (or 6pm in cities) Monday to Saturday, and often 11am to 5pm Sunday.

Restaurants Lunch noon to 2.30pm, dinner 6pm to 9pm or 10pm; in small towns and villages the chippy (fish-and-chip shop) is often the only place to buy cooked food after 8pm.

Public Holidays

Although bank holidays are general public holidays in the rest of the UK, in Scotland they only apply to banks and some other commercial offices.

Scottish towns normally have four days of public

holiday, which they allocate themselves; dates vary from year to year and from town to town. Most places celebrate St Andrew's Day (30 November) as a public holiday.

General public holidays:

New Year 1 & 2 January

Good Friday March or April

Christmas Day 25 December

Boxing Day 26 December

Telephone

The famous red telephone boxes are a dying breed now, surviving mainly in conservation areas. You'll mainly see two types of phone booths in Scotland: one takes money (and doesn't give change), while the other uses prepaid phonecards and credit cards. Some phones accept both coins and cards. Payphone cards are widely available.

The cheapest way of calling internationally is via the internet, or by buying a discount call card; you'll see these in newsagents, along with tables of countries and the number of minutes you'll get for your money.

Mobile Phones

The UK uses the GSM 900/1800 network, which covers the rest of Europe, Australia and New Zealand, but isn't compatible with the North American GSM 1900. Most modern mobiles can function on both networks – but check before you leave home just in case.

Though roaming charges within the EU are due to be entirely eliminated in December 2015, other international roaming charges can be prohibitively high, and you'll probably find it cheaper to get a UK number. This is easily done by buying a SIM card (around £10 including calling credit) and sticking it in your phone. Your phone may be locked to your home network, however, so you'll have to either get it unlocked, or buy a pay-as-you-go

phone along with your SIM card (around £50).

Pay-as-you-go phones can be recharged by buying vouchers from shops.

Phone Codes & Useful Numbers

Dialling the UK Dial your country's international access code then 44 (the UK country code), then the area code (dropping the first 0) followed by the telephone number.

Dialling out of the UK The international access code is 00; dial this, then add the code of the country you wish to dial.

Making a reverse-charge (collect) international call Dial 155 for the operator. It's an expensive option, but not for the caller.

Area codes in Scotland Begin with 01xxx, eg Edinburgh 0131.

Directory Assistance There are several numbers; 118500 is one.

Mobile phones Codes usually begin with 07.

Free calls Numbers starting with 0800 are free; calls to 0845 numbers charged at local rates.

Time

Scotland is on GMT/UTC. The clocks go forward for 'summer time' one hour at the end of March, and go back at the end of October. The 24-hour clock is used for transport timetables, but plenty of folk still struggle to get the hang of it.

The time difference between Scotland and some major cities is:

Paris, Berlin, Rome	1hr ahead of Scotland
New York	5hr behind
Sydney	9hr ahead Apr-Sep, 10hr Oct, 11hr Nov-Mar
Los Angeles	8hr behind
Mumbai	5½hr ahead, 4½hr Mar-Oct
Tokyo	9hr ahead, 8hr Mar-Oct

Tourist Information

The Scottish Tourist Board, known as **VisitScotland** (☑0845 859 1006; www.visitscotland.com), deals with inquiries made by post, email and telephone. You can request, online and by phone, for regional brochures to be posted to you, or download them from the website.

Most larger towns have tourist offices ('information centres') that open 9am or 10am to 5pm Monday to Friday, and on weekends in summer. In small places, particularly in the Highlands, tourist offices only open from Easter to September.

If you want to email a tourist office, it's townname@visitscotland.com

Travellers with Disabilities

Travellers with disabilities will find Scotland a strange mix of accessibility and inaccessibility. Most new buildings are accessible to wheelchair users, so modern hotels and tourist attractions are fine. However, most B&Bs and guesthouses are in hard-to-adapt older buildings, which means that travellers with mobility problems may pay more for accommodation. Things are constantly improving, though.

It's a similar story with public transport. Newer buses have steps that lower for easier access, as do trains, but it's wise to check before setting out. Tourist attractions usually reserve parking spaces near the entrance for drivers with disabilities.

Many places such as ticket offices and banks are fitted with hearing loops to assist the hearing-impaired; look for a posted symbol of a large ear.

An increasing number of tourist attractions have audioguides. Some have Braille guides or scented gardens for the visually impaired.

VisitScotland produces the guide *Accessible Scotland* for wheelchair-bound travellers, its **website** (☎0845 859 1006; www.visitscotland.com/accommodation) details accessible accommodation and many tourist offices have leaflets with accessibility details for their area.

Many regions have organisations that hire wheelchairs; contact the local tourist office for details. Many nature trails have been adapted for wheelchair use.

Disability Rights UK (☎020-7250 3222; www.disabilityrightsuk.org; 250 City Rd, London EC1V 8AF) This is an umbrella organisation for voluntary groups for people with disabilities. Many wheelchair-accessible toilets can be opened only with a special RADAR key, which can be obtained via the website or from tourist offices for £4.50.

Disabled Persons Railcard (www.disabledpersons-railcard.co.uk) Discounted train travel.

Tourism for All (☎0845 124 9971; www.tourismforall.org.uk) Publishes regional information guides for travellers with disabilities and can offer general advice.

Visas

➡ If you're a citizen of the EEA (European Economic Area) nations or Switzerland, you don't need a visa to enter or work in Britain – you can enter using your national identity card.

➡ Visa regulations are always subject to change, and immigration restriction is currently big news in Britain, so it's essential to check with your local British embassy, high commission or consulate before leaving home.

➡ Currently, if you're a citizen of Australia, Canada, New Zealand, Japan, Israel, the USA and several other countries, you can stay for up to six months (no visa required), but are not allowed to work.

➡ Nationals of many countries, including South Africa, will need to obtain a visa: for more info, see www.ukvisas.gov.uk.

➡ The Youth Mobility Scheme, for Australian, Canadian, Japanese, Hong Kong, Monegasque, New Zealand, South Korean and Taiwanese citizens aged 18 to 31, allows working visits of up to two years, but must be applied for in advance.

➡ Commonwealth citizens with a UK-born parent may be eligible for a Certificate of Entitlement to the Right of Abode, which entitles them to live and work in the UK.

➡ Commonwealth citizens with a UK-born grandparent could qualify for a UK Ancestry Employment Certificate, allowing them to work full time for up to five years in the UK.

➡ British immigration authorities have always been tough; dress neatly and carry proof that you have sufficient funds with which to support yourself. A credit card and/or an onward ticket will help.

Women Travellers

Solo women travellers are likely to feel safe in Scotland.

The contraceptive pill is available only on prescription; however, the 'morning-after' pill (effective against conception for up to 72 hours after unprotected sexual intercourse) is available over the counter at chemists.

Transport

GETTING THERE & AWAY

Flights, tours and rail tickets can be booked online at lonelyplanet.com/bookings.

Air

There are direct flights to Scottish airports from England, Wales, Ireland, the USA, Canada, Scandinavia and several countries in Western, Central and Eastern Europe. From elsewhere, you'll probably have to fly into a European hub and catch a connecting flight to a Scottish airport – London, Amsterdam, Frankfurt and Paris have the best connections. This will often be a cheaper option anyway if flying in from North America.

Airports & Airlines

Scotland has four main international airports: Aberdeen, Edinburgh, Glasgow and

Glasgow Prestwick, with a few short-haul international flights landing at Inverness. London is the main UK gateway for long-haul flights. Sumburgh on Shetland has summer service from Norway.

Aberdeen Airport (ABZ; ☑0844 481 6666; www.aberdeenairport.com)

Edinburgh Airport (EDI; ☑0844 448 8833; www.edinburghairport.com)

Glasgow Airport (GLA; ☑0844 481 5555; www.glasgowairport.com)

Glasgow Prestwick (PIK; ☑0871 223 0700; www.glasgowprestwick.com)

Inverness Airport (INV; ☑01667-464000; www.hial.co.uk)

London Gatwick (LGW; www.gatwickairport.com) London's second long-haul airport.

London Heathrow (LHR; www.heathrowairport.com)

Britain's principal international airport.

Land
Bus

Buses are usually the cheapest way to get to Scotland from other parts of the UK. The main operators:

Megabus (☑0900 1600 900; www.megabus.com) One-way fares from London to Glasgow from as little as £8 if you book well in advance (up to 45 days). Has some fully reclinable sleeper services.

National Express (☑08717 818178; www.nationalexpress.com) Regular services from London and other cities in England and Wales to Glasgow and Edinburgh.

Scottish Citylink (☑0871 266 3333; www.citylink.co.uk) Daily service between Belfast and Glasgow and Edinburgh via Cairnryan ferry.

CLIMATE CHANGE & TRAVEL

Every form of transport that relies on carbon-based fuel generates CO_2, the main cause of human-induced climate change. Modern travel is dependent on planes which might use less fuel per kilometre per person than most cars but travel much greater distances. The altitude at which aircraft emit gases (including CO_2) and particles also contributes to their climate change impact. Many websites offer 'carbon calculators' that allow people to estimate the carbon emissions generated by their journey and, for those who wish to do so, to offset the impact of the greenhouse gases emitted with contributions to portfolios of climate-friendly initiatives throughout the world. Lonely Planet offsets the carbon footprint of all staff and author travel.

TRAIN FARES

The complex British train ticketing system rewards advance planning, particularly on long routes. A one-way fare from London to Edinburgh, for example, can cost over £150, but a fare purchased well in advance, at off-peak times, can be as low as £30. Regional fares in Scotland have a lot less variation. In this book we have quoted fares that fall somewhere in between the cheapest and most expensive options.

Car & Motorcycle

Drivers of EU-registered vehicles will find bringing a car or motorcycle into Scotland fairly easy.

The vehicle must have registration papers and a nationality plate, and you must have insurance. The International Insurance Certificate (Green Card) isn't compulsory, but is excellent proof that you're covered.

If driving from mainland Europe via the Channel Tunnel or ferry ports, head for London and follow the M25 orbital road to the M1 motorway, then follow the M1 and M6 north.

Train

Travelling to Scotland by train is faster and usually more comfortable than the bus, but more expensive. Taking into account check-in and travel time between city centre and airport, the train is a competitive alternative to air travel from London.

East Coast (☏03457 225 225; www.eastcoast.co.uk) Trains between London Kings Cross and Edinburgh (4½ hours, every half hour).

Eurostar (www.eurostar.com) You can travel from Paris or Brussels to London in around two hours on the Eurostar service. From St Pancras, it's a quick and easy change to Kings Cross or Euston for trains to Edinburgh or Glasgow. Total journey time from Paris to Edinburgh is about eight hours.

ScotRail (☏08457 55 00 33; www.scotrail.co.uk) Runs the *Caledonian Sleeper*, an overnight service connecting London Euston with Edinburgh, Glasgow, Stirling, Perth, Dundee, Aberdeen, Fort William and Inverness.

National Rail Enquiry Service (☏08457 48 49 50; www.nationalrail.co.uk) Timetable and fares info for all trains in Britain.

Virgin Trains (☏08719 774 222; www.virgintrains.co.uk) Trains between London Euston and Glasgow (4½ hours, hourly).

Crosscountry (☏0844 811 0124; www.crosscountrytrains.co.uk) Runs trains between Wales and southwest England to Glasgow and Edinburgh.

GETTING AROUND

Public transport in Scotland is generally good, but it can be costly compared with other European countries. Buses are usually the cheapest way to get around, but also the slowest. With a discount pass, trains can be competitive; they're also quicker and often take you through beautiful scenery.

Traveline (☏0871 200 22 33; www.travelinescotland.com) provides timetable info for all public-transport services in Scotland, but can't provide fare information or book tickets.

Air

Most domestic air services are geared to business needs, or are lifelines for remote island communities. Flying is a pricey way to cover relatively short distances, but certainly worth considering if you're short of time and want to visit the Hebrides, Orkney or Shetland.

Airlines in Scotland

Eastern Airways (☏0870 366 9100; www.easternairways.com) Flies from Aberdeen to Stornoway and Wick.

Flybe/Loganair (☏0871 700 2000; www.loganair.co.uk) The main domestic airline in Scotland, with flights from Glasgow to Barra, Benbecula, Campbeltown, Islay, Kirkwall, Sumburgh, Stornoway and Tiree; from Edinburgh to Kirkwall, Sumburgh, Stornoway and Wick; from Aberdeen to Kirkwall and Sumburgh; from Inverness to Kirkwall, Benbecula, Stornoway and Sumburgh; and from Stornoway to Benbecula. It (as Loganair only) also operates inter-island flights in Orkney.

Hebridean Air (☏0845 805 7465; www.hebrideanair.co.uk) Flies from Connel airfield near Oban to the islands of Coll, Tiree, Colonsay and Islay.

Bicycle

Scotland is a compact country, and travelling around by bicycle is a perfectly feasible proposition if you have the time. Indeed, for touring the islands a bicycle is both cheaper (for ferry fares) and more suited to their small sizes and leisurely pace of life. For more information, see http://active.visitscotland.com and the **Sustrans** (www.sustrans.org.uk/scotland/national-cycle-network) pages on the National Cycle Network.

Boat

The Scottish Government has introduced a scheme called the Road Equivalent Tariff (RET) on certain ferry crossings. This reduces the price of ferry transport to what it would cost to drive the same distance by road, in the hope of attracting more tourists and reducing business costs in the islands. This has been permanently adopted on routes to the Western Isles, Coll and Tiree and is being trialled for Islay, Gigha, Colonsay and Arran. Fares on these crossings have been cut by around 40%, and initial signs are that the scheme has been successful, with tourist numbers up by 25% to 40%. Expect it to be adopted for other west coast islands during the lifespan of this book.

Caledonian MacBrayne (CalMac; ☎0800 066 5000; www.calmac.co.uk) Serves the west coast and islands. Comprehensive timetable booklet available from tourist offices.

CalMac Island Hopscotch offers more than 20 tickets, giving reduced fares for various combinations of crossings; these are listed on the website and in the CalMac timetable booklet.

Island Rover tickets allow unlimited ferry travel for £59/85 for a foot passenger for eight/15 days, plus £275/410 for a car or £138/207 for a motorbike. Bicycles travel free with foot passengers' tickets.

Northlink Ferries (☎0845 600 0449; www.northlinkferries.co.uk) Ferries from Aberdeen and Scrabster (near Thurso) to Orkney, from Orkney to Shetland and from Aberdeen to Shetland.

Bus

Scotland is served by an extensive bus network that covers most of the country. In remote rural areas, however, services are more geared to the needs of locals (getting to school or the shops in the nearest large town) and may not be conveniently timed for visitors.

First (www.firstgroup.com) Operates local bus routes in several parts of Scotland.

Postbuses (www.royalmail.com) Minibuses, or sometimes four-seater cars, driven by postal workers delivering and collecting the mail. There are no official stops, and you can hail a postbus anywhere on its route. Although services have been cut severely in recent years, it's still the only public transport in some remote parts of Scotland.

Scottish Citylink (☎0871 266 3333; www.citylink.co.uk) National network of comfy, reliable buses serving all main towns. Away from main roads, you'll need to switch to local services.

Stagecoach (www.stagecoachbus.com) Operates local bus routes in many parts of Scotland.

Bus Passes

Holders of a **National Entitlement Card** (www.entitlementcard.org.uk), available to seniors and disabled people who are Scottish citizens, get free bus travel throughout the country. The youth version, for 11- to 26-year-olds, gives discounted travel, and SYHA members receive a 20% discount on Scottish Citylink services. Students do, too, by registering online.

The **Scottish Citylink Explorer Pass** offers unlimited travel on Scottish Citylink (and selected other bus routes) services within Scotland for any three days out of five (£41), any five days out of 10 (£62) or any 8 days out of 16 (£93). Also gives discounts on various regional bus services, on Northlink and CalMac ferries, and in SYHA hostels. Can be bought in the UK by both UK and overseas citizens.

Car & Motorcycle

Scotland's roads are generally good and far less busy than in England, so driving's more enjoyable.

Motorways (designated 'M') are toll-free dual carriageways, limited mainly to central Scotland. Main roads ('A') are dual or single carriageways and are sometimes clogged with slow-moving trucks or caravans; the A9 from Perth to Inverness is notoriously busy.

Life on the road is more relaxed and interesting on the secondary roads (designated 'B') and minor roads (undesignated), although in the Highlands and islands there's the added hazard of suicidal sheep wandering onto the road (be particularly wary of lambs in spring).

At around £1.30 per litre (equivalent to around US$8 per US gallon), petrol's

FERRY LINKS WITH NORTHERN IRELAND

CROSSING	DURATION	FREQUENCY	FARE PASSENGER/ CAR (£)
Belfast–Cairnryan	2¼ hr	5-6 daily	29/90
Larne–Cairnryan	2hr	6-8 daily	28/96
Larne–Troon	2hr	2 daily (late Mar–early Sep	28/96

Car-ferry links between Northern Ireland and Scotland are operated by **Stena Line** (☎08447 70 70 70; www.stenaline.co.uk; passenger £20-29, driver plus car £99-150) and **P&O** (☎08716 64 20 20; www.poferries.com). Stena Line travels the Belfast–Cairnryan route and P&O Irish Sea the Larne–Troon and Larne–Cairnryan routes.

The prices in the table are a guide only; fares are often less than quoted here.

expensive by American or Australian standards; diesel is about 8p per litre more expensive. Prices tend to rise as you get further from the main centres and are more than 10% higher in the Outer Hebrides. In remote areas petrol stations are widely spaced and sometimes closed on Sunday.

Driving Licence

A non-EU licence is valid in Britain for up to 12 months from time of entry into the country. If bringing a car from Europe, make sure you're adequately insured.

Hire

Car hire in the UK is competitively priced by European standards, and shopping around online can unearth some great deals, which can drop to as low as £12 per day for an extended hire period. Hit comparison sites like **Kayak** (www.kayak.com) to find some of the best prices.

The minimum legal age for driving is 17 but to rent a car, drivers must usually be aged 23 to 65 – outside these limits special conditions or insurance requirements may apply.

If planning to visit the Outer Hebrides or Shetland, it'll often prove cheaper to hire a car on the islands, rather than pay to take a hire car across on the ferry.

The main international hire companies:

Avis (www.avis.co.uk)

Budget (www.budget.co.uk)

Europcar (www.europcar.co.uk)

Hertz (www.hertz.co.uk)

Sixt (www.sixt.co.uk)

Road Rules

The *Highway Code*, widely available in bookshops, and also online and downloadable at www.gov.uk/highway-code, details all UK road regulations.

Vehicles drive on the left. Seatbelts are compulsory if fitted; this technically applies to buses too.

The speed limit is 30mph (48km/h) in built-up areas, 60mph (96km/h) on single carriageways and 70mph (112km/h) on dual carriageways.

Give way to your right at roundabouts (traffic already on the roundabout has right of way).

Motorcyclists must wear helmets. They are not compulsory for cyclists.

It is illegal to use a hand-held mobile phone or similar device while driving.

The maximum permitted blood-alcohol level when driving is 80mg/100mL (35mg per 100mL of breath); this is slightly higher than in many other countries.

Traffic offences (illegal parking, speeding etc) usually incur a fine for which you're allowed 30 to 60 days to pay. In Glasgow and Edinburgh the parking inspectors are numerous and without mercy – never leave your car around the city centres without a valid parking ticket, as you risk a hefty fine.

Hitching

Hitching is fairly easy in Scotland, except around big cities and built-up areas, where you'll need to use public transport. Although the northwest is more difficult because there's less traffic, long waits are unusual (except on Sunday in 'Sabbath' areas). On some islands, where public transport is infrequent, hitching is so much a part of getting around that local drivers may stop and offer you lifts without you even asking.

It's against the law to hitch on motorways or their immediate slip roads; make a sign and use approach roads, nearby roundabouts or service stations.

Tours

There are numerous companies in Scotland offering all kinds of tours, including historical, activity-based and backpacker tours. It's a question of picking the tour that suits your requirements and budget.

Discreet Scotland (☑07989-416990; www.discreetscotland.com) Luxurious private tours in an upmarket 4x4 that range from day trips from Edinburgh to full weeks staying in some of Scotland's finest hotels.

Haggis Adventures (☑0131-557 9393; www.haggisadventures.com) Offers fun backpacker-oriented tours, with longer options taking in the Outer Hebrides or Orkney.

Heart of Scotland Tours (☑01828-627799; www.heartofscotlandtours.co.uk) Specialises in mini-coach day tours of central Scotland and the Highlands, departing from Edinburgh.

Hebridean Island Cruises (☑01756-704700; www.hebridean.co.uk) Luxury small-boat cruises around the west coast, Outer Hebrides and northern islands.

SINGLE-TRACK ROADS

In many country areas, especially in the Highlands and islands, you will find single-track roads that are only wide enough for one vehicle. Passing places (usually marked with a white diamond sign, or a black-and-white striped pole) are used to allow oncoming traffic to get by. Remember that passing places are also for overtaking – pull over to let faster vehicles pass if necessary. It's illegal to park in passing places.

Mountain Innovations

(☎01479-831331; www.scot-mountain.co.uk) Guided activity holidays and courses in the Highlands: walking, mountain biking and winter mountaineering.

Rabbie's

(☎0131-226 3133; www.rabbies.com) One- to five-day tours of the Highlands in 16-seat minibuses with professional driver/guide.

Scot-Trek

(☎0141-334 9232; www.scot-trek.co.uk) Guided walks for all levels; ideal for solo travellers wanting to link up with others.

Timberbush Tours

(☎0131-226 6066; www.timberbush-tours.co.uk) Comfortable small-group minibus tours around Scotland, with Glasgow and Edinburgh departures.

Train

Scotland's train network extends to all major cities and towns, but the railway map has a lot of large, blank areas in the Highlands and the Southern Uplands where you'll need to switch to road transport. The West Highland line from Glasgow to Fort William and Mallaig, and the Inverness to Kyle of Lochalsh line, offer two of the world's most scenic rail journeys.

The **National Rail Enquiry Service** (☎08457 48 49 50; www.nationalrail.co.uk) lists timetables and fares for all trains in Britain.

ScotRail (☎08457 55 00 33; www.scotrail.co.uk) Operates most train services in Scotland; website has downloadable timetables.

Costs & Reservations

Train travel is more expensive than bus, but usually more comfortable: a standard return from Edinburgh to Inverness is around £50 to £75 compared with £30 to £50 on the bus.

Reservations are recommended for intercity trips, especially on Fridays and public holidays. For shorter journeys, just buy a ticket at the station before you go. On certain routes, including the Glasgow–Edinburgh express, and in places where there's no ticket office at the station, you can buy tickets on the train.

Children under five travel free; those five to 15 years usually pay half-fare.

Bikes are carried free on all ScotRail trains but space is sometimes limited. Bike reservations are compulsory on certain train routes, including the Glasgow–Oban–Fort William–Mallaig line and the Inverness–Kyle of Lochalsh line; they are recommended on many others. You can make reservations for your bicycle from eight weeks to two hours in advance at main train stations, or when booking tickets by phone (☎0845 755 0033) or online.

There's a bewilderingly complex labyrinth of ticket types. In general, the further ahead you can book, the cheaper your ticket will be.

Advance Purchase Book by 6pm on the day before travel; cheaper than Anytime.

Anytime Buy any time and travel any time, with no restrictions.

Off Peak There are time restrictions (you're not usually allowed to travel on a train that leaves before 9.15am); relatively cheap.

It's always worth checking the ScotRail website for current family or senior offers.

Discount Cards

Discount railcards are available for people aged 60 and over, for people aged 16 to 25 (or mature full-time students), two over-16s travelling together, and for those with a disability. The **Senior Railcard** (www.senior-railcard.co.uk; per year £30), **16-25 Railcard** (Young Persons Railcard; www.16-25railcard.co.uk; per year £30), **Two Together Railcard** (www.twotogether-railcard.co.uk; per year £30) and **Disabled Persons Railcard** (www.disabledpersons-railcard.co.uk; per year £20) are each valid for one year and give one-third off most train fares in Scotland, England and Wales. You'll find they pay for themselves pretty quickly if you plan to take a couple of long distance journeys or a handful of short-distance ones. Fill in an application at any major train station. You'll need proof of age (birth certificate, passport or driving licence) for the Young Persons and Senior Railcards (proof of enrolment for mature-age students) and proof of entitlement for the Disabled Persons Railcard. You'll need a passport photo for all of them. You can also buy railcards online, but you'll need a UK address to have them sent to.

Train Passes

ScotRail has a range of good-value passes for train travel. You can buy them online or by phone or at train stations throughout Britain. Note that Travelpass and Rover tickets are not valid for travel on certain (eg commuter) services before 9.15am weekdays.

Central Scotland Rover Covers train travel between Glasgow, Edinburgh, North Berwick, Stirling and Fife; costs £36.30 for three days' travel out of seven.

Freedom of Scotland Travelpass Gives unlimited travel on all Scottish train services (some restrictions). all CalMac ferry services and on certain Scottish Citylink coach services (on routes not covered by rail). It's available for four days' travel out of eight (£134) or eight days out of 15 (£180).

Highland Rover Allows unlimited train travel from Glasgow to Oban, Fort William and Mallaig, and from Inverness to Kyle of Lochalsh, Aviemore, Aberdeen and Thurso. It also gives free travel on the Oban/Fort William–Inverness bus, on the Oban–Mull and Mallaig–Skye ferries, and on buses on Mull and Skye. It's valid for four days' travel out of eight (£81.50).

Glossary

For a glossary of Scottish place names, see p256.

bag – reach the top of (as in to 'bag a couple of peaks' or 'Munro bagging')

bailey – the space enclosed by castle walls

birlinn – Hebridean galley

blackhouse – low-walled stone cottage with thatch or turf roof and earth floors; shared by both humans and cattle and typical of the Outer Hebrides until the early 20th century

böd – once a simple trading booth used by fishing communities, today it refers to basic accommodation for walkers etc

bothy – hut or mountain shelter

brae – hill

broch – defensive tower

burgh – town

burn – stream

cairn – pile of stones to mark path or junction; also peak

camanachd – Gaelic for *shinty*

ceilidh (*kay*-li) – evening of traditional Scottish entertainment including music, song and dance

Celtic high cross – a large, elaborately carved stone cross decorated with biblical scenes and Celtic interlace designs dating from the 8th to 10th centuries

chippy – fish-and-chip shop

Clearances – eviction of Highland farmers from their land by *lairds* wanting to use it for grazing sheep

Clootie dumpling – rich steamed pudding filled with currants and raisins

close – entrance to an alley

corrie – circular hollow on a hillside

craic – lively conversation

craig – exposed rock

crannog – an artificial island in a *loch* built for defensive purposes

crofting – smallholding in marginal agricultural areas following the Clearances

Cullen skink – soup made with smoked haddock, potato, onion and milk

dene – valley

dirk – dagger

dram – a measure of whisky

firth – estuary

gloup – natural arch

Hogmanay – Scottish celebration of New Year's Eve

howff – pub or shelter

HS – Historic Scotland

kyle – narrow sea channel

laird – estate owner

linn – waterfall

loch – lake

lochan – small *loch*

machair – grass- and wildflower-covered dunes

makar – maker of verses

Mercat Cross – a symbol of the trading rights of a market town or village, usually found in the centre of town and usually a focal point for the community

motte – early Norman fortification consisting of a raised, flattened mound with a keep on top; when attached to a *bailey* it is known as a motte-and-bailey

Munro – mountain of 3000ft (914m) or higher

Munro bagger – a hill walker who tries to climb all the *Munros* in Scotland

NNR – National Nature Reserve, managed by the *SNH*

NTS – National Trust for Scotland

nyvaig – Hebridean galley

OS – Ordnance Survey

Picts – early inhabitants of north and east Scotland (from Latin *pictus*, or 'painted', after their body paint decorations)

provost – mayor

RIB – rigid inflatable boat

rood – an old Scots word for a cross

RSPB – Royal Society for the Protection of Birds

Sassenach – from Gaelic 'Sasannach': anyone who is not a Highlander (including Lowland Scots)

shinty – fast and physical ball-and-stick sport similar to Ireland's hurling

SMC – Scottish Mountaineering Club

SNH – Scottish Natural Heritage, a government organisation directly responsible for safeguarding and improving Scotland's natural heritage

sporran – purse worn around waist with the kilt

SSSI – Site of Special Scientific Interest

SYHA – Scottish Youth Hostel Association

wynd – lane

Behind the Scenes

SEND US YOUR FEEDBACK

We love to hear from travellers – your comments keep us on our toes and help make our books better. Our well-travelled team reads every word on what you loved or loathed about this book. Although we cannot reply individually to your submissions, we always guarantee that your feedback goes straight to the appropriate authors, in time for the next edition. Each person who sends us information is thanked in the next edition – the most useful submissions are rewarded with a selection of digital PDF chapters.

Visit **lonelyplanet.com/contact** to submit your updates and suggestions or to ask for help. Our award-winning website also features inspirational travel stories, news and discussions.

Note: We may edit, reproduce and incorporate your comments in Lonely Planet products such as guidebooks, websites and digital products, so let us know if you don't want your comments reproduced or your name acknowledged. For our privacy policy visit lonelyplanet.com/privacy.

OUR READERS

Many thanks to the travellers who used the last edition and wrote to us with helpful hints, useful advice and interesting anecdotes: Sain Alizada, Tracy Armstrong, Massimo Cocci, Sapideh Gilani, Noemi Gnadinger, Christoph Lehner, Roz Machon, Jill Mordaunt, Ruth Mueller, Ada Pianezzi, David Sillars, Silvia Stals, Bryan Thomas, Marie-Claude Vinette

AUTHOR THANKS
Neil Wilson

Many thanks to all the helpful and enthusiastic staff at TICs throughout the country, and to the many travellers I met on the road who chipped in with advice and recommendations. Thanks also to Carol Downie, and to Steven Fallon and Keith Jeffrey, Steve Hall, Russell Leaper, Brendan Bolland, Jenny Neil, and Tom and Christine Duffin. Finally, many thanks to co-author Andy and to the ever-helpful and patient editors and cartographers at Lonely Planet.

Andy Symington

Many thanks are due in many places, but firstly to Jenny Neil and Brendan Bolland for a big welcome and cracking cemetery stay and to Juliette and David Paton for guaranteed warm and generous hospitality. Old mate Hugh O'Keefe was grand company on the Highlands' winding roads, while John Campbell brightened an Unst evening. Gratitude goes also to Eleanor Hamilton, Cindy-Lou Ramsay, Riika Åkerlind, the Jackson-Hevia family and numerous helpful folk met along the way. Big thanks to Neil for coordinating and Taybank pints, and cheers to James, Cliff and the LP team for a top organising job.

ACKNOWLEDGMENTS
Climate map data adapted from Peel MC, Finlayson BL & McMahon TA (2007) 'Updated World Map of the Köppen-Geiger Climate Classification', Hydrology and Earth System Sciences, 11, 163344.

Illustrations pp50-1, pp96-7 and pp182-3 by Javier Zarracina.

Cover photograph: Smailholm Tower, Borders region; David Lyons/Alamy

THIS BOOK

This 8th edition of Lonely Planet's *Scotland* guidebook was researched and written by Neil Wilson and Andy Symington, who also wrote the previous two editions. This guidebook was commissioned in Lonely Planet's London office, and produced by the following:

Destination Editors James Smart, Clifton Wilkinson

Product Editor Tracy Whitmey

Book Designer Wibowo Rusli

Senior Cartographer Mark Griffiths

Assisting Editors Katie Connolly, Carly Hall, Anne Mulvaney, Charlotte Orr, Simon Williamson

Cover Researcher Naomi Parker

Thanks to Sasha Baskett, Brendan Dempsey, Ryan Evans, Anna Harris, Claire Naylor, Karyn Noble, Luna Soo, Ellie Simpson, Angela Tinson, Lauren Wellicome

Index

Map Legend

Sights

- Beach
- Bird Sanctuary
- Buddhist
- Castle/Palace
- Christian
- Confucian
- Hindu
- Islamic
- Jain
- Jewish
- Monument
- Museum/Gallery/Historic Building
- Ruin
- Shinto
- Sikh
- Taoist
- Winery/Vineyard
- Zoo/Wildlife Sanctuary
- Other Sight

Activities, Courses & Tours

- Bodysurfing
- Diving
- Canoeing/Kayaking
- Course/Tour
- Sento Hot Baths/Onsen
- Skiing
- Snorkelling
- Surfing
- Swimming/Pool
- Walking
- Windsurfing
- Other Activity

Sleeping

- Sleeping
- Camping

Eating

- Eating

Drinking & Nightlife

- Drinking & Nightlife
- Cafe

Entertainment

- Entertainment

Shopping

- Shopping

Information

- Bank
- Embassy/Consulate
- Hospital/Medical
- Internet
- Police
- Post Office
- Telephone
- Toilet
- Tourist Information
- Other Information

Geographic

- Beach
- Hut/Shelter
- Lighthouse
- Lookout
- Mountain/Volcano
- Oasis
- Park
- Pass
- Picnic Area
- Waterfall

Population

- Capital (National)
- Capital (State/Province)
- City/Large Town
- Town/Village

Transport

- Airport
- Border crossing
- Bus
- Cable car/Funicular
- Cycling
- Ferry
- Metro station
- Monorail
- Parking
- Petrol station
- S-Bahn/Subway station
- Taxi
- T-bane/Tunnelbana station
- Train station/Railway
- Tram
- Tube station
- U-Bahn/Underground station
- Other Transport

Note: Not all symbols displayed above appear on the maps in this book

Routes

- Tollway
- Freeway
- Primary
- Secondary
- Tertiary
- Lane
- Unsealed road
- Road under construction
- Plaza/Mall
- Steps
- Tunnel
- Pedestrian overpass
- Walking Tour
- Walking Tour detour
- Path/Walking Trail

Boundaries

- International
- State/Province
- Disputed
- Regional/Suburb
- Marine Park
- Cliff
- Wall

Hydrography

- River, Creek
- Intermittent River
- Canal
- Water
- Dry/Salt/Intermittent Lake
- Reef

Areas

- Airport/Runway
- Beach/Desert
- Cemetery (Christian)
- Cemetery (Other)
- Glacier
- Mudflat
- Park/Forest
- Sight (Building)
- Sportsground
- Swamp/Mangrove

OUR STORY

A beat-up old car, a few dollars in the pocket and a sense of adventure. In 1972 that's all Tony and Maureen Wheeler needed for the trip of a lifetime – across Europe and Asia overland to Australia. It took several months, and at the end – broke but inspired – they sat at their kitchen table writing and stapling together their first travel guide, *Across Asia on the Cheap*. Within a week they'd sold 1500 copies. Lonely Planet was born.

Today, Lonely Planet has offices in Franklin, London, Melbourne, Oakland, Beijing and Delhi, with more than 600 staff and writers. We share Tony's belief that 'a great guidebook should do three things: inform, educate and amuse'.

OUR WRITERS

Neil Wilson

Coordinating Author, Edinburgh, Central Scotland, Northeast Scotland, Inverness & the Central Highlands, Northern Highlands & Islands Neil was born in Scotland and, save for a few years spent abroad, has lived here most of his life. A lifelong enthusiasm for the great outdoors has inspired hiking, biking and sailing expeditions to every corner of the country. Researching this edition took him from the country's most westerly point at Ardnamurchan Lighthouse to its most easterly at Fraserburgh, and to every corner of beautiful Perthshire where he now lives. Neil has been a full-time author since 1988 and has written around 65 guidebooks for various publishers, including the Lonely Planet guides to Edinburgh and Scotland's Highlands & Islands. Neil also wrote most of Plan Your Trip and the Scotland Today, Scottish Larder and Scottish Culture essays.

Andy Symington

Glasgow, Southern Scotland, Southern Highlands & Islands, Northern Highlands & Islands, Orkney & Shetland Andy's Scottish forebears make their presence felt in a love of malt, a debatable ginger colour to his facial hair and a love of wild places. From childhood treks up the M1 he graduated to making dubious road-trips around the firths in a disintegrating Mini Metro and thence to peddling whisky in darkest Leith. Whilst living there, he travelled widely around the country in search of the perfect dram, and, now resident in Spain, continues to visit very regularly. Andy also wrote the Golf planning feature, the History and Natural Scotland essays and the Survival Guide.

Published by Lonely Planet Publications Pty Ltd
ABN 36 005 607 983
8th edition – Feb 2015
ISBN 978 1 74321 570 8
© Lonely Planet 2015   Photographs © as indicated 2015
10 9 8 7 6 5 4 3 2 1
Printed in China

Although the authors and Lonely Planet have taken all reasonable care in preparing this book, we make no warranty about the accuracy or completeness of its content and, to the maximum extent permitted, disclaim all liability arising from its use.